THE
MEDIEVAL
EUROPEAN COMMUNITY

Donald Matthew

Reader in Modern History, University of Durham

B.T. Batsford Ltd
London

R.W.S.
magistro dilecto

Malcolm: Why are you silent?

Macduff: Such welcome and unwelcome things at once
'Tis hard to reconcile

Macbeth IV, 3

First published 1977
© Donald Matthew 1977

ISBN 0 7134 3254 3

Printed in Great Britain by Thomson Litho Ltd., Scotland
for the Publishers B. T. Batsford Ltd, 4 Fitzhardinge Street, London W1H 0AH

CONTENTS

PREFACE

The author's preface is addressed directly to those who open this book, uncertain whether to read it or not. Professional historians are in no need of the author's assistance when assessing the book as a whole. Other readers will be content to discover by sampling whether they are sufficiently interested to read to the end, whether they assimilate information easily or only with effort, and whether the time or energy expended is worthwhile. But there will be some potential readers who need a preface to persuade them to read on.

This book is intended for those who wish to understand better the nature of the European community and who believe that history may help them to do so. I do not venture to estimate their numbers; I am certain that they are many. Some will still be at university, looking back in order to contemplate the future with less dread; they will, however, have some guidance from their teachers. I hope there may also be readers outside the universities, where there is woeful ignorance and prejudice of all sorts about the European middle ages, actively encouraged by the 'media'. There will be young graduates still trying to advance their education in a profoundly unfavourable environment. There will be some with many years' experience in both private and public affairs, able to take the long view, and not deceived as to what qualities are required for the conduct of human affairs. There will be some, still, who think it no more than their duty to take notice of all that has some bearing on the process of making men civilized.

The book was conceived some years ago in England for the English public. Earlier in this century, there was an understandable emphasis in English history teaching on the tradition of insular superiority and commitment to the responsibilities of empire. In recent years, changing circumstances have brought both these elements into question. It is natural that more attention should be given in the future to the history of England before colonial activity began overseas, and especially to the nature of England's relations with the continent of Europe, when they were accepted as necessary and desirable.

The theme of European development in the period before 1500 obviously deserves attention on the continent itself; perhaps its significance for world history is sometimes overlooked. Even in those parts of the world where its legacy is not highly valued it is important to know how it was that Europeans, from being backward and dependent, achieved by their own efforts a dominant role in world affairs. This book is therefore concerned with that period. Western Europeans made their first bold attack on the much more civilized Muslim world at the time of the Crusades and won a few victories by the effect of surprise. The Muslims regrouped their forces so successfully that they eventually captured Constantinople from the Christians. The capture of this great city at any earlier date might have meant the permanent subservience of Europe to the east. In 1453 it signified much in the Levant, but in Europe it meant little. Europeans had by then devised a manner of life that did not depend upon the activities of one great governmental centre and were indeed on the point of not only discovering another world beyond the reach of Islam, but of finding that their own achievements were capable of making them powerful all over the globe. Somehow, in a matter of three or four centuries, the peoples of this small continent mastered their own inadequacies. The story of how they did so should be better known everywhere, not merely in Europe itself.

Such a vast topic has in fact been poorly described. 'Medieval' historians have tended to prefer the earlier period and leave it to be understood that, after the achievements of the 'high' middle ages, decline was inevitable. 'Modern' historians have traditionally relied on the 'Renaissance' to start up their engines. For many reasons the period concerned presents unusual technical problems for historians required to be proficient in many languages and familiar with many peoples and traditions. In one book there can be no question of doing justice to all the aspects that matter. I have not tried to be too systematic, but to explore the subject as lecturing, teaching, research and general reading have prompted me. I have benefited from travel on the continent as well as from the interests of my pupils and the learning of my colleagues. I am grateful for all those experiences that have enlarged my understanding of the past and the enjoyment of the present. In particular I wish to record my appreciation of all those who have personally never failed to astonish me, since they have proved that human nature, however carefully studied, constantly surpasses rational calculation. Finally I would like to thank Professor C. N. L. Brooke for the encouragement he has always given to this project, from the time when it was no more than a prose version of some lectures, down to a recent draft that he was kind enough to read and comment on.

Letcombe Regis   **Epiphany 1976**

1

SURVEYING
THE FIELD

Geographically Europe is notable for the length of its coastline in pro-portion to the size of the landmass. Contrast the northern shores of the Mediterranean with those of Africa in the south: from Anatolia in the east, through Greece, Italy and round to Spain, the shore-line is immensely extended by great peninsulas thrust into the sea, not to speak of the numerous islands, especially in Dalmatia and in the Aegean, which huddle close to the European shores. Northern Europe also has remarkably indented coasts, numerous fertile islands, including Ireland and Britain, with peninsulas like Brittany and Scandinavia well supplied with harbours. The inhabitants of Europe have often found the interiors of the continent unfavourable for cultivation, preferring to settle near the coast and journey by sea. Historically, however, after the collapse of the Roman empire and particularly after the later Muslim conquest of Africa and Spain (and then of the islands as far east as Sicily), Western Christians had been frightened off the Mediterranean sea: it was in this period that the populations expanded further up in the mountainous regions, in isolated places of refuge. To the north, at the same time, the seas were at the mercy of Vikings—dreaded pagan pirates. Then the pressure relaxed: Scandinavia was converted to Christianity and raiding petered out; and, in the south, Normans established a Western Christian bastion in Southern Italy and Sicily. Europeans had recovered confident access to both seas by 1100.

Over the years contact developed by water between the northern and southern systems. Regular sailings of Venetian and Genoese ships to the north had by the fourteenth century united European commerce. Goods from the markets of Cairo in the east travelled through the straits of Gibraltar to the towns of the Low Countries, where Hanse merchants exchanged them for furs brought from Novgorod the Great above Lake Ladoga. Not content with this routine traffic mariners began to venture out beyond the coastal waters of the continent to discover Madeira and the Canary Islands. In due course these explorations led to the rounding of the Cape and spurred on the discovery of America. Confidence at sea was the main secret of European predominance in recent world history, for the penetration of the great continents hardly began before the nineteenth century. Until then the European supremacy in the world depended upon their technical capacity to maintain links round the whole earth by these fragile vessels at the mercy of winds and seas. The basic lessons in sailing the open seas, making charts, navigating by the stars and using the compass were learned in the period covered by this book, between 1100 and 1500. This is not its theme; but it does set out to explain how the timid Europeans who first appeared out of their hiding-places about 1100 had become by 1500 the confident and aggressive Europeans who could conquer the New World and hold the rest in thrall.

The importance of the sea to Christians should cause no surprise.[1] No other religion so often resorts to the imagery of the sea: the central part of the church-building was likened to an inverted ship—the nave; fishing recurs as an image in the Gospels of the process of evangelism; the fish itself became a symbol of Christ. But the importance of water in the history of Europe has perhaps been underestimated: modern histories have been chiefly written by sedentary scholars of the continental mainland. For since the discovery of America, though Europeans as a whole depended on shipping for their status in the world, their continent has been dominated by several great territorial states, whose navies in Europe served only to further contintental ambitions. The development of these states grew out of the needs of Europe at the time, needs which had, however, only become apparent because of the earlier growth of great maritime interests. Take, for example, the Baltic in the fourteenth century, where affairs were manipulated principally by Hanse traders in the great ports while rulers of the inland territories, like the kings of Poland or Scandinavia, struggled to recover control of the coasts. By 1500 the great days of independent maritime free towns all over Europe were finished. The greatest of them, Venice, survived for a time, but only by conquering territory on the mainland which kept its neighbouring enemies at a distance. The great territories of the European dynasties, the Valois, the Habsburgs and the others, have in turn given way to national states and interest in history before 1500 has tended to focus on the obscure origins of those nations, which has also prevented due recognition of the real significance of water for European history earlier. The sixteenth century marks for Europe not only the transference to the world stage of the earlier maritime concerns, but the end of a period of remarkable freedom for maritime powers in

European waters. The disappearance of the great maritime republics coincides with the consolidation of dynastic empires. These empires had not been a long time agrowing: they took root only from the fifteenth century. The period of four centuries here considered should not be therefore interpreted as a great conflict of interests between the sea and the land, but it is between these two extremes that interest swings. The period begins with the new access to the sea after 1100 and closes with the appearance of powerful territorial states by 1500, and the concomitant extension of maritime ambitions to the whole world.

1. NORTHERN WATERS

Instead of beginning this survey of Europe by considering the states, we shall therefore start with the waterways. In the absence of controlling authorities, men had much easier and more direct access to them they have enjoyed since. Journeys overland for travellers, pilgrims merchants were slower, more hazardous and costly than journeys by water; whenever possible men took to boats to travel by sea or river. Admittedly they were often frightened of the sea, but this did not deter them. We shall try to consider Europe as they could have done envisaging relations between the powers as seen from the water. (No contemporary surveyed the continent in this way but the schematic map of the world made at St Sever in the eleventh century shows clearly enough how much importance was accorded to the seas and rivers which divided up the land mass and offered possibilities of penetration into the heart of the continent.[2]) We can thus try to consider their problems, as they could have done themselves, those men of Venice, Barcelona, London or Lübeck who then thought more of traffic overseas than of the doings of their own lands. In this way we shall at least avoid the anachronism of supposing that men in this period laboured only to produce the states of modern Europe.

(i) England

England might seem an ideal place from which to view the continent from the sea, but the English are more introverted now than their legends make out. Their attitude to the continent has been shaped by two crucial experience since the sixteenth century: the Reformation, and the responsibility of colonial empire. The Reformation did at least have some bearing upon continental history itself and for a long time stimulated zeal for intervention, but eventually the religious settlement left the English with an ignorant hatred of the Church of Rome and indifference to continental Protestantism that encouraged splendid isolation. Subsequently her naval superiority gave Britain such responsibilities round the world that the English were culturally closer to their colonies than to their nearest continental neighbours. Condescension to the inferior peoples across the seas became ingrained and the English adopted the same attitude to the continent as well. Such recent experience ill equips the modern English to understand that period of English history when involvement with the continent, France in particular, was taken for granted. From the Norman Conquest (1066) to the English defeat at Castellion in Gascony (1453) is almost four centuries, almost the four centuries covered in this book. The English share in French history has been badly explained by historians of both countries. The English have adopted the view that England was well rid of French territory, which expresses their preference for isolation. Let us see if we can do better than this.

English history begins with the Roman conquest of Britain. When the Romans withdrew, its history is confused until the link with Rome was renewed by the mission of Augustine in 597. From then until the Reformation, the English link with Rome was one of the stay-ropes of English life. This involved a journey overland which took nearly a month on foot one way, but it was a well-beaten path throughout the middle ages. For a time those links were threatened by enemies from the north. But during the tenth century England reacted vigorously against the menace of Viking invasions and established a powerful monarchy that subjugated the alien colonists and defied the pirates. It lay however at the heart of the Viking system, the only great landmass across their waterways. Their command of the seas became such that they claimed the prize of the kingdom and under Canute England became the centre of his Scandinavian empire. This state did not endure. Canute himself represented the last stage of the nerve racking pressure put upon England since the mid-ninth century; but as that pressure subsided, so it became possible to construct a different political society, the Anglo-Norman kingdom, which from 1066 to 1204 bestrode the Channel instead of the North Sea. When the king of France conquered Normandy in 1204, the king of England retained possessions in south-western France and England mariners then moved into closer contact with Biscay. When these possessions too were lost, the English easily slipped further out across the great Atlantic. Over the centuries the focus of English attention thus moved from the north, to the east, south and west.

England and the continent
English attention to the continent may for this period be analysed geographically in three zones: (i) the lands across the straits; (ii) the land to the south-west; and (iii) France as a whole.
(i) England's crucial position in the northern waterways enabled the united monarchy of the tenth century to intercept traffic obliged to pass up and down through the straits between Dover and Calais, since there was no

comparable political power on the other side. Shipping, however, was increasingly anxious to gain access to the continental ports just north of the straits in the Low Countries, for by the eleventh century Flanders was already becoming an area of particularly dense settlement in towns. The industrious weavers of cloth needed both raw materials and victuals which came from ever further afield. The expansion of the Low Countries in this period is itself part of the process of developing Europe's waterways. The major internal waterway of Europe is the Rhine, which then supported a great number of independent cities, bishops and princes. As it approached the sea it opened out into a vast plain, where the inhabitants could trap the produce of all Europe as it flowed down the great river. Other produce came along the coasts from Denmark and the Baltic or from Brittany and beyond, to the south.

The Low Countries were not only densely settled but much divided politically, for it was hardly possible for the German emperor or even his duke of Lower Lorraine to keep control of all their abundant energies. The most prominent of all the lords was the count of Flanders, nominally a vassal of the king of France but practically independent. Count Baldwin v was uncle to the French king Philip i and father-in-law to William Duke of Normandy. After the Norman conquest of England (1066) the kings aimed to cultivate friendly relations with the counts, from whose territories they drew the majority of their hired soldiers. Concern about conditions across the straits has remained a permanent feature of British foreign policy.

The English naturally favoured the existence of many small competing states in the Low Countries, which gave them opportunities to intervene and obtain a foothold, if required; above all they hoped to prevent the appearance of a united state which could challenge English power across the sea. As the other monarchies of medieval Europe began to gain confidence in their powers, however, they were far from willing to leave unchanged this position in the Low Countries. The king of France in the late thirteenth century thought himself strong enough to take over the county of Flanders (1297). This provoked violent opposition from the Flemings, who encouraged the king of England to intervene actively to keep out his French cousin. The king of France in fact never succeeded in taking over this county, but his near relations, the dukes of Burgundy, eventually did. Faced with this powerful bloc the English not only lost their possessions in France; they had for the first time to deal with a difficult situation on the continent. Only the Reformation and the revolt of the Dutch against Habsburg rule gave them back a little of their old sense of security, though they lost even Calais their last foothold on the mainland. The Habsburg power to challenge the English represents the end of an era: the old freedom of the waterways had become a less significant force in European politics than the possession of great lands, rents and numerous soldiers. It is easy to see how England could play a major role in Flanders as long as maritime assets counted most, by exploiting the political uncertainties of the region for three centuries. The appearance of a consolidated state with greater resources put an end to a phase of history not only in the Low Countries, but for England as well and forced the English into unwonted isolation.

English involvement with Flanders had become closest when English security against the Vikings focused attention on ships descending from the north through the straits. About the same time, the English also became alarmed about the potential dangers of cooperation between the Vikings and the Normans, whose dukes were of Scandinavian ancestry and whose reputation for Christian pieties had not in the early eleventh century cancelled out other influences. The marriage of King Aethelred to Emma, the duke's sister (1002) was designed to attract Normandy away from northern alliances; though it did not prevent the Normans from harbouring Scandinavian raiders, it was in other ways so successful that even the Danish Canute as king of England found it prudent to marry Emma after Aethelred's death, to discourage Norman support for Aethelred's sons. After Canute's death the Normans did renew their interest in England. Eventually it came to a showdown between the Normans and the Scandinavians; the Normans won. The Norman kings wedded English interests irrevocably to the affairs of France and made the Channel, not the North Sea, the watery centre of their concerns. In practical terms the Channel crossing is both shorter and less stormy, but this cannot be more than part of the answer.

The management of the Anglo-Norman kingdom was tauter than in Canute's empire. Norman lords with lands on both sides of the Channel went to and fro between them and took for granted the existence of regular communications. Throughout the twelfth century the association was consistently maintained, and renewed if broken. The concerns of the Channel mattered to both sides too much. King John of England could not however prevent, from England, the king of France, Philip II, from occupying the duchy and most of his other French lands north of the Loire (1204). It was the most energetic action of any French king of his dynasty and the first important proof of the power of a great territorial lord to stretch out towards the shore. French control of the Norman coast did not give them control of the Channel, but once Norman sailors began to compete instead of cooperating with the English, the English had to fight to retain their old position. However, the king of France had less time for and interest in the Channel ports than the king of England, who depended on his to cut a figure in the world. For since, after the loss of Normandy, the king of England also retained his interests in south-western France, in Poitou, for a time, and in Gascony, his major concern was to keep his lines of communication open down the Channel. He did not intend to lose all his advantages. least of all to the king of France.

(ii) English links with Bordeaux began through Henry II's marriage to Eleanor of Aquitaine (1152) but until the loss of his other French lands, the king of England showed little personal interest in Gascony. Henry III sent his son the Lord Edward there in 1254, and arranged for him a marriage with the king of Castile's sister, in order to cover Gascony from the south. In their disputes with the king of France over Gascony the kings of England could therefore invoke remoter allies. The English interests in Biscay naturally indicated friendship with Castile, which the French for their part aimed to break. Their opportunity did not come until Pedro the Cruel provoked his bastard half-brother Henry of Trastamara to rebellion. Henry seized the throne and Pedro sought the help of the Black Prince at Bordeaux, during a lull in the Anglo-French war. The Black Prince won a notable victory for Pedro at Najera (1367), but Henry nevertheless eventually prevailed with the help of the great French captain Bertrand Du-Guesclin (1369). Thereafter the Castilian fleet operated in Biscay on behalf of the French, most notably when Pembroke attacked La Rochelle in 1372. Obviously links with Bordeaux became much more vulnerable once a hostile navy operated in the area. Richard II's uncle, the Duke of Lancaster, married Pedro's daughter and campaigned for the recovery of Castile from the Trastamaras. Though unsuccessful, the English helped to stiffen Portuguese opposition to Castile which enabled their kingdom to keep its independence. Portugal remained a grateful ally of the English and the help of her fleet compensated for the loss of the Castilian. By such means the English enlarged their knowledge of the politics and the waters of north-western Europe.

English information about Castile did not go very deep. They took no interest in the problems of the wars with the Muslims, the rivalry with Aragon, the drive towards the Mediterranean or the unpeopled south, which in the long run produced the imperial power of the sixteenth century. When contacts between England and Castile were first made however, Castile was still a predominantly northern European kingdom, settled just to the south of the Cantabrian mountains, with its ancient capital at Burgos and its main centres in the north, with interests in selling raw wool, as England did, to Flemish industry. The great pilgrimage centre of St James at Compostella attracted hundreds of English visitors, sick but cheerful, sailing out of western ports. How different the medieval and modern English images of Spain!

(iii) Between Flanders and Spain lay France, which the English king regarded as the principal stage for his continental appearances. As Duke of Normandy he had been at least as powerful as the king of France until 1204. As Duke of Gascony he had been accepted by King Louis IX in the Treaty of Paris (1259) as one of the great peers of France. No English king contemplated accepting anything less if he intended to keep his throne. The position proved to be irritating and bold kings in the fourteenth century campaigned either to take over the monarchy as a whole (Edward III professed to believe he had better dynastic rights to the throne than Philip VI) or to settle for the outright concession of Gascony. Such terms were at last arranged after the king of France had been captured in battle by the Black Prince, but they could not be carried out (1360). The English king could not secure that independence for Gascony he thought indispensable. He continued to defend his title but thereafter he fought a rearguard action. There are many unusual features to this affair. Firstly the inability of the French king to dislodge his Gascon vassal until the mid-fifteenth century contrasts with his power to remove him from Normandy and Anjou. True, the latter were both much more vulnerable to forces mustered in Paris. On the other hand the English king found it easier to keep up his ties by water over a much greater distance from England than Normandy. Remote contact was easier for the English by water than for the French by land. This being so, the king of England could assail France from the sea wherever he could secure a foothold, from Flanders in the north (1341), Normandy (1355-6, 1415), Brittany (1343), La Rochelle (1372) round to Bordeaux. The Breton campaign is a good example of how Edward III could exploit a dispute about the ducal succession to intervene and weaken the Franch champion. It leaves unanswered the question as to why the king of England attached so much importance to defending Gascony. Its riches and its trade in wine, even the king's prestige: could they be worth so much effort and expenditure?

Contrary to what might have been supposed, the most aggressive of English kings abroad were the most successful at home. The un-enterprising came home to face political crises and there is no reason to believe that English domestic affairs suffered from neglect while the kings concentrated on France. The great men of the realm showed no reluctance to follow kings on successful expeditions. The Commons might decline to be interested in the king's wars when asked to pay taxes, but that was politics. Archers were found in the country; merchants grew rich as royal suppliers; patriotic fervour flared up when French shipping raided coastal towns. The war remained the king's war and not a national one; all the same there are no signs of popular discontent with the war. The opposition to King Richard II complained rather that campaigns were mismanaged and the war not prosecuted with sufficient vigour. When Henry VI's minister, the Duke of Suffolk, opted for peace, thinking the war had become futile, he was executed by common sailors (1450).

Apart from defending the king's duchy, the war with France kept that kingdom weak and enabled England to play a major part in European affairs on a par with France, which was larger, richer and more populated than England. As duke, the king of England could also reasonably act in concert with other peers of France, the count of Flanders, the duke of Brittany and the king of Navarre, who together had an interest in preventing the king of France from becoming too strong for them. The great magnates of France in fact fought to preserve the kind of kingdom in which they could act independently; when the English resistance collapsed, France rapidly became a great centralized state, which could keep England out in the cold. The English kings did not act spitefully towards France, for they had ample proof in Gascony and Flanders, as well as elsewhere, that their view of French affairs commanded popular support. They also saw that the English position in Europe depended on French weakness and that their only real strength was their mobility at sea.

The international outlook of the English in this period is reflected in their facility in languages. English may have already become the language of the sea in the twelfth century;[3] but ties with Rome and France gave the Englishman a natural interest in at least two other languages. English, the mother tongue, served domestically; for all business at law, at court, in the towns, French would have been more common, since men of social rank employed it exclusively well into the fifteenth century. Latin church services probably made certain Latin phrases familiar and justified the use of Latin for all solemn occasions. England's setting in the seas gave the English access to the continent and made an important difference to their outlook: no self-satisfied stay-at-homes they.

Nor were the English or their king then mainly preoccupied there with economic advantages or the protection of commercial interests. Italians provided the principal commercial services for England, particularly from the fourteenth century. English transports could not rival them and played no significant part in shipping goods from the Mediterranean until the sixteenth century. Even less did they ply northern waters. The king himself by parliamentary grants of tunnage and poundage derived valuable revenues from taxes on shipping and had every interest in protecting the approaches to Southampton and London for the Venetian galleys and the Bordeaux wine-shippers.[4] Similarly the king of Castile kept a watchful eye on the approaches to his ports. Within Biscay merchants travelled securely and developed their own commercial codes enforced in the tribunals of the chief commercial towns. Prosperity increased in the whole area because conditions made it possible not only to produce important quantities of raw wool, wine or Biscay salt, but also to convey them safely great distances by sea to certain markets, unimpeded by political controls. The best guarantee of this system became the Anglo-Castilian alliance designed to keep France in check. As long as it worked, the English could roam at will.

During the period discussed in this book English interests on the continent were concentrated on the Low Countries and places further west and south, and no events of importance occurred in that sector without exciting English concern. To the north and east, this was not so — so the northern sector must now be examined on its own account.

(ii) The North

English trade with the Low Countries and places further north remained in the hands of German shippers till the sixteenth century. The various towns from which they came gradually grew into a trading federation, the Hanse, which accepted a common code of commercial practice, without thereby forfeiting their municipal independence. Wherever they operated, however, they left little scope for the activities of the English king, or indeed any other royal authority (until the dukes of Burgundy began to dictate the terms on which they could continue their trade in the Low Countries). This area effectively comprised all the seas to the north of the straits of Dover. When they ventured into Castilian waters they met a stern rebuff from the king (1420).[5]

The inability of the northern kings to master these merchants in the period here studied is one of the more remarkable features of it. The Scanadinavian empire of Canute in the eleventh century might have become the basis for a great maritime power, but it broke up. Denmark lost most by this and found no adequate answer until all the shores of the narrow channels between the North Sea and the Baltic could be recovered for a single ruler. For this to be possible, territorial rulers had first to learn how to manage their territories and master their vassals. In the meantime all those who could take to the sea escaped their supervision and made their own way in the world. The Vikings themselves had been fearful as pirate merchant-men, and sought no advantages from Scandinavian kings. The monarchies that succeeded Canute in Denmark and Norway set about developing their resources in land and discouraged the dispersion of aggressive talents, for once at sea Viking warriors were no help to their kings. In these now peaceful seas, the merchants of the German towns along the shores and rivers could operate without hindrance. Their own princes had generally more pressing occupations than protecting or controlling these men. Not until the mid-fourteenth century did the kings of Denmark realize how powerful this association of merchants had become.

The Hanse association of towns had no common institutions and they were united only by common acceptance of a corpus of commercial law enforced by merchant courts, of which the chief, and court of appeal, had been set up in Lübeck before 1300. A similar situation in Biscay had produced a codification of customs called the *Roles d'Oléron* about the same time, but had not promoted an association of towns like the Hanse capable of combining if necessary against the great kings,[6] for the kings of England and Castile provided adequate protection. Why then did something similar not occur in the north?

In the first place it is probable that the merchants had already developed a greater capacity to act independently. Until the thirteenth century there was a central depot of Baltic trade at Visby on the island of Gotland. To this centre came traders from all over the area, Swedes, Finns, Russians and Germans, bringing with them their valuable goods, amber, furs and jewels for sale. This kind of trading in fairs declined in the thirteenth century particularly as a consequence of the Tartar invasions of Russia, which left only Novgorod as an important Russian trading centre in the north and shifted the focus of trading interest further south and west.

Secondly, the political situation in the Baltic itself favoured urban independence. As the great princely houses in Germany, Poland and Denmark disintegrated, the loss of political stability obliged German traders to look after their own interests, particularly as German pressure on the Slavs to the east and north was intensified. The collapse of the nascent Polish kingdom was not directly the work of the Germans, but the fault of dividing the great regions of Poland amongst the children of the king. Pomerania, which provided the most important strip of coast left to the Poles, not only lost contact with the kingdom but became divided. Western Pomerania was acquired by the Danes, then by Brandenburg. Eastern Pomerania with the great port of Gdansk was also much coveted; recaptured by the king of Poland in 1294, it was ceded by a successor to Brandenburg who sold it to the Teutonic Order in 1309. Not surprisingly the later fortunes of the Polish kingdoms were remade from the interior—particularly from the capital in the south Cracow. Till then little resistance could be offered to German encroachment in the north. Not that Germany was itself a united force. The kings' political involvement in Italy diminished their power to intervene on the northern frontier. Henry the Lion, Duke of Saxony, took an interest in the Baltic and favoured Lübeck as a port for his dominions in 1157, but his successors at Brunswick lost access to the sea. Lübeck became a 'free city' of the empire (1226). The prince of Brandenburg was mainly interested in extending the lands of settlement across the Oder. The Teutonic Order, installed by the Polish duke of Mazovia to combat the pagan Prussians (1246), gradually built up a territory along the coast, encouraging the foundation of German trading settlements. Defeated at Lake Peipus by Alexander Nevsky, the northern limits of their influence were fixed at Narva.

Amongst these political figures, the Danish king was the most powerful, as ruler of the Baltic, controlling the islands of the Sound, Jutland and what is now the southern part of Sweden. It was there that his position was weakest. The Swedish nobility further north were mainly interested in Finland and the frontier with the Russians. After a turbulent start a new royal Swedish dynasty, established in the late thirteenth century, effected a union of kingdoms with Norway for Magnus Ericson (1318-55), which also drew Norway away from its natural bent towards the Atlantic. Such a powerful Scandinavian kingdom could not avoid conflict with Denmark, particularly in wresting away her lands in southern Sweden. The Swedish nobility with such territorial objectives could only encourage Hanse merchants to weaken the Danish enemy. After the death of Magnus and his son (1357) however, the Danish king Waldemar IV immediately attempted to recover lost ground. Some Swedes preferred Magnus's nephew, Albert of Mecklenburg. Waldemar's daughter Margaret subsequently worked for the union of all these territories under her great-nephew, Eric of Pomerania, which came about when he was recognized as the union king of Kalmar (1397). The appeasement of these political disputes threatened to deprive the Hanse of the position built up piece-meal in the fourteenth century, which could only have been salvaged by unprecedented cooperation between the towns involved, an effort that proved too great. Scandinavian history in the fourteenth century proves, however, that formerly disparate political elements groping towards a common life and attempting to find a single solution could eventually succeed where townsmen failed. Only while these experiments continued, the Hanse towns could, indeed had to, fend for themselves.

The Hanse[7]
By 1300, when Lübeck had become the dominant town of the group, there were about twenty towns in the Baltic which enforced a common code of commercial law, together with Hamburg to the west of Jutland. The German colonization of the interior opened up eastern Europe for exploitation. The most important products were grain, iron-ore, salted herrings and timber which descended the rivers to the Hanse ports of Pomerania, Prussia, Livonia, Curland and Riga. These bulky goods were shipped from the Baltic to the Low Countries where they were in demand.

The chief difficulty was the power of Denmark to hinder and tax this traffic through Danish waters. The organization of the convoys could be intelligently planned in Lübeck within sight of Denmark and the city became the chief mind in the league.[8] Merchants no longer needed to travel personally with their produce when writing and credit had become common in business. But the trade had to be protected and common policies to be agreed on.

The Hanse needed to develop no permanent institutions capable of coordinating their joint activities. The towns were far apart and could not expect to establish territorial links. As maritime republics they were proudly independent and their common interests were only assured by the presence in each town hall of great merchants with common trading concerns. The greatest of the Hanse successes was the defeat of Denmark in 1367 and the dictated peace of Stralsund, which was secured by alliance with the Swedes and Norwegians; by this they obtained guarantees for their trading position in Sweden, liberties there for the Cologne confederation of towns (the Western branch of the Hanse) and influence over Denmark. This peace provoked Margaret into planning the union of the princes and nobles against the traders. For Margaret saw that if the political territories could be united, the Hanse would lose their power to play off rival interests in Scandinavia. She worked for a union of the three crowns, which was in fact achieved by her great-nephew Eric of Pomerania. He was elected king of Norway in 1388, conquered Sweden in 1389 and became king of Denmark — the union king of Kalmar (1397). Precarious and ramshackle, this monarchy nevertheless served its purpose and more or less lasted until Gustavus Vasa led Sweden to independence in 1523. The existence of the united monarchy obliged the Hanse to reorganize their league so as to give Lübeck real authority over the other towns in order to conduct war against the Danes. The Hanse could still blockade Denmark. This had a depressing effect upon the Swedish mining industry and provoked a popular rising against the Danish king in 1434. The Hanse thus got the terms they required as late as 1435, but the writing was on the wall. Everywhere great princes were learning how to harness their strength.

At the same time the Hanse towns were struck down internally by objections to their patrician governments, as conditions of trade became more hazardous. In the late fourteenth century, there were ominous signs of protest against patrician rule, notably in Brunswick (1374). Hanse patricians elsewhere were alarmed by such onslaughts on their fellow merchants, but they had little power to intervene and trembled for fear of similar disturbances in their own towns. Rostock and Wismar duly experienced them in 1407. In 1408 Lübeck itself succumbed. The tight control which the patricians exercised on behalf of the security of the town's trade exasperated the other citizens. By the time these troubles were resolved, the Burgundian dukes in the Low Countries had so established their political power that they could curtail free trade and impose unwelcome conditions on foreign merchants. This was the final blow. The Hanse association did not utterly collapse at once, but its power to manage affairs in the northern seas had been sapped. The towns made their own terms with new masters who took on the responsibility of keeping the seas at peace. The king of Poland-Lithuania, with the united forces of two peoples, pushed back the Teutonic order, received the submission of the Prussian towns (1435) and of Gdansk (1466). The Hanse surrendered its powers over the Baltic to the 'union' kings of Poland and Scandinavia. Many of the towns accepted the change phlegmatically. In many ways the territorial rulers were able to provide better protection for commerce, particularly over land. The Polish landowners were just as eager as the Germans to sell their produce. The experience of German influence in the Baltic had played its part in bringing Scandinavians and Poles to realize the need to improve the order of their dominions. The period of German Hanse expansion falls within the time limits treated in this book and exemplifies many of the leading themes in it.

(iii) The Low Countries

Between the areas of Hanse domination in the north and English 'imperial' activity to the south, traffic and attention focused on the Low Countries, which lay at the heart of the system. Townsmen and traders knew that the greatest industrial and commercial activity of Europe was concentrated there.

The Low Countries were divided by a confusion of authorities. The linguistic border between French and German rambled through these lands but defined no national groups. Politically, some territories belonged to the empire, and others to the kingdom of France. For centuries the direct intervention of either king was minimal. The counts of Flanders, in the kingdom, confused even this frontier by acquiring the county of Hainault in the empire, and it was symptomatic of growing French power in the thirteenth century that King Louis IX was able to separate these two counties again and subject the count of Flanders to the sole authority of the king of France, by an arbitration award over disputed inheritance within the count's family. Flanders was the most prosperous of all the Low Countries in the thirteenth century, with numerous great towns. One of them, Bruges, became the most important financial centre of Europe, so that in the next century even Italians, though they managed the principal banking houses of Europe, established their offices in Bruges.[9] The great Flemish towns generated considerable prosperity, but they were too close together to have any chance of establishing 'city-states' on the Italian model. They needed the resources of all Europe to keep their activities going — conquering a mere adjacent county would have been quite inadequate anyway. Competition for materials and markets created conflict within the towns as well as against rivals, and townsmen could not easily devise means to assert themselves for long against traditional authorities. The count of Flanders was able to cultivate the friendship of urban interests neglected by the governing 'patriciate' of the towns, which, outraged by his interference, appealed against him to his overlord the king of France. The king gladly took advantage of finding himself with a party called, after him, the Leliaerts. When he overran the whole county, this roused the fury of the Clauwerts, who rose and massacred the French troops at Bruges (1302). Politics of this degree of complication were still unusual at this period.[10]

The king of France was at this time the greatest king of Europe. He dared to oppose the pope himself. His defeat at the hands of the burghers was a great disgrace for him, which he was unable to expunge. As early as 1288 Philip IV had been unable to exclude the duke of Brabant from taking the county of Limbourg, which he coveted, and his subsequent failure to make good his claims on Flanders confirmed the situation. The Low Countries were not to be dominated by the king of France. This left the situation very open, but it exacerbated the competition, rather than soothed it. The towns themselves took advantage of the political stalemate but they were not able to build permanently. They could assert themselves in rebellions, or by treason, as when the men of Ghent invited Edward III into their midst and persuaded him to cover their actions by taking the style of 'king of France' (1340). Edward III had no objection to taking advantage of their desperation, but he had no intention of encouraging their republican principles. By appealing to him, the townsmen showed the limits of what they could do without the princes. At this period the great princes of the Low Countries were so nicely balanced as to leave the towns some choice, but when this impasse was broken the current moved in favour of the greatest families, not of urban autonomy; in the long run, the Low Countries were united and governed by one great family, the dukes of Burgundy.

While the authority of the king of France was challenged, the German kings could intervene themselves to some effect. Several Lorrainers were elected to the throne of Germany in the thirteenth century. The last of them was Count Henry of Luxembourg, whose family acquired Bohemia and became a very great power in Germany. His successor, Louis of Bavaria, took an interest in the affairs of the region. He married the daughter of the Count of Holland, whose domains included Frisia, Zealand and Hainault, and all these lands eventually passed to the imperial Wittelsbach family. To oblige his father-in-law, Louis declared all these lands to be independent of the empire, not because he was disinterested in them personally but to indicate that an 'autonomous' state had to be recognized. At the end of his life Louis was involved in a struggle for the empire itself with Charles of Luxembourg-Bohemia, and Charles, in order to counteract the effect of the Wittelsbach territories in Lorraine, duly declared his own ally there, the duke of Brabant to be, likewise, independent of the empire. Within a few years, as a matter of fact, Charles's own brother succeeded to this duchy. Two of the greatest families of Germany had thus acquired two independent duchies in the Low Countries and expected to compete for supremacy.

Meanwhile, on the French side of the border, the situation of the count of Flanders also improved dramatically during the fourteenth century. Instead of being hounded by the king as Count Guy had been by Philip IV, the count was cultivated as the French king's most cherished northern vassal. He was encouraged to accumulate great estates for his family within the kingdom, rather than cold-shouldered. The counts arranged marriages to secure the reversion of the greatest inheritances. Count Robert married Yolande for the county of Nevers; their son, Louis de Nevers, married Jeanne for the county of Réthel; their heir, Louis, married Marguerite, daughter of the king of France, Philip V, for Artois, long coveted, and the Free County of Burgundy; their son, Louis, married one of the two heiresses to the duchy of Brabant. He had only one daughter to succeed him and she was in 1369 the most desirable heiress in Europe. The king of England, faced with the prospect of another war with France, angled for her marriage to one of his sons, in order to get another foothold in the Low Countries. Charles V of France was not surprisingly prepared to pay a high price to keep out the English. He proposed the candidature of his youngest brother, Philip, surrendered the Somme towns to round off the count's domains and in effect conceded that autonomy to Flanders which Brabant and Holland had secured from the empire, by allowing the count to set up his own *parlement,* the Audiencia (1369). By this date therefore, the affairs of the Low Countries had passed into the keeping of junior branches of three of the greatest dynasties: Wittelsbach, Luxembourg and Flanders-Valois. It was no longer a question of intense rivalries between very local communities, but a struggle amongst princes with great resources, ambitions and persistence.

In a predominantly aristocratic world, princes who knew their own minds and could muster their forces had little difficulty in putting distracted townsmen in their place. In the north, the management of great lands gave the princes experience of men and the handling of affairs on a scale quite beyond the competence of a town. The processes of government were assimilated to the management of a great estate and kingdoms inherited like property: this was the 'political theory' of the princes. For a time they had been thrown off balance in the urban resurgence of the thirteenth century, but in the Low Countries themselves, at the very heart of European business, the great princes discovered how to effect a powerful re-entry into history, instead of fading away like anachronisms. The period of this book closes when politics had once more become predominantly a concern of rulers, and when urban independence had collapsed in its very stronghold, the Low Countries of the dukes of Burgundy.

Before leaving the waters of the north for those of the Mediterranean, one further point should be made. The emphasis upon the north and the Low Countries would have seemed right and proper in the fifteenth century, but it apparently needs some justification now. Since the nineteenth century there has been a strong historical tradition of stressing the importance rather of Italy and the Renaissance for the future of Europe. More will be said of this later. At this point it is sufficient to remark that the economic activity of the Low Countries was fully matched at the time by the achievements of painters and musicians. This was recognized even in Italy. It is true that Michelangelo personally did not like the emotional style of Flemish religious painting. What is significant is that he knew of it and had to take it as seriously as his own work.

Whether or not Europe subsequently made more use of Italian achievements in the arts (which were by 1500 still little known north of the Alps) it must be conceded that the contributions of Italy, however great, did nothing to restore to Italy itself the lead in European affairs. No one begrudges Italy her cultural achievements, but there is no denying her political suffocation. The most important innovations in European history continued to come in the north, where already in this period the nervous determination to create several centres of activity and to make the most of unfavourable circumstances had already scored some success. The great princes of northern Europe though laid low by events earlier in the period overcame their limitations. Where there had been numerous spirited adventurers risking their luck on the waves, kings moved in to concert a new harmony. Whereas the Mediterranean became divided into two opposing camps—Habsburg and Ottoman—European history embarked upon a series of adventures launched from the great arc of northern states from Portugal to Castile, France, England, the Low Countries, Germany, Scandinavia, Poland and Russia.

2. THE MEDITERRANEAN
Since the appearance of Ferdinand Braudel's magisterial book (1949) the

study of the Mediterranean as a whole has needed no further justification. For the purposes of the present survey we may begin with the late eleventh century, when, as explained earlier, Catholics from the north first planted their standards in southern Italy, where the Muslims had faced only Greek opposition in the past. We are here concerned with those four centuries when the Christians had not to fear the Muslims at sea. The freedom to sail the length of the inland sea in that period enabled the crusading states to be supplied by Italian transports, Italian cities to prosper and adventurers of every kind to swarm between Gibraltar and Constantinople.

Despite the activity in the northern seas, the more important and better educated Europeans of the north, then as now, turned naturally to the Mediterranean not simply for fun or from greed, but in search of culture and civilization. These terms sound modern and pretentious; yet they have meaning. The barbarians of the north who had received the Christian gospel came to Rome as the seat of the Apostles, and lived to admire the vestiges of an older order, which they attempted to reanimate with their less grandiose imagination. From the east and south too, the Muslims settled in the Mediterranean as heirs of the Roman world in Syria, North Africa and Spain, and though the language of the Koran made them indifferent to the literary traditions of Greece and Rome, in other respects they may be considered better disciples of the ancient world than the Christians.

The most obvious point from which to view the Mediterranean as a whole would seem to be Italy, which is not only central but almost forms a bridge on which men may step from Europe into Africa with only two narrow sea passages. The rival claims of Spain as a bridge between the continents have to meet the objections of her more westerly situation. If, for a moment, we do consider the picture from Spain itself, we shall see how irresistibly the current of interest runs towards Italy.

(i) Spain

Looking at the atlas, Spain may appear a united country; but in a period when water was the simplest means of transport and men thought politically in terms of people rather than lands, Spain did not take shape as one unit. From diverse settlements seeking the best access to the sea on four separate fronts, the states were kept apart by the arid mountainous plateau of the interior.

Until the mid-thirteenth century there were only two Spanish powers interested in the Mediterranean (for Castilian access to that sea only began with the capture of Cartagena from the Muslims in 1263 and this did not become an important base of naval power until the reign of Pedro the Cruel 1349-69). Muslim power was based on the force of the Berber tribesmen of North Africa and their main naval concern was the protection of the straits of the Gibraltar, which guaranteed the hold on Andalusia. The strongest Spanish naval state was the Catalan empire, with its centre at Barcelona. It was fundamentally maritime in character and grew out of the activities of the towns stretching both sides of the Pyrenees from Provence to Valencia. Early in the thirteenth century the house of Barcelona which had been deeply involved in the feudal politics of the northern part of this region surrendered its interests there to the nominal suzerain, the king of France, as a consequence of the Albigensian crusade against Provençal heretics. The count of Barcelona, James I, who was born in Montpellier, happened also to be king of Aragon, a small, arid, mountainous and unprofitable kingdom which offered him no attractive prospects. Instead, James conquered the Balearic islands and the Moorish kingdom of Valencia from the Muslims and launched the Catalans upon the seas, though the Catalans lost their ambition to destroy the Muslim hold on the straits, once Castilians appeared in Murcia. Instead they bargained for trading privileges in North Africa and sought political influence to the north and east.[11]

For two centuries these peoples cut an important figure in European politics. Modern writers tend to obscure their significance by calling them Aragonese. James's son, Pere II, married Frederick II's granddaughter and was invited by the Sicilians to claim the throne from the unpopular Charles of Anjou. In this way the Catalan connection was extended to Sicily which remained in the family. When the great war to vindicate this acquisition was eventually stilled (1302) the Catalan company took ship for Greece where it eventually conquered the duchy of Athens (1311). This Catalan colony endured for most of the fourteenth century. Despite some anxieties about Castile in the Spanish peninsula, the long-lived Aragonese king Pere III (1336-88) also expended great efforts to conquer Sardinia and Corsica. In the fifteenth century the war of succession to the kingdom of Naples at last enabled King Alfonso the Magnificent to reunite Sicily and Naples. Though separated again for two generations after his death, by division of the family inheritance, in the sixteenth century the kingdom of the Two Sicilies passed definitely into the keeping of Spain and its dynasties. By starting in Spain we have arrived in Italy all the same.

(ii) Italy
Italy does not bend only south; it bends to the east as well, so at first sight it seems at the very heart of Mediterranean affairs. It enjoyed there a similar role to that of the Low Countries in the north. Both lands had been formerly part of the middle kingdom assigned to the emperor after the partition of Charlemagne's lands (843). Above all, both lands, at the

extremities of the great European route, through the Alps and down the Rhine, Mosel or Meuse, were unusually densely packed with towns. Many great cities jostled for place in the Po Valley. Further south they were more spread out, but Tuscany alone could boast of Pisa, Lucca, Siena, Florence and Arezzo. Rome, the greatest city of all, was a spectacular ruin with no industry other than tourism, but it never lost its fascination for the most disillusioned visitors.

The many towns implied intensive industry and trade in every article. Independence and pride demanded politicial autonomy though this was costly to maintain. Italian towns won their municipal self-government from the emperor in the twelfth century. When he ceased to appear in Italy they fought amongst themselves for dominance. By the fourteenth century, the republics could only preserve their own independence by absorbing their weaker neighbours and thus creating principalities, which for the most part abandoned republicanism for dynastic tyrannies. The great maritime republics, Venice, Genoa and Pisa, became parts of territorial states, only Venice being rich enough to conquer her own territory instead of being absorbed by others. Such had also been the fate of the towns in the Low Countries. In Italy likewise there was no tradition of political unity, except that provided by the Roman Empire. No barbarian invaders ever obtained possession of the whole of it, because the Roman imperial government, from the time of Justinian, had always maintained its foothold, with the ultimate intention of staging a comeback. The Lombards in Italy had not therefore achieved the trick of the Visigoths in Spain or the Franks in Gaul, and left no fond memory or noble example of a united Italy to valiant princes. Charlemagne and the Ottonian emperors of Germany claimed the Lombard lands in Italy but did nothing to extend their rule to the southern seas.

In the late eleventh century the Norman armies under Robert Guiscard did exactly this. They swept away every vestige of Greek imperial government, though they took over its methods on their own account. For the first time the whole of Italy (and Sicily too, recovered from the Muslims) belonged to Catholic princes — and began to share in a common political and cultural life. The western emperors immediately aimed to secure the submission of the new Norman lordships in the south, but this was delayed until the late twelfth century. Even the pope could not command the political services of the Normans, though they offered him the religious loyalty of their dominions. Italian history was profoundly changed by the Norman acquisition of the south, and the creation of 'the Kingdom' (Regno) as it came to be called. The four centuries that elapsed between the proclamation of the kingdom in 1130 and the sack of Rome in 1527 are without any doubt the most glorious in the whole history of Italy (including that of the ancient world), and snears which can be made in England about 'the relevance of the middle ages' cause astonishment in Italy.

The Norman rulers in the south had the gift of using the talents of their various Greek, Muslim, Lombard and Norman peoples to promote a highly original community. The force of their example and the fruit of their labours drew into Italy after them a succession of rivals, German and French, which went on intermittently throughout Italy's more glorious years, until Spain, combining maritime power in the south with territorial power in the Alps, obtained both ends of Italy and checked foreign invasions. The Norman Regno not only bore a considerable part of the responsibility for attracting foreign invaders into Italy and disturbing domestic politics thereby. Its own ability to resist the German emperors also stiffened the resolve of the towns in the north and the will of the popes to reduce the emperor's powers in Italy. As a result, the peninsula showed no signs of consolidating politically and in the eyes of those who judge by national standards the tiresome inability of the Italians to unite politicially invalidates their claim to importance. The political divisions in this period prove rather the ability of the peninsula to support a boundless variety of political units and forms as well as to bear the weight of foreign invasions without breaking. The burden did gradually force a reduction in the number of the great states, but without imposing such an abject surrender as entrusting only one man with the task. Intense local patriotism and the stimulus of having many different units to juggle with made Italy an exciting land of political opportunity, not only for Italians but for fascinated (and unskilled) visitors from the north.

Urban Italy
Instead of studying these centuries of Italian history with an eye on a unification that never came, it is more sensible to notice what did grow. For example, three cities, Milan, Venice and Florence, came to extend their city bounds to embrace great districts and regions subject to their capital and the more important question is why it was these cities, and not, for example, their rivals, Pavia, Genoa or Siena, which succeeded in doing this.

Before the growth of such states, with frontiers and administrations, Italy had chiefly flourished at sea. For its area Italy has the longest coastline of any modern European state. The interior is generally mountainous and often unsuitable for cultivation. The local inhabitants perched uncomfortably but in safety on hill-tops. They owed their civilization to peoples from the sea, Greek, Etruscan and Carthaginian. The land is not easily penetrated by water, though the plains of the Po, Adige, Arno, Tiber and others provide suitable terrain for roads. Without the sea, however, Italy would remain poor. In the eleventh century most of her greatest cities were the independent ports like Venice, Pisa and Amalfi which lived by trade with the east, often still in closer touch with the empire at Constantinople than with the west. The only important exceptions to this rule were Rome and the episcopal cities of the north which the German kings used as centres of administration.

The first great Italian state of the twelfth century, the Norman kingdom, owed its size and strength to seapower, which enabled Guiscard and his brother Roger to capture Bari from the Greeks and Palermo from the Muslims. Seapower took them also into Dalmatia, the Balkans and to Tunis. In the thirteenth century it was the turn of Venice, whose ships transported the Crusaders to Constantinople and won Venice the colonies of the Aegean which constituted her empire till the seventeenth century. Her rival Genoa contested her superiority for two centuries. Both states had at the time negligible territories in Italy. Their power, riches and influence came from the sea and it was to the sea that the great inland industrial city of Florence urgently sought access, at Pisa, once it had been humbled by the Genoese. Without the commercial enterprise of these ports, Italy could never have supported the great industrial towns like Florence and Milan, which depended on the importation of raw materials for their workshops and supplies for their populations. As long as the ports could pump into Italy the supplies so sadly lacking in her barren mountains, the future prospects remained good, for Italy developed the riches of craftsmen accustomed to the best quality of all kinds, particularly in cloths, the principal article of medieval industry.

There came a time however when expanding cities began to compete so intensively with one another for foreign markets that each one strove to impose its power over rivals. Soldiers, from beyond the Alps if necessary, were called in and alliances made with the princes of nearby territories. Success itself provoked opposition, as when the power built up by the Visconti family in northern Italy eventually forced Venice to abandon the isolation of the lagoon and conquer its own territorial state. Seapower which had given Italy the possibility of a richly developed city-life could not prevent such consequences. The sea did not lose its importance, but maritime republics without territories could not remain independent. The power of the French and Spanish armies in Italy after 1494 demonstrated the importance of finding the soldiers and keeping them on the battlefields. As in the north, and for the same reasons, seapower ceased to be adequate support for independent states.

In the meantime the sea had opened men's minds to possibilities and uncertainties; it demanded skill, as well as daring and independence. These qualities gave medieval Italians the incentive to rely on them-

selves, venture everywhere and try anything. They were the great entre-
preneurs, in banking, insurance, long-distance trade; the great craftsmen,
steelmakers, furnishers of fine cloth: they learned to collaborate for
business though they preferred to operate in families. Government could
do little to help them at sea, though the government of Venice built the
galleys to be hired by traders. The laws of the sea had to be enforced by
merchants themselves. They took on the management of their towns,
with the usual consequences — friction amongst patrician families and
discontent from those excluded. As in the north, such conditions opened
the way for political authorities better able to appease social and personal hatred, particularly for the enforcement of territorial laws modelled,
indeed borrowed, from Rome. By the fourteenth century every major
city in Italy had become in its own eyes the sovereign successor to Rome.
Gone were their fears of the emperor and his laws: the city was an empire
unto itself.

By its commerce, industry and small political units Italy differed
essentially from the ancient Roman empire, but neither Italians nor
their visitors from further north could fail to be reminded in the peninsula of ancient civilization and what it represented. Italy was strewn with
the most amazing examples of ancient buildings. The presence of the
(Greek) imperial governments so much longer in Italy than elsewhere in
Latin Christendom had kept alive a more serious interest in and understanding of the imperial past. The universal bishop of the Catholic
church in Rome himself insisted upon the traditional Roman values of
order and universality. From the twelfth century, some of the best
educated men of all Europe frequented Italian universities to study
Roman Law. Dante, the great Florentine, advocated the revival of the
universal empire. In the fifteenth century scholars and artists worked for
a revival of classical culture. Distorted and transformed, the achievements of the past spoke more meaningfully to men's minds in Italy than
anywhere else in the Latin world.

Looking back, northern Europeans tend to give thanks to the Italians
for their revival of ancient studies. At the time, however, the Italians
were not of course resurrecting the dead. The Roman empire still refused to behave as though it had ever died. A Christian emperor reigned
at Constantinople until 1453; and for as long as the empire endured,
even only nominally, the Italians at least were never in any doubt about
its importance, both culturally and politically. The Norman states,
before they became a unified kingdom, began to conquer the Balkans
and aspire to Constantinople. Venice, Italy's richest city, which had
practically no Italian territory before the fifteenth century, possessed a
valuable empire in the Aegean from 1205. Not all Italian states could
individually participate in Greek politics, but ruling families from Mont-

ferrat, Savoy, Florence and Barcelona could not refrain from looking to the new Rome. Nor were princes farther away unmindful of it; to them, Italy was a stepping stone further east, for it was the crusading states of the twelfth century which were the major concern of European international politics.

Crusades and plans for crusades constantly drew western attention to the plight of eastern Christians, Greeks included. Western attitudes to Constantinople became more and more ambivalent. The Normans and the Crusaders who seized the city in 1204 thought themselves more worthy heirs of Rome than the Greeks, but it was in Constantinople that they claimed their inheritance. Experience of the Latin empire (1205-61) increased the mutual dislike of the Latins and Greeks for each other's religious discipline. Western emulation of the Romans was combined with scorn for the actual title-holders. Even at the height of Italy's enthusiasm for Greek culture in the fifteenth century, the Italians upheld the religious superiority of the Latin church, and by imposing a political formula of union with the Greek church (1439) ensured that the Orthodox population of the empire would prefer submission to the Turks. Centuries of uncertainty about the future of the empire had encouraged many adventurers and major powers from the west to play with the idea of the conquest of Constantinople, but in the end they all refused to accept the necessary conditions of success and thus made way for the Ottomans. Interest in Ancient Rome became for the West a cultural asset, not a spur to imperial ambition: politically Constantinople had no lessons to teach the Latins. Great though Italian achievements are in this period, therefore, they must be seen in the context of the Mediterranean as a whole. It is in fact not even in Italy but in the east that the main problems of Mediterranean history lie at this time.

(iii) The Roman Empire at Constantinople

At the end of the eleventh century, the principal power of Christendom was exercised by the direct heir of the Roman empire at Constantinople: the western areas of the empire which had submitted to the barbarians lived only in his shadow. The capital city had been chosen in the early fourth century as the centre of the Hellenistic world. It had a fine harbour fit for a government that united the peoples of the Mediterranean sea, it was easily defensible with a short wall across the isthmus between the Golden Horn and the sea of Marmara. It commanded the major highways from Europe into Asia and the straits that linked the Black Sea (terminus of the Asiatic caravan routes) and the Mediterranean. It overlooked the numerous cities of the East and threatened the major enemy of the Roman world, the Persians, No finer capital could have been found in the Mediterranean. For more than a thousand years the city showed considerable resilience in defending Christian civilization against numerous enemies. In the west however this achievement meant very little until the eleventh century, when Christians in the west regained access to the Mediterranean by the expulsion of Muslim settlers and sailors and by the conquest of the eastern emperor's lands in Italy.

By the time the emperor was defeated in Anatolia by the Seljuk Turks in 1071, he had become aware that for the first time military ability in the west had attained a potentially useful level. The first emperor of the new Comneni dynasty, Alexius, decided therefore in his predicament to negotiate for western Christian reinforcements against his Muslim enemies. Westerners already served in the imperial Varangian guard, but Alexius's proposals seem to have involved something more in the nature of regiments under western leaders of their own.

When substantial armies of men did arrive in the east, stirred up by the papal appeal for crusaders, Alexius found that they had been inspired with personal ambitions to recapture Jerusalem and the Holy Places from the infidels, which made them unwilling to serve as mere auxiliaries of his empire. Amongst them Alexius already knew the Normans as usurpers of imperial lands in Italy and he distrusted their intentions. He was wary too of the enthusiasm of the more naive crusaders with their greater devotion to the Holy Places than to the safety of the empire. The western and the eastern Christians could collaborate, but they showed from the first very different reactions to the problem of the threatening infidel. For the crusaders the defence of the Christian empire had little appeal. Passing through the royal city on the way to Jerusalem they were inevitably impressed by imperial power and riches. From quite early on some of them were tempted to seize Constantinople for themselves, in the belief that such resources in their own hands would be more selflessly expended for the Holy Land. Of the dangers for Christianity of weakening the political state of the 'Greek' emperor they had no thought.

Under the Comneni emperors the empire held firm; they even managed to reap some advantage for themselves from the Crusades. However, the next Greek defeat in Anatolia, at Myriokephalon in 1176, destroyed the dynasty and produced a crisis in which even Greeks did not scruple to defy the capital. The independent state of Cyprus under Isaac Angelus in 1191 sheltered Crusaders well-informed about court intrigues and rival parties in the capital. When the fourth crusade was launched in 1204 Greek refugee princes solicited western aid for their own political ends.

Invited to bring about what had long been secretly desired, exasperated Western soldiers soon rid themselves of tiresome Greek pretenders and hopefully set up their own Latin empire in Constantinople as a base for their operations against the newly consolidated Muslim power of Syria and Egypt. True to their own western political ideas, however, the Latins divided the captive empire amongst their own leaders, assigning the largest single share to the Venetian state which had supplied the ships for the expedition. Some Greek princes managed to salvage fragments for Orthodoxy; and eventually one of the Greek dynasties, the Palaeologi, was able to recapture the capital from the Latins in 1261, but the empire was never recovered as a whole. Some of the fragments, under both Catholic and Orthodox princes, for long retained their independence, while the Turks made no immediate gains in the thirteenth century from the weakness of the empire. To survive at all the Palaeologi emperors, who kept the empire going for nearly two centuries, had therefore to contend with many different powers, and this left them scant opportunity to play their traditional role as Christian champions against Islam.

In these circumstances Constantinople appeared to be the prize of endless rivalries between ambitious rulers. Strong enough to resist capture by all but the greatest, but constantly exposed to danger, Constantinople had in the past offered important benefits—a model of sophisticated government and examples of refined culture to impress western barbarians. The fragmentation of the empire had reduced the splendours of Constantinople, court included, and diffused its benefits, its stock of holy relics included. The last cultural renaissance in the Greek world began, significantly enough, not in the capital, but in the provincial city of Mistra; this literary and philosophical learning rapidly penetrated the Italian courts and those of Frankish Greece. Constantinople itself had not withered. It sheltered Italy's first Greek professor Manuel Chrysoloras and his Italian pupil Guarino of Verona in the first hopeful decade of the fifteenth century. But it was no longer, even for Greece or Orthodoxy, the sole cultural light. As for government, the secrets had been lost; anyway the busy Latins seemed to have no interest in learning them. They were stumbling upon devices of their own which adequately served their limited requirements.

The greatest days of Christian Constantinople were over. In spite of some brilliant episodes the history of the late empire entered a long crisis. For western visitors, the empire lost its special claim to consideration; politically its divisions made it very similar to such western lands as Italy; religiously its resistance to the Latin dominance made some Latin Christians openly declare their preference in the fifteenth century for Muslims against Greeks, treacherous and schismatic.

There has been an understandable tendency to blame the Latins for the fate of the empire, which they seized in 1205, could not defend, and would not succour except by demanding Greek submission to papal supremacy. There is no doubt that from the time of Alexius Comnenus's appeal for Latin help, the empire could not dispense with help against the Muslims and that the Christian West was the most obvious source for it. All the same the responsibility for its ultimate collapse cannot be laid principally upon the Latins, whose brute strength would never have broken so much in 1205, if the orthodox world had not itself lost confidence in the imperial mission. The Comneni emperors have been blamed for making too many concessions to their aristocratic supporters and thus losing the strength of the free peasant armies. The new significance of military cavalry would have anyway given the aristocratic soldier an advantage over traditional infantry forces and while the Comneni lived the centrifugal tendencies of 'feudalism' were held in check.[12] More significant perhaps was the new sense of religious orthodoxy that made the Greeks keener to preserve their church than their state. While Palaeologi emperors continued to conciliate the popes in expectation of adequate reinforcements into the mid-fifteenth century, their subjects rallied behind religious leaders. In the end they preferred to lose freedom under a Muslim government in return for being allowed to run their own ecclesiastical affairs and reunite the Orthodox churches, under the patriarch of Constantinople. Responsibility for the long crisis at Constantinople thus cannot be laid at any one door.

The future of the Levant remained a major problem in European affairs for nearly three centuries. The Ottomans were only the ultimate beneficiaries. Before their final triumph there was hardly a political power which did not take an interest in this question. The revival of the Greek empire in 1261 for Michael VIII had been possible because of the rivalry between Venice and Genoa. Genoa supplied the Paleologi with the ships necessary for their re-conquest in return for free trade in the empire (which broke the monopoly enjoyed by Venetians since 1204), sole rights in the lucrative Black Sea trade, and possession of Smyrna. Three years later, Genoa's defeat in Sicilian waters enabled Michael to cast off these feeble allies and restore Venetians to favour. The government gave up maintaining any Greek fleet at all in 1268 so that the future of the city of Constantinople was obviously vested in the western sea powers. Angevin control of Naples (1266) was promptly followed by the occupation of Corfu in 1267, which threatened the Epirus. Frankish princes of the Latin empire who feared Michael's power in Greece encouraged Charles of Anjou's ambitions. Michael could deal neither with the Franks nor with Charles directly, but he participated in a successful intrigue to wrest Sicily from Charles's grasp for the benefit of Pere II, king of Aragon (1282). Michael VIII had some limited success in the Balkans, with the recovery of Greek Macedonia; however, this only drove the Bulgars to accept a Serb ruler and there was no restoration of orthodox unity under the Palaelogi emperors.

After Michael's death in 1282, the disappointing reign of his son Andronicus II (1282-1321) suggested the imminent disintegration of the empire. The Albanians appeared upon the scene and occupied parts of the Epirus. Andronicus's use of Catalan mercenaries when peace in the west deprived them of employment introduced the Greeks to a violent and merciless enemy that battened on the empire and gloried in the occupation of the duchy of Athens for three-quarters of a century. Andronicus married two Catholic wives, Irene of Montferrat and Anne of Hungary, and his court reflected the ideas and manner of the west more than it cherished the traditions of the empire. Andronicus showed sufficient concern for the future, when his oldest son Michael died in 1319, to propose the succession for his second son Constantine, because Michael's heir Andronicus was frivolous and prodigal, but the latter violently asserted his claims in a civil war lasting six years. During this war, the Turks occupied the imperial lands around Nicaea, and all the expectant predators — Bulgars, Serbs, Italians, Franks and Venetians — intervened on their own account. In 1341 when Andronicus III died, civil war broke out again between the partisans of his infant son John V, in the care of the empress Anne of Savoy, and those of the chief minister, John VI Cantacuzene, which was not appeased until 1354. In these wars the Ottomans served both rivals in turn.

Hemmed in by so many disrespectful neighbours, the Greek emperors, whether they aimed only to survive or hoped bravely to reconquer the old empire entire, had no need to harbour idle fears of a future Muslim victory at Constantinople to focus their attention on the need for vigorous leadership and undivided counsels. No one can underestimate the difficulties that stared them in the face, or despise the resilience of the Palaeologi family that somehow kept the emperors in the forefront of Greek political life, even when reduced to extremities. These virtues are however in the same class as those more pitifully shown by the Latin emperors of Constantinople who maintained the fiction of power by perpetuating the mere title from 1261 until 1383; they sprang from an exaggerated esteem for family right, personal honour, military pageantry and the powers of diplomacy. They are emphatically not the virtues of imperial government, Roman, Greek or Ottoman. A political sense of the real power needed to preserve the empire seems to have eluded even those pathetic puppets who pretended they pulled their own strings. The Greeks who recovered Constantinople had only done so with some Catholic support and could not do without it: they had therefore to accept the partition of their empire.

Lulled into a sense of security by the remoteness of powerful enemies, they all settled down to steady and trivial disputes amongst themselves. The Greeks had to be content with the token of imperial sovereignty. In practice the princes, Greek and Latin, behaved and thought very similarly. The Greek emperors often married Catholic wives and the Latin princes spoke Greek like the natives. An anxious and disillusioned Frank of the early fourteenth century hoped to rouse his contemporaries from their complacency by recording the great deeds of valour performed by their Latin predecessors against the perfidious Greeks: this is the chivalrous history of the Latin conquests in Greece down to 1302 — the Chronicle of the Morea.[13] Such a work however appealed so intensely to the peoples of all countries that versions of it appeared in Italian and Greek as well, suitably modified to spare Greek feelings. The translation was the more necessary because some Franks understood only Greek. The author's purpose was frustrated by his own success: he provided both Franks and Greeks with a new bond through their familiarity with chivalrous literature.

(iv) The Balkans

This somewhat cosy atmosphere compares unfavourably with a much more desperate struggle in Serbia to revive the power of Orthodoxy that came into its own in the mid-fourteenth century. The initial reaction of the parts of the empire to the death of the emperor Manuel in 1180 was to set up local governments. If this was what happened in Greek Cyprus it is hardly surprising if the Bulgars and Serbs did the same. This independence was encouraged and patronized by the Latins and the popes, though they never became popular in the Balkans, where indigenous religious traditions provided rulers with more support than Latin assistance could. Despite a glorious history of resistance to Constantinople before 1018, the Bulgars showed little capacity to exploit the weakness of the Greek empire or papal friendship after 1180. Instead, the kingdom fell apart, the east to the Tartars of the steppes, the west increasingly subjected to the Serbs, who disputed for control with the restored Greek emperors.

The failure of the Greeks to restore the unity of the Orthodox world reveals their basic political weakness better than any account of their half-hearted relations with the Latins. The new Serb state created by Stephen Nemanja, great Jupan of Rashka (1186) was resolutely Orthodox and persecuted the Bogomil heretics; his two sons completed the process of independence by becoming respectively king and archbishop, when the Latins set up their own empire and patriarchate at Constantinople. After the Greek restoration in 1261, magnificent Greek ambassadors were sent to the Serb court in 1264 and reported how mean and rustic it seemed to them;[14] but the Serbs were not overawed by the revival of Greek authority at Constantinople. Instead they borrowed administrative forms, taxation, policies and the taste for luxury and ceremonial which spurred on the ambitions of later rulers. Milutin (1282-1321) conquered Macedonian Skoplje from the Greeks and made it his capital; his successor, Dushan, defeated a combined Greek and Bulgar army in 1330 and went on to proclaim himself emperor in 1345.

Dushan was the greatest Serb king and, after he had been crowned emperor of the Serbs and Greeks at Easter in Skoplje in 1346, even the monks on Mount Athos acknowledged him. The empire did not survive his death in 1355, but he came nearer to making himself the greatest king of Orthodoxy and heir to Constantinople than any Greek ruler of the century, even if the capital eluded his grasp. The Greek half of Dushan's empire was the more important and inspired his ambition to replace the Palaeologi, but this does not diminish the significance of the fact of Serb power with its careful preparation of the final climax. The Serb aristocrats were favoured with territorial grants and groomed for positions of dignity. The Serb church, like the Russian, lived through its most glorious and vigorous phase. However, within a generation of Dushan's death the Ottomans swept aside all remnants of Serb independence at Kossovo in 1389; at Nicopolis in 1396 the Serb contingent fought for the Muslims against a Latin crusading army.

Beyond the Serb frontiers, the rulers of Bosnia, who had defied even Dushan, naturally aped his policies: Tvrtko was crowned king of Bosnia and Serbia in 1376 and modelled his rule on Constantinople. Bosnians had however no clear interest in or idea of the Greek empire. The territory of Bosnia comprised Herzegovina taken from Serbia (1325), Dalmatian islands seized from Venice, and Croatia, acquired temporarily from Hungary. Numerous Bogomil heretics complicated the religious pattern, but the proximity of major Catholic powers like Venice and Hungary strengthened the Catholic party. The rulers of Bosnia struggled rather to create and preserve their own identity without offering any credible foundation for another Balkan empire. Beyond Bosnia there was only Hungary, the greatest Catholic power in Eastern Europe, and later Christian champion against the Ottomans, which found itself unable to collaborate with the Orthodox sects. When its own forces were directly engaged alone, they proved able to hold out temporarily in siege warfare, as at Belgrade, but by that time the Ottomans controlled all the Balkan peoples and eventually Hungary too fell.

The Orthodox states, despite their brave front, never showed any inclination to cooperate with one another or with Catholics against the Ottomans. Greek example had the unfortunate consequence for other Orthodox peoples of encouraging distinct states to set up their own ecclesiastical authorities. This might have intensified local patriotism with religious zeal; in practice it destroyed the unity of the organized church in the Balkans and this tended to encourage mystical forms of devotion which viewed political problems with indifference. A Serb emperor with his own Serb archbishop found it difficult to reimpose Comneni-type unity in church and state on all his subjects; the Greeks despised the Serbs and took it for granted that only a Greek should occupy the seat of the patriarch. The Serbs were certainly unfortunate that Dushan died leaving a child as his heir, for an hereditary monarchy might have consolidated Serb unity and given it the will to resist Ottoman attacks. In the absence of a single ruler with a simple dynastic interest to focus his ambition, the Balkan peoples had no means of defence except personal heroism.

None of the major Catholic powers of the Mediterranean were ill-informed or uninterested in the Christian Levant. The affairs of Greece had come to involve them all: Venice, Genoa, Anjou-Provence, Naples, Sicily and Aragon-Barcelona. In addition to these powers in the West there were the important island states of Cyprus and Rhodes, both formerly parts of the empire that had fallen into Catholic hands. Cyprus became after 1195 a kingdom for the exiled Lusignan kings of Jerusalem; Rhodes became the headquarters of the Knights of the Hospital after the Egyptian conquest of Syria (1309). The possibilities of the Aegean continued to attract other adventurers, like the Catalan company that seized the duchy of Athens in 1311 or the Navarese company that overran the Morea (1382-1402). The Venetians for long continued to defend the Catholic outposts in the Mediterranean; the richest island, Crete, was not lost until 1667. In the meantime, Greece and the Aegean was an area for opportunists, grabbing as much as they could for themselves, and determined to prevent anyone from taking the lot.

By inclination anyway the Catholic powers in the Levant maintained their power by sea. The Greeks had no fleet to speak of after 1180; the Egyptians let the Venetians monopolize Mediterranean commerce; the Genoese traded in the Black Sea. Trade and Muslim good-will was what these maritime republics cared most about. The strongest Catholic base on the mainland was the Morea, practically another island. The most northerly Catholic state in the area was the marquisate of Bondonitsa. Between this and the nearest Catholic state of Hungary stretched a road 500 miles long in the hands of unfriendly Orthodox powers. To hold the Balkans for a Christian empire certainly required a military authority strong enough to hold down the population and to maintain a long line of communication in very difficult terrain. No Catholic power in contemporary Europe had yet devised the means to do this and none of the eager contenders in the Mediterranean could have done so.

Precarious those links across the sea might seem, but they were more durable than a permanent state in the Balkans. Western Europeans already showed their preference for the safety of the fortified harbour and the easy escape by water to the routine work of policing hundreds of square miles of a landed empire in the Roman manner. Confident at sea they discerned no potential rivals there. As for the empire, they hardly attended to the problems of the indolent monarchy on the Bosphorus; the land bridge between Europe and Asia, served no Latin needs at all. The Western colonists in the Aegean were allowed two centuries to develop a sense of their responsibilities through their new acquisitions. They could hardly complain when the Ottoman Turks, within fifty years of their appearance in Greek history, had summed up their chances and decided to run the risk of provoking the numerous Christian powers to unite against them in another crusade. In fact the Ottomans were able not only to consolidate a territorial state, but then to push their enemies into their boats and take to the sea for themselves — the true heirs at last of the imperial Romans.

(v) The Mongols

Constantinople had been awaiting an imperial master for three centuries. When the empire had begun to collapse after 1180 the great Seljuk Sultanate of Roum, the principal author of Greek defeat at Manzikert and Myriocephalon was the potential candidate for this role. Any moves in this direction had in fact been prevented by the advent of a stronger power still, the Mongols, who suddenly appeared from the Asiatic steppes and overwhelmed all the peoples who resisted them. The bases of their power were remote but they continued to influence events from a long distance even after the withdrawal of their most westerly contingents. The future of the eastern Roman empire thus came to depend not merely upon the contending princes of the empire or on its perimeter, but also upon the major powers that lay beyond.

Latin Christians realized this immediately; both the pope (1245-47) and the king of France (1253-55) sent intelligence missions to the Mongol leaders to assess the possibilities of finding allies against the Muslims, despite the destruction the Mongols had caused in Latin Christendom and their occupation of lands in Christian Russia.[15] The results were not as satisfactory as they had hoped, but contact once made with the Far East opened the way for a century of regular visits by missionaries and merchants. This enormously enlarged men's ideas of the world they lived in; a Latin writer about 1332 offering advice in the formulation of policy towards the east already thinks on a global scale: arguing for the existence of the antipodes he concluded that the Christian peoples amounted to less than a tenth or twentieth of the population of the world: the Latins began to measure the real dimensions of their problems in the east.[16]

By that time there were Latin colonies on the Crimea, at the end of the great route across the steppes from China and until the expulsion of the Mongol dynasty from China in 1368, the existence of missionary churches in Peking, and in India too, kept alive the hopes of those Christians who lived closest to the Muslim powers and who did most to stir up Western enthusiasm for crusades. After the collapse of the Mongol dynasty in China, the power of the Tartars further west remained. Christians could not hope to gain anything from them after their conversion to Islam, but they continued to play a part in the history of Constantinople. The Ottomans who had overrun the Balkans and repulsed Western Crusaders (1396) faced no obstacles in Europe to the conquest of Constantinople, but this was in fact postponed for a full half century by the Turks of Anatolia. Fearing for their own independence they called to their aid the great Tamberlaine of Samarkand who defeated his fellow-Muslim, Bajazet I, at Ankara in 1402. This gave the city of Constantinople more hope than the West had provided for two centuries—yet illusions persisted. The geographical bases of Mongol and Tartar power admittedly precluded their rulers from taking any direct interest in Constantinople for themselves, but they had no intention of allowing any other military power to seize it either. The Mongols' influence on Levantine affairs may be considered more closely from two different points of view, for while they were directly responsible for the shadow cast over Russia for more than two centuries, their effect on Islam as a whole is rather a different story.

(vi) Russia

Mongol pressure upon the affairs of eastern Europe bore most heavily on Russia, the Orthodox state second only to the Greek in importance and the one which subsequently appropriated the traditions of Constantinople in both church and state by calling Moscow the third Rome. No other Orthodox power should have more naturally succoured Constantinople, but in the period of greatest need Russia was politically isolated from the Black Sea by Mongol occupation of the steppe. The Mongols had seriously weakened Russia by the great raid in which they had destroyed Kiev (1237) and advanced as far as Silesia (1241) before receding again. As a direct result of this shock the Russians became divided into three distinct groups: the Ukrainians, with a centre at Kiev, the White Russians, with a centre at Minsk, and the Great Russians, for whom Moscow became the chief city. All these three groups submitted to alien suzerainty of some kind, Polish, Lithuanian or Mongol. The Great Russians made the most of their opportunities and emerged from a long period of difficulty as the masters of a new kind of Russian state, but these struggles obviously rendered them powerless to intervene directly in the affairs of the Greek church and empire. All the same they probably had some effect, for during the fourteenth century Russian monks on Mount Athos established a living link between the Orthodox churches of Russia and the Balkans. A knowledge of conditions in Russia played their part in developing the attitudes of Orthodox churchmen elsewhere.

Kiev, the ecclesiastical metropolis of early Russia, had become after the recession of the Mongols the capital of a Catholic kingdom, whose ruler Daniel received his crown from Pope Innocent IV (1253). After his death the Mongols reoccupied his lands but the connexions with the Latin world were renewed when Galicia passed into the keeping of the Polish king after the 1330's.[17] By that time, the leader of Russian orthodoxy had not surprisingly left Kiev. He came to rest in Moscow (1308), where he expected the religious loyalty of all Orthodox Russians. Moscow became the religious centre of Russia before political unity was thought of. In 1343 it already had at least 28 churches. Monasteries flourished in the surrounding countryside, under the inspiration of famous monks like Sergius, who founded the Troitsa monastery 40 miles north-east of Moscow (c.1335) and the favourable economic situation enjoyed by church land encouraged donations and peasant settlement. The monks built churches, favoured painters and contributed to religious literature. It was a period of new spiritual intensity in prayer and meditation. The influence of the monks and churchmen upon the ordinary population cannot have been counteracted by any secular exhortations.

Though Moscow was already important in the early fourteenth century for linking the two great river systems of Russia together, politically it was the least considered principality when Alexander Nevsky's sons divided his estates. It was owing to the church's reputation there that the princes of Moscow gradually enhanced their position; they also obtained the menial and dishonourable service of acting as the Mongol's chief tax collector, and this helped them to secure pre-eminence amongst other princes. The luck of dynastic succession provided Moscow with a mere nine rulers in three hundred years — an average reign of 37 years — and this gave exceptional stability to their government. No religious person in the whole Orthodox world could fail to admire the resilience of Russian Christians, despite the loss of real political independence, and a mood of religious quietism spread over other parts of orthodoxy as well. Orthodoxy, which had been the Christian community previously most strongly marked by devotion to its imperial destiny, began to discover an alternative approach, no less encouraging for the most devout. The religious independence of the Russians was shown in 1439. When their Metropolitan rashly concurred in the diplomatic reunion of the churches at the Council of Florence, he was repudiated and a new Metropolitan set up in his place. The Russian patriarch had thus already become the main pillar of uncompromising Orthodoxy and confident of his power to uphold it, before Constantinople fell to the Turks (1453). However, during the long agony of the Greek empire, the Russians had been unable to defend the Orthodox states or church, and it was only just before the final Ottoman victory that Moscow clearly showed its potential.

(vii) Islam

Concern for the impact of the Mongols upon Christendom must not obscure the fact that when the descendants of Ghengiz Khan moved west, Islam had suffered much more seriously, if only because it was much more exposed. No Christian city of comparable importance was totally destroyed, as Baghdad was in 1258, when the Caliphate was brutally suppressed. The Muslim rulers of Egypt best weathered this storm. They patched up their forces and returned to the attack, picking off the surviving Christian outposts of Syria as mere incidents in their efforts to push the Muslim frontiers back to a line of defence in the desert. By 1300 Egyptian recovery was complete; a truce with the Mongols was sealed by the conversion of the Mongol rulers of Persia to Islam. Once the major political forces of the Middle East were in the hands of the Mongols and the Egyptians, no other power was allowed to emerge between them which could have threatened Constantinople. Egypt was nearer to the great city than the Mongols but Constantinople did not need to fear an Egyptian attack across Anatolia; the new rulers were too cautious to renew the Islamic assault on the ancient enemy.

However, no careful observers of the political situation in the area underestimated the significance of the Egyptian position for the future of Christian influence. The Western presence in the Holy Land had originally exploited the mutual hostility of Egypt and Syria based upon religious differences between the Fatimid rulers and the Orthodox Sunnis. The Western victories had duly inspired a religious revival in Islam, which enabled Saladin to effect the military reunion of Syria and Egypt in 1171 and in due course to recapture Jerusalem (1187). Subsequent western assaults in the Holy Land had to be made against Egypt. The fifth crusade (1219), the first crusade of St Louis (1250), the belated and brief conquest of Alexandria (1365) tackled Egypt head on. Western pilgrims to the Holy Places steadily reported on the strength of the Egyptian rulers, dreading Egyptian victories whenever war came, as they believed it must.

The Egyptian empire of this period demonstrated to both Christians and Muslims the renewed vitality of the Muslim world. It steadily eroded any earlier Latin confidence in their power or destiny as the chosen hands of God for the liberation of his oppressed churches. Not since the distant days of the Ummayyad caliphs at Damascus or Cordova had Christians observed such an impressive Muslim state. Saladin himself, the author of this greatness, inspired Christian awe and admiration. The emperor Frederick II owed his appearance in the Holy Land to friendship with Saladin's heir Al-Kamil (1218-38). When the Ayyubid dynasty failed in 1249, it was succeeded by an outstanding line of slave-sultans — the Mamlukes, who ruled until the Ottoman conquest of 1517. For all its decadent and violent elements, this improbable, even dishonourable, dynasty sponsored as brilliant a flowering of civilization as the Islamic world has known.

The second founder of the state was Baybars (1260-77), who repulsed the Tartar Hulagu from Syria (1260) and also extended his dominion over the Berbers and over Nubia. He reorganized the administration, built great mosques and schools, enforced Orthodoxy and appointed caliphs. The slave army, which comprised Mongol and Turkish units, provided the force and leadership, but was far from being a mere military machine. Egyptian prosperity depended upon its control of the commercial passage between the Red Sea and the Mediterranean, so Baybars gave attention to the digging of canals, improving harbours, regular postal services and commercial treaties, even with Christians like the eager Venetians. Fragments of the magnificent hospital built in Cairo by the Sultan Qala'un (1279-90) and the restored mausoleum of the same ruler survived to show the exquisite refinement of the new dynasty. Fourteenth-century travellers like the Muslim Ibn Battuta or the Christians, James of Verona or Frescobaldi, were moved by the size and opulence of the great city of Cairo, and the flourishing condition of the countryside.[18]

Al Nasir (1298-1308), luxury-living but able, was the last of the great rulers of the first slave-dynasty, the Bahri Mamluks. The local army captains, the emirs, usurped the place of the sultans; the coinage was debased. High taxation, and the Black Death, provoked serious disturbances. A second Mamluke dynasty—the Burji (1382-1517)—inspires less admiration than the first, but nine able sultans ruled for all but ten of these years, giving new life to the country. The arrival of the Portuguese in India in 1497 deprived Egypt of its long standing monopoly over the Red Sea trade, and within a matter of years the dynasty succumbed to the new Ottoman power which had developed to the north. Albuquerque's bombardment of Aden in 1513 came just before the Ottoman conquest and demonstrated how necessary Ottoman protection had become.

(viii) The Ottomans

The Ottomans were the most important as they are the most familiar of Europe's Muslim neighbours, but, after centuries of occupation, their religion has kept them remote and alien. They have some claim to be considered the most credible modern heirs of the Romans, but this has not made them any more acceptable to Christian Europeans; they even succeeded in turning the Roman baths into an exotic Turkish institution. The secret of the Ottoman success lies in their anomalous position as Europeans without the Christian religion, as the only Muslim peoples with a permanent foothold in Europe, owing their initial success to employment as mercenaries by Christian rulers and their long term rule to their neutrality in the religious disputes of Christendom.

The Turks are neighbours still unknown to most Europeans. Their reputation in the nineteenth century for decadent government or atrocities against Christians is likely to mislead and prejudice examination of their earlier adventures. Their final capture of Constantinople and the reconstruction of a great empire based on the city brought them a distinction coveted in vain by many earlier Muslim rulers, but it was not secured without incurring opposition from jealous Muslim rulers, frightened of losing their own independence. The Ottomans had to fight hard for their victories and they had to start all over again in the fifteenth century after Tamberlaine had shattered their first empire.

On both occasions the Ottomans obtained control of the Balkans first, so that the eventual capture of the capital did no more than round off the conquests. Their enemies were not overwhelmed by surprise, as they had been by the Mongols, or overawed by established greatness, as they were in the case of Egypt. Repeated attempts to defeat the Ottomans were made and frequent opportunities to attack them recurred. Christian opposition to them could hardly have been given longer to try its best, and it is extremely unlikely that Christian forces could have made any greater efforts than they did. The Ottomans prevailed in the end because they offered the best possibility of a settlement in the whole area affected. However regrettable it may seem from the Christian point of view, it represented the total inadequacy of Latin Christendom to meet the needs of the peoples who had looked to Constantinople for government for over a thousand years. Since these same Latins within a century won command of a world position beyond Islam, it is even more extraordinary to see that they had failed so near at home: how can we explain the Ottoman success and the Latin failure?

The Ottomans derived no advantages from the Muslim great powers. They owed everything to their native ability to turn the confused situation in the Greek empire to their own advantage. They had however to postpone their triumph until the great powers—the empires of Tamberlaine and Egypt—were too weak to interfere against them. This conclusion should not diminish Ottoman achievement. The Ottomans began as casually as many another group which came to make its fortune within the limits of the Greek empire. At that time the great Seljuk Sultanate of Roum, the principal author of Greek defeat and the most obvious beneficiary in Asia Minor, had broken up into ten minor principalities. The Ottomans were only trying to salvage something for themselves from the wreck of Turkish fortunes when they took Brusa (1326), Nicomedia (1328) and Nicaea from the Greeks, during the civil war over the succession in Constantinople. From this secure base so close to Constantinople in north-west Anatolia, the Ottomans expanded into Muslim areas and conquered the Qarasi in Isauria (1334-36). But they were chiefly active in the Christian world. Their leader Orkhan married a princess of the imperial family and they were used by rival Greek emperors John VI Cantacuzene and John V as trusted auxiliaries. They could not have failed to be impressed by the civilization of Constantinople; their intimate part in its affairs gave them an insight into its weaknesses and aroused their ambitions. Their religion admittedly placed a barrier between them and the Europeans, but on a secular basis the Ottomans found no difficulty in mixing in Frankish Greece, where admiration of military exploits inspired the most cultivated type of literature. In the late fourteenth century the same kind of subject-matter appeared in the earliest Ottoman work of Turkish literature — astonishingly enough a poetic history of the deeds of the Greek hero Alexander: Ahmedi's Iskender-name. Nothing could more convincingly demonstrate how much the Turks accepted their own place in chivalrous European society.

The Greeks had no hesitation about employing the Ottomans against their Orthodox enemy Dushan, and these campaigns opened the eyes of the Turks to the internal disputes of the Balkans and gave them experience of the difficult countryside. After Dushan's death (1355) the Turks showed a new interest in the possibilities opened up to them in Europe. They occupied Gallipoli (1357) which protected their crossing from Europe into Asia, and the new 'sultan' Murad I (1359-89) moved his capital from Brusa to Edirne (or Adrianople) in 1366. A western crusade under Count Amadeus of Savoy in the same year did nothing to dislodge him. Murad won a great victory against the Serbs in 1371 on the Maritsa river, and annexed Serbian Macedonia. Before his death, the Turks had advanced into Bulgaria, taking Sofia in 1386; they effectively destroyed the Serb state at Kossovo (1389). Murad's position was already such that, after Maritsa (1371), he could exact tribute from the Greek emperor at Constantinople. The commanding position of the Ottomans towards Constantinople is adequately illustrated in the instructions given to an ambassador setting out from Venice in the 1390s as to what he should do if he found the imperial city already in Turkish hands. Murad also extended his Asiatic dominions as far as Konya, the old Seljuk capital. He was no longer dependent on the weaknesses he could exploit, but took the initiative on his own account. He could dispense with the tricky alliances that local political interest promoted. On both sides of the sea he offered the advantage of having a single purpose—to unite lands exposed to futile rivalries, to eradicate local oppressors and to provide strictly disciplined forces.

The Turkish army was no doubt fearsome. The sultan had a personal bodyguard of slaves established in 1330, presumably on the model of the Mamlukes in Egypt, distinguished by its headdress (a conical cap of white felt) and its religious fervour: the warriors of the faith, 'Ghazis', in constant warfare with infidels, even when acting as Christian auxiliaries. Only later, after the conquest of Serbia, did this special corps receive additional members, originally captured Christians, later specially recruited boys, to become the new force, *Yenicheri,* the Janissaries of history. The religious dedication of the Turkish armies owed much to the fervour of the men of Islamic learning recruited as teachers by the Ottomans in the *medrasas* of Asia Minor.[19]

The Serb peasants seem already to have welcomed the Ottomans as their deliverers from the new lords imposed on them by the Serb princes. The lords had been intended to help the monarchy, but their rivalries after Dushan's death undermined Serb resistance. No doubt it would be naive to exaggerate the social advantages the Ottomans brought with them, but it is obvious that the new rulers had no interest in leaving Christian aristocrats as great landlords. The land registers of the fifteenth century showed the Ottoman government consistently opposing the formation of great hereditary estates and relying on an impersonal administration, staffed with well-educated officials.[20] The Ottomans' chief advantage, however, lay in their complete detachment from the religious quarrels which dominated their subject people; given their supreme political power, they could tolerate many different religious practices without themselves incurring any *odium theologicum.* It is not difficult to believe that the sense of purpose and dedication shown by the Ottomans very rapidly convinced their new subjects of the advantages to be gained by peaceful submission. Proud aristocrats would naturally refuse to do this, but their own powers of resistance depended on the loyalty of the tenantry, and for various reasons this was rarely forthcoming.

When Murad I died in 1389 the conquest of Constantinople was still many years away, but the Christians were not responsible for postponing it. The Ottoman defeat by Tamberlaine at Ankara (1402) was the really unexpected event that saved the city for another half-century. The Greek emperor Manual II (1391-1425) did try to turn the divisions between the sons of Bajazet I to his own advantage: ironically, he himself helped the eventual victor, Mahomet II, who realistically made sure of his position in Anatolia before turning against his brothers Suleyman and Murad in Europe. Suleyman, like so many Frankish princes before him, enjoyed the pleasures of a small court and a native (Serbian) wife. Mahomet I reintroduced and stiffened the purest Islamic elements. The Ottomans could not rule in Europe alone, or by European means, even if their chief territories were there. After Mahomet I had reconstituted the unity of the empire, his son Murad II (1421-51) recreated it in the style and extent of his namesake. This was the sultan whom the Burgundian lord, Bertrandon de la Brocquière, saw in 1432 at Edirne and describes as 'a little short thick man with the physiognomy of a Tartar. He has a broad and brown face, high cheekbones, a round beard, a great and crooked nose, with little eyes; but they say he is kind, good, generous and willingly gives away lands and money.' La Brocquière himself admits that Murad had in fact 'met with such trifling resistance from Christendom that were he to employ all his power and wealth on this object, it would be easy for him to conquer great part of it.'[21] When he died in 1451, only the capital Constantinople remained to fall to his eager son Mahomet II.

(ix) The Crusade

Muslim pressure in the east was not disregarded by the Catholic powers of the west, but it is symptomatic that the princes of the Avignonese obedience were less successful in their military expedition to defeat the Ottomans in 1396 than the king of Castile was in his diplomatic embassy to Cairo, begging for the release of the imprisoned Lusignan king of Armenia Leo V.[22] The fact is that the West could never command military resources equal to those of the Ottomans.

In attempting to explain the ultimate Ottoman victory, what stands out is the Ottoman control of both landmasses, Anatolia and the Balkans, and the steady parallel expansion into the interiors of both. It is difficult to see how any Christian power could have rivalled this. Admittedly the Anatolian Turks were as weak and divided as the Christians in the Balkans, and a successful onslaught in Asia Minor did in fact secure Christian control of Smyrna (Izmir) for many years after 1345, but the Christians could not be parted from their ships. Catholics were characteristically uneasy so far away from their real friends and they clung to the shore and their escape routes. This also meant that the loss of Anatolia to the Turks, which had followed the Greek defeat at Manzikert and had never been reversed, permanently weakened Constantinople. Whatever temporary advantages the Comneni emperors enjoyed in the twelfth century depended upon their determination to prevail at sea.[23] Once the Greeks lost this too, not to one sea power but to the many competing groups based in the west, they lost their only means of patrolling Asia Minor and confining their most blatant enemies. Real resistance to the Turks was left to the powers directly involved, like the Venetians and Hungarians, who had their own mutual hostilities to indulge for control of the Dalmatian coast. Such Catholics fought for tangible assets and moved cautiously to consolidate local interests; they were not much moved by the idea of a Christian cause, which alone might have smothered animosities within the camp.

Throughout the fourteenth century there was much talk of crusading. There were also several expeditions, even some successful ones, like the capture of Alexandria by King Peter of Cyprus in 1365. Several thoughtful writers considered how their own western societies could be reorganized to improve their crusading potential. In the early fourteenth century Ramon Lull campaigned with some success for the study of oriental languages and theology as part of the work of repulsing Islam, but the very idea of greater intellectual effort betrays a certain flagging of military confidence. The papacy, despite other obligations, creditably maintained the tradition of reminding Catholics of their Christian brethren overseas, down to Pius II who died at Ancona in 1464, vainly awaiting his crusaders. Catholic Christendom needed a secular leader capable of sustaining the effort required. After Louis IX's crusade of 1248-54, the king of France was the most favoured candidate for this role, but proposals to enhance his power and prestige for this purpose did not meet with universal approbation. Nor did the advice offered by eastern experts always command confidence in the king's council, as when it was suggested that Constantinople should be recaptured by the Latins first. The kingdom could not bear the strain put upon it, particularly once the king of England, from Edward III's time on, campaigned in France. This deprived eastern Christendom of its best chance of succour. It would be unfair to disparage these efforts to face up to responsibilities. The Greeks who could not reunite the orthodox world had no right to berate the west for its divisions.

Modern writers who regard the failure of the west to reanimate the crusade as proof of the decline of religious enthusiasm miss the real significance. More enthusiastic and successful military expeditions could not have made Catholic government any more popular or acceptable in the east, while the inability of the west to raise an effective army demonstrated not the decline of the religion but the collapse of the idea of military might as a basis for power. Western religious interest in the east had from the first concentrated on Jerusalem and the Holy Places; even over the twelfth century the Latins developed no recognition of the value of the eastern empire as such. Repulsed from the Holy Land, they disciplined their disappointment as well as they could, without reconsidering their new position in the front-line of opposition to the Muslims.

Later, the Emperor Manuel II could not persuade even the Venetians to assume direct responsibility for the defence of Constantinople. Christians further west might be more susceptible to rash enthusiasm for a holy war, but they were more ignorant, less exposed to danger and far more fickle; anyway mere enthusiasm was not enough.

Western Europeans had no need of land in the east to colonize, only of certain products obtained from their island colonies or by trade. Their populations were not large or rich enough to provide and support standing armies and they had no means of managing them or any concept of what to do with them. The fitting out of ships was expensive enough but was justified as remunerative investment. When the colonies were cut off, the Latins, scarcely dismayed, made alternative arrangements. These vivacious seafarers gave scant attention to the conditions of their own survival in the Levant or how, for want of force, they could have used more guile to keep the Muslims of Anatolia divided. Above all, they would not accept a real Christian leader to maintain the struggle with persistence. The need for a Western leader, or rather general, particularly impressed Fidentius of Padua who was entrusted by Pope Gregory X with plans for a new crusade at the Council of Lyon in 1274. His treatise, presented to Pope Nicholas IV in 1290-91, is found only in a fourteenth-century manuscript containing military treatises from Rome and Constantinople, a context which emphasizes the significance of Western disunity.[24] With the Ottoman empire established at Constantinople, the era of free maritime activity in the Mediterranean was over and the power of the political state reestablished. At this point therefore this survey of the Mediterranean is complete. It now remains to consider briefly how the continent of Latin Europe should be considered in this same period.

3. WESTERN EUROPE

The lack of western unity did not, as it turned out, make it an easy prey for the Ottoman conquerors of the east: the west enjoyed a different kind of strength. The collapse of the Greek empire certainly did nothing to stir the ambitions of any emperor of the west to revive claims to sovereignty. The west had completely lost all sense of empire as a form of government. The emperor's attributes were in fact assumed by the pope, who wielded a spiritual sovereignty. Whatever its imperfections this differed totally from the emperor's. The substance of imperial law was enforced all over Europe by sovereign princes of exiguous territories. The image of empire as burnished in Constantinople, which had once fascinated the west, had as little appeal in 1453 as the Greek reality. This was due to developments in the west more than to the misfortunes of the east.

The triumph of the Ottomans at Constantinople demonstrated that in

all Christian Europe there was no power able to organize a great territorial empire of the Roman type, as the Turks could. Instead of one great
universal empire, the boast of Europe became the many viable states
each quite capable only of mastering their own regions; they were not
only individually unequal to the burden of empire but collectively unwilling to unite their forces. The memory of Rome had mesmerized the
barbarian successor states for centuries, but none of them had ever
learned how to restore the empire. Though unequal to the task, these
barbarians devised no alternative political model, but reverted again and
again to the Roman example as the only one possible. It is only during
this period, and as part of the process alluded to already, that an entirely
new kind of political community arose in the west.

(i) The Empire

The situation in the twelfth century still bore the marks of the collapse of
the Roman empire in the west in the fifth century and the barbarian
attempts to revive it. Each barbarian state started with the difficulty that
real political power could only be exercised in one region of the former
empire, but their natural ambitions to lord it over one another goaded
them to emulate the Romans, particularly because in Constantinople
they could measure the effectiveness of a political authority claiming
Roman origin. Their rivalries were to some extent made possible by the
fact that Constantinople protected them from Asia for centuries. When the
Roman defences were by-passed, barbarian states showed no general
capacity to oppose invaders. The Muslims entered Spain and rapidly
destroyed one of the barbarian kingdoms of the west; the Magyars were
only repelled by the Saxon emperors. The Vikings from the north brought
additional destruction, particularly on the few havens of peace in the
barbarian world — monasteries. But in due course the new barbarians
settled down to conquer or cultivate the land, just as earlier barbarian
marauders of the empire had done. Even these later assaults on their
kingdoms had not stimulated any real cooperation between western rulers.

By the eighth century, however, the Franks had attained to such preeminence in Gaul that they could not avoid responsibility for assuming
leadership of the opposition to both Muslims and Vikings. Regarded by
the clergy as their surest defence, the Frankish leaders were persuaded
to see themselves as reincarnations of the great Old Testament kings or
of Christian emperors like Constantine. Brought into Italy by popes who
needed protection from the Lombards, when the emperor at
Constantinople would no longer assist, the Franks were laden with the
burden of empire before they received the benefits. The revival of the
Roman empire in the west by the coronation of Charlemagne (800)
shows both the power of the clerical imagination and its traditional

content. The barbarian king no doubt lent himself willingly to their grandiose projects. Yet neither the clergy nor the emperors then or later can ever have had a clear conception of what the Roman empire had been or what was needed for the empire's restoration, even if the idea of the Roman empire, as a universal government in the west, maintained its fascination for centuries. A nominal empire existed for more than a thousand years (it was only suppressed when Napoleon created his own version of European unity) and therefore played an important part in shaping expectations of government, however different it turned out to be from the Roman empire itself, in both time and space.

All the same, emperors encouraged the learned (that is the clergy) to collaborate in reconstructing the empire from their knowledge of letters. Emperors with more or less personal enthusiasm tried to turn their peoples into Romans with the naivety (but not the determination) of Peter the Great transforming his boyars. During the first and Carolingian phase, the Vikings played havoc with the clergy, so it was not until the Saxon emperors revived the scheme that continuous progress was achieved. The territorial basis of the empire had by that time, however, shrunk considerably: the western Franks never acknowledged the suzerainty of the 'German' emperor. All the same, he was ruler of the largest 'state' in the west, including many different peoples, requiring at least three royal crowns, and steadily expanding towards eastern Europe, where the tenth-century emperors earned their reputation as new Romans by defeating the Magyars and persuading their eastern neighbours to settle down within the Christian context. Hopefully too they turned to extend their rule in Italy until on both fronts the German emperors should meet the real emperor of Constantinople. The German empire of these years has still not received its due from historians, except in Germany, and promotion of its reputation there may have hindered its recognition elsewhere. The Roman past and the immediate future of the empire after the investiture controversy (1122) combine to make the imperial efforts look puny and inadequate. Yet the German emperors showed far more imperial sense than the much-studied Carolingians, repudiating the tradition of division amongst sons to keep their territory together, pursuing intelligent policies from one generation to another and consistently integrating the educated (through the bishops) into their administration. They certainly looked back to Charlemagne and east to Constantinople for guidance in their task, but the German empire was no eclectic imitation. Its building and painting (tell-tale signs) indicate that it drew upon Rome for inspiration with a serious sense of purpose and a clear grasp of essentials.

The empire was almost universally acknowledged in the west, leaving aside only the kingdoms of Spain, 'France' and the British Isles. How was such a state envisaged by contemporaries? For Rome, law and citizenship had been basic concepts. In this empire a man's law was personal and his day-to-day affairs were regulated by traditional customs, with which imperial interests were rarely concerned. The emperor concentrated on the larger issues. His duty to defend his people meant above all fighting the pagans, like the Magyars and extending his rule amongst them. The German emperors sought to extend their sway in the east against the Slavs and in southern Italy against the Muslims. Under his sway, the only common 'citizenship' was given by baptism. As Christian emperor, his main policy was to carry out the religious and moral duty imposed on him by God to help forward the divine plan.

The unlettered emperors in the west had to listen more attentively than the emperors in the east to those who claimed to know what the divine plan involved. The bishops exercised the chief local responsibility as the imperial representative, a role for which both their education and the empire's sense of purpose predestined them. So much the legislation of fourth-century Christian emperors had required of them; in practice, as in fifth-century Gaul, they had been obliged to go even further. Once the empire tried to function again, as under the Ottomans, the bishops found themselves saddled with public burdens. In the fourth century some of the most idealistic and conscientious aristocrats had become Christian bishops; in the eleventh-century empire, the emperors inspired or demanded a similar service of their own family and those of their great aristocrats. In the key cities of the Rhineland, of the Alps and of northern Italy, which formed the core of the empire, a succession of able and devoted clerical servants began to make the idea of empire serve barbarian Christian society. In this context it is understandable that the emperors could not allow the bishop of Rome himself to remain aloof from this Roman revival.

(ii) Rome

Rome was on the periphery of imperial territory and the emperor rarely resided there for long, if at all; in his absence the greater Roman families managed the affairs of the city and its bishop on their own account. The best the emperor could do was to install loyal German bishops at Rome to counteract local influence and to use the authority of the Roman See to advance the reform of the Christian world. One of these German bishops, who became Pope Leo IX, in a short but remarkable pontificate (1049-54) shook off the local incubus and carried the assertion of Roman universality to councils in France and Germany. Rome itself and the pope thereafter claimed a share in the affairs of the new empire. But Christian respect for the pope extended far beyond the frontiers of the German empire; moreover the traditions of the Roman See accorded western emperors scant importance; in Rome it was believed (erroneously) that Constantine had abandoned Rome to the pope when he left for Constantinople, a belief that prevailed as long as Constantinople remained Christian. In Rome, the emperor could seem most honourable when unobtrusive and at arm's length, to be summoned when required.

Only for a brief period did the German empire and the reformed papacy live in harmony. It was inevitable that those who drew upon such different traditions of the Roman past should dispute so acrimoniously about their roles. Compromise and cooperation were possible, had both sides not believed so implicitly in their own rightness and in their own mission. Within a generation the west was exposed to a controversy between the emperors and the popes which proved decisive for its subsequent history (1075-1122) the so-called investiture controversy. German emperors fought obstinately, even nobly, for what seemed plain good sense — the traditional authority of the emperor which Christ himself had accepted by his birth and death. In modern terms they fought for the state and the power of the big battalions. It seemed as obvious then as it often seems now. The popes fought with resilience for what they called the spiritual power — the right to criticise the way power was exercised by appeal to the moral law. They relied on their ability to frighten men with their future in the next world, they invoked ancient learning no less impressive for being, sometimes, spurious, and they muddled their enemies by verbal arguments that left men of strength stammering like fools. In fact a conflict of this kind did not remain upon an elevated plane of controversy. All the actors put into it more or less of their personal, self-interested concerns. Yet the conflict so rapidly transcended the original parties and continued over so many years, that it is not misleading to focus attention on the abstract question. In real terms men had to choose between whether they would work for the restoration of the Roman empire as inaugurated by the Germans, with all the traditional respect for Rome, or whether they would create a new Roman order directed by the pope, dedicated to the furtherance of the spiritual goals of Christians, hitherto never realized — a hope, but a risk.

The conflict did not continue: as men must live they had to compromise, but at the Concordat of Worms (1122) the moral victory lay with the papacy, which steadily improved its position at the empire's expense. Its detractors would say that the victory of the papacy was hardly a vindication of the spiritual power. Contemporaries were slow to see this, because for them the term 'spiritual' had not then acquired its unworldly meaning. The defeat of the empire was much more obvious. It had been obliged to give up its unique position of strength, to acknowledge the existence of another Roman tradition and in practice to lose the undivided loyalty of the bishops. In retrospect the empire may seem to have deserved its fate. If the state's purpose is to further the divine plan, its direction will inevitably be taken out of secular hands. If it has only 'secular' purposes, what attitude should it adopt to spiritual societies in its midst, claiming divine inspiration? It can only tolerate them if it is prepared to abandon the familiar claims of states to total loyalty.

Till the twelfth century no human society had done this. All political communities had decided the religious practices of their members. There had been total cooperation between the servants of the gods and those of the state. In the twelfth century, the west embarked upon the most original adventure in history — the attempt to create a framework in which men could fulfil their public duty but at the same time pursue their spiritual goals, adopting a dual allegiance which had to be acceptable to both their civil and religious leaders. This is a hard thing to achieve and is never attained once and for all. It meant the greatest surrender by the state, which was not accustomed to making allowances for independent interests. It also came to require restraint by the spiritual power, in case arrogant demands totally discredited its reputation.

The history of the west is basically a history of these conflicts, which are its peculiar speciality. Its point of departure was this initial demonstration that the empire was not to be the kernel of the new Europe, as had seemed natural, not because of the inadequacy of its territorial basis, but because its basic appeal to the Roman past had been taken over by the papacy. The meaning of Rome in the west became 'spiritual'. The *idea* of Roman unity proved to be of more practical value to Europe than the attempt to bring back the practice of empire. The political consequence of this has been that the west remains to this day fragmented amongst many states. Every dominant power that might impose unity on unwilling Europe has been feared and opposed. Europe has been powerful in the world, but never, so far, as a unit. This makes it difficult to define the nature of its unity, particularly in modern times.

(iii) Papal Europe
In this period, however, the unity attained beneath the spiritual aegis of the Roman bishop provides such a definition. This Europe was Catholic or Latin; the clear distinction drawn between them and eastern Christians, like the Orthodox, has already been shown. The contrast was an important aspect of the creation of Catholic unity. The call from Constantinople for western help came at the time of the dispute between emperor and pope, and it was the pope who took up the cause of the eastern churches. He found in it not only the means of demonstrating his powers in the whole Latin church, particularly in the Gallic non-imperial part, but also a way of extricating the papacy from the impasse in Italy, which the conflict with the emperor had created. The first crusade

renewed that willing cooperation between the popes and the 'French' which had brought about the revival of the empire under Charlemagne, who became in legend the Great Crusader. The Muslims called the crusaders 'Franks'.

The expansion of these loyal Catholics overseas gave the papacy its first taste of more than western jurisdiction. The Catholic presence established in Eastern Europe (Poland and Hungary) and even further away extended the sway of Roman obedience beyond the limits of the old Roman world. The organization of the Scandinavian church by the (English) Cardinal Nicholas Breakspear (1152) brought parts of Europe unknown to the ancient Romans into the obedience of the Roman church. Recovery of old Roman lands in southern Italy was followed by the more gradual reconquest of Spain. In the fourteenth century there was a Franciscan archbishop at Peking. As the area of Catholic jurisdiction grew, the pope became an increasingly important figure in the Christian church as a whole, while the western emperor gained nothing from these extensions of Christendom.

To the east the Greeks, who were the principal supporters of a different tradition of church government, had either to submit to Catholic teaching on the Petrine primacy or accept non-Christian rulers; either way Catholic doctrine appeared to be the only independent Christian truth. Though 'Free' Christendom later shrank in size, as the Muslims recovered their strength, its catholicity remained unadulterated and, as a consequence, Christendom has appeared in the world at large mainly in its Latin forms. Christianity has therefore come to seem an exclusively European religion. This equation has recently had unfortunate connotations for Christianity, but for a long time it gave the west a significance and a purpose. From the twelfth century the Latins strove for the realization of the kingdom of heaven, giving up the idea that this world could be united under any earthly lord. The real work of advancing God's kingdom was left to the Christian clergy, whom the kings protected in their several dominions, but the clergy belonged in spirit to one great ecclesiastical ministry with an elected autocrat, the vicar of St Peter, who sat in the seat of the apostles Peter and Paul, Christ's own vicar — the pope.

Chiefly by this means, the papacy had become by the end of the twelfth century responsible for directing the affairs of Christendom as a spiritual whole. Because of his place at the head of the clerical hierarchy, the pope could use the clergy everywhere to advance his policies. For many priests, clerical privilege came to matter too much, but on balance there is no doubt that once secure from secular oppression, the clergy under the pope set out to implement the second stage of their reform programme: the total conversion of the lay-world to Christ.

Human nature is neither perfectible nor uniform and the millennium did not arrive, despite some remarkable achievements in the thirteenth century. The period after 1300 is often represented as a decline. The clerical society, however, continued to manage its own affairs, under ever closer papal scrutiny, while at the same time fostering more intense lay piety. In due course laymen became critical enough of the clergy to bring down the clerical society—at the Reformation. The creation and continuance of the papal monarchy of Europe is however the dominant characteristic of Western European history for about four centuries. Some ambiguity may be involved in describing this monarchy as spiritual, but no deception is intended. Clearly, whatever its material assets, the papacy never exercised universal political power in the generally recognized sense (though it had its own estates, like other churches of the day). Its authority was religious and moral and generally commanded respect: in this sense its government was spiritual.

No comparable institution is known. The unity of the west under this direction did not bring about the elimination of other differences. It was a visible unity sustained by the educated persons of the church—the clergy, who used one language (Latin) and were formed by one system of education. Their formation gave them an *esprit de corps* and distinguished them from the others, who were expected to listen and obey. Even after the Reformation destroyed the formal aspect of clerical unity, Europe continued to be held together as a learned community—the importance of being educated, being *literate* as a qualification for entering the European elite, has never been lost. And it is from the privileged ranks of the literate that must come most of the records on which all history is based. Understanding them aright is the next part of our task, and for the middle ages this means assessing the place of education in a predominantly unlettered society: the survey of the field of study is complete.

2

SETTING THE HISTORICAL RECORDS IN THEIR CONTEXT

The survey of four centuries of European history presented in the previous chapter was designed to suit modern tastes and needs to see events in perspective. No person living at the time could have seen events in such a way and contemporary patterns of thought would have encouraged quite a different approach to history. It is indeed unlikely that persons then living would even recognize their own times from the account set out above. How legitimate is it to take evidence from contemporary witnesses and serve it up in this modern style? Aren't modern historians too inclined to imitate the King of Brobdingnag? He listened politely, even scrupulously, to the puny Gulliver, with his enthusiastic drivel about what he knew best; then he propounded 'many doubts, queries and objections upon every article' and used the same evidence to put Gulliver's country in a quite different, and disreputable, light. The modern investigator, faithful to the rationalist tradition of scholarship, arrogantly and rudely demands answers to predictable questions about religion, population, kinship patterns and political outlook, forcing witnesses with quite different stories to tell into bewildered confessions. The purpose of this chapter is to break away from this tradition of culling answers to our questions and listen to what the witnesses from this past themselves wanted to say. What is the story of their records? Can the evidence itself give us some insight into their manner of thinking? Can we go on to use it in some modern manner, useful to ourselves but without captious intention of turning their testimony against them? Could we, to take one example, learn to enjoy medieval tales of lecherous priests as jokes against 'father-figures' or foolish husbands, instead of twisting them into evidence of anti-clericalism and ecclesiastical corruption, as humourless reformers, and historians, have been doing for centuries?[1]

Most of the evidence about the past that can be used for historical purposes comes in writing. The interpretation of it for this period is made more difficult by the fact that medieval Europe was predominantly composed of illiterate people, and more significantly still, that even the most powerful secular leaders in it had no need to be literate and often were not. In modern times, this would be a reproach; the problem for us is to imagine how a society could once accept leadership of such a kind. Moreover, it puts learning itself into a light, that is strange for us.

Educated men then performed important services for their contemporaries, but they were neither leaders nor heroes. Historians are prone to forget this, because they are themselves so dependent on writers for their evidence about the past. Inevitably history books overemphasize academic, administrative, legal and controversial issues, the concerns of the narrow group of educated persons, at the expense of those matters in which the majority were actually interested. At the beginning therefore some attempt must be made to see this written material against its proper background of an illiterate society and assess how that society could function more than adequately with only minimal use of writing. This has to be done, paradoxically, by drawing on written evidence, but the writers have made it quite plain how their world was. Chaucer himself tells us that though he took such delight in books that no game could induce him to leave them, yet in summer he too gave them up:

> *Whan that the month of May*
> *Is come and that I heare the foules synge*
> *And that the floures gynnen for to sprynge*
> *Farewell my book and my devocioun.*

(Prologue to the Legend of Good Women).

What did Chaucer do when he did not read or write? This is the question we must consider for the great majority all the year round. What was life like for those who had no interest in books at all?

1. TRADITIONAL SOCIETY

Barbarian society had for centuries before the conversion to Christianity done without writing, and, after it, the clergy vainly attempted to make books seem important. They laboured to provide the barbarian languages with alphabets, and translated religious works into these vernaculars for the benefit of laymen. They took a surprising interest in the pagan stories and poetry of the barbarians, and wrote some of it down, if only in modified forms. Such works read to the young Alfred stimulated him to learn his letters. This was no easy matter. Charlemagne was an accomplished linguist who spoke Latin as fluently as his native German and understood Greek; he never mastered the art of writing, though he kept 'writing tablets and note books under the pillows on his bed so that he could try his hand at forming letters during his leisure moments'.[2] Charlemagne himself, the commanding figure of Europe in his day, wrote nothing. Historians are dependent on his clerks for their knowledge of his thoughts and actions. In his day, barbarian society still saw no need for its leaders to have a formal education in reading and writing, not even in the vernacular. Such schooling was fit only for the clergy. This means that all the basic skills of barbarian society—agriculture, instrument-making and warfare—could be transmitted without the intermediary of books.

Most barbarians were raised in small communities and few of them ever strayed far from their villages. They learned to speak from their kin and neighbours, and beyond the limits of their spoken dialect they would feel themselves to be amongst foreigners. Within the community they expected to find all the essentials for life and play. Trade with other districts, though never negligible, could not be relied upon for basic necessities of food, clothing and tools, and these therefore had to be produced in the community. Its well-being depended upon the division of labour and cooperation. Every village contained diverse elements: a priest, a smith, a charcoal burner, ploughmen, foresters, pigmen, cow-herds, spinners, weavers—so many talents according to the exploitable resources of the local environment. Occasionally craftsmen, like smiths, might wander about in search of employment, but in general villages must have expected to function by finding the skills required within themselves. Probably occupations ran in certain families. Those that prospered might think of sending a son to train for the priesthood; those that did badly might oblige sons to take humbler occupations. It is unlikely that individuals had much choice and there was no need of formal learning to acquire the skills required.

Men must then have accepted the differences of work and consequent status as facts of nature, and did not therefore consider them to be improvable. Seeing no possibility of arranging things otherwise, they took inequality in their stride, particularly because the community, as a small working unit, had no reason to prize social equality: its prosperity depended upon cooperation between the most diverse occupations. It was something of a matter of chance if a man became a ploughman; it required no greater natural ability than keeping pigs. To this extent social differences in rural communities were always arbitrary. Moralists called attention to the changes of fortune that could make a noble into a slave by the whims of war. To judge from the oldest surviving evidence, the barbarian laws, there were only two main social categories in barbarian society: the slaves who had no legal rights and the freemen who did.

Within the category of freemen several social groups were distinguished and this had a direct bearing upon their variable military obligations. It may be that the differences had originally grown out of military rank, for they were expressed in terms of blood-money paid for their deaths, presumably according to their respective military values. Differences of social degree continued into the thirteenth century and beyond, to determine the liabilities of freemen to furnish arms in proportion to their resources: men who could afford the most elaborate weapons and armour and horses belonged to the best society. Differences of military equipment did not divide a society so much as enable it to provide better for general defence. While they make men self-conscious as to rank, they also promote solidarity and cooperation between soldiers, particularly in the face of the enemy. So, as men cooperated to win a livelihood from their environment, they also naturally undertook to defend it in person against outside enemies, raiders, thieves, even government officials, when there were any. Though the women worked with the men there was not much scope for feminine refinements; it was a masculine world in the sense that masculine values prevailed in it, because of the military situation.

All freemen had the duty or right to bear arms in their own defence or on behalf of their family or property. There was no state to give them protection. Lords, who were left to organize the military defence of the locality, were certainly not expected to defend each man's own homestead. As long as this attitude persisted, men earned respect from their fellows chiefly and in the last resort only by their ability to defend themselves. A man of worth knew how to fight with the weapons of war and did not hesitate to use them. If a man intended to retain the respect of his peers, or even to keep his own self-respect, he was obliged to consider fighting to the death any insult regarded as a slur on his virility or integrity. These societies living constantly in expectation of attacks on life and property were in one important sense individualistic, since every man had to be prepared to fight for himself and prove his worth and right to be respected. In this situation society as a whole was committed to upholding the values of martial prowess. Men sought as allies those able to help them in fighting. They valued the personal commitment of one man to another and devised ceremonies of blood-brotherhood to create bonds as strong as those of kinship.[3] More commonly, men found protectors or lords and entered into pledges of mutual loyalty.

Violence was endemic in barbarian society and only tamed with difficulty. The early laws show that the payment of blood-money was already used to discourage the vendetta, but it took a long time for it to disappear from the greater part of Christendom. Public authorities did not begin to enforce other means for detecting and punishing murders until the twelfth century. It was natural that in the meantime and for long afterwards men accepted the need for self-defence and that free-men expected to carry weapons for this purpose.

All social ranks were equally pugnacious — townsmen no less than nobles; in Italy they fought out their local disputes with enthusiasm as long as citizen armies lasted. The violence of the non-noble population is less frequently remembered than that of their social betters. Law-reports nevertheless reveal that individuals could be cruel, and commit unprovoked and spontaneous crimes in their personal quarrels. In one of the best documented of all medieval murders, the victim had intervened in a quarrel to help the provoked party, but was immediately attacked and mortally wounded.[4] No virtue attached to peaceable behaviour or meekness in the face of authority. The history of the period is strewn with examples of horrible excesses. The brutal massacre in Jerusalem when it was captured by the crusaders in 1099 is famous. Blood-thirstiness persisted. It has even been said that thirteenth-century picture books exhibit a crude pleasure in slaughter.[5] Loyalty and cooperation were reserved for the familiar members of the local community: to the outside world it was natural to show ferocity.

Social Values in a Man's World

The notion of personal worth and the need to defend it, if called upon, by using violent means, lost hardly any of its force throughout these centuries. It was not only totally alien to the civil conceptions of the ancient world but equally repugnant to Christianity itself. The medieval clergy could do little about it except to preach humility and piety. They did not approve of the freeman's basically pugnacious self-reliance, except when partisan zeal ran away with them. Nor could the existence of a military aristocracy help much to restrain human belligerence in the other ranks of society. If anything, high spirited noblemen tended to cultivate a tendency to become reckless in battle. Later on they continued to esteem brave cavalry charges in the face of cannon, though by that time much of their own natural savagery had already been purged out of them. If they rushed into battle it was the effect of their own un-disciplined excitement at the chance to emulate their noble ancestors by showing indifference to personal danger. Great nobles of the fourteenth century, for all their refinements, perpetuated heroic traditions of a remote past. It was in these circumstances quite natural that Marshal Boucicault, a chivalrous hero, should excite wonder still in the late fourteenth century for his sheer personal strength.[6] Not all problems could be resolved by fighting. Intermittently men of religion were called on to arrange truces and negotiate peace, but men did not in general lose confidence in their strong right arms. The clergy themselves leave us in no doubt that the world outside the cloister was in chaos and prone to disorder.

The men of power in the world, the nobles, had to be more militant than the rest if they were to enjoy eminence in it, but to be noble involved more skills than fighting. Blood, or ancestry, obliged them to live up to the reputation of their ancestors and this meant being open-handed and cordial with their friends and dependents. For the most part even great men were constantly surrounded by their familiars, members of their households and kinsmen. Brought up in such company, they found friends and companions without searching far. In the French romance, the *Mort du Roi Arthur,* the great friends of the narrative were in fact cousins. Great men were regarded by others as members of distinguished families, rather than as individuals in their own right, and this must have had its effect on the way they thought about themselves and their obligations. They were rarely, if ever, alone, and cannot have sought or valued occasions for it. At home men had specially comfortable quarters for their own wives and women, but otherwise it was taken for granted that living and sleeping would be in proximity. In fourteenth-century Northumberland all the men without social distinction lay down and slept in the great hall, after dinner and music, in conditions not now paralleled even in army barracks. On pilgrimages the men of the company lived very close together with strangers, brought by their religious zeal into temporary fellowship, not expecting differences of treatment according to their wealth, all equally vulnerable to the hardships of the journeys, particularly at sea, and unable to take refuge in private rooms or quarters.[7] These conditions of physical sociability were only gradually changed. Not until the fifteenth century did even the townsmen of London and Florence begin to build houses with separate rooms for different people. By the sixteenth century Castiglione, the Italian courtier, can mock the old men who remembered that until they were twenty they had slept with their mothers and sisters without any impropriety.[8] People in those days simply did not know what it was to be alone.

If these conditions prevailed physically, it is difficult to believe that it was without effect on their emotions. It would have been pointless for men to restrain their impulses in public in order to give vent to them in private: they could have had no expectation of finding private moments, except in prayer. Their friends were the companions of everyday, not intimate sharers in their griefs and joys. Emotional reactions were more spontaneous, because there was never a better occasion than the present to show them.

Great men, far from enjoying the privilege of more privacy, were in fact least able to escape the obligations of their rank. Lordship had originally been a matter of finding a personal protector, but this had so much changed that by the twelfth century a man was likely to inherit his lord from his father or with his land. The commitment between lord and vassal continued to be made, as before, in person and defended by the personal loyalty of both sides, but it was not a 'personal' matter in the modern sense at all. A man could not refuse to do homage, or deny its implications. He was obliged to assume the burdens of his estate to lord and tenant alike, and though carried out by virtue of his own sense of loyalty, his acts were more those of duty than of choice. There is no reason to suppose that much emotional capital was invested in these social formalities. On the other hand, in such a context of personal commitment acquired by force of circumstances, there was no room for 'personal' inclinations at all. Indeed it may be proper to conclude that the distinction between public and private character then had no meaning. In fighting the same openness and sense of duty were found. The noble man proved himself by his personal courage, meeting enemies in battle, and challenging his friends in tournaments. Enemies met with invincible determination rarely if ever took personal action to provoke hostitilities. The Muslims in the *Chanson de Roland* are fought as enemies of the faith; in the heroic sagas an inherited vendetta or a complicated feud lies behind the resort to violence. Men had no right to refuse their destiny and the obligations they incurred. When honour was satisfied, compensation could be arranged amicably, marriage alliances entered into, enemies received as guests. There were no schools to inculcate historical lessons about national enemies from one generation to another, and, when the immediate fighting was over, there were no personal grudges against victors or conquerors.

The noble man was lavish not only with his money, but with his whole person and property, holding nothing back. He was expected to be hospitable to his friends, guests and dependents. There is no need to suppose that he condescended to the vulgar if he enjoyed bear-baiting, acrobats and vulgar jests along with the rest of the company. There was no snobbery about pleasure. Likewise he was expected to be open with his feelings of affection or hatred, not to cultivate stoic composure or aristocratic aloofness.

Modern critics are often disconcerted by certain features of this masculine society which are now thought very unmanly. Twelfth-century monks, for example, wrote in terms of effusive affection to one another, sometimes to men they had never met.[9] The account of the affection between Abbot Ailred of Rievaulx and his monks likewise suggests an unexpected kind of monastic community.[10] The sentiments of the letters have been explained away as literary conventions, and monastic friendship as a thin disguise for sexual sublimation. They seem rather to express an entirely different conception of human relationships, in which genuine affection between men was positively encouraged, rather than barely permitted. The heroes of the *gesta* embraced *bouche sur bouche.* Henry II greeted his trusted barons with a kiss and Becket dreaded the import of his specific exclusion from Henry's embrace.[11] These signs of friendship persisted for centuries and still have not entirely disappeared everywhere. To take an example from the fifteenth century, when deference to women had already begun to change men's views of what was seemly; the great quarrel between the dukes of Burgundy and Orleans was appeased (briefly) by elaborate ceremonies of friendship—riding together on the same horse, mutual offering of delicate morsels at a formal banquet and sleeping together in the same bed.[12] These were not residual rituals; they were the actual modes of conduct between friends. Shakespeare himself took it for granted that a few years later, at Agincourt, the wounded York should embrace the dying Suffolk with extravagant tenderness. In a society where men were always together, their strongest feelings were shown to one another.

This was not a matter of chivalry or nobility. In unrefined circles too, men were less inhibited than they are now expected to be. The *Manière de Langage* is a conversational manual in French written for English students of the late fourteenth century. The author provides dialogue for commonplace occasions. Two students go up to bed in their lodgings and settle down together with good humour:

> 'Move over there. You are so cold I can't bear you to touch me.'
> 'Let's get some sleep for God's sake. I need it. I've not slept a wink these past two nights.'
> 'The devil. You are warm enough now you are sweating so much... Bill, you have a fine smooth body. Would to God I was as smooth and nice (nette) as you are.'
> 'See here, Pete, don't touch me, I beg you, for I'm so ticklish.'
> 'Well then, Bill, I will give you a good tickle.'
> 'For God's sake, man, cut it out. It's time we got some sleep.'[13]

No modern manual could assume a similar degree of friendly foolery without arousing suspicious comment. Churchmen never tried to discourage the display of affection or associate it, as we do, with 'perversion'. Not that sexual perversion was unknown, though evidence for its incidence is in the nature of the case difficult to come by. It has been alleged, for example, that the poems of Villon indicate that it was a common practice in the criminal underworld he frequented,[14] which is not unlikely, but certainly no guide to what was acceptable in the rest of society. But there, it is important to realise that the show of friendship did not then excite unfavourable comment as implying something else. It was part of the way men behaved in their own very aggressive and masculine world.

Their interest in showy clothes was of a similar nature. Not for them the disciplined preference for unobtrusive uniforms. They revelled in gaudy and elaborate dress, as most soldiers did until the middle of the nineteenth century. Monastic writers of the twelfth century who chose the sober black or white habits of their orders disapproved (or envied) the taste of soldiers in the world for silly fashions, elaborate clothing and long hair. St Bernard himself tried to persuade them that their clothes actually hindered their military effectiveness, by impeding their movement, and that their long hair impeded their ability to keep a look out.[15] Those who indulged these tastes were compared to Sodomites, which was intended to be a generalized allusion to the city of vice, not to sexual perversion in particular.[16] Laymen remained impervious to these criticisms. In the fourteenth century the fashion changed. Instead of long flowing skirts, men wore skin-tight garments on the lower half of the body that emphasized their contours, while the upper part's basic form was concealed beneath exaggerated padding on the arms and shoulders. The monk of St Denis was so horrified by the suggestive character of these clothes, about 1346, that he said they looked like entertainers *(jugleurs)* and was not surprised that God had sent the king of England to punish the French at Crécy.[17] Clerical hostility to flashy clothes contrasts strongly with their indifference to the show of affection, but should not be written off as eccentric. By intention, the indulgence of vanity and extravagance was more reprehensible. The history of taste in clothing had been little explored; still less its psychology. The style of men's clothing in this period was of a piece with the behaviour expected of them by their contemporaries. They were not ashamed or frightened of giving themselves away. It was a man's world, but it was not tight-lipped or bowler-hatted.

The celebration of men's qualities, particularly the martial virtues of courage and cunning, was left originally to the poets of the *chansons de geste* and the heroic lays. Though the texts we have of these come from the Christian period, the basic story elements of some of them, as well as the genre, are far older. Whatever originally historical event lies behind them has been transformed into literature. The poets and the audiences valued them no less for that. These heroic poems were declaimed or chanted to the accompaniment of the harp on occasions of public feasting, to commemorate historical deeds of such public importance as the slaying of monsters, tribal enemies, or later, as in the *Chanson de Roland,* the enemies of Christendom. They must have stirred general enthusiasm as the heroes grappled with their doom and vindicated the struggle of heroic men against the forces of evil. The stories came from no books and the poets received no bookish education, though the versions we have betray the bookish education of the scribes. They came from the society of warriors who remembered the great deeds of the past and inspired themselves to emulate such heroes in the future. The stories were not mere diversionary entertainment; they were a source of psychological power in battle. At Hastings, William of Malmesbury reports that the *Chanson de Roland* was intoned before battle to inspire the knights with martial spirit.[18] While the battles raged, the drums and the warcries kept bravery at pitch: music served in war,[19] and the arts themselves were not necessarily peaceable.

The talents which counted in this society clearly had to be learned, but there is nothing to show that formal means were required for training men to perform their tasks, not even to fight; it was taken for granted that men would pick up what was needed from their kin or neighbours. Since freemen owed their status to their military arms, they must have been proud of their abilities and quite unashamed of their illiteracy. They probably had little respect for the clergy's values and still less for the clerical ability to read and sing, since professionally the clergy would not fight for themselves but relied on the protection of others. Whether a layman fought, traded or ploughed, he had nothing to learn about his profession from the clergy's books, and, not surprisingly, there is not much to be learned from the books about these occupations.

2. THE CLERGY AND THE USE OF WRITING

The western barbarians when converted to Christianity had no written culture of their own, though they had an oral literature transmitted from one generation to another, possibly by professional bards, as was certainly the case in ancient Ireland. After their conversion, barbarian societies subsidized literate persons, especially in monastic communities, where books were studied because of their importance to religion. The Bible and service books for the liturgy had to be understood and copied, and this obliged the clergy to learn the Latin language. To make the religious texts intelligible, they studied other Latin books; this rarely inspired a love of learning as such. Outside the monasteries Christian laymen still acquired no appreciation of reading and writing. They could participate adequately in liturgical services and without embarrassment, since gestures were still as important as words: only the clergy needed to understand the services in a literal sense.

If books in barbarian society began by being no more than indispensable for religious purposes, they acquired much greater consequence, as instruments of civilization, as soon as barbarian kings aspired to conduct their affairs in the Roman style. Kings in touch with the empire at Constantinople realized this very quickly. but it was not until the Frankish conquest of Lombardy (774) that appeal to the books became common, and the clergy, who alone knew the language of books, more

influential. The revival of the Roman empire in the west (800) encouraged this, for knowledge of the Roman past could only come from
books. Monks and bishops were expected by the Carolingian emperors
and their successors to provide a plausible justification for their empire.
They were reduced to drawing on the Augustan poets, like Virgil, or
St Augustine's *City of God,* for inspiration. Rulers had their own grasp
of the political realities of government, but their higher inspirations, in
politics as much as in religion, had henceforward to be found by learning.

The later Carolingian bishops, left to their own devices by the slump
of the empire, also learned from books how Ambrose and other great
bishops of the fourth and fifth centuries had borne the burdens of
government. An interest in historical bookish learning with a secular
purpose thus established its utility. The empire at Constantinople, which
became better known in the west from the tenth century, confirmed
western impressions that books and learning had an important part to
play in the process of being civilized and in the restoration of Roman
greatness. Then, from the late eleventh century, the learning of the
clergy was developed, especially to create a clerical society under the
bishop of Rome. Since this needed secular confirmation, they wrote
special laws, privileges and charters for themselves, and got rulers to seal
them. At first, rather self-consciously, the scribes justify this constant
recourse to writing because it was still unusual. Charters open with a
phrase to the effect that since human memory is liable to error and of
short duration, solemn grants of land, or privileges (nearly always to
churches) had been put in writing. What for contemporaries was an extra
precaution, a piece of evidence of intention rather than fact, has become
for us the sole historical proof. Given their character as records of events,
the charters were treasured by the clergy, for their evidence of rights
which might be challenged when all living witnesses were dead. They
were deeds of eternal validity. Monastic care of charters has since made
it possible for historians to collect them and to enlarge understanding of
the kings or others who granted them. Kings originally kept no records
of their own grants for office use. For want of anything better, historians
have to make these charters yield information about the processes of
government or law. The scribes had no inkling of this future use.

From about 1200 there is a very noticeable increase in the habit of
regular record keeping, not only by clergy but also by some secular
governments.[20] In England the limit of legal memory was fixed at the
time of Richard I's coronation, when it was literally within human
memory, and thus typical of the contemporary system of dating. In due
course it would have been necessary to revise this date every generation.
However, the compilation of legal registers or rolls made this unnecessary. By the early years of Henry III's reign, English government officials

could refer to a body of legal, financial and administrative records that grew steadily more bulky. This gave them a much longer sense of continuously developing time than had ever been available before. The same process may be observed elsewhere.

Some popes had kept registers of their letters in the past, but only intermittently. The arrival of the new importance of system in Rome may be gauged from the survival of continuous official registers after 1198 when Innocent III became pope. The earliest systematic survey of papal sources of revenue — the *Liber Censuum* — was compiled *c.*1192; more orderly administration of the material aspects of papal responsibilities therefore began about the same time.[21] A little later comes a new sense of what was needed in church law. The popes had played a leading part in deciding the new law of the church since the late eleventh century, and disputes had been taken to Rome for decision from all parts of Christendom, yet it had been left to the practitioners of the law to note papal judgments and modify the rules of law accordingly. These collections of papal 'decretals' were not officially promulgated until 1234. This is an important moment not only for the church but for the history of government. By this time the church had established a model of what orderly administration did: 'Roman' government implied keeping records.

From the church it passed to others through the use of clerks and bishops in secular administrations. It is known that some French royal charters were preserved before the time of Philip Augustus, since they were lost in the king's luggage after the battle of Fréteval in 1191. However, until the reign of Louis IX (1226-70) the royal archives appear to have comprised only detached pieces of parchment, not enrolled copies of charters or letters. Then some sense of orderly record keeping did appear. The most remarkable of these are the great judicial registers, the *Olim*, which start after his return from the Crusade in 1254. The town governments of Italy, like Venice and Florence, also began to take better care of their administrative records. The kings of Aragon kept registers of their affairs from *c.*1300. The careful Pere III (1336-89) organized separate registers for distinct branches of business.

The consequences of record-keeping for making governments tidy, routine and conservative only gradually became obvious, but from the first the compilation of records for reference purposes created extensive employment for conscientious scribes and capable literate administrators, who had to be drawn from the ranks of the clergy. The increased use of writing in secular affairs automatically enabled them to improve their relative standing in society at large. Over the succeeding centuries, they were primarily responsible for making the use of writing and books more common and even necessary accomplishments for laymen too. In this sense they made all men of any pretension into clerks — what could be called the clericalization of society. In the twelfth century, literacy was still a minority, professional qualification; from then on it steadily became more common. The invention of mechanical means for multi-plying copies of the word in the fifteenth century met an existing demand. From Europe the assumption that all men of ambition and ability should be encouraged to read and write has spread to every other human culture. Illiteracy has become a reproach. It is now sometimes difficult to remember in Europe itself that languages were originally only spoken and most of them never written at all. If Europe at this time moved from a situation in which writing was for the most part only in Latin to one in which every spoken language might be written down, we are dealing with a society that is changing its fundamental attitude towards writing as such. The original professional writers, the clergy, were entirely responsible for this change.

The rapid growth in the use of writing during this period is itself an historical fact of the greatest significance, as will appear in the course of this work. For the historian it means also that no earlier period of the past is better documented. Written material is more bulky, more varied and more explicit than ever before. The danger, however, is that its real limitations may be overlooked and the historian over-estimate his own power to deal effectively with it. For the first time the historian advanc-ing through the past comes across such voluminous records, particularly of government and official business, in every European tongue that he could never hope to master it all or even take stock, let alone learn all the necessary languages. The bulk of it is however made up of admini-strative or legal records. Patient historians have reconstructed from them the machinery of governments and shown how they worked, but even in our own day history is not concerned only with the rigmarole of administrations, and at that time the bureaucrats interfered even less in most men's affairs. Moreover the official records themselves deliberately set out to create an impression of orderly serene and confident manage-ment. We have always to remember, in dealing with them, that by their nature they deflate the excitement of events. Bulky government dossiers may still impress the naive. Historians have to bear in mind the limited functions of government, let alone of writing, when assessing these laboriously composed records.

The talents required for keeping routine records at the time hardly encouraged clerks to become historians themselves, so that it is not sur-prising if their professional preference for orderly procedures made them casual about the exceptional events of interest to the historians. Mercifully, there are other more lively sources of information about the past. Can it be a coincidence that just when the education of clerks is being most improved to equip them for office jobs, the writing of histories and chronicles was more or less abandoned by them to the more traditionally educated monks or taken up by the barely educated literate townsmen?

Whatever their nature, the written material used by historians continued in this period to be compiled by observers, not by the principal actors in events. These actors used in their own writing offices clerks formed in church schools (it was cheaper that way), and took no interest in training their own, so that reports of their activities reach us only in forms of words originally designed for very unsecular purposes. In order to understand the rulers, we have first to study the education of their scribes. What had they been trained to notice and to do? Did their schooling sharpen their vision of important issues?

Schooling

Medieval education made no attempt to stimulate the development of every kind of human talent or interest: only a limited number of talents mattered there. Schooling is now so much taken for granted that we often miss its essential character of disciplining men for society's benefit, since even the modern concern for individual development is itself really only an expression of our society's insatiable appetite for innovation; it offers rewards to the exceptional individuals with valuable skills, not to the talent of everyone. Medieval education was likewise offered to only a few boys showing aptitude for careers where reading and writing had become indispensable. The cost was met from ecclesiastical revenues. The training was the equivalent in bookish terms to the apprenticeships served by craftsmen and had nothing to do with 'education' in the modern sense. Since all the books used were in Latin, the preliminary courses were devoted to laying a foundation of Latin grammar; once this was mastered, Latin opened the way to understanding all known book-learning.

Some criticism of the effects of Latin literary education upon Western Europe in recent centuries is well founded. Take as an illustration for this period a letter written by Conrad, bishop-elect of Hildesheim, to his cathedral church describing what he had seen in Italy during his journey south with the emperor Henry VI on the way to the conquest of his wife's inheritance in Sicily (Conrad was the imperial chancellor).[22] Any description of the peninsula is rare at this time; this letter was also written at a moment of exceptional historical interest, but Conrad is not himself concerned either with geography or with history in the making. His letter explains enthusiastically that he has at last seen with his own eyes what he had formerly only heard about at school. His first surprise in Italy was the insignificance of the Rubicon river which Julius Caesar crossed after so much hesitation. His next important comments are devoted to Sulmona, Ovid's birthplace, where he heard of some miraculous trees into which Phaeton's sisters had been metamorphosed after his death. Travelling down through Italy (bypassing Rome), Conrad stopped to admire and comment on the places associated with the classical writers and mythology, reserving his most extensive comments for Naples and the marvels there attributed to Virgil, philosopher and magician. He makes no more comment on the beauty of the landscape than the description of the slope of Mount Etna where Ceres left Proserpina as 'munitus et amoenus'. There is remarkably little allusion to Christian history. The longest is an aside on the apostle Paul's shipwreck at Capri (which he mistook for Mitylene), as a result of which the local inhabitants had been endowed with the miraculous power to kill poisonous animals by spitting at them.

Travellers' impressions of foreign lands are not numerous for this period, least of all for Italy, a land which attracted many visitors then and has since inspired an extensive travel literature. As a description of Italy, or as an account of Henry's journey, Conrad's letter is a disappointment. Yet it serves to show how the influential clergy's attitude to Italy was framed chiefly by the Latin literature of the schools. This admittedly inspired them to go and see the places there mentioned; once there, they were obviously most struck by the great buildings of the past they saw. It is also proper to notice that they invariably assumed that characters of literature, like Aeneas or Achilles, were historical persons associated with real places. Conrad hints at doubts about the stories he has been told, but the letter is written to strengthen the faith of the clergy of Hildesheim about the marvels in the books. Conrad has seen what sounded trivial or incredible *(frivola et incredibilia)* and his letter was intended to silence any of his readers who had doubts.

The letter from the bishop to his clergy concentrates on the intellectual interests of the educated persons of the day. At the time of its reception, the clergy certainly obtained news of public events and other interesting details by questioning the actual messenger, so the letters should not be read as meaning that the bishop or his clergy were indifferent to everyday realities. But their education did not prompt them to think that such occurences deserved to be written up. The letter indicates the utterly unhistorical outlook of educated persons. Without a sense of history, how could they have even been aware of their own historical situation?

This bookish education also had consequences for their attitude to the natural world around them. There is no reason to suppose that men were in general any less interested in the natural world than they ever have been; most of them lived in direct contact with the natural order and needed to follow the seasons and the stars more closely than urban life now encourages, allows or makes necessary. The unlettered pagan neighbours of the ancient Romans presumably possessed considerable practical knowledge of plants, animals and the seasons simply in order to carry on their activities, but their combined knowledge, had it been written down, could not have compared in quality with that of the Hellenistic world which survived in book form. Only snatches of this learning were preserved by the monks as guardians of ancient books. They had only limited use for it. Perhaps the most useful were the herbals, in which the learned could recognize the medicinal plants and see the use of cultivating them in the monastic garden.[23] Though much scorn has been devoted to the unwholesome concoctions prepared from medieval recipes, some of their herbal potions had medical value and the books encouraged the view that learning about the properties of some natural products had potential value for the health of mankind. The work of Dioscorides was adapted from its Mediterranean homeland and some plants were introduced from the south into northern monastic gardens. Such works were transmitted in the company of other works of supposed medicinal value and this included some recipes using animal products, though, in general, animals were not an important source of materials for potions and charms.

Admittedly the clergy did have books about animals, and these were so popular as to be made available in vernacular translation for laymen. Bestiaries contained descriptions of animals, mainly exotic, and often illustrated. This literary genre appeared in the late Roman world of Syria or Egypt at a time when the allegorical method had taken firm hold there, so that animals only interested educated persons because they exemplified certain virtues or indeed religious doctrines. The longest of all the *Physiologus* allegories is devoted to the panther, who symbolized Christ. The medieval beast-books were not written to record observed behaviour, or indeed out of interest in familiar animals at all. This did not in itself inhibit the clergy from taking realistic note of the few animals which might prove useful, but the probable effect of such books was to prevent them thinking rationally about the animal species.[24] The whole world and all the objects in it were considered to be so many pointers to the world of the spirit. Those who could read were expected to learn from the wisdom of the books how to interpret the mysterious signs of nature. There was no suspicion that Nature had laws of her own or that the species had any autonomous reason for their existence. Everything in the world was certainly there for man's benefit, and, if this was not always as clear as it might be, it was the duty of the learned to discover what it was.

There was some change in the twelfth century, when the clergy took up the new opportunities for travelling into formerly Muslim lands, like

Spain and Sicily, to discover books and teachers from whom there was much to learn. As the case of Conrad of Hildesheim shows, travelling itself was insufficient to have opened men's minds. Like the scholars, crusaders and merchants began to visit many strange lands, not only in Islam, but beyond it, and some practical knowledge of foreign lands found its way into books, but mere travel was not educative. The fate of geography was to become popular as a storehouse of fabulous stories; these did nothing to change the basic categories of men's thinking about the whole world. And if scholars learned little by travelling, they were as slow to learn from their Muslim teachers about 'science'. Translations into Latin from both Arabic and Greek texts made available the scientific corpus of the ancient world hitherto neglected in the west. By the mid-thirteenth century the process was complete, but scholarly acquisition hardly mounted an impulse to do research. One of the most original minds of the twelfth century was that of the scholar-traveller, Adelard of Bath, who wrote the *Quaestiones Naturales*.[25] In this work he attempted to use his learning in an original way, but it was not sufficient to change the general scientific outlook of his day. He tried to answer 76 scientific questions (such as why the ruminants lie down hindquarters first and rise forequarters first, why some animals see better at night and why the sea is salt) not by quoting earlier authorities but by reasoning from first principles. Though not perhaps a very fruitful method, it was unusual at the time. For the most part, however, clerical curiosity then and later was concerned with gathering more information, which was merely incorporated into an existing pattern of understanding. The only improvement was that Greek and Arab sources of information were better than the earlier Latin works.

When the works of Aristotle became available, particularly the physical works in the translations of Michael Scot in the early thirteenth century, they prompted a more intellectual curiosity.[26] The Dominican Albert the Great was certainly interested in natural science and made some advances in the subject. Roger Bacon showed an attractive enthusiasm for scientific knowledge and technology, and a typical Franciscan exuberance for futuristic inventions that did not commend him to many of his contemporaries. During the thirteenth century, the new texts of Aristotle brought many Latin scholars to a more inquiring and systematic approach to the natural world. New information was absorbed into elaborate encyclopaedias. Certain textbooks written in this period, like Sacro-Bosco (Holywood) on the Sphere *c.* 1230, or Grosseteste on Optics, remained in use for centuries. For somehow the impetus ran down. In the fourteenth century, apart from a continuous interest in Oxford and Paris in the physics of motion, there was much less scientific activity than a century earlier. This was mainly

because, having digested the novelties into its own educational programme, the scholastic world had not in fact changed its basic character.
Information was still sought in books and differences of opinion between authorities debated in logical terms. Some new observations of
the natural world were made, and some corrections to older books
proposed, but most scholars modestly preferred the weight of authority
to their personal opinion, and disapproved of Bacon's invective against
revered names. They did not think it any part of their duty to supersede
the best books of the past and on their assumptions it is difficult to
believe they could have found a better guide than Aristotle. So they
concentrated on expounding him. Scholastic learning turned on commentaries, not on innovations.

There were very few practical advantages brought by these studies
except perhaps in medicine and in the star-tables compiled by Muslim
astronomers which were made available from the late thirteenth century.[27] Understanding celestial phenomena continued to elude contemporaries because the chief authorities, Aristotle and Ptolemy, disagreed
and could not be reconciled. When such great men had demonstrated
the inadequacy of human intelligence to penetrate the heavenly mysteries, Christian scholars naturally concluded that such matters were
too difficult for them to resolve. What else could they do? Contemporary
interest in the stars came to rest upon elucidating the omens of the
conjunctions of births and leading events: even merchants calculated
the astrological advantages for business transactions.[28] The measure of
science was its potential in practice, a view no less often heard now than
believed then. Men had no rational grounds for believing that knowledge
of natural science had any potential for transforming the natural order.
They regarded science books as satisfying legitimate curiosity. The
stars turned in their courses and the wild beasts roamed unmolested —
what was the use of closer study than that?

Clerical education was in its own way excessively concerned with the
application of knowledge. It therefore cultivated those subjects that
could obviously serve their own bookish preoccupations. Whereas
there was no practical application for book learning about science,
books had value for understanding the things of the spirit and the life in
the church which attempted to live by spiritual standards. Bookish
authorities disagreed with one another, but not so radically as to discourage intellectual efforts to harmonize them. For this scholars needed
an intellectual tool to cut through the morass and therefore logic
became the basic subject matter of the university schools. Like Latin,
logic had very practical uses in the church's affairs. The most sophisticated higher learning of the clergy was their study of the church's
law, which justified the clergy's effective independence and defined the

limits of their power in the lay-world. Not surprisingly this attracted the most ambitious and successful clergy. Drawn though that law was from sources of diverse historical origin, the law excited no historical curiosity. Like logic it rather encouraged a positive desire to sort out tangles, establish rights, vanquish opponents and rely on authorities. This attitude was also extensively cultivated in theological questions.

The pagan origins of their intellectual disciplines provoked these clever men to do something more sophisticated than a mere declaration of Christian doctrine. They saw the value of expounding it in a way compatible with pagan learning and acceptable to every rational man. The number of dialogues composed to explain Christianity to philosophers, Jews or Saracens reflects a twelfth-century interest in exploring the possibilities open within monotheism and a genuine desire to pin down the specific superiority of Christianity over the others. Abelard's dialogue in this vein showed no weakness for reconciling different speakers by some philosophical subtlety; he proves how much Christianity could borrow from other systems and then advance additional insights of its own. This superiority lay in the assessment of the role of men in the created order, since God had become Man, a truth revealed in Christianity as nowhere else. By this means men had been redeemed and individual salvation had become possible. This was the key issue and involved a new probing of the nature of the soul, its understanding, its will and its association with the body and, at a more general level, the problem of the created order and its relation to the creator who was no part of it. On these issues turned the debates of the schools. The virtue of clear definition was brought from logic into theology, and both disciplines were developed in the twelfth century, particularly to resolve the internal inconsistencies of scripture and the contradictory opinions of the commentators. For a time in the thirteenth century a further stimulus to theology was provided by the discovery of ancient scientific writings that initially could not be squared with revelation. All the books were assumed to be somehow basically compatible, so the brightest minds of the day did their best to demonstrate this by drawing logical distinctions and by ingenious interpretation.

For two or three centuries universities played the major part in shaping the intellectual outlook of the educated, the clergy and the lawyers, and some appreciation of the nature of the studies pursued there is indispensable. How much high-minded intellectual subtlety filtered through to the students from the *cathedra* of the great doctors is dubious — on the analogy with modern philosophers, perhaps little more than the pretence of sophistication. A few devoted disciples learned much; for the rest, students picked up a learned vocabulary, a general sense of what the exercises were all about and a style of arguing. Some of the clergy at the universities went on to popularize this learning in sermons, or in 'encyclopaedias', so it was not esoteric learning for the universities alone. Modern scholarship has barely as yet assimilated the work of the greatest scholastic doctors and is still far from understanding how their teaching altered the general outlook. But it is safe to assert that this schooling, however ingenious, did nothing to diminish the emphasis upon verbal definitions and logical argument which were the hallmarks of university men. The active and aggressive clergy all came from the schools. The pugnacious attitude they took there over questions of rights and doctrines encouraged them to continue debates and arguments when they left the schools for the market place. They niggled in the law-courts and engaged in polemic from the pulpit, never doubting the power of words to say all. One of the best illustrations of how much their sharp, sceptical minds differed from those of the uneducated comes in the questions the university men put to Joan of Arc at her trial in Rouen in 1431.[29] How did she know it was St Michael who had appeared to her? How did she know he spoke the language of angels? How would she know, if the devil appeared to her in angel's form, that he was not a good angel? Does she know if saints Catherine and Margaret hate the English? Was God with the English when they were successful in France? Why does she have angels painted with arms, feet, legs and clothes? Did she kiss or embrace saints Catherine and Margaret? Did they smell good when she was embracing them? Did she feel any warmth? Did she embrace them in the lower or in the upper parts? The records clearly reveal the preoccupations of learned men in dealing with popular religious aberrations. This gap within fifteenth-century French society is certainly more significant and more certain than the alleged collaboration of the judges in framing a political trial in religious terms: such a theory only panders to the modern prejudice about the real primacy of politics. The arrogance of university men in dealing with Joan is bad enough. The superiority of modern critics who see in this only the hypocrisy of the judges shows that intellectual arrogance is no less common now than then.

The Writing of History

We are now in a somewhat better position to understand how educated persons approached the business of writing history or compiling historical records. It might seem a comparatively simple matter to record historical information for posterity. The clergy, however, had in fact very little interest in the instruction of future generations about their own times. Even today, we are not well placed to know either what the future will want to know about our present or what events of our present will 'then' look significant: our present will in fact look different at different future times.

Our writing of history and the present compilation of records to serve for that purpose presupposes a certain scheme of historical development — the belief that history can at least show how the present has taken shape, what 'forces' are at work in it, and even, within limits, what kind of future is being prepared. The passage of time seems like a conveyor belt on which events are already set out, the present arranged in a pattern determined by what is past and the future, just discernible, from what is now in view. In the twelfth century there was no need to project the passage of time in this way because the beginning of time, its course and its end were already known — by revelation. Within that scheme, it was not uninteresting to record outstanding 'events', but what was outstanding was clearly established by other means than are used now to select comparably important events. Moreover, these events had no need of explanation in terms of 'cause'; they could be described as though they were sudden eruptions on the geological scene. Any remarkable event, human or natural, attracted naive interest. It is from jejune records of such happenings — the chronicles — that historians derive some of their most basic knowledge of the period.

This attitude to historical events basically owed something to most men's upbringing in a society without books. Knowledge about the immediate past came from conversation with older contemporaries. Human memory was comparatively short; and it was unlikely to be more than anecdotal. Without records it is difficult to retain an exact memory of the sequence of events, let alone to understand relationships between them. Human memory alone gives men a very erratic sense of the past and a curious assessment of human wisdom. Rulers who heard about the deeds of their ancestors formed no coherent impression of their policies or of the reasons for successes and failures. At best human memory picked out exemplary, or humorous, incidents. A charter from Normandy records that Duke William, conferring land on one of his monasteries, pretended to jab the hand of the abbot with a knife, a playful gesture intended to make the occasion memorable for those who witnessed it.[30] Whether men acquired much wisdom from the memorable occasions they witnessed may be doubted. They only needed such information as would be useful when, for example, they were asked in a law-suit to say what had happened. Human memory was a storehouse of precedents, particularly useful in disputes of law, and occasionally called upon also to supply information about family ramifications and points of social etiquette.

Instructed men had, however, one model of historical writing devoted to a great theme: the Bible; this had important consequences for their historical outlook. It was a sacred text which explained by revelation what could not be known by other means: how the world began, the nature of the historical experience as God's intervention in time to redeem the human race, and how the world would end. The incidental historical information in it about ancient peoples and places also had its uses. The northern races, when they were belatedly introduced to it, drew on it to provide themselves with Biblical ancestors for their tribes or kings, and so to find a niche in sacred history: in those days too history had a small part to play in giving men a sense of how they fitted into the great scheme of things. By the twelfth century Biblical interpretation had a long tradition behind it, but it was theologians, not historians, who laid down the rules of interpretation. Hugh of St Victor advised students not to be too impatient with all the incidental historical matter in the Bible; only by first assimilating the literal sense of these histories could they lay the foundation of the more interesting and spiritual interpretations to come: the allegorical, the anagogical and the tropological.[31] The mere literal account of what happens was in the twelfth century only the first level of meaning, to be superseded, as soon as mastered.

It is not surprising if the subsequent development of scholastic theology had even more unfortunate consequences for historical writing. Aristotle himself had despised history as a discipline, since it was concerned with particulars, one thing happening after another without any other connexion than mere chance. He found even poetry more philosophical since it dealt with the generalities of human nature, and with only one action at a time. Scholastic historians were avid collectors of anecdotes and painstaking compilers of universal histories, but since they had no historical sense whatever, they allowed perhaps even more room than their monastic predecessors for the popular legends of the past. Confident of the scholastic approach to theology, they had certainly less understanding of the nature of the history of salvation than the monks who had imbibed their theology from the Bible. The scholastics broke the Bible up into chapters and verses, to facilitate quotation; though this greatly extended scholars' familiarity with the text of the Bible, fragmentation weakened their grasp of the nature of the scriptures. Their monastic predecessors with their placid commentaries upon whole Biblical books, Job, Ezechiel or the Song of Songs, had in this been the better scholars.

The consequences of the theological approach to history can be gauged from one of the most thoughtful writers of the twelfth century, Otto of Freising. His *World History,* like most medieval chronicles, begins with the Creation, because the purpose of chronicles for their readers was to survey the whole of human time. Otto, bolder than most, concluded his chronicle with the Day of Judgment, the course of which had been revealed in scripture, and which he thought could not be far off.[32] Modern historians have little use for this work. Most of it is derived from earlier authors; much of the account of his own times is devoted to the expansion of the monastic orders, as a fitting prelude to his last book on the last days. Otto of Freising was a bishop, uncle of the Emperor Frederick I, a scholar and a much travelled man. Instead of deploring what he has omitted to tell us of what we are interested in, we ought to appreciate in him one of the most profound historical thinkers of the twelfth century. In this work we see how contemporary events appeared to a reflective and educated person of the time. His purpose and his perception in writing history are different from ours. To use the information he gives, we must see what part it played in his whole work; his conception itself casts more light on the twelfth century than his mere information.

In his other historical book, *Gesta Friderici,* Otto frankly tells us that his purpose is to write a joyful history.[33] When writing therefore of the unsuccessful second crusade he deliberately chose only one episode to relate, which proved to his mind how favourably Providence always looked upon his nephew Frederick: many crusaders were drowned when heavy rains flooded the valley where they were camping, but Frederick, who had pitched his tent on the hillside, was saved. Otto does not pretend that the second crusade had been anything but a failure; he passed over disastrous episodes with the remark that they were well-known and recorded by others. Now his selection of historical material seems extremely arbitrary; Otto would have justified his procedure by appeal to theological, not historical, criteria. For him the Bible was the model— the most complete, and authoritative history book he knew. The historical events worthy of note in the present had to seem to him outstanding in the total context of human history from the creation to the end of time: he was not interested in the trivial—only in the significant.

The medieval chronicle remains one of the most important sources of medieval history down to the age of printing. It was intended to provide a complete view of significant happenings and it gave men a much vaster sense of human time than anything previously known. Their source books of the past enabled them to fit into their scheme of things all the known people of the world—the Jews, the Greeks, the Trojans and the Romans, and themselves. The past was for them heroic and glorious, the present a decline. They had no sanguine expectations for the future of the world. The writers who brought existing chronicles up to date by recording the events of their own times varied considerably in their assessment of what events deserved notice in this cosmic context. There was nothing incongruous about notices of natural disasters or local catastrophes, when there was no means of knowing for certain the proportions of comparable events elsewhere. The compilers of such chronicles probably also satisfied their own idle curiosity and indulged a certain gossipy interest in great events, from which as historians, clerical or lay, they were usually excluded. Only from the fourteenth century did a somewhat different genre appear. More in the nature of political memoirs, such works concentrated on personal experience, so the motive for writing them tended, as now, to be apologetic. However useful these may be as sources for modern histories, they were not 'histories' in the medieval sense.

Chronicle writing as such was never a very popular activity, and the number of surviving manuscripts does not encourage us to think that such works were widely read. A few popular histories sufficed to give such information about the past as the present cared to know. On the whole men were quite content to accept legends about the past rather than facts; they often still are. It did not matter to them that Charlemagne had not in fact gone to the Holy Land on crusade; he ought to have done and was generally believed to have done so. Since there was no general concern to ascertain the truth about the past, the materials for the study of this period were usually composed by men lacking the basically critical and sceptical approach, now normal. The lack of comparable information also meant that most persons were blithely unaware of the problems of biased reporting. They did not dubiously check their own annals against those written elsewhere, as modern scholars must. In any one centre the local version was trusted implicitly —there was no reason for scepticism. Clerical librarians would see no reason to stock many accounts of the same episode, and readers certainly imbibed the view that essential information about the past was simple, certain and not very interesting, until worked up by moralizing. And for their purpose they had no reason to doubt details of wonders, for example, however improbable in themselves.

Modern scholars using monastic chronicles are struck by their limitations. Consider first their selective presentation of the facts, of which a striking instance occurs in the Saxon history of Widukind, describing how the German king was acclaimed emperor by the soldiers on the field of battle in 955. He completely ignored Otto's papal coronation in Rome in 962 of which he can hardly have been ignorant.[34] Widukind made his choice of significant event and treated the empire as a Roman and military institution, not an ecclesiastical one: this worries modern scholars who find Widukind's attitude lacking in candour. His readers in Corvey are unlikely to have noticed his bias or distrusted his scholarship. They did not compare his text with other histories; they did not have them. Often historical works were copied out uncritically simply to equip a library with the best sources, and readers naturally preferred a single chronicle that began in the beginning and went on to the end; a universal historical encyclopaedia, even if the sections were copied from different sources. Over the years chronicles tended to get longer and fuller. The monk of Chester, Ranulf Higden, wrote a *Polychronicon*, which, with its continuation, takes up nine volumes of the modern printed edition.

The real interest of these historical compilations lay in the individual event which was thought to exemplify some other truth: to show a great act of God or some moral principle. If moral truth is the essence of the matter, however, literary heroes like Aeneas, Charlemagne and Arthur might be made even more effective examples simply because they were not trammelled by obscurantist, historical detail. Concern for the trivialities of their daily lives and social context, their styles of clothing, their speech, even their religion, was more likely to distract attention from the essentials than add anything of importance. Since for us such details are what most bring the past to life, we are constantly disconcerted by medieval indifference to them. There was no sense of what was 'anachronistic'. Thus Cola di Rienzo's idea of reviving the Roman tribuneship in the fourteenth century seems to us fanciful and utopian, yet it filled Petrarch (the scholar of the time most expert in Roman history) with the utmost enthusiasm. It was agreed that history had a slight edge over literature as a source of inspiration to great deeds and for this reason the heroes of literary epics and romances were presented as historical, rather than mythical; but the moral standards of both genres came from other 'sources, and not from any historical interpretation.

This point is worth further elaboration. The life of Cola di Rienzo was written by an anonymous Roman chronicler within a few years of the principal events described: Cola's political prominence in Rome for a brief period of seven months in 1347.[35] The course of his career could have become clearer to anyone writing a little later, like this chronicler, and generally sympathetic to Cola's cause and intentions, had he been possessed of what now passes for 'historical' sense. The author is an authority of considerable value; he writes as a contemporary, even as a witness; he seems to have presented the sequence of events correctly; he rarely allows his attention to wander from Cola himself. Such an episode in modern times would receive a great deal of intensive study and profound analysis of how the demagogue lost power. Attempts to explain the disaster would consider relevant factors, from Cola's unstable personality to the power basis of the political forces in and out of Rome. The chronicler makes no attempt whatever to understand the situation from the inside in this way. He does not speculate as to how Cola reacted to his difficulties or misjudged the situation. There is no sense of political engagement, of an inevitable course of events, or of the 'human drama'. If ever he tries to explain the events he describes, he does so simply in terms of the degeneration of Cola's idealism to the point where he became a 'tyrant'. The author assumes that this decline requires no other cause than the moral collapse of Cola himself.

The modern historian cannot dispense with this invaluable direct evidence, but he will probably feel somewhat uncomfortable about the chronicler's explanations. He may think he ought to suggest some more 'plausible' ones of his own. Such a course is, however, fraught with difficulties. What reasons are there for assuming that there was in fact some course of events to be analysed in modern political terms, which the simple chronicler missed? Is it right to suppose that there have always been realistic men of power ready to size up the situation in politics and do battle in modern style, whether they were observed to do so or not? On what grounds would we be justified in believing that the chronicler's 'moralistic' preoccupations made him blind to the real 'political' issues? So far as we know, the chronicler himself delivered the most considered opinion of the whole episode. He went to the trouble of selecting and recording information about the events, and a few years later tried to see them in perspective. He was an educated man, but since he wrote in the Roman dialect, not in Latin, he expresses Roman opinion, rather than that of the aloof clergy. As a man who bothered to write up these events at all, he must be accepted as altogether unusual for his interest in public affairs. He shared Cola's nostalgia for the great Roman past and his hopes for restoring it. Why should such a man have failed to notice the obvious, if it was staring him in the face? In his account the great Roman families and those of the Campagna hardly seemed worldly-wise. Their actions seem to be the unreflective response of great barons stamping their feet in bad temper, because Cola had originally caught them napping.

The chronicler's descriptions are of a piece with his explanations: they belong to a world with a different conception of 'political' society, behaviour and analysis. If he believed that the project for restoring Roman greatness had foundered on the reef of Cola's ambition, it had likewise been Cola's belief and his enemies' fear that inspired moral leadership was likely to be sufficient to revive the real authority of the Roman people throughout Christendom. Had men in the fourteenth century had any possibility of making cool 'political' calculations, they would have regarded Cola's hopes as absurd from the first. It is therefore because the chronicler focuses our attention on the moral issues that he exposes so clearly the nature of political thinking in the fourteenth century. Small-town personalities were convinced that idealism and the Roman *genius loci* would conquer the world as Roman armies had once done. Any modern attempt to dress up this episode as an important 'proto-revolutionary' movement would wrench it out of its context and distort its historical significance. The chronicler's own interpretation of the events should not be explained away: it lays bare an important truth about all his contemporaries.

For centuries men in general were brought up to conceive all public affairs in moral terms. This did not make all powerful men moral, but it hindered them from thinking that their actions might be 'justified' by 'history'. The moral rules were based upon scriptural revelation and on the abstract reasonings of the ancient philosophers. There were no lessons to be learned from the reading of history, not even practical good sense. History had some limited use, in particular to illustrate moral principles in action: it showed that virtue was rewarded and vice punished. Modern histories in fact often show the reverse to be true, so that medieval histories seem to us more like falsifications of the facts of life. It would, however, be wrong to suppose that medieval historians deliberately told lies. The true facts that mattered to them were the moral truths, not the confused record of events. The episodes that they selected for insertion into their histories were deliberately chosen because they seemed to offer clear proof of their general moral beliefs. What would be the point of remembering muddled and uninstructive episodes?

There could not be any question of recording everything and musing over its historical significance. History was conceived of not as a 'science', but as a branch of literature. And as today it is possible to accept moral standards from some outside source and use literature only to illustrate them, this was then the function of history too. This being so, how could the public figures themselves envisage their actions otherwise? Could they suppose they would in some way be 'vindicated' by history, or imagine themselves as performers in an historical situation? Could the actors have understood their own parts differently from the way their historical observers did? Chroniclers reporting historical events in moral terms are not just imposing some personal literary slant of their own; they reflect also the current educated conventions of their own day as to the proper judgment of public events. The framework of their general scheme of historical understanding was supplied from religion. In these circumstances, history could not acquire intellectual autonomy, and contemporaries did not understand how to leave behind them the kind of evidence which can be used to write it. Records kept to preserve a memory of the exemplary cannot provide materials for a complete picture of social life, any more than routine record-keeping can.

The moralistic outlook engendered by the clergy's own education was, admittedly, not spread uniformly everywhere, either in the clerical community or outside it. The most intransigent and advanced opinions canvassed in the universities, then as now, were obviously neither known to nor shared by other clerks, let alone by ignorant laymen. The question is not so much whether all men believed what learned men taught, but what other intellectual positions could even exist? When the opinions of the learned were rejected by others, it was not because of any appeal to a different set of argued beliefs or principles. William Rufus was a ruler unpopular with the clergy of his day, but he was too hostile to their basic approach to imitate them by arguing. He just did what he wanted. It is not easy to catch the echoes of lay reactions to the clergy and their views. However, for the thirteenth century there is the spirited account of his own life written by King James I of Aragon, which demonstrates both spontaneous piety and a headstrong determination to have his own way, even in religious matters. For example, he appears to be defending his own position from attack when he writes of a Saracen who aided him in the conquest of Majorca that 'I call him an angel, for though a Saracen, I have no doubt that God sent him to us; and he stood us in such good stead that under the circumstances we likened him to an angel'. Moreover it is clear that James did not see much to distinguish his prelates from his own barons; he represents them as no less greedy, warlike and foolish.[36] In general, however, it is probable that, except over those matters where laymen had particular reasons of their own to disagree, they believed the most learned men they knew, as is still the tendency today. Laymen were probably less curious than the clergy anyway. Book learning did not matter enough to them, except for what concerned their souls' weal.

On this issue the clergy were not only well instructed but intolerant, while laymen had no reason to doubt that the clergy offered them better religious instruction than they could have found anywhere else. Christianity gave them a new religious confidence in the destiny of men in the universe, in the benevolence of God and the dependence of the natural order upon its creator. The central teaching of Christianity affirmed that men were not inevitably alienated from God but had the means of access to him through the sacrifice of Christ and the ministry of the church. Christianity did not need to appease the malevolent spirits, because the real spiritual battle had already been won: the only problem was to bring all men to realize this truth. Hence the function of the educated, the clergy, was to disseminate the truth as widely as possible, not to preserve their own superiority by keeping others in ignorance.

As part of their work in this respect, the clergy brought the vernacular languages into regular use for devotional reasons, though the liturgy itself remained in Latin. Pious laymen valued these works and began to write their own. Facility in the use of writing encouraged them to use it more often for secular purposes too. Historians, who have by the fifteenth century a growing body of evidence about the way laymen thought, can cease to rely on the clergy alone for educated opinion. At the time too, the literacy of laymen no longer made the clergy indispensable for the transaction of laymen's literate business. They were happy to withdraw to their own religious affairs and leave the management of the world to others, whose experience of public affairs often makes their writings more useful to historians. The clergy themselves seem to recede from the stage, as though the world itself had become more secular.

Probably the reverse is nearer the truth. The vernacular works for and by laymen show that they had become more high-minded, pious and moralistic than their lay predecessors. From the fourteenth century some laymen had begun to assimilate clerical Latin learning. Dante is an early example of such an educated layman. If laymen ventured to criticise the clergy and the church, it was for devout, not secular, reasons. We know that earlier laymen had also been critical of the clergy, even when they did not leave explicit evidence of their dissatisfaction. Yet if the laity as a whole had become more pious as they became more literate, what explanation may be offered for the frequent abuse of the clergy found in their work? It is insufficient to listen to this new siren song and assume that anti-clericalism implies widespread disaffection with the clergy and a rejection of the church's teaching. The trouble rather was that naive laymen called for reforms and perfection without delay, bold with suggestions, like all idealists without power. Since laymen knew they had themselves no means of effecting changes, it cost them nothing, but the ill-will of some clerics, to denounce abuses.

The clergy as a whole were, however, irritated by this criticism. The church was better run by them than it had been in the days of the barbarian monarchies; their privileges were necessary to protect their autogestion. They knew that perfection was not possible and that criticism was often malicious. They also liked to ascribe it to heretical opinions since this made it easier to discount. So they tended to react with much exaggeration to criticism, and the disputes have therefore a certain unreality. There is no evidence of general discontent with the church's ministry or its intellectual supremacy. The clergy were still on the whole able to claim privilege and survive unscathed, and if it looks weak for them to fall back on privilege, they did so because it was the easiest way out of a tiresome situation. Contemporaries did not share modern impatience with this and call it prevarication. It was accepted that privileges and procedural formalities were the appropriate way to deal with awkward problems. It was the only civilized alternative to fighting: the clergy, who never fought, were inevitable 'offenders' in this way. There was nothing reprehensible about appeal to the letter of the law. The clergy owed their prominence to their success in winning privileges for their whole order and there was no good reason why these should be surrendered, since society was still led by men with less education, conscience, even competence in managerial affairs. No one wished to fight the old battles over again. This did not preclude continuous skirmishes in the no-man's land between clerical and secular jurisdictions, which were invariably debated with the fiercest and most virulent arguments.

The clergy, if they wrote of public affairs at all, always paid close attention to disputes touching their order and spent a disproportionate part of their energy on their grievances in such campaigns. Historians have to make allowances for the prejudices of the educated; it is still true today that the good causes of liberal sentiment get 'unrepresentative' reporting space in some newspapers. Their education also encouraged the clergy to despise lay opinion on the most erudite questions of the day, and like experts everywhere, when attacked, they took umbrage. They could never be entirely in sympathy with laymen or secular matters. This can be taken into account, once it is detected for what it is. In the final analysis, however, it must be remembered that the clergy, whatever their faults, were no more completely out of touch with their own times than the educated ever are. They belonged to no closed caste. Once celibacy was enforced, as it was from the twelfth century, they had to be recruited in lay families and were brought up initially in lay company; they were not, as monks had once been, offered as children to the church. In some respects they continued to provoke criticism because they continued to behave more like laymen than saints. They liked fine clothes, rich food and the company of women. Some of the most dedicated of them gave more and more attention to living in the world in order to improve the quality of laymen's religious lives and their educational attainments. The clergy were partial observers of the world, but they were not completely out of reach. The strongest proof of their influence was that they eventually succeeded in converting all men to the view that reading and writing were universally valuable accomplishments. When they had done this, they willingly gave up their earlier monopoly of these skills.

3. THE LAW AND THE LAWYERS

In barbarian society men had managed to settle their quarrels amongst themselves without the help of men learned in written laws. If there was pleading in the courts it was not done by experts but according to ritual formulae every freeman had to utter on his own behalf. The oaths he swore on the Christian Gospels were none the less taken in the aweful sight of God and he had to find others prepared to swear with him in the divine presence. If he could not find neighbours or friends to vouch for his trustworthiness and found himself alone, he might be put to the supreme test and have to vindicate himself in the ordeal — the appeal to God to demonstrate the truth of his testimony. In some parts of Europe men fought their personal accusers to prove their rights; elsewhere the ordeal lay in carrying a hot iron or submitting to the test of water. Whatever else is tested, there is no doubt of the fortitude required. A man who could endure such pain had either a clear conscience, or supreme self-control. There were probably few cases that went so far — but the ultimate sanction demanded friendless suspects to prove heroism, which convinced everyone.[37] The formalities of the court did not depend upon the solemn trappings of the learned world. The court was managed by 'amateurs', law-worthy men who knew the precedents and judged their neighbours according to the traditional rulings of customary law. There was no legal book-learning and no use for writing. Accused men needed not advocates but kin, lords or neighbours to vouch for them and swear with them in respect of the accusations. Most offences were committed by known or suspected persons of the vicinity. Cattle raiding, which involved outsiders, would be pursued by the whole community and summary justice carried out immediately on offenders when caught. In England if men were found murdered and there was no kin to accuse or suspect, the district was fined as a punishment or as an inducement to winkle out the offender. Local communities aimed to be self-sufficient legal units and developed customs of their own. Before 1100 the edicts of kings and churchmen had made only formal inroads into this system — reserving certain crimes for special sittings of the courts, demanding a certain frequency of meetings, without attempting to provide alternative courts or different procedures.

The clergy had been responsible for breaching this system when they demanded the right to manage legal business concerning clerks, or 'spiritual' disputes. They gathered their own laws into book form and began to expound them in special schools. They borrowed concepts of law from Roman jurisprudence, like appeal to written statements of law, the use of written evidence in court and judgment by men learned in written law. They pioneered new forms of finding the truth by inquest and argument. Through their obligatory part in the ordeal-procedure they were able in due course to discredit it all together. Their anxieties about their property rights made written instruments as evidence of legal transactions in land more acceptable. They obtained special courts of their own for judging the clergy, but they were not of exclusive advantage to the clergy. They acquired a predominate interest in legal business of concern to laymen, not by abuse, but by defending the rights of individuals to free choice in marriage and testamentary bequests. Learned in Roman and canon law, as landlords of churches and monasteries, they provided courts for their vassals and tenants and they continued to serve on royal commissions of justice, from chancellors downwards. Clerical influence on the concepts and practice of law was therefore persistent and pervasive. Traditional justice did not die out all together or at all in some places, but from the twelfth century it was seriously dislocated by the clergy.

Rulers saw that they would only retain respect for their own courts if they adopted some of the improvements made possible by the new approach to law-finding. Twelfth-century kings who opposed the clergy's demands for total independence of their jurisdiction did not hesitate to protect their own legal rights by using bishops and abbots in their administrations; nor did prelates generally refuse to serve on partisan grounds. No attempts to create an entirely alternative system of royal justice were made, so clerical improvements were grafted into traditional practice. Kings were slow to devise new laws and means for enforcing them. The result was spasmodic and piecemeal secular reaction to the growth of clerical law and legal learning. Kingdoms had no common laws as such, except what cases or procedures kings reserved for themselves.

Learned civil law, as studied at the time, inevitably appeared to subject kings to the authority of the Roman emperor, which naturally pleased and encouraged the German king, as much as it alienated the others. Its more 'civilized' procedures did not thereby recommend it to secular landlords. King James I of Aragon records that in a case in his court the spokesman of the count of Urgel referred scathingly to the specious pleading of the learned advocate on the other side 'which you learned in Bologna'.[38] Secular law would have floundered on in this way had it not been for the voices that broke through at a political level, demanding improvements.

This did not come about from a concern for the enforcment of law and order, as might be casually assumed. The criminal law remained highly primitive. Savage in its punishments of those who defied the tight-knit communities of the past — thieves, gangs, outlaws — all those in fact without neighbours to vouch for them, the desperate and the dregs of the population to whom no mercy need be shown, the law repressed crime on the assumption that criminals were like animals to be exterminated. Violent murders were of course perpetrated by respected persons too, in political and family disputes, but these were not at first considered reprehensible in the same way, because it was taken for granted that in such cases the injured parties would retaliate or use political power. In fourteenth-century Italian towns where the vendetta remained endemic, it was not from lawyers that remedies could be found: but in politics. It is improper to conclude that it was a matter of 'class-privilege' if such murders went unpunished. The notion of crime had then a different meaning from that which it has since acquired. In those circumstances, it seemed right that justice should be summarily enforced by the crudest means which hardly allowed lawyers to interfere.

Changes in secular law grew rather out of the need of the most prominent members of twelfth-century society, the militant knights and barons, to establish unequivocally what their rights in land were and to devise courts of law in which they could be defended. In effect therefore they abandoned their former reliance upon warfare to defend their interests. Their 'rights' were too multifarious, and often intangible: how could a feudal lord make good his claims on a vassal in possession of a fief? Few lords were not also themselves vassals to other lords. There were also disputes as to the respective rights of lords and kin to a dead man's property, and arguments about those of collateral kin as against heirs in the direct line. Concession of lands and rights had in the past proceeded without recourse to writing, and terms were often in dispute. No estate however small could in feudal conditions be the 'property' of any one person; here was room enough for dispute. Feudal grants were by nature life-tenures, but by the twelfth century all freeholders took it for granted that their children had claims to inherit. In a world of diminishing opportunities children could no longer make their own fortunes so parents prepared the best future for them they could. Lords requiring services were not unwilling to take on an active son in his father's place, so primogeniture of succession suited them best. However, regular inheritance of estates, if it became customary, threatened to annihiliate the lord's right to the reversion of land. His formal position could be protected by the exaction of dues for entry into the succession, but amounts were fixed arbitrarily by the lord and became a source of grievance. Disputes about such matters simmered throughout the twelfth century. In England, where they were at the centre of political arguments, the barons were not able to force the king to define them until 1215.

Until the twelfth century the land had been the obvious and direct source of most men's livelihood and the traditional expectations of all parties had been protected by local custom whatever it was, known and declared by the neighbourhood. Outright ownership of land was a concept unknown. Kings, churches, lords, peasants, squatters and townsmen all drew on the land in proportions established by usage, influence and dignity. The idea of 'property' had more meaning in mercantile communities disposing of commodities and where these flourished, as in urban Italy, the revival of Roman Law was welcomed for its protection of such rights. The extension of the idea as such to land was impracticable, but there were advantages in it for those who could convert their rights into something more substantial by finding new rules of law to protect their titles. Kings who could call upon the services of learned clergy had to become the source of this better law.

They naturally began by trying to exploit their advantages for their own particular benefit, but their direct vassals, who suffered from this, proved powerful enough to place limits on royal oppressions. Barons and knights began to use their political power and draw what help they could from churchmen's books of law to sort out conflicting claims in land. Gradually a body of doctrine appeared and those who could force new courts to take cognizance of their grievances became in effect communities with their own laws, as privileged as the clergy. In England, which developed such courts precociously early, the significance of this was rapidly lost because the king's courts offered to protect the seisin of every freeman, only a limited number of people in the twelfth century, but a formula capable of great extension later on. Even so the vast majority of men were not able to plead in the king's courts, or bothered that they could not, for they continued to enjoy the benefits of traditional customary law in their own localities. Not until the common-law courts had devised new rules of land-law for freeholders did important legal disabilities begin to appear for the 'non-free'.[39]

The new law or privilege for freeholders produced its own learning and its professional exponents and these constituted the first secular professional group of persons, with learning enough to challenge the idea that the clergy had a monopoly of it. For several generations their competence was of a very limited and technical kind: mastery of the intricate system of pleadings involved in disputes about land, which distinguished the procedures of these courts from the old. They made themselves indispensable to the land-'owning' class and this had a decisive influence upon the character of their rules, their social standing and their political outlook.

They helped in at least three distinctly different ways. First, with the law of succession itself. As 'owners', owing little but nominal services to lords, the possessors of estates intended to use them for the benefit of their own families. Where primogeniture prevailed, they had to devise legal means of creating 'estates' for younger children and daughters. Elaborate precautions were made to keep the inheritance in the direct family and it became the pride of any man of consequence to found its fortunes and so perpetuate his memory. This curious attitude drove fathers, in the absence of sons, to promote the chances of their daughters by finding distinguished husbands for them. Already in the early twelfth century, Henry I of England, after the death of his legitimate son, showed almost desperate concern to perpetuate his policy in France by marrying his daughter to the count of Anjou and working for her eventual recognition in England. His barons were hostile to these schemes and Matilda did not much take to her husband. Henry was indifferent to objections and persisted with his plans for reasons of his own: his life-work should not be allowed to crumble after his death. Henry's example is the more instructive in this regard, that he made no attempt to secure this objective by working for the succession of one of his bastards, like the able earl of Gloucester. Although Henry's own father was a bastard and had become duke of Normandy in 1035, a century later the barrier had been raised against illegitimacy. For twist though fathers might within the confines of the rules, they were denied the right to provide for their natural children from their lawful estates. Inheritance of land was accepted with reluctance by society as a whole, and only on condition that the rules were stringent.

In these conditions there were both advantages and disadvantages for women of high society, but from the legal point of view their interests were subordinated to the projects of their fathers, husbands and sons. They had to be cosseted against the influence of unwelcome suitors and the attentions of inferiors. Churchmen defended their technical right to free consent to their marriages and supervised both the ceremony and the legalities long before the emergency of the property laws. Secular lawyers later came to jib at ecclesiastical jurisdiction in such matters and procedural disputes added to the legal complications. Insistence on the rights of landownership for their families did not necessarily serve or promote family affection. Whatever emotional advantage derived from it by particular landowners, the lawyers, looking after those interests for them in the courts, certainly stood to gain most in the long term.

Second, although owners worked frantically to keep lands in the family, the penalty of failure to produce heirs was that their ownership made it possible to sell their rights in the market, an advantage that unscrupulous owners might exploit on occasion for personal reasons and which legal contrivances to tie up estates by entails could never totally eliminate. The possibility of buying estates of land on the market for cash did not immediately enable a swarm of rich merchants to enter the landowning class, but from the twelfth century their numbers did grow. In England, purchasers of land were accepted into the 'feudal' pattern of landholding by the statute of *Quia Emptores* (1290) which admitted that in practice lords could not prevent the alienation of land by vassals. Whereas in the past the granting of estates to newcomers had been allowed exclusively by concessions of fiefs on conditions, for the future newcomers could expect to purchase lands outright like any other commodity. It would be too much to say that the still exceptional purchase of land totally undermined older attitudes but it was not without influence in encouraging all landowners to think more in terms of market values, if only for their produce, and to change their views about the nature of their relationship to the land and those who dwelt on it. Cling though they might to the concept of property for their families, the legal implications of winning independence of lordship opened the way to treating land like any other item of property, such as chattels. In dealing with outsiders, as well inside the family, lawyers provided the services of clerks and notaries, drawing up contracts of sale, loans and fictitious suits to facilitate the owner's exploitation of his rights for personal advantage.

Third, there are the consequences for those who had become the tenants on the land, whose rights, though undoubted, were not to be protected by public law, but only by local custom, and the more vulnerable on that account. Landowners did not immediately, or in all cases, set out to exploit their legal advantages over peasants to force them to work longer or pay increased dues. Nevertheless, there was a marked change in the attitude of proprietors towards their land, which encouraged them to think more frequently in terms of improved returns, where there was a market to stimulate production. This might result in legal disputes with tenants defending customary ways; it might only introduce more managers and officials to supervise the estates. From the thirteenth century records survive in ever greater numbers to show how landowners expected to profit from the new rules and particularly from the availability of a new group of men trained to look after their interests. The English royal 'Pipe Rolls' of the twelfth century illustrate how closely accounting and law were already linked for the king's advantage, and the seigneurial records of a century later prove too that better accounting and more legal training went together.[40] In both cases the accounting procedure was conceived as the means of making officials answer for their charges and obtaining all that the lord was entitled to, rather than as an exercise in calculating profit or loss. Texts written to instruct officials in their responsibilities occur in manuscripts with other legal matter: a smattering of legal learning, if no more, was invaluable.

In all three aspects of landownership men with legal learning, the 'lawyers', became the principal agents of the proprietors, in the great issues of law, in devising negotiable instruments and in the simple management of the property. For these occupations, various levels of competence were required, but the need of some training was undeniable and the opportunities for men of ability to become important and wealthy attracted many men of good—as well as of humble families—to obtain the necessary qualifications. Landowners with no formal education of their own, who distrusted the advice of churchmen in matters of business, placed their confidence in their legal advisers. No professional man, certainly not the physician, was so often consulted. Great tracts of history must be written from the documents left by these professional men—formal, lengthy, often tedious though they are. The lawyers worked together, dedicated to pursuing the goal, overcoming every obstacle and never subject to impatient irritation. From the first, such professionals were also found in governments, since the growth of administrations everywhere originally depended upon the use made of them for judicial purposes. If governments had to devise courts and procedures to meet these needs, they called upon those known to have special skills for it. One way or another, professional lawyers came to be the men of business, helping to frame rules of law as well as to apply them— partners in legislation as well as advocates and judges. Knowing the rules, they advised the powerful and the rich; their subordinates, clerks and notaries, composed the written instruments of sale, lease, contact or use: both managed any ensuing litigation for their clients.

For several centuries to come officials principally concerned with public affairs were educated as lawyers. No effort was made to cultivate urbanity, sublime ideas or consideration of human virtues. The study of the law promoted sharp memories, concern for precise detail, exactitude, precedent and authority: it encouraged ever more elaborate record-keeping and phrases designed to cover every eventuality. It began to oust reliance on the memory of man, ancient custom or the appeal to God. It established written rules, precise formulation, written testimony, subtle distinctions. But there could at first be no question of subjecting children to these uninspiring studies, unless they were intended for a legal or a business career.

The change came in Italy. In the cities there, where the landed aristocracy could not as such exercise their traditional functions of government, the supreme magistracies were nonetheless occupied in rotation by professional lawyers, drawn from the 'best' families. Amongst the leading organizations of any major town, the men of the law came first in dignity, by virtue of their birth and education. The public law of Italy was originally, as elsewhere in Europe, a matter of local custom. When imperial government in Italy collapsed after the death of Fredrick II (1250), public life entered a critical phase in which authority had to be improvised. The intellectual world of the time, dominated by theological interests, had no conception of a civil society or its ends, and in the Italian context the clergy enjoyed no special respect as men of learning. They suffered other disadvantages: in general they were less lavishly endowed than their northern brethren, and those few who had managed great country estates were penalized along with other rural magnates by the towns. The clergy also might incur political oppro-brium as suspected creatures of the pope, particularly later while he was absent in Avignon. The makeshift political authorities depended essentially upon the lay magistrates who put their learning to practical use. Only law could provide men with an understanding of the nature of public right, as well as of personal status, rights, duties and mutual obligations. This law was not, however, that found in customary law, for this lacked any corpus or text of comprehensive insight into these matters, but in the Roman law books.

The rules of the Romanists were rapidly adapted in the late thirteenth century to make them useful to town governments who had hitherto been suspicious of rules implying imperial authority.[41] Most Italian towns already elected each year a *podestà*, the man of power, to act as impartial magistrate in their turbulent affairs. Even if he did not become master of the town, his manner of doing business could not be ignored by the real masters, who accepted the same standards or orderly and meticulous record-keeping by learned clerks and notaries. It is principally to the law graduates of the universities of Italy—Bologna, Padua and Perugia—that we owe the composition of the surviving records of these towns; the statutes, the regulations, the minutes of council meetings, the histories and chronicles, in which may be followed attempts to turn the political chaos following the collapse of established authority into the administrative order lawyers advocated and managed. The law was used against the country nobility, the churches and other towns. Cities found a use for services of the 'Roman imperial' lawyers as advocates and magistrates. Roman Law had been the sovereign's law: hereafter, those who could enforce it acquired sovereignty. Even the most respectable pro-papal cities began to obey the emperor's law, not in his name, but in the name of their city. With the professor Bartolus of Sassoferrato (1314-57) installed in Guelf Perugia, the new interpretation of the law became academic orthodoxy.[42] There was no further need for cities without formal recognition by the emperor of their powers to dread visits from German emperors, however weak, in case their *de facto* independence were called in question. Civil government was carried on beneath the nominal lordship of upstart rulers. Lacking the traditional authorities of northern Europe and cast adrift on stormy political seas, Italians found their bearings by reviving ancient learning associated with a glorious period of the peninsula's past.

Humanist Education
In Italy the study of law first opened the way to a much more educative programme of studies. From the fourteenth century, lawyers there showed increasing interest in reviving the study not only of law, but of Latin language, literature and history. In due course this developed into the programme of humanist education which, when adopted elsewhere in Europe, provided the framework of lay education until the

present century. The new education for laymen grew naturally out of the enthusiasms of educated lawyers, like the Paduan humanists, Mussato and his circle, or Petrarch, a notary's son, who had studied law at Montpellier and Bologna.[43]

· Italians were trying to strengthen the links between themselves and the heroic past. Dante had advocated the revival of the empire as the only solution to the continuous civil war of Italy, but at that time he did not emphasize that this empire had been formerly based in Italy: the German King Henry VII was for him undoubted emperor. Dante's contemporaries for the most part did not share this enthusiasm for the empire. However, two generations later, the figure of the emperor loomed less fearfully and Italian self-confidence had become greater. Petrarch and his friends indulged their historical imaginations with less anxiety about the present state of the empire. They considered questions of particular concern to Italians alone, neglecting the later history of the empire for discussion of the political problem underlined in Cicero's writings: the growth of Caesarism in the late Roman republic. Quite apart from the intrinsic interests of this period of Roman history for citizens of fourteenth-century city state republics, the early humanists from Petrarch onwards found their Latin authorities, particularly Cicero, even more rewarding as models of Latin prose composition.

Italy did not as a whole possess a common literary culture in the fourteenth century. Dante had himself discussed the great variety of spoken versions of Italian used in the peninsula in his *De vulgari eloquentia*. Some of them were used for the composition of love poetry, but not for official purposes. Poets might also write in Provençal itself, and French was often used for prose works in the thirteenth century, as in Brunetto Latini's *Tresor* or Marco Polo's *Milione*. Dante wrote mostly in his own vernacular, Tuscan, and this example was important for those who wished to imitate his style: in the *Commedia Divina* Dante composed a major work of literature in his own dialect of Tuscany, and there was no comparable poem in the whole of Europe. This poem was the object of study, commentary and public exposition: it was known even to the less educated and cited by them. It gave Tuscan a standing as a literary language which it would not otherwise have enjoyed. Looking back it therefore seems to us strange that Petrarch did not adopt Tuscan as a prose medium. Instead, he set about a renewal of the study of Latin as a language, not of churchmen, but as the language of history, of public affairs, of eloquence and dignity.

So the Italians embarked upon an experiment in education and scholarship that had the most far reaching consequences. Petrarch had no doubts about the rightness of making Latin the medium of expression. It was the language Italians had spoken and it was the one written language they could all understand. (A fourteenth-century Tuscan commentary on Dante had to be translated into Latin to be understood in Lombardy.)[44] It had an important prose literature of its own (which Tuscan had not). Above all it was the language of the great men, which the new Italians were incited to imitate. In the educated circles of the day, where his clerical and legal acquaintances had all learnt the rudiments of the language already, there were no initial grumbles about its difficulty or antiquity. All that Petrarch encouraged them to do was to give up writing the pitiful Latin of clerical hacks and to compose with the polish and eloquence of Cicero.

At first the new programme depended upon the scholar Petrarch and his friends. They hunted down manuscripts and laboured to produce sound texts which could, a century later, be produced on the printing press in such numbers as to meet the demands of all Europe. After Petrarch came the schoolmasters, who opened up schools where young laymen, and women, could learn the art of writing elegant Latin — and Greek too, for good measure. The basic subject matter, politics, history, rhetoric and morals, had nothing of the professional aridity of clerical education: it led to no specialized careers as such. It offered a preparation for any one of them and it was an accomplishment in its own right. Such an education was particularly suitable for the affluent citizens of northern Italy, from families enjoying political or social prominence. It gave them at least familiarity with the greatest days of their own country's past, taught them something of the complexity of public affairs and inculcated the sound moral lessons of the ancient philosophers. Incidentally it tended to focus their common attention upon matters of secular importance, which left religious issues to their private attention and to their confessors.

The revival of the ancient programme of education also stimulated interest in the theory of education, as found in writers like Quintilian and Plutarch. From the Greeks in particular the teachers picked up the value of physical training, so the young gentlemen and ladies were not brought up to be only intellectual prodigies: the programme was much more comprehensive. At this point of course the books fail us, for it was not until the mid-sixteenth century that Hieronymus Mercurialis wrote a book to advocate gymnastics on the Greek model.[45] With him the whole programme of a nobleman's upbringing entered into literary form; the books had achieved total victory.

4. EDUCATION FOR A SECULAR WORLD[46]
Already in the twelfth century, heroic society and the primitive solidarity of fighting men had begun to contend with disruptive influences. The old military virtues continued to be esteemed, particularly

by the nobility who cultivated them most, but even they had to adjust to different conditions. The most disturbing feature was the growth of towns, which not only introduced a style of life quite distinct from that in villages, but interfered with the villages as well by attracting country immigrants, and drawing village production into a market economy as money began to percolate into the countryside. Villages remote from urban centres remained most impervious to these changes, but even those which profited least from the new possibilities were unable to resist them altogether. The tight-knit, self-contained community broke down. In every place the consequences of this were different and the historical evidence precludes any detailed description of it. Nevertheless the main lines may be roughly drawn.

The departure of villagers for the towns required them to adjust their traditional expectations to a different social organization and it introduced them to the need for learning new skills as craftsmen, traders or shopkeepers. Eventually this encouraged the growth of guilds of craftsmen to regulate, amongst other things, the conditions under which the skills would be taught to apprentices, in order to keep up the standards of the craft. In the towns, jostling for influence in local affairs also encouraged some men to acquire the rudiments of an education in letters, if only to deal with the clerical and episcopal authorities entrenched there. From the thirteenth century many towns provided schools of their own, often with secular teachers, where the pupils at least learned their letters and basic arithmetic, if they did not advance far enough to learn Latin grammar.[47] The development of clerical education ran parallel to this, but its specialized character made it unsuitable for most laymen. As we have seen, it tended to wrap the clergy in protective abstractions and, from their writings, little may be gleaned about lay education itself.

The towns and the clergy reacted to the dislocation of the old society by creating little enclaves of privileged sanity for themselves. This course was obviously not open to the traditional military leadership, whose expectations were also disturbed by the new conditions: they could not opt into privilege without forfeiting their leading role. They continued to remain responsible for keeping society together. They saw that this could no longer be done on a purely local basis. The adjustments that they had to make are clearly indicated by our sources. For them too, some better preparation for adult life became desirable, not because they were 'privileged', but because they were most in need of guidance: appropriate training was sought for.

Noble boys, who went on being trained as warriors, to fight with swords, to ride and to go to battle, found as they grew up in European society that the possibilities for campaigning had been drastically curtailed by the pacification of the eleventh century. Internal feuding was frowned on. Men of energy had to seek their real adventures far away, in Spain or in the Holy Land. At home their parents and their lords, however, expected or required them to subordinate their impulses to the wise schemes of maturity. The children resented these irksome restrictions. They found that their upbringing, which prepared them to fend for themselves, was something of a cheat. When old enough they were expected to serve the purposes of their family, not to pursue adventures of their own. The increasing burden of family responsibility bore down on the children and turned them into dutiful and obedient servants of the family goals. In military matters this is aptly symbolized by the growth of heraldry from the twelfth century. Whereas eleventh-century knights had borne their own personal and whimsical advices on their shields, in time these were replaced by the ever more elaborate family quarterings that proclaimed the individual's place in his family tree. The effect of these frustrations on young nobles was already clear in the early twelfth century when Orderic Vitalis put into the mouth of Robert Courthouse, son to William the Conqueror, a remarkably rebellious speech complaining of his father's discipline and asking for adequate funds to prove himself a generous grown man.[48] The speech is apocryphal but it is intended to express a plausible explanation for Robert's restlessness under his father's expert political management of the duchy. Children of Robert's generation vented their resentment against indulgent, sensible, parents by lavishing gifts on frivolous entertainers or by dashing away on rash and desperate adventures to prove themselves to themselves: the first crusade came opportunely. There were fewer opportunities that they wanted. The second crusade was a more elaborately planned affair that ended in the failure to take Damascus. It discouraged further efforts and it was more than forty years before the last cooperative effort, inspired by the hope of recapturing Jerusalem from Saladin. Such ventures required careful planning, political negotiation and large fortune. They were not even suitable occasions for the display of heroism. Succeeding generations had to be coaxed out of their wish for adventures and learn how to cope with the real problems.

Society therefore subjected its favourite children to unwelcome restraints, and they reacted accordingly. In the 1130s when few changes in the preparation of young nobles had occurred, hundreds, if not thousands, of young men of good family rejected their unattractive prospects by personally choosing the hard way of entering the new Cistercian monasteries, where in loving comradeship they expected to attain to a new spiritual life. The Cistercian reform made a point of refusing to accept young boys offered by their parents to the monastery, as had previously been the case, and emphasized the need to make a personal mature choice. Orderic Vitalis himself, who had been given to a Norman monastery by his father, even ventured to accuse him of acting more like a step-father in sending one so young away to an alien land.[49] Orderic probably knew from his own experience the unhappiness of a life lived without personal satisfactions, and it seems to have been only later in life that he found intellectual consolation in scholarship and history after making friends with an older monk. Orderic appreciated how young men could respond in such numbers to the Cistercian call, for it was his generation that first began to realise how little real freedom there remained to mettlesome young men hoping to prove themselves by their own brave deeds. Churchmen, celibates themselves, offered what outlets they could, like the military orders and the crusades, but society which was stampeded by Cistercian impetuosity made few other concessions to youthful irresponsibility. Christian influence on secular life could not be kept out all together, but it was at first rather formal, as in the ceremonies of knighthood. Secular leaders realized that the social order they presided over obliged them to keep churchmen, like other groups seeking corporate privileges, on a short rein. They wished to teach their children how to curb their own impulses if their 'class' was to remain in command.

The new costliness of war, like the new idealism, required leaders to keep their heads and hold a balance between their emotions and their reason. They framed their policy for the future by considering the probable interests of their children. They hoped to effect it by alliances with other families and by cooperating with others of similar background. In the past the rough equality of soldiers in the field had prevented the emergence of distinctive ranks amongst the nobility. Slowly this was replaced by a nobility highly sensitive to gradations of rank. This was later on elaborated by kings who wished to enhance the dignity of their courts on ceremonial occasions by a concourse of nobles, correctly placed. They devised titles of distinction from the thirteenth century; the earliest were those devised for the king's son: Edward I had been no more than the Lord Edward before his accession, but his son became Prince of Wales in 1284; in France, the style 'Dauphin' was adopted later still. Titles of dignity, which came to flatter noblemen for royal purposes, prove that effectively noblemen had by then become courtiers. This process had taken a long time.[50]

Already in the twelfth century, noblemen had begun to frequent one another's company, and to mix less with their social inferiors from their own localities. They did this initially for reasons of common political interest, though it acquired a social value. Either way, it was desirable for their children to learn how to behave and do business with others of their own particular rank. It became more difficult to enter this society without the right background, and the acquisition of mere military skills was not sufficient. A young man had to have manners fit for courts, *courtoisie,* and this had to be learned somehow, not simply from his family, certainly not in the village. It was probably best to start a life of service in a baronial household. Given the right opening, a young squire might rise to serve the king himself. The essential purpose of this noble training was to create a sense of social cohesion amongst the persons of distinction with whom rested the management of regional or 'national' society, by bringing them into frequent contact with another. There was no formal subject-matter of their education and no formal means of teaching it. By putting young people together, in the company of their elders, particularly of the women (who had little else to do) they would learn the *mores* of their own social class. Even the young men eager to engage in military sports had to learn how to bend their inclinations to the demands of peaceable polite society and particularly to mixed company. The ladies came to expect better manners from the men and brought up their children by those standards.

The new importance of women in European society from the twelfth century depends upon a number of auxiliary factors like the less imminent perils that had formerly swept their sons out of reach and onto the battlefields much younger. The clergy also had an impact on the status of women, not merely by their moral stand, but through their enforcement of rules about the need for consent to marriage. As a consequence, women were more often separated from the company of lewd and ignorant persons and subjected to the close supervision of their fathers and husbands. Allowed only the company of other women, they were shut up in special quarters where they lived a refined life of their own, quite distinct from that of mixed company and ribald humour. Men were admitted to these 'courts' on conditions of light-hearted severity if they proved that they were not boorish like their social inferiors, but able to talk with wit and subtlety. The earliest courts spoken of are those of Eleanor of Aquitaine and her daughters in the second half of the twelfth century. Such ladies succeeded in coaxing men from their blood-sports and beguiling them with the charms of poetry. There were probably always men like the warrior in Castiglione's *Courtier* who refused to dance,[51] and preferred to compete for the ladies' favours, where possible, by exercising their martial skills in the lists. Young women too may have found this more exciting. But feminine support on those occasions did not dispense men from courtly behaviour, address in conversation, wit in repartee, delicacy of allusion, mastery of verse and music. There was no place for learning these accomplishments except by frequenting feminine company.

Book learning as such probably had no important part to play in the education of these young people. However, since poetry and story-telling were common in these courts, it is possible from such works of literature to derive some impression of what went on in them. When gentlemen began to read and acquire books on their own account, it was still chiefly 'romances' that proved popular; alongside their devotional books they kept books containing military or chivalrous material, such as the stories of Arthur. Whether they read them or only heard them, they probably acquired, or at least reinforced, their social ideas or ideals from such sources. The question of how deeply fictions may mould actual behaviour is still being debated, but before considering that, it is as well to begin with the romances themselves.

The medieval romance has provided us with the word, as with the concept of the romance, a story of adventure concerned with the attainment of true love. It has been the main theme of European literature ever since the twelfth century cast off the long spell of the heroic saga and concentrated the imagination on the love-story. This break was itself important. In the heroic lays, the encounters of the heroes, however fantastic, had an earnestness that craved to be taken seriously. The romance is by contrast a wilful fiction. It has to be plausible, but it does not need to be cast in the real world. A clever author can create his own fictional world; the reader will happily believe in it if it appeals to his imagination and his emotional desires. Either way there is no deliberate intention to mirror social reality: rather, on the contrary, to project as reality the hidden longings of the young in heart. Fiction appears when the wish to live in the imagination had become a social necessity for those unable to achieve their real ambitions in the world. The birth of fiction as an art form is obviously an historical fact of some significance.

It is certainly striking that the creative phase of the romance came in the period between *c.* 1160 and *c.* 1230 while the clergy were actively engaged in establishing their own clerical society. This often brought them into opposition to secular authorities, and their moral ascendancy over lay society as a whole suffered in consequence.[52] The romances bear few overt signs of the Christian church; even the Grail stories, whatever their meaning, drew upon mystical inclinations that were not strictly compatible with Christian teaching. Yet the difference between its romantic outlook and that of epic poetry suggests that, in a fundamental way, Christian teaching has at least broken the pagan spell of fatal doom. The characters of fiction choose their own paths. In the *Mort du Roi Arthur,* Arthur admittedly dies, but there is no sense of fatality about this: it is no more than a necessary conclusion to the cycle. Arthur slays all his enemies before being carried away to his own pious end. Released from fates beyond their control, these fictional characters make free choices in which their passions are subjected to their wills. Their lives become purposeful by their moral actions, just as they are punished and rewarded according to their deserts.

The stories also assume that monogamy has become the standard of polite society and that the lady ought not to act dishonourably: this often creates the action out of the lover's frustrations, for it exacerbates his passion and tends to sublimate it from lechery into love. The stories are not gutless. The pleasures of the flesh, like the military set-pieces and indifference to slaughter, are frankly acknowledged: the victory of puritanism and squeamishness is not complete. All the same the social context assumed by the romances is one in which the churchmen had already scored some success. Marriage has become a major social hurdle to be negotiated and combat must be justified. The influence of the clergy on the romance is undeniable, even if the literature as a whole did not reinforce Christian morals. Instead it taught a standard of chivalrous behaviour.

The romance proper first appeared in French in the courts of northern France *c*. 1160. The stories were taken from the books known to the clergy, about Alexander, Troy, Charlemagne and Arthur. It was composed to be recited in a distinctive rhythm, not, like the heroic lays, to be sung. The personal culture of the author in devising new situations, adventures, dialogues or diversionary interludes played a large part in the success of his story, as of the genre itself. New authors added fresh episodes, particularly about characters of previous tales only mentioned but not elaborated upon. Reading earlier versions, the learned author tried to improve upon them; even if he did not, he had not to fear accusations of plagiarism: his audiences did not know his sources and valued only his own lively versions. More commonly they listened than read.

There is a dearth of evidence about the authors themselves. Every author left clear traces of his own individual talents in his work, but society was slow to recognize the new significance of authorship. Romance literature begins with the formal lyrics of Provençal poetry in the early twelfth century and the personal idiosyncracies of their authors stand out in their experiments in verse forms and distinctive tones. Such genres rapidly became too stylized to be analysed in personal terms; later authors used them only as a means of discovering their distinctive literary manner—the way best suited to them as writers. However, the diffusion of these distinctive literary forms in thirteenth-century Italy, immediately stimulated there an almost modern craving to read autobiographical information into such personal poetry. This brought about the composition of summary biographies of the Provençal poets, which created a new literary genre: so before 1300 there is a literature about authors.[53] The author has by then become a person of interest in his own right, independently of his works. (During the same century, King James I of Aragon himself wrote his memoirs, mainly of his military and political achievements; his descendant Pere III did the same a century later. If to be a writer had become a matter of consequence, persons of consequence could also write.)

The romantic writer may seem far in spirit from the clergy, but he grew from the same stock. The contrast of matter is certainly more striking for a modern critic than for a medieval one. The clergy had learned how to assimilate and interpret the most unedifying stories in classical poets. The allegorical interpretation had long since transformed understanding of the Biblical Song of Songs. The stories that romancers drew from their sources and worked up by their imaginations never remained merely sensual. If they appear shameless, and took man's nature for granted, recognizing both his animal and his spiritual aspects, the author's task was to lead men from the lower to the higher. So, medieval critics praised the *Roman de la Rose* for its morality. Not until the fifteenth century were certain episodes misunderstood and denounced. Once literal-minded critics ceased to read it as an allegory they were shocked by its depravity, and this has of course earned it admiration in still more recent times.[54]

The author himself expected therefore that his audiences would be sufficiently sophisticated, or at least familiar with the genres, to interpret them correctly: the audiences did not just enjoy a story—they had to find the message. Of course the story mattered but the author prided himself even there on the personal *finesse* he showed in his version and hoped to be admired as he deserved. His audience needed discrimination and culture for this. The narration exploited the techniques of classical rhetoric; the conflicts between reason and passion echo scholastic debates; the composition of formal verse for recitation tested a learned author. The clerkly authors not surprisingly composed poetical debates about the respective merits of the clergy and knights as lovers, in which the clergy were triumphant. In their view literature was the way to win a lady's heart and they polished their verses to please a cultured mistress. Such refinement demanded an intimate setting. It was not suited for performance in the great hall of heroes or to stir the enthusiasm of the intoxicated company. In Dante's famous story of Francesca da Rimini, she and her lover discovered their passion by reading together alone from the book.

This literature first appeared in French and was rapidly adapted into every European vernacular. German poets first took up the themes and made them indigenous in early courtly Staufen literature. Elsewhere they spread chiefly as mere translations. The Arthurian matter was known to the Catalan nobles in the early thirteenth century. King Haakon of Norway commissioned vernacular prose versions of the romances to bring his country out of its provincial isolation in 1226. The Arthurian stores were rendered into Dutch, English, Leonese, Italian, Latin, Hebrew and Swedish. Wherever the audiences assimilated these courtly refinements, they came to share in the outlook of the refined nobility.[55]

The gist of the subject matter was the relationship between the sexes. It is not difficult to see how these stories appealed initially to feminine audiences. The woman is always the prize and the object of the man's affections and the stories of love overcoming every obstacle had an obvious attraction to young women sighing for romance in a society where they were married off by their menfolk with scant regard for their feelings. The situation looks rather different from a young man's point of view, whether he be the clerical author who cannot hope to fight and win a lady, or the young squire whose wife will be found by other means (for the knights of the period seem in practice to have become increasingly concerned to find rich or influential wives, rather than marry for love). For him, the most interesting part of the story was the long sequence of adventures that led up to the dénouement. Gentlemen, denied military adventures except in tourneys, and tied to polite society, welcomed tales in which knights won favours by battle. They could all the same have regarded them as parodies of the real thing, for experience taught that in real life, ambitions and actions were framed by more substantial and exalted concerns than the mysterious pursuit of love. The earlier heroic poetry had here been more realistic. Men fought for pride or family honour not for women. In the romances the knight's own pride had sometimes to be sacrificed for the lady, as in the famous incident of Lancelot being humiliated by having to ride in a cart. The stories have more obvious appeal to the ladies. Perhaps in some sense they compensated them for their social passivity, allowing them in fiction to become the principal inspiration of knightly endeavour.

The fiction that men's battles and adventures were inspired by love of women[56] has nonetheless its own implications for the young men. The adventures were not concerned at all with the realistic details of strange lands or of fighting. Knights are always happiest when dealing with mere monsters or other knights. Only too often however they have to cope with magic, malevolent hosts, mysterious forces and bewitchment, where steadfastness and moral courage serve better than martial prowess. In this sense the stories are not concerned even with the attainment of true love, except allegorically. They are stories which show how men are tested in their moral characters through their military skills. They have to prove themselves acceptable to their ideal in combat with rivals or spirits. They set off from a familiar, joyful base, the court of King Arthur—with its friendly society of like-minded equals. Soon they are alone, left to their own devices, starting at every sound, beguiled and bewildered. The men are less concerned with the lady, who is the mere prize of victory, than with the adventures that will lead to her, adventures that befall without rhyme or reason, in which the knight's real qualities will be put to the supreme test.[57] Fight as he may, some slip may bring him down. More important than the purely military skill and combat there is the persistent implication that only the right choice for the right motive will save the day.

The interpretation of these romances is not without its problems. The stories are obviously not intended to be works of social realism in the manner of the nineteenth-century novel: even in the fourteenth century it would have been quixotic to emulate the knights of romance in person. However, the audiences must have known how to respond to the stories as both fictions and guides to conduct, for there is no doubt that certain knights were regarded as exemplary and taken as such by young nobles. In the absence of any 'historical' models of conduct, it would not be surprising if at the time characters of fiction were used in this way. It is comparatively easy for us to distinguish between the historic Nelson and the fictional Captain Hornblower. We know how to keep what is real and what imaginary separate in our minds, but this distinction then had little meaning. It was commonly believed that Arthur was as historical as Alexander or Charlemagne, and the stories told of historical characters could as easily be told of the others. A writer like Froissart was as happy to write history as romance. For contemporaries therefore both genres supplied stories of equal applicability. If men have more recently tried to learn from history, it was then natural to expect to learn from the fiction, which passed for history. There was obviously no intention of learning political wisdom.

Something could profitably be learned about social etiquette, but more influential still was the general outlook of the romances towards society and social relations which fostered, if it did not actually create, social and moral values in gentle knights and ladies, who had no other guides except those of the church.[58] This code of conduct mattered in some ways more than the church's, certainly at first. Richard I was himself raised in a very early chivalrous court, and if he answered the papal call to the crusade, it was his secular ideals of knighthood that made him admire Saladin. He is said to have proposed a marriage alliance between their two families as an expression of their relations, though his sister refused to consider it.[59] Richard's code of honour laid down recommendations for conduct. Chivalrous heroes were expected to live up to their ideals, not to realize their potential as people: the delineation of character as such is not important in the romances. The romances in this respect mirror current beliefs about human motives and the plausibility of human action, for readers could have made nothing of these fictions if the heroes had not seemed to them to be real. If by modern standards their actions are often arbitrary and out of character, it is obviously because consistency of personality had no more meaning for author or readers than plausibility of circumstances; in the real world, as in fiction, men were expected to respond to circumstances in an admirable way, not to be 'themselves'. If this was the expectation, men probably attempted to regulate their reactions to events likewise. They reacted to events spontaneously, like heroes of romance fulfilling their duties. They did not think of the personality as self-determining, cultivate their own idiosyncracies or observe those of others. The creation of individually discreet persons was no part of the author's task. On the contrary he showed contemporaries a moral map of human life, with temptations to be overcome and virtues to be practised.

The thirteenth century was the period when the romance made its strongest impact. Its secular idealism took root and has continued to flourish. It spread throughout Europe a taste for high-mindedness, noble gestures, refined ladies and dedicated knights. It was so much of a challenge that the clergy had to campaign against its implicit snobbery. They devised a new kind of didactic literature, moralistic and pious, which later on challenged the authority of chivalry. Nonetheless the romance survived. It found its way through to all classes of society by means of prose paraphrases even though the literary refinements were here pared away to leave only the sentimental frame of the story intact.[60] The romantic element suffused all secular literature of the period. It inspired another literary genre, the traveller's tale, when Rustichello of Pisa, who was a professional writer of romances, happened to be a prisoner of war in Genoa in the company of Marco Polo. The latter recounted his exploits in China to his fellow-prisoners in the traditional manner. Had Rustichello not perceived the interest of these tales, and written them down they might never have been recorded, for mere journeying could not make a book. That depended on the romancer, who turned the stories into the kind of adventure readers appreciated. As fabulous tales, Polo's adventures aroused interest, which as memoirs they would never have received. The connexion between the traveller's tale and the romance is proved in Fazio degli Uberti's *Dittamondo* (1350-68), which refers to the places of the Arthurian lands, as though they did exist. much as maps of Tolkien's fairyland may be bought now.[61] The idea of geographical representation was easily assimilated into literature and

Laurent de Premierfait (*c.*1400) claimed that Jean de Meung had painted a true *mapemond* of all celestial and terrestrial things in his *Roman de la Rose.*

Similarly the romance transformed history writing. The process of turning historical events into literature comes so naturally to us that we are hardly aware of what is involved by it, but at a time when clerical history-writing had little to commend it and fictions passed for history, it took some time to bring about. Long after the crusade of St Louis, the Sire de Joinville delighted the company at the royal court by telling anecdotes about the king; it was only in extreme old age that he was persuaded to write them down. His vernacular life of the king, the first of its kind, retains some of its original flavour as oral recitation. With Joinville there is however a marked taste for the historical over the fabulous, and this may represent a sign that the fourteenth century increasingly favoured romantic histories rather than historical romances. Muntaner and Froissart are the best writers of this kind of vernacular history. To the same period belong such incidents as show kings attempting to revive the glorious days of King Arthur, like the construction of round tables by Edward I and Edward III for their knights. At the same time, this is also a sign that the audiences were taking their literature for history and missing their meaning as fiction. It was such attempts to bring the make-believe to life which in the long term discredited the romances altogether.

The idealism of the romances had, however, originally provided the young nobles of both sexes with a form of schooling for their emotions and manners. For the historian, the romances are therefore evidence of the noble and chivalrous outlook. It is not important whether contemporaries 'lived up' to these ideals, provided their own social behaviour was influenced by them. Persons regularly exposed to such courtly entertainment could not avoid some softening of their social behaviour. The upper classes found in this literature a projection of an idealized life suited to their standing and their aspirations. Those who had no contact at all with these literary conceits immediately gave themselves away for lacking in courtesy, that is not knowing how to behave to ladies and in society.[62] Despite the obvious differences of rank in earlier society, there had been nothing to correspond to this social barrier in the past. For the first time young people had to be educated in the elaborate rules of conduct for their class.[63]

The promotion of genteel society in a few privileged places did not immediately open an unbridgeable gulf between persons of good birth and the rest, but the drawbridge was raised and lowered at the discretion of the well-born. As long as they continued to direct political activities, they could not withdraw from social contact with their inferiors. The ladies might be isolated from coarse company, but the men continued to enjoy the pleasures of a man's world, as in hunting and sport. As landlords, they perpetuated the tradition of hospitality to tenants and patronage in their districts. Their great halls gathered in dependents, vassals, domestics, herdsmen and neighbours. Gentlemen were not turned into milksops by literature. Though the stories of the romances became common knowledge in late medieval Europe, particularly through vernacular prose versions, they had by that time already had their chief social effect in dividing the refined from the vulgar. The courtly style of life excluded the latter from that familiarity with great men which had once been taken for granted. In the place of the vertical divisions between territories of distinct speech, Europe was divided horizontally into those who knew the meaning of *courtoisie* and those who did not. Book education had once been a form of technical learning for the clergy. Only when adapted into lay society could it become, instead, a means of defining classes in terms of their 'culture'.

5. THE UNWRITTEN EVIDENCE

For the most part it is impossible to write historically about the great majority of humble men at any time, since they leave no record of their thoughts and feelings. But some unlettered men have left their historical evidence: artefacts which may be used to shed some light on the un-educated. In the past such objects were studied as part of archaeology, before this term came to imply buried remains. The archaeology of the middle ages is for the most part above ground, and surprisingly well preserved. Medieval churches and castles, with their furnishings, together with domestic housing and town-plans, are still familiar features of Europe even now. Some of them stand out prominently and justify the confidence of their builders that they laboured for eternity. Defaced, abused, restored and gawped at, they are often best served by neglect, like our own lanes and hedges. They are part of that diminishing legacy which our creative forebears have left us. The present is often lost in wonder that men could make mere pots to last. Modern appreciation of these objects is still limited. Modern archaeologists are now more concerned with shifting tons of earth to uncover the unknown. And there are the prejudices that either medieval implies inferior (since the term is often used pejoratively without reference to a particular period at all) or alternatively the term is used to convey some sickly religious con-cept and to invite mindless admiration for lofty spires, soaring Gothic or luminous stained-glass. The romantic medievalism of the nineteenth century's reaction against industrial soullessness has of course abundant reason to flourish in the present too. Unfortunately such nostalgia is singularly ill-suited for appreciating one of the most constructive periods of the European past.

The archaeological monuments are amongst the most obvious and impressive products of this age, and it is impossible to envisage the period without them. Before men open a book of history they already have in their mind's eye a picture of a castle, monastery or cathedral, perhaps of an illuminated manuscript, a church-wall painting, or tympana or gargoyles from a church. In modern style, it is easy to assume that what is seen tells something about the period in which the work was produced: projecting awe, sublimity, grotesquery, or savagery. This simple use of art to illustrate modern prejudices needs to be carefully controlled. What is read into these visual impressions depends more on the viewer than on the artist or his times. Medieval works of art appeared idolatrous to Protestants and had no attractions for most eighteenth-century taste. If they speak now as art, it is especially because the surviving majority are no longer seen principally as religious objects. This may not matter when assessing their 'aesthetic' value, but it does when arguments are drawn from their effects now to their historical meaning. The solemn awe inspired by Gothic cathedrals completed in the nineteenth century, swept clear of colourful trappings, pictures, statues, set up with pews and massive organs, does not help in the appreciation of medieval cathedrals, which were always in a state of suspended building, swarming with people of every kind about their business in the town's principal permanent building.

To put works of art into their social context, it is necessary at least to consult contemporary writers. Most of them, the clergy, gave little attention to works of art, even of their religious buildings. They praised builders and attributed the glory to the enterprising bishop or abbot, not to his architect or master mason. They liked innovation or novelty and tried to get the best of the new men to carry out the work. They had no respect for the old as such, and cheerfully destroyed to rebuild, bigger and better. (This did not preclude conscious imitation of the recognizable grand manner of Roman or Carolingian predecessors, when they wished for other reasons to adopt imperial styles. The reforming papacy in the eleventh century thus consciously revived the styles of the fourth century as part of its programme. But there was no preference for antique 'styles' as such.) Medieval building styles changed constantly. We may ourselves date the construction stylistically almost to given decades. At the time contemporaries certainly had no inkling that they were building in one 'Gothic' style. Nor did they notice the difference between Romanesque and Gothic, which is both the most obvious and the most baffling phenomenon for us. At best, writers noticed the contributions of exotic workmen, Greek or Saracen; a chronicler of Wimpfen *c.* 1280 records how the new basilica was built there *opere Francigeno,* by a

Parisian architect, which is so easily explained in modern terms as the reception of the 'Gothic' style in Germany, that it is useful to note that the sentence continues with the architect making window-columns *ad instar anglici operis* with great labour and at enormous expense.[64] The observer on the spot was not interested in 'style' but in workmanship. Thus contemporary descriptions of buildings, though generally brief, concentrate upon the practical aspects of the building. What seemed most important was the dispositon of the shrines. They had no photographs or realistic drawings of other buildings to compare with their own and they were so very easily 'reminded' of a famous prototype of their church in Rome or Jerusalem, simply by association of religious ideas, that they did not even require churches of the Holy Sepulchre, for example, to be round.[65]

The power of buildings or pictures to move the beholder is often attested. Matthew Paris himself is praised for the *subtilitas* of his power to model in gold, silver and other metal, and in painting he was believed to be second to none in the Latin world, but enthusiasm is usually for the technical accomplishment.[66] Abbot Suger is the medieval connoisseur who comes closest to speaking of aesthetic appreciation. He wrote extensively of his improvements and beautification at St Denis, and there is a somewhat vulgar tendency to concentrate on the money he had lavished on materials and workmen, particularly on the gems he accummulated by gift and purchase. His approach to aesthetic ecstasy is not through the work of artists but in contemplation of these jewels of which he knew the mystical properties. 'When—out of my delight in the beauty of the house of God—the loveliness of the many-coloured gems has called me away from external cares and worthy meditation has induced me to reflect on the diversity of the sacred virtues, transferring that which is material to that which is immaterial; then it seems to me that I see myself dwelling, as it were in some strange region of the universe which neither exists entirely in the shrine of the earth, nor entirely in the purity of Heaven: and that by the grace of God, I can be transported from this inferior to that higher world, in an anagogical manner'.[67] It is difficult to argue from such a text that the abbot appreciated art as such. At best, when speaking of improvement to the altar of St Denis he says that it was as admirable in form as in material, so that certain people *could* say *'materiam superabat opus'*, but his own preference is clearly for rich material; his splendid *operarii* of stained-glass windows are singled out because they cost him seven hundred pounds; he says nothing of their artistic merits.

The remarks of the educated clergy are thus meagre. Perhaps they are untypical. But how could the uneducated, great or small, who commissioned or regarded the churches or their decorations find better words or a more refined approach? What did the craftsmen themselves think they were doing? Did they infuse into their works a personal, or a collective, piety? Even if they did, this might have been only incidental to their workmanship, which they carried out modestly according to their skills as craftsmen. Without special commendation from his patrons, or social encouragement, the craftsmen could have at best taken only a personal pride in his work. Surrounded by others working in the same tradition, he cannot have regarded his work as exceptional, as it may seem today when only a few examples of it survive. Perhaps he produced with the same unpretentious skill of the eighteenth-century craftsmen in wood, furniture makers and carriage makers, quite unsuspecting that their work, hundreds of years later, would be acquired for museums, and put on a par with classical statuary. Some artists clearly had a higher opinion of their own worth. A few twelfth-century sculptors proudly incised their names for posterity: by the fourteenth century, architects boldly 'signed' their own work—but painters did not generally sign their paintings until much later. The surviving texts on the subject of the arts are few and unsatisfactory, but they warn against attributing too much to medieval works of art. The evidence of the texts helps to reconstruct the world these works of art were intended to serve.

From the twelfth century the 'artists' who achieved personal fame and social consequence were the architects—internationally reputed stone-masons, who preserved the secrets of their power to build on a huge scale and direct the largest public works then executed. This revival of stone building went far beyond recovery of a lost Roman art. Inspired by the religious leaders of the day, most notably by Suger, they first created high buildings of unprecedented majesty. Lofty, stone-vaulted, full of light, rippling from bay to bay towards the choir, encouraging the faithful to press forward to the sanctuary, they were, as God's houses, calm and eloquent of the rationality of the supreme Geometer. These were men made in God's image—creating marvels out of stones of the earth. These architects were actually men of learning, with the necessary knowledge of geometry, of mechanics, as well as manual skills, the tricks of the trade.[68] In a famous sermon of the thirteenth century, the preacher Nicholas de Biard dares to express his sense of scandal that such artisans could be allowed to supervise without taking off their gloves, like worldly bishops.[69] Intended as criticism, his saying is proof of their dignity. By their plans and advice the great churches rose lofty and light to stand for eternity upon the slenderest pillars.

The architects supervised all aspects of their buildings: the windows were glazed and the niches filled with sculptures by their subordinates. Their finest works were commissioned by churches and towns; the glory was attributed to God, for they served the Christian community as a whole.

This was still the artistic condition of Italy *c.* 1400, as may be gauged from the discussions about Milan cathedral that brought many famous international architects together.[70] There is no question of these sublime managerial intellects using their position to win recognition for the other 'arts'. Whereas Romanesque buildings had needed decoration, Gothic buildings expressed the purest principles of architecture; wall-space for painters was reduced, and then even stained glass banished, to let the day in to light up the architects' designs. The supremacy of the architect made the painters and sculptors redundant, and reduced them to executing decorative work or smaller portable objects, like panel paintings and prayer books. Such objects had no 'artistic' value and could be easily replaced or superseded — much more easily than the architects' buildings, which could not be knocked down and rebuilt in each new generation.

In modern terms however the artist *par excellence* is the painter: the terms are almost interchangeable. It is easy to see that the ability to draw, to make plain in pictures, accords the painter a respect second only to the writer, if indeed the priority not be in the reverse order. In the thirteenth century a jongleur's poem in praise of painters boisterously celebrates their skill in a tone, which, if mocking, is none the less complimentary. It is the kind of burlesque that the painters themselves could have well enjoyed singing in their cups, boastful but humorous. The poet likens every deceiver to the painters, who know how to create illusions. Even the peasant who puts the finest logs on the outside of the bundle is a 'painter': how much more so writers and advocates with their fine words. Those who paint their trade finest know the most tricks.[71] This recognition of the painters' talents is a commissioned piece, not disinterested praise.

The literary author not unnaturally put it differently: when King Arthur saw the room where Lancelot had painted the story of his love for Guinevere, he did not fully understand what he saw until he had read the verbal explanation painted into the picture. For him painting had not in the thirteenth century become an autonomous form of communication, but even the author recognized that Arthur noticed the pictures first and read the text second.[72] But pictorial elements crept into the books, not as mere decoration but as intellectual aids. The book page itself, as in complicated legal texts with glosses, had to be much more carefully designed by expert calligraphers.[73] Matthew Paris was both writer and draughtsman. He drew pictures in the margins of his work not just to decorate but to depict more clearly and concisely. He drew Henry III's show-elephant from life, without perhaps altogether succeeding in escaping from the drawing style he had learned from books. He was also an early designer of maps, so he had a precocious sense of how to use design or illustration as an aid to understanding.[74] By the end of the century, Richard de Furnival took it for granted that men would learn from both words and pictures.[75] The passion for pictorial representation developed beyond the stage of mere illustration to the point where it could dispense with words altogether. This was dependent upon a profound change in educated opinion about the nature of reality itself.

Until the fourteenth century, men in general believed that the only realities were the matters of the spirit and that books from the past were the main sources of information about them. Painters had nothing better to do than provide images to help men visualize what they could *not* see directly with their eyes.[76] Painters used traditional pattern-books to help them draw, and relied on conventional symbols like Peter's keys to show which saint they had painted. They had no interest in direct observation of nature and not surprisingly later critics supposed they could not draw.

From the late thirteenth century, certainly as one of the consequences of the revival of Aristotelian studies, the visible world began to claim their attention. The later emphasis of Scotists and Ockhamists on individual objects at the expense of abstractions diverted even learned attention to the importance of specific detail. Painters drew beasts and flowers from life and their paintings were filled with people and places, some of which may still be identified. The oldest view of Florence appears in a fourteenth-century picture. Siena is lovingly depicted in Ambrogio Lorenzetti's frescoes of Good and Bad Government in the council chamber of the town hall. The oldest surviving portraits are those of the fourteenth-century kings of Aragon, of John II of France (died 1364) and of Richard II. The physical appearance of an individual's physiognomy has become a matter of significance. This does not imply that man lost interest in the soul, only that they were more attentive to naturalistic details. The fact that the details were incorporated into religious paintings may obscure the fact of change. The harrowing details of the Crucifixion paintings were obviously not records of contemporary events; they stirred up the devotions of the faithful the more effectively by appealing to their direct experience of intense emotion: grief, suffering, even malice. Observation had become part of the painter's technique, but it had not yet modified nature of his art—to present ideas and concepts visibly. The work of art retained its place in a scheme of life or ritual and had no aesthetic significance of its own (though hanging in modern art galleries such works are inevitably treated as though they did). In the fifteenth century, such works by Flemish masters passed for the summit of artistic achievement, even in Italy, at a time when Italian painters were carrying through even more far-reaching changes.

It is understandable how pictorial representation could do more than books to record appearances and give knowledge of what things looked like. Photography which has made it unnecessary for painters to serve this purpose has confirmed the usefulness of visual record. In the fourteenth century this discovery was new and it was the painters who made it seem indispensable. There were many possible applications of it: portraiture, anatomical illustration and many uses in both science and technology. These opened a way to the understanding of the world that owed nothing to books and everything to careful observation of nature. The sum of human learning was no longer distilled in words alone. The accurate picture, too, would last for ever and record what man had seen in a mere moment of time. And draughtsmen could do more still, as in the making of maps, for no man would ever see the land spread out as it appeared there. The problem here was to combine picture-making with accurate measurement: two very different skills had to be combined. Accuracy in direction or orientation was essential if charts were to be useful to navigators; it is for nautical maps that precision first appears, already by the late thirteenth century. Early in the fourteenth century there are attempts to depict the geographical look of some lands, notably in Venetian maps of the Adriatic and Levant.[77] In the sixteenth century it was the painters who were commissioned to project maps of their countries on the walls of council chambers. In our own day the visual projection of geographical maps is so natural that we forget how schematic any pictorial projection had been until the new techniques showed the way to something both accurate and beautiful. Without it maps would have remained much more diagrammatic — projects of intelligence, rather than of observation and manual skill.

During the period of European history discussed in this book, the written word established itself as essential for public business, but became thereby a basic skill of only elementary significance, for those with aspirations to public notice. By the end of the period something more significant still had occurred: the supremacy accorded to the artist. Portraits, domestic stone buildings, and the instruments of work and comfort, all products of men's hands, give historians evidence, and in abundance, about aspects of past life formerly quite obscure. Out of sight of the scribes, European society had been transformed by the activities of persons at first without pretension to historical fame, men of whom it may be said that they have left no memorial, but whose activities have the first claim on historical attention.

3

MUNDANE BUSINESS

'To study the laws of history', wrote Tolstoy, 'we must completely change the subject of our observation, must leave aside kings, ministers and generals and study the common, infinitesimally small elements by which the masses are moved. No one can say how far it is possible for men to advance in this way towards an understanding of the laws of history; but it is evident that only along that path does the possibility of discovering the laws of history lie; and that as yet not a millionth part as much mental effort has been applied in this direction by historians, as has been devoted to describing the actions of various kings, commanders and ministers and propounding reflections of their own concerning these actions'.[1] A century later we may look back on the devoted labours of historians who have applied much mental effort in this direction, and if the results, for this period, remain meagre it is because Tolstoy did not seriously consider how it would ever be possible to study the common, infinitesimally small elements.

Every man may in fact contribute his mite to the accumulated historical heritage, but if his contribution goes unrecorded, it is impossible to distinguish his from that of others, and even in aggregate the contributions of whole generations may not receive their due if there is no one to put the achievements into writing. For the written evidence of the past remains the best: the most precise, and the most informative. Granted the purpose of writing and the interests of writers before the sixteenth century, the dearth of information about the daily lives of the majority of Europeans for many centuries should cause no surprise. Modern critics who appear to regard it as incorrigible snobbery to focus historical attention on the thoughts and deeds of exalted persons must stop to consider how suitable evidence for those of others can be found, let alone the inherent difficulties of interpreting it. What can be known at all is very little: England fares better than most European countries. The evidence about such matters is always specific to time and place, and generalization about regions, countries, classes, decades or centuries rests upon uneven foundations. Modern educated interest in the subject constantly expects only broad views to fit modern theories. What evidence there is points to the fact that in the past there was no belief amongst the educated then that life in society is, or ought to be, man's prime concern.

1. MEDIEVAL SOCIAL THEORY AND ECONOMICS
The word *socius* was in constant use, and fellowship with equals much valued. The concept of *societas* extended no further than real fellowship. Indeed it is only recently that society has come to mean something larger than the social group to which men had access for the purpose of conviviality. The indiscriminate companionage of modern society empties the term of its essential meaning. There was no medieval term corresponding to it except *humanitas.* This had currency amongst the intelligentsia, who were, however, in general, as narrow in their own academic loyalties as their contemporaries were to their *societates.* Working in close proximity and enduring personal rancours, for the peace of their own group men harboured distinctly hostile attitudes to the next village, profession, class or country. There could be no view of the whole, except in religious terms, let alone a suspicion that taking thought might effectively modify the whole structure of human life. The existing social relationships were explained as the consequence of man's sin.

From one end of the middle ages to the other, the clergy were sure that God had intended men to be free and equal: Gregory the Great on men's natural equality is cited by Francesc Eximenic in the fourteenth century. A German writer of the mid-fifteenth century deplores the attitude of those Christians who say of others 'You are my property' when God had freed all men.[2] Social differences derived their force from past oppressions. It was difficult to do much about them, since men were wicked and would not cease to oppress one another in the future. Nevertheless it was meritorious to undo them by acts of mercy. This was what the commune of Bologna considered in 1257 when it bought the freedom of all those in servile condition from their masters by a memorial, duly called *Paradisus,* from the place where God had shown his original intention of giving men the most perfect freedom.[3] There was no awareness that the mere passage of time in any way modified the existing social patterns. Frequent complaints about degeneration from earlier standards or about the reversal of fortunes imply at best that moral revival alone will restore the proper order and virtue maintain it. Actual observation of society duly reinforced the clerical explanations of the human condition: there was ample illustration of wickedness and abundant room for improvement.

It was rare to consider how society might be reformed on the grand scale. Fate spared one early manuscript of the elaborate projects made by Pierre Dubois at the beginning of the fourteenth century for the total reorganization of the Christian kingdoms. Here is a visionary much to modern taste, gleefully adjusting all the crucial parts of the kingdoms for the great enterprise of launching a united crusade. Though he did his best to secure recognition and employment, in both France and England, his contemporaries ignored him.[4] The practical difficulties of implementing his proposals were of course beyond contemporary resources. Dubois' ideas, however idiosyncratic, are derived from a view of human nature quite untroubled by historical determinism, blithely assuming, like those following Rousseau, that human societies are products of men's wills and may be reshaped with confidence, at least when so noble a venture as the crusade is at stake. By his religious purpose, however, even Dubois fails to meet modern expectations of a radical reformer.

As to any attempt to make a survey of such a specific problem as the national economic interest, there is nothing before the mid-sixteenth century, when an anonymous pamphlet *The Discourse of the Common Weal of this Realm of England* appeared.[5] However partially executed, this represents an important advance in the powers of human abstraction to consider the social whole. The anonymous author of the *Libel of English Policye,* a poem written c.1436, attempted something much more limited in reviewing the interests of English trade, arguing against foreign carriers and for the importance of defending Calais against the duke of Burgundy: a partisan pamphlet.[6] Speakers in the Venetian and Florentine council chambers must have also tried from time to time to establish what the 'public interest' required in any given emergency, but all such talk also reflected the speaker's own personal experience and prejudices. In the absence of any theory about how to represent the town's or kingdom's productive interests, such attempts to frame policy are more interesting for their intention than for their proposals. The need to close ranks in self-defence and to devise common policies rather proved that the time was past when merchants would venture on their own in open competition. If some merchants sought power and influence to advance their own interests, the effect was to damage the affairs of rivals. Others preferred to rely on friends or exclusively on their kin. The realization of what governments could do had not dawned, and in practice the 'state' was used blatantly by particular interests for their own advantage.

If contemporaries failed to provide general views of society and economy, modern scholars have demonstrated remarkable ingenuity (increasingly so recently) in the compilation of statistical information designed to enable us to take the global view for ourselves.[7] These studies, when their fragmentary basis is remembered, may yield valuable insights, but they must not obscure the fact that those described in statistical terms lived and worked in total ignorance of the significance of figures. Neither kings, nor merchants nor clerks were in a position to calculate, even as well as we are, so their activities were conducted in the light of other factors. The principal European source of medieval statistics is the Domesday Book, produced in England in 1086, and describing the estates of the king and his barons by counties. Already so named in the twelfth century, it was a book to excite awe, but it inspired no successors. Modern scholars derive little profit from reading it without the statistical aids or the indices provided by a succession of painstaking students, so that we can now assess the relative wealth of the king, his barons and his churches (the king's is declared to be 17 per cent of the whole). Though much used in the medieval royal exchequer, no one there ever attempted to concoct tables of figures from it, because its chief use at the time was to provide information about each estate, not grand totals. Modern historians of the Day of Judgment will of course analyse the saved and damned, by age, profession and income bracket; medieval writers concentrated on individuals.

This attitude may also be found in the earliest sets of financial records to be made or kept in England and France. Royal officials, sheriffs or *prévôts,* gave account of their charges, two or three times a year. The English records go back to 1130 and become continuous from 1155. French records are much more patchy and the oldest dates only from 1202.[8] They reveal a persistent, indeed niggling, scrutiny of official revenues and expenses. Yet there is no surviving record of any annual review of the whole financial position. All the various account rolls in meticulous detail were preserved separately; if there was one financial minister to the king (which was not always the case), he was not apparently required to make any financial statement about the past or prepare estimates for the future. The king of France was pragmatically more anxious about the place of deposit for his real money: it was kept with the knights of the Temple in Paris until 1295 and again between 1303 and 1307; only finally transferred to the Louvre about ten years later. During this time the king's government also obtained considerable additional sources of revenue and developed its financial administration accordingly. Even so, no actual statement of estimated revenues and expenses is known to have been prepared for the king until 1332 and no further enquiry of this sort was made until 1344 when the situation had drastically deteriorated.[9] Later, when French royal finances were salvaged by resort to taxation, separate administrative machinery was set up for this, which made assessment of the overall situation even more difficult. In England despite a precocious interest in financial record keeping, the oldest surviving attempt to present a coherent review of royal revenues and expenses comes from Lord Cromwell, minister to Henry VI.[10]

If kings knew or cared little about the workaday totals of their revenues, even less should they have cared about the totals of population. Domesday has been used as a basis of calculating the total population of England in 1086 at 1½ to 2 million. It is assumed to have risen steadily until the fourteenth century and then, after falling seriously, to have climbed back to its earlier height by *c.*1500. The losses caused by the Black Death provoked many attempts to encourage emigration from less devastated areas, but no idea of compiling a census. The story of how King David had presumed to count the number of his people and incurred punishment from God for it circulated as a popular tale in the fourteenth century and strengthened clerical opposition to exact counting. Ignorance of numbers could be surprising. In 1371, when the English parliament intended to raise fresh taxes, the king's lay ministers assumed there were 40,000 (instead of 8,600) parishes in England, though the 17 bishops in the lords had the means of computing the numbers accurately by consulting their archdeacons.[11] It is true that, for purposes of taxation, registers of assessment were compiled, but they are not as easy to use for demographic purposes as they could have been. Significantly, the unit that mattered then was the household. The surviving ones from Paris can be used to prove that over the years from 1292 to 1313 the number of taxpayers actually declined, leaving the more influential citizens to settle amongst themselves the individual assessments: the government was emphatically not interested in the numbers, but only in the payments; it had not the machinery to exact petty sums from all citizens liable and preferred to be sure of its total.[12] Similarly in England after 1334 the king settled for fixed grants of tenths from the laity and fifteenths from the clergy.[13]

General scrutinies of the financial resources of private citizens were feared. In republican Florence, governments had to promise to destroy tax registers once the taxes were collected so that assessments had to be made afresh each time taxes were imposed. Not until 1427 did the Florentines adopt a tax-reform that established the total assets of each citizen, from which regular taxation could be exacted.[14] In most countries taxation, however enduring, was always treated as a temporary imposition, only justified by urgent necessity. For ordinary expenses governments were after all assigned revenues on lands. After more than a century of recurrent taxation in connexion with the French war, the English parliament was therefore gratified to be told by Edward IV in 1467 that his ordinary revenues sufficed and that he could dispense with parliamentary grants, indeed with parliament altogether.[15] Kings enjoying their own revenues or seeking to share those of others either way lacked the means of knowing their kingdom's total resources and the motive for trying to consider the economy as a whole.

The general absence of figures or concern to supply them must have had consequences for the manner of doing business. There are, for example, manuals of merchant practice from the late thirteenth century which distilled essential practical wisdom of businessmen for general benefit; but each merchant dealt in total ignorance of matters now deemed essential. They knew nothing of their rivals' business affairs or accounts, for there were no company statements, or stock exchanges. They could anticipate variations in the price of foreign monies according to seasonal business, but there was no international telegraph or prices on the international markets to guide them. In individual cities, it is doubtful whether merchants derived much advantage from collective solidarity. Florentine business diaries, composed to warn the next generation of the family, recommended extreme wariness in all affairs and putting no faith in their own governments, for though managed by businessmen they might be rivals or enemies.[16] Though the great patricians of Venice acquired a reputation for tight-lipped devotion to the public cause, lesser merchants maintained a lively sense of commercial rivalry, as shown in an amusing account of the 'race' between two transport galleys bearing pilgrims from Venice to the Holy Land in 1484.[17] Merchants had very little to help them in their individual enterprise, apart from what their relations or trusted agents and friends could add to their own talents. The Polos travelled as a family team to the far end of the known world, relying on their wits and trusting the strange people they frequented, without hope of rescue if imprisoned, or vengeance if murdered. Their business was an adventure and it is not surprising that the earliest merchant manual surviving, from Pisa, included the elements of astrology. Its ultimate recommendation was to rely on *seny* — cautious good sense; it was the most important quality in business.[18]

A few clerical writers, like Peter Comestor,[19] bestowed some attention to business but the nature of their education gave them little help. It took a modest 'clerk', Bonvesin de Rippa, a schoolteacher from Milan, to produce the most original educated contribution to medieval 'social science'.[20] He thought he was inspired by God to do honour to his city by modestly counting up its resources. It was an enormous labour at the time and one which amazed and disconcerted his contemporaries. With only a list of churches to guide or inspire him, Bonvesin de Rippa counted the gates on the public streets (12,500) (presumably barricades for protection at night), covered squares or markets (60), the length of the wall (10,141 cubits) and its height (38 cubits), its 6 main gateways, and 10 posterns, 200 churches (and 480 altars), 120 belltowers, 200 bells and so on. He assesses the city population at a total of 200,000, which needed

1,200 moggia of grain a day to eat. He includes a notice of the 28 physicians and of more than 70 schoolteachers. This numerical curiosity goes further than a mere desire to impress by figures, for he took great pains over many years to glean his information. Some of his figures are calculations or estimates based upon careful thinking, which do him great honour. His work was not appreciated as it deserved and other writers excerpted from him carelessly and disdainfully, so that his statistical information, cut up and wrong, survived chiefly as additional pieces to marvel at in the uncritical and bombastic works of more distinguished clergy like the Dominican Galvano della Fiamma. The latter more certainly represents the general opinion of the times in finding Bonvesin's concern for numerical calculations rather fanciful. The daily business of living had therefore in general to proceed without attention to numbers. This no more prevented lively concern for making money in real coins than ignorance of higher mathematics spoils a bookmaker's profit.

One other modern aid to thinking, diagrammatic representation, was also defective and only in exceptional use. There were some maps. From the late thirteenth century navigation charts survive for the practical use of mariners in the Mediterranean. Some early fourteenth-century maps already show a power to project plausible geographical shapes on paper, and map painting and design progressed pictorially over the next two centuries. For most persons interested in travel, however, itineraries giving the number of days' journey in words or in a diagram of the ribbon-road kind remained for long in more common use. Only gradually could men begin to think of acquiring mental images of the shape of other lands.[21]

We must imagine the daily experience of men deprived of the mental props of figures and diagrams in different terms from the ones we use. By dint of taking thought to improve our daily lot, the ordinary, not to say the trivial, has acquired a prominent part in our thinking lives. In those days, although much more vulnerable, men took little thought how to improve their lot, and turned to other things, no doubt for a variety of reasons. They were not so different from us in some ways. They feared death and tried to escape from the contamination of the plague, but they could not fear old age: not many of them lived long enough. The clergy steadily denounced their unbridled sexuality, which they appear to have enjoyed without humbug or coyness. The celibacy of the clergy may have soured their judgment, but men living constantly in the vicinity of animals had no doubts about their own animal natures and suffered from no false modesty, or illusions about the divinity of men. Modern anxieties about health, cleanliness and the impulses of nature were not unknown, but had no power to mesmerize even the educated, amongst whom education consistently fostered preoccupation with spiritual redemption. On those matters they tended to concentrate, not hypo-critically averting their eyes from the sordid world, but persuaded that nothing could be done to improve it, as indeed is likely. The limits of their endeavours were set by the size of the societies they felt they belonged to. The largest and most powerful of these was the church—which offered them most inspiration. The least was their working community within which they operated as best they could in ways inherited from their elders. If they improved on their inheritance, it was not by inten-tion, but incidentally.

2. RURAL LIFE

Most men were raised and worked in the countryside, which was the scene of visible collective efforts. It was not the place of work for a few specialized workers, nor a retreat for tranquil pleasures. The life of the whole community obviously depended upon the conscientious labours of cultivators, and due if brief acknowledgement of this is regularly made.

The most attractive and positive attempt to describe the functioning of society as a whole, and the part played by every member of it comes in Jacobus de Cassolis's allegory of the game of chess (1300).[22] Even if only cultured laymen were able to appreciate the game, they could acquire an insight into the complex nature of civil society and the part valuably played by every member of it, in terms of a familiar game. Jacobus justified from *Genesis ii* his view that the earth was the source of man himself and his natural habitat: 'The earth is the mother of us all, because in the beginning of all life we were fashioned from it and we shall have the earth for our final resting place.' A special responsibility, almost an honour, therefore, rested upon the great majority of men who worked it and made nature yield her fruits—ultimately natural increase was the only real source of wealth. 'The lives of the greatest and the best men are in the hands of those who labour the soil.' Jacobus assumes that the peasants will fulfil men's expectations without dishonesty or compulsion. It was obviously to everyone's advantage to obtain the maximum yield from the land; the peasant did not need to be whipped on or brow-beaten. Jacobus recommends him to worship God, respect the law and scorn death: through him the whole kingdom is provided with the necessities of life. The peasant knew his value to society and, since there were never enough men to go round, every man was indispensable. Cultivators can never have been so numerous as to lose their strictly economic value. Even on the extreme assumption made by a few scholars that the total European population rose in the late thirteenth century to a level unequal to the resources in land, this can have had a depressing effect on the peasantry only in some parts of western Europe: Spain remained short of people; in Italy at this time communes were weakening the nobility by forcibly emancipating their serfs and raising their status; in eastern Europe inducements were being offered to attract new settlers. Any notable increase in village populations was met by extending the cultivable lands or by emigration to towns or new areas. It is unwarranted to consider the conditions of the rural population in terms of a rural proletariat. Differences of class, wealth and function could excite hatred and disapproval, but the favoured groups had no power or means of oppressing their labourers. Where the seigneurial regime was most firmly established, the peasantry had also proceeded furthest with collective agriculture, ploughing, reaping, grazing and pasture. Within this legal community, traditional rights were known and enforced by them in their courts, albeit under the lord's aegis. The rights to homesteads and land were protected. Lords had no power to evict and no interest in doing so.[23] The consistent effort required for agriculture hardly made the labourers' lot idyllic. Even without the predominantly legal records of violence, cheating and oppression, the roughness of country life can be imagined.

The clergy are our chief source of information and comment about rural life: though most of them were themselves country-born, they were not inevitably sympathetic. The successful ones turned their back on it and cultivated higher things, for they had no doubts that it was nobler to cultivate *animos* (souls) than *agros* (fields) and they turned 'villein' into a term of opprobrium and scorn.[24] A French clerical poet of the fourteenth century who satirizes the peasantry, with some bitterness asks why God allowed villeins to live so well: eating beef and getting drunk daily on the best wine, although they hated Him for not giving them what they asked and grumbled equally about fine weather and rain. The poet would have preferred to see villeins, whom he says were no better than animals, going on all fours, naked like their beasts and eating thistles and thorns.[25] Here their simplicity is presented in a less flattering way, in accordance with the polite standards which emphasized the crudity and stupidity of the peasants, though the same tradition shows that craftiness nevertheless earned them exasperated respect. The Aragonese Franciscan Alvaro Pelayo's work *De Planctu Ecclesiae* contains more ponderous and less useful information. He lists every known sin ever attributed to rustics by any book he knew.[26] This can hardly be used as though it were a description of daily life. No attempt was made at the time to describe country life and medieval writers are not easily made to answer modern questions. The country clergy, who might have been more charitable towards their parishioners, rarely bothered to write and are chiefly remembered for their own misdemeanours which earned them rebuke from their betters.[27] So too, in literature and in sermons, the honest labourers who receive commendation for their efforts are none the less blameworthy. The Franciscan preacher who pitied the oppressions they suffered singled out four principal causes for their eternal damnation — their laziness in neglecting the divine offices, their theft of corn or land, their willingness to commit perjury for money, and their drunkenness.[28] The clergy often complained too of matters that affected them in particular, like the reluctance to pay tithes. But accusations that they encroached on their neighbours' land by crafty ploughing and the maxim that when in doubt peasants split the difference properly remind us that the conditions of agriculture simply remained somewhat crude.

The cultivation of the soil requires particular attention to local conditions in climate and land. Improvements were made as a result of experience rather than learning. The quintessence of Roman agricultural knowledge in the Mediterranean region was available in literary form in Virgil's *Georgics* and in Columella's treatise, but it is doubtful how useful such works could be in improving the conditions of cultivating northern Europe, where the climate was ruder and the soil heavier. New lands were constantly being won from the forests and marshes. The increase in population had much to do with this and the effects were most notable in northern Europe. Improvements in Italian agriculture came from the thirteenth century with drainage schemes in the Po valley, and later, when rich citizens took an interest in improving agriculture, as in Tuscany. On the other hand, it was at this period that southern Italy began its steady decline, as disafforestation played havoc with the water systems. Generally speaking, however, the development of agriculture owed less to the investment of capital than to the cooperative labours of the peasantry, and bore most fruit in the north, in lands which the Romans had not occupied or could not improve. The hope of better lands had driven on the Germanic invaders, and their traditions kept alive the model of the free peasant, though historical information about agriculture depends on the records of lords, which emphasize (quasi-) servile obligations. However, whether the peasants cooperated on a large estate or in a village community, it was by working together in the confines of their little world that they subdued nature to their wills. Men, and women too, worked at their different tasks. Village children soon proved useful.[29] The stories of Joan of Arc's childhood as told to her judges show her minding the sheep with her friends, though she found opportunities for other matters nearer her heart. The most intensive agriculture in the north involved the use of large open fields operating a two- and then a three-field rotation, and this imposed cooperative cultivation and communal decisions about ploughing, reaping and gleaning. Common meadows and other pasture rights had to be protected, boundaries set up, ditches dug, cattle-thieves pursued and local disputes settled by common agreement. It was difficult to introduce novelties, though the change-over to the three-field system was effected in these conditions.

How these village communities were managed is largely a matter of speculation. Documents refer to decisions being reached, even at the lord's insistence, by the locals. When the Abbess of Essen wanted to know what her *schulteti curtium* ought to leave her when they withdrew from office, the ancient custom was declared by the *heymanni, litones, coloniet iurati*. For many purposes these communities having no regular organisation or spokesman, they simply improvised what was necessary on occasion. The men of Dithmarsch found a hero, but not a leader, in bold Rolf Brickensohn when they fought against the lords of Schleswig and Holstein to defend their liberties. The bishops of Bamberg at the same time allowed the village of Eggolsheim bei Forsheim the privilege of having its own sworn council, seal and banner.[30] What villages expected and were prepared to fight for varied greatly; there were no general theories, only ancient customs; what was traditionally the case was accepted without complaint. Abuses and oppression there must have been nonetheless, but most allegations of seigneurial oppression are too vague or too idiosyncratic. An interesting dispute over hours of work in the vineyards of Auxerre went to the Paris *parlement* for settlement. The nature of the dispute is not clear but the law upheld the rights of the town's inhabitants to oblige the labourers to spend the whole day in the vineyards, perhaps because of the civic charter. The labourers complained of having to work the whole day in the sun and claimed as ancient custom their right to withdraw at noon. It was alleged that they repaired to the tavern, to tennis or to their own labours, but their case is not fully stated.[31] It proves however that such day-labourers, whatever the ultimate outcome, were sufficiently independent to drive the townsmen of Auxerre to seek special privileges and courts of law against them.

The village community was not composed of equals. If estates were held there by great lords they would be frequently absent, leaving stewards anxious to get the best service possible, if not always by the gentlest methods. The resident priest occupied a prominent position in the community. What the villages made of his services is unknown. The church itself was the most permanent building in every village, as may still be seen from many surviving early village-churches, though it would be misleading to judge their influence then from their modern state. It is difficult now to credit that the clergy had frequently to forbid the use of churchyards for dancing. How can we now imagine the nature of the garth where St Cuthbert protected a stag seeking sanctuary?[32] The survival of pagan superstitions associated with the seasons may be presumed, but this is without much significance, for the church had certainly secured the suppression of the grossest pagan practices, like the fertility dances. The revival of such a ceremony in late thirteenth-century

Scotland was sufficient to excite scandalized comment.[33] For the rest the church blessed rogation days. Belief in the supernatural at least brought high and low together. Helinand of Froidmont, the Cistercian courtier of King Philip Augustus, told a story of the Count of Anjou's charcoal-burner who saw the devil ride at night and naturally informed his master so that they could both enjoy the spectacle on the next full-moon.[34]

The building of mills, water and wind, was the most costly of rural improvements; apart from the costs of construction, millstones were very expensive.[35] Millers too were persons of consequence and the rights of mills were strictly enforced. Villages also found use for the services of many specialized trades from charcoal-burners to shepherds. Villages probably needed a smith for the repair of their tools. Cultivators, even of open fields, were not all equally rich. Some had more strips, more animals, and later, more cash, than others. How in practice, and on what occasions, did men of different kinds combine for the diverse obligations of justice, cultivation, hunting, charity, marketing or warfare? In the absence of any strong pull on their affections and interests from outside, it seems likely that they lived as a community much as villages still do in many parts of the world, and which, though rarer in modern Europe, is still very obvious in rural Greece. Seen without prejudice, each village community combined many talents to win a reasonable increase from nature, devising its own social and political organization to deal with the inevitable human conflicts generated by life in proximity and in common.

Given considerable inequality and respect for tradition, it might seem that the lowly were condemned to a life of misery without hope of improvement. In fact there was more scope for change than the generalizations allow for. A constitution of the Emperor Frederick I foresaw the case of the rustic who acquired arms and became a knight. A German poem by Seifried Helbling at the end of the thirteenth century discussed the case of the peasant's son who became a knight, much to the chagrin of one born to the rank.[36] As time passed and the nobility closed its ranks to interlopers, there could have been a growing sense of class conflicts. On several occasions in the late fourteenth century, peasant uprisings brutally demonstrated their hatred of the nobility. The best known incident is that of the Jacquerie. After the disastrous battle of Poitiers, the nobility were accused of cowardice, and some of the peasants of the Paris region then exacted vengeance, taking advantage of the nobles' temporary unpopularity. One clerical writer was sympathetic to the miseries that provoked the outburst, but the peasants forfeited respect by their indiscriminate massacres.[37] Similar incidents elsewhere usually ended in ruthless repression because the peasants lacked reliable leaders who could unite and restrain their dispersed forces. In favourable situations, however, peasant forces more than held their own. Inspired by religion, some of the Bohemian peasantry proved capable of military organization and beat successive waves of conventional troops sent to destroy them after the Council of Constance (1417-34).

Even more enduring were the efforts of the Swiss to obtain real independence from their feudal overlords, the counts of Habsburg. The conditions that favoured them were exceptional, but detract in no way from the significance of the achievement. In the fifteenth century the Swiss were the best soldiers of the continent and won grudging recognition from the other peoples. Their popular style of government over the centuries earned them dislike, and fear as well; even now, when their values are held in more general esteem, there is an unattractive inclination to belittle them. It is not without interest that the most extended treatment of the subject of 'class conflict' comes from the well-born Cantor of Zürich, Felix Hämmerlein, in the mid-fifteenth century. His dialogue on nobility and rusticity inevitably shows the marks of his Swiss background, his support of the Austrian counts and his dislike of the Swiss for their persecution of the clergy.[38] His erudition, literary, theological and legal, accounts for a great deal of the matter, even when, after reviewing the whole history of the question, he finally reaches the point of discussing the current situation. The criticisms made of nobles by the *Rusticus* concentrate on the abuses of power and force, often at clerical rather than peasant expense, and state boldly that what the nobility can get away with on account of rank would be punished as crime in others. The peasant cites distinguished knights of the past and contrasts them to the nobles of the present, inevitably concluding that there had been a serious deterioration. The noble's attempt to repudiate the charges and denounce the rustics makes even the *Rusticus* of the dialogue impatient with his irrelevance. The dialogue is a tedious compilation made up of quotations, references to law books and to earlier chapters by way of amplifying the matter. Even so there is a gleam of good sense about the rustic's resigned account of human failure that is notably absent from the noble, who is reduced to denouncing peasants for their dabblings in necromancy.

Hämmerlein saw the opposition between the two classes first and foremost as a canon lawyer and therefore advocated a mutual recognition of their need for one another and assumed that concord could be established. His dislike of the Swiss peasantry could have inclined him more to the side of the nobles, for he was well-born himself. Instead, he was inclined to be indulgent towards the peasants and denounced the nobility for their pride, abuse of responsibility and lack of charity. This emphasis may indicate not that the nobility were more in need of, but only that they were more likely to read and profit from, such works. Yet the same belief in their mutual need of one another also appears in William Langland's ideal picture of the peasants working while the knight wards off their enemies and enforces justice.[39]

Hämmerlein's manner of presenting this dialogue underlines the inability even of an educated writer with a contemporary interest in the question to discuss the matter realistically. When he is not using books, he recounts anecdotes and his evidence has no persuasive power in modern terms. His authorities were bound to be ancient authors, however oblique their contributions; his anecdotes are always tangential and never demonstrate the real point at issue. The training of a canon lawyer in the learning of his century as a whole (he is alleged to have had a large private library) admittedly did not go far to helping him understand the great social conflicts of his day, but it is unlikely, in that case, that anyone else 'understood' them better. The rebellious peasantry needed no more than abuses and the occasion to stir them to arms. Why should they bother to study the question more deeply than he? Thinking little about social and more about the moral and religious problems, contemporaries blamed not the 'system', but human sin. If their life seems to us wretched and mean, contemporaries would have agreed. The condition of the great majority demonstrated the truth about the fall of man. Only those who somehow escaped from the common lot and enjoyed wordly glory might venture to believe in some other truth: they were those most in need of constant reminders about the frailty of human hopes and lives. Special efforts had to be made to bring such proud men to recognize their need of God. As the social differences became more obvious, so religious teaching and painting more ghoulishly insisted that death was the greatest equalizer. And the pitiless frescoes of kings, popes and bishops in hell, intended to frighten the great, perhaps also gave the poor some satisfaction and pandered to their sentiments of revenge.

Changing circumstances
Against this ground base of peasant cussedness must be set the continuous improvization in response to the natural environment and the economic situation that kept agriculture as Europe's liveliest industry. Down to the early fourteenth century agriculture itself generated its own productive forces; when adverse natural conditions and the plague undermined the old confidence and growth, agriculture became more passive, responding to the fluctuating demands of towns for immigrants and grain, at the mercy of market forces it could not control. Over the centuries the rural scene was far from being uneventful. The sequence of events may be hidden from us without being any less important. Major innovations like the invention of the horse-collar and the subsequent use of horses for ploughing in the place of ox-teams passed unnoticed by

chroniclers: such events happen at different times in different places and only deserve notice when further consequences flow from them. The horse ceased to be a rare beast for a special class of warriors between the twelfth and fourteenth century. A Franciscan report from India about 1300 comments that there by contrast only kings and great barons had them. The horse, though stronger, was a costly animal to keep in the country — much less economical than the ox because it needed oats to keep it alive in winter. The increase in its numbers therefore indicates the superior ability of European agriculture to sustain life for men and beasts.[40]

The most direct aspect of agrarian colonization was the steady expansion of Western Christendom throughout the twelfth century. Thereafter expansion was limited in direction, as in the extensive German settlement east of the Oder after 1250. This expansion coincided with an increase of total population which had perhaps been building up since the ninth century. Documentary evidence earlier than the twelfth century is slender anyway; by that time expansion was probably already slowing down. Fences were then being put up to protect reserves of game and timber. Such protection did not prevent further inroads, but the brake had been applied. There were not enough Christians to cultivate the new lands won from the Spanish Muslims in the thirteenth century, and tracts of southern Spain became a great transhumance for thousands of Castilian sheep, clipped to supply the Flemish cloth industry with raw wool. Cistercian settlement in neglected Yorkshire valleys produced, almost by accident, exportable surpluses of wool. England, which had been famed for her good grain lands in the eleventh century, began to acquire her more familiar reputation as a land where the wool paid for all. Thus old lands could also be improved by the exploitation of new resources in response to new demands.

The writers of the twelfth century exhale a spirit of contentment with nature. Latin poets found again the classical tone of the pastorals, without their latent paganism. God favoured men's efforts to make nature fruitful and men could therefore rejoice unaffectedly in their blessings. Twelfth-century sculptures present the twelve months of distinct rural occupations, with the ensuing rewards in grain, wine, pigs and logs.[41] Europe is not the only region of the world where a clearly defined annual cycle marks off the years as the seasons come round, but its temperate climate rewarded regular and continuous efforts to win increases from nature. Improvements, generally speaking, came to be expected, and exceptional disasters regretted rather than anticipated.

Evidence of these successful endeavours comes from religious sources, but the religious had themselves not much wisdom or learning to contribute to the enterprise. The biggest monasteries, like St Denis, or the famous centres of pilgrimage, like Mont Saint Michel and Santiago de Compostella, certainly acquired great knowledge of the world from their merchants and pilgrims. It is unlikely that this stimulated any economic ambitions. Monastic landlords used their authority to impose reforms, but it is probable that the settled habits of life that they practised and the peace to which they were entitled had more to do with the steady improvement of their properties than their books did. They concentrated on the improvement of their lands to increase the yields needed for their numerous local obligations.[42] Surpluses could be sold on occasion. Only in the thirteenth century did the increased reliability of commercial exchange stimulate a more businesslike concern to produce for the market rather than for consumption, in some favoured places.

To this century belong those works which best sum up medieval wisdom about agriculture: Walter of Henley's treatises on husbandry and Peter Crescenzi's guide for improvers.[43] These handbooks are intended for managers, or, over their shoulders, for landowners. They demonstrate what rational calculation and good sense could contribute to the improvement of the soil, with tips about animal husbandry, and the use of fertilizers like dung and marls. The prudent overseers of great estates dutifully compiled registers of tenants and statements of customs, lists of rents due, which have become the staple sources of information about rural life. They are hardly the best sources from which to gauge the workers' point of view: management is a white-collar occupation. Crescenzi's handbook remained popular and was frequently printed in the fifteenth century, which suggests that little real improvement in technique occurred after 1300. The learning of the thirteenth century, petrified in writing, may itself have done something to sap innovations as the routine managers moved in. Better management was the most that could be hoped for; there was little place for capital investment. In fact improvements only came much later on from the new interest in animal breeding and in new strains of plants.

As so often happens, however, just when the winds appeared to be set fair, a succession of disasters broke, at least over western Europe. Whether agricultural stagnation had already set in remains an open question. But there is no doubt from the records of the arrival of unexpected problems, like the unprecedented falls of rain in 1314, 1315 and 1316, which sufficiently account for the great Flemish famine,[44] or the recurrent ravages of the Black Death which crippled the power of the population to recuperate. The fuller records of the fourteenth century immediately create a much more gloomy picture than the earlier ones. How far should they be pressed to a conclusion about deteriorating meteorological conditions? It is not by chance that fuller records mean more disasters. Before newspapers existed, men did not imagine how many horrors were perpetrated daily.

The increasing amount of information reflects the fact that Europe, being more united, had access to more news; becoming dependent upon stocks of food commercially, it was more important to be well informed about conditions everywhere. In the past, without expectation of supplies from outside, many communities succumbed to famine without leaving a ripple in any record known to us. From the fourteenth century this was no longer so. Merchants, and the chroniclers after them, took a practical interest in news as relevant to their business. Giovanni Villani, the Florentine chronicler, duly noticed the great famine of 1315 in northern Europe and the profit Italian merchants made from sending Apulian and Sicilian corn to places where the price of grain was high.[45] The town chronicles that multiplied in Germany and Italy from the late thirteenth century just as naturally attended to new social catastrophies or commercial opportunities as came within their ken, as clerical writers of the same period who saw no point in accumulating yet further evidence of human misery settled down to exploit the existing stock of examples.

The chronicles have all been pressed into service to describe the onset of the great plague of 1347-8. It remains very difficult to assess its incidence and long-term consequences. Villani reported that Florence suffered from plague less in 1347 than in 1340 (he must be referring to two different diseases), but he spoke too soon: he did not himself survive the 'Black Death'. Modern calculations of the number of deaths have been extravagant. The most recent medical opinion therefore holds that in England, in the comparatively densely populated region of East Anglia, as in the larger towns affected by it, the 'Great Pestilence may possibly have destroyed as much as one third of the population; in the rest of England and Wales, it is extremely doubtful if as much as one twentieth of the population was destroyed.'[46] Still, there is no doubt of the impact of the disaster on contemporary imagination or that it made a great difference to economic activity. Survivors had to carry on and adjust as best they could. Begetting new children was only a long-term solution, since recurrent epidemics constantly frustrated the best intentions. After the initial shock, contemporaries noted a tendency to pursue pleasure frantically, while there was still time: modern historians catch an echo of the impulse to return to normality. It is hard to take the onset of the plague as a real turning point in economic history. It demonstrated that Europe formed already one economic unit, that variations in any one economic factor could seriously upset all and that there was no escape in town or country from the economic consequences of this mutual dependence.

The plague festered in the great towns. Carried to Europe originally from the Crimea aboard a Genoese galley, it spread chiefly from port to port and along the waterways, settling into towns where the population was most dense and living in such premises as harboured the black rat, since the fleas carrying the germs were parasites of that animal. The chances for avoiding the contagion were therefore good for those who lived in stone buildings and in country districts remote from main routes along which rats might inadvertently be transported. Since proportionally greater numbers of townsmen succumbed, surviving tradesmen had to attract immigrants from the country to take the empty places. Countrymen determined to take advantage of their opportunities and this aroused grave anxiety about the dearth of husbandmen and the rising cost of labour. Perturbations of the population ratios between town and country had never been so universal as in the second half of the fourteenth century and there was no easy means, or rapid, to restore the balance. Fluctuations in the town populations not only affected countrymen; they unsettled country activities which had been confidently carried on for many years on the assumption of a steady urban demand for grain, vegetables, wine and other comestibles. Adjustments to the changed level of demand could not be made all at once; it was supposed that former conditions would be quickly restored. There was anyway no means of estimating future demand, even when the picture became clearer. Apart from the moralizings of the clergy and the wooden attempts of lords to exact their traditional dues, there was no source of wisdom to deal with the problem. There was therefore an uncontrollable outburst of frantic attempts to obtain personal advantages. Some lords offered higher wages to tempt labourers into their service. Others tried to use laws to control wage levels. Many landlords surrendered their direct interest in cultivation and rented their lands to farmers for money. Peasant farmers could still produce saleable surpluses for local towns, but the great towns of the north relied upon the grain from Eastern Europe, which had suffered less from the plague and where the dominant lords tightened their grip over the formerly free peasantry in order to keep up production. The greatest Italian towns, anxious about feeding their own fluctuating populations, tried to consolidate their hold on the countryside. By conquest, purchase and harassment of the local nobility, townsmen acquired their country estates and stocked their town's granaries.

Fierce competition between rival interests was not new in the late fourteenth century, but it had never been so universal or so desperate. The victors became the prominent aristocrats and cities of the fifteenth century, but there were many more victims. Only a handful of Italian cities out of the many communes of the thirteenth century retained their real independence. In England and France, the few princes of royal blood managed to perpetuate aristocratic pretension, but since they could not restrain themselves from competition amongst themselves for control of the crown, they engaged in self-destructive frenzy. While public attention is naturally fascinated by these great spectacles, what of the country peasantry? Attempts to peg wages by legislation were doomed to failure owing to the shortage of labour. Countrymen could not resist the lure of the towns, which were thronged with day-labourers as well as beggars and parasites. Those who remained behind did so to improve their position. In England they leased land from noble lords and worked them as yeomen families. In Italy, they accepted crop-sharing agreements from citizen landowners. Some land went out of cultivation altogether, as demand for grain declined over all. The less good lands were left for sheep. The new methods of agriculture on a more intensive scale produced grain surpluses: bread prices (in terms of silver) tended to fall for the rest of the fourteenth century. Peasant farmers may not have made great profits, but they began to live better. In England a peasant farming a mere 40 acres (a virgater) could expect to produce a saleable surplus in an average year and market towns about 15 miles apart gave him a convenient outlet for this. The temptations for individual farmers to produce for the market affected the attitude to the land. Formerly profit had been the lord's concern. With leaseholding the peasant himself took an interest in profitable production and schemed to consolidate his holdings and work it with his family or a few hired men. Langland satirizes the hired labourers who demanded fresh meat and fish fried or baked and hot from the oven: men therefore with a sense of their own worth, not humiliated labourers.[47] Wills and inventories begin to record the accumulation of peasant property. After the plague it looks as though the opportunities for personal enrichment had increased, at least for those who would work: for part of their opportunity was the enormous increase in the numbers of those who discovered how to batten on to the general prosperity and live as beggars or ruffians with little effort.

The new agricultural pattern which emerged depended upon the assumption of a market in agricultural surpluses, as the 'excessive' population moved out of the countryside and into the towns. To this extent urban demand now set the pace for agriculture, instead of being merely parasitic upon it. In real terms it meant that money circulation entered into every crevice of the agricultural world. It was this that soured the affluence of country life.

The treasurer of the English king in 1178 reported as past history the days when peasants had paid their royal dues at Winchester in pigs and chickens, but payment in kind was not everywhere commuted for money, or at once.[48] In Italy the widespread practice of crop-sharing *(mezzadria)* became more extensive at a time when Italians acted as bankers and coiners for much of Europe. As long as lords remained themselves interested in agricultural production, they preferred to exact labour services and resist peasant pressure to take money instead. After 1350 they more frequently took money from the peasantry. Both sides needed it and calculated in it.

Money does not grow on trees. It is minted by great men, especially kings, who were not always overscrupulous about respecting its purity if they could make a quick easy profit by debasement. It percolated into the countryside from the towns, where prices in the markets responded to supply and demand, not to the costs of production. Agricultural communities were ill-equipped to deal with the disruption of the familiar patterns of life, which in other respects retained their vitality. There was still abject dependence, for them, on natural increase as well as expectation that diligent labour would be duly rewarded. Such considerations lurked in everyone's mind, but they did not suffice. The villages could not prevent the attraction of young men into the towns, or the lure of purchasing fineries in the market. Villages became less self-reliant and benefited from the work of skilled artisans. In some places the cloth industry moved into the countryside to benefit from water-power and avoid guild restrictions on labour. The country community disintegrated, as monetary wealth openly engrossed some villagers and depressed others. Money was flaunted, particularly in attire. One preacher even noticed how much care the poor gave to the dress of their children, while the rich neglected theirs, a paradox that intrigued him.[49]

The greater availability of money had the most disconcerting effects in the country where it had no traditional place. By modern standards, of course, the rot did not proceed very far, but there is no need to exaggerate the effects in order to perceive how baffling the phenomenon appeared at the time. Land itself was more frequently the subject of money deals, leases, purchases and mortgages. Estates were still mainly acquired for social and domestic advantages, but those who paid over money for land also had a real concern for its revenues. New owners regarded lands as businesses or as investment and thought about improvements, better management, consolidation of holdings, reduction of unsatisfactory commitments, more tools and less labour—so many sources of potential grievances quite alien to the calculations of old-fashioned lords dealing with a collective workforce. Peasants owing money-rents risked eviction if they fell behind on their dues, no longer adequately protected by the custom of the manor. Money which had been an occasional intrusion into the lives of twelfth-century cultivators became an unavoidable necessity. It brought them many anxieties and they found no other strength than their own ingenuity. Against the greed of the lords, how much help were the exhortations of the clergy or manorial custom? Money stimulated enterprise. Villages near great towns could specialize in market gardens, orchards or raising animals for the slaughterhouse. Activity in the countryside became more diverse as it became richer, but the old social strength of the village community had begun to crack.

3. TRADE

The Arab writer Ja'far ibn'Ali al Dimishqi wrote before 1174 a treatise on the beauties of trade, concluding 'that it was the best of all gainful employments and the one most conducive to happiness. The merchant attains to easy circumstances, he is a gentleman, and however rich he may be he does not have to live ostentatiously as do those who have to befriend the sultan'.[50] This self-satisfied recommendation comes from a society in which commerce across deserts peopled mainly by nomads mattered far more than agriculture, as a means of life, culture and prosperity. Christendom was not necessarily less advanced economically than Islam because it did not endorse this individualist approach. However, Francesc Eximenic, in his voluminous advice offered to a great Catalan nobleman, describes merchants as the life and treasure of the republic: the land where they flourish is always full, fertile and in fine fettle, they are good to the poor and the strength of all business.[51] Nearly a century later, another Spaniard, Rodrigo, Bishop of Palencia, remarked in his *Mirror of Human Life* (1468) that without navigators and merchandise, practically the whole of human intercourse would perish. No province or city could suffice unto itself; all things necessary and useful for life are borne easily and conveniently by the efforts of seamen.[52]

Christendom continued for centuries to be a predominantly agrarian society, supporting much more complex and integrated social patterns than Islam, and accepting trade for reasons of general advantage, since it secured the interchange of essential produce between specialized regions. It is not of luxuries or exotic goods that Rodrigo speaks. He thinks rather of the redistribution of salted North Sea cod, Rhenish and Bordelais wines, Breton salt, or oil and rice from the Mediterranean: and this comprises only trade in foodstuffs. Thousands of persons were engaged in such operations without leaving more written evidence behind them than bills of lading. Seamen, like ploughmen, are not likely to bother with writing. Columbus is the earliest navigator whose words have survived (though only in extracts and paraphrase), but he wrote as a visionary who was anxious to convince others about the nature of his discoveries; about those he was basically wrong. Seamen were perhaps naturally curious about strange lands and peoples. Some of Vasco da Gama's crew asked to be put ashore to study native customs off the coast of Africa. But as they did not commit their observations to writing what they learned did not add to human knowledge.[53] Traditionally tellers of tall stories which could not be verified and might therefore be true, sailors probably fed the imaginations of many European peoples about the remote inhabitants across the seas; they did not increase general enlightenment.

The most detailed glimpse into a seaman's life comes from the commonplace book of Michael of Rhodes who signed on as a oarsman in the Venetian galleys in 1401 and by steady promotion became captain of a vessel for the first time in 1421, retiring from the Venetian navy only in 1443. In 1434 he began to compile his book, giving an account of his own career, together with information useful for sailors: prayers, astronomical tables, standing orders, aids to navigation, notes about tides and soundings, portolan charts and an original treatise on ship-building, as well as an account of life aboard a galley. As a Venetian he was also interested in business and set down some problems about oriental merchandise, though he seems to have developed his mathematical curiosity for its own sake, and revels in solving his problems by algebra.[54] This reveals very intellectual and serious interests in a sailor for the first half of the fifteenth century. Michael took his profession seriously as he navigated between the Levant and the North Sea, but he was not interested in describing the peoples he visited, or the merchandise.

The best known medieval traveller's tale is Marco Polo's *Il Milioneo* the astonishing account of life in China as lived for more than 20 years by one who was more nabob than merchant.[55] Historians value Polo's work highly for its direct testimony about Central Asia and the Far East, but its considerable popularity in the fourteenth and fifteenth centuries rested upon its store of incredible wonders, a literary genre that encouraged the fanciful imagination more than wanderlust. Polo himself was avid to see exotic sights, with a keen eye for the fauna of strange lands. Though his elders had originally travelled for business to Peking, they were not narrow-minded or in a hurry. They appreciated their special privileges of access to the Mongol court. In this they showed the traits of the Venetian more than the merchant, travelling like the gentleman merchant of the east, described by al Dimishqi, and not like later businessmen under the protection of their country's gunboats, who snatched profits without palaver. In western Europe, in general, merchants enjoyed less status than in the Orient. Nevertheless Buonaccorso Pitti's memoirs of his spirited life as a merchant abroad *c.* 1400 proves that he was familiar with the French royal princes and that they gambled together. Wealthy merchants who continued to travel on business could expect at least the same consideration as would today be accorded a commercial diplomatic attaché. Philippe de Mézières describes Lombards and foreign merchants as the best of all possible spies, because they had access to the courts of kings and princes and made friendships there on account of their dealings in precious stones.[56] No good comes of imagining medieval merchants as humble termites constructing a new order to overwhelm feudalism.

The cities of Europe boasted of townsmen of great social preeminence.

The patricians of Cologne owed their wealth to trading though as they were so 'backward' as not to take bookkeeping seriously, the details of their business are now lost.[57] Modern impressions of merchants' activities are chiefly derived from Italian sources—like the surviving archives of the merchant of Prato, Francesco Datini,[58] and the several handbooks of mercantile practice, which distil the practical wisdom of commerce for easy reference. Such evidence tends to emphasize the businesslike aspect and obscure the context in which business was carried on, though Datini's letters show the domestic tone of his vast business affairs. The handbooks themselves with their basic word-lists in Arabic, Cuman, Turkish and Persian indicate how much Levantine merchants had to deal directly with strange peoples in their main business of acting as middlemen between the Orient and northern Europe. Sailing in convoy both in the Mediterranean and later to the north reduced the dangers to be expected from pirates; all the same, merchants had no compunction in those days about protecting themselves and their cargoes. The merchants had therefore great need of qualities not disclosed by manuals or documents; they were not dependent on a high standard of book learning or rational calculation, however useful both might be as adjuncts in business. King James of Aragon reminded his barons that all the cities and citizens of Aragon and Catalonia knew as much of war as the barons did.[59]

The handbooks remain the most important guide to the practice of commerce as a whole;[60] they imply a commerce between different lands, as Rodrigo of Palencia himself understood it. Merchants need to bear in mind differences of language, coinage, weights and measures, customs duties and tolls. They are told what merchandise to sell and what to buy and even, sometimes, how to recognize good quality merchandise. Trade was not limited to luxuries, precious stones and silks. The Genoese station at Caffa in the Crimea exported alum, bought at Phocea, an essential ingredient for the European cloth industry. (No alternative source of this was found in the west until 1460, when it was discovered, providentially according to Pope Pius II, in the papal states at Tolfa.[61]) The Black Sea supplied timber, hemp, pitch, beeswax, tallow, furs and skins. Even 'spices' were not luxuries. They were sources of dyes, medicaments and preservatives. In the Mediterranean itself the great ports, Naples, Barcelona and Marseilles, dealt in local produce, oil, wine, rice and grain, and redistributed it along the shores. Venice brought cotton from Syria and North Africa to supply the South German cloth industries, and imported grain, wine and oil from Crete and its other colonies to supply the landless city—one of the largest in Christendom. Italy is a predominantly mountainous country and there was no doubt about the superiority of the sea for commerce. Once at sea, Italians travelled as far as their ships could take them. Apart from natural disasters, over which the increasing expertise of navigators gave some control, the greatest danger was presented by pirates, against whom the merchants had to be prepared to take personal action.

At sea there were no toll duties to increase the cost of transport and it has been calculated the *c*. 1300 transport by land cost bulk for bulk twenty times what it cost by sea. The merchant had to consider the basic cost of fitting out a ship, paying freight charges and the sailor's wages. The more valuable the cargo, the greater the profit. It was obviously preferable to load spices than grain, salt or wine. Mediterranean galleys varied considerably in size. The ordinary fifteenth-century galley weighed 150 to 250 tons—Venetian galleys of the same period could weigh up to 700 tons. In these great hulks, merchants could stow many times over the quantities of produce they could send across the Alps on a mule's back. By the early fourteenth century Italian merchants sent regular convoys from the Mediterranean through the Straits of Gibraltar to England and Flanders, even to Norway.[62] Eximenic says that those galleys were smaller and stronger and better adapted for battle. They had to contend with heavier seas as well as pirates.

Trading centres were most numerous at the two ends of Europe's commercial axis, from central and northern Italy through the Alps and down the Rhine, which roughly divided Europe into two. The great concentration of Italian towns is somewhat deceptive. It depended upon the adventitious advantage of geographical position that made northern and central Italy Europe's bridgehead to the Mediterranean, to the Crusading states and to Oriental commerce. It was north of the Alps that the Italians found their principal markets for what they acquired in the east, pumping their merchandise up the Rhône, across the Alps and down the Rhine, and it was the northern waterways fanning out from the Alps that brought Paris, London, Bruges, Augsburg, Prague, Cracow and the Hungarian plain within easy reach. In the thirteenth century they travelled north to their customers in the Champagne fairs conveniently situated for the French, Lorrainers and Germans in the peaceable lands of the greatest count of eastern France. Already by 1218 their attendance was so regular that they could stipulate repayment of loans for the following year.[63] A century later, regular sailings from Venice and Genoa had brought merchants to the northern ports, especially to Bruges, so that it was in Flanders that merchants met to do business, as overland journeys to international fairs declined in relative importance. The European money market had its centres successively in Bruges, Antwerp, Amsterdam and London, never in Italy.

Venice and Florence were outstanding places of economic activity, where prosperity depended on northern business. Venice supplied raw materials and highly specialized products such as Murano glass; Florence was more industrial, specializing in finishing northern cloth and needing to import wool or cloth from the north; Milan was preeminent as an armament centre, well placed to extract iron from the mountains and distribute swords, armour and artillery to the north. Italian merchants derived great advantages from their experience in the Levant and maintained their commercial lead to the sixteenth century. Many Italian merchants extended their commercial contacts in the north by first taking on responsibilities as collectors of papal dues. Handling large sums in northern cities, like Paris, they assumed the role of bankers. Merchants of traditional Guelf cities like Siena and Florence had these duties thrust upon them, because the papacy had no better agents to care for its northern assets. The nature of Mediterranean trade, with its seasonal bulk-buying of basic commodities and the regular convoys, also stimulated the development of credit facilities. At certain times of the year many merchants were trying to raise loans to buy oil or equip galleys, and investors realized by the fourteenth century that there were regular variations in the value of moneylending. The risks involved in sea-freight, or commerce with Muslims, who were beyond the reach of Christian morality or military retaliation, inspired efforts to provide cover by insurance against loss. They attempted direct negotiations for trade treaties; several of these survive for the North African trade of the Catalans from the late thirteenth century.

As the details emerge from the surviving scraps of information the ramifications of European commercial activity became dimly discernible. There had never been any period when trade had ceased altogether, but it is clear from the conditions of international trade even in the thirteenth century that, as long as it involved personal travelling to annual fairs, overland, with mule-packs and no better coinage than silver pennies, it remained a mere supplement to local self-sufficiency.

From the twelfth century, charters repeatedly record the desire to increase facilities for commercial exchange by setting up weekly markets and annual fairs where traders could be sure of protection under the aegis of some respected authority, particularly of a famous saint or a great monastery. The importance of some annual fairs, like the famous Lendit fair of St Denis, ultimately rested upon the assumption that commerce, except at the most local level, would be unreliable for the rest of the year. The sense of occasion which these fairs generated may be caught in the charter for the fair of Passion week at the Abbey of Romans in the Dauphiné, *c.* 1240. The list of dues collected by the monks evokes an impression of the motley crowds of people, animals, carts and merchandise that crammed into the little town: sheep, goats, lambs, bulls, cows, asses, pigs, horses, mares, mules passing over the bridge, leatherworkers, smiths, fishmongers, butchers, pastry-makers, cloth-merchants in wool and silk who paid no dues; the drapers, mercers, apothecaries, fur-sellers, smiths, saddlers, who did. The most astonishing variety of skins of horses, calves, gazelles, vultures, foxes, panthers, whales, stags, chamoix, goats, horses and asses, white and coloured, smooth and hairy, of products like mustard, wax, iron and copper, lead and tin, pepper, cloves, cumin and ginger, enabled the local inhabitants to acquire in one week the stocks they might need for a whole year, or more.[64]

By the end of the thirteenth century there existed the technical means of providing more continuous commercial facilities by bulk transport of goods by sea from one end of Europe to another. This did not suddenly put an end to commercial fairs, but it considerably modified ordinary experience of trade and encouraged more reliance upon it. The revival of maritime commerce in the Mediterranean began earliest, but since Venice only acquired colonies in the Levant in 1205 and the Balearic islands were not conquered by James I of Aragon till 1238, this is only a few years before the first signs of the developing Hanseatic league and the expansion of the Teutonic order into Prussia began the commercial exploitation of the Baltic. These two streams of commerce flowed together about 1300.[65]

The *conjoncture* could hardly have been worse. It was a period of Muslim resurgence in the east; ambitious military adventures by great kings disturbed the peace on land, and exposed rich merchants to confiscation or forced loans and eventual ruin; allegedly the impetus to agricultural expansion declined and the populations were certainly cut back by plague in the succeeding century. Royal adjustment of the coinage and arbitrary measures to influence economic activity added to the muddle. There was no political power which embraced the whole economic unit. The papacy which presided over its moral values had no practical solutions to offer and no useful advice. The resilience of the economy in the circumstances proves how strongly the pulse beat. The technical means of improvement, though they brought incidental troubles of their own, really expressed the fact that the European economy had found a new kind of articulation: in themselves they could have done nothing had they not served, in particular, to redistribute essential products from one specialized region to another. This represents the end of local self-sufficiency and the arrival of a potentially dangerous dependence on the power of commerce to provide food for men's mouths and work for their hands. It means the growth of great cities living on riches gathered from many lands. It was in the late thirteenth century that many towns began to plan the extension of their town walls on a huge scale; when they were finished decades later, they far exceeded the need of the population reduced by plague. It means the concentration of production in suitable regions on the assumption that it will all be sold: grain in Eastern Europe, wine from the Bordelais. Perhaps the guaranteed supply of fine wine in England also acted as an incentive for the improvement of the poor men's beer: hops were introduced at this time as flavouring. City populations relying on their powerful provision merchants for supplies earned their keep by industry and expected to export their products and exchange them for others. The expansion of specialized skills in this way rested on the assumptions that trade would do the rest and that natural conditions were sufficiently reliable, both to allow the transport of essential goods at regular intervals and the production of raw materials in distant lands out of sight.

Much of Europe continued to flounder on economically, as before, largely self-sufficing, eking out with occasional sorties to fairs. Yet increasingly the outlying regions were brought within the scope of a system that intensified specialization as commerce grew more confident. The pace of the economy was set by those areas where the towns were biggest and most numerous, where commerce fed the needs of industry and whole populations wilted when it failed. The erratic course of the economy on these uncharted seas should cause no surprise. Human misery was not deliberately willed; aggressive measures, taken to defend threatened interests, were the acts of frightened men entirely ignorant of how to improve matters in the general interest. Disasters of all sorts intervened to upset reasonable expectations. Crops could fail, ships sink, wars cause devastation and rulers play havoc with money values. Entire populations, like those of Flanders, were at the mercy of circumstances, even if the majority did not realize this and took them too much for granted. Had they seen them as historians can, they would have been no better able to control them. The boundaries of their economic lives lay far beyond even the spiritual jurisdiction of the pope, who commanded no respect in Egypt or the Mongol empire, out of which the Black Death itself had come. Merchants, had they been of a philosophical disposition, could have worked out the lineaments of the problem. Most of them probably did as Giovanni Villani and thanked God, if they were themselves spared. The workmen in the towns, without experience of trade, found themselves deceived in their customary expectations and naturally blamed crooked merchants for raising prices, grasping industrialists for pegging wages or arbitrary kings for debasing the coins. In their turn they struck out for themselves and used their force of numbers when all else failed. The economic ills of the fourteenth century brought waves of measures designed to defend injured interests. They generally made matters worse. It was fortunate, but unforseen, if Edward III's attempts to control wool exports for fiscal reasons had the unintended advantage of encouraging the English to turn from the production of raw wool for foreign looms to domestic cloth-making; even this boon naturally did not please the Flemings.

Money
The new economic situation required, already, a grasp of the detailed complexity of the whole European economy and only the vaguest recognition of this was then possible. For all parties, the image of rural life with its visibly integrated division of labour, respect for nature and natural increase as the justifiable profit of honest toil combined to frame the basic approach to economic thought. This was not unjustified. Rural Norfolk, taxed in the fourteenth century by tenths, yielded five times as much as the tax of one sixth raised in the many towns of the country. The intrusion of money into a still predominantly natural economy jarred upon the feelings and the intelligence of the majority. It would be easy to find literary examples proving that men have called money the root of all evil since the beginning of time, but the other evidence of the insidious effects of money by the thirteenth century gives the literary expression more immediate point.

The Italian share in Levantine trade prompted Italian governments to revive a gold coinage in Christendom. Frederick II began this with the *augustales,* as much an assertion of his succession to Roman emperors as a claim to equality with his Muslim contemporaries. The stamp of Muslim approval for the Florentine *fiorino d'oro* is recorded by Giovanni Villani with obvious satisfaction. When Villani was serving on the Priorate (the Florentine government) he picked up from a fellow prior a story of how impressed the king of Tunis had been by the quality of the first florin he saw, enquiring about the inscription and place of issue, from this merchant, then in Tunis.[66] James of Aragon records in detail the efforts he himself took to track down the forgers of gold coins, struck in imitation of the Muslims, but in the names of the Christian kings of Spain.[67] The new coinage had to be of international repute. When all these Italian advantages have been considered, it is even more striking that Bruges became the real financial centre of fourteenth-century Europe.

The gold coins, florins, ducats, francs, and eventually the English angels too, represented the need of the European economy for a more convenient means of exchange than silver pennies for large transactions. Against that standard in gold, all other money transactions had to be measured. Louis IX, when striking this new coinage, restricted the circulation of his vassals' coins to purely local use.[68] In the thirteenth century this condemned them to disappear. All men buying in fairs and markets were obliged to use coins of international standard. There were never enough of these for everyone's need.[69] The new coinage made it necessary to look for untapped sources of precious metals. The principal new sources of supply from the fourteenth century were Bohemia and Hungary, whose rulers were amongst the greatest princes of the day.[70] The quantity of ore available fluctuated and affected the price. Princes without opportunities for mining dabbled in alchemy, or borrowed from those who kept supplies of ready cash. Philip IV's bankers, the Templars, were unscrupulously accused of abominable crimes, tortured to death and executed. The coins were of various sizes and purity: expert services in establishing their market value were indispensable, for the value of coins fluctuated not only according to their intrinsic content but in relation to the market demand of particular currencies with the specialized banking houses. Bankers had to be tolerated by all those who dealt internationally, including the church, and abstruse questions of high finance were therefore considered moralistically—allowing the bankers reasonable profit on exchange transactions.

The church had particular responsibility for the activities of men of money because from the mid-thirteenth century its own functions depended upon the facility with which credit could be supplied in Italy against the dues to be collected in the provinces, particularly from the French and English.[71] The effects of money upon people and communities were as obvious then as now, and the church could not ignore a social factor of such blatant importance. Operating within a predominantly agrarian economy with the philosophical works of antiquity as their chief guide, the teachings of the church could not fail to be conservative and hostile, with some justification; if the purpose of money is chiefly for the benefit of exchange, it should not be hoarded. In the economy as a whole men were impressed by the importance of natural fecundity as the source of profit and remarked that money was barren. Objections to money-making came also from considering the motives of moneylenders, whose principal concern seemed to be guaranteed certainty of profit. In contemporary terms, the moneylenders were accused not only of avarice but of lack of charity. The church's criterion should not be caricatured. Provided an investor stood to lose his investment if the enterprise failed, he was equally entitled to share in the profit: the objections were to the idle rich who did nothing but make others work for them, demanding, in return for a loan, a steady percentage proportionate to the time the loan lasted: usury.[72] How effectively the teaching and the penalties imposed actually hampered business activity we cannot say. Usurers repented on their death-beds sufficiently often to become laudable examples to others, while disguised loans show that shame-faced efforts were made to conceal activities generally disapproved, though moral theologians were well aware of such subterfuges. More important however is the evidence that usury, when it did occur, played little part in developing the European economy, since moneylenders preferred to help aristocrats, whose political power offered some hopes of a guaranteed repayment of loans even if they were squandered on luxuries rather than lend money to enterprises with doubtful prospects.

The growth of money values was obvious and ugly in this period. There were no invisible assets, except in Italian ledger books. For the most part money accumulated in coin or was converted into items of conspicuous extravagance, fine clothes, furs, jewellery, which critics from the fourteenth century found improperly worn by persons 'out of class'. This curious comment shows how much contemporaries assumed that apparel was not a matter of what money could buy, but appropriate to social standing, occupation or quite simply social order. Money upset the fitness of divisions that continued to exist, though blurred by ostentation. Money in fact had become a source of great confusion, because, though a general measure of what could be bought and sold, men at the time did not think that everything and anything had its price. They subscribed in fact to a different set of values and found money false as a measure.

There has been much ill-judged comment on the church's economic doctrines. Christian writers such as Langland with no academic axe to grind subscribed to the same views. Christian sentiment as a whole abhorred the buying and selling of men's lives. Judas Iscariot was the greatest traitor known; he had sold his lord for 30 silver pennies. This is not merely the reaction of rural simpletons. It is a belief that human society should not be dominated by the power to put a price upon everything. This power grew in spite of objections, but it never achieved sovereignty, as it since has in some parts of the world. In opposition to it hardened the feeling of proper social status and the ideals of chivalrous virtue. The nobility did not live up to the ideal, but they stood for it and so checked the power of money to take command. The respected values required good breeding as well as education which could not be had by money alone. As these values became self-conscious, the richer politicians and greater merchants were themselves absorbed into the class of gentry, thus reinforcing the nobility. Eventually, aristocratic disdain for trade put the seal on the social inferiority of merchants, of which the earliest sources betray no signs. Modern economists may deplore medieval moralizings about the evils worked by money, but socialist ideals inspire similar criticism of materialism. The intelligentsia of those days were churchmen and accepted their learning from the books. These could not offer much guidance, but they did assume that men had a higher calling than to make money. The most respected source proclaimed that men had been made by God to cooperate with nature in making the earth more fruitful: they believed that money feeds neither the body nor the soul and bears no fruit.

4. TOWNS

The barbarians who inhabited Roman cities found little use for them. On the continent Christian bishops continued the ancient association with their cathedral cities but all the chief functions of the ancient city as a centre of administration, schooling and commerce slumped with the empire itself. Out of barbarian society with its rural background developed the reinvigorated agriculture and the social hierarchy it could support — the military aristocracy. By the twelfth century social and political power was vested in them — the nobles and the kings. From these rulers towns had sometimes to extract recognition by force; and if towns won back for themselves a prominent part in European affairs, for centuries they remained overshadowed by the traditional military aristocracy. Yet the occasional conflicts between towns and lords did not express latent class-war. Lords could also found new towns for their own advantage. Disputes concerned specific privileges in particular towns, like the imperial right to nominate officials in the Lombard towns.

The place of towns in the whole social order must be kept in perspective. Most of them had fewer than 10,000 inhabitants. Not more than a dozen towns in the whole of Europe could muster numbers in the region of 100,000. The rural populations heavily outnumbered the townsmen. The overriding importance of the land explains the continued aristocratic preeminence. The problems of the towns from the twelfth century turned on their ambiguous relationship to the country. The intensification of rural activity had itself generated the need for concentrated settlements where markets, artisans and merchants could satisfy rural demands. The increase in population, the specialization of regions and the possibilities of greater sophistication and luxury enabled towns to justify their independent existence. How independent could they be? They needed country produce, and could not sever their links with the country. They needed legal institutions to protect merchants, property and commercial contracts, which had to have confirmation from the existing authorities to be effective. They desired conditions favourable for the transportation of merchandise over great distances: royal and ecclesiastical sanctions were worth having. Only towns with defensible positions on the coast and prepared to organize urban resources in defence of cargoes at sea could be totally independent: these were few. Each town had to compromise as best it could between its need of the 'established' powers and its wish to manage its own affairs.

The formative phase of this development all over Europe in the eleventh century is, as usual, sparsely documented. As the Viking raids died down, commerce emerged from its piratical chrysalis. Kings and churches accepted obligations to defend merchants, which diminished their former self-reliance. King Canute, who began as a Viking and ended as a pious Christian ruler, negotiated commercial advantages for his subjects in England with the emperor in Rome (1027).[73] The churches of France promoted the truce of God to still local warfare: merchants were specifically included along with widows, orphans, pilgrims and rustics, as defenceless strangers entitled to respite.[74] Local bullies who had plundered travelling merchants began to recognize that taking regular tolls on growing business would be more rewarding and less offensive. Merchants passed on tolls, harbour dues and wharf fees to their customers and appreciated the facilities of shelter and protection they got in return, together with advantages over rivals and interlopers. Merchants on the move were not the stronger party in negotiations with local nobles, but they found allies in towns, amongst powerful local figures, often themselves with landed estates, who took the lead and bargained for better commercial terms from potential oppressors. Towns needed sufficient powers to create an institutional framework for commercial transactions, particularly to cope with disputes. Merchants travelling on business could not be easily fitted into a system of law-finding by compurgation and ordeal, which had its rationale amongst small communities of neighbours. They needed quicker justice, more summary methods and adequate compensation against theft of their articles.[75] Only urban residents of consequence could obtain these concessions and enforce them; all over Europe the first town governments were entrusted to such citizens. In London the wards were governed by aldermen, men of social rank equivalent to sheriffs in the shires. On the continent the ruling officials, particularly in the south, were often called consuls, in grand imitation of the Roman republican constitution. Towns boasted of their ancient heritage and ingeniously invented distinguished founders to prove their derivation from Rome. Some went back still further and claimed Noah, Hercules or Trojan heroes as their original founders.

The distinctiveness of the institutions and manner of life in towns may disguise their real relationship to the world about them. Despite all pretence otherwise, the towns of this period owed little to ancient example and everything to their part in the economic life of the country. Paris and London flourished as commercial cities long before kings came to reside in them frequently. Towns, walled off from the world outside, did not at first aspire to exercise general administrative functions. New towns did not grow up, as in ancient times, as civilizing centres, but to serve market needs. In this connexion it is significant that the vernacular words then adopted to describe these settlements, town, stadt, burg, ville, are etymologically derived from less sophisticated settlements. Once transferred to fit the new towns, they have continued to be used till the present; likewise, in general, the centres they described have remained towns until now. When the towns were new, contemporaries were not so much struck by their novelty (for which recourse to a Latin word would have been required), as by the way they grew naturally out of a familiar economic and social context. So towns proliferated in some areas more than in others, with no regard to administrative factors, as had been the case in the old empire. Northern Italy and the Low Countries were the principal regions of growth. In the Low Countries there was in consequence a very inadequate provision of bishoprics, based as they had been on the administrative units of the Roman empire, since at that time, before the appearance of the towns, it was an underpopulated area of marsh-dwellers. The extremely uneven spread of towns directly plotted the economic energies of the times. This had considerable political importance. The kings of France had only cathedral cities to contend with, except in the area extending north of Paris into Flanders. The Spanish kings took over and extended a system of government more like that of the Roman Empire, in which the towns and their bishops were at the heart of local administration. In the western lands of the medieval empire the number of towns was very much greater and far exceeded the number of episcopal centres. The dependence of townsmen upon local conditions meant that these variations of political context played a major part in their individual histories and explains why generalizations for European towns as a whole are few.

From the twelfth century, contemporaries were extremely conscious of the nature of the differences between life in town and country. A record from Cologne in 1181 gives a rare glimpse of a young man's feelings of distaste for the country: he sold his holding *(feodum)* in order to remain permanently in the busy city.[76] Cathedral schools attracted young, enterprising and independent clergy who appreciated the animation of the towns. In Wace's poetic description of the Arthurian Carlion he picks out the bustle of the townsmen as characteristic of urban life. The town itself created an environment suitable for continuous labour, whereas the country worked according to seasonal rhythms, responding to the changing length of the days and the quality of the weather, wet or fine. Towns gradually broke down natural limitations. From the fourteenth century, the invention of clockwork began to make possible the division of the day into constant units. Townsmen ceased to work by the seasons. Louis XI authorized Parisian glove-makers to work till ten at night by the light of candles, though they began at five in the morning: there is not much sense here of 'natural' hours for work.[77] By modern standards, mechanization of life had taken only a few tentative steps forward, but contemporaries found even this 'progress' a matter of wonder. In towns men began the process of creating their own environment and, in each one, satisfying every imaginable need.

The earliest poetic descriptions of the town single out the advantages of the site and its natural beauty with comments as to the fertility of the surrounding region in game, fish and cereals.[78] Bonvesin de Rippa begins his description of Milan, placed between wonderful rivers, with an ecstatic review of its bountiful supplies of fine water and its healthy fresh springs of benefit to the digestive system. The stylistic development of this literary genre led in particular to complacent dilation on the remarkable number and quality of the imposing constructions of the towns—first the walls, their length, height and strength, the gates, the markets, the palace and the courts of justice, the temples or churches. Eximenic, who discusses whether the town should be square or round or other shapes recommended by philosophers in their writings, suggests an ideal layout for the buildings, with the cathedral in the centre, with a great open square in front and a flight of steps leading up to it, so that persons being looked for could be easily seen. He recommends paying attention to the prevailing winds before deciding on the location of hospitals, leproseries, brothels, fulling mills and drainage outlets, so that the whole town should not be contaminated by bad odours. The construction of the town and its buildings could not often be carried out according to one man's rational recommendations and the results were therefore wide open to criticism, but every construction in the town necessarily bore the marks of some human intelligence and effort.[79] The city expressed the ambitions of the community and the ideals of its life in common. Educated men could draw inspiration from an existing tradition, since the city was already idealized in Christian thought, and heaven itself conceived as a city, Jerusalem the Golden. Likewise classical literature hymned the praises of city life, particularly of Rome. But whereas for centuries these sentiments had been appreciated only by learned men, by 1200 Europe had once again discovered what city life actually meant.

The limits of the town were normally, if not always physically, marked out by town walls, so that admission and departure could be closely checked, or even refused at night or at the approach of enemies. The histories of enough towns are known to make it seem probable that the first enlargement of the town walls beyond the limits set in the dark ages came in the twelfth century, and that a mere century later they were then extended a second time to incorporate the many new suburbs. The period of rapid growth was therefore in the thirteenth century. In many towns the limits then drawn sufficed until the nineteenth century, for by the time the building of the walls was finished, they already exceeded the needs of populations, reduced by famine, disease and warfare. These great new cities were not crammed to over-flowing with tall houses and narrow streets, pullulating with people, as they became later, when populations rose again. The new walls enclosed many great open spaces, like those for markets, while numerous religious foundations, of friars, of hospitals and other communities, each had their cloisters and gardens to admit space, air, and light into the town.[80] The Florentines re-organized the layout of the streets of the town in the early fourteenth century and took steps to improve the hygienic arrangements, public latrines, fixed sites for slaughterhouses, street lighting, as well as to enhance its beauties, with new buildings, street paving and the realign-ment of buildings. Most surviving medieval towns bear witness to the townsmen's interest in the amenities of their town. Though the centuries have obviously preserved the best and not the most squalid construc-tions, the records also show a consistent interest in improving the town, whenever it had the resources to do so. Town councils sometimes took over from the clerical chapters the responsibility of building the cathedrals. Streets were paved and regularly cleaned.[81] If the town was started from scratch, as the thirteenth-century foundation charter of Mirepoix demonstrates,[82] the plan could be regularly devised, but in the nature of the case most towns grew up fitfully around existing churches or fortifications that permanently affected the town's layout. The interest shown by the citizens in the appearance of their town comes out clearly in the protests made in Avignon against the canons of St Agricol who planned to enlarge the *pavis* of their church in the second half of the fifteenth century. They gave various grounds for objecting—hygienic, military and aesthetic and concluded that '*ex hoc difformaretur totus aspectus publicus resque publica in immensa lederetur.*[83] When James I of Aragon punished some traitors, citizens of Montpellier, by pulling down their houses, as was usual in such cases, he made an example of a few and spared the others, to save the appearance of the street.[84] A different concern for building is shown by one of the oldest surviving regulations for the city of London, Fitz-Aylwin's ordinance, which defined the safe distance between houses to prevent the spread of fires.[85] Medieval town regulations also prove the existence of public bathing facilities, from the twelfth century. They were popular and had an un-savoury reputation as places of debauch, but they were not closed down on that account until after the reformation in the sixteenth century.

The earliest buildings in stone and brick were the churches and the bishops' palaces, all rebuilt in the latest styles from the twelfth century. There followed the friars' great churches to accommodate the crowds attracted by their preaching. Suburban parishes also required new churches. The expansion of city governments made other permanent buildings necessary, especially in Italy, where numerous transitory officials needed accommodation and offices. Town-halls were constructed there from the early thirteenth century. The guild-merchant of the governing group had its own hall and later on the trade guilds eventually built halls and other buildings for their own uses, social and charitable. Private houses and shops filled up the urban site with permanent buildings, though in the north these remained of wood often until the seventeenth century. The construction of stone *torri* for Italian city families can be traced back to the eleventh century; the more spacious *palazzi* only appear three or four centuries later.

All this building activity and in such a confined space was new in the 'barbarian' world. Since the end of the Roman Empire there had been no general desire for building in stone, so that, when the art was revived, it was natural that the masons should be thought of as emulating the works of the legendary Romans. They organized their trade and skills accordingly to meet the renewed demand for Roman civilization, the ways of cities. From the visitors' handbooks to twelfth-century Rome, it is obvious how much impression was created by the enormous city itself, its walls and the remarkable constructions behind them — the imperial palaces, baths and places of amusement: the Colosseum, the hippodrome as well as the many churches, which so bewildered them by their numbers that guides tried to make each one of them memorable by some little anecdote.[86] On their return north, pilgrims retained very muddled impressions of the great city. From their point of view, building in stone itself was sufficiently remarkable to demonstrate 'Roman' character. The new towns of the north, by their cluster of buildings, were to that extent therefore like Rome. Towns on or near Roman sites thankfully utilized the ruined Roman buildings as quarries. Elsewhere the cost of transport encouraged the use of local stone wherever possible, and masons learned how to make the most of its virtues and developed local styles accordingly. In other regions, without stone, the art of brick-baking was revived and builders likewise learned how to use bricks and devised appropriate regional styles.

This might seem to make for dull uniformity, but contemplation of homogeneous groups of towns, like those of the Cotswolds or in Tuscany, does not bear this out. Individual towns never lacked their distinctive qualities. No modern visitor confounds the different Tuscan hill-towns; he recognizes Massa Marittima, Volterra, San Gimignano, Siena, Montepulciano, Arezzo and Pienza for the individual places they are. At that time, all towns offered even more distinctive signs than age has spared, bristling with many more towers of churches and noble families than San Gimignano still boasts. From a distance every town displayed its own unique silhouette. The individuality of the greatest Italian towns, Milan, Florence, Naples or Venice, eludes no modern visitor and in modern Britain the differences between two such similar ports as Liverpool and Glasgow are still unmistakable. If modern towns are generally thought to lack individuality, it is only the recent use of brick and concrete that has robbed them of distinctiveness — once their very essence. Throughout this period, when towns first grew and flourished, the unique aspect of every town could be literally perceived from its own buildings and their relationship to one another. Living constantly in their shadow, townsmen accepted the town as a self-contained microcosmos serving every human need. How difficult it is for us to realize what life in a town once meant, now that life in towns has become a misery and towns themselves are despised as places of work to be left as quickly as possible: eyesores inflicting universal blight. Yet with our more terrifying and ugly loyalties we misjudge the intensity of civic patriotism, as it once was, and pronounce their urban rivalries only quaint.

Each town not only proudly bore the physical signs of its individuality: it lived its distinctive way of life according to the most important of its occupations, social groups, wealth and environment. The early thirteenth-century chronicler Guillaume le Breton already picked out specific Flemish towns for their characteristics.[87] Townsmen initially interacted with men of their own speech, that is the members of their own families, their friends and workmates. Other relationships were temporary. If they looked beyond their immediate circle for any sense of community, it was the town they chose. The modern tendency to call them all *bourgeois,* pitting them against the 'feudal' order, misses the significance of their attachment not to middle-class values, but to those of their own particular *bourg.* The effect is sometimes ludicrous. Eximenic the learned Franciscan takes infinite pains to prove that the city of Barcelona was older and in every way finer than Tarragona, not hesitating to trot out the most improbable legends about its foundation by Hercules hundreds of years before Rome and Roman Tarragona were heard of: Barcelona, he says, is 'mils e plus bellament edificada que ciutat que home sapia al mon.'[88] Patriotism can go no further; it certainly made no attempt at objective comparisons.

Fortunately these sentiments also inspired some notable literary descriptions. One of the earliest comes in William Fitz Stephen's account of London, which he inserted into his life of Thomas Becket, on the tenuous grounds of their common citizenship. Conventional enough in his opening sections on the site, its churches, its defences and its supplies of fresh water, Fitz Stephen becomes more expansive as he considers the pleasures of London life, its public eating house on the Thames, its Friday horse-market and gymkhana: already at this date, he gives an affectionate description of London sports 'since it is expedient that a city be not only an object of nobility and importance, but also of pleasure and diversion'. The character of the city comes out decisively in this earliest description of it.[89] No less apposite is the earliest description of Paris *c.*1332 written by Jean de Jandun, who lavishes his attention on the amenities of the city—academic, royal and sophisticated.[90]

Loyalty to the town was nurtured by frequent defiance of neighbours. The cavalcade of soldiers about their serious duties or in colourful procession excited the highest fervour in all patriots and until the fourteenth century able-bodied townsmen were expected to defend their city and assault its enemies, so the soldiers were not alien forces paid by oppressors. One of the finest passages in Bonvesin's account of Milan is the description of the standard chariot around which the battles raged: the ark of the covenant of the medieval communes. When the threats of war died down, the repressed internal animosities of the townsmen erupted into life. All towns were divided into wards, quarters or *sestiere* in which the local armed bands were raised. Rivalries between different sections roused serious passions, even more then than they still do in Siena, when the *palio* is run. The town itself, though sealed off from the outside by its walls, thereby bottled in together the heterogeneous elements of which civic society was composed.

If the struggle for independence united all townsmen, what happened once this was secured? Surrounding countrymen had submitted meekly to 'natural' lords, but the towns owed their freedom to defying them. To take the place of the lord, magistrates had to be chosen. From the first there were distinguished families expecting to take on these burdens. Their sense of rank was well developed by the twelfth century. Great families in Cologne protested against the admission of a mere monied plebeian into their favoured monastic foundation, St Pantaleon.[91] They cared even more for their monopoly of civic office. They had taken the lead in defying the former established authorities and naturally assumed the new responsibilities in the town. They organized the sworn communes and ran the town. But they had not the same 'moral' claim to perpetual leadership as 'feudal' nobles and kings. They had to justify their government by their success in satisfying enough powerful local interests. These were often difficult to reconcile and impossible to bully. Practitioners of the same trade and skill were more often rivals than comrades. Not until the thirteenth century did brotherhoods and guilds go far to appeasing dissensions and creating harmony within professional or parochial limits. It took time to discover if the 'town' as a collectivity had common interests and was prepared to construct appropriate institutions to look after them. Few towns were in the situation of Venice, isolated in the lagoon and obviously dependent upon importing its food and its prosperity up the Adriatic. The population there accepted the need for a tight-lipped government under senior patricians with experience of the Levantine trade. Similarly in Lübeck, the great merchants, who master-minded the convoys in the Baltic and through Danish waters, controlled the city council, at least until the fifteenth century.

Towns dependent on commerce understood the need for political discipline best, but the biggest towns, with the most specialized industries, always contained many diverse and some industrial elements. Venice itself had shipbuilders, fitters and artisans, all potentially bent on improving their own lot. Many elements co-existed with ill-grace and found it difficult to recognize their mutual dependence. Yet Milanese steel-workers, using iron from the mountains between Bergamo and Brescia, or Florentine cloth finishers, working on imported woollen cloth, both also needed the services of importers and shopkeepers. There was constantly trouble about terms of service, costs and wages. The least skilled parties invariably came off worst, because they were easily replaced by other men coming into the towns and willing to accept any jobs. The chances for the humblest to improve their position only in-creased for a generation or so after the 'Black Death', when all workers were in short supply. The strongest groups were the great merchants who imported essential articles from far away, and the owners of the workshops, particularly in towns which specialized in one product. Between the two extremes, management and workers, came the local shopkeepers whose commerce extended no further than the town's natural catchment area, but whose distributive services became more conspicuously necessary as town populations grew. The management of all these different affairs by the town government could not be an easy matter.

There was no theory of politics to help. There was no understanding of the principles of how to establish a government 'representative' of the different interests, or one capable of acting in the 'general' interest, let alone strong enough to enforce the 'general' will against self-righteous opposition. Solutions to the problem of government came in each town by arrangements which suited the most powerful elements. The compro-mises and alliances, which suited some, infuriated others. Unruly townsmen were tamed by force; the intransigent were driven out all together into exile. Since the forces of repression—the police or the militia—were rudimentary and inadequate, the government could only work if it concentrated on the minimum and left the townsmen for much else to manage their parochial or industrial affairs themselves. There were party labels, like Guelf and Ghibelline, which suggest an ideological bond between members of the different groups, but there were no party programmes or doctrines or, in general organizations. Once a party took power and had taken revenge on its enemies, it rapidly disintegrated, as the factions within the party lost interest in a united front.

Until the end of the thirteenth century, the political difficulties within the towns, though serious, were rendered more manageable by the favourable economic situation. The eminent families of the town maintained their leadership in the affairs of the commune, but the growth of population eventually transformed the nature of their responsibilities. It made the need to secure adequate food supplies and access to raw-materials imperative if industry was to flourish. Towns competed politically and commercially; military expenses began to rise. Dissentient groups in the towns, which had begun to form their own craft guilds, showed their discontent with the established patrician governments and both sides sought what allies they could from other towns or princes. For about a century, from *c.*1280 to 1380, towns became the centres of considerable political activity and debate, which give an almost modern aspect to their histories.

Political theory, though in practice of little help, significantly reappeared as an intellectual interest in this period in urban Italy. Originally this grew out of the scholastic appreciation of the works of Aristotle, which were retranslated into Latin by William of Moerbeke and commented on by Thomas Aquinas *c.*1260; only in Italy were important discussions of political theory made in the succeeding three generations: Giles of Rome, Dante Alighieri, Agostino Trionfo and Marsilio of Padua. Both Dante and Marsilio took up politics in search of a solution to Italy's problems of disorder: Dante, by hoping to restore the empire, which he attempted to justify in mainly secular terms; Marsilio by denouncing the pope and canvassing a revival of city-state politics, inspired by Aristotle. Marsilio's work acquired an evil reputation as a revolutionary book, but its radical programme and theoretical character rendered it useless to townsmen in search of political wisdom. The level of political sophistication in the towns is more faithfully reflected in a much more popular work, Brunetto Latini's *Treasury,* a thirteenth-century encyclopaedia.[92] It summarizes the conventional views of educated citizens, covering in one volume everything of importance. It culminates with politics, the most noble and exalted science and the most noble task on earth, since politics includes generally all the arts needful to the human community.

Latini gives a plausible, if unhistorical, account of how human political society arose from the need to deal with the covetousness and the pride of the strong. Houses were built, towns enclosed with walls and ditches; customs, laws and rights common for all men were established. It suited men to have lords, but the form of lordships permitted many variations. Kings, counts and castellans passed their lordships to their children; the pope and emperor held office only for their own lives: others like mayors, provosts and *podestà* held office for only one year at a time; papal legates and secular judges were appointed for a fixed period. Latini's interest in office from this account shows an odd concern for formal differences in the period of appointment, rather than awareness of differences of substance. After such preliminaries, he turns immediately to the government of towns, since politics naturally meant for this Italian the government of cities. He again called attention to the existence of two main types. The first was found in France and in other countries subjected to royal lordship or other perpetual princes where the government was sold or farmed out to the highest bidders. These were of little value to the townsmen *(borjois)*. The second, in which he was mainly interested, occurred only in Italy, where the citizens, the townsmen and the communes of the towns elected their magistrate *(poeste)* as their lord, according to his usefulness, for the common advantage of the town and all men subject to it. Having reached this stage in the argument, some discussion of political questions might be expected, but Latini has in fact exhausted his interest in the subject. He trails off with the commonplace assertions that all lordship was ultimately assigned by the pope and that government was founded on the three pillars of justice, reverence and love. His analysis thus becomes moralistic. If this is the best a man of learning could do, it is improbable that citizens who held office by rotation for short periods gave political theory more thought than this.

Impressions of how towns adjusted to the mounting difficulties of the late thirteenth century are most usefully drawn from the urban histories of particular places. Very few towns, compared to the total number, nursed 'schools' of historians, but it is significantly from this period that citizens took more extended interest in keeping a record of their city's affairs. There is probably some connexion between an interest in history and experience of dissension. Histories have undoubtedly played an important part in trying to fix an image of the 'homeland', its glorious past, its 'principles' and its great future, particularly when the community seems otherwise racked with conflicts, uncertain of its values and in search of its 'identity'. The earliest of all civic chronicles comes from Genoa in the mid-twelfth century. It was composed by one of its great noblemen-citizens, Caffaro, and records the deeds of the Genoese (himself included) in the Holy Land, enlarging on their heroism and valour, with a view to stimulating local pride and patriotism. It was also intended to discourage partisanship and internal rivalries and to show how much they damaged the city's reputation and weakened its capacity for distinguished action. Caffaro's chronicle was continued under official sponsorship, because it was hoped that such histories would serve to promote the moral unity of the town seething behind its walls.[93] In other cities too, the compilation of chronicles was often entrusted to the town clerk, who also looked after the town archives. It was part of the business of government to edit the city's history and remember what was significant for the town as a community.

It was in Germany and Italy that urban history was most cultivated, because the towns there fostered their own historical outlook. However, even in Germany, there were no more than ten principal cities where continuous interest in historical events kept the chronicle tradition alive: Cologne, Mainz, and Strasbourg in the Rhineland; Lübeck, Brunswick, Lüneburg and Magdeburg in the north; Nüremberg and Augsburg in Bavaria.[94] It is also notable that the tradition was best maintained in those towns where the clergy had important centres of learning. The townsmen adapted an existing learned concern for historical record-keeping. Likewise in the Low Countries, the clerical traditions of Tournai, Liège or Cambrai explain the interest in history, whereas there was less urban history writing in the commercial towns, Bruges, Ypres and Ghent. The Franciscan 'annalist' of Ghent left a spirited account of the great popular reaction to the interference of the French king in the Low Countries, but by the time he wrote, in 1307, he was already fearful that the memory of the great deeds of the townsmen in defeating the French nobles was fading away.[95] The comparative neglect of urban histories in the great centres of the Low Countries has had its effect. The struggles of the towns against the king and the count, like their involvement in the Anglo-French war, are best known to history from the accounts of outsiders, the clergy in particular who did not always share the civic enthusiasms of the townsmen, whereas in Italy urban histories were more sympathetic to political independence.

In Italy municipal history had a distinguished course which culminated in Machiavelli's *History of Florence:* this draws attention to the marked political interest always shown. The struggles of the towns against the emperor had inspired some annalistic writing even in twelfth-century Lombardy, but the texts become more numerous and interesting in the thirteenth century. Florence had no native chronicler before Sanzanome *c.*1200, nor did Venice until the middle of the century. These consistently republican cities produced histories written in the vernacular. The most famous of them is the chronicler Giovanni Villani, who crammed miscellaneous incidents into his lively record. He was the model Florentine, in touch with the known world, always curious, alert and interested, constantly varying the content of his chapters. His contemporary in Venice was the Doge himself, Andrea Dandolo, who wrote in Latin, supporting his history with *pièces justificatives,* as might have been expected from a great Venetian lawyer. Whether the writers concentrated on past history, like Dandolo, or on keeping up the contemporary record, like Villani and his brother, Matteo, the effect of these histories is to bring to life again the patriotic fervour found in their communities and to promote a sense of the city's continued essential interests.

From such histories it is also possible to see how at least a few of the greatest cities coped with the problems of expansion and, in the fourteenth century, with deteriorating economic conditions. The old patricians who had ruled often had to cede to demands from newcomers, particularly of better organized professional groups, for a share in the municipal government. In Flanders, the patricians attempted to use the king of France against their count, only to find that the lesser townsmen were provoked into taking up arms against them and their French allies.[96] In Italy, patricians fearful for their power also turned for support to military captains, and by this means many towns found themselves subjected to the government of despots. The chronicles themselves show how the cities that retained their own independence were driven to annex those of their neighbours: civic glory for Florence was felt as humiliation in Arezzo or Pisa. In this respect it is misleading to contrast the survival of republican forms of government in some places with the growth of despotisms in others, though this was the way contemporaries often represented it in their propaganda. Those cities that were strong and rich enough to become 'capital' cities did so; the rest sank to 'provincial' status. By 1380, a few Italian cities had become the nuclei of territorial states; the rest had ceased to count. But either way, the era of municipal independence was over, for even in the great capitals government had to be conducted for other purposes than the interests of the local inhabitants. The need to secure supplies of food and raw materials had initially made it necessary to look beyond the walls, but military defence, diplomatic alliances and the effects of competition for diminishing resources had transformed even the basic economic problem.[97] The responsibilities of government fell increasingly on those citizens who had the time and ability to take a broader view of local problems and who expected to enjoy office long enough to deal effectively with them. This means the end of the old municipal regimes everywhere, as well as urban autonomy.

The effect of the new system was to bring about a new relation between the town and the countryside itself.[98] Townsmen living within territorial states with fortified frontiers could move beyond the city-walls, acquire country lands and try to improve their productivity, terracing the hillsides, draining the marsh, planting vineyards and orchards, and raising fresh vegetables for their own use or for the market. The country nearest to the great towns attracted both investment and settlement. Townsmen began to enjoy their spells in the country, in summer or for retirement. Those who had created human settlements in a setting of stone and brick proceeded to 'civilize' rural communities. Formerly the country had been the preserve of the factious noble families, who had been the victims of urban resurgence from the twelfth century, whether they lived in the towns or not. By the fifteenth century, the townsmen themselves had colonized the countryside. Some noble landowners survived the changes, but most had disappeared in the troubles of the fourteenth century. The towns had originally expected simply to create a network of town governments, but the result was more like the creation of a few great principalities, ruled, sooner or later, by hereditary despots. They were not rooted in the country like the old nobility, but in their own way they had restored the bond between the town and the country, this time in the town's favour.

This balance created the circumstances in which the modern European consciousness has emerged — the possibility of what a European regards as civilization: life in towns. The town itself was the focal point. All specialized skills required for a civilized life could be found in them, supplied by local masters for persons able to discriminate amongst them as to quality. Within the towns the great merchants and bankers, by their professional connexions in other towns on the great trade-routes, were able to make their own contributions to the supply of internationally desirable goods, and to acquire what was needed by their fellow townsmen. In the smaller towns the contributions and demands were less varied and less diffused than in the greater, but they too had their place on the great network. Such a system had not existed in ancient Mediterranean society with its independent city-state tradition, bucolic countryside and 'international' links provided essentially by the Roman imperial administration and army. The modern European state system had no fixed centre, provided better status for the countryside and gave more initiative to the townsmen, at least until the Industrial Revolution destroyed civilization in the European sense. For a few centuries, while the balance between town and country was maintained, Europeans made some of their most important contributions to the history of the world.

5. CRAFTSMEN
Towns were primarily places of concentrated activity by men of many different occupations, but evidence for the ordinary population is, as usual, sparse. The number of trades in any one place was always great. In mid-thirteenth century Paris, an official enquiry into the customs of the different trades disclosed the existence of a hundred. At that time, these trading associations still had no formal rules, charters or written agreements. The royal provost gathered sworn statements from leading members of the organizations, which show that there were nonetheless effective regulations for managing their common affairs, including election of trusted guardians to supervise the trade. These established norms of apprenticeship and hours of work, though they did not fix wages or prices.

The statement made by Master Fulk of the Temple as to the rules of the carpenters, which had been handed down from their predecessors, shows that even in an unwritten form they could be quite detailed.[99] At the time such customs were still little preoccupied with protecting corporate interests against interlopers or customers; they reflect confidence in the prospects of economic prosperity. Craftsmen did not see themselves as struggling to maintain a standard of living, only to practise their particular craft according to established usage.

The first need of the townsmen was for adequate supplies of comestibles. Shopkeepers and men in the carrying trades as well as some great merchants in wine or oil were all essential for provisioning the town and they formed an important proportion of the total population. But when the needs of the belly had been served, the next most important activity was the adornment of the person. Great numbers of craftsmen were continuously busy, clothing the body from crown to heel. The Nuremberg register of 1363 which listed 1200 'masters' shows that there were more persons engaged in clothing than in any other branch of the city's business, apart from service industries.[100] In a remote past there had once been a time when men had relied on local homespuns to satisfy their needs, but self-sufficiency lost its virtue in a commercial society, where merchants could tempt every one with some article of clothing. The importance of clothing transcended the requirements of decency. Underclothing was little used and layers of garments had to be worn in winter for warmth in unheated houses. More important still, clothing was the most conspicuous sign of social station and occupation. In great cities men were pointed out by their clothes as natives of different countries. The importance of clothes may seem surprising in an age where their functions have been much curtailed, but in other circumstances, a different set of criteria prevailed. The clothing trades utilized an enormous range of basic materials from the coarsest to the most costly. The royal enquiry into the trades of Paris in 1250 recorded no less than six different groups making headgear alone: in felt, cotton, peacock's feathers, embroidery-work, studded with gold and pearls, with makers of flower-chaplets in season. Fabrics woven in the great centres of Europe found ready markets all over the continent and could therefore be refined for every known purpose and supplied for a range of customers. Furs, skins, leather all served, as well as the woven fabrics, wool, cotton, linen and silk.

Some idea of the sheer variety of objects in such demand that there was a market for them even secondhand can be derived from the list of merchandise disposed of by the Rigattieri guild in Florence in the early fourteenth century:

'Old clothes and skins, all kinds of cloth for the use of men and women, of all colours and used for whatever purpose, linings and edgings of fox-skins, new and old lambswool linings, linings and edgings of squirrels, new and cleaned, new and old quilted materials, ornaments of gold and silver, feather-beds and bed-clothes and other woollen cloths, linen cloths and underclothes, coarse cloths, old and new, serge materials used for bed linen, bench-covers, bedspreads, tablecloths, old and new Irish serges, jewel-boxes, chests, benches and all room furnishings, mattresses etc., decorations of all kinds, lengths of buckram and linen, used waistbands, old and new linings of all kinds for men and women's use, cloths for covering horses, all kinds of canopies and sun-blinds, leather bags and cloth bags, bindings in cloth and leather for psalters, piled-cloth and mattress covers, old and new, all kinds of women's gowns and all cloths for priests and friars and in general all kinds of clothes and adornments for men and women, including ornaments of fur, gold and silver, beds with their furnishings, and all furniture and furnishings for interiors, and all woollen and linen cloths for the use of men and women or in their houses or rooms of all kinds and for making old and new doublets.'[101]

Customers were eager to take advantage of what skilled men could do, but it was probably the craftsmen themselves who took the initiative in constantly devising improvements, variations in quality and other innovations. Competition with other trades or other towns sharpened their ingenuity in the production of both raw materials and garments. Clothes were made to measure, since there was no ready-made clothing trade, except in secondhand goods.

On the one hand there was an intimate relation between the man and his tailor, glovemaker and hosier; on the other, the specialization of trade assumed that the basic materials could be obtained internationally. In these circumstances the weaving of cloth could become a matter of general European importance, to be organized on commercial scale, because of the size of the potential market.[102]

The early history of the weaving trades is obscure, but it was certainly not until the twelfth century that they became significant internationally. As late as 1135 a curious episode related of weavers in Cornelimünster shows that they were still regarded with disdain as outsiders. They were made to pull a model ship westwards to Aachen and the Duke of Brabant himself had to intervene on their behalf. The monastic chronicler of St Trond was mystified by the bullying attitude of the townsfolk and expressed sympathy for their misfortunes, since they were poor men who only worked hard for their families.[103] In many other parts of Europe in the twelfth century there were important groups of weavers, living apart from other townsmen, probably in depressed conditions. Such men were so often suspected of unorthodox religious opinions that the word *textator* was used as synonymous with heretic. Possibly the nature of their occupation at the loom encouraged conversation and speculation on matters less easily pursued in the noisy business of building or manufacture.

Cloth manufacture was not organized on a large scale. In a great cloth town like fourteenth-century Ghent, with a total population of *c.*50,000 inhabitants, there were not more than 4,000 weavers and 1,200 fullers working for many different firms. By medieval standards these numbers were important and required a high degree of organization, but they preclude modern descriptions of such industry as 'capitalist', though there are inevitably certain features that could be arbitrarily picked out as similar. Equipping a textile workshop clearly required some capital, since workmen had to be provided with looms, fulling-mills, spindles or flyers. The difficulty is to know to what extent a mere skilled master of his craft could be prevented from setting up his own workshop for want of money. The evidence does not support the view that the capital required was ever so great as to inhibit this. The small scale of operations, the constant modifications in technique, the readiness of masters to retire and masters' widows to sell or remarry constantly opened up new opportunities. The cost of equipment does not itself seem to have become a drag on enterprise, though this does not preclude disappointments at a personal level.[104]

Improvements in machinery and tools were not confined to this branch of industry. In this society there could be no reliance on slave-labour, even in the countryside, and there was therefore every incentive to devise more mechanical aids. Beginning with the harnessing of wind and water power, or using it more effectively, men went on to design horse-collars and to exploit horses for agriculture, which put an end to their formerly exclusive military use. Even the wheelbarrow had once to be invented and prove its simple effectiveness. Communications were improved, particularly by the building of stone bridges across rivers.[105] Also at this period the wheel was adapted for spinning and clockwork made its first appearance. In due course this changed men's means of calculating the passage of time and led to ingenious contrivances both useful and amusing which fascinated contemporaries. They borrowed devices from their Islamic neighbours—the crank-shaft, the abacus, 'Arabic' numerals. Europeans displayed at this stage their bent for conserving effort and expense. The regular use of machinery encouraged constant modifications to improve on it, to save scarce and expensive labour. The demand for metal tools meant greater exploitation of the metal-extracting industries and experiments with steel-making. Progress could not be continuous but it was cumulative and by the fifteenth century

Europe had acquired valuable experience of many basic industries. Regional differences remained. Indeed specialization emphasized them, but the international market distributed skills and products over an immense area. The reputations of some industries and towns gave them international acclaim and set the highest standards for the whole continent.[106] The obvious, if disagreeable, proof of this can be seen when the Portuguese sailed into the port of Calicut with their firearms in 1497. They could challenge the Orient on its own ground by their use of 'gadgets'.[107] The same civilization produced the printed book and the anatomical drawings of Leonardo da Vinci and Vesalius. The casters of cannon were also makers of bells. Attention to detail and taking pains to get it right were the qualities required for the mastery of all the 'arts'.

The building industries may be taken to illustrate how the adaptation of Mediterranean civilization to the darker and cooler north (when this became an active concern from the twelfth century) stimulated the ingenuity of artisans in a way that had not been necessary in the south.[108] The Romans had not modified their building styles when they moved to the north. From the twelfth century the new builders in stone deliberately raised higher constructions, to let in the light. This immediately gave the glaziers a new role. The most obvious difference was that northerners spent more time indoors than southerners, who did their business in the streets. Northern constructions were not predominantly of stone, despite the significance of the revival of stone buildings. For centuries, northern Europe remained a region of timber houses and this gave employment to a great number of different crafts and craftsmen. There were various qualities of wood in use and artisans were skilled in making the most of these not only in building, but in panelling interiors for extra warmth, and in furniture. The Paris carpenters' trade included men who made doors, frames, barrels, wheels, carts, ceilings, coaches, ships as well as turners and panel-makers. Chairs were still reserved for the use of kings, bishops and professors; even judges sat on benches, like the whole company assembled at meals in great halls. Chair-makers were not therefore working at a commonplace craft, but for special persons; their skills were appreciated accordingly. The northern interiors as shown in Flemish pictures were crammed with domestic objects made by artisans of various sorts; the ever burning hearth is surrounded with the new variety of cooking utensils, terracotta and pewter; the walls were covered with panelling or tapestries for comfort and colour; the tables laid with forks as well as knives; the beds made with linen sheets. Life was normally conducted within doors and everything needed lay to hand. Contrast with this the austere interiors of the Florentine house, sparsely furnished, designed for warm weather with airy rooms, tiled floors and occasional pieces of furniture. It was the craftsmen with their handiwork who made it possible to live a comfortable life in the north. Objects could be purchased at modest prices by many, because they were produced in adequate quantities by capable artisans relying on a steady demand for their services.

The organization of craftsmen

The expansion of urban activities in the thirteenth century, and the increase of town populations and of the numbers of craftsmen can only be explained on the assumption of constant recruitment from the countryside. As immigrants entered the town, they settled initially in those streets where certain craftsmen had already established their trades and where the newcomers found appropriate employment. At that time nowhere did clusters of tradesmen exercise influence in the town comparable to that of the formal divisions — parishes, wards or quarters, of which the town had long been composed. Geography still mattered more than the professions. The small size of these districts presumably helped immigrants to adjust to life in the noisy and busy towns, which as a whole must have bewildered them on first arrival from country villages. The districts were units of more familiar proportions. Each one of them still mustered its own military contingents, under its own standard-bearer, a man of good family, whose patronage was the chief means of preferment. Defending the town-wall or fighting in the militia, new men quickly found comrades. Such glimpses as we have of life within the town wards suggest tight-knit local solidarity.

In the thirteenth century the town populations were easily stimulated by the religious passions and enthusiasms of the period, heretical and orthodox. The preaching of the mendicant orders won them many friends amongst urban workmen, which enabled them to set about eliminating some wrong-headedness and ignorance. They stirred up the religious life of the old town parishes. New associations of neighbours, called brotherhoods or fraternities, were created to promote better social relations and perform works of charity, care for widows and children, attend funerals of members, as a sign of respect, and celebrate the patronal feasts of their communities.[109] Gathered in the parish churches or later in special chapels, the fraternities attempted to realize a more profound expression of their Christian faith in common than had been required in the days before St Francis. It was in its way an adaptation to the towns of a manner of social solidarity natural to village life and therefore in tune with the needs of the most recent immigrants.

The idea of the fraternity was taken over by tradesmen for their own professional organizations. Through collective worship and attendance in the guild chapels on feast days and for funerals, they promoted social solidarity within the trade. They appreciated the advantages of these associations so well that guilds of masters attempted to prevent inferiors or employees from imitating their example. The guilds were intended from the first to serve the interests of the members. If the public came to benefit by the insistence upon quality or prices, this was incidental. The guilds set out to prevent outsiders from practising the craft in the town. They restricted admission to the craft, fixed the number of 'masters' and the latter, or some of them, supervised the craft's interests, adjudicated in trade disputes between members, and defined the terms of apprenticeship. In the same spirit, their contemporaries amongst the university teachers were setting examinations for students and restricting admission to their own ranks by awarding degrees of bachelor and master, to keep up the standard of their profession as much as to defend their own status. The guilds or *universitates* enforced high qualities of workmanship. This did not discourage ingenuity or hamper innovation. The crafts gave artisans confidence to develop their skills in a practical, but virtuoso manner. They gave their energies to the solution of the difficult problems of the trade, as may be judged from the surviving examples of their work as goldsmiths, sculptors, artists and glaziers. Their skill came from the practice of the craft from apprenticeship onwards. They owed little to books, but they were proud of their calling and claimed the title *magister,* like men of learning. Italian lawyers were said to have given up using the title *magister* for this reason and expected to be called 'doctor' as proof of their intellectual superiority.[110] By the fourteenth century, nonetheless, the judges and notaries of Florence were obliged to admit representatives of the craftsmen to a share in the great public offices of the town. If it had not been for the guilds, it is inconceivable how such a degree of equality could have been attained, for the guilds which initially promoted the internal harmony of tradesmen became the means whereby they forced the whole community to take note of their interests.

Everywhere in thirteenth-century Europe, there was real progress in the organization of craft associations, despite endless variations in objective and degree of success. Some craftsmen were never to be weaned from their street loyalties, because they saw no advantages for themselves in better organization. But there were few important industrial activities that did not force craftsmen to take note of the effects of the economy outside the town on their own prospects. They desired to use their guild spokesmen to represent their views to the local authorities, still in the hands of the notable families. There were perhaps few cases like that of Florence where guildsmen actually forced through a change in the constitution to obtain power for their members; in London such an innovation, though it was tried between 1352 and 1384, did not last. Whatever their share in local power politics, the guilds had by the fourteenth century become influential corporations of important citizens with definable interests that authori-

ties could not ignore. Their chief purpose became restrictive and defensive as the favourable conditions of an earlier period changed. Limiting
the number of masters only became desirable for the whole community
when all the candidates could not be absorbed. As the guilds became powerful, they realized the advantages of a select membership, and they used
their professional organization to keep out interference by the local
authorities in their own affairs. They were very self-conscious of their
own importance and dignity. If they did not run the towns themselves,
they distinguished themselves in its society. The trades of Chartres commissioned stained glass windows in the cathedral to demonstrate their
pride, as they still do. Guildsmen in Strasbourg took over the direction of
the building operation of the whole cathedral. Later craftsmen staged
religious plays for festivals which illustrated both their piety and
their taste for public spectacle. The guildsmen of London who could
not abolish the ward structure of city politics achieved their objective in
the fifteenth century by setting up liveried companies and reserving the
mayoralty to members of them.[111]

The common activities of craftsmen and their pride in their skills gave
them special ways of life, even a jargon of their own, the esoteric vocabulary of their 'mystery', which contemporary writers noticed as professionally significant. It is easy for modern critics to see literary examples
as mere stereotypes, but they were rather embodiments of ways of life
that were distinctive. The exclusiveness of their attitudes sometimes
astonishes. This comes out, for example, in the chronicle of Augsburg,
written in the sixteenth century by Clemens Jäger. He wrote the history
of the town from the weavers' point of view, out of gratitude to the
burgomaster, a weaver, who had found a place for him on the town-
council. He began with the battle of Lechfeld against the Magyars (955)
in the belief that this had seen the beginning of the weaver's guild, and
then jumped forward to the heroic events of 1368, when the guildsmen
had overthrown the old civic order. This event he compared, pointedly,
to the Roman revolution against the Tarquins. His work concludes with
lists of guildmasters and of the weavers who had been burgomasters.[112] It
was not difficult to promote group loyalties when they were as potentially
partisan as this, but does such a history inspire local patriotism for the
city, or only for the weavers' guild? Men clung to the narrowest loyalties,
because they were the most sure. Medieval towns, however passionately
they rejected outside interference, never lost a sense of their own profound divisions.

Eximenic divided the inhabitants of towns into three categories. The
first were the patricians, the social equals of knights *(cavallers)*. The
second were those without nobility who nevertheless had great riches in
the towns: the judges, notaries, merchants and substantial drapers. Only

in third place came the craftsmen, silversmiths, smiths, shoemakers and cuirassiers, whom he describes not as citizens but as inhabitants and neighbours *(vehins)*. With them he lumps others not to be considered citizens either: pilgrims, journeymen, servants, freedmen and former slaves, all necessary for the well-being of the city, but no more entitled to the name of citizens than such denizens of the city as cats and dogs.[113] It is hard for us to imagine how Barcelona was the greatest light of Spain when the contributions of the craftsmen were so dismissed, but it is typical of Eximenic's time that he thought the city's honour was embodied in the pompous distinguished citizens who processed on public occasions and ran its affairs. The London chroniclers of the fifteenth century thought similarly when they described the solemn reception of kings and foreign princes by the leading members of the city in their finery: it is against such a background that the liveried companies could emerge as the real disposers of civic power.[114] Dignified and discreet, they united against persons of lesser consequence, but in the historical records they often look more like an operatic chorus, shouting hurrahs and bravos, than men of action, even when they enjoyed real influence in city councils.

The London chroniclers who came from such circles attribute no significant activity to them and themselves betray so little sign of political intelligence or ambition as to raise justifiable doubts about whether their fellow citizens, with even less interest in history, could have been more sophisticated.[115] In Paris it is something of the same story, with great figures of the court or university as substitutes for businessmen:[116] so the medieval town makes its dignified bow. Did this façade faithfully reflect the essential smugness of the late medieval town? The light on Savonarola shows, however, that even such worldly-wise citizens, as late fifteenth-century Florentines, appear to be no less volatile and passionate than their ancestors.

It would be a mistake to read into the urban and industrial history of this period a belief that towns nurtured a type of person out of sympathy with the country, the nobility or the church. Towns were complex societies of many elements, most of which may be only hazily discerned in the records. The records themselves, particularly those of the legally trained notaries, who kept the official minutes and wrote the histories, are often too formal to admit how rustic town-manners could be. It took a clerk in depressed and provincial Arezzo to report that an irate citizen had shown his contempt for the authorities by showing them his bare backside.[117] For the most part, the records try to maintain a dignified tone, unsuited to the bustle and violence of urban life in this period. Drawn from the country and eventually restored to it, townsmen too were earthy and excitable, the workers of the world who responded in their own way to the teachings of the church, but unavoidably out of sympathy with men educated to books. They were men of action who laboured and laughed without a care for what should be said of them after their deaths. More important for them than their historical reputations was their own future in the great hereafter.

4

THE
CITY OF GOD

'It is only with the aid of history,' Nietzsche says (thus not from his personal experience) 'that the scholar succeeds in summoning up a reverent seriousness and a certain shy respect towards religion; but if he intensifies his feelings towards it, even to the point of feeling grateful to it, he has still in his own person not got so much as a single step closer to that which still exists as church or piety: how much naivety, venerable, childlike and boundlessly stupid naivety there is in the scholar's belief in his superiority, in the good conscience of his tolerance, in the simple unsuspecting certainty with which his instinct treats the religious man as an inferior and lower type which he himself has grown beyond and above, the little presumptuous dwarf and man of the mob . . .'[1] Those who easily fall into the way of despising religion may from the history of this period learn how much attention thoughtful men once gave it and encouraged others to give it; if this in itself may not do much to weaken contempt for religion, it should undermine excessive modern confidence in the opinions of the educated. If educated opinion as such is ever worth the intelligent man's attention, it will mean taking religion at least as seriously for this period as he is expected to take the preoccupations of the intelligentsia in the present.

Nietzsche believed that history could help the scholar to appreciate religions of the past, but it can't unless that past is seen realistically and not projected as a romantic image, like Catherine Morland on her way to Northanger Abbey expecting to see a grandiose edifice and experience an eerie thrill.[2] By historical accident, religion and the church do not carry in the twentieth century the meanings they did 'in the middle ages', though they do still have more meaning than 'myth' or 'temple'. The church of this period became a privileged, powerful and centralized institution into which were recruited the most idealistic, the best educated and some of the most ambitious men of those days. The 'church' provided education, 'social security' and programmes of reform, as well as religion in the modern sense. The modern state has stolen most of the church's 'programme' in order, of course, to commend itself particularly to those who have discarded 'superstition', but it has not been able to dispense with superstitions and rituals of its own. It offers political promises instead of religious aspirations and provides or allows its own substitutes for ritual and faith: hire-purchase for indulgences, package tours for pilgrimages, motor-cars for holy images, disc-jockey patter for ceaseless prayer, materialist complacency for divine intervention. In these ways men are no less 'religious' now than they were then. The historical problem is not therefore to 'understand' how men could once be so superstitious and to pity them their poverty, ignorance or barbarism. The historical problem is rather to see how educated persons could at that time, as at no other, not merely champion existing beliefs, for they usually do that, but rather forge such powerful bonds amongst themselves across the whole of western Christendom as to erect a privileged institution for all men of literate culture. This secured for them unprecedented social status, yet also justified itself, and won general, if not total, goodwill, by appealing to the better side of human nature and directing its loftier aspirations.

For the most part these achievements are still despised. 'Art and architecture', lifted out of their religious context, are treated by modern unbelievers as merely aesthetic activities. Works of literature are read as part of the vernacular canon or ransacked for socially realistic detail. Protestant theologians are sedulously protected in their colleges from knowing anything about the history of the church between the Age of the Fathers and the Reformation. Roman Catholics have wallowed in the spectacle of undisputed papal power and tried to justify the pretentions of the post-Tridentine church by the achievements of the past. Recent appeasement of sectarian rivalry at the academic level is likely to be cheated of its historical fruit in the future because of the increasing ignorance of Christianity itself shown by the young: 'Only with the aid of history'. . . .

Christianity appeared in the Roman Empire at a time when civilization had attained one of its highest levels, and became the prevailing religion because the achievements of civilization did not satisfy the best minds and aspirations of the Romans. Until it became the authorized religion it was obviously in no position to sap the strength of the empire; within a century of that, after the barbarian incursions, whatever of the empire survived was saved by the efforts of the church; it is churlish to accuse it of not preserving more. In fact religion had more to offer men than the empire itself by 400, as was rightly seen by Dostoevsky in *The Brothers Karamazov*. This moral superiority of religion gave the church a self-confidence that only deserted it long after the Reformation. The barbarians were absorbed into the church without showing any special interest in the incidental advantages to be derived from civilization: city life, general education or public law. They valued the church for its religious teaching. Were it not for the fact that the Christians had already converted the Romans and Greeks, city-dwellers and philosophers, this barbarian acceptance of Christianity might be explained as the consequence of their simplicity and ignorance. As it is, there is no reason to doubt that the barbarians accepted the best news they had about religion and unaffectedly followed its injunctions.

Christian writers had no reason to record information about the pagan religions abandoned by the barbarians so that it is difficult to know what beliefs the new religion had to oppose. However, it is certain that the barbarians had no access to any comparable body of religious thought and no scientific or philosophical knowledge adequate to counter a religion that had already outmanoeuvred Hellenistic philosophy and science. This did not mean that some barbarians did not put up a stiff resistance to Christian religious teaching, but only that, in the long term, they had no intellectual resources capable of repulsing it. The new religion opened up a prospect of the power, unity and benevolence of God that could have come from no other source. In place of wilful, sulky gods needing appeasement, Christians proclaimed one God, who had, out of compassion, become Man and suffered once, and for all men: the God of Salvation.

The religion of the highly educated cities of the empire was thus grafted into the northern European countryside of illiterate people, and their descendants became in due course the chief witnesses to the Christian religion. No such radical adaptation has taken place anywhere in the history of the church. Though it could not happen without loss of sophistication and refinement, by their conversion the barbarians nevertheless joined the history of civilization: their monks wrote books to prove it. Religion was not only the basis of their future bliss; it formed the ground plan of their lives.

The new Christians could not help but change Christianity. Unlike the early Christians of Roman cities, they showed little taste for learned controversies and sectarianism. Barbarian kings worked for the conversion of their whole people and most Christians accepted as a matter of course that the whole community should practise one religion. This identity of practice is a primitive or barbarian feature. It had not been characteristic of Christianity even in the empire, where emperors had met steady resistance in many Christian circles to the imposition of imperial orthodoxy. For centuries barbarian kings, once their peoples were converted, had no difficulties in maintaining the allegiance of the

Christian populations. Barbarian Christians were fervent and aggressive; they forced the extension of their religion among other peoples. They were generally successful against other pagans whose religions were not sophisticated enough to stand up to Christianity. Attempts to browbeat the schismatic Greek Christians or the enigmatic Muslims were not successful. Christian intolerance has earned itself an evil reputation, yet has an attractive side. The barbarians fought for their God because fighting was what they believed best demonstrated a man's worth and devotion.

They also showed concern for the spiritual welfare of people less blessed than they, in contrast to the imperial Christians who had preferred learned controversies inside the imperial frontiers to converting the barbarians without. Like clumsy boys, the barbarians could not imagine any kind of conduct or belief superior to their own, and amongst other people with their outlook their no-nonsense approach won them lasting converts, if only in the long run. The Romans had never thought it possible to extend the benefits of civilization outside the empire and the Roman Christians had likewise kept their religion to themselves. The Germans who had lived near and amongst literate Romans for centuries did not learn how to write their own language until Christian missionaries provided them with an alphabet. Not until a century after the Catholic conversion of the Frankish king Clovis did Gregory I send a mission to England intended as much to recover a lost province of the empire for Rome as for Christendom. Before England itself was totally converted, however, these Saxon Christians were eagerly attending to the conversion of their brethren across the seas, the Frisians and the Old Saxons, and the new barbarian Christians have never since ceased to carry the good news they have acquired to all men within range, however unwilling. Christianity was good news which barbarian peoples carried to others without the trappings of civilization; with them Christianity learned to run on its own feet, without the crutches of Hellenistic thought.

The acceptability of the new religion in this context could not depend upon its purely intellectual merits; fortunately its advocates were remarkable men. The new Christians and potential converts seem to have been impressed even in spite of themselves by heroic saints able to vanquish familiar enemies: hunger, weariness and lust; saints who subdued their bodies and demonstrated the power of God's grace to help men through adversity. The saints were often called athletes of Christ and their asceticism appealed to the age in much the same way as dedicated sportsmen, climbers, athletes and swimmers who pound the body into submission earn popular respect now: they prove something important about themselves and human nature: that men do not live by bread alone.

1. MONASTERIES

Most of these saints lived celibate lives alone or in community, subduing desires that all men find somewhat shameful but almost irresistible. Contemporaries who admired their strength of will and acknowledged their own inadequacy were attracted by their example into communities, to find the discipline and the fellowship that would enable them to attain similar self-control. From the end of the Roman empire the attraction of monastic life for men of exceptional determination and independence constantly renewed and enriched the life of the church. Conditions in the world may have been unusually disturbed, but this is hardly a sufficient explanation, for it becomes even more surprising that men who abandoned self-defence could survive and receive generous support from their secular fellows. Monasteries even became treasure-houses needing protection by the great kings of the day and were duly pillaged by the powerful, as by the pagan Vikings. For centuries therefore their very existence demonstrated the self-sacrifice of the whole Christian community that supported them.

Monasticism came into the Latin church from the east, and only in the late fourth century, on the eve of the collapse of the empire. It is unlikely that it would have obtained such an influential position in the life of the church under more settled conditions of life, but the peculiar conditions of Western Europe in the next millennium gave Latin monasticism a special boost. Small groups of monks striving for self-sufficiency in the bare essentials of life managed to salvage more for the spiritual life than the bishops who had in effect become officials of imperial government in the fourth century. How could the western bishops, unaided, have coped with the pagan barbarians, once converted? The barbarians had too little Roman sophistication to value the bishops as administrative officials or great teachers. Where the Christianity of the empire had needed to be articulate, philosophical, learned and skilled in debate, none of these qualities made any impression on the barbarians. For the ministry to the people, the miraculous interventions of the saints, living and dead, seem to have mattered more than any attempt to teach barbarians about the historic foundations of Christianity.

For a time there was some danger of thinking that books had no value at all, in a world that normally did without them. Earlier Christian scholars with scruples about pagan learning, who thought it better, or safer, not to read authors capable of corrupting their purity, bequeathed these scruples to other, less sophisticated peoples. Bolder barbarian spirits forged ahead confident that what was valuable could be extracted and the poison antidoted. The Christian religion owed much to the Roman empire, Hellenistic thought, Judaic religion and prophecy, all of which had to be 'understood' to 'explain' it. In the Roman empire, living experience and formal education had taken Christians a long way towards this; with the end of the empire these facilities dried up. Fortunately by the fifth century scholars like Jerome and Augustine had reduced most of the necessary explanatory matter to the size of 'books'. The barbarians had only to use these digests as convenient summaries, never even guessing how much else had been lost. The amount of learning required to read and copy these books and to expound their teaching to novices remained very limited; it was certainly not necessary for every Christian. It was a task for monks who had only to acquire a small library and keep up the scholarly tradition by teaching child oblates.

For centuries the tradition of monastic learning provided the barbarian peoples with the most essential and elementary benefits of civilization. Only monks cared anything for books — service books, Gospels, Scripture-commentaries or the elementary textbooks of grammar and science for the novices; learning as such was never their main purpose, which was prayer. Neither in Greece nor in Egypt had monasteries originally been intended for learning, but in the context of barbarian Christianity, those who renounced the world for Christ became the principal ministers of the church, and of civilization and learning too. The monastic assumption of the burden of civilization changed both learning and monasticism. Communities of monks could take root in Ireland, England and Germany, where there was no imperial legacy to build on. Monks there came to provide all the services demanded of the Christian minister: they were bishops, missionaries, priests, scholars as well as monks. Monasticism which began in the desert as a means of escape from the cares of the world became in the west the principal means of transmitting religion and culture to barbarians.

Monastic involvement in pastoral work and in learning came about in the peculiar conditions of the western empire, and their religious purpose did not deflect them into a course of pursuing learning for its own sake, nor did the barbarians themselves aspire to learning as such. Nevertheless the connexion made between monasteries and the survival of some purely secular learning in Latin civilization, even if originally only valued as a help in elucidating the sacred mysteries, has left a permanent mark upon western education. In due course the clergy became the guardians of all book learning, Christian and pagan; they nurtured the idea of imparting to the undoctrinated what soul-healing truths they had distilled from the best of it. The rest of pre-Christian culture could be forgotten. From this approach to education is also derived of course, the modern belief in the value of universal education.

There was no need to wait long for monastic Christian learning to flourish. Within two generations of its conversion, Northumbria had monasteries adequately stocked with enough books to instruct Bede, the barbarian scholar who made the most significant contribution to the learning of the church for several generations. The nature of those contributions reveals his limitations. Bede was essentially a painstaking compiler, of exceptionally penetrating intelligence. He set out to understand the sacred texts of scripture and the holy institutions of the church by reading the works of others, sensibly sifting and arranging his learning for the benefit of less systematic readers. No other scholar came near equalling his achievement. Even at its best, barbarian learning remained conservative and restricted.

Plentifully endowed to relieve them of material anxieties, monasteries dedicated within to prayer, learning, austerity and the celebration of the liturgy, nevertheless excited enough greed outside to become the victims of barbarian disorder without. The history of monasteries was far from uneventful. Despite all the troubles and persecutions, however, monasticism constantly reasserted itself and in the disturbed conditions of western Europe it came to be taken for granted that monastic observance most tested Christian devotion. To contemporaries, monks lived the model Christian life. However few joined such institutions, they were the most dedicated of all Christian people; their prayers to God on behalf of the others offered the best chance for all men in the next life. This impression is of course derived from monastic writers, but they also refer frequently enough to those who scoffed at their pieties to show that, although there were critics, there were no alternative theories of how to lead the ideal life. Those who rejected the monastic ideal simply enjoyed the temporary pleasures of this life in expectation of eternal damnation: grasshoppers who preferred immediate satisfaction to eventual bliss.

Once the Carolingian emperors had prescribed the rule of St Benedict of Nursia for general use, most western monasteries regarded him as their exemplar. Although the Benedictine rule provided for the total obedience of the monks of each house to their abbot, so that in theory each house was autonomous and self-sufficient, by the eleventh century there were a number of common characteristics. Lay patrons encouraged the institution of large monasteries with many monks, rendering sonorous service to God with great solemnity. Such monasteries needed plentiful endowment and servile labour; the biggest often received lands widely scattered across Europe. The reputation of the monastery at Cluny for its religious zeal had caused it to become responsible for an enormous congregation of houses, each one no longer autonomous but ruled by a prior appointed by the abbot of Cluny himself. This pattern of monastic life affected even other houses not formally members of the group. In the monasteries of Christendom there was sufficient uniformity of discipline and custom to create a common sense of their unity. In their separate houses monks felt themselves to be part of a great international brotherhood. These were ideal conditions for promoting historical interests, not only in local affairs, but in notable deeds performed all over Europe. On account of these monastic historians the lives of monks are better known to us than those of any of their contemporaries.

The monastic community lived together under a spiritual father (abbot), and was dedicated entirely to the spiritual life. Delivered from the obligations of the present world, individuals without families, possessions or even wills of their own, they praised God in splendid buildings with magnificent ceremonies without parallel in the Latin world, living the life expected in Heaven, working, singing, praying and talking, without thought of secular reward. Monasteries had to designate a few monks to be responsible for their public life, and these men were obviously deeply involved in economic cares and social commitments. However, comparatively few valiant men were needed to manage wordly affairs, and the activities of toiling abbots and their assistants were as little typical of monasteries as the activities of modern universities if judged by what their administrative officers do.

The monastic communities of the eleventh century may seem like attractive havens of rest, tempting men in search of a comfortable life; we should not underestimate the challenging nature of these institutions. Peter Damian, the Italian ascetic, found the ordered life at Cluny arduous. Orderic Vitalis, sent as a child to St Evroul and brought up in the monastic life, appears to be impressed by the hardness of his lot, even while accepting it dutifully.[3] Monasteries were not easy places to live in and tested a man's devotion. These communities were not hives of identical simpletons performing in unison. They were recruited from the most ardent spirits of the best families. Their individuality had plenty of scope in the discharge of their different obligations to the community, in their eventual departure as abbots elsewhere, in their reputations for sanctity, in their fraternal quarrels, or in their pious resignation. As soon as we can see a monastic community from the inside (as Christ Church, Canterbury in Eadmer, or Bury St Edmunds in Jocelyn of Brakelonde) we see what a varied collection of men and minds went into a community and how individual each monastery was. The monks never claimed a monopoly of spirituality, though they have left more proof of their success and their zeal than the other clergy. Bishops and laymen sometimes derided monkish pretensions, but in general the monks set their contemporaries high spiritual standards and attempted to live by them. At best lax houses needed more discipline and inspiration.

Monastic reform

Nothing therefore better reveals the profound change that came over the Latin church than the altogether unprecedented experimentation in new monastic styles of life from the late eleventh century.[4] For rather more than a century religious idealism took the form of proposing new rules of eremitical and coenobitic life, usually of greater austerity than the Benedictine. The careful search for rules of life could hardly be pursued without scrupulous regard to the teaching of previous generations. The boldest and most individual reformers sought support from the past. Benedict, as the key figure of the Latin monastic tradition, had to be interpreted afresh. The most famous and extensive reform was that of Cîteaux. The Cistercians began in a Benedictine monastery at Molesme, where they found the accretion of custom had obscured the nature of the rule itself. The novelty was to try and recover the stark simplicity of the original rule by taking it literally. Contemporaries did not always appreciate how much the Cistercian 'interpretation' itself became a wilful insistence on rigour which literally repudiated the essential Benedictine rule of autonomy, for though the aim was to live strictly by the Benedictine rule, each house was so closely supervised by the 'order' from outside, that it introduced a spirit quite alien to the rule; in effect with its ascetic standards and its hierarchical organization, Cîteaux devised a monastic rule distinct from that of Benedict.

The nature of the dispute may be characterized from the emphasis put by the Cistercians on wearing undyed habits, and refusing to use drawers or furs, because they were not prescribed in the rule. If Peter the Venerable's defence of Cluniac customs and laxities seems to deal with matters of trivial detail at needless length so do all the great controversies eventually shrink into insignificance. Peter adequately disposes of Cistercian arguments for asceticism, by appealing to the rule itself: *Haec ergo consideratio penes abbatem.*[5] Where Benedict had left the application of the rule to every abbot's discretion, this basic principle of the rule itself was rejected by the Cistercian enforcement of the rule according to the letter. This literalism was not unusual in the twelfth century and could prove a double-edged weapon in the demand for reform.

The dispute between the Cluniacs and the Cistercians over the proper way to live by the rule of St Benedict should not be misinterpreted as a conflict between the conservative and the progressive, or the decadent and the reformed. In Peter the Venerable's understanding at the best it represented the conflict between the compassionate and the impatient new vigour that commanded rather than recommended perfection. The Cluniac monasteries continued to flourish even as Cistercian foundations multiplied. The number of combined 'Benedictine' monks therefore increased dramatically and they continued to rise to high office in the church as bishops and popes. As Otto of Freising came to the end of his world history, he saw it culminating in a period of great monastic expansion. Yet the split between Cluny and Cîteaux in fact marked the end of the great era of monastic history. There was no longer any real certainty about the model of Christian perfection. Whilst the monks argued amongst themselves, those looking for the perfect life began to strike out along unexplored paths. Otto of Freising calls attention to one of the most astonishing changes, when, regretting the internecine war between Henry IV and his son Henry V, he argues that at just such a wicked time, other soldiers went to Jerusalem (on Crusade), a movement that produced in time the military orders *vita et conversatione non milites, sed monachi videantur.*[6] Hitherto the monks had been the steadfast critics of soldiers, men of blood. The *milites Christi,* renouncing the world, had sought to overcome the real enemies, of the soul, in the cloister. Bernard himself had advocated seeking Jerusalem in the monastery rather than overseas, but he had eventually come to approve the military orders and preach the crusade (1147). When monasticism became only one of several means to salvation (however much its superior merits were lauded), the whole attitude of the church towards the notion of Christian perfectibility had changed.

The tremendous vitality of the twelfth-century experiments indicates the depth of religious resources, but the disconcerting effect on the life of the church should not be minimized. Admittedly all new reformers, however original they had to be to establish a novel order, claimed to draw upon some earlier rules and guidance. However, their very inventiveness in the twelfth century betrays the lack of any single authoritative source of guidance, such as the papacy supplied in later centuries. There was no formula of a religious order to rival Benedict's, but already in the late eleventh century the 'rule' of Augustine of Hippo for diocesan clergy was revived and made to serve a variety of purposes, since it gave some disciplined framework for a new kind of Christian service, not 'outside' but inside the lay-world. Significantly enough it was Pope Urban II, preacher of the first Crusade, who invoked Augustine's name, along with that of Jerome, Gregory I and his own eponym, Urban I, when approving the foundation of the convent of St Ruf in Provence. He claims that the church proposed two ways of life for faithful Christians — the first, for stronger souls ascending *ad montis altiora,* namely monks, was flourishing adequately (Urban had been prior of Cluny and had no reason to suppose that the Cluniac order would soon be under attack). The second may, however, need revival — it was the lesser way for souls living a canonical life, redeeming their daily sins *lacrimis et elemosinis* within the rule of their original founder, Urban I and the others. Urban's rule did not survive, but Augustine's did and over the next fifty years it was adapted for many different purposes until it had crystallized into a variety of rules and customs governing many communities, of which the most numerous were the houses of Augustinian canons.[7]

The use of revered names and texts in these 'monastic' controversies does not thereby conceal the fact that for about fifty years Latin Christendom was stirred up by the most idealistic and uncompromising members bent on establishing new communities or experiments in religious life. Saint Norbert (d.1117) began as a preacher, travelling like a layman and borrowed from both Augustine and the Cistercians when founding the order of Prémontré. Another German, the learned Bruno of Cologne, ingeniously combined two quite different traditions of monasticism, introducing a community of hermits. His Carthusian order has best preserved to the present its original inspiration and spiritual level.

Like the Cistercians, most of these reformers appeared within the boundaries of the kingdom of France, often beginning as hermits. Communities of admiring followers gathered round, for whom provision of rules of discipline eventually had to be devised. Robert of Arbrissel, at Fontevrault, founded one community for both men and women (living apart) to regulate such a manner of life as had grown up naturally. Gilbert of Sempringham began a comparable experiment in England *c*.1130. Though there is no need to doubt the propriety of their rules or discipline, the very idea of mixed communities shocked monks of the traditional kind and in its own way it is symptomatic of a totally new willingness to think out the institutional life of perfection afresh. The experiments were in part able to extend the religious life into sectors of lay-society immune to the old monastic influence, which had clearly drawn mainly upon the support of great men able to endow and protect them. The Cistercians took in peasant-monks as *conversi,* who worked the estates as members of the community, however inferior. The canons did a variety of work, preaching, academic and charitable, which indirectly, if not directly, stiffened the standards of the secular clergy of cathedrals and parishes in contact with the laity. The military orders enabled the most violent men to serve the church's purpose.

Gradually from these various diverse and often squabbling parties the church as a whole found that, instead of recommending a life of total renunciation, it had marked out several ways of Christian perfection, and was well on the way to thinking that the present world might be redeemed for Christ and not simply abandoned to the devil. Instead of emphasising Christ as the devil's foe, reformers proclaimed Christ as the Christian's friend, sorrowing and suffering; this inspired a sentimental piety far removed in spirit from that of the steadfast victor over the world, formerly celebrated by the monks.

Tears and love flow constantly in their prayers and letters. Bernard of Clairvaux commands an impressive range of personal emotions that he poured out to his monks and correspondents. Disciplined by sanctity and life under the rule himself, he nonetheless released a new flood of personal emotion that had very disturbing consequences. In many ways he was essentially a monk of the traditional kind, but he raised it to a higher pitch of emotional intensity by virtue of his Cistercian inspiration. He believed that religious perfection could be found in the monastic community where as brothers the monks lived emotionally the life of the heavenly Jerusalem. Though Bernard increasingly interfered in all the affairs of the Latin church, even without being invited to do so, his fundamental belief was in the power of monastic life alone to place men on the road to salvation, in the company of others earnestly seeking enlightenment. In a life of prayer and spiritual companionship the soul would rediscover its lord. Bernard supposed that progress in the church meant the infinite extension of the monastic system and in his lifetime more than three hundred Cistercian houses were founded, half of these from Clairvaux itself. Thousands of young men flocked into the monastic orders devised in the two generations after 1090. The Cistercians themselves rejected the oblation of infants and all reformers appealed to young men at an age for making up their own minds. The challenge to contemporaries was therefore dramatic.

Hitherto, monks had for the most part been recruited in infancy while most young people were clearly not brought up with more than a token of respect for religion. They were certainly not expected to be pious in the world — only when they left it. Orderic Vitalis reports the efforts of a baronial chaplain to correct the ribald frivolity of royal soldiers by telling stories of military saints, mostly, significantly, from the east such as Demetrius.[8] The new emphasis on the choice of a religious vocation placed the onus upon the individual and his right and duty to choose for himself. For a brief time men had freedom — what should be done with it? What else was there? Outside the church there was no call to service more demanding than the claims of a lord on his vassal. Few kings had adventures to offer, though in Spain there were regular opportunities to fight the Moors. Elsewhere, as in Germany, royal service had become a matter of duties and benefits, with no vision as yet of the extensive royal kingdom to serve the public good. Within the church, religious idealism was not yet hitched to a remote or abstract ecclesiastical conception.

In the twelfth century the variety of orders offered a wide initial choice to the novice; there were presumably many young men of enthusiasm and spirit, like Ailred (of Rievaulx) at the court of King David of Scotland, who were eager to give their lives to the most

challenging ideal. Emulation drove clergy with reputations for holy life
to embrace more austere discipline, and monks to abandon orderly
houses for a more arduous life elsewhere. Authority took no part in
stimulating conversions. Lives of saintly reformers constantly assert that
the choice of the religious vocation was an individual decision, often
taken against the advice of parents or friends, and pursued in spite of
early disappointments and setbacks.[9] The proliferation of novel rules
emphasizes how little existing institutions measured up to contemporary standards and taste. The number of disciples prove how much
men craved to find communities capable of bringing them spiritual
peace: thousands of persons eagerly accepted religious service, when the
way was pointed out. The monastic recruit was presumably, as Dostoevsky put it, 'a young man of our own times, that is honest by nature,
demanding truth, seeking it, believing in it, and, believing in it, demanding to serve it with all the strength of his soul, yearning for an immediate
act of heroism and wishing to sacrifice everything, even life itself, for
that act of heroism.' The wonder is not that the young responded
ardently to the idealists of the twelfth century, but how our own century
has failed to find ideals worthy of its youth.

2. DOCTRINE AND DISCIPLINE

While the most pious and conscientious Christians were seeking perfection in unregulated ways, the ecclesiastical authorities were powerless to impose discipline. Reformers neither sought episcopal
confirmation of their rules, nor felt the obligation to do so, until the
community was viable. The Cistercians themselves had no papal confirmation of their rule until *c*.1119 when the order already comprised
several monasteries.[10] The papacy had in the past occasionally issued
privileges when required, but the conflict with the emperor after 1075
had diminished its influence in Germany, weakened its power outside
Italy and distracted attention from its universal obligations. The suspension of authority during the period of religious experiments may
have helped reformers by leaving them in peace, though they flourished
most in Burgundy and northern France, which suffered little from
episcopal paralysis in those years. Probably more important was the
positive encouragement given by the papal reformers to popular excitement for reform. In certain Italian cities, like Florence and Milan, this
won them support there against the emperor. Whatever refinements of
language reformers used, they were popularly understood to advocate a
ministry of chaste, unworldly priests. Local advocates of drastic reform
did not therefore always wait for episcopal and papal authority and they
thus provoked violent opposition. Fervent Christians did not suppose
that legal niceties or ecclesiastical obedience mattered more than the

moral perfection of the clergy. Many were swept along by an intransingent enthusiasm for restoring the apostolic life which was preached by unlicensed persons, clerk and lay, to the scandal of the establishment. Gregory VII was properly horrified to hear that the bishop's own men of Cambrai had burned an enthusiastic uncompromising preacher, though he could not do anything more than ask the bishop of Paris to order an enquiry and excommunicate the offenders.[11]

While the disciplinary powers of the church remained lax, there is evidence to show that a number of self-appointed apostles and prophets stirred up popular enthusiasm against the churches and the priests. Papal invective against unworthy priests, though aimed at imposing a model ministry, had also served to inflame popular hatred against all the unworthy. The followers of Peter of Bruys expressed their contempt for the sacramental priesthood *in toto* by rejecting such parts of the church's ministry as the eucharist, baptism of children, prayers for the dead. They were accused of advocating prayer in taverns.[12] The evidence for popular reformers is spasmodic but suggests that the excitement of the church's life in these years helped to stimulate action and eccentricities not easily controlled by the bishops.

The schism between popes Anacletus II and Innocent II in 1130, which brought the latter to France and the Cistercians into 'political' activity, released a new wave of popular religious commitment. A runaway monk, Henry, who had roamed in the same territory as the monks of Cîteaux and the reformer Bernard of Tiron, acquired an influential following in southern France, 1135-45, and was accused of denouncing the virtues of the ascetic life and forcing monks to marry. The opponents of these preachers who have left accounts of them naturally concentrated on their 'errors', not on explaining their success, though it seems probable that the doctrinal, credal or dogmatic elements that were discovered and denounced in their preaching in fact mattered much less to them and their followings than they did to the authorities. Learned persons were anyway most interested in doctrine (and claimed a monopoly of preaching it); the undisciplined enthusiastic reformers somewhat bewildered the authorities, who tried to explain their errors by isolating specific dogmatic failings. The authorities, being committed themselves to exciting changes, had once simplistically assumed that all reform would promote their cause. When undeceived, they turned their dogmatic intelligence against these unreliable allies. (In recent years we have seen revolutionaries similarly denounce 'splinter' groups for their 'deviations'). In a candid letter to Bernard of Clairvaux the Premonstratensian Everwin, provost of Steinfeld, reports his puzzled reactions to those calling themselves Christ's poor. These people were burned by the mob in Cologne for their unorthodox efforts to practise the apostolic life with no possessions, by prayer, fasting and hard work, having their own bishops *viri periti;* they went joyfully to the stake as martyrs showing a fortitude hardly found amongst orthodox Catholics, living and dying therefore as witnesses of the true church.[13] For men like Everwin and Bernard, themselves pioneers in the new religious life, it was disturbing to realize that not all fervour, however admirable, would lead to a general improvement of religious life: somewhere 'lines' had to be drawn. Where? and how?

At this stage in the history of 'heresy', however, there is no evidence that erroneous teaching owed anything to alien teachers, un-Christian 'dualism', or indeed cared much for doctrine at all. Error commended itself, as always, as 'truth', not perversity, and what earned it support was the popular view (not only of the twelfth century) that it was more Christian, not in the clerical sense, but because it embodied either the ascetic or the exalted tradition popularly ascribed to the New Testament. These men had certainly acquired their ideals from the church; they simply did not accept the interpretations of it offered by the authorized preachers. Heretics won acceptance by virtue of their own exemplary conduct, as popular Christian standards saw it. The popular idealism of the age reflects, like the monastic zealots, a literal belief in the injunctions of the Gospels, 'sell all that thou hast', and that the devout neither marry nor are given in marriage, but will be like angels.

The appeal to Biblical inspiration in the first half of the twelfth century was made as naturally by Bernard, as by 'heretics', with equal good faith and for equally subversive reasons, Bernard was no doubt the more learned and more scrupulous interpreter, and the later distinction between saint and heretic is justified, but at the time it was not quite so simple to recognize the good or to convict the bad, because the state of Biblical criticism and of legal discipline were themselves in a state of radical reappraisal. These subjects will therefore be considered in turn.

Biblical study
Western society has still not found a single book comparable to the Bible as a source of authority, yet able to open up a whole world of experience.[14] It was a sacred text drawn from some of the most ancient authors known, which spoke to the questions of the hour—the destiny of the human race and the spiritual goals of individual men. However, the Bible and revelation are not as obvious or clear as they may seem on first sight; even if the majority of Christian people had some knowledge of scripture there were obvious differences of interpretation amongst them. This suggested that there were misrepresentations to be swept away by study. Thoughtful persons were disturbed that the scriptures could be so diversely interpreted. They could not believe an inspired

work to be at variance with itself or capable of misleading individuals. Not unnaturally they hoped to be able to establish an authoritative meaning to prevent the spread of errors and so unite their own society in its essential beliefs: it fell to the 'intellectuals' to show the basic harmony of the revelation.

In the process the sacred text was analysed to discover its real teaching about such practical matters as the propriety of infant baptism or the suitability of the married state for devout and faithful Christians, let alone the profound problems of the nature of evil, and whether the creation was the work of God or Satan. In the process of theological exposition, teachers drew heavily upon their conventional education when it came to defining terms like sacrament, to comparing texts, and deducing principles. But behind all the didacticism lies a simple belief in the integrity of Scripture, its comprehensive character as a source of every necessary article of faith, its consistency with itself, even if super-ficially discordant, and ultimately its divine inspiration, a wonderful revelation of truths so deep that men's superficial rational intelligence could never have found them unaided. It was no part of the problem to engage in historical research into the texts or rediscover their original significance. Quite the reverse. Each statement of Scripture became a self-contained unit with its specific meaning—a tag to be cited with crushing authority—often to modern minds out of context and incon-gruously. The scriptures of the clergy, holy and patristic, were atomized; the separate pieces were used for the construction of quite different pictures, as the learned men grew more confident of their mastery of the texts and their right, or power, to make use of them.

The schools where this was done later became places for training preachers to refute heretics, but they did not grow in the twelfth cen-tury for that reason. They owed most to the general movement for the improvement of the clergy, and particularly to the efforts to create conditions for more learned communities in attendance on bishops, in colleges of secular and regular canons. Benedictine monasteries, for long the only and limited institutions of learning, rarely had much to contribute to the new scholarship. The post-Conquest English monas-teries, for example, though well-supplied with books, did not make much use of them.[15] The new orders of monks seeking better conditions for contemplation naturally had little interest in learning as such. The Carthusian monk following in Bruno's way, devoted some of his time to individual erudition, but had no pupils and he had no taste for learned discourse or debate. The greatest intellect of the late eleventh century was the monk Anselm, abbot of Bec and archbishop of Canterbury, but his theological reasonings owed little to the traditional kind of monastic learning and anyway inspired no school.

Benedictine learning in the twelfth century did still have religious possibilities. No writer showed better than Bernard of Clairvaux himself how deeply the words of the Latin Bible could become part of a man's thought and utterance, but in Bernard, Biblical study was pursued in a spirit of contemplation which stirred a kind of prophetic utterance, transported and transmuted by Bernard's own loving fervour for every soul he met, in need of encouragement or reproof: there was no scope here for the pursuit of intellectual understanding and in Bernard the monastic community retains its traditional place as the real context of the spiritual life.

The schools

Making every allowance for Bernard's position, it was unfortunate that he refused to face the awkward facts about the apparent incompatibility of texts and the need to find an objectively commendable manner of dealing with them. This was the problem that Peter Abelard (1074-1142) faced without flinching. His contempt for the intellectual standards of his day is shown by his reference to the 'conventiculum', called the Council of Soissons, that had condemned his work on the Trinity in 1121 because his intellectual inferiors had imposed on the papal legate *quia . . ille minus quam necesse esset litteratus fuerat.*[16] In 1121 Abelard had few supporters outside the rank of his own disciples. Over the succeeding generation such eager young men, not attracted by the cloister and monastic reform, opened up a new profession within the church. Though Abelard himself was obliged to give up his teaching in the schools and seek refuge in several different monasteries — St Denis, St Gildas de Rhuys, his own foundation of the Paraclete and finally at Cluny, driven out of the world more by the envy of other teachers than by his affair with Heloïse, he was the pioneer, the first great teacher in the schools, expounding, explaining and above all disputing *rationabiliter* against other teachers.

In his famous history of his own misfortunes (or more properly his *epistola consolatoria*) Abelard related how his students asked him to make them understand difficulties in the texts; he reports how he dazzled the students of Anselm of Laon by his brilliant explanation of the obscure book of Ezechiel. Abelard was born into a tradition with a revered text that he had no wish to overthrow, but he set out to understand the revelation. He took the words of the texts and tried to establish the essential meaning by comparing them. He used the discipline of logic to help him with definitions, distinctions, qualifications in theology. Of course, this could not help him to rediscover a message obscured by the text, for it emphasized the significance of every word as the bearer of meaning. Yet the processes of logic themselves encouraged him to imagine the nature of theological coherence, from which could be deduced the real principles he needed to know: the rules of life, for a generation in search of perfection and certainty. His most original work was an unfinished treatise on ethics. But his most influential writing was the *Sic et Non* (1120-26) in which he expounded a method for conciliating texts for and against. He showed how both sets of propositions could be true and thus by human reason 'save' the reputation of Scripture at variance with itself. The differences of theological opinion found not only in the Bible but amongst the 'authorities' had disturbed teachers before Abelard, but no one before him had so confidently seen how to resolve them by developing the techniques of logical thought.

From his time, logic became the new intellectual discipline for as the students wrestled with the most serious problems of their world — order in the present life and salvation in the next — logic became through theology and law the basis of medieval education.[17] These three do not now live in intellectual proximity and they are all austere subjects not immediately attractive to most students. From the seventeenth century the preeminence of logic in the medieval schools has aroused general scorn; modern attempts to revive it don't command general assent. The world then appeared to be in disorder: logic showed how human intelligence could bring order out of chaos. Admittedly, the earliest logicians barely looked at the world around them. They had for long been satisfied with Boethius' textbooks and his translations of Aristotle and Porphyry. But as they applied their learning to the contradictions and inconsistencies of scripture, they perceived the value of all Aristotle's works so their chief intellectual discovery was the corpus of Aristotle, translated from both Greek and Arabic versions, gradually extending their notice from his logical works to include his scientific and metaphysical ones: an unforeseeable development still incomplete in the twelfth century.

Aristotle was the teacher of them that know, but they were not immediately tempted to follow the philosopher along unfamiliar paths. It is said that Adam of Petit-Pont, a Parisian logician, thought Aristotle the only master worth study as early as 1130. A generation later, however, John of Salisbury, the most learned man of his day, still found Aristotle's *Posterior Analytics* puzzling. The main concern of the schools remained logic and John of Salisbury himself reports both its popularity, and its wide applicability, in the *Metalogieon* of 1159.[18] This intellectual discipline had thus attained its maturity in just over one generation since Abelard's *Sic et Non*.

The desire to understand with the rational mind, and to establish the validity of the understanding by a clear process of reasoning, which makes the demonstration irrefutable, obviously differs totally from the thirst Bernard knew and ministered to. Whereas it seemed to Bernard, as to others since, perhaps unfairly, that intellectual understanding was not only insufficient to satisfy the human soul but also threatened to damn it beneath intolerable intellectual pride, for the schoolmen understanding became their main concern, as it has remained. Though only very recently have teachers professed to take no interest whatever in the moral conduct of their pupils, from the first the schools renounced the coddling characteristic of the cloister. Bernard of Clairvaux was a steady opponent of Abelard's whole approach to theology, because it taught Biblical study by argument and did nothing to help men live by its saving truths. The old monastic study had concentrated on Biblical exegesis and absorbing the words of the Latin Bible into a life of meditation and prayer: the new desire for logical management and exposition tore the Bible to shreds and rearranged them in an order that pleased the human mind.

By 1150 Peter Lombard, later bishop of Paris, had composed his Sentences.[19] This work was used for the next four hundred years in the schools to expound the Christian religion systematically, beginning with the nature of the Trinity—the Godhead itself, then turning to the creation, the incarnation (the work of redemption) and finally to the means of grace, the sacraments of the church. Whatever its defects as Biblical criticism, it was the new style in Biblical study, designed to elucidate the meaning of the relevant texts in a system of rational belief. It was this desire for human understanding of the divine mysteries according to the light of human reason that Bernard found sacrilegious. Yet this commended itself to the best minds of the later twelfth century. Despite Bernard's objections to Abelard and his method, the attempt to draw the line in these matters and condemn what lay behind it as heresy ultimately failed.

The new confidence in the power of the intelligence to cope even with theological questions is one of the most important developments of the twelfth century. The intelligence is not in fact either omni-competent, or universally useful. Few men are well-endowed with it. The virtues attributed to it or derived from it did not encourage holiness, or Christian charity. Developed in special schools, the new learning sapped the intellectual talents of the provinces, dioceses and monasteries to concentrate it in a few great centres. Here famous teachers impressed contemporaries with their own cleverness, but left many scholars wondering about the real nature of man. Within the Christian soul, the teaching of such men themselves appeared to open a great conflict between the disciplined intellect and the unruly emotions, while the schools, unlike the cloister, offered no regular discipline to the young. French vernacular literature after 1160 developed a novel taste for adventure stories in which characters regularly debated with themselves about their ideals, their duty and their feelings, conflicts dressed up to interest and amuse lay noblemen by learned clerks exposed to academic learning. So, transmuted, the problems of the schools became familiar in other circles too.[20]

Whereas there is no difficulty in seeing the nature of the change, it is far less easy to explain its origins and analyse the appeal it made. Why did Abelard's disciples so thirst to understand? These young men lived in times of great religious aspirations, and were surrounded by ardent spirits in search of perfection and salvation, but can it be said that circumstances stimulated the intellect? Could the emotional fervour of the 'possessed' have the effect of sharpening the edge of the rationalists' mind? Nor does the use to which schoolmen's learning was subsequently put cast light on the origins of the movement. Abelard was not interested in heretical misuse of scripture or even inspired by earlier scholastic writers of controversial theology, like Berengar of Tours, or Anselm. The later application of 'logical' methods to problems of administration and government indicates only mediocre academic enthusiasm; the use of learned men in the English royal administration suggests that patrons there had little time for the theories of the clerks and subjected them to hackwork. In France, where these studies were best developed, application mattered neither at the beginning nor at the end. The dispute between the emperor and the pope which inspired much polemical writing and legal study in Italy and Germany barely ruffled the intellectuals of France. Bishop Yvo of Chartres (1091-1116) admittedly produced two influential works of canon-law. His systematic exposition in the *Panormia* was valued both for its practical utility and for its intellectual ideas about how to draw distinctions between authorities and separate general rules from particulars as to time, place and circumstances.[21] But Yvo is an isolated case. The French went no further with the development of the new rules of canon-law and if his intellect stimulated others in his generation, it is significant that it did so, not in law, but in logic and theology. We are forced back to the mainly intellectual outlook of the scholastics, and this is certainly borne out by their subsequent history. They were from first to last interested in the intellectual techniques of logic and applied it to the principal intellectual problems raised by their religion; they never deliberately sought applications for their learning.

The intellectualism of the schools is involved in the very notion of 'understanding'. What did this mean? It certainly did not involve understanding of a modern kind, scientific or historic, by general law or temporal origin. It grew out of the problems of interpreting the books written in a foreign, bookish language, originally only intelligible by the grinding study of grammar and of the rules of literary composition, Rhetoric. Latin words were easily reified in this context and the best minds of the day gave themselves to the manipulation of these words like so many mosaic stones. They could arrange them in intelligent order, treating them as things; words as products of the human mind and voice were obviously clues to human understanding, if they were not the names of real things themselves. There was at the time no conception of human understanding of nature in the modern sense of acquiring secrets as to how to harness the forces of nature for human benefit. Understanding the universe could at best be only a matter of learning how to speak about it correctly. The basis of human science was therefore the intelligent use of speech itself.

Legal discipline

The promotion of studies of law in the late eleventh and early twelfth century is more easily explained. Its source in the disputes about papal reform, its use in drawing lines between catholics and heretics, monks and canons, clergy and laymen, its outcome in the creation of an effective papal *plenitudo potestatis* — all these aspects indicate its obvious historical importance, even if, perhaps more than the abuse heaped on scholastic theologians, the later execration of the canonists has since discredited their achievements. Churchmen knew that their Latin speech made them Roman citizens in a universal Roman empire, with a right to that order, peace and law which the empire had stood for. But at the time there was in fact no experience of such an institution. From its knowledge of the Roman past, medieval Christendom as a whole preferred to fasten on to the idea of order, not the reality of the empire as it had by then become. Christendom had to devise its rules and ultimately a new form of government to enforce them, with only an intellectual concept of Roman unity to guide them.

The obvious model for such a law was the imperial law of Rome itself. The codes of the late Roman empire were specially useful even to reformers, for they demonstrated plainly how much emperors had laid upon bishops to make peace between Christians, and judge disputes. Read in the conditions of the eleventh century, these old imperial rules served to enhance the bishop's role. No serious study of Roman Law had occurred in the West after Justinian's codification (*c*.530) until the eleventh century and, when the German emperors encouraged it, it served their pretensions to rule as Caesars. The original impetus for the reform of the Roman church had come from Emperor Henry III who expected Rome to take on its responsibilities for the whole of Christendom. The tradition of imperial, barbarian and Carolingian Christianity had developed on the assumptions that the churches would receive protection from rulers. Till the eleventh century churchmen were mainly agreed about the attitude to be adopted towards the secular power. All the clergy had been brought up to expect clerical solidarity in submission to kings. Differences of opinion within the clerical ranks followed from the adoption of controversial policies. When reformers broke with this tradition, how could they justify their opposition?

Their idea that there had been an ideal state of Christendom when the law of the church had been agreed and enforced had no historical foundation: it was a mere act of faith. There was no lawbook to tell them what church law was, and there never had been.[22] Of course in the past, particularly after the collapse of the Roman empire in the west in the late fifth century, and again after the distintegration of Charlemagne's empire, individual bishops, reformers or scholars had compiled their own books of legal precedents taking texts from the Bible, conciliar decisions, papal letters and indeed, when in need, making blatant forgeries. Precedents were lifted out of context, but in good faith, to provide at least the moral support of law when imperial authority was wanting. These existing private compilations were what reformers had to use. Gregory VII, a Roman churchman, naturally sought historical precedents in the records of his great Roman predecessors for his intransigence in daring to reprove and depose the Emperor Henry IV. When these had proved inadequate the defects were in fact supplied from those spurious collections of 'decretals' composed in ninth-century Gaul, which passed at the time for authentic papal letters. This is notorious but it proves that even if the Roman church itself had not taken the initiative, churchmen elsewhere in need of authorities would have also supplied them in Roman guise.

After Gregory VII's death popes were more often suppliants for support north of the Alps than imperious prelates — yet the church did not despise Roman weakness. It had too much need itself of the idea of what Rome might be. Diversity of opinion about such solemn matters as the church's constitution could hardly be tolerated. The truth had to be established without delay. For two generations either side of 1100 the major intellectual task of Christendom was thus to rediscover its basic rules, arrange them and evaluate them, and then teach them so that all the clergy could agree on fundamentals. This was what the study of canon-law provided. In the disputes with the popes, both sides turned to the books and records, not for mere curiosity, but expecting them to reveal what the rules of a well-ordered church had been, before being overthrown by ignorance and disorder. The purpose was to restore those rules and prevent them ever being abandoned again, by enforcing them with the correct institutional powers. Such a conception of the past golden age to be brought back once and for all by heroic endeavour seems quaint to us. We believe in a process of continuous change with standards constantly adjusted by social developments. Against the predominantly religious preoccupations of the age, with the belief that God's purpose had been revealed in all its essentials, such relativism would have been inconceivable.

The conflict between emperor and pope itself revealed profound disagreements about the nature of that past ideal state. The emperors who appealed to Roman imperial law, as in the Code of Justinian, to justify their stand in church government, had no need to be ingenious, even if they were challenged by the difficulties of understanding the texts themselves, which had come out of a different social order. On the other hand papal supporters disinterred a vast amount of historical material that was not, on the surface at least, consistent with itself. The texts of the fathers and church councils, which were sifted for guidance about the rules of the church, provided contradictory rulings. Somehow or another their differences had to be explained away and the church's true teaching set forth. Neither side could be deeply satisfied with the results of its appeal to the past — it did not give the obvious answers expected. The papal reformers had to wrestle more with their discoveries, being determined to make the best of them and devise a means of cutting through the contradictions, since they were challenging the existing and traditional system and had therefore to propose an alternative. As educated persons they already knew something of the nature of arguments and how to resolve them: their classical education taught them the arts of understanding the text (grammar) of persuasion (rhetoric) and of arguing (logic). Gradually out of these individual efforts there emerged more systematic surveys of the whole ground, as the schools of law compared the precedents, judged their relative value and arrived at a reasonable academic solution to every point of law. By 1140 the divine law had been surveyed and arranged by a monk of Bologna, Gratian, and this became the basic textbook of a new kind of professional education. From all over Christendom students came to Bologna to learn the divine law.[23] They carried back their learning to their own lands. In place of the individual bishops managing as best they could, the new professionalism created a body of international law with experts able to enforce it.

Gratian's *Concord of Discordant Canons,* usually called the *Decretum,* was in many ways more influential than Peter Lombard's *Sentences.*[24] It was the basic textbook of lawyers, the greatest professional class in medieval Christendom for four centuries, whose activities and decisions had more practical consequences for more Christians in their life and dying than any other. To describe it as a law-book hardly does it justice. Before theology itself had been systematically expounded, Gratian had succeeded in mastering the mass of historical research undertaken in the three or four previous generations and arranging it intelligently. His purpose was nothing so crude as to digest and epitomize. The book was intended for serious churchmen aware of the difficulties of reconciling authorities, and answering the arguments of opponents. So Gratian not only arranged the texts, but set them in a context of problems and discussed their effectiveness in establishing conclusions. His own reasonable summaries as to the state of the law in the light of these precedents and arguments carried conviction by virtue of his authority as a great teacher, but they were not in any sense final or official. His text inspired commentaries and new problems. His conclusions sometimes aroused dissatisfaction. The law-schools and the Roman curia were involved in constantly improving on their text. The training required to master both the book and the commentaries demanded talents of a very high order: the sharp logical mind of the schools; the gravity and piety of a theologian; the dispassionate rationality of a judge. The divinely established rules of Christian society, as culled from Holy Writ, from the inspired utterance of the Holy Spirit in church councils and from learned teachers, were no less holy for being arranged according to the wit of man.

The book is divided into three very unequal parts. About a quarter of the text is given to the first part, significantly entitled Distinctiones, concerned with general principles of law, rules pertaining to bishops and the discipline they were obliged to enforce. The longest part of the work, the second, dealt with the disputes to be settled in the courts, relating to the bishops, the clergy, the monks' part in diocesan affairs, heresy, excommunicates and matrimonal disputes. This included an elaborate little treatise on the rules of penitence. The final section dealt with the rules for the proper celebration of the sacraments, which involved dealing with some questions normally considered theological.

The arrival of the textbook signified in fact the establishment of a regular form of legal instruction at Bologna, a great Italian city admirably situated on the great routes north-south and east-west of northern Italy, where the jurisprudence of the Romagna came closest to the pro-papal territories of Tuscany. To this school came not young ardent disciples in search of intellectual enlightenment, but beneficed clergy seeking professional qualifications for obtaining ecclesiastical posts of influence. The new canon-law was quickly disseminated throughout Christendom and its value demonstrated in public affairs.

The new rules, universally acceptable and applicable, showed up local anomalies in the existing customs of the churches. The clergy in general aimed to eliminate these. They were the principal beneficiaries of the law which defined their status. The law was their own law—their privilege, which some powerful rulers like Frederick I (1152-89) or Henry II (1154-89) initially intended to curtail. In all their disputes with one another, or with the secular powers, the clergy claimed to be judged by this code alone. They themselves also presided in clerical courts to judge laymen, accused of offences against the laws binding on all Christians—over marriage or death-bed bequests for example. Only because the laws were thought to be old did they command respect; but the universal enforcement of standard rules by standard process all over Christendom was new. This gave the clergy a sense of their common standing against all others that abolished nation and language. It even threatened to abolish social distinctions. Rulers were able to impede the recruitment of serfs into the ranks of the clergy, for that would have destroyed their servile status, since the new rules accorded all clergy privilege. Bishops found a new solidarity with priests and it probably became easier for the humbly born to become bishops. The reforming movement's first success was to establish a clerical community subject to its own laws and courts and ultimately protected by an international clerical hierarchy whose idea it had been. By the end of the twelfth century, rulers who denied the clergy their rights could expect to be forced to answer for their offence. The efficacy of this protection was unprecedented. Without big battalions the clergy had become powerful, and all over Christendom the same rules applied to all its spiritual persons: over this clerical body the pope ruled as sovereign.

3. THE PAPACY

The need of Christendom for the papacy was felt long before the means were found to make its decisions effective: through law. Appeals to Rome for aid would have remained desperate and intermittent had it not been for the law and lawyers. Sorting out sound laws from abusive customs had taken them only so far. In the new conditions of the twelfth century the old laws needed clarification, amendment and refinement. Popes summoned synods and councils where many obscurities could be cleared up, but this was not sufficient. The most sturdy churches expected privileges or special favours, like right of access to the pope when their oppressors, lay and episcopal, defied anathemas. Far from accepting the new universal rules, every church worth the name made claims to special treatment. Only a living head could keep the peace when the law could not. Even had the churches been less litigious, the nature of the church's growth in the twelfth century had made a final court of appeal indispensable. Take so simple an issue as tithes. Christian liability to pay tithes to the church had been generally enforced by the lay powers since the tenth century, but in any one place there could be many deserving representatives of the church with a plausible claim to receive, if not all, at least some, of the tithes. Who was to decide their relative merits? And what should be tithed? If new lands were cultivated, could the cultivators bestow their tithes at their own discretion or did certain churches have prescriptive rights? The assignment of reasonable revenues for the actual incumbent could be left to the bishops in ordinary circumstances, but what happened if the patrons of the churches were monasteries directly subject to the pope? The new religious orders were so numerous that they got in one another's way and appealed to the pope. It can hardly be a coincidence that Gratian discussed the binding power of papal privileges to dispense with general rights in the context of a dispute about tithes between two monasteries both claiming papal authority (Causa 25). Powerful ecclesiastical corporations hoping to establish their legal rights in the courts did not rest content with local decisions and forced their problems on the Roman curia.

The popes were not altogether content to be plagued with litigious clergy. From the time of Gregory VII they had constant political anxieties in Italy and with the emperor. Alexander III (1159-81) who was the first important canon-lawyer to become pope—he was, according to Robert of Torigny, the most learned pope ever—had to attend almost daily throughout his pontificate to legal business, though he too had considerable political problems, and more often lived in exile than in Rome. His decisions in the curia contributed over twenty years to building up a case-law for the church to supplement the textbook and its commentaries. Lawyers for the sake of consistency realized that these decisions should be noted and absorbed into their learning so they began to collect these papal decretals. In turn these were sifted and arranged and eventually published by papal authority in the following century. It is easy to see how the apostolic see became involved in this legal business, but it did not grow inevitably from the papal office itself. In the past, popes had had occasion to rebuke immoral conduct; not until the twelfth century was there regular machinery for invoking papal anathemas or making them effective. In other words the papal government of the church was new. Neither the ancient origins of the papacy nor historical hindsight should obscure the extent to which a radical transformation occurred between the death of Pope Gregory VII in 1085 and that of Alexander III in 1181. The sovereign court was overwhelmed by requests to settle controversies.[25] Gregory VIII tried to refer back to local bishops legal suits about assets worth less than 20 marks. Innocent III exhorted bishops to spare the papacy and attend to their own responsibilities. The papacy tried to harness the judicial resources of the provinces by delegating cases to those who could make minute enquiries on the spot. Litigants were not to be satisfied with anything less than Rome itself: in the provinces, diffidence inhibited, as envy frustrated, attempts to decentralize. The papacy could not prevent the curia from being inundated with business. It was not Rome that demanded this business, but the body of Christian clergy in general.

Churchmen mastered the speaking and writing of Latin as the most important part of their basic education; and this enabled them to be at home in any part of Latin Christendom. Monks, teachers and students roamed without intellectual barriers. At no period in European history has the intelligentsia been more restless or more travelled, making friends in many lands and acquiring by experience a sense of the unity of the church. In one sense Christendom already had an obvious focus in the pope at Rome, but the twelfth-century clergy did not then automatically and obediently turn to Rome, for monasteries like Cluny or Cîteaux made a powerful appeal to their sense of loyalty, just as Paris left an unforgettable mark upon the clergy who flocked there. The pull of purely local affections constantly incited individuals to defend their own church against neighbours and rivals. In the 1170s Thomas Becket's bones at Canterbury made his own church a place of power more effectively than his stand in life had served the general ecclesiastical interest. Rivalries between churches were not conducted with good temper or tolerance, as the outraged criticisms of Roger, Archbishop of York, by his former colleagues at Canterbury show. In a sense the parochial loyalties and disputes which made them such passionate defenders of local rights drove them individually to seek approval from the supreme tribunal in Rome itself. Monasteries and churches that refused obedience to the local bishop happily submitted to papal supervision and gloried in their special relationships. Until the late twelfth century Rome had only spasmodically intervened in local affairs when required, leaving the existing loyalties to Cluny or Cîteaux untouched.

From the time of Alexander III the lawyers had themselves taught the higher clergy and their own clients in the courts to look to Rome. As they worked on their own legal procedures and the hierarchy of courts, they naturally found the need for a sovereign tribunal, just as in arguments about principles they needed to know who would pronounce final sentence.[26] Given the respect shown in the west to the see of the apostles Peter and Paul and awe of Peter's Vicar as bearer of the keys of Heaven and Hell, the lawyers did not hesitate in designating Rome as the final arbiter in all disputes. The forms and definitions they devised came from the law-books of the Roman empire, their models of jurisprudence, which inevitably distorted their interpretation of the pope's role. The attributes of empire were applied to the pope; he was invested with *plenitudo potestatis,* and there was no human authority superior to him. This preserved the coherence of the ecclesiastical institution. Final decisions about every matter of human concern could therefore be given by this authority without fear of contradiction. This

Roman legalism was foisted upon the papacy to suit the western church.

The different developments of the life of the church considered in the previous sections grew out of the zeal, concern and initiative of hundreds of individual Christians inspired and caught up in the enthusiasms of their contemporaries. By the end of the twelfth century, however, there was a slackening in the pace of discovery: the territory of Christian experience had been marked out, the principal routes signposted and orderly government under which the new resources could be thoroughly exploited came to seem the primary need. Administrators acquired respect and power. To qualify for office, routine learning counted for more than spiritual inspiration.

Christendom did not lack existing administrative forms. The Roman empire of Diocletian had been divided into dioceses and after Constantine bishops became the executive officers of imperial Christianity. The collapse of the empire left them with considerable local responsibilities which they discharged as best they could within the barbarian kingdoms. The conversion of English and German peoples extended the system all over Christendom. Bishoprics were however of variable size and endowment. Over the centuries bishops had compromised with the secular authorities, as organizers of local justice and military contingents. From the first, church reformers had sought to elude episcopal discipline as too arbitrary, unreliable and uneven. Cistercian monks who began by dutiful submission to local bishops so rapidly became an international order far more powerful than the diocesan that this part of the programme was dropped. For many purposes the diocesan unit continued to serve for local supervision of parish churches, but by the twelfth century there could be no question of bishops exercising total authority there. Each diocese was riddled with independent ecclesiastical corporations. Nor were the Christian kingdoms any more acceptable as ecclesiastical units, though some ambitious prelates like the archbishop of Canterbury aspired to 'national' patriarchates. Concessions had to be made to diverse local customs as in England, Hungary, Sicily and Castile, because churchmen could not in practice ignore royal power, despite their general theory about the inferior place of laymen in the church. Their attitude may look weak, but it was realistic to satisfy rulers with some show of the respect they expected. At the same time the clergy pressed as far as possible for observance of the rules of the universal church, and whatever local loyalties some clergy showed their rulers, they felt even more personally about the rights and dignity of the clerical estate.

For much of the century the papacy itself had been at odds with the German king and Roman emperor. Alexander III had been obliged to live on the charity of others—he had taken refuge in the kingdom of France, like so many of his predecessors, and relied on the Cistercian order for political support which was effective even in Frederick's own lands. The papacy's need of allies, however willing, had hardly put it in a position to rule. The papacy had remained a preeminent but not peremptory leader of the church. At that time, too, Barbarossa himself had made a spectacular revival of the empire, which entered its finest period; he had Charlemagne canonized by his imperial anti-pope and the empire was thereafter deemed 'sacred'. In dealing with Barbarossa's most powerful contemporary, Henry II, the pope had, however, been able to secure something more than a token submission after the murder of Becket (1172). When, five years later, he came to terms with the emperor too at Venice, he could take some satisfaction for the success he had achieved for the interests of the clergy against the most powerful rulers of the day.

Alexander had no additional revenues, arrogated to himself no new powers of appointment, commanded no special reputation for holiness, allied with no military and no political power.[27] Yet the papacy he presided over became the basis for an authority able to dispose of resources as extensive as any secular state. On the legal basis of his plenitude of power, the pope could exercise additional functions as required. Whatever the pretensions of the Holy Roman Empire, it was the pope who actually presided over an assembly of nearly 300 representatives of all Christendom at the Third Lateran Council of 1179, as visible demonstration of his universal rule. The emperor was not present and could never have summoned a comparable representative body. From this time forward the papacy began to govern with increasing confidence a steadily more submissive church.

The creation of a clerical *respublica* within or beside the existing public 'authorities' of Christendom was of no obvious benefit to anybody but the clergy themselves. The growth of heresy amongst the most literate laymen of Christendom and the attitude of ordinary laymen to the church in the late twelfth century, well attested in a number of different ways, suggest that while the clergy had concentrated on improving their own status, the state of religion in Christendom as a whole was far from healthy. So after 1177, the papacy had to combat the alarming signs of discontent with the church and churchmen, using its new authority over the clergy to initiate and enforce reform. Christendom needed both leadership and inspiration.

4. THE NEW SOCIETY

The Third Lateran Council that met under Alexander III in 1179 is less celebrated than the Fourth which Innocent III presided over in 1216, but it already adumbrated the same programme. The papal church was not ruled by autocrats, but by lawyer-administrators through conciliar decisions. The disputes within the clerical fold that had sapped its strength and reputation were to be avoided by clear definitions of powers and functions. Those who refused obedience to this eminently rational and human *ecclesia* would suffer anathema and outlawry, and if they refused submission they would pay the ultimate penalty. The church itself did not, of course, shed blood, but Christian princes gladly took on the responsibility of eliminating heretics. The first kings to do so were the Emperor Henry VI and Pere I of Aragon in 1197.

The new church was to be tidy and disciplined. The lawyers took over from the exalted monks and preachers who had dominated the religious life of the proceeding century. Unauthorized preachers were excommunicated. All monks were confined to their cloisters. No doubt the lawyers and administrators intended to be of service to the monks in defining their ranks and status, and securing for them those conditions of life in which their essential virtues of contemplation and prayer could be practised. The result was in fact disastrous for the real influence of monasteries in the church. The enforcement of the new rules of canon-law severed the monks from all their old and familiar associations with the world. The proliferation of the specialized orders of canons and teachers deprived the monks of multifarious obligations they had undertaken in the past. Under the new rules, the monks became those persons dedicated to God who chose the hardest way of prayer and contemplation. They lived in communities with no obligations to minister to outsiders, to teach, preach or study. Their spiritual energies were entirely devoted to God's service; in less idealistic terms, they were bottled up without possibility of escape. In effect the monks were thus being 'defined' according to the intellectual ideas and ideals of the educated, particularly of the lawyers and the administrators. The final indignity for the Benedictines was to have imposed upon them by Lateran IV a form of provincial organization clearly inspired by Cîteaux.[28] Thus even the special relationship with Rome had not spared them the loss of their treasured autonomy.

The same council also required all future monastic innovators to adopt one of the many existing rules. The decision does not seem unreasonable. After more than a century of innovation, it seemed likely that the profitable paths had already been marked out. The mind of the council indicated however a conservative intention. There was no enthusiasm for enthusiasm and no historical awareness of what had taken place or what the consequences of the decision might be in the future. These churchmen lived in a world which they thought could be reasonably administered according to the newly established rules. After centuries of abuse the church, having reestablished its basic principles, had only to leave the lawyers to enforce them for all to be well. Innovation would be a hindrance. For what we see as twelfth-century experiment had been interpreted at the time as no more than a return to the principles of the past.

The history of the monastic orders from the thirteenth century therefore makes sad reading, not because of the abuses, but because the nature of the monastic ideal had been so defined as to shift monks into gentle backwaters.[29] Monastic reformers might have approved the peace they had won to devote themselves to prayer, but those who in the past had been seen as the only example of Christian renunciation assailed on all sides by unholiness, now became the unremarkable exponents of only one pattern of Christian living—not even so praiseworthy in the new settled conditions, since the church guaranteed their peace. Later centuries drew no strong spiritual inspiration from the monks they never saw except when let out on secular business. Locally, monks probably earned respect, even if records almost invariably call attention to disagreements and criticism. Significantly, proposals from extremists that they should be disendowed, though symptomatic, did not carry conviction.[30] These uneventful institutions must have retained the general confidence of their contemporaries in the worthiness of their aims. Yet of their effective role in shaping the church characteristic of earlier centuries, almost nothing remained; monks might enrich church but they were no longer essential, as the protestant churches later showed. The church had taken a direction in which monks could only limp along in the rear.

To some extent their earlier successes had deprived them of their *raison d'être*. The original experiments in monastic life that had begun with the Cistercians and ended with the Franciscans were all marked by a revulsion against the power of wealth or comfort which choked the spiritual life. Successive reformers embraced simple austerity; they undertook to settle in waste or unpropitious places which decreased in number as Europe became wealthier; so they were driven even further by their ideals to the fringe wastelands and ultimately to the urban down-and-outs. The religious founders never anticipated the astonishing success of their projects: the waste blossomed; the reformers' own physical efforts and their exhortations to the rich helped to bring the condition of all Christian peoples to public notice. Having done their work well, such orders lost not only their public utility, but their very means of preserving their ideals in the original context. Orders that impressed contemporaries for their idealism were naturally patronized to the point where they became well-endowed in land, and then they attracted recruits of a different calibre with no personal knowledge of the founders. Success stimulated a new wave of even greater austerity. Landed estates to support religion were accepted even by the Cistercians; but once cultivated, land became a responsibility which was burdensome to the truly devout. Endowed generously in the past they had served in so many different ways, the monasteries retained the burdens of managing estates and revenues, given to God for ever, but were deprived by the church's new rules from appearing to deserve them.

The records of their administrative cares, though disappointing in many ways, carry their own commentary. In a sense the problem was not new in the late twelfth century. Peter the Venerable at Cluny had accomplished important administrative reforms as an integral part of his work as abbot. The need for reforms in monastic administration in the early twelfth century are in fact a counterpart for the older, established houses of the demand for a totally new start expressed by the Cistercians. Abbot Suger of St Denis rather smugly records his own administrative achievements in raising the revenues and yields of his monastery's lands, though this famous essay in management culminated in the passages describing the marvellous new buildings and shrines on which much of the money had been spent.[31] Thus administration was not at that time a self-contained virtue, of modest ambition and reasonable enterprise. The burden of property for monks is perhaps most bleakly revealed by the collapse of the brave Cistercian attempt to renounce all property and rights in order to work their own living from the land. After 1130 they began to accept even grants of tithes. The popes showered them with privileges and exemptions. The lawyers showed how exceptions could be justified and how general principles could be reconciled with special cases. Walter Map satirizes the callous greed of English Cistercian abbots less then fifty years after their first appearance in England.[32] Whatever brave new worlds the Cistercian monasteries had seemed to Ailred in his youth, the mood of saintly friendship he fostered was soon dissipated by the comforts of prosperous sheepfarming.

By the end of the twelfth century, the management of these varied and numerous religious corporations naturally attracted to the orders men of different spiritual outlook, aiming to preserve, not innovate. Genuine independents like Francis or even Waldo of Lyons could not be fobbed off with the prospect of serving others' ideals. There were many to follow them in the call to ever more total renunciation, for the administrative church, which depended upon cool, intelligent management, was incapable of inspiring religious men; on the contrary they loathed its compromises, riches and worldliness. Disciplined by the canon lawyers, monks still seethed with exaltation and those who could not break out of their institutions responded to apocalyptic prophecy, when in the far south, the Cistercian abbot Joachim of S. Giovanni in Fiore in Calabria (d. 1202) produced his 'third' gospel, the most heady drug available in the next century.[33] In the religious passions of men, who in a worldly sense happily entrusted their welfare to political popes, the power of medieval religion can still be measured. Against this background, the success of the friars may seem warranted.

The Franciscans

The most original and influential of the later religious orders was the Franciscan, the Minorites, the little brothers.[34] The turbulent history of its divisions and rivalries cannot diminish its greatness; though they suggest how little the highest aspirations could do in the increasingly complex situations facing men of God. Francis's original intention had been a literal imitation of Christ himself. This radical return to first principles has been frequently advocated since, though never again with equal simplicity—the idea has become rather obvious. To do so in the thirteenth century implied a total rejection of the whole Christian pattern of holiness as it had developed for more than a thousand years. It was in its way presumptuous; it was also an act of desperation—there could be no other way—and it demanded total renunciation and dependence on God. There was nothing overbearing in Francis's understanding of his role. His simplicity overcame the doubts of the great pope Innocent III and his programme was duly approved. Francis tried to live with his brethren entirely spontaneously without such rules as had fettered and corroded earlier reforms. Unhappily this was no solution; his movement could not function without rules, and it was institutionalized out of recognition within twenty years of his death. This is not simply the fault of those who could not live up to the founder's basic ideals. By developing the order in a way apparently clean contrary to his instructions they nevertheless found the only possible means of preserving anything at all of his vision. As much could be said of the transformation of Christ's teaching in the church.

It is worth commenting on three points insisted on by Francis, which had to be set aside. He himself was a layman who never advanced beyond the order of deacon; the Minister General Haymo of Faversham in 1242 forbade the recruitment to the order of anyone not a priest or a clerk. Ministry in the church by the thirteenth century could not normally be conceived of without priestly ordination. Francis himself could refuse the honour and talk of the service of holy jesters—but Francis's desperate attempt to save the church from the clergy was shrugged off as an eccentricity; the clergy themselves had no difficulty in proving that they were indispensable and the sole authorised spokesmen of God. Secondly, Francis had profoundly distrusted education and book-learning. Amazing stories were told of his violent reactions to seeing his brothers with devotional works of their own. Francis hated the pride of the learned; he saw that simple folk were taken in by their pretensions and led astray

by their egoism. Yet even before he died in 1226 the brothers began to
recruit heavily in academic circles, where the best minds of the day only
too keenly felt the nub of his criticism. Such learned recruits with the best
will in the world could not break with learning as easily as Francis. Nor
could the early Franciscans resist the force of the Dominican example,
which ran parallel to their own, yet for whom learning was seen from the
first to be an essential part of their teaching mission. Within a few years
of Francis's death his brothers had schools in each of the principal universities of Europe. Franciscans participated in all the academic quarrels
of the century. Was the world worse for the insights they brought to
theology and philosophy, even if it was a strange perversion of Francis's
original intention? Francis had wished to show harvesting peasants an
example: this was no less necessary in the schools. The directness of
Franciscan religious response had much wider application than Francis
himself had supposed. Lastly, there was the problem of poverty—
the most important of all and the one which remained the deepest
source of disagreement within the order itself, and the basis of criticism
from without.

Francis thought that Christ and his followers had come to serve and
save the poor. He believed that only by becoming poor himself could he
fulfil his duties as a Christian. He expected his brothers to beg for what they
needed, learning the humility, dependence and degradation known only
to the poor, in order to promote the blessedness of giving on the other-
side. It was the complete opposite of the seigneurial monastic virtue of
charity, for which great endowments had been justified. Francis's reading
of the Gospels was not the only one possible; but his interpretation was
becoming popular at the time; many other religious persons of his
generation responded likewise, though not all were as obedient to the
authorities of the church as he. Within and without the church these men
clearly pointed to the great stumbling block that riches had become for
religion. Riches had corrupted the church itself. Men pointed to the
greed of the Roman curia, the avarice of the Cistercian abbots, the
ostentation of princely bishops. The wealth of merchants and the luxury
of lords threatened to stifle their religious life. They became indifferent
to their own spiritual welfare, and to the precarious existence of their
penniless fellow-Christians; they imagined they could bargain for whatever
spiritual gifts they wanted with their ill-gotten gains. This problem has
had a long history since the twelfth century; at the time it was fairly
new. Hitherto the predominantly self-sufficient rural economy of Europe
had made money, that is liquid assets, of little serious concern in the
world at large. The open-handed lord was expected to have an in-
exhaustible supply of riches to give away to his vassals. Noblemen had
been generous and their goods were splendidly wasted away. Their money

was not for purchases for self or for sensible investment. This became less and less true during the twelfth century. Religious men were shocked by their contemporaries' love of barren silver. Those who suffered most from shortage of money protested loudly about what money could buy.

It was in the great cities of the continent where these protests had the most general religious effects, particularly in those of southern France and northern Italy. Religious and moral protest against corrupt rich worldly prelates ripened into popular heretical movements increasingly alienated from Christian teaching altogether and functioning independently, with or without their own 'bishops'. Official reactions were excessively nervous. Even orthodox Christian leaders of protest like Waldo were condemned along with heretical ones when they declined to stop their unauthorized preaching. A jittery church worried more about obedience than its own reputation. In many dioceses of southern France the ecclesiastical authori--ties thus found themselves isolated amongst whole populations. Energetic teachers then arrived from the Balkans and found it easy to extend their own doctrines to the disaffected. In Francis's lifetime the established church was in some places in southern France fighting for survival. The church fought for what it believed were the essentials of the Christian religion, and took the view that only the authorized clergy had the right to preach. It frowned upon the extremism of the uninstructed laity; lay enthusiasm was only tolerated under tight clerical supervision. It was an important turning point for the church. The clerical movement for church reform had long been popular because it looked like inaugurating the perfect Christian society. When the clergy put the maintenance of their own dominance first and turned on critics of the hierarchy, much popular enthusiasm melted away.

Francis who refused the priesthood was, for all his eccentricity, one of the few reformers who never wavered in his obedience. The grateful church seized upon his reform and this gave it the chance to retain contact with the humblest layers of society. The order had nevertheless to be adapted for the church's purpose. At first it was seen to be important that the Franciscan emphasis on poverty should be respected. Not until a century after Francis's death did Pope John XXII, exasperated by the recent acrimony shown between rival groups, categorically declare in 1323 the doctrine of the absolute poverty of Christ to be erroneous, thus ending a century of confusion.[35] But in the meantime, whatever the official position, the order had in fact been encumbered with decent housing, educational facilities and pastoral responsibilities. Nominal ownership of the property was vested in others but this was mere subterfuge. The enthusiasm of pious laymen overwhelmed the Franciscans with lavish support. Friaries and churches were forced upon them; their leaders were promoted to bishoprics and cardinalates; friars became royal confessors and advisers. Their religious zeal received all the encouragement and patronage which the thirteenth century was accustomed to bestow on worthy religious enterprises. It was useless to protest that such patrons failed to understand Francis's intentions. They had no doubt that they understood; they were persuaded that they would have made an equal fuss of Christ had they been alive in his time and never allowed him to suffer and die. The established religious enthusiasms of the age inevitably missed the profoundest level of this religion. They could not however stifle all the merit of the new movement. The Franciscans did become the missioners amongst the poor, did preach the Gospels in the highways and did play an incalculable part in reconciling the underprivileged to the new religious order in the church.

These 'monks' differed radically from the older established orders. They were not vastly endowed with landed estates and supported by serfs and servants. They lived on the fringe of the town, dependent on the charity of the townspeople they ministered to. The ordinary clergy could not rival them in popularity. Lacking the special protection of the papacy, they could do little but abuse the friars. University men like William of St Amour and Jean de Meung in the *Roman de la Rose,* both Parisians, indulged in extravagant and filthy invective. These criticisms and the quarrels within the order grew in the fourteenth century.[36] They were accused of avarice and immorality, abuses which grew naturally out of their ease of access and familiarity with their charges. A lot of the criticism was inspired by jealousy and rivalry; much of it might be true; much else might be wickedly ironic. Yet the continued support of their churches, the bequests made by dying penitents and the splendid revival of the Franciscan order in the fifteenth century show that the Franciscans did not deserve all the obloquy heaped upon them by petulant critics like Wyclif.

The friars turned their attention to the urban scene. The established monastic orders had grown up in a different world, and the continuing strength of the monasteries was derived from the fact that Europe remained a predominantly rural society. Yet as the towns were the important new centres of restless idealistic people, who desperately wanted a more spiritual religious life, the friars provided the most important guidance they ever received. In the Rhineland cities, communities of devout women found Dominican friars to preach to them and direct their religious lives. These experiments in the devotional life were not monastic in the earlier sense. The communities were not permanent, nor necessarily contemplative and not subject to fixed rules. They represented novel attempts to lead devout lives in community, yet in touch with the world. They indicate that the laity could still improvise forms of religious life and not settle into institutions in the traditional sense. They are to that extent what Francis might have approved. Within these centres there grew up a body of vernacular religious literature, especially sermons or works for meditation, which provide the best evidence of the religious aspirations of the next two centuries.

The official church was suspicious of these communities and their beliefs, for it had by this time settled what it thought necessary for the religious wellbeing of Europe and itself saw no need of these unregulated bodies. It is difficult for those with fixed ideas about society to tolerate those who seem to call basic assumptions into question. In modern socialist states governments similarly persecute even harmless groups of individuals who by living with independent ideas betray their indifference to doctrines the government holds dear.

The orders of friars in many crucial respects stood monasticism on its head. Instead of withdrawal from the world they deliberately courted it. Despite the conventional reservations imposed by authority, they also implicitly recognized that salvation was possible for laymen in the world and that neither monastic vows nor clerical ordination were indispensable for leading the religious life. By sermons and in the confessional they expected all Christians to serve God in their calling. As long as this teaching was not pushed to exaggerated lengths and not used to discredit the existing clerical hierarchy, it was tolerated by authority. The many medieval writers who may seem to be teaching 'a priesthood of all believers', were not persecuted because they did not intend such a belief to be used to bring down the whole structure.

Dissidents
The diffusion of 'heretical' belief in some parts of Christendom comparatively well supplied with towns and poor artisans is not easily distinguished from the concomitant evidence of popular hostility to the lazy and corrupt clergy, or from enthusiastic preaching by unauthorized but inspired teachers, or from the blatant rejection of clerical morality noticeable, for example, in the aristocracy. The ecclesiastical authorities disliked all these aspects of disobedience and were perhaps too alarmed to consider carefully how much wiser it was to separate their enemies than brand them all as heretics. But the clergy themselves claimed a monopoly of teaching, so all that taught by others was potentially and probably wrong. Since they were themselves, and increasingly so, preoccupied with intellectual problems of belief and given to defining them in words and formulae, they naturally analysed the 'inspired' statements of the unauthorized preachers and found them wrong in doctrine. And attacks on the sacraments or the unworthy priests were condemned as heresy, for they could be proved wrong from Gratian and Lombard, whereas the criticisms were, of course, not intended to be refined statements of scholastic belief but to echo scriptural censures.

Information about 'Cathar' heretics in the south of France after 1167 (when allegedly the disaffection of the masses was first seriously reinforced by 'Bogomil' teachers from the Balkans) comes from orthodox Catholic critics, mostly writing much later, with doctrinal problems in their minds. Whether 'dualism' or Manicheanism as doctrines appealed much to the masses or mattered much to the teachers is more difficult to be certain of, than the fascination it had for Catholic polemicists. Their position is not unreasonable. Dualist positions are philosophically unsatisfactory, and certainly incompatible with the theological emphasis upon God as Trinity, God as Creator, God as Incarnate and the church as dispenser of sacramental grace. The theologians had no difficulty in dealing intellectually with the Cathar teaching and at the important meeting in 1178 in the presence of the papal legate the Cathar bishops turned out to be unlearned and unimpressive in debate. Yet the heretics continued to persists in their beliefs and practices, survived the Albigensian Crusade of 1209, the introduction of the Holy Inquisition and still worried the persecuting bishop of Pamiers who became pope Benedict XII in 1334.[37] It seems very unlikely that the principal attraction of heresy could ever have been intellectual statements of belief. Its teachers were by all accounts steadfast in their faith, ascetic in their conduct, recommending extreme puritanism in morality and a life of poverty and austerity which contrasted sharply with the clerical concern for endowments, status and show. The clergy had been fighting for recognition of privilege, no doubt with the best intentions of using their advantages as a necessary basis for their attack on secular abuses; they were in no position to deny that they were in the 'Cathar' sense 'worldly'. At this point therefore those who had accorded reformers popular support in the past, in expectation of the dawning of an apostolic age, had to choose between recognising the newly privileged clergy as the sole artificers of the 'apostolic' Roman church, or risking a life of renunciation which would expose them to censure as heretics. The Franciscan movement might have saved men from making this agonizing choice had it not been divided on the issue of poverty throughout the same period as the Cathars suffered persecution under the Inquisition.

Unsophisticated, that is unclerical, Christianity, has always expected marvels from its religion and demanded holy men as its representatives. As Montaigne put it much later: religion should make men better, and the improvement must be visible. By the late twelfth century the clergy, having won the right to dispose of the church, had still not convinced the poor or the powerful that they were holy. Indeed the church they ran had deliberately locked up the holiest out of sight, on the plea that isolation from the world would save them from temptation. If the poor were impressed by self-confident preachers and 'non-conformists' were often able to proselytize because the clergy had as yet done little for the religious improvement of humble people, the signs in 'upper-class' society too of indifference to religion, ignorance of its teaching, rejection of its values, are much more serious proof of the church's failure. In the nature of the case, the evidence is indirect and literary, and contrived for a purpose other than historical reporting. Nevertheless when Aucassin in the famous tale rails against his lord because he has lost his Nicolette, he mocks paradise as a fit place for old priests, beggars and down-and-outs and brazenly prefers hell with its elegant priests, fine knights slain at tourneys, freemen and brave sergeants, beautiful fine ladies with their two or three lovers, gold and silver, harpers and minstrels, provided he can go there with Nicolette.[38] The author's irony is transparent, but the message is nonetheless clear. Fine people preferred the pleasures of this life to the values of the church.

Whereas in ecclesiastical charters great men appear as benefactors or repentant sinners, quite a different impression emerges from the literature composed at this time by men of letters, often themselves clergy, for noble entertainment. There the nobles pursue ideals quite at variance with Christian teaching. They are concerned with refined feelings or with their own personal worth and valour. The clerk Andreas composed a famous dialogue *c*.1184-5 to explore the character of passionate love. The author admittedly concludes by advising against it; all the same the appearance of such a book, the statement of the ideal and even the attempt (generally judged unconvincing) to reject it all indicate that a new, non-Christian ideal had won some converts.[39] At the present time, it is not difficult to see how men without transcendent beliefs or moral imperatives are forced back upon themselves to find their ideals in personal integrity, the attainment of pure emotion or in intense personal relationships. The exploration of these strictly human ideals reached its peak in late twelfth- and early thirteenth-century literature. The Tristan and Isolde story has retained its power to stir the European imagination. The finest exposition of the theme is Gottfried von Strassburg's poem of *c*.1210. There is no mistaking the importance of passion to Gottfried, despite his recognition of its essentialy sad outcome. Tristan's name itself implies the hopelessness of love and Gottfried's *Prologue* expresses the ache of human life in which he that never had sorrow of love never had joy of it either. Gottfried is not alone in his generation with his celebration of the power of human love — the troubadour and minnesinger poetry express feelings that must have played an important part in the sentimental life of their contemporaries and stirred emotional depths which the church had not then plumbed. This first great wave of vernacular poetry appeared in the period of clerical organization between popes Alexander III and Gregory IX. It betrays a state of emotional agitation amongst the upper-classes, which proves them to have been no less remote from established religious values than the more blatant opposition lower down. If the nobility did not much care for vulgar protest movements this was because as great lords their ideals of high-mindedness demanded nobility of soul and decorous emotions. The literary legacy was not forgotten, but when the second wave appeared with Dante or Chaucer it carried the moral teachings of the church without ambiguity. What had happened?

5. THE CHURCH'S MINISTRY TO LAYMEN
Faced with so much evidence of secular dissatisfaction with the church, the clergy and the pope gave earnest consideration to how they might remove hostility and harness talents prostituted for other purposes to the glory of God. The achievements of churchmen in doing this do not seem to be adequately appreciated, because churchmen naturally did not perceive how much ground they had gained, only how much remained to do. Yet looking back on the eve of the Reformation in the sixteenth century, a church historian could have taken legitimate pride from the spectacle. Paganism and 'humanism' had virtually disappeared. The revival of classical 'humanism' in Italy meant something different, and had the most pious and moral intentions. The towns of Christendom had been converted by religious fraternities. Florence in the late fifteenth century, perhaps potentially the most secular city of Europe, hung for a time on the words of the inspired Dominican friar Savonarola. Preaching, moral instruction, pious pamphlets proliferated. Whatever its impact, religion had never been so well propagated, so well supported or so uncontested. In the circumstances the reforming clergy could dare to tear the ecclesiastical fabric to pieces, in order to promote a still greater intensity of religious understanding. Before turning to the superstructure of the church which tends to overshadow all discussions of it, some attention should therefore be given to the real problems of lay-conversion.

Preaching
Though by 1200 the old religious paganism had vanished, the church had not done more than recruit a clerical army for the final assault on lay values. Some clergy, like their modern counterparts, placed their hopes on more instruction. Not for nothing was the famous philosopher Aquinas suspected in some quarters of falling into the error of believing that if men knew what was good they would pursue it. Admittedly the teaching of lay-people in the barbarian past had been neglected. In the twelfth century the bishops still bore the main burden of preaching, but they were in fact already saddled with political and administrative duties. Where heretics appeared, they were answered in kind rather by

famous catholic preachers, like St Bernard, and other Cistercian abbots who preached in the south of France. The canon of Osma, Diego Guzman who founded the order of Preachers to combat Provençal heresy, first provided the episcopate with a professional preaching force, and the Franciscans rapidly expanded the teaching side of their mission with papal encouragement. From the late twelfth century, there was a new interest shown by clergy of all kinds in the problems of preaching. Formal sermons to educated persons being less suitable for many audiences, the new preachers considered how to instruct by using even vulgar tales to make their points. Increasingly preaching became more common, more effective and more attractive. It is well-known how long sixteenth-century reformers could harangue the crowds — but the taste for public eloquence had been acquired much earlier.[40]

It is not possible to deduce from the text of a sermon the impact it had when delivered though it is probable that few heretics were converted by Dominican preaching. Instead the friars became responsible for hunting down heretics and incurred popular hostility for their part in persecution. Preaching probably had more effect on the lukewarm than on the hostile; at all events, it continued, though this does not mean that it was either as frequent or universal as reformers believed to be necessary. In every generation, there arise optimists who believe that human nature needs no more than a dose of preaching to cure its weaknesses. It is, however, I think, to the church's credit that preaching then seemed to be more of an extra than an essential. As a body the clergy worked perhaps most conscientiously to establish a resident ministry in every Christian community, to endow it and protect it and ultimately to improve the quality of the ministers by what means they could.

Parishes
The idea of a resident priest serving every settlement of Christian territory for so long seemed the most natural form of Christian mission that even now it is difficult to realize how late it developed even in the context best suited for it: the agricultural village. This system grew haphazardly out of the expectations of the community and the generosity of many benefactors, not from any united ecclesiastical campaign to provide village churches everywhere. Building churches had gone on fitfully throughout Christendom from the time of the original conversion; at first of wood, only later of stone. The great Celtic crosses were put up at a period when Christians did not expect to assemble under cover. In northern Europe, permanent stone buildings in the Roman style were, to start with, exceptional luxuries. When they became more common it was to shelter particularly venerable places and saintly relics. In southern France, the cathedral church of St Sauveur at Aix-en-Provence was

itself so small that it could hold only ten persons according to the arch-bishop who, in 1070, decided to make it more spacious.[41] Laymen of special standing probably took for granted the desirability of building a shrine on their estates as part of their obligations, but it did not follow that they expected to secure a permanent priest. The church was used only intermittently and did more honour to the saint venerated there than service to the faithful. But as monasteries maintained continuous prayer on behalf of their benefactors from the ninth century, it is probable that the local churches likewise satisfied villagers' desires for the advantages of regular celebration of the mass. Carolingian laws enforcing the payment of tithes by all Christians imply the existence of a local clergy. The early eleventh century witnessed an extraordinary spate of church building, which continued for many years. The life of St Altmann bishop of Passau (1065-91) records that whereas almost all the churches of his diocese had been of wood and unadorned, by his efforts almost all had been rebuilt in stone and supplied with books, paintings and other ornaments.[42] In the more inaccessible parts of Christendom, the churches then built have survived to the present as the most positive evidence of the simple nobility of contemporary piety. Elsewhere rebuilding and extensions have modified the appearance of parish churches, but there are few places which do not still show some evidence of the eleventh- or twelfth-century buildings. Churchmen played their own part in stimulating and financing this building operation, but the bulk of it came from lay benefactors great and small.

Far from receiving unstinted thanks, they were almost immediately assailed by the most ardent clergy, for presuming to interfere in the management of clerical affairs. The reformers report the grossest abuses: that clergy should pay patrons for ecclesiastical appointments they likened to the sin of Simon Magus. They also saw that lay patrons had no power or interest to prevent clerical marriage, or the subsequent inheritance of churches. In the interests of a more exemplary clergy, they tried to deprive the laity of their rights to church patronage. Many laymen, duly abashed, then handed over their churches to monasteries, as the most respected spiritual corporations, for in the eleventh century neither the parish priests nor the bishops yet seemed the obvious per-sons to receive those endowments.[43] There was good sense in the reformers' programme, but its merits should not blind us to the advantages of the old. Though abuses could occur, for the most part the laity had had personal reasons to provide adequately for the church and secure the regular services of a priest. There is no evidence as to whether the married or hereditary priest of the village seemed unacceptable to the villagers. Nor do we know where lay patrons or monasteries found their priests. Presumably they selected some sufficiently respected laymen in the village and duly had him consecrated for the service of the altar. Some monasteries probably deployed monks in some parishes.

Secular priests

All this was changed as a result of the campaign launched to secure a better qualified, celibate parish priesthood, protected by their ecclesiastical superiors against the lay proprietors of churches. At the same time monks were firmly returned to the cloister and a barrier erected between the monasteries and the parishes. The new pattern had clearly emerged by 1200, though anomalies survived in some places. Reformers had no need to build churches or endow them. Their problem was to use existing arrangements to provide a pastoral ministry directly answerable to the episcopal administration, and diminish the influence of the lay patrons, whose ancestors had originally built the churches and provided for their upkeep.

The clergy were the first professional group of medieval Europe to enjoy benefits of laws different from those of their neighbours. Gregory VII in a famous passage emphasized that all those ordained to the service of the church were of more account than any layman, even a king, for in a Christian community those who served the needs of the soul had precedence over all earthly dignity.[44] Such a radical programme could not be carried through in its entirety. Yet, in the process of trying to do so, the church at least succeeded in winning for priests, as such, a general respect never previously theirs. Some theologians like Hugh of St Victor went so far as to treat bishops as priests, with some additional powers; to raise priests to the dignity of bishops accorded them a very high standing. There was a price to be paid for this dignity and privilege. The clergy had to give up their wives and concubines and live as celibate as monks: no easy task in their exposed position.

The earliest surviving papal decrees against the married clergy date from as far back as 1075. Thirty years later they had still had little effect in England, where the diocesan administration was nevertheless comparatively effective.[45] Only during the twelfth century did the new ideals gradually gain ground by virtue of several contributory factors, the energy of the bishops, the appeal of the new religious idealism, the changing expectations of the laity and better preparation for the parochial ministry. The most important factor of all was the new enforcement of the legal distinction between laymen and clergy. The clergy were assigned to the jurisdiction of the ecclesiastical courts, where they were subject to a distinctive body of law. Brushes with secular authority about the limits of clerical exemption from secular processes of law occurred, as in England between Becket and Henry II, but gradually the principle was generally conceded everywhere.[46]

Conscientious bishops worked to secure a minimum annual salary for the resident priest, from the legal recipient of the church's revenues — the rector or the monastery or other clerical establishment. It is significant that they showed such concern to secure adequate material support; they showed no comparable anxiety as to the possible unworthiness of these ministers.[47] As patrons lost their power to do more than present candidates to the bishop for induction, the bishop could supervise their fitness and their celibacy. Bishops and officials apparently regarded these means of scrutiny as adequate.

The Fourth Lateran Council showed what expectations the bishops had of parishes by prescribing annual confession for all Christians before the resident priest *discretus et cautus*.[48] The village priest was not then expected to preach. His basic duty was sacramental. To this was added the duty of moral supervision and guidance. Both duties steadily enhanced his standing in the community. The purely sacramental conception of the priesthood had only crystallized in the twelfth century. Alexander III still thought priests could be degraded from their office for misconduct and so lose their sacramental power. Only after his time did the church extend to ordination, on the analogy of baptism, a sacramental character which once given left an ineffaceable mark. A priest could still lose his earthly office, or jurisdiction, but once marked as a priest, a spiritual power had been conferred upon him by the words and ritual of the rite of ordination (1231).[49] The unworthiness of the minister, his immorality even, had no power to hinder the efficacy of the sacraments he bestowed. Far from encouraging them to indulge their wickedness, such a doctrine strengthened priests to lead lives dedicated to the sanctification of souls, threatening direct consequences in the next life for those who inadequately fulfilled their duties. If the priests had any power to move laymen by their teaching on heaven and hell, how anxious they must have been on their own account. Education never achieved comparable power for graduates, though they did their best to exalt their own calling. Mere training thus counted for less than the responsibilities of office.

The priesthood became the most respected rank of Christendom, and all Christians intended to defend the holiness of the office by denouncing shortcomings in office holders. Priests enjoyed protection in the tribunals of the church; they had to be physically perfect and legal freemen. They were the chosen Judges in the new Israel. They had no families; the church had therefore to recruit the best men it could find in every generation. However rotten some of them may have been, in general the respect for sacramental religion by the sixteenth century shows that they had generally proved their value. The sacraments of the thirteenth-century church were most regularly celebrated by priests, not bishops (for whom were reserved only the occasional duties of confirmation and ordination). The laity were admitted to the church by the priest in baptism, married before him, absolved by him in confession, fed by him in the eucharist, anointed by him at death and buried by him in the church's graveyard. The priestly office to bless and make holy mattered far more than any verbal instructions he could give. The special emphasis put upon the eucharist and the real presence of Christ in the elements of bread and wine, originally emphasized in 1215 to counteract heretical teaching, placed the priest at the living centre of the religious community.[50] Priestly vestments, making the sign of the cross, genuflexions, all visibly enhanced the solemnity of the occasion without making impossible intellectual demands on uninstructed people. The priest himself bore the burden of the service and the thirteenth-century liturgical books combined for the priests' use the various elements of the service which had formerly been celebrated in the greater churches by a variety of clergy, bishops, priests, deacons, readers and choirs. The village priest in every place was expected to perform all these functions himself. The result may have been lacking in dignity or coherence, but the availability and regularity of the service more than compensated for this.[51]

The importance of a sacramental rather than a teaching ministry is often overlooked by modern writers who take pride in learning as such. In the circumstances of the thirteenth century, it made sense for the church to emphasize the sacramental aspect, which not only had more obvious significance for unlearned lay people, but pointedly demonstrated the church's essential religious teaching to an age riddled with 'spiritualist' heresies. The created order was made by God; bread, wine, oil, and sexual intercourse itself could be made holy by the church.[52] There could hardly have been a more effective repudiation of Cathar errors and of the ideals of 'pure' love.

Despite the obvious practical importance of education for the priesthood, there was no universal significance attached to a superior education except by those who had it, and in the sixteenth century divided Christendom still did not define priests or ministers according to educational qualifications. However, some kind of educational improvement for the clergy occurred over the three centuries between 1216 and 1517. Even in the most backward parishes, the village priest needed a little learning. He needed to give some basic instruction to them, even if preaching was not very important. Though thirteenth-century bishops (themselves often distinguished scholars) had no great regard for their clergy's learning, this could still have been adequate for the needs of the parish. Robert Grosseteste bishop of Lincoln (1235-53) required no more of his priests than that they teach the village children the Lord's prayer,

Ave Maria and how to make the sign of the cross. Archbishop Peckham's Lambeth Council of 1281 prescribed more elaborate instruction, given four times a year by every priest, in the articles of faith, the ten commandments, the evangelical commands, the seven works of mercy, the seven deadly sins, the seven principal virtues and the seven sacraments.[53]

Other than learning how to read and write, these parish priests originally received no training to equip them for the task of understanding the Scriptures. How much they knew depended directly upon how many years they studied, for there could be no real question of country priests accumulating books of their own or reading for themselves. Priests needed only some service books and manuals to guide them in their arduous roles of defining sins, and giving advice to parishioners in making proper confessions.[54] They needed ever better preparation for their roles because the strain put upon the priests was considerable. Bishops denied them the company of wives; they lived without companions or helpmates, exposed to the temptations of the village, in everyone's confidence, but expected to be themselves above reproach: model Christians, the source of sacramental power. The priest had no monastery to help him and even if he maintained a clerical establishment of deacons or curates this could only have added to his responsibilities without diminishing his cares. The lay patron is not likely to have given him much spiritual or psychological support; the lord of the manor he may often have met, but more likely on difficult occasions when he acted as spokesman of the parish. The priest had indeed to be a discreet and careful person, able to keep his own counsel, to uphold the dignity of his religion and to be the servant of the whole community; answerable only to the diocesan officials who came to extort dues and to censure errors. Increasingly therefore the conditions of service made it inevitable that more training should be provided, though uniformity was not prescribed until the Council of Trent.

As conditions varied enormously it is impossible to describe in detail what facilities there were for all potential ordinands to obtain basic education. The popularity of learning suggests that there were more than enough tonsured clerks visiting the schools. The authorities limited their anxieties to postponing priestly ordination until the ordinand had obtained a benefice. The problem as they saw it was not in recruiting the educated but in finding them posts.[55] Records may distort the truth because competition for lucrative benefices could still leave poorer churches without well-qualified priests. Still, there were certainly more clergy than there were parishes and this created an unprecedented system of a two-tiered ministry; many endowments could support a salaried vicar and an absentee rector, since the latter often preferred to continue his education with an eye to ecclesiastical advancement.

Boniface VIII's bull *Cum ex eo* (1298) at last encouraged bishops to authorize the concession of parish revenues to young clerks, so that they could obtain a university education before returning to be ordained priests in charge. England was lucky to have two universities of its own in the thirteenth century. France had only one big university for clergy at Paris. This also served most of the empire as well, until a new university was founded at Prague in 1348; others followed in the lands of other princes after 1378. The increase in the number of institutions offering superior instruction improved the chances for parish priests to obtain a higher education. Chaucer's poor parson was 'a learned man, a clerk'. Endowments of colleges at the universities from the mid-thirteenth century began to encourage longer study for students without other resources. By the end of the fifteenth century Oxford had already become a university of colleges. On the continent, other universities also sported numerous colleges, though this is sometimes forgotten because, outside England, college tutors never obtained control of university government. Though the direction in which education was moving may certainly be traced in general terms from these observations there was obviously no steady universal improvement in the educational standard of the priesthood.[56] Lesser schools were clearly thought to be inadequate, but they must have continued to provide the best part of some clerical educations and for the illiterate or the barely educated, such parish priests, as unpretentious pastors, may have served their flocks usefully in both town and country.[57]

Their inadequacies were to some degree anyway compensated for unsystematically by the rich variety of extra-parochial organizations, such as the friars, and less reputably by the pardoners. The regular contact between different areas caused by expanding commerce and industry, which enabled heresy to spread, no less effectively brought most rural villages into familiar contact with neighbouring market towns with their greater churches, market-cross preachers and religious gossip. They could supplement the minimal services of the rural priest with knowledge of how religion was practised elsewhere, the new devotions, rosary beads, the use of prayer-books, prayers for the souls in purgatory, the pilgrimages to Jerusalem and Compostella. Medieval parishes were highly self-sufficient communities, but few of them were cut off from contacts outside. Christendom was densely sown with religious communities, monastic, canonical, collegiate, many older than the parish churches themselves. The number grew to saturation point and by the fourteenth century reforming effort inspired renewed calls for improvement, rather than new foundations. Whatever the faults of the system, it is difficult to believe that those in need of spiritual counsel could not find it more easily by the fourteenth century than they could at any earlier period. Like the modern state, the medieval church was an institution set up to serve the needs of mankind, and dutifully supplied all that an institution can do. It could not make men perfect, but it pointed out the ways.

6. UNIVERSITIES

Universities were not the only corporations *(universitates)* of their day. It is only the abolition of other guilds that has left them looking unique (and vulnerable). The use of a familiar word, like university, also threatens to inject into the medieval institution a totally misleading set of ideas. This has not been helped by a modern scholarly interest in the revival of learning in the twelfth-century schools, or in 'humanism'. Universities did not appear until the thirteenth century — an institutional consequence of the developments of learning in the twelfth century, for which the university was not responsible. The university grew up only when the teachers (Paris) or the students (Bologna) organized its members to defend common interests, with forms of association, purposes and procedures similar to those of the guilds which enabled illiterate lay men to protect skills of value, sought after by many. It was not learning, but corporate professionalism, that created the universities.

The famous history of his own misfortunes which Abelard wrote in 1132-5 reveals that the intellectual activity of early twelfth-century Paris was carried on with the minimum of institutional forms. The chancellor of the cathedral maintained a school, but it was possible for teachers to attract students to unofficial lectures and the students were free to come and go, following teachers where they went, with no concern for authorities. Abelard's less famous contemporary, Hugh of St Victor, who contributed much to the intellectual life of the period, was an Augustinian canon, shut out of the extravagant rivalries of the secular masters without any disadvantages for his intellectual development. The many religious establishments of twelfth-century Paris may have helped in some way to make the city an intellectual centre, but the best teachers were attracted to the life there because it was also a big city, combining commercial bustle with royal patronage, where life was freer and more stimulating. St Bernard was properly concerned about the effects that certain teachers had upon their pupils by exposing them to scriptural studies in these conditions. The teachers seemed to indulge in captious criticism and encourage impiety. The dangers which the new learning represented for the church were in fact averted in the thirteenth century, when the universities were organized to exclude frivolous or improper teachers from doing just this. The processes of learning were taken out of the hands of individuals, setting themselves up, as Abelard had done, to startle and provoke, and vested in a corporation.

As late as 1179, the Third Lateran Council supposed that bishops' schools everywhere would continue to serve Christendom's essential needs for learning. Alexander III instructed the bishops' chancellors, as nominal masters of the schools, to grant without charge the degrees of *licencia docendi* (when students had shown that they had learned enough to be able to teach others). At that stage the actual teachers still had no influence in such matters. Within thirty years the situation changed radically, because the teachers, in Paris, insisted on taking over the process of graduation from the chancellor. The teachers required proof of the students' abilities, tested by themselves in examination, and they combined to refuse permission to teach to those who did not meet their tests. They successfully pushed the bishop's chancellor aside and organized the university for themselves. Had there not been students eager to acquire their skills, they could not have established this control over learning; it was not however learning itself, but their own capacity to act in concert that mattered. The teachers intended to treasure the accumulated tradition of learning and to transmit it to others, in such a way as to preserve it from travesty by impostors. Students who mastered the 'mysteries' of this craft would themselves be allowed to teach, and graduation conferred public recognition of their competence by those best fitted to know. University discipline thus replaced the more informal procedures of the past, when aspirants had merely attended and absorbed the lectures of famous teachers and 'graduated' at the chancellor's discretion. The university was also determined to suppress teachers who did not belong to their 'guild' — hence their ferocious opposition to the mendicant professors who infiltrated into Paris in the middle decades of the thirteenth century.

University men intended to manage their own affairs and used the papacy, as other bodies of clergy had done, to exclude interference by the local bishop. If erroneous opinions were detected in their midst, they had every interest in silencing it themselves, lest more powerful authorities be tempted to intervene. Universities were thus not places of unregulated speculation. They taught established disciplines in conventional forms. Like other craftsmen, they innovated to improve on the tradition, but they were brought up to respect their masters. The procedures of the 'student' university of Bologna were obviously different in many ways, at least until the city began to endow professorial 'chairs'. But the idea of forming an academic corporation is common to both, except that in Bologna it was the students from outside Bologna who had to organize their own defence against the local authorities in order to defend their right to learn and coerce the teachers into giving them a thorough training.

The exclusive character of these corporations does not recommend

them to modern idealists. No more do the content and form of its preferred disciplines, logic, law and theology, which are at best minority
interests, at least in insular English universities. In this period, the skills
they exercised and taught were far from being traditional or rudimentary. In the past the learning of Latin composition by the study and
imitation of classical authors had been the essential part of learning. The
Latin stylists of the twelfth century, whose own poetry briefly revived the
literary possibilities of Latin, belonged to a recognizable tradition going
back to classical writers. There could be no objection to the use of pagan
learning here for buttressing Christian teaching and supplying any gaps
in its perfection. A scholar's Latin education introduced him early on to
pagan writers and poets and their teachings were familiar. Such
frivolous authors as Ovid were taken seriously and interpreted solemnly.[58]
Scholars did not really understand classical paganism and they were
quite uninterested in it as an alternative system of belief. Peter of Blois
was already lamenting that these literary studies no longer earned men
their dues.[59] Even before 1200, mere literary and linguistic studies of
this old-fashioned kind were abandoned by university teachers to grammar schools. The 'arts' faculty concentrated instead on logical studies.
Their importance was such that by 1260 the university of Paris was
effectively run by the Arts Faculty, in spite of the ancient eminence of
the theologians.

University students in arts spent most of their time of study on books and
debates ultimately concerned with problems about the nature of human
knowledge and the grounds for religious faith, even if they did not pursue
advanced courses in theology, which were very long. Since the students
were generally of independent means, expecting to obtain preferment in
the church by their connexions and not necessarily proposing to continue
their studies with subsequent courses of law, the arts training seems to have
been valued for its own sake. It trained the mind to think clearly and
systematically, how to assess arguments, to expose flaws and to crush
opponents; it also trained the memory, developed mental resource and
imparted self-assurance. Graduates could exercise various responsibilities
quickly and effectively, but there is no proof that graduation had become
indispensable for preferment or that higher education became popular for
that reason. Indeed the numerous recruits that the friars made in the
universities in the 1220s and 1230s prove how many idealistic students were
not eager to seek ambitious offices.

Logic was the foundation of medieval education because it concentrated on the nature of words and the reality hidden in them.[60] Logic was
the science of making reality out of verbal constructions. Its most elementary form was to prove that any object must be either 'a' or 'b' and proceed
from there. Such dilemmas were not settled by appeal to reality but by the

rules of logic. The method could only be applied to verbal statements and was particularly suitable for the discussion of incompatible statements found in books. Since history and science necessarily dealt with individual facts, not with classes of objects, its main application was in theology and law, which dealt with a definable number of problems in terms of statements taken from divergent authorities and there was reason to expect progress in resolving them by logical arrangement and discussion.

The greatest master of logic was Aristotle, so that until the seventeenth century the universities were mainly devoted to the exposition of his teaching. In the Christian context however this could only be done with such reservations as Christianity imposed. This state of affairs rather puzzles us but it explains the fascination of university education in this long period. It posed the fundamental problems of human knowledge — on the one hand Christian conviction, overwhelming and certain; on the other, rational demonstration. The great masters proposed various solutions — synthesis where possible; where not, they could try to use Aristotle's metaphysics as a model for supplying Christianity with its own metaphysical buttress, or diminish his stature by showing that his science had only trivial earthly significance incapable of undermining faith. Teachers laboured to test the nature of rationality, to formulate religion reasonably and to salvage for religion all that reason could not do. There was no Thomistic monopoly in the schools, as in the neo-scholasticism of modern Catholicism, so the debates of the schools were open and exciting for the students. The schools did not generate much interest in natural science or advance modern thinking, despite the use that might have been made of Aristotle's scientific work. These texts were too difficult for them.

Interest in Aristotle had begun with his reputation as a logician. Not until the early thirteenth century did his scientific works become known and no real progress could be made with understanding them at first without help from Arab sources, particularly from Averroes, whose pioneering work (which was only done in late twelfth-century Spain) inspired no interest amongst his fellow-Muslims. Aristotle in this company not surprisingly excited theological suspicions. The theologians were still powerful enough in Paris to obtain a ruling from the cardinal legate Robert de Courçon that Aristotle's scientific works should not be lectured on (1213) and this ban was still in force in 1231. As so often, this kind of irksome restraint incited the most fervent Aristotelians in the arts faculty to protest. It was not however the artists who salvaged Aristotelian science. It was very much the work of the Dominican Albert the Great, who made an extensive study of all Aristotle's work, particularly while he was at Cologne where he raised his pupil Thomas Aquinas in this tradition. Only under the protection of these Dominicans did Aristotle in his entirety become a respected thinker. His works were re-translated directly from the Greek by William of Moerbeke and Aquinas's commentaries and later works tried to demonstrate the compatibility of pagan philosophy and revealed religion.[61] By 1250, Aristotle had become a major teacher for the first time since his death.

In this intellectual society of rationalizing scholars, there was no question of doubting the Christian revelation all together. This does not invalidate their learning. Underlying faith in the Christian revelation did not inhibit fierce controversies, denunciation of errors declared or implied in professorial lectures, or strong appeals by university teachers to ecclesiastical authorities, especially the pope, for tolerance, on intellectual grounds, of suspect teaching. One school of thinking was accused of preferring Aristotelian rationalism (or Averroism as it was called) to revelation, but, even if the charge were just, most scholars were not interested in exploring a purely rationalist or scientific programme of research, as modern students of Aristotle might suppose. The original interest in Aristotle had been as a master of thinking about the meaning and use of words and statements. There was no reason to believe that experiments would improve human knowledge; the soundness of this view was confirmed by the strictly mathematical advances of the seventeenth century.

Though Aristotle did not tempt scholars away from their Christian allegiance some of them certainly regretted the Aristotelian incubus, and would have been happy to rely more completely on the sacred texts. Yet to justify their attitude they relied on Aristotelian logic, demanding more logical and precise proofs and demonstrating the real logical limitations of rationalism itself. Franciscan teachers of the fourteenth century, who encouraged the simple faith of ordinary Christians and castigated the intellectualisms of their opponents, stood very close by intention to the position of Bernard of Clairvaux two centuries earlier when denouncing Abelard for scrutinizing Holy Scripture with critical and intellectual doubts. Aristotelian studies had done little in two centuries to undermine Christian belief.

The superiority of Christian revelation, that is essentially the teaching of the Bible, in European society was not therefore a matter of general uninformed public opinion, but the convinced belief of the best educated persons of the day, who in the absence of cheap printed vernacular bibles were responsible for teaching it to their contemporaries. St Bernard who had no Aristotelian learning to counterbalance his Christian beliefs shared with St Bonaventura, who did, a profound belief in the power of the Scriptures to guide men through their most serious difficulties. Thus the crown of scholastic achievement was theology: knowledge of the things of God. Modern condescension towards this science is misplaced. The clergy could never have taken the passage of their historical time as the promise for future progress, as the modern intelligentsia has done. Nor did the study of the universe offer any hope that learning could penetrate the secrets of nature: only God as creator, not man, could understand that. Concerned first with themselves as men, they lived without fear of the universe, even though they did not understand it, and concentrated on trying to explain their own mysterious eminence in it. Convinced that they were more than flesh and blood, they believed that their spirits must have an origin with God beyond the tangible world and therefore a destiny in a life beyond the grave. They taught that the death of the individual should be accepted without bitterness, and argued to what extent the after-life would depend on merit in this. They accepted more naturally than we do, for all our science, that mankind formed one family before God.

During the thirteenth century clerical learning made a remarkably complete job of replacing alternative views about any subject with a Christian one, drawn from the whole range of extant learning: Biblical, Greek or Arabic.[62] It was the age of the encyclopaedias which synthesized all learning, exuding confidence in the soundness of these taxing disciplines and the power of logical construction. Aquinas and Dante Alighieri, from their different standpoints, never doubted the power of Christian learning to produce even a theory of state-power, for every object had its place in the realm of knowledge: nothing existed in isolation. Christian scholars had begun to measure themselves for the first time against the whole of ancient learning. Their eagerness began to flag as the problems of the texts, the un-Christian character of Aristotle's thought and the inherent difficulties of the scientific programme he outlined loomed up in their real magnitude. The confident conflation of scriptural revelation and philosophical truth disintegrated.

The investigations and speculations of the theologians by the end of the thirteenth century undermined the earlier confidence that all learning contributed to the understanding of God. Some theologians like John Peckham had always been understandably suspicious of the more audacious attempts to assimilate the teachings of the pagan Aristotle and his Muslim commentator, Averroes, into the Christian syllabus. By 1277 the more extreme Averroistic teachers in the university of Paris had laid themselves open to charges of heresy. In the ensuing showdown the more conservative teachers succeeded in extending this net, to include, for example, some propositions culled from Thomas Aquinas.[63] After 1277 university teachers had to be much more wary than before not to incur censure. The conservatives grew more confident that there were specifically Christian truths which could not be and did not need to be, supported by arguments drawn from pagan writers, whose mere plausibility depended on logic or pure reason. The truths of God had been given by revelation and were not open to human scrutiny.

The Franciscan writers of the fourteenth century defended orthodoxy with the most rigorously logical demonstrations of the inadequacy of human reasoning about God.

At first sight this intellectual reaction may seem regrettable, but it is hard to believe that Aristotle and other philosophers, rightly understood, do provide an undisputed basis for Christian theology or that closer familiarity with Aristotle's work justified the innocent enthusiasm of such thinkers as Albert the Great and Aquinas. It is also doubtful whether the Christian religion could in the long term derive any further advantage from the support of natural theology. The Franciscans, more in touch with popular religious attitudes, shared the belief in religious experience as a personal emotion: for them the essence of religion was the personal response of the individual soul to God. They were far from believing with Aquinas that the human soul was essentially intellectual in composition.

The nature of this university learning explains why it remained of such limited interest and led neither to other studies nor to greater extension of numbers. It settled into that kind of professional security described so amiably by Jean of Jandun *c.*1330 and which has been characteristic of universities for most of their lives, except when stampeded by demands for making them perform admirable tasks for which they are quite unfitted.[64] Clergy who were exposed to these new intellectual forces at the universities owed to their training in the new logic much more intellectual restraint than could be expected in the untrained laity, where manifestations of religious zeal were more spontaneous, less learned, more popular. The people wanted more devotions, rituals, pilgrimages; they expected surges of religious emotion not the discernment of spiritual values behind the veil of nature. A gulf began to yawn between sophisticated religious learning and the more emotional demands of the laity. Some educated writers began even in the fourteenth century to castigate the clergy for their abstruse learning. Petrarch detested the logic-chopping of the schools. He sought his religious and moral stimulus by intelligent reading from cover to cover of the works of great minds like St Augustine. Later Italian humanist writers, usually pious conservatives in religion, naturally turned to the edifying moral writers of pagan antiquity in search not of 'humanism' but of the moral reinforcement of their faith, just as the intellectual demands of Aquinas or Ockham had led them to the pagan Aristotle.

7. THE ORGANIZATION OF CHRISTENDOM

To talk of *the* medieval church misleads because instead of the diversity of church life from one parish to another and from the simplest country church to the most complex religious order, it evokes a picture of uniform conditions controlled by the papacy, which was held responsible for the system. In a very limited sense this was true in the fourteenth century and again by 1500 and the attacks of the reformers were therefore directed at the curia: the ecclesiastical superstructure that held the whole together. Reformers, though abusing the papacy, in fact paid it the compliment of supposing it more powerful than it was, just as the uniformity of abuses itself proved how much the papacy had been able to accomplish in the centuries of its dominance. The medieval church in the singular implies a church run by the Roman curia. To this structure of ecclesiastical government we must now turn. The papacy was the ultimate beneficiary of diverse movements for reform in the twelfth century, because it seemed obvious that the creation of the new Jerusalem on earth should come about in all parts of Christendom equally. Since the only way to do this was to provide a central authority which could treat all provinces uniformly, it became natural to look to Rome from which centralization in Europe had come in the past. There was no other European tradition of government. The papacy provided what was required and went beyond this in taking the initiative and pressing others to assume their responsibilities. Its own duties were already clear to St Bernard in the middle of the twelfth century. From him comes the earliest use of the key phrase *plenitudo potestatis* in connection with papal authority and in his exhortation to Pope Eugenius III, the *De Consideratione,* Bernard already warned the pope of the possible evil consequences of the church's government losing popular respect as it became less remote and more familiar.[65] Attitudes of naive veneration for the successor to the prince of the apostles hardly survived the experience of papal government. By the end of the century popes were more frequently spoken of as *vicarius Christi,* another phrase of Bernard's, than *servus servorum dei.*[66] There was no disputing the ultimate superiority of papal sovereignty and popes no longer hesitated to act energetically from their new found legal strength.

The growth of papal institutions proceeded slowly and in response to a host of circumstances that were to a considerable degree unexpected. After 1200 the existence of a central figure in the church obviously modified response to events. The greatest of popes, Innocent III, may be described as ambitious, but the effect of his pontificate was not merely due to his personal qualities. The responsibilities of the office in due course made it certain that a man of the right qualities would be forced to use his opportunities. During the course of the thirteenth century the preeminence secured by the Roman church in the Latin west, through the general appeal made to its authority, came to be worked up theoretically by the canon lawyers, but since earlier Christian tradition had given two principal sources of decision—the pope and church councils

—thirteenth-century popes did not hesitate to call councils. Four major councils sat at the Lateran (1215), Lyon (1245 and 1274) and Vienne (1311). The meetings outside Italy which made it easier to obtain effective representation from all over Christendom emphasize how much they served the general interest more than the papacy in particular. The councils played their part in giving advice, promulgating doctrine or demonstrating the church's unity. But regular central institutions were necessary to the church for its ordinary functioning, so the curia became indispensable. It might seem to us that a fixed place of government was essential, because we cannot conceive government without the weighty ministries of bureaucrats with their records and their daily routine. The papal curia tried hard to stabilize itself at Rome, the bishop's see, the only traditional centre of empire. Yet even in peaceful conditions, the curia voluntarily left Rome in the summer months for the cooler hilltowns round about, and more often conditions were so uncertain that the papacy was not always in political command at Rome during the thirteenth century. Clearly it had to be a major concern of papal policy to obtain uncontested and continuous occupation of Rome, but popes were frequently disappointed and their secretariat had to cope with an itinerant curia. It was able to do this because for some time to come the business of government emanated from the pope himself and it was not primarily concerned with the administration of territory. As long as the popes dealt mainly with the spiritual problems of all Christendom it was in some ways to their advantage to have no permanent home of their own.

For want of fixed locality the popes had to rely upon the security of their own clerical establishments.[67] The principal members of this were the cardinals. As the papacy had grown closer to the affairs of northern Europe in the twelfth century, it had recruited many of its chief advisers and officials from all over Christendom. By the 1180s however the inconvenience of such a heterogeneous body outweighed the advantages of having a cosmopolitan front. Instead of promoting distinguished men at the end of their careers, popes from Clement III onwards preferred to recruit younger men from the Roman aristocracy to provide a reliable cohesive group of working cardinals, who could also use their family connexions to promote the papacy's political interests in Rome. The rule on papal elections (1179) required a majority of two-thirds of the cardinals to elect the new pope and the new ministerial cardinals tended to choose one of their own kind. Cardinals were appointed for life but they acquired no real independence of the popes and in this respect they were unlike either the members of the royal courts or of the ancient Roman senate, to which respectful contemporaries compared them. In this remarkable organization, with no fixed seat, no certain territory and universal responsibility, the pope was the only person with a recognized office, to which he was elected, often at an advanced age, usually after many years' experience of curial business.

The college of cardinals had no agreed powers; the pope consulted them individually or together as he pleased. In practice they shared in all the work of the popes, listening and settling legal problems, advising on canonizations, rules for religious orders, the authenticity of documents, serving as ambassadors and legates, acting as 'ministers' of the chief departments of state. It was these men, and their staffs who constituted the papal curia, a word that came from the feudal courts of the north in the twelfth century and replaced the older local terms— though it was in fact very unlike any royal curia known at the time. No other court was entirely composed of educated bachelors preferring the use of writing and records to warfare. The curia began to organize its affairs in the tidy and formal way of intellectuals. The writing office, the chancery, which had been a necessary part of the pope's establishment from the beginning, showed the first signs of the reforming movement when far back in the mid-eleventh century it had been reorganized and its documents remodelled in accordance with the practices of the German imperial chancery. The enormous increase in its business over the next century had introduced departmental practices and routines, which were codified by the chancellor, Albert de Morrac (1178-87) who became Pope Gregory VIII. Innocent III drew up new rules, and issued instructions for trying to limit forgery and from his pontificate the chancery showed a new determination to preserve its records.

Resources
Shortly before this the papal chamberlain compiled the earliest known record of all the dues and payments owed to the pope with the charters proving his rights. This record promises a kind of programme to make payment more certain but papal resources and expenses remained precarious throughout the thirteenth century. These problems were faced when they came. German and French kings at different times tempted the popes to give up their temporal claims to revenues in return for a regular income from them. Popes declined to become royal pensioners and preferred the independence and the trouble of collecting their own rents. From Innocent III onwards this involved the popes in damaging political connexions with rival emperors who promised to hand over to the popes the lands in central Italy which had been assigned over the centuries to St Peter, but never totally obtained. These negotiations resulted in campaigns and activities that were not always popular in Christendom. The bill to be paid for the desired universal

jurisdiction in the church only then came in for payment. The curia could not live on air. To live from fees and *ex gratia* payments was demeaning and uncertain. The alternative to the management of a papal state of its own was dependence on one of the greater powers of Christendom. The papacy's problem only magnified that of the humblest priest in the church. Spiritual services regularly performed needed a man who could live from the offerings of the faithful, as the landlord's private chaplain, or from his own freehold. On balance there was not much doubt what the best solution should be.

The papacy was able to finance its business by calling upon the resources of the whole of Christendom. From the mid-thirteenth century therefore, the papacy was no longer in the position of trying to satisfy the requirements of others, but made its own demands upon Christendom on the strength of its rights. This development is very important for the history of the west and it is remarkable that it was so little contested. Protests might be made about specific requests but there was no general denial that the papacy had rights: in fact the papal government of the church had become accepted. Grumblers and critics did not moderate their complaints out of consideration for the papacy's real needs and usefulness: they hoped that increasing papal demands would be met by economy and reform. (Faced by the increase in bureaucracy in twentieth-century England, the public do not blame their own increasing expectations of government but hopefully assert that waste and indolence in the offices explain its elephantine proportions.) Criticism at the time should not be read therefore as objections to the papacy.

Clerical appointments

At the level of demand the papacy directed its chief attention not only to extracting money directly, but also to subsidizing its own staff by appointing them to vacant benefices all over Christendom. Accusations of papal abuses tended to concentrate on this, because, in addition to the genuine needs of humbler clerks, there was the greed of the more influential for wealthy sinecures. It must be pointed out however that the accummulation of offices, often without serious responsibilities, was not peculiar to the Roman church, or the Christian church at all. It was universally practised and expected.[68] Howls of disappointment went up from the unsuccessful, not from the righteous. Moreover, the chief reason for accumulation was the enormous number of clerical posts for which endowment had been provided with nominal obligations. The piety of earlier centuries had set up prebends in cathedrals and collegiate churches on a scale in keeping with the patron's standing and his hopes of eternal salvation. The papacy might be excused for thinking it right to appropriate some of this superfluous clerical wealth for the general benefit of the universal church, and it invoked the supreme authority for Christendom vested in its office to do this. Likewise the generous endowment of country clergy often exceeded the needs and expectations of the rural ministers and could be assigned to those doing a useful job in the central offices of the church. Had the resources assigned to the church over the whole west been more easily utilized for the whole church's needs, and as time and circumstances required, the papal actions would not have seemed justified. Central government of the church did what it could to make the most of the total resources in the light of its unique information. Only at the centre can the total needs of the whole community be assessed and its resources in men and money calculated. The critics were the unsuccessful candidates, the local interests that had been brushed aside, the descendants of lay patrons who protested about the injury to their ancestral rights. There is no reason to believe that such persons would have been more honest, less partial or less greedy.

The papacy did not immediately lay claims to make all the principal appointments in the western church. The first general declaration of the papal right to reserve nominations to benefices left vacant by the death of the incumbent at the curia was not issued till 1265 by Clement IV, and the codification of papal rights to appoint to benefices was more or less complete when John XXII issued the bill *Ex debito* in 1316. The constant requests at the curia for benefices, particularly from such patronless clerks as university graduates, kept the curia busy for centuries. The university of Oxford which appreciated papal patronage for its graduates thus deplored the statute of Provisors passed in the English parliament (1351) in the interests of lay patrons. This much publicized act of national protest against Rome in fact served only a particular vested interest. The university, no less than the pope, was an interested party, and it is probable that, between them, these last two better understood the general needs of the church in their day.[69] And even royal attempts to hoist assiduous ministers into bishoprics were generally managed by papal provision. Popes had no reason to make royal enemies unnecessarily, yet at the same time they had no need to give in on every occasion. Given the possibility of bishops finding suitable working substitutes in the diocese, there was no objection to promoting worthy and distinguished men to the titles and emoluments of high office. It would also be self-defeating to make all clergy abandon the arena where they were most useful to the church as a whole, for the local ministry of their diocese.

Clerical taxation

Papal taxation of the clergy was a more sinister danger. The clergy had first been asked, then required, to pay contributions for the needs of the

Holy Land, which had a moral claim on western Christendom. If taxation was justified for holy wars, crusades preached against even Christian enemies of the church, the disobedient or the schismatic, again justified asking the clergy to help the supreme pontiff. The problems of assessment and collection involved finding the right balance between effective local collectors, who knew the clergy's resources and could coerce reluctant taxpayers, and the more reliable, impartial papal collectors, Italian bankers or curial employees. Moreover clerical taxes had to be turned eventually into armies and equipment, matters better managed by lay princes. The papacy tried to tempt princes into supporting their political policies by offering them a share in the clergy's taxes, with the further advantage that the princes acquired an interest in securing collection. At this time rulers had still no regular right to augment their revenue by taxation for warfare, (because vassals expected to fight in person and only paid to be excused). Henry III (1216-72) raised only four aids from his barons in forty years for specific needs, but he received monies through papal grants of clerical taxation, without ever actually taking a step towards the conquest of Sicily—their ostensible purpose.

This exercise of papal power to tax its 'subjects', the clergy, not only gave kings the experience and advantage of taxation, it also fatally encouraged the papacy to embark upon expensive political commitments because it could so easily slip into regular use of this device. Taxation had been intended as a desperate last resort in case of war, but war became easier to bear once ready cash could be obtained. Warfare, however, obliged the papacy to rely upon faithful princes, since it had no military forces of its own. Once papal policies clearly came to depend upon lay support in this sphere, its future as a purely spiritual institution was in jeopardy. The papacy reasonably argued that its spiritual independence was compromised by temporal insecurity.[70] Unfortunately, excessive concern for temporal politics could destroy the papacy's spiritual credit. By the end of the thirteenth century the papal position in Italy had become so dependent on the indulgent attitude of the king of France, the strongest prince of Christendom, that popes could not imagine how to do without it. Many contemporaries were exceedingly alarmed by what they saw, proposing schemes for purifying the church which had nothing to commend them but their naivety. Such criticisms must not be misconstrued. The most outspoken English critic of the thirteenth-century popes, Robert Grosseteste, Bishop of Lincoln, protested that his criticisms were not aimed at the papal jurisdiction as such. Indeed Christendom remained united in its loyalty to the idea of Roman order until the sixteenth century. Despite notorious cases of controversy, their respect for logic made medieval churchmen submit to

Rome; in the famous words of Boniface VIII, 'there was no salvation outside the church'.[71]

Papal achievements

The popes were not irresponsible about their powers. They took their legal responsibilities very seriously and used the services of lawyers professionally trained not at Rome, but in Bologna, the centre of legal studies. There were no matters of major importance in Christendom that eluded their supervision. Popes did not rashly set about overturning traditional rules or authorities and dared to threaten rulers only after insolent provocation. The papacy had duties to the clergy and to God and intended to obtain respect from Christians: it had no reason to doubt that they would eventually submit rather than suffer eternal damnation. The pope had no other powers apart from his spiritual jurisdiction and if the papacy triumphed it was because the body of clergy and laymen put their spiritual welfare before all else.

Coolly considered, the success of the papacy is a cause for astonishment in the modern world. It is impossible to conceive of the modern intelligentsia making effective use of power, even if they could work together and agree on doctrine. The papacy eventually went beyond the requirement of the lawyers in exercising the power they accorded it, and found the means to articulate this power in every part of Christendom—even if it did not obtain equal success everywhere. General confidence in its disinterested pursuit of the church's good increased rather than diminished throughout the thirteenth century, as the branches of its power became more powerful and complicated. No other religious organization has ever been able to command such obedience and the papacy has left a profound mark upon European history. Success, and protests about the size or corruption of the curia, did nothing to arrest the process. The papacy was not discredited by the parasites who lived upon it. It provided the nearest the middle ages ever came to knowing about effective government and this at the improbable hands of the clergy in combination with the Roman families.

On this theoretical basis, in response to practical demands, the papacy built a jurisdiction that has since been roundly criticised, and not only by protestants. Instead of seeing how much it fell short, credit should first be given to what it had achieved. The twelfth century had set out with confidence to achieve an ideal Christian society. As the ideal began to take practical shape, some illusions had to be shed, but in as much as it proved possible to secure total respect for the clerical estate and enforce spiritual issues in clerical courts by enlightened principles, important inroads had been made into worldly power. The new clerical organization as a spiritual state had then used its power to enforce more religion, raise standards, improve education, settling, as such practical institutions must, for what is possible rather than what is best. The apparatus of the 'state' inevitably identified its own survival with the best interests of the whole. It is not obvious that dismantling the structure and starting again from simple idealism would have achieved more. The fact is that, as soon as movements are successful, they need to be superseded, because the institutions created to consolidate reform have by then acquired prestige and a vested interest in self-preservation. For centuries men will continue to put up with the real inconveniences, sensing how inadequate the alternatives are. The late medieval church earned many hard words, often justified, but it is necessary to see it as a whole. Its unity is most worthy of commendation, particularly in a time like the present when the divisions of the world into national sovereign states (never so numerous as now) make a mockery of parallel attempts to promote human unity. Medieval Christendom lived at a conscious level in a single community, the Church, and the genuine responsibilities of the civil power were as immediate and trifling as local governments now are. The educated, at any rate, lived, thought and acted in a universal church and turned naturally puzzled eyes on those who opposed it.

The structure of the late medieval church is so often thought to have been in need of reform that we overlook the extent to which religious life flourished; indeed it had never been in such abundant supply. There was a brand to suit everyone from the most ignorant and the most weak to the most austere, ascetic and ingenious. Since the thirteenth century the campaign against dualist heresies, like Catharism, had deliberately chosen to emphasize the reality of the Christian concern with the world God had created and His Son had saved. The story of salvation was enacted in mystery plays trundled round the cities in carts and staged by mechanicals. Churches were decorated with instructive pictures portraying in lurid detail the torments of the damned and representing the saving works of saints in realistic fashion. Churches were not so much noble monuments designed to lift the soul to soaring contemplation, but labyrinths of chapels, passages, in each of which the various episodes of the Christian story had their appropriate stage. Worshippers must have wandered from one chapel or picture to another constantly receiving new impressions of wonder and veneration, hardly lifting their eyes to a single remote God but comforted by the multiple witnesses of familiar aspect who had shown the way to overcoming feeble human nature. Medieval religion presents to us a confused, disruptive picture of agitated emotion. Reformers itched to set it right according to their own ideas. But it was a church that suited most people to perfection. It fostered a credulous piety and confident faith, capable in some people of inspiring saintly virtues: a religion for the people that the better educated, clerical and lay, began to despise.

The need for reform

Criticism of the centralized church invariably concentrates on the neglect of the local responsibilities: yet it is the normal result of central govern- ment. If the requirement is uniformity, control must pass out of the hands of the people on the spot who are best able to run their own affairs. Men of talent were attracted to the centre where they took on the duty to serve the whole to the detriment of the particular. The springs of local action were fed into the mainstream, and they became dependent on the ebb and flow of the great tides: local authorities looked expectantly to the best minds in Rome for instruction and resources. But centraliza- tion is more like a great inner sea receiving abundant supplies of living water and generating no energy of its own to pump them back where they are most needed. The best talents of the medieval church were first cul- tivated in the small religious community, then drawn to the centre. The main channels of preferment remained wide open; it was the failure of the centre to irrigate the provinces that ultimately discredited the papal system.

The parish priests or others concerned with the pastoral ministry have left no records of their dissatisfaction. The better educated, the ones who rose to be bishops or distinguished scholars, lamented most. Two possibilities lay open to them: either to work personally as bishop or teacher for reform; or alternatively to obtain influence at the highest level in order to instigate universal reform by decree. Despite good work at the personal level, the structure of the medieval church from the twelfth century fatally tempted reformers to concentrate on gaining influence, much as the structure of the modern European state has tended to depreciate the value of individual acts of charity and encouraged the view that human nature may be reformed more quickly by politicians or by legislation. The most able and the most idealistic churchmen continued to obtain high and influential posts in the church, because educational attainments continued to earn scholars recognition.

Installed then in positions of power, what could be done? Bishops could carry out their duties scrupulously, but they could not afford to demand a higher standard of education from their clergy than the general level of ability allowed, otherwise parishes would have been without pastors altogether. They could not from their own resources adequately improve the priests' stipends: nor is it certain that richer livings would have attracted better priests. The 'church' was perhaps too richly endowed as a whole, but the wealth was concentrated in institutions that were least in need of it by the fourteenth century. No Jeremy Bentham then arose to survey the church's needs and reallocate revenues. Not only is the idea itself obviously absurd for the time, it contradicted the real ideal of Christian giving. If Dives failed to use his resources to comfort Lazarus, he was the ultimate loser. At the time, little sentimental pity was lavished upon the miseries of Lazarus in this life. The church, even had it tried to face the problems of redistributing its resources, would never have been able to carry them through, because the laws of property maintained by the lay courts would have intervened. Grasping laymen did later seize monastic lands. Neither the church, nor the church's interests were served better as a result. Wyclif's arguments for the lay patron's rights to reoccupy monastic lands were not believed in the fourteenth century and refuted by the events of the sixteenth. Indeed in the 'reformed' churches, the problem of the inequality of endowments has still not ceased. Critics and reformers harp dolefully upon the vices and ignorance of the clergy. Allowing for the worse (in some dioceses the very worst) it is nevertheless certain that over the three centuries, from 1215 to 1517, the parish clergy had consolidated their role, served their parishes, steadily forced up the standard of public worship, increased the endowment of religious building, shrines and decoration, and improved their own educational attainments to keep pace.

Surveying the diocese a new bishop would also discover that though parish priests were his responsibility, the religious life of the diocese

and well-connected clergy, monasteries, friaries, his own cathedral chapter often, over which his powers were surprisingly limited. Many institutions were directly subject to the pope; others had powerful friends amongst laymen; the bishops could easily find themselves frustrated by interfering secular lords or Roman prohibitions. These institutions armed themselves with privileges intended to frustrate episcopal initiative. By the late middle ages the laws of church and state tended to protect every institution worthy of the name, leaving its affairs in its own hands subject only to ultimate papal supervision. At the beginning of the period when the rules of law had not been so exactly defined, there was more room for manoeuvre, but from the first the new rules had been worked out so as not to offend important and distinguished churchmen. The twelfth-century reformers made a clean sweep of some abuses such as communities of hereditary married canons or lay abbots, but the great monasteries of the past, enjoying exemptions from episcopal control and visitation in later centuries, had been too powerful and respectable in the twelfth century to be brutally subjected to a new and rational scheme of church government. There may even be some element of calculation in the readiness of canon lawyers to extend the idea of direct papal sovereignty over such great churches, for this prevented bishops from consolidating the dioceses in their own undisputed hands and left plenty of opportunities for papal interference. At least till the thirteenth century the papacy itself probably had no mischievous intentions of this kind, for the policy had grown up in a haphazard way, as quarrelsome parties had appealed to popes to intervene on their behalf. Popes had tried to please and pacify; in this way they had become indispensable.

The trouble was that no part of medieval Christendom could function in isolation; reforming intentions anywhere could not help but convulse the whole community. At the same time, in so complicated a structure no one scheme or reform ever commanded universal approval. Eager and sincere reformers were as surprised then, as now, to discover that their pet programmes even roused waves of emotional defence for the worst abuses, less on account of newly discovered merits but because the spirit of reform itself behaved like a vengeful angel spurning deeply cherished attitudes of mind. The reformers at the institutional as well as the personal level were therefore often dashed by considerable disappointments and since reformers are bound to speak out to get attention and support, their disappointments cry aloud from the written records. Hence the need to appreciate the benefits of abundant and exuberant Christianity for the uninstructed.

5

LAY DOMINION

Reflecting on the French Revolution, Joseph de Maistre called attention to a feature of political society particularly significant in the history of medieval Europe, though, as should be expected for his day, he derived his insight from the history of the ancient world:

> 'It is very far from being true that everything that can be written is written; there is even in every constitution always something that cannot be written and that must be left behind a dark and impenetrable cloud, on pain of overthrowing the state. The more that is written, the weaker is the institution, the reason being clear. Laws are only declarations of rights, and rights are not declared except when they are attacked, so that the multiplicity of written constitutional laws shows only the multiplicity of conflicts, and the danger of destruction. That is why the most vigorous political system in the ancient world was that of Sparta in which nothing was written.'

Unfortunately, when nothing at all is written about law, nothing is known long afterwards, and what may be a strength for the state is a disaster for the historian. Sparta, which rejected writing, owes its reputation to Athenians. Medieval governments, which dispensed with writing, only become known to history from the records of the clergy, who never tired of airing their own grievances. When they demanded privileges, they stirred up the earliest medieval controversies; likewise they inspired political reflections based on the clerical learning about history and the Bible when rulers asked them for political programmes. Pious kings who adopted their suggestions found that they could be carried out only by taking into their service many clerks. These professionals changed government from the management of men into the administration of things. Increasingly the business of ruling appeared to involve the keeping of rolls (read, files), the passage of documents from one office to another in search of seals (read, initials) and a constantly expanding number of clerks (read, bureaucrats). Such notions came new in the thirteenth century, but they have gone from strength to strength ever since. What did the king's traditional companions, his warriors, make of all this? Can the activities of clerks have ever seemed to kings themselves the essential business of rulership? It was part of the trappings of monarchy — the part supplied by the clergy. However much they came to value these ornaments kings had not originally been laden with them. It is necessary to begin by trying to penetrate the nature of political power before the clergy began to insinuate attitudes of their own.

1. BARBARIAN SOCIETIES

There can be no question of supposing that laymen themselves originally took a strictly 'secular' view of authority. De Maistre himself believed that there was a mysterious core to every constitution, necessarily veiled, and this opinion would certainly have been endorsed in primitive times. It has been said of the ancient Germans that for them the law itself always had a cosmic aspect: that it was the supporting pillar of the building of the world, such that the collapse of right order sealed the fate of the world itself.[1] And, just as the 'law' expressed a mystery, so too the kingship had a priestly character. Titus Livy described how the military state of Romulus had to be supplemented by Numa with a spiritual basis of law and religious observance. The barbarian kings before their conversion to Christianity discharged special religious obligations for their peoples; some were descendants of gods; others were 'priests'. When Christian missionaries arrived, it was from the kings as religious leaders that they received protection, and, as Bede's account of the early English church amply demonstrates, the kings, if not priests of the new church, were its indispensable patrons. Could kings have ever coldly calculated the purely 'secular' advantages of religious conversion? Did Clovis the Frank weigh only the political possibilities of winning over Gallo-Roman support when he decided to accept Catholic baptism? Did Penda of Mercia refuse it, in case it damaged his political goal of Mercian hegemony in seventh-century England? Though the historians of the barbarian kings were clergy, who ascribed religious rather than political motives to them, it is probable that kings, who already had religious responsibilities, were only doing what was expected of them when they made religious decisions.

Christianity, which owed much to them, did little to undermine the religious implications of kingship even if the specific content of religious teaching was changed. Missionaries with doubts about the priestly character of kingship found it expedient to promote the cult of saintly rulers, while they referred to biblical precedents, like David and Josiah, for allowing kings to intervene in religious affairs. From the eighth century they revived the Jewish practice of anointing kings and improved on this with coronation ceremonies. The coronation was made by the clergy themselves into the most solemn ecclestiastical occasion in a barbarian community. When papal reformers in the eleventh century dared to claim that the king nevertheless remained a 'mere' layman, their Christian protests were unable to shake public faith in the religious character of kingship. Since such faith did not originally stem from Christianity, it could, if necessary, survive its disapproval.

In barbarian society fighting was no more a purely secular business than kingship. War had its own gods. Warriors did battle with their enemies in heroic encounters on which the gods pronounced judgment. In courts of law, well into the Christian period, disputes would come, by decision of the judges, to battle, in which God vindicated the just party.[2] The clergy, who ministered in battle or in the ordeals of the court, might commend humility rather than courage in these great contests in God's sight, but they too believed that God spoke in the outcome. Later, specifically Christian wars, like the Crusades, were fought for the church and were expected to obtain divine approval, and victories by the *paynim* had to be accepted likewise, if only with bafflement, as divine punishment on Christian sins. Warriors themselves may have continued for a long time to see in these encounters occasions for heroism, rather than righteousness, as with Roland at Roncesvalles, for in their eyes, it was no slur to be called a man of blood: it was a title of honour and this too has its mystical aspect. The clerical horror of bloodshed and warfare has never been more widely accepted than it is now, so it may be salutary to remember that as late as the nineteenth century a progressive writer such as Proudhon could still write seriously of the 'mystical' element in warfare.[3] It is likely that, in addition to the mystical thrill of combat, there was a frankly sensual pleasure in contest to the death. If such a feeling had once disgraced the Roman gladiatorial displays, there was no element of public entertainment about bloodshed in this period and it would be perverse to regard battles as depraved simply because men enjoyed fighting. They aroused the same excitement as modern sporting contests, carried to extremes. In a violent society all men knew how to defend themselves, and all were 'sportsmen' ready to take up the challenge.

Barbarian society, both before and after the conversion, built its social and political organization upon the general commitment to warfare. But this foundation began to crumble under the consequences of barbarian success. The Carolingian empire was in origin the culmination of barbarian ambitions to overcome all other tribes and incorporate them into one great whole. In tenth-century England similarly, the centuries-old conflicts between the different kingdoms were arrested by the united monarchy of the house of Wessex. Violence did not cease abruptly, but it was contained. It was transferred to the frontiers, against the Welsh and the peoples of the north, while the kings tried to settle civil society and impose ways of keeping the peace. On the continent, wars were launched against the Muslims and in eastern Europe against the pagans by the new Ottonian emperors. Within these states the assumption that kingship implied warfare was sapped by a new requirement that great kings preserve peace and guarantee justice within the extended realms they governed.

The most sophisticated kingdom of Latin Europe in the eleventh century was the German empire, and, as it began to grapple with the problem of keeping secular allegiance in the new conditions, it turned to the bishops for advice and assistance. Yet, while King Henry IV was trying to deal with lay opposition in Saxony, he was stabbed in the back by Gregory VII, who demanded the total loyalty of the bishops to the spiritual body of the church. The opposition to Henry IV naturally expected to make common cause with the pope, but in fact alliance between the clergy and the nobles could only be temporary. The pope's moral attitude to politics was highly exasperating. Just when Henry IV seemed to be at the mercy of the opposition, he sought absolution from the pope at Canossa in 1077; secular lords found it incomprehensible that the pope should give way.

It was nevertheless significant that the king-emperor found himself attacked at once by both the nobles and the clergy. Till this point, the nature of royal power had not been scrutinized — as De Maistre observed, rights are only declared when attacked, and in this case it was the clergy who forced laws, as declarations of right, into writing. The clergy were at first the most determined critics of the monarchy, for, however conservative by temperament, they applied an inflexible moral yardstick to royal actions. Their education and their spiritual duties made them self-conscious as a group within the kingdom. They had a definite concept of their duties, a test of their doctrines in canonical writings and some capacity to transcend the limits of the kingdom by appeal to the pope. Even when the papacy itself hung back, for political reasons, reformist clergy like Becket were prepared to resist kings, demanding privileges of law and courts of their own. The idea of such private enclaves was attractive to others. In due course, townsmen, even feudal barons, would also demanded confirmations of 'privilege'. Since the first problem was to formulate the demands in words, the clergy were bound to be pioneers in knowing what to ask.

Kings did not quail before these challenges, because they knew their rights were rooted in the pagan past and watered by centuries of Christian teaching; they had no intention of allowing their branches to be lopped off without protest, and soon discovered how they could take advantage of divisions within the clerical camp and waverings in Rome itself. Gregory VII's general onslaught against all secular rulers had not persuaded all the clergy, because many of them appreciated the practical assistance pious kings still gave to particular churches. They rejected Gregory's view that kings were inferior to exorcists in the spiritual hierarchy. After Gregory's death in exile, his successors in the papacy also found it expedient to get firm political support where they could, in order to ensure their main objective, which was emancipation from the emperor in Italy. This gave other kings their chance. When William Rufus quarrelled with Archbishop Anselm about the rights of his crown and saw no reason why he should spell them out just to please his vassal, Pope Urban II proved much more anxious to keep on good terms with Rufus than to take Anselm's side; there was after all no risk that Anselm would desert the Roman allegiance.[4] Later on and nearer at home, the papacy was also obliged to confer approval on the new Sicilian monarchy of Roger II, because it could not prevent him from uniting the Norman lands of southern Italy.[5] Kings commanded military forces and even the papacy had sometimes to bow to their power, however reluctantly, if it could not find a military champion prepared to submit permanently to its direction.

The monarchies were therefore reprieved: kings won recognition of their *de facto* power, in return for which they were prepared to concede some clerical privileges. The clergy were on the whole thankful they could revert to their traditional policy of praising and serving rulers, since in some ways they were more in need of protection than ever before. The reformer's plan to improve the spirituality of the church by keeping it away from contact with men of blood had the unforeseen consequence of putting it at the mercy of such men of blood, like kings, who would fight the bloodless men's battles for them. The idea that the spiritual and secular could be neatly severed was absurd enough and in practice most men of the eleventh century were rightly sceptical about how to separate the spiritual from the secular. Take this passage from William of Poitiers' account of William the Conqueror, which sets out to do this, but quickly proves it was impossible: 'Although he divided his time between warfare and administration, the things which we call secular affairs, this excellent prince spent his greatest effort on spiritual matters; even when he was on campaigns, he never forgot his fear of the eternal majesty. In foreign wars and in the suppression of rebellion, plunder and brigandage he served his country. Indeed nobody could ever say that he undertook a war which was not just. Who would dare to suggest that a good prince should put up with traitors and brigands? By his punishments and by the laws which he made, Normandy was freed from thieves, murderers and wrongdoers. The truce of God was observed. The cause of the widow, the poor man and the orphan found in him an attentive audience, a sympathetic defender and an impartial judge. Through him villages, castles and towns enjoyed security of their rights and possessions.'[6] No passage could more conclusively demonstrate how much the king's attention to secular affairs was the layman's means of discharging his spiritual obligations. The clergy themselves saw kings as men of power who acted to preserve the peace and create conditions in which the clergy could live and work more effectively. The king, as the Lord's anointed, was specifically entrusted with this work. Kings were beholden to churchmen for this concept of their function, and did not therefore lack for ministers to help them discharge it.

The fact that the clergy eventually rallied to the kings did not of itself do much to wean secular lords too from their rebellious attitudes to the monarchies of the late eleventh and early twelfth centuries. They naturally did not need to think of the king as their special defender in the same way as clergy, for as men still able to stand up for themselves, the king was not for them the sole source of peace and order. They were not mere disrupters of royal or clerical attempts to find peace; they had a positive role of their own to play, and they brought to the task quite a different set of assumptions about the nature of the civil community. Their ideas were most thoroughly worked out in northern France, because the king there had lost the initiative and could not become the nucleus of order. Real power had passed into the hands of the counts, descendants of the Carolingian officials who, together with the bishops, had been held responsible for the business of the empire. These men exercised all the imperial rights within their territories, unhampered by any vestigial religious obligations. Unable to command moral obedience, they devised effective alternative forms of political association in their own regions, by establishing personal ties with great men who would become their vassals. Their need to develop personal followings in this way was accentuated from the early eleventh century by the ability of quite small men to erect fortresses or castles, built of stone (or, more commonly still at this date, a timber construction with a wooden palisade) and to defy the count's authority. The counts drew lesser men into their service by offering them lands and thus reduced the enclaves of defiant rebellion. When building up their vassal strength, counts may have followed some generally understood principles about making such concessions, though our mainly clerical sources of information (considering always their own advantages rather than political realities) do not allude to any. Counts must in general have acted to see that no one vassal became too influential or indispensable; perhaps favours were adjusted exactly to the value of services rendered, or only to the dignity of the recipient; there were certainly, also, some impolitic rulers who learned the dangers of favouritism or reliance on filial loyalty. The nuances of political life are lost to us, but there is no reason to doubt that the lords of the eleventh century understood them perfectly well at the time. This lay society of lords and vassals struggled to reconcile conflicting interests. More and more, some counts managed to enlarge the areas of their jurisdictions, by absorbing the counties of others and giving themselves grandiose titles such as marquis or duke to indicate their importance. Gradually northern France was marked out in great regions of power. Conflicts within were appeased by the princes and warfare relegated to the borders between them as they fought, with declining effectiveness, to expropriate their neighbours. In time the struggles died down. Counts resigned themselves to secure by marriage what could not be achieved in war. Out of this strictly military society there also emerged a programme for peace.

Military interests were in the eleventh century uppermost in their thoughts. They did not bother with titles of honour. The terms baron and knight were used indiscriminately; it was prowess rather than status that mattered. As men of action they had little time for the clergy or for writing. The most pious founded monasteries or became benefactors of them, entering the cloister themselves only to pass their last few days with their monks. They gave property, as they received it from their lords, by ceremonial acts in public assemblies, not by charters, though these might be concoted afterwards by monks distrustful of the integrity of founders' kin to respect bequests. The barons of the period were distinguished soldiers, who fielded their own contingents, which they recruited either from the family lands or from the honours granted to them by greater men for that purpose. It was partly the need to replenish the ruler's stock of dispensable lands for granting to vassals that drove him into wars against his neighbours, just as it was natural that the most successful counts could for that reason expect to attract the services of the most distinguished barons. But when the forces were well matched, further conquests came to an end.

The history of the feudal principalities has suffered from prejudices against factious barons defying royal jurisdiction. The barons should be seen to have supplied for themselves a form of government that the king did not; given his still magical and 'imperial' legacies, he could not have done so well. For nearly two centuries the king of France enjoyed little more respect than any count. For a time he could not command more obedience within his royal domain than his counts could in their counties. Despite his weakness, his great provincial neighbours did not try to suppress the monarchy, or usurp his place. Barons were disobedient and disloyal on occasions, but they found their own use for the monarchy. If they needed advice, peace or aid, they applied to him, as 'president' of their federation. Even by sympathetic inactivity the king could remain master of the situation. His own forces were not negligible and in combination would deter powerful neighbours. He needed very little real political power to hold the ring, as long as the principalities were well-balanced. However, the Norman conquest of England which so strengthened Normandy reduced the monarchy in France to a very low level of activity. Even then the Norman duke could not hope to extinguish it in his own favour. When Henry I invoked the help of his son-in-law, the German Emperor Henry V, against King Louis VI in 1124, the latter found eager contingents pressed upon him from every side.[7] In France the barons went furthest towards making the monarchy superfluous, but it was not in France that they caused the king most trouble. This was because in a country the size of France, the principalities managed with the minimum of royal government for many centuries. The king and the barons were not forced to engage in constitutional dialogue there. It was in England that a political structure had to be built out of the umpromising materials of 'feudalism'. There, a powerful monarchy in a small territory provoked strong baronial objections. This forced the kings to compromise. Out of the discussions that ensued, England began to forge a political society.

2. THE ANGLO-NORMAN MONARCHY

The Anglo-Norman monarchy was the earliest European institution to meet the challenge of both clerical and baronial opposition successfully and to create an effective monarchy of an entirely new pattern. Since the pattern owed more to the barons' feudal ideas in the first instance it is sensible to begin with them.

Normandy was one of the last French duchies able to engage in aggressive wars beyond its boundaries, but hemmed in to the south by Anjou, with Maine as a buffer county for them to fight over, individuals sought adventures far away in southern Italy and in Spain. The Normans could not take Le Mans and keep it, but their military prowess was sufficient to overcome peoples outside France not practised in their kind of warfare, and their greatest success was the expedition led by the duke himself to England.

Normans esteemed military talent and generalship above all else. Their model king was the heroic but benign Charlemagne of the *Chanson de Roland* who deferred to his barons. Later, they approved of the distinguished but politically ineffectual Arthur, as described in the romances. They favoured in practice a rough military society. A king like Rufus was as popular with his soldiers, as he was deplored by his monks.[8] But kings who intended to cut a great figure in the world had also to reckon that the brute power of men could be used to defy them. Management of his 'barons' was the king's crucial political problem, particularly when the conquests were over and the 'settlement' began. The Normans who expanded easily enough into England had there to learn political behaviour. Successful conquest itself turned soldiers into English 'land-owners' and they were obliged to arrive at a new understanding with the kings there.

William the Conqueror was not a reformer or a revolutionary. In his relations with the church his government stood faithfully in the Carolingian tradition, though he did not rely, like his German contemporaries, on the inspiration of books or clergy in the business of 'secular' government. He was original for his time in using the relationship between himself and his vassals to obtain political advantages as king. To some extent this was a second-best policy, adopted only after the collapse of his original hopes of building on the basis of the Old English monarchy. By 1086 English land 'owners' had been so effectively eliminated from political society that even the churches had passed into the hands of Norman bishops and abbots, sitting uncomfortably in the places of Dunstan of Canterbury or Wulfstan of York. The king had then to rely almost exclusively on his Normans. They were not in the Conqueror's time famous for their discipline. Normandy had no tradition of strong government and William trusted his own talents rather than his officials when he decided to make the bond of lord and vassal the basis of his political community. He was a good lord to those from whom he expected and exacted obedience: this personal morality served the monarchy well.

It is an illusion that there was any established feudal 'system' existing in Normandy to be introduced at one fell swoop into England in 1066. The inchoate forms of feudalism gave the Conqueror and his sons the possibility of moulding them in their own political interests, as opportunities arose. The system obliged the king to entrust lands to faithful vassals. If they rebelled against the king, as frequently happened, the king could assert his royal right to take back the fiefs, but he could not simply keep them, enlarge the royal domain and run them through paid officials. Such lands were in due course ceded to others, no less able than their predecessors to rebel against royal authority, even if kings naturally hoped that they would be more loyal. There was no question of dispensing with this feudal system. Kings did not fear the risks and they valued the advantages. Grants of land were the essential means of attracting and keeping the most powerful and energetic men of the kingdom in royal service. 'Government' depended upon their loyalty.

Though the Norman kings had inherited a remarkably competent form of financial administration, capable of collecting impressive sums of money in taxes, even the existence of such officials could not dispense the king from delegating other responsibilities to vassals. He operated on the assumption that, together, he and his vassals owned the principal stock of the kingdom. They trusted one another to carry out their obligations in a comparable manner, with mutual goodwill. This did not preclude a great deal of argument and selfishness, but it ruled out any intention of depriving barons of all effective power over their lands and their own vassals.

The Conqueror's concern was to make all stiff-necked men, English and Norman, bow down to his lordship. By their homage the king may be said to have become the ultimate landlord of all England, but this emphasis upon land-ownership did not appear in the eleventh century. A century later it might seem as though the Conqueror had imposed a single pattern of landholding by a homogenous group of royal vassals in a single generation. Late-twelfth-century legal theory made no allowances for the actual historical developments. The terms of post-conquest tenures were ill-defined and confused by old English survivals. Rules about inheritance, the rights of widows and children, the dues of wardship and relief were uncertain in 1087 and were only gradually defined in response to political circumstances. The great families of the Conqueror's day did not all survive the reigns of his sons. However, although the rules were changed and new families emerged, it remains true that the Conqueror did introduce an enduring scheme of landownership. A small landowning class from across the Channel was brought into England, where it was inextricably caught in a web of complicated tenures, at the mercy of a system of public law-courts unfamiliar to the Normans themselves. By English tradition the king had authority to manipulate the machinery of justice in royal and local courts; the Normans who held land in England could not therefore dispense with the king or his law. On the contrary, they found even under the Conqueror that there were advantages for them in appealing to the king to intervene in their legal affairs, and in the next century baronial demands for royal justice became the principal means of augmenting royal powers. By twelfth-century standards England was elaborately governed because the kings had exceptional influence in the legal business of their vassals.

Baronial dependence on the king who controlled the courts and the terms of tenure initially gave the king an 'unfair' advantage, which the Conqueror's sons had no hestitation in exploiting. Their father had secured the compilation of a register of titles to land — the Domesday book — which could be used as a guide to vassals' assets when estimating capacity to pay reliefs or other dues. The abuses of the system by Rufus already provoked a reaction and the next king, Henry I, had to begin by placating the barons with promises to give up his brother's oppressions and accept the restraints of law and custom. In fact over his much longer reign, Henry turned out to be every bit as grasping as Rufus. When he died leaving the succession in dispute, many barons took the opportunity to pin the new king, Stephen, down. From these reactions it is possible to gauge baronial views about the functions of kingship and assess what they could do to impose their ideas. They had only the crudest means at their disposal. Kings could be induced to swear oaths and grant charters. If the king went back on his word, what could the barons do but rebel? It was a desperate remedy, unlikely to succeed unless enough barons could agree on a joint enterprise. This was difficult. They were jealous of one another and eager to turn the grievances of one party to their own personal advantage. Kings became adept at not alienating all the barons at once. Rebellions occurred nonetheless and even as expressions of impatient baronial bad-temper, they were in the twelfth century effective reminders to the king of the limits of baronial tolerance. It should not be supposed that the kings were really more calculating than their barons. Both sides had a lot to learn about keeping cool. Over several generations the barons slowly grasped the basic elements of political life and kings learned the rewards of self-restraint.

The chief advantage which the barons had for learning to respond to the king politically was the recurring opportunity to choose between rival candidates for the kingship. They had individually to make calculations, weighing up the merits of the candidates, judging the better right, or opting blatantly for the regime better able to protect their interests on both sides of the Channel. The political choices open to them may not seem substantial, but they were enough to develop in them a sense of political responsibility unparalleled in the twelfth century. Elsewhere there was no generally accepted doctrine of hereditary monarchy, but in practice nowhere outside England was the succession so consistently a bone of contention. It was this that deferred the consolidation of the hereditary character of the English kingship, until the barons had made clear their 'conditions'. The profound political reason for this is probably that the barons instinctively refused to admit the inheritance of such a powerful institution as the monarchy of William the Conqueror. In France, the barons had no qualms about accepting the virtual inheritance of the Crown (though cautious kings until the thirteenth century only secured this by crowning their sons in their lifetime, which avoided the dangers of asserting an hereditary claim), because the monarchy was hardly more than a great fief and treated as such. The monarchy in England struck the barons as far too dangerous to be 'inherited' without considering political conditions.

Their distrust of it is shown as early as 1075, when the Norman Earl of Hereford shared in a conspiracy with the Breton Earl of East Anglia and the English Earl of Northumbria to divide all the honours of England amongst themselves.[9] The critical attitude of the baronage towards the kingship reappeared at the Conqueror's death (1087). The uncertainty about the succession excited some discussion as to the advantages of William Rufus, who took the throne, as against those of his older brother Robert, Duke of Normandy, who had many supporters. The outcome in England was closely related to the situation in Normandy. Once Rufus had taken control of the kingdom, he disputed Robert's undoubted rights in Normandy as well. In 1100, when Rufus died, Robert's absence on crusade naturally facilitated the succession of Henry I in England, but even so Robert's claims were not passed over in silence. Like Rufus, Henry I once secure in England, could not resist trying to impose himself on the duchy as well. He defeated Robert in 1106 and for the rest of his reign managed to hold on to both lands, despite the constant opposition of Robert's supporters and those of Robert's son, William Clito, whose prospects became much brighter after 1120 when Henry's own son William was drowned. Until the Clito's death in 1128, Henry's hopes of a peaceable settlement of his estates after his death must therefore have been slight. The death of his son had made that problem acute. Although he had many bastard sons, Henry aimed to perpetuate his line through his only surviving legitimate child, his daughter Mathilda, widow of the German emperor, Henry V, and known as the Empress, whom he forced to marry the unpopular Count Geoffrey of Anjou in 1128, regardless of baronial objections.

On Henry's death in 1135, it is hardly surprising that the barons rejected Henry's arrangements. His favourite nephew, Stephen of Blois, seized the throne. Like his predecessors, Stephen began by making formal concessions to secure recognition and turning promptly to Normandy. Unlike them however he was not able to keep up the struggle, let alone win it, by campaigning on the continent. He fell back on England and it was there, rather than in Normandy, as in the past, that the supporters of Stephen and Mathilda fought out the war of succession. In 1141 he was captured at the battle of Lincoln and almost supplanted as ruler for a few months by Mathilda. Though he was restored, he never completely recovered authority in the whole kingdom and the English baronage learned in this reign about the disadvantages of a king unable to govern. They had found Henry I too arbitrary and apparently welcomed the chance to play off the rivals in 1135. By 1153 they had learned that disorder was more of a liability. The greatest vassals could of course, impose their regional power and protect their own supporters by taking on the king's responsibilities there. This merely doubled their own work.

The lesser barons discovered that, without the king to appeal to, they were at the mercy of the great. Both groups were disillusioned about the chances of profiting by disputes about the succession. When Stephen's son Eustace died in 1153, the barons induced the king to recognize Mathilda's son Henry of Anjou as his heir and, when Stephen died the next year, Henry actually became king, making no further concessions and fearing no rivals: the first king to have stepped into his predecessor's shoes without mishap since 1042.

While uncertainty about the succession gave the barons some room for political decision-making, the Norman kings' concerns on the continent gave them more still. Rulers with wider responsibilities than England had to adjust their policies 'at home' to their commitments 'abroad'. England was a rich kingdom, where the king had many estates and the right to money-taxes. The kings had an undeniable interest in exploiting these financial resources for ambitious and contentious policies elsewhere. At the same time, the king's frequent absence from England indicated that he was much less worried about the loyalty of his vassals there. Nor did he show any desire to impose uniform political institutions in all his lands. While absent himself, the existing administrative arrangements of England were able to develop independently. The growth of royal government in twelfth-century England owed much to these factors — the size of the royal domain and its character, the king's confidence in his English vassals and servants, the emergence of a native tradition in administration, all in turn affected by the fact that the king himself only made spasmodic visits to England to galvanise his officials into greater activity. The constant royal presence would not necessarily have been more of an advantage. Stephen, driven out of Normandy, did not thereby become a more effective king in England. The king's main function was to preserve the peace between his barons. If he could not do this on the continent, he had to do so in England; there was no alternative role to play as 'administrator'. The royal administration in effect improved when the king was out of the country.

Henry I consolidated the achievements of the Norman Conquest administratively. The financial machinery, already in place before the Domesday book, was improved in the next generation. The court of the exchequer makes its first definite appearance under Henry I, to check the payments of the royal dues by the sheriffs and to record their outstanding debts, year by year. One roll of account still survives to indicate how closely the sheriffs were supervised. For the most part, judicial administration was left to local courts of the manor, hundred, shire and honour, but the long list of royal pleas incited the king to check that he lost nothing of his dues from such sources. His zeal in this respect was not designed to provide better justice for all his vassals.

The English had to be self-reliant while their kings were away and this gave them some experience of government, which enabled them to judge their rulers better. Though they were docile under Henry I, they found many features of his government oppressive, and they hoped to live more freely under Stephen. Deceived in these expectations, they came to appreciate the advantages of effective royal government provided its rigours could be softened by making it more sensitive to the interests of the governed. The succession of the new kings had been treated as a suitable occasion for a show of gracious concessions. Henry I had issued a detailed coronation charter promising to remedy the barons' grievances against Rufus. But coronation charters had turned out to be inadequate means of binding rulers. Henry I had blatantly disregarded the terms of his own. The turmoil under Stephen was in part due to the excessive concessions he had made to meet baronial demands; anyway it destroyed the advantages of having secured charters. What was required was some means of securing loyal cooperation between the king and his barons, since the king could not govern without their confidence and they could not dispense with a man able to dominate their rivalries. The barons needed to spell out what they expected of good lordship, not necessarily in a charter, but by plainly showing what they regarded not as a royal right, but a tyrannous imposition. After half a century's experience, first of royal oppression and then of royal incompetence, the English barons by 1154 had much clearer ideas about what kind of kingship they wanted.

Henry II

Henry II claimed the crown of England as part of his inheritance and never made it his central concern. No king of England had ever had greater possessions or more wide-ranging responsibilities. Rebuilding the authority of the English king, was only one of the many consequences of his reign, and may not even have been planned at all. If it was, it was not from any particular concern for England. Henry was a politician, who responded instinctively and without hestitation to events, as is most obviously shown by his marriage to Eleanor of Aquitaine, his senior by more than ten years, as soon as she became free. He took on his public duties with the same instant determination. In this he was perhaps somewhat typical of other twelfth-century rulers nervous of being overtaken by hostile forces. Henry knew how to exploit the weakness of others to the full; he never allowed his enemies time to prepare themselves against him. He took his occasional falls like a good rider and was ever ready to leap back into the saddle and return to the fray. His main interests were all in the immediate, not the remote future. His main preoccupations were not institutional, but his inherited lands and his family. He provided for them with exemplary generosity; only one of his bastards was pushed, in some desperation, into the church and the daughters were all married off well. His main political difficulties were also caused by his sons, not his vassals, because his sons believed they had the right, as they had reason, to challenge his exercise of power: it seemed to them too that they were engaged in a family matter and did not fear to rock a political edifice.

The king's principal obligation to his vassals was to provide them with a forum for the settlement of their legal disputes and by Henry's time it was clear that the king would have to do more than his grandfather to meet these requirements. Henry I had been mainly concerned to exact all his own legal rights. Henry II created a new form of legal administration to serve his whole baronage. In effect this reduced the activities of the greater feudal courts and opened the king's courts to all freeholders, whether they were royal vassals or not. This was not done to satisfy the king's thirst for power — he had too many other interesting things to do — but to meet the demand for better government. No freeman was excluded from sharing the privileges of royal legal protection, formerly reserved to the king's direct vassals. As soon as he became king he took steps to inject more life into the existing courts, instructing feudal courts to do justice or lose their jurisdiction. All freemen were able to obtain a royal instruction, or writ, from the king's chancery to facilitate the process of law in the ordinary courts. Church courts too were scrutinized and attempts made to curtail their criminal jurisdiction. Sheriff's courts were suspended while special judges came on eyre to do justice in the king's name. The most surprising feature of Henry's legal reforms is the extent to which use could be made of customary procedures within a completely new system of law. The single most important novelty was the use of royal writs to initiate legal action of many different kinds. The little writ secured a crucial place for written documents in law, though there was no use of written evidence in the pleadings and no formal court records were kept, at least under Henry himself. The reform did not therefore imply the presence of many learned clerks or the penetration into common law of learned clerical concepts. It was a new law for lay affairs, that made a modest bow in the direction of writing.

Why were Henry's reforms desirable? We may surmise that they were, from the rapidity with which they were accepted. Henry's freeholders were chiefly anxious about the legal oppressions they might suffer from their immediate lords pressing claims to services and dues, or refusing to accept their heirs to feudal estates. Henry perceived what was required and, since we are told that Henry had a very subtle legal mind, it is not difficult to believe that he even took a personal share in devising remedies to the abuses. He made no direct assault on his barons' courts and endeavoured to make them share in the burdens of litigation and work more effectively. Since the barons had become powerful enough to browbeat their weaker tenants in their courts, it might have been sufficient for the king to offer their vassals his services to induce the barons to proceed more cautiously. However, the outcome of the royal reforms was eventually to deprive feudal courts of their most significant business; all the barons and the freemen were brought into direct dealing with the king's courts and were thenceforth interested in the king's law and changes in it. This made possible the political society which produced Magna Carta and later attempts at baronial intervention in government.

At this point the reconstruction of feudal government owed much to what Henry could borrow from churchmen — the use of a clerical bureaucracy and written records for his affairs. No previous English king had made such extensive use of the better educated clergy in his government, partly, of course, because it was not until the improvements in clerical education during the twelfth century that many potentially useful men became available to serve the king as well the church. Henry II was himself well-educated and he surrounded himself with educated persons. Not all of them were clergy, but all were impressed with the clerical values of learning and literacy. In discussions at court, in the administration, on commissions of inquiry and justice, clergy were always prominent and did not need to be in a numerical majority to be listened to with attention. The English bishops were no more successful than Becket in turning Henry II into a meek instrument of ecclesiastical policies, but they were happy to work with him because he fulfilled their requirements of kingship to perfection. Chroniclers of the reign, like the dean of St Paul's and the abbot of Mont Saint Michel, concurred with the royal treasurer in approving his actions. And for the first time, a royal clerk began to keep an account of the king's deeds, year by year, which lays bare the scale of royal activity.[10] Henry did not tyrannize the church. He dominated secular society in such a way that churchmen were able to enjoy in peace the special status they valued. For this they were grateful. They repaid the king by carrying out dutiful services, not just in his counting house, or on the bench, but in his writing offices as well: the chancery became the seat of the royal administration, issuing letters and writs to make the king's government serve his suitors: and the first of the prominent chancellors was Thomas Becket.[11]

It may seem somewhat perverse to stress Henry's cooperation with the churchmen when his reign is perhaps best known for his quarrel with Becket. The notoriety of their quarrel depends upon the survival of a great dossier of letters, mainly written from Becket's side, in which Henry inevitably stars as the villain. While the archbishop in exile had nothing better to do than concentrate on resolving the controversy, it must be remembered that Henry's attention was not absorbed by this episode. The very years of the Becket affair are marked by a succession of royal acts that initiated the new style of 'literate' government. They begin with the Constitution of Clarendon, published in January 1164, continue with the Assize of Clarendon, January 1166, the Cartae Baronum, spring 1166, the great eyre of the summer of 1166, the commission to the eyre of 1167 (entrusting the judges with the enforcement of the Assizes of Clarendon), and culminate in the inquiry into the conduct of the sheriffs in 1170. Apart from the first of these, no connexion can be traced between them and the Becket affair. The archbishop's exile appears to have no bearing upon the course of royal government. These measures cannot as a whole be described as a programme of royal tyranny carried through while the king's chief critic was out of the kingdom. The legal reforms met a public need for better justice. Moreover, the royal innovations all assume that the king could rely on the loyalty of many churchmen to serve as ministers, clerks and diplomats, never so numerous as in these years. The period of Becket's exile was less one of conflict with the church, than one in which churchmen and church methods became an integral part of the king's own government. Becket tried to save 'the church' from royal control: that was a cause of his own. Most of his fellow churchmen took the view that it was better for the church to accept the king's invitation and share in his affairs, preferring to imitate Becket's own example, when, as archdeacon of Canterbury, he had been the king's chancellor.

How had Henry been drawn into this bureaucratic path? His case exemplifies the view that it was disputes about ecclesiastical rights which precipitated royal action to strengthen secular royal government itself. Though he had come to the throne claiming to be in no wise bound by the acts of Stephen (whom he chose to regard as an interloper) he made no attempt to ascertain what the 'rights' of his grandfather Henry I had been, as might have seemed sensible after twenty years of disuse. In 1154 such a course would have been unusual, but excusable. When nine years later Henry did order an enquiry into the customs of his grandfather's day, it was, significantly, with regard to ecclesiastical matters, because churchmen had driven him to it by their taste for definitions. Henry took from them the idea of definitive written statements, and was prepared to use it for his own purposes: no wonder the clergy were scandalized.

In October 1163, the king held a great assembly at Westminster to discuss the affairs of the realm, at which the archbishops of Canterbury and York fell to squabbling, as was their wont, about precedence. They had both recently attended the council of Tours where the pope had also had to find seating arrangements that did not offend their dignity.[12]

Roger of York had already been archbishop for nearly ten years and had no wish to recognise the imperious claims of his recently promoted colleague Becket to 'primacy'. After this council the king obtained a written statement of the ecclesiastical customs of the realm and when this was ready the bishops were asked to swear on oath to uphold them: the Constitutions of Clarendon published in January 1164.[13] The nub of the statement was that disputes should not be carried beyond the archbishop's courts without royal approval (the only place they could have gone beyond that was the Roman curia). There is not much doubt that in general the customs were stated correctly, so that objections to them were not based on errors of fact but (i) on the king's committing them to writing in the first place, and (ii) on the king's insistence that the bishops take an oath to observe them.

The second point may seem rather captious, but the king was here combining an outrageous novelty with traditional practice. In feudal society oaths sworn to uphold ancient custom were taken without compunction because customs were not explicitly spelled out word for word. When these customs were put into writing, the bishops feared that their oath committed them to a more punctilious adherence to the form of words. Bishops had no objection to taking oaths to be honourable and true, particularly if they could cover their obligations to the church, by adding the clause saving their order (which Henry II refused to accept), but they would not undertake on oath to act in specific ways. They did not even swear on oath to keep the commandments of the Gospels and they found Henry's insistence on swearing to the customs intolerable and humiliating. Frankly they did not even approve of putting customs into writing, for this froze them into precepts so that they ceased to be customs. Customs might be tolerable as long as they could change; once accepted as 'law' however justified in themselves, they threatened the church's own legal system. Writing was to be used by them against kings, not vice-versa.

If we can appreciate the force of their objections and appreciate their reluctance, we may more easily perceive the novelty of Henry's move, though it raises a very difficult problem about the king's intentions. It is clearly absurd to suppose that in 1164 the king was merely falling back upon his policy of claiming the customs of Henry I, without suggesting why he had delayed such important definitions till that moment. Had he been waiting, as some historians have thought, for the death of Archbishop Theobald before taking such action, it would have been more reasonable to act either in the long vacancy at Canterbury 1161-2 or at least to be ready to impose the terms when Becket became archbishop. The only possible provocation for Henry's customs was the Council of Tours, in May 1163, in which Henry could have observed the formal promulgation of church laws in writing, and the consequences for England when the two archbishops returned to settle the differences between their sees. The principal issue by the summer of 1163 had become the attempt by Canterbury to secure the canonization of Anselm, a move that was challenged by York. The pope had dodged the issue by delegating the decision to an English council, without deciding which of the two archbishops had the better right to preside over it.[14] In these circumstances the king had to find a means of putting their quarrels on ice. He also saw in the conciliar decrees an example of the clergy making new ecclesiastical laws and thought he might define old customs in writing with equal justification. Then he made doubly sure by asking his vassals to swear on oath.

The Constitutions of Clarendon are the first attempt by a European secular government to give written authority to customary practices and thus establish basic unchanging laws which should supersede 'customs'. Such a short step is less timid and tentative than it seems. Henry II was himself a highly educated and intelligent ruler, with extraordinary energy and resource. He forced English government upon a headlong course with extreme precipitation. Because he was in haste, he gathered up the use of writing and the services of the clergy at an early stage into business of government that was still predominantly feudal and illiterate. This caused the English government to acquire its juridical framework so much earlier than that of other northern European monarchies, that it was saved the excessive accumulation of paperwork, which later clerks brought into the administration. In the twelfth century writing had still only limited use.

3. LITERATE MONARCHY

If Henry II's government found a use for writing and for clerks, his political attention was still nonetheless engrossed by his relations with secular persons. The problems of all twelfth-century rulers were to reconcile local men of power to the royal office. Prelates were never more numerous than lay magnates; if they appear to loom larger in history this is only because they put their opinions into words sooner. Their example did however prove infectious. Contemporaries began to see the advantages of verbal definitions of privilege because the clergy showed that this was the way to force rulers to meet their objections. In England, John's confirmation of ecclesiastical privilege in January 1215 preceded the grant of Magna Carta in June. In Germany, Frederick II treated with the combined ecclesiastical princes in 1220, several years before conceding privilege to the secular princes in 1232. Secular business was always more important to rulers than the ecclesiastical, and the chief importance of the clergy's use of written charters was that they showed laymen how to do the same. This changed the nature of secular government as a whole.

The traditional monarchies of warriors were transformed into kingdoms where specific groups of privileged persons, clergy, princes and townsmen obtained written undertakings from their kings, that their 'rights' would be protected; in return, they were prepared to bolster up royal authority. It was the source of their own legal status and it became the only means whereby any conflicts amongst the privileged groups could be settled.

In these monarchies, the clergy played a very distinctive role. Instead of establishing only one Christian society ruled by the pope, as some twelfth-century reformers had planned, they came to terms with kings determined not to surrender their powers. The clergy did not regard this as a total defeat, but as a more realistic means of securing their main ends. Appeal to history showed that God's purposes had been served by Christian rulers, such as Constantine, Theodosius and Justinian. Beyond them lay the traditions of the kings of Israel as known from the Bible itself. It was a hard question to know whether royal power came direct from God; it seemed more likely to churchmen that it was mediated by the church, through the coronation ceremony, which publicly conferred that power. However, kings, once crowned, were divinely authorized, they ruled for the advantage of all Christian people and the clergy were bound to submit to them, if they expected to benefit themselves from order and law. The pope might take a firmer line with errant kings, but from this time he did not lightly think of deposing rulers and reserved this ultimate weapon for the emperors alone.

Beneath the authority of the universal church, therefore, many kingdoms could spring up and prove the utility of their limited functions. The kings owed their crowns to the ecclesiastical ceremony and it is from a treatise on royal coronations that a list of European kingdoms may be compiled.[15] These were the Christian states known to the fourteenth century. The author began, still, but properly, with the emperor in Constantinople, whom he believed to be crowned. The emperor of the west was, however, said to be crowned three times over. Though this was somewhat theoretical, it certainly established his superior dignity. Some kings, following the Carolingian tradition, were admittedly anointed as well (France, England, Jerusalem, Naples and Scotland), but most were only crowned, so this was the real test of kingship. The list is somewhat fanciful, but impressively comprehensive nonetheless: Armenia, Serbia, Cyprus, Hungary, Bohemia, Poland, Sweden, Norway, Denmark, the Irish kings (! of Connaught, Munster, Meath and Ulster) Castile and Leon, Portugal, Navarra, Aragon, Sardinia, Majorca and Sicily. These kings did not necessarily have crude military power, but they were accorded status. They were the authorized and benevolent heads of state, like figures in fairy stories, handing out prizes and suffering personal misfortunes. Few of these kings were engaged in serious political occupations like 'expanding their power' or 'reforming their administrations'. They presided with dignity, at best, over many semi-independent authorities, piously respectful of their ruler, as God's choice.

Instead of eagerly rushing in to denounce immoral rulers, the clergy saw that it was more sensible to offer kings their own advice, and more to the purpose, their services, in order to forestall kings failing to do their duty. The kings, who found some clergy took too strong a line on the theory of kingship, appreciated the positive contributions they could make in government. Thus the association between throne and altar served both parties. It was not improper that kings were taught to believe that they would answer to God for their office or that churchmen were encouraged to serve the public interest of the kingdoms and not left to sit smugly in sacerdotal privilege. In medieval Christendom, churchmen had to perform duties equivalent to those discharged by the intelligentsia for the modern state, which would be nowhere without their *servitudes et grandeurs:* the rationalist philosophers who invented it, the bureaucrats who serve it, and the schoolteachers who encourage the young to believe in it. All these had their medieval counterparts. The services of the clergy in secular affairs, though often represented as an abuse or an affront, may even seem natural and desirable if it is remembered that the modern state has only earned a reputation for benevolence by seizing from the churches responsibility for education, hospitals, almshouses and poor-relief, because it was the church which has made them seem indispensible to civil life. The thirteenth-century 'state' which the clergy served was very different in character from the modern one; rulers had no ambition to extend the field of their activities into concerns of the church and were happy to borrow clergy for their administrations: nor did it bother them that the church had a monopoly of training learned clerks.

His coronation oath committed the king to defend the church, punish the wicked and uphold peace, mercy and justice: vague terms that served their purpose in turning a feudal magnate into a public person. How could the churchmen be of most help to the kings in discharging these obligations? Their most considerable contribution came in the staffing of the greatly enlarged administrative apparatus of government, which kings developed to improve their judicial services and to harness the resources of their kingdoms for more effective warfare against evildoers at home and abroad. Enforcement of justice was not a royal monopoly; the king only guaranteed that justice would be done. But, by opening his court to the privileged, the king encouraged resort to it by influential and determined litigants. This encouraged the growth of royal justice, learning and judicial ingenuity. The learned clergy had much to contribute and supported extensions of royal authority which seemed to offer more equitable justice. Thanks to them the courts of justice became learned and literate. The clergy appreciated more than secular lords how vulnerable their lands and persons were to secular pressures and strengthened the king as much as they could. Unwittingly they were drawn into creating an apparatus of state which would eventually trap them more cruelly than the traditional kingships of the past, because they had sold away their power to defend themselves.

The survival of written records tends to obscure the fact that royal palaces continued to be overrun by laymen attending to the king's person, his household, his stables and his messages. Despite the numbers of lay officials and servants, the clergy had two incontrovertible advantages over laymen for certain kinds of post. First there could be no question of sons of clergy claiming some right to succeed to their father's office, as commonly happened in the case of laymen; the new clergy were celibate; employing them delivered kings from the problem of servants who used office to benefit their families. Second, the clergy could be 'paid' by the assignment of ecclesiastical benefices, of which the king had a reserve in his gift. In effect, they cost the king nothing; the church paid for the king's servants, so that, though laymen could, of course, acquire the skills of clerks and notaries, clergy were preferred in those functions. Great prelates served on embassies and courts of legal inquiry. The drudgery of routine business fell to humble clerks, whose assiduity could in due course earn them the dignity of a bishopric, for they brought to their offices a conscientious desire to give satisfaction within the narrow compass assigned to them. Henry II's treasurer, Richard Fitz-Nigel, took pride in the scrupulous fulfilment of his charge, without further thought about how the king spent the money gathered in by bureaucratic effort. He became bishop of London. He is the twelfth-century clerk who wrote the only description of a government department — a remarkable instance of how the clerks were serving the monarchy.

4. THE EMPIRE

The numerous small kingdoms of Europe have so engrossed modern historical attention that there is some danger of forgetting that in the twelfth century the only secular state of universal significance was still the empire. It was by far the largest state territorially. It occupied the heart lands of Christendom. All the kingdoms, with the exception of France, were found only on the periphery and had no power to dispute the emperor's preeminence. The empire had the most glorious traditions and far-reaching pretensions. Some of its rulers, like Frederick I or

Frederick II, outshone all their contemporaries in personal dignity and prestige. In retrospect the empire has been treated as a problem. Nationalist historians in Germany regretted that the brilliant promise of the Staufen did not result in a national state, like France. The nefarious consequences of taking the French example as a model for nation-building distorted German politics throughout the nineteenth century and prejudiced assessment of the medieval empire. Until the late eleventh century, there had been no alternative political theory for the whole of Europe. The Germans inherited the empire from the past and had been proud to succeed the Franks, the Greeks and *their* predecessors as wielders of the universal state. Not until the quarrel with the papacy were serious doubts first cast upon the emperor's role in Christendom. Reform raised the possibility of a spiritual government, in which the emperor was a mere executant of papal instructions. Few emperors stomached the implications of this, even if lesser monarchs had fewer inhibitions about compromise with it. Emperors fumbled in devising an alternative theory; their indecision weakened their credibility, as they tried to perpetuate the old and discredited tradition, yet come to terms at the same time with the undoubted power of the popes. Barbarossa tried to turn Charlemagne into the founding father of the Holy Empire and obtained canonization for his predecessor from his anti-pope in 1165. Frederick II revived the memory of the universal claims of his Roman predecessors. Even after his death and that of his son (1254), the Germans still did not abandon the concept of empire and work instead for a German kingdom, though this seemingly reasonable solution was indeed advocated by Humbert de Romans, the canonist, at the Council of Lyons in 1274, because the empire *quasi ad nihilum est redactum*.[16] The empire proved more resilient than he expected.

After the triumphant revival of the empire by Otto I in 962, the Germans occupied the leading place in European affairs and in relations with the papacy. The empire comprised three distinct kingdoms, the East Frankish kingdom, Burgundy and the kingdom of Italy conquered by Charlemagne from the Lombards in 774. What did the 'empire' mean to its German proprietors? The Roman past might convey something in the Rhineland or south of the Danube, but most of Germany had no historic links with Rome, nor even with Charlemagne, who had travelled no further east than Saxony and Bavaria. 'Germany' as a concept had no precise meaning. There was no common Germanic hero, as Clovis was for the Franks, to act as a barbarian royal prototype for a later kingdom. Germany was not united by its past. It was because it was still growing as a 'community' until the fourteenth century, that it was convenient to use the idea of the Christian empire to provide it with a respectable framework for its activities.

It is not the diversities of Germany that need to be stressed first. The other kingdoms of the empire — Burgundy and Italy — were no less composite in character. Yet whereas those kingdoms did in fact disintegrate during this period, Germany did not. It willed to survive as a community, in spite of its heterogeneous composition.

Germany

The core of the Carolingian empire had been the Rhineland. Successive German kings of other dynasties fostered the imperial traditions of Aachen, Frankfurt, the great Rhineland cities and bishoprics. Their hold on Italy, which had originally depended on access up the Rhine, through Swabia and through the province of Salzburg into the march of Verona, had been strengthened by the acquisition of the kingdom of Burgundy in 1037 and the county of Burgundy by Frederick Barbarossa in 1156. Under the Swabian Hohenstaufen therefore the empire comprised not only the expanding East Frankish realm, but also most of the Middle Kingdom, as defined by the Verdun agreements of 843.

Although as a matter of fact the Staufen empire was disrupted principally by the attitude of the papacy, it is arguable that an empire centred on Swabia would have found difficulty anyway, as German interests expanded eastwards. When the Emperor Conrad III went to the Holy Land in 1147, the Saxons, who had once shared the imperial dreams of the Ottonians, conducted their own crusade against the Wends. Later under their duke, Henry the Lion, they put their own ambitions in northern Germany before those of the empire and emperor in Italy. There was an inherent problem about maintaining the traditional universal empire together with an expansive, colonial movement.

The story of German expansion in eastern Europe has not been popularly understood and has been wilfully misrepresented by nationalist passions in recent times. The advance into Bohemia brought the Slavs there into permanent association with the empire. The later penetration of Silesia by the Luxembourg rulers of Bohemia gave the empire an important non-German element there too. The Teutonic Order, which consolidated its hold on the Baltic littoral in the fourteenth century, brought other non-German peoples into the 'empire'. But the Germans too were on the move as settlers, as well as 'exploiters'. The present state of East Germany itself, between the Elbe and the Oder, was colonized and annexed by Germans in the period between 1134 and 1250 when the march of Brandenburg was established. Such key cities as Lübeck and Hamburg only became imperial cities at this same time. This gives some measure of the concern in Germany for 'imperial' expansion and explains their comparative indifference to the Italian imperialism of the southern Germans. How could any single ruler hope to hold together all the divergent interests of the Germans?

The diversity was not merely one of old and new lands. The old lands also knew of rivalries going back centuries into the pagan past, like those which divided Lorrainers from Swabians and Bavarians. And new differences came to divide the Germans. The traditional divisions of Germany in the tenth century had been duchies, supposedly of tribal, that is racial, origin, which the Ottonians had begun to undermine: the last independent duchy, Saxony, was broken up in 1180. The administrative divisions that replaced them were the counties. These had been used under the Ottonians in particular to provide local powers for bishops (the chief officials of the empire before the papal quarrel) and most extensively applied in lands where the emperor was strongest, like Swabia and Franconia. The disputes with the papacy and the parallel growth of opposition to bishops in some towns, compromised the success of this policy which never succeeded in imposing a complete comital system. By the twelfth century too, feudal ideas of landholding jurisdiction and dependent vassaldom had penetrated deeply into some territories, particularly those most influenced by the Carolingians, that is Lower Lorraine and Bavaria. This accentuated the differences with northern Germany where, in Frisia and Saxony, there were no original feudal institutions. Frisia remained a land of free peasantry, where justice was enforced in a public court, not by feudal lords, and armies of foot-soldiers still effectively took the field. So the formulae of Frankish feudalism had no general currency in Germany and the ceremony of homage could be seen there as a sign of humiliating servility.

Germany was also a land without uniform legal institutions; there was no body of public law until Frederick I's reign. The emperors made no general attempt to impose public peace on a countywide basis in the Länder until 1235 so that in the meantime what was necessary had been improvised locally either by powerful princes and landowners or by the existing courts, sometimes at the hundred or parish level, usurping jurisdiction from absentee counts. By the early thirteenth century some of these territorial laws were sufficiently crystallized to attain written form. The most important of these was the (East) Saxon code, the Sachsenspiegel of Erich von Repgow (1221-24), written at a time when the Staufen empire was still a powerful force for centralization. It therefore recognizes the place of the king as the supreme judge in legal matters. It proved to be a popular and exemplary work all over Germany. Friesland, which had no prince of its own, had nevertheless before 1200 also formulated statements of some of its customs and maintained an authority to preserve them — the Upstalsborner Bund (1231). During the thirteenth century the compilation of written laws for the territories consolidated local feeling around the idea of maintaining agreed custom and laws, and this arrested the process of legal disintegration and reduced the chance of Germany becoming a federation of villages. In Germany, as in Italy, the towns proved most capable of maintaining their independence, but increasingly here too, laws were borrowed by one town from another so that families of town-law, of Cologne, Lübeck or Magdeburg, reduced institutional differences between them. Germany was however less a land of towns than of countries (Länder). The spread of country-land-laws did not create uniform *land* institutions. In the more highly feudalized lands, the powers of the count and his officials diminished the participation of the others; elsewhere, as in the Tyrol and Baden, peasants attended meetings of the local *landtage,* in which judicial business was despatched. In public business, therefore, Germans behaved very differently according to their locality.

Nor did the language help. If a modern nation usually owes its unity to its common language, the problems of creating a common written language out of diverse forms of the spoken dialects do not seem to be much appreciated (even if critics are sensitive to the significance of differences of pronunciation for causing social barriers). Princes encouraged a courtly German literature under the Staufen emperors, which admittedly gave Germany a common language, based on the Bavarian-Swabian dialect and used even by northern authors for literature and social refinement. Low German dialect, though written, especially in town chronicles and charters, never became a means of 'literary' expression, except significantly 'outside' the empire, in fourteenth-century Dutch. What linguistic unity Germany had at a cultural level was dependent on the work of the Staufen period. Courtly literature consolidated earlier efforts to produce literature of secular interest, and it did so without drawing exclusively upon the French *roman courtois.* But there were limits to its usefulness. The vernacular language did not serve politically for documents until 1235 when the Mainz Land Peace was published in German;[17] even the Sachsenspiegel was originally written in Latin. German was not in regular use in the archives of the imperial court until the fourteenth century. In fact the retention of Latin not merely perpetuated the traditions of the Roman empire; it was the only language universally used and understood throughout the German kingdom; the Germans were the true heirs of Rome.

The Staufen empire[18]

Against this confused background, we should not underestimate Frederick I, Barborossa, (1152-90) though he was defeated in Italy and thwarted in Germany. He still towered head and shoulders above all his contemporaries in the twelfth century. Europe did not then measure its rulers by the numbers of their battalions or their gold reserves but by dignity, prestige and personal distinction. By all these standards Barbarossa easily outshone his rivals. This need not mean that he was satisfied with the empire he succeeded to. He was the first German emperor to live in the period of intellectual renewal and papal leadership in the church. He sensed that new forces could work for good or ill in the empire. Though the intellectual advantages may seem to lie already with France by 1152, Frederick had as distinguished a group of courtiers as any more western king: Otto of Freising, his uncle, one of the finest historians of the twelfth century, Rainald of Dassel archbishop of Cologne, his chancellor, Anselm of Havelberg the theologian, and the important professors of Roman law at Bologna. His son Henry VI was a distinguished poet in whose era German chivalrous poetry attained an unprecedented height and outclassed its nearest poetic rivals, the troubadour poetry of Provence.

The Staufen empire was in its time more brilliant that the kingdoms of the Capetians or Plantagenets, though, unlike these latter, it did not survive for more than a hundred years. The Staufen dynasty did not overreach itself by grasping too much power. The chief reason for its collapse was the implacable hatred vowed by the papacy to the Staufen dynasty. As the lustre of the empire under Frederick II grew, the popes, particularly Gregory IX and Innocent IV, came to believe that the papacy would lose its real independence if the universal state continued. It is therefore beside the point to argue that the empire was fundamentally flawed in not becoming an hereditary monarchy like the other states of Christendom. In 1274, after all the dangers of elections had become manifest, Jordan of Osnabrück, the enthusiastic German publicist, could still write that 'Non enim convenit, sanctuarium Dei id est regnum ecclesie jure hereditario possideri'.[19] The dignity of the empire, as well as papal interest, dictated election in every generation.

All the same, the Staufen, like their successors, were not blind to the advantages for their own families of an hereditary monarchy however unusual this still was: in 1152 the French king had no son to succeed him and in England, the claims of Stephen's son were set aside in favour of those of Henry Plantagenet, who had consistently defied Stephen. Rulers realized the personal advantages for their own houses and had no need to be exhorted to work for their children's succession. Frederick's son Henry VI succeeded him unchallenged in 1190. And Henry's son Frederick would certainly have succeeded him without question in 1197, but for his youth and for Innocent III's interference. The following ten years showed that Innocent had nothing to gain from trying to pick a docile candidate of his own, for the Welf Otto IV, chosen as rival to the Staufen in Germany, proved every bit as troublesome in Italy as his predecessors. Innocent III repudiated him and sent the young Frederick to Germany for election. Frederick secured the election of his son Henry as his successor in 1220, admittedly by making concessions—but these did not inhibit the young Henry's government. If in the long run the Staufen did not build an hereditary monarchy it was not for want of trying. It might on the contrary be argued that they had pursued this objective so successfully that Pope Innocent IV himself had to swear to exterminate the whole brood of vipers. In their own way, the Staufen did provide, as long as they could, the advantages of leadership and continuity offered by one family. They linked together their own lands by a personal bond, just as their contemporaries, the Plantagenets, did in the west.

Frederick Barbarossa married Beatrice of Burgundy and revived the meaning of empire in those lands. His own duchy, Swabia, lay at the centre of his power—Strasbourg lies about half way between Utrecht and Verona or between Magdeburg and Lyon. The most troublesome part of the empire was in northern Italy, where, since the loss of imperial control over bishops (1122) and the rise of independent town communes, the emperor found no secure basis for support. The popes were not in his time utterly opposed to the revival of imperial government, for the spread of heresy had shaken papal self-confidence, even at Rome itself. However, popes could not on that account refuse to countenance alliance with the emperor's rebellious Lombard communes. Frederick I overconfidently espoused the cause of the papal candidate he thought more subservient to himself in the disputed election of 1159. Thus a local problem became a schism in Christendom. Frederick's Italian policy was in the long run unsuccessful. He had to acknowledge Alexander III and recognize the right of the communes to elect their own officials. Frederick's position in Italy was not irremediably compromised and the chance of improving it came when the king of Sicily died without sons in 1192, leaving his aunt Constance with the best claim to the succession. She was already married to Henry VI, who made good his claims in 1194. Thus he realized the ancient imperial dream of extending the bounds of the empire throughout the whole of Italy, which had eluded the Carolingians and his German predecessors. The kingdom of Sicily was technically a papal vassal-state, but the papacy exercised no prerogatives there until 1197 when Henry VI died, leaving the custody of his son Frederick to the pope. This made papal intervention in the kingdom feasible for the very first time. Cheated as a boy of the empire, Frederick nevertheless retained the loyalty of the Germans who educated him in Sicily until eventually in 1213, at the age of nineteen, he became master of the lands and rights of both his mother and father.

Frederick II is not known to us through the account of a sympathetic biographer as Louis IX is. He is often therefore presented more as a figure out of sympathy with his time, more at ease with his fellow rulers in Islam than with the Christian kings, and more interested in the companionship of men of secular learning than in the advice of his bishops. It is probably wiser to remember how conventional Frederick II could be instead of building upon the gossip of hostile contemporaries.[20] Like Louis IX, the emperor found time for his own interests: his treatise on falconry establishes him as a sportsman-naturalist acceptable in the masculine · company of both Christian and Muslim societies. The haughtiness, that we associate with his zeal to revive the Roman empire in all its glory, came as much from his parents, the arrogant Henry VI of Staufen and the Junoesque Constance, heiress of Norman Sicily. Whatever wishful thinking he may have indulged from time to time, he seems to have behaved in each of his lands, Germany, Italy, and in his Sicilian kingdom as was expected of him, not attempting to do more than custom allowed, but using his authority, as his contemporaries did, to make the most of his royal position. In spite of the hostility shown by the papacy, his dominions did not show unusual disloyalty till his very last years and had his son not died within four years of him, the empire might well have survived. It was not inevitably doomed. It did of course present rather a different problem from the kingdoms of England and France. In particular it is not so easy to see how Frederick might have combined both his northern and southern kingdoms into an effective whole without alienating the papacy which disliked and feared Frederick's abilities as a ruler.

Geographically, it might seem inevitable that the papacy would resist the unification of the peninsula under one lord; even so, individual persons and single events also helped to influence the outcome. For the project had existed potentially from the time of Henry VI's marriage to Constance in 1186 and this too was only the final stage of a policy pursued by the western emperor for centuries, intermittently at first, but with some persistence in the twelfth century, to make the authority of the western emperor acknowledged in the old Byzantine provinces of southern Italy. The effect on the papacy could have been anticipated, yet the popes, though wary, did not consistently oppose it altogether, *a priori*. Innocent III, when desperate to find a rival to Otto IV, could only think of Frederick of Sicily and the sole safeguard he obtained was a promise that when convenient Frederick should set up his son in Sicily and separate it from the empire; this basic arrangement, though modified, was confirmed by his successor Honorius III. This would still have left the pope in a very uncomfortable position, but popes saw no alternative at the time. Only with Pope Gregory IX (1227-41) did the papacy move to a position of irreconcilable enmity, when Frederick proved that he would not be the obedient minister of papal aims.

Frederick II was the last great emperor, because he was the first king to show he had a mind of his own and would not be directed by the pope. For though Frederick may personally have been inspired by the imperial title he bore, it was not as emperor that he found the strength for opposition to the pope, but in the kingdom of Sicily, where he built upon the work of his Norman predecessors. This kingdom had been brought into being when his grandfather Roger II, forced the barons of southern Italy and Sicily into feudal dependence, though behind this lay some centuries of political institutions in the previous Muslim and Greek administrations. Roger had himself also learned from contemporary Constantinople. This enabled Frederick to exploit his resources in a manner quite without parallel elsewhere in Europe, except in England. The Sicilian kingdom had wrested reluctant recognition from the papacy but had rapidly fallen prey to adventurers from the north, of whom the Staufen were the latest, the greediest and the most successful. Under Frederick II these resources were for the first time made available for a ruler of ability with ambitions beyond the frontiers of southern Italy. Under Gregory IX, Frederick II was the only king able to master resources of men and money for royal purposes without needing papal assistance in the government of his realm. Gregory feared a king who would never be one among many defenders of the church. The kingdom must be wrested from the empire.

Frederick II was almost, if not quite, master of Italy as well as Germany. His weakest point was that he could not dispense with papal recognition and was unable to create his own popes. After Gregory IX's death, he failed to secure the election of a papal candidate favourable to him. He altogether lost control of the papacy when Innocent IV slipped out of Italy and settled at Lyon. This was technically still an imperial city, but he was safe there from the emperor and close to French protection. In Lyon, Innocent IV decided to excommunicate and depose Frederick, provoking the election of inadequate anti-kings in Germany and looking for a suitable prince to conquer the kingdom of Sicily. For a time the prospect of an English king of Sicily deceived both the popes and King Henry III of England, until in 1258 the baronial revolt brutally put an end to these illusions. Peace between Henry III and Louis IX opened the way for Louis's youngest brother, Charles of Anjou, ruler of Provence in the right of his wife, who was inveigled into Italy in 1264. Louis IX had for a long time resisted these entanglements, so that when Charles eventually departed it was without imposing forces. All the same he swept all before him in the battles of Benevento (1266) and Tagliacozzo (1268) and the papacy was then faced in Charles with as formidable a rule of Italy as Frederick had been. Charles as ruler of Provence and Sicily sufficiently over-awed the whole peninsula.

As if to demonstrate the papal dilemma, the cardinals proved unable to find a replacement for Pope Clement IV (died 1268) until 1271. In these circumstances the new pope, Gregory X, saw no alternative to reviving the empire if the balance of forces in Italy was to be restored and the new Sicilian king checked. The papacy had moved full circle.

The German federation

In the years since his predecessor Innocent IV had called on the Germans princes to overthrow the Staufen, the only part of the empire which had obstinately retained some respect for the past was Germany, or more accurately the German princes, and so it was to them that Gregory appealed in 1273 when Richard of Cornwall, the nominal emperor died. The German monarchy could never have survived the extinction of the Staufen dynasty had it not been for the determination of the princes to preserve it. Innocent IV had found minor princes to take the royal title — he was powerless to defend the monarchy as such. The result of their insignificance was that in 1257 there were only 'foreign' princes who aspired to the title; the king of Castile whose mother was a Staufen, and Richard Earl of Cornwall, a relation of the Welfs. At this point a group of electoral princes made its formal appearance as a committee entrusted with the task of choosing a new emperor.[21]

Within the complicated network of German political society, some great men built up powerful units by taking into their hands local jurisdictions and privileges obtained from kings, such as the right to strike coinage, collect tolls, hunt or fish in protected areas and to fortify castles. The beginnings of princely power in this sense may be traced to Frederick Barbarossa's reign. The charter for Austria (1156) became a model for other princes, like the powers granted to the bishop of Würzburg (1168) or to the archbishop of Cologne over Westphalia (1180). In this way the emperor assembled in Germany a comparatively small number of princes through whose sworn loyalty to himself the empire was held together. It was an attempt to use a Frankish form of royal feudalism to unite Germany.

At first concessions were made to individual princes as special favours, but after the death of Henry VI in 1197 and the confusion about the succession, rival candidates had to make more far-reaching concessions. When Frederick II became king in 1212 he was obliged to confirm such grants in return for recognition. Frederick like his Staufen predecessors intended to secure the imperial title for his son and he bought confirmation of the 'hereditary' right from the ecclesiastical princes in 1220. This was the first time that concessions had been made to a 'class' of princes and it served as a precedent for a privilege to the secular princes in 1232.[22] As in England, the self-conscious churchmen had led the way in obtaining royal privileges and creating a basis of common agreement, which enabled the princes to see their common interests and not stress their personal differences. The creation of this princely element under Frederick II did not blatantly hinder the emperor in his lifetime. After 1254, when the last Staufen emperor Conrad IV died, a new responsibility obviously fell to the princes, as the only formal group capable of taking on the empire. At the imperial election of 1257 the group of princes left seven of their number to speak on their behalf — the three Rhineland archbishops (Mainz, Cologne, Trier), the Count Palatine of the Rhine and the three major secular rulers of the centre, Saxony, Brandenburg, and Bohemia. This is the first formal appearance of the 'college' of electors. In 1257 the four Rhineland electoral princes felt most strongly about the continuation of the empire and they elected Richard of Cornwall because of Rhenish links with England and Richard's Welf family connexions. The 'German' kingdom then showed that it could act without a king or dynasty and that it continued to will its own collective existence.

Not all the territories of the empire wished to recognize the elected king. Richard had no authority outside the Rhineland, where the strongest sentiment for the empire could be found. If the wider concept of empire was to retain any meaning, it was obviously desirable to command the loyalty of the German princes further east, where despite the vacuum in the monarchy, the energies of the German peoples were still overflowing. The most powerful prince in this area was the king of Bohemia, Ottokar II, who took advantage of the weakness of the monarch to seize the lands of Austria and Tyrol after the death of the last duke, and who hoped to succeed Richard as king. Ottokar's ambitions were frustrated by the other German princes who could not accept him as their ruler, probably, above all, because as a Czech he did not seem to them acceptable as German king. All the same it is true that Bohemia was becoming the major state of central Europe: it was one of the principal European sources of gold and silver, its mining resources were already opened up and new towns beginning to flourish. (Thwarted in the empire, Ottokar's immediate heirs still had energy enough to turn on Poland.) However the manifest importance of winning central Europe for the empire in 1273 made it necessary to find a new king from the imperial west capable of defeating Ottokar. This was Rudolf of Habsburg, Count of Aargau. In 1276 he took back Austria and Tyrol, granting them to his son Albert. He became the first of several kings chosen in the west who moved firmly into central Europe and made their families permanently powerful by this means. Whatever intentions Rudolf may have had for going to Italy were swallowed up by the absorbing concerns of Germany itself, concerns not unknown under the Staufen. Moreover in the process

Rudolf found himself transformed from being the head of a small county family with its bases in Swabia and Alsace, into the head of a powerful dynasty based on Austria which was not badly placed for imperial advance into Italy as well. Rudolf's heir Albert was however more attracted by the possibility of succeeding to his northern neighbour in Bohemia, just as the Bohemian king himself had been involved in claims to the kingdom of Poland and the lands of Silesia. The control of Bohemia was becoming a vital question of German politics.

Forced to accept the facts of imperial weakness after Frederick II's death in 1250. 'the Germans' had nevertheless continued to vest their confidence in the idea of the empire. The electoral college is sometimes accused of holding back German unity; it would be truer to say that it kept the Germans together within the only existing framework they had. The commitments of emperors outside Germany admittedly diminished after 1273, but they were never totally renounced. If the idea of empire survived best in German lands it was because the Germans remained most loyal to the concept and because it had over the centuries become the best means of keeping the Germans in particular together. They had only to glance at the chaos of Italy, in the absence of an Italian kingdom, to foresee the dangers in store for Germany if even the notion of empire was abandoned. The consolidation of Germany as the surviving 'rump' of the empire involved serious modifications in the style of imperial government; the more German it became, the less interest was taken in it by the other nominal parts of the empire, like Italy. However, the adaptation of the empire for German purposes gave the Germans a permanent interest in the imperial idea, which others, at the time, rather mistakenly, despised.

5. THE KINGDOM OF FRANCE

According to Joannes Teutonicus, *c.*1215-20, the king of France was still *de jure* subject to the Roman emperor because the emperor was *princeps totius mundi.* He recognized that in the various *provinciis* of the empire there were *diversi reges sub eo constituti sunt,* but those who would not recognize their place in the Roman empire would lose the benefits of Roman law, such as inheritance.[23] It did not occur to him that other laws might guarantee inheritance or that acceptance of part of the Roman legal doctrine might not demand submission to the Roman emperor. This opinion is somewhat strange since Innocent III in the effective vacancy of the empire had granted the king of France, Philip II Augustus, the privilege *Per Venerabilem* of being 'emperor' in his own kingdom (1202), though it concedes perhaps Joannes's main point that to be sovereign it was necessary to be emperor. In practice the emperor Frederick II (1212-50), the last great emperor to assert himself in

Europe, never attempted to subordinate the French kings to his empire. He owed his own triumph over his Welf rivals to the Capetian victory at Bouvines in 1214. Philip Augustus, however, took no chances and obtained from Pope Honorius III in 1219 an order suppressing the teaching of Roman law in Paris. For him, Roman law was still an instrument of imperial pressure. One of Philip IV's advisers, Pierre de Belleperche (died 1308) was still of the theoretical opinion that the emperor was *de jure dominus cunctorum* and in such a legal age, this admission was significant.

If the theoretical situation of the French monarchy looked precarious in the thirteenth century, historians might well pause before assessing how powerful really was this monarchy, that had been held for over two hundred years by direct descent in the same family. Philip II himself felt the monarchy strong enough to dispense with the traditional ceremony of crowning his son while he was still living, a device that had secured the succession for the previous seven generations. In practical terms, the monarchy of Philip II more than doubled the size of territory directly subject to the king by the conquest of Plantagenet lands and the acquisition of estates in the south which brought the king of France to the Mediterranean sea as well. Within a century, royal ambitions had extended French government to fiefs long independent, like Flanders, and to territories of the empire like Lyon which had never been part of the kingdom before. The growing confidence of the French monarchy throughout the thirteenth century enabled it not only to try and capitalize its own feudal assets, but to draw into its wake the insecure western fragments of the empire.

Gerard d'Abbeville in 1265 declared that royal power is 'potestas sublimior, et maxime regni Franci quia sicut dixit capitulum Rex Francie superiorem non cognoscit'. The emperor Richard of Cornwall would not have challenged the real supremacy of Louis IX of France, who had been invoked as arbiter in the quarrel between Richard's brother King Henry III of England and his barons in 1264. Louis had not set out to make France the greatest state of Christendom, but, after the collapse of the Staufen empire, greatness was thrust upon France, and with it new responsibilities and ambitions, for which the kingdom was ill-prepared.

The strongest feature of the monarchy was the ruling dynasty, which had by the thirteenth century developed a unique consciousness of its obligations and instilled throughout the kingdom a respect for the royal office as an inherited charge above the reach of baronial ambition. The full significance of this achievement may not be realized, if the institution of hereditary monarchy be taken as normal. The Capetians were the only dynasty before the thirteenth century to succeed in keeping the monarchy in their undisputed hands; it was only their exceptional success which established this as an example for all European monarchies. From the time when Hugh Capet had his heir Robert crowned in 987 the coronation was nothing more than a device to establish the same rights over the monarchical office as the great feudatories claimed over their fiefs. Likewise the king's effective power was confined to his own estates until the time of Philip Augustus, and the royal domain was no more than a great fief. The dynasty at first had not grasped after greater responsibility. Kings quarrelled frequently with their heirs and allowed personal rancour to threaten the continuity of the crown. Henry I fought his father Robert II and Philip I alienated the affections of his son Louis VI.

Respect for the kingship outside the royal domain depended particularly upon the loyalty of some of the bishops who invoked the king's help in their disputes with local feudatories. The abbey of St Denis nurtured the idea of monarchy through the eleventh century, as a special part of its own tradition about Denis, who was regarded as the the apostle of the Gauls. The monastery perpetuated the memory of the great Merovingian and Carolingian kings who had endowed the monastery richly, far beyond the limits of the Capetian royal domain. Capetian protection of the church of St Martin at Tours also enabled them to call upon the loyalty of the clergy there who kept alive the sense of the national mission of St Martin to the Franks. The traditions of the church of Rheims also emphasized links between the coronation of the Capetians and the original mission of the Frankish king Clovis, baptised by St Remy of Rheims. Around the French kings of the eleventh century there circulated heroic poetry which nostalgically celebrated the exploits of Charlemagne and gave the Franks some inkling of their national destiny. Enlarging upon these legendary elements, Abbot Suger of St Denis, a friend of King Louis VI, who was regent of the kingdom for Louis VII while he went on crusade, not only rebuilt his abbey church to enhance the reputation of his saintly patron, but also by his writing established at St Denis a tradition of royal historiography. Thus the monarchy could draw on several streams of sympathy that flowed, not from their personal merits and achievements, but from the aspirations of the great clergy and nobility.

The twelfth-century monarchs were hardly great heroes; the monarchy's survival seemed doubtful. Louis VI (1108-37) spent his reign in ceaseless campaigning on his own royal domain to subject the minor nobility to obedience, exploits which even Abbot Suger could not invest with heroic proportions. Louis VII (1137-80) went on crusade, but did not leave one heroic exploit worthy of being recounted by the monk of St Denis who accompanied him. At best he could be commended for his sagacity and prudence. Unabashed by the failure of the army at Damascus in 1148, Louis stayed on in the Holy Land to make the round of the Holy Places and on his return to France showed his unflagging zest for religious journeys by pilgrimages to Le Puy, Compostella and Canterbury. His son Philip II also went on crusade, less by inclination than by force of the superior example of his fellow rulers, Barbarossa and Richard I. He did not distinguish himself there and hurried home, where he aroused distaste for his intrigues to secure the capture of his enemy Richard by the German king. Louis VI at first showed little concern for the succession. He reigned eight years before marrying at the age of forty. His son Louis VII obviously worried more about the future, and he is not to be blamed if he reigned 28 years before the birth of his son to his third wife. Until the birth of Philip II in 1165 and the conquests he made from the Plantagenets in 1204, the future of the Capetian monarchy continued to look more problematic to contemporaries than it does to historians. Philip II himself had no son until 1198 and his concern for the reputation of the monarchy was not strong enough to deter him from repudiating his wife and living with another woman despite the censure of the church.

The king of France certainly enjoyed unique respect within the kingdom, even if he did not enjoy real power outside his domain lands. The king was perpetual president of a group of great dignitaries, clerical and lay, who for the most part managed their affairs without recourse to the king.[24] The consolidation of these principalities had proceeded throughout the eleventh century when the kings themselves had had to fight to uphold even their local powers. The most important of them were the counties of Flanders, Vermandois, Champagne, Blois-Chartres, Anjou-Touraine and Normandy. The conquest of England gave the duke of Normandy such preponderance after 1066 that he could be regarded as the most dangerous of the king's vassals. The dukes were on the whole docile, except when provoked, but they had commitments so different from other French counts that they avoided anything more than the most perfunctory respect to the French king. As kings themselves they found it irksome to acknowledge feudal vassalage to the Capetians and tried to dodge the crucial ceremonies. The power of Normandy weighed upon the politics of the Loire valley in particular. French kings supported Anjou against Normandy for possession of Maine, in an effort to prevent Norman dominance. These calculations were overturned when Henry I made an alliance with Anjou. His grandson Henry Plantagenet thus acquired all the lands of England, Normandy, Anjou, and Blois, and also had the gall to marry Louis VII's divorced wife Eleanor and take on her lands of Poitou and Aquitaine as well. Louis VII lived in his own kingdom in the shadow of a much greater king, of more energy, intelligence and ambition. Henry never tried to appropriate the French crown, and had he done so, the other feudatories of France would have opposed him. All the same, Louis VII was excluded from west France and could only intrigue with Henry II's wilful sons or fall back on the support of Champagne, the county of his third wife Adela, mother of Philip II, and on Flanders.

It suited the feudatories to have a royal court to resolve their quarrels and foster their grandiose illusions, but monarchy made no real impact on the kingdom. France was at this time bursting with creative energy — religious literary and economic — but it derived no inspiration from kings. Apart from Suger at St Denis no chroniclers kept an interested eye upon royal activity, for there was none. The royal court itself kept little note of its own doings. The accounts for 1202 show that the king's officials were regularly called to court; the king kept some copies of his most important grants, and from the time of Philip Augustus the business of the monarchy comes within historical scrutiny. No regular record was kept of the activity of royal clerks on rolls or in registers, as was the case in England from the 1190s and throughout the thirteenth century the chief royal clerk was a mere keeper of the seal and not dignified with the title 'chancellor'. But the king of France, in spite of the considerable limitations of his power, had two incontrovertible advantages over his Plantagenet enemies: he enjoyed the unquestioning obedience of his own family, and his revenues were more than adequate to his ambitions.[25]

A new phase opens with Philip Augustus. He owed his resounding success to the blunders of John, whom he had recognized as Richard I's successor in 1199 in preference to the youthful Arthur. Arthur might have seemed a more pliable candidate than John, but the cunning Philip realized that John in opposition would be more dangerous than John the committed vassal. John did not take long to provide Philip with an excuse to summon him to the royal court to answer the complaints of his barons (as it happened from the Limousin March), and when he failed to appear Philip confiscated his lands. John had intended only to secure nominal recognition of his contested claims from the king; he had in fact forfeited his moral independence. There was nothing extraordinary about Philip's procedure. At first only the power of his vassal made the case exceptional; but when he very swiftly followed up the sentence of the court, drove John out of Normandy and annexed his lands, a complete revolution was accomplished. A similar situation had brought about the exile of Barbarossa's chief enemy Henry the Lion, John's brother-in-law in 1180, but Barbarossa had not been able to obtain possessions of his lands, which had passed to the princes. Philip kept the Plantagenet lands and added them to the royal domain, lands rich in both money and talent. The king of France at one stroke disposed of his chief enemy and doubled his resources. After ten years of effort, John lost all hope of recovering them. The vast league he organized to oppose the Capetians was defeated at Bouvines in 1214. John himself was not present but he had staked and lost all by his own diplomacy. No one could have guessed that Philip would prove so successful or John so incapable of defending lands previously loyal to his father and brother. Philip should have been astonished at his own luck. He personally was not covetous. He declined to intervene in southern France against Albigensian heretics; nor did he, as his son Louis VIII did later, deprive John's son Henry of Poitou, while the king was still a minor and unable to defend it—an act of un-Christian aggression. Between 1204 and 1229 the French monarchy came into an impressive inheritance of lands and responsibilities that gave it unchallengeable authority over all the princes of northern France and capacious lands in the south as well: two *sénéchaussées* in Carcassone and Beaucaire. This gave the king a direct interest in the affairs of his vassal, the count of Toulouse. Philip Augustus first used consistently the title *rex Franciae* in place of *rex Francorum* from 1204. The change brought about in the monarchy in one generation was therefore unprepared and enormous. It remained to be seen how the dynasty would cope with these new responsibilities.

The first king to succeed his father without preliminary coronation was Louis VIII. He died after three years, leaving these problems to his infant son, Louis IX (1226-70) and his widow, Blanche of Castile, granddaughter of Henry II. Louis VIII also left a large family to be provided for, with instructions about how to do this from the now vastly extended domain. So St Louis was brought up to face political problems of an unprecedented nature with little traditional wisdom to help him.

Louis IX presided more than forty years over this new France.[26] He was by all accounts the most unworldly of men, but no saintly imbecile. He gave the French monarchy a sense of unassuming superiority which hardly ever betrayed it. The king of France held the kingdom together almost by his presence alone, assembling the new pieces and supplying the fervour and the articulation that enabled them to live together in one body politic. His vassals had nothing in common with one another except their relation to the king and the state had therefore only one institution: the monarchy. Louis did not make this monarchy out of nothing, but he gave it a shape and purpose quite different from the monarchy of feudal association that had grown up in the eleventh and twelfth centuries and of which Philip Augustus was the last and greatest representative. After his death, as a canonized saint, Louis continued to be the patron of France and of the dynasty.

St Louis' monarchy was based upon the religious duty of the king as God's representative to govern. The French monarchy normally worked in close cooperation with the church and the papacy. Occasional quarrels were not allowed by either side to get out of hand, as even the trifling disagreements between emperors or popes often did. This religious function of kingship was nothing new in itself, but Louis IX wore the traditional cloak of religious kingship with a difference. His mother Blanche of Castile had moulded him to be the traditional pious ruler his father had been; only in the course of the 1240s and 1250s did his own particular qualities begin to show him as a man of greater resource and devotion. He was increasingly carried away by the demands for practical Christianity made by the friars in the thirteenth century, and more than any of his predecessors or contemporaries he attempted to realize the demands of the Christian religion in the practice of his government.

Modern investigators may expect the king to have been more active, as though fussiness could have helped society to better governance at the time, but the king had little to do. He could for this reason devote much of his time to planning and conducting campaigns against the infidel: against Egypt in 1248-54 and against Tunis in 1270. Louis IX still thought of his duty as king more as an obligation to assist Christendom as a whole than as limited obligation within his own kingdom. Not that he neglected the latter. A general inquiry into administrative abuses before he first left France in 1247 demonstrated his eagerness to do his duty, and disclosed how little his subjects had to fear from his officials.[27] When he planned a second expedition twenty years later, he was told by the Sire de Joinville, no less, that he should rather concern himself with his obligations at home and not abandon the kingdom. Joinville himself came to see that there was much to be done at home. The king's barons required him to attend to their common interests, even if Christendom itself should suffer because of it.

This may seem to be putting narrower secular loyalties before wider Christian ones; yet this is to oversimplify. The notions of Christian responsibility were also changing and in a sense the commitment of all rulers to the interests of their dependents likewise reflected the in-fluence of Christian teaching on their more immediate duties. Chris-tianity was becoming more practical and less visionary. Louis IX lived in both worlds. There was nothing reckless about the painstaking care he showed preparing his crusades. The very effort he put into them subse-quently discouraged others who saw that even such great preparations brought no success. Yet the power of organization shown in preparing fleets, victuals and allies and then in transporting, feeding and leading thousands of Frenchmen across the seas demonstrated in itself what the monarchy could do. For less distant goals and idealistic motives such forces could subsequently be assembled by other French kings.

The Crusades and the Inquest may be considered in their different ways as traditional expressions of royal piety. Louis's most surprising innovation was to attract to his court learned friars, Dominicans and Franciscans, who were clearly consulted by him about what they thought a king ought to do and who wrote several treatises for his edification.[28] The literary form was admittedly already familiar, but no other medieval king had so many religious writers engaged on political speculation. This interest may have encouraged the new Latin translation of Aristotle's *Politics* and therefore also stimulated Aquinas's work and the rediscovery of Political Theory as a subject. Aquinas, like other religious writers who took up the question of politics, could not accept that the state had any intrinsic value of its own, because men had an ultimate spiritual destiny and their life on earth affected this. Nevertheless, the ruler was bound to organize the life of his people to make it easier for them to live righteously in this world and so attain beatitude in the next. While the state was a distinct society, subject to the ruler's control, he himself was bound to seek instruction from the church about this ultimate and spiritual goal, which was that of all men. One of Louis IX's advisers characteristically made use of Bernard of Clairvaux's treatise for Pope Eugenius III on papal government, advising Louis to restore peace to the world, to regard his office as a service, not a lordship and to remember that he was only a poor member of the body of which Christ was head. Other advisers set out to provide more detailed advice. The most interesting of them was the polymath Vincent of Beauvais, a Dominican who wrote encyclopaedias and who had been court lecturer in Louis's royal monastic foundation at Royaumont. He tells us that it seemed useful to him to collect together in one volume, but divided into distinct chapters, what he could find in books relating *ad mores principum et curialium,* so that his intention was not merely to cater for the prince, but also for his officials.[29] Vincent knows precisely the men for whom the king is concerned — he specifies princes, knights, counsellors, ministers, *baillis, prévôts* and others, both those resident at court and administrators of public affairs in the provinces. Louis's concern for government went beyond a conventional sense of his responsibilities. He and his team of Dominicans found very little already written in the books to be of any help. Obviously, no one had considered the special duties of the men of court before. These writings are however full of pieties and like Louis's own instructions written for his children, especially his heir Philip III, they stress moral rather than practical issues. Louis' advice to his son on such secular matters as the desirability of having good *prévôts* and *baillis* and making frequent enquiry about them and about the officials of the household, is earnest rather than acute and typically he urges him to refrain from war *sans trop grant conseil* and to imitate St Martin by making peace *au plus tost que tu pourras.*[30]

Apart from the teaching of churchmen, Louis also tried to learn from the example of his predecessors and to leave suitable evidence of his own reign for his successors to profit likewise. To Louis' reign belongs a great collection of historical material used in the *Grandes Chroniques de France* and probably inspired by the king's wish to compile a comprehensive historical work on the French monarchy until the time of his grandfather Philip II.[31] (Oddly enough, he took no steps to have the life of his father Louis VIII written up and this was only done long after his death when the record of his own reign was already written.) Histories of this kind were designed to be exemplary, and not to keep records for their own sake, but Louis IX did also take steps to preserve records and transactions of his own reign. His grandfather's important archives, and his own, were lodged in the Sainte-Chapelle, his sumptious religious foundation at the heart of the royal palace in Paris. This formed the nucleus of the *Trésor des Chartes* — the select muniments of the monarchy.[32] Louis's interest in the past also had a monumental aspect, for he rearranged the tombs of the kings in St Denis to demonstrate the two races of Charlemagne and Hugh Capet, lined out on separate sides.

Louis expected to take advantage of family sentiments for his own government. The political power of the apanage princes (from *apanamentum,* provision for princely livelihood) began with Louis IX, when, under the terms of his father's will, he provided in 1237 for his younger brother Robert, the county of Artois, their grandmother's inheritance. His next brother Charles also founded an important branch of the family. His apanage was Anjou, Touraine and Maine (1241), but after his marriage to the heiress of Provence (then still part of the empire) in 1246, his attentions were diverted to the south. He went on to conquer the Staufen kingdom of Naples in 1266. His dynasty extended its grip to Hungary (though it lost Sicily). Its importance in the Mediterranean was such that in 1270, Charles was able to deflect Louis' own carefully prepared crusade to Tunis. The French kings inevitably worked out even their 'foreign' policies in association with their family.

The apanage system, on a more modest scale, was continued by Louis IX's successors. No attempts were made until 1366 to introduce clauses limiting the inheritance of these estates. They were considered a natural and beneficial means of promoting family sentiment. There was no thought of dismembering the kingdom. Louis IX's younger son, Robert of Clermont, married the heiress of Bourbonnais in 1272 and founded a princely estate, which became a duchy in 1327, got the status of a peerdom in 1328 and was constantly being added to: the county of Forez (1372), the lordship of Beaujeu (the Beaujolais) in 1400, Thoire-Villars (1402-3) and the duchy of Auvergne (1416). The Bourbons were the last great independent princes of France, and they brought their lands back to the monarchy only when their descendant became King Henri IV. The years of warfare did not impede the family's ability to expand nor give them unfair opportunities to do so. It depended essentially upon the goodwill and complacency of the royal dynasty towards its princely relations. There seemed to be no danger of disloyalty and this case indicates how the system could work well by unloading local responsibilities onto faithful kinsmen. Family sentiment was the only bond that kept them together and in case this tended to diminish over the generations it had to be fostered by more concessions and by intermarriage. The size and the standing of the holdings tended to grow at the expense of other families. The extended Capetian family thus became a cluster of princes, well-endowed from the new lands particularly from those won in the early thirteenth century. The new monarchy drew strength from the loyalty of the apanage princes, since their personal relations to the crown brought their principalities under royal aegis, without involving the king directly. In return the kings could not seriously contemplate trying to undermine the princely independence of apanage lands, not at least for some time to come.

With these religions, moral and sentimental ideas to guide him, we must suppose that Louis IX hoped to carry out the obligations of kingship. None of his contemporary monarchs did more. The functions of government in the mid-thirteenth century were still extremely limited, as may be judged from the four aspects of rule discussed by the jurist Odofredo.[33] They are described, significantly, as the royal 'rights' — over taxation, law, the church and the public interest — a list that becomes increasingly vague.

(i) The vaguest of all was the defence of the public interest, which justified royal action in emergencies, that is intermittently. The idea of the *res publica* clearly came to Odofredo from Roman Law, which was still treated with suspicion in thirteenth-century France. Its possible use may however be judged from a treatise on homage written by Jean de Blanot *c.*1250.[34] He gives a hypothetical, but possible problem which would face the vassals of the duke of Burgundy if the latter summoned them to help him against the duke of Lorraine at the same time as the king of France summoned them to help him against the king of Germany. Blanot argues that the vassals are bound to the duke both by the tie of homage and by the jurisdiction he has over them. They are not bound to the king of France by homage, only by reason of his general jurisdiction as king of France. Nevertheless he upheld the superior right of the king, borrowing his principles from Roman law when he says that a summons to the greater court excludes the call to the lesser; the German threat to subdue the French crown affects the *bona totius patrie* or *bonum publicum* which is therefore a more important matter than the neighbourly dispute of the dukes; he concludes that although the duke's claims are double and the king's only single nevertheless one *ratio efficax* can defeat two less good reasons in law. The notion of the public good also appears in Beaumanoir's work.[35] Philippe de Beaumanoir came from a family holding a fief of St Denis and he himself served as a royal official in a number of different places for nearly twenty years. His systematic exposition of the customs of Clermont-en-Beauvaisis was written in 1283 when he was in his thirties after only three years' experience as *bailli* for the count. It reveals a mind of exceptional lucidity, independence and enlightenment, such as would be a credit to any government servant. Yet there is not the slightest sign in his work or attitude of anything corresponding to a royalist or centralizing tendency. He expounds the local customs of Clermont without betraying dissatisfaction with their traditional character or lack of learned authority and has only the slightest acquaintance with the principles of Roman law. He anticipates that men could live in peace and adequately deal with malefactors themselves. His main concern was the dutiful enforcement of the customs of the region, declaring without surprise or regret that no two *chasteleries* in the kingdom had the same customs. There was some borrowing of rules in cases of difficulty, but even here Beaumanoir made no place for royal activity. He sees it mainly as a curb on the exercise of private rights brought into operation only when the urgent necessity of dealing with problems of the common good justified royal action. The crisis over, private rights would be resumed. Beaumanoir has no need for the state except in time of war. The state is a contraption for saving desperate situations without normal remedies.

(ii) Royal protection of the church meant allowing clerical privileges, but Louis IX did not suppose this meant total surrender of traditional royal rights to supervise, make appointments, raise matters with the pope directly, or intervene against heretics and infidels, as a dutiful son of the church. From the point of view of the extension of royal government, Louis' concerns for the church were most important for establishing precedents for taxing the clergy for his crusades. This had become so ingrained that his successor, Philip III, was able to pay for his campaign against Aragon in 1285 from a papal grant of a tenth on the French church.[36] The war was called a crusade because the king of Aragon had taken up arms against the pope's candidate for the Sicilian crown. At the time the church was more easily taxed than any other part of society and if papal permission were obtained it was comparatively simple to set the machinery in motion. French kings took for granted this papal approval and eventually forgot it was necessary.

(iii) Royal rights over taxation were obviously important, but as long as kings could more or less make ends meet, they were not interested in improvements to the management of their financial affairs or in finding better ways to raise money than those traditionally practised.[37] In the late thirteenth century, the king had still only a small office as counting-house, the *chambre aux deniers* with a staff of five clerks. Four officials (one a layman) called *maîtres des comptes* sat to scrutinize the accounts at special times and the regular office which was housed in the royal *palais* in the city of Paris under Philip IV came to be called the *chambre des comptes*. This was a court in the same sense as the English exchequer. Twice a year, as in England, the accountants put up their table covered with drugget (*bure,* which gave its name to bureau, much as the English checkerboard gave its name to the exchequer) and those responsible for collecting the king's money came and presented their account and paid in the surpluses. The *chambre* had therefore in the course of duty to confirm, approve and record all royal orders affecting his finances: royal foundations, purchases, sales, exemptions, so that the king should lose nothing of what he was entitled to; it checked on royal pardons for fines, confiscations and tax exemptions, the royal mintings; its decisions on all financial matters had the force of legal judgment, as the exchequer did in England. The presence of specialized clerks, accountants, assayers, copyists and others on these occasions had not made the office impersonal. The king presided at a session of the court as late as 1286 and the accounts were still checked on occasion by temporary commissions of great prelates or nobles having no permanent connection with it. Accounting procedures remained informal and the king evinced no great interest in reforming it. The royal attitude to money continued for many years to be irresponsible, on the one hand casual, on the other arbitrary. Philip IV took extra money where he could and showed some concern about the place of deposit for his cash, shifting from the Temple to the Louvre (1295-1303) and back again, but the accounting office, the *chambre,* continued to do the paper-work. The extension of business in this field admittedly obliged the bureau to expand: by 1338 there were ten *maîtres* and nineteen clerks, but this was modest growth compared to what happened in the court of the parlement.

(iv) The real growth of the monarchy must be measured in terms of the royal success in discharging the most important of its obligations, to do justice. Legal institutions developed unobtrusively under Louis IX. By the time of his death, the king's concern for justice had become institutionalized in his court of parlement, where great matters could be discussed and settled. It was the king's high court, to which all men of the kingdom could appeal for justice. To make its judgments effective became the principal proof of the king's political ability. Seen from a distance the king's success in converting the informal proceedings beneath the oak of Vincennes or in his bedchamber into court proceedings capable of being conducted without the king at all, may seem the most important aspect of St Louis' reign, but at the time his own presence in the kingdom inspired a confidence which was more significant than any institution.[38] His style of kingship became the model for his successors. It was not so much the practice of justice, but the king's evident belief that justice mattered which reassured the thirteenth century.. The king's attitude to this duty commanded respect. The English barons themselves trusted him to arbitrate between them and King Henry III (though they were disappointed with his judgment, 1264).[39]

Louis had a horror of war between Christians. On his own estates he forbade his subjects to fight one another, as legal custom allowed, in judicial matters. In 1254 when he returned from crusade he modified procedure in his court so that in civil cases instead of the judicial duel a form of inquest should be used. This was generalized in his famous instruction to his judicial officials 1259-60 which explicitly says: 'we forbid throughout our domain all battles or duels in all suits.., and in place of duels we put proof by witnesses and documents'. This certainly did not put an end to judicial duels throughout the kingdom; Louis's powers as king were limited and he could not enforce this rule outside his own domain. The very nature of the document — an instruction to his own officials — proves that he was unable to obtain general consent to an *ordonnance.* Even in Clermont de Beauvaisis, where Louis's son was count, the king's instruction had no validity. Beaumanoir shows that the nobility continued to enjoy the privilege of private war in which their families might well become involved; the only limits were those imposed by customs — or as we might say by a code of honour. Nothing may seem more surprising to us than that the manifest will of St Louis on such an issue was flouted, but Philip IV, who had his grandfather canonized, rescinded it altogether. Louis's most famous legal reform was ineffective, and only from the late fifteenth century did private war subside, as noblemen consented to bring their quarrels to the courts.[40]

This shows that the king of France was sovereign only in his own domain. There he had power to change law and custom, even if he could not get the consent of his subjects; but outside his domain he had no such power. The king's first duty was to his own particular domain — men for whom he provided regular courts of justice like any other lord. This royal court also acted however as a court of appeal, for those who claimed that they could not get justice from the court of their own lord, or for those who accused the other court of having broken the law and summoned its judges to the king's court to answer. After 1260, since the king's court had repudiated trial by battle, such appeals were also dealt with by the inquest system. This means that the court required a new type of trained lawyer to investigate, ask questions, write reports and keep records. The king's court began to develop rapidly under the influence of such men.

Within a generation the king's parlement had transformed the public notions of law and justice and the king had acquired the first great institution of state that made the French monarchy a power in the land. He could not force all his 'subjects' to change their customs, but once he had a court of appeal, with its own 'modern', intelligent and reasonable procedures, he could not prevent aggrieved persons appealing to his court or in any conscience allow those pleas to go unheard. The kings of France from St Louis relied on the benevolent reputation of their courts to tie the kingdom together. Like his nephew Edward I of England, St Louis began the foundation of a new state based upon justice. The growth of the institution was in its own way Louis's fulfilment of St Augustine's demand that the state should be founded in justice, if it was not to be considered a mere lordship of violence.

Kings provided a final court of appeal where claims for justice from provincial tribunals could be heard, and disputes between the great princes themselves were settled. Louis IX had strengthened his claim to suzerainty over important fiefs of the monarchy. His arbitration in the case of the Flemish inheritance had severed French Flanders from its imperial lands. The Treaty of Corbeil had secured French control over Montpellier. The Treaty of Paris with Henry III brought Gascony too within the scope of the king's right to hear appeals from his vassals' courts. After Louis' death the effective action of his parlement was directly enlarged by the incorporation of the estates of Alfonse of Poitiers, count of Toulouse in 1271 and closer to hand, by Philip IV's government of Champagne and Brie in his wife's name after 1285.

The parlement was the most important of the royal institutions of the new monarchy after Louis IX and it rapidly developed its own machinery and its own specialized servants. In 1278 two members of the parlement were appointed to hear complaints and to decide whether to issue letters authorizing a lawsuit. Such cases did not necessarily take place in the parlement itself: they could be heard in the court of Paris — the Châtelet, or in the 'county' by the king's representatives — the *baillis* or *sénéchaux*. The number of judges appointed to hear these preliminary complaints rose from 2 to 4 in 1296 when the king set up the court with its traditional title *Requêtes* with a special sign manual: two clergy and two laymen sitting daily from dawn to noon even during vacations (they lost their stipends if they arrived late). By 1345 the court was composed of 8 judges: 5 clergy and 3 laymen.

Assuming however that a case was made out and went forward to the parlement there was a good chance that the matter would require to be investigated. After 1278 a special court of *Enquêtes* came into being. This was the busiest part of the parlement. There were 8 members in 1291; 40 — by 1345: 24 clergy, 16 laymen. The court functioned in two parts.

When an inquest or enquiry was required the members went to collect testimonies and examine written evidence—this work was accomplished by the *auditeurs* or *rapporteurs* or *commissaires.* The relevant evidence was then transferred to the *regardeurs, jugeurs (rapporteurs,* 1345) who gave their conclusions in writing. At this stage, the case was ready either for judgment or pleading. The court of *Enquêtes* was able to deal with most criminal and civil matters concerning the ordinary people but it was not omni-competent. Certain suits were reserved for the *Grande Chambre,* the greatest and most dignified part of the parlement, which dealt with criminal cases, involving bloodshed or liable to corporal punishment, and civil cases affecting bodily honour, inheritance or great persons, ecclesiastical and lay, and pronounced decisions *(arrêts)* on the *enquêtes.* Bishops and abbots were released from sitting in the court after 1319. In 1345 its members were 15 clergymen and 15 laymen, with three presidents. The evolution of the parlement did not stop there, but by March 1345 it had achieved a certain stability and had established its own special traditions, style and division of labour, defined in Philip VI's *Ordonnance.* As the highest legal tribunal in the land it had become a new factor of importance in political life, fixing norms of legal action and thus acting as a brake upon royal initiative. The king's court could facilitate the task of royal justice, but also hinder the king's arbitrary will.[41]

Those who served in the king's lawcourt were naturally zealous to establish the supremacy of this court over the provinces. The difficulties of doing this became obvious during the reign of Philip III (1270-85) and rose to their height under Philip IV (1285-1314). Some were of a technical character. When the county of Toulouse reverted to the crown in 1271 the king set up a special committee of the parlement to deal with its affairs, since its law was written, not customary, and there was no place for training Roman lawyers in northern France until 1312.[42] It was found necessary to supplement this work of the parlement in Paris by other means and in 1303 the king decided to hold a judicial parlement in Toulouse itself every year. Much more serious were the difficulties which arose in cases where the provincial princes resented the interest taken by the parlement in hearing cases on appeal from their own courts, on the grounds that they had refused to do or give justice. At first the parlement was cautious in attending to such appeals. When the citizens of Ghent appealed to Philip III's court against the count of Flanders because they could not get justice in his court, the parlement twice rejected their appeals and sent them back to Flanders. The king's relations with his vassals were based upon trust and goodwill and he could not afford to upset their feelings by insisting on his judicial rights. Some political adjustment was called for to protect great princes from the numerous enemies who could attempt to use the royal court for their own purposes. Edward I, as duke of Gascony, accepted the need for the Paris court and retained legal proctors to defend his interests there, but Edward, who took his duties very seriously, also began to suspect that appeals to Paris were pursued more to thwart the effectiveness of his court at Bordeaux than from genuine dissatisfaction with his tribunals. However, both the parlement and the king became increasingly eager to take advantage of these appeals, since they weakened Edward's independence and built up royal support in the remote duchy. So long as the direct government of provinces remained in the hands of great princes, of the royal blood or not, the appellate jurisdiction of the parlement was the king's only real means of influencing events there. Under Philip IV, the members of the king's parlement became notable defenders of his rights and advocates of his political programmes; they were eager to test their theories in the courts and follow up decisions with force. They did not therefore draw back from declaring Flanders or Gascony confiscated when the royal vassals defied the jurisdiction of parlement. The future of the monarchy would turn on the power to implement these decisions.

When in 1294 Edward I refused to recognize the parlement's ruling on the Norman fishing dispute with Bayonne seamen and the court declared him contumacious, and his duchy forfeit, war broke out. This also involved Flanders, the one great independent fief left in northern France. Parlement using the pleas of such restless subjects as the patricians of Ghent decided to assert royal sovereignty over this rich territory. The count himself had become politically more feeble after the partition of his lands by the arbitration of Louis IX; the greatest of his urban subjects had already perceived the advantages of direct dealings with the king. They had been rebuffed by Philip III, but his son, Philip IV, eager and rash, thought that the appeal for justice against the count gave him the ideal occasion for finishing him off. It appeared to be at least as good an opportunity as his namesake had found for driving John out of Normandy.

In the long term, the appearance of a royal court of this kind indicates that an important step forward had been taken to curtail the jurisdiction of traditional courts. However, at the time, opposition to royal justice was not the work of benighted reactionaries, defending anachronistic powers and vested interests for Justice was not a royal monopoly. As late as the fifteenth century a treatise on the justice administered in the highly centralized duchy of Normandy showed that there were then, still, three distinct levels of high, middle and low justice. High justice covered the powers of the official *(bailli)* having cognizance of murder and theft with authority to *trayner et ardoir* together with execution of all writs, plaints and complaints. Middle justice covered the case of the seneschal with power to capture and hang provided that the suit only lasted one day; otherwise the case passed to the judge who only handed over the convicted felon for execution. This kind of privilege was proved by the presence of a gallows, which had to be maintained; the lord of such justice also had power over weights, measures and market disputes (except *haro,* reserved for high justice). Low justice accorded only the right to enforce collection of dues and revenues owing in the lordship, including disputes over damage caused by roaming livestock, as well as blows between men, provided there were no dangerous cuts and no blood drawn.[43] The royal courts of the thirteenth century had therefore no exclusive right to enforce 'the law' and it was taken for granted by all landowners that they had responsibilities in this field. They did not contest the king's right to provide an ultimate tribunal to hear appeals for want of justice, but they became highly critical of suits in parlement seemingly prosecuted to bring local courts into disrepute and to mock their jurisdictions. The great princes, including the apanagists, were loyal to the king, but they did not conceive of their loyalty as committing them to a centralized monarchy. However significant the centralizing institutions may seem in retrospect, it is necessary to remember that it was in precisely the same period that provincial sentiment also began to take more definite shape. Within the old royal domain itself, a number of distinctive regions of customary law put their rules into writing. It could well be that the activities of the parlement itself prompted this wish defend local rules.

In a sense the enlargement of the monarchy to contain parts of southern France subject to written law indefinitely deferred the possibility of providing any unified legal basis for the kingdom as a whole. The southern French were of different speech, literature and culture to those of the north, who had brought with them unpopular religious discipline still resented by some sections of the population well into the fourteenth century. By keeping such different peoples in the kingdom, the kings condemned themselves to preside in a state of motley character. If the north was more homogenous, little progress was made even there towards reducing the legal differences between districts. To some extent this could only come about after the formulation of local laws, when lawyers could use the texts to compare rules and practice to reveal what common ground existed. Not till the late fourteenth century did Jean Boutillier take the first step towards a general customary law for northern France, in the *Somme Rural c.*1370-92. The *Grand Coutumier* was compiled by Jacques D'Ableiges, 1387-89. In the sixteenth century however there were still 60 general provincial customs and 200 local ones recognized by the lawyers. No wonder if as late as 1607, Loyseau wrote of the wish to subdue to the uniformity of a single law, the provinces subjected to the authority of a single king.[44] Though the king's justice had acquired rules and experience of its own, which would eventually modify the law of the whole kingdom, the difficulties of creating a united French government in the absence of any 'common' law should not be underestimated. In these circumstances the ambitions of the Parisian lawyers to rush through a centralized administration of justice may seem premature rather than commendable. The lawyers and the kings grasped after a coherent principle, but the basis for their power was inadequately constructed.

6. THE COMMUNITIES OF THE REALM

The two greatest monarchies of thirteenth-century Christendom were far from being effective administrative machines for all the peoples within their borders. The king of France had eventually to fight to uphold the jurisdiction of his court of law; the king of Germany was at the same time handing out royal privileges of justice to princes strong enough to demand them; in the long term, the consequences of this difference have left visible traces in the present structures of the French and German states. In 1300, the French bid for centralization smacked of unwarranted innovation in France itself. All over the rest of Europe, whatever the urgent need of government, it still seemed natural for local communities to defend themselves, with or without a royal umbrella to shelter them all.[45] The functions of the best governments were limited; because for most purposes men still governed themselves in their local communities.[46] The modern state is first and foremost for us an apparatus to preserve 'law and order', because it is now considered uncivil to defend ourselves; we are now all as the clergy then were — at the mercy of the government. But most men then still provided basic security within their own group, to the point, where even a single town might be portioned out amongst several distinct jurisdictions of lords and corporations, such as privileged churches. In this situation 'the rule of law' meant for them not something less, but something different. Above all it meant that the enforcement of order could not rest with a few officials, but upon the active participation of the majority of the population. In England, for example, all countrymen were members of tithings, groups of ten, who answered for the good behaviour of their members. In fourteenth-century Italian towns all able bodied men in regular occupations bore arms in defence of their town, as the modern Swiss still do.

Defence of life and property was managed in the most local units and most men lived entirely within societies of familiar members, according to the local customs of their neighbourhood — what Beaumanoir calls *chastelries* — no less well known and observed for being unwritten. The 'masses' of those times were not manipulated and managed by a few oppressors.[47] The majority, making a livelihood from the land, relied on their neighbours, in an arduous routine of cooperative effort. They had to act together for sowing and harvesting; they had to deal with disputes in their settlements about boundaries, grazing rights, ditching and hedging; they had to pursue cattle-thieves from outside, search for strays and round up beasts pasturing in woods and commons. In what sense could they be in need of government from outside? The arrival of some official in their locality was more likely to mean trouble, expense and interference. It was not for countrymen that government was to grow.

The towns were also self-regulating, with their own rules, if not always under their own independent authorities. These rules had to be different from those of the countryside to suit the activities of the community—supervision of buying and selling, problems of riotous assembly where the mob might muster its terrible, transitory strength, and against outsiders, the defence of the walls and gates. Towns discontented with the traditional authorities always demanded permission to run their own affairs: they pressed for royal charters which allowed them to do more for themselves; they wanted less, not more government from on high. By walling themselves in, they became visibly isolated units of local administration, where 'freedom' prevailed.

There were some persons in the kingdoms, not able to manage their affairs entirely within the circumscribed limits of town or parish who needed help from 'government'. Merchants venturing along the highways between towns required royal protection, against robbery, ambush or unlawful tolls. Offences along royal highways were amongst the earliest which kings reserved for their own special attention. The effectiveness of royal action inevitably depended upon the reliability of the king's local officials or vassals in respecting royal commands. However, merchants, like other travellers who benefited from effective actions, contributed nothing themselves to the peaceable managements of the areas they passed through. The chief agents of effective government in local communities, were, as might have been expected in an agrarian society, the 'landowners'. These were not the actual cultivators of any one locality, but those with legal rights in more than one place, whose concerns to protect them against one another were as inadequately served by the village byelaws as by the remote courts of kings.

The landowners
Anxiety to define every free man's rights in land developed as the possibilities of acquiring additional lands diminished. There had been a long period when western Europeans lived without fear that the amount of land available would be inadequate. By the second half of the twelfth century there are already signs that the military aristocracy could no

longer expect to augment their lands. Kings, who had to give up fresh conquests, enforced their rights against their vassals. Ventures overseas became more rare. After the Second Crusade of 1147-48, great kings could not expect to win even glory by them; if they stayed at a home to manage their affairs, their lords did likewise. All those who could, tried instead to cope with the growth of a money economy, the cost of weapons, armour and fortification, by wringing more from their existing assets. They became more careful in granting lands to vassals, demanding due services. Churchmen showed the same concern to define the nature of their rights in church land; tithes had been paid for centuries, but there had never been more competition amongst churches to obtain them, nor more exact definition of what should be tithed and how tithes should be divided. The numerous disputes before the papal court prove how niggling these could be.

The church's laws were fixed internationally, but for others defining the rights of landlords became a matter of local custom. In few cases did kings themselves impose or participate in nationally agreed rights for landownership, except in the case of tenants-in-chief. Only in England did the reforms of Henry II, building on the uniquely uniform system of landholding established after the Norman conquest, create a 'common' law for all free men. In most of Europe the laws of landowner-ship were 'common' only in the limited areas of agreed custom. The 'frontiers' of these areas were determined in large measure by those of the feudal principalities between the mid-eleventh and mid-thirteenth centuries. Agreement about customs was secured when vassals realized it was impossible to resist their lords' burdensome demands altogether. When they agreed on how to define respective interests, in effect they endowed their regions with distinctive customs. Not every local *seigneur* could turn his own *chastelrie* into a self-contained district of customary law or county, even if he tried; he had in the end to share with his fellows in a community of agreed custom. The limits of each of these jurisdictions were defined during the eleventh and twelfth centuries. For example, the dukes of Normandy had to fight on their southern border to retain the loyalty of the family of Bellême, who had important assets further south, and would have preferred to remain totally autonomous. It is even possible in the case of Normandy to define rather narrowly at what point the limits of custom were drawn, because districts brought under ducal control after 1080, retained their own customs. Norman customary law, though distinctive by that time, was not however formulated in writing until *c*. 1199, much modified, of course, after more than a hundred years of purely oral tradition.[48]

Areas of custom, once defined, thereby acquired a certain interest in maintaining their political unity. It suited the *seigneurs* to submit to the 'count' and his law, because most of their estates, scattered within his 'county' were covered by the same customs, (which is not to say that the lord was spared great efforts to secure their political subservience, as Louis VI was obliged to do in the Ile de France). In the duchy of Aquitaine, on the other hand, where the duke was unable to keep the duchy together, numberous sub-ordinates there consolidated discreet territories of their own; having no estates spread over the whole duchy, they had no interest in a ducal law.

Feudal dues and reciprocal rights between lords and vassals were an important part of what customary law had to define, but the need for rules was felt all over Europe about the same time, even in places where feudal tenures were not all that common, such as Germany. There, too, the old customary laws of the duchies failed to meet the new concern about rules of 'ownership' and new rules were formulated within the existing political structures, whatever they were. Friesland, which had no duke, acquired its own customs by *c.* 1200. Saxony, or rather east Saxony, the rump left after the separation of Westphalia (1180), was the first German *land* to have its customs put into writing, by Erich von Repgow (1221-24). In the late thirteenth century, the division between Upper and Lower Austria introduced by Ottokar II (d. 1276) left its mark on the customs there, while the Tyrol was the *land* defined by the allegiance of Count Meinhard II (1246-64).

The customs of any one region in effect defined the terms on which the landowners recognized one another as members of the same 'political' community. How they 'deliberated' for purposes of declaring these rules cannot be decided from the written statements themselves (where there are any). No doubt there were disputes and arguments about law, since there were no authoritative books to settle the problems. Men had to rely on precedents and their own 'concepts' of 'feudal' or 'tribal' custom then centuries old, which offered diverse regulations in different parts of Europe.

Customary law was intended to establish agreed rules within any given political unit, whether the tenures were feudal or not, as to the respective rights of lords, vassals, kin, wives, widows and children. The positive rules of law given by so many different customs cannot be reduced to a simple formula, but they were in general designed to do two things: (i) to keep the peace by protecting occupiers from tiresome legal suits, and by penalizing the use of self-help in disputes about ownership; and (ii) to define the rights of children to succeed to parental possessions and thus protect the future peace too.[49] Sometimes books could help in improving upon the definition of feudal law. In Italy men naturally made use of Roman law, then newly rediscovered: the earliest *Libri Feudorum* occur in the *Obertina,* and its basic elements were derived from the cases a Milanese judge reported to his son, who was studying Civil Law at Bologna (1137-58)[50]. But Roman laws of 'ownership' could hardly be applied neat in the twelfth century, however useful they were in other ways. The rules of feudal law had to satisfy all the parties with diverse 'rights' to any one piece of land, or dues from it, not only in the present, but for the future. Feudal grants were originally conceded only for life or for a limited number of generations, but by the twelfth century, even a life expectancy had become a 'right' which a feudatory desired to transmit to his heirs. Siboto, Count of Neuburg, expressed his anxiety (1165-74) about the future interests of his sons in the various fiefs he held of the bishop of Passau, the count Sulzpach of Salzburg, the count palatine, the bishop of Trent, the marquess of Freiburg (Chreiburch) Wazzerburch and many others, when he besought his faithful men and his friends and relations to act promptly to prevent his various lords reentering his benefices after his death so that 'nullomodo filii sui possunt eis eripere et sic perdetur.'[51] Inheritance of the father's estates was by no means guaranteed by 'law', for, as Joannes Teutonicus wrote in the early thirteenth century, inheritance was a right under Roman law which had no general validity at the time. Conrad Otto of Bohemia and Moravia thus made an important concession (1189-91) when he allowed his people to alienate their own lands: this charter is the oldest written statement of Bohemian customary law.[52] All those who could establish their right to enjoy such a privilege in effect became the 'landowners', the 'nobles', the men of consequence in Bohemia; the rest enjoyed only local rights whatever they were. The landowners, however, then assumed the right to speak as the *universa Boemorum gens* and their status and privilege was established before the kingdom was set up in 1212 when Frederick II confirmed their right to elect to the kingship. Thus the Bohemian nation, represented by the landowners, was as a legal entity older than the kingdom or the (royal) dynasty of the Przemyslids (1192-1309). This 'nation' defended the laws which protected its rights; loyalty to Bohemian custom gave the nobles moral support in their later opposition to both king and church.[53]

Those who claimed to hold their lands by the customs of the land—its common law—were freemen. It followed that those who did not succeed in upholding these claims, lost this law and were considered servile—though this only means that they were protected by the rules of their own local estate (usually a seigneury, or lordship) as declared by their own neighbours. In 1220 Roger of Kirkley cited Henry de Vere before the royal justices for breaking into Roger's house and burning down his barn. De Vere countered this by claiming that Roger, was his villein, and had improperly married off his daughter without approval; for this reason De Vere had broken into the house. To establish Roger's status, the justices asked him if he had attended the meetings of the county court regularly. When Roger claimed that he had, the question was put by the rules of common law to the twelve *liberi et legales et discreti homines* who settled such problems by English custom.[54] Villeins were not entitled to common law and the judgment of the county as a whole, but only to that of their neighbours. Cases like this bring out the difference between the free and the unfree in thirteenth-century society.

Since the purpose of establishing common rules of law was directly related to the concern of all who could to define their obligations to the lords, particularly over dues, in money or service, and not with the drudgery of regular working routines on an estate, the peasants in general dropped away from attending the public courts.[55] The freemen within any one common region of law were left to uphold the freedom or liberties they enjoyed by that law, attending the courts in which disputes were settled by the judgment of freemen, discussing modifications of customs and joining protests against encroachments on their liberties. Political discussion and activity, in as much as it existed at all in the thirteenth century, turned therefore on the laws by which freemen lived.[56]

The different written versions of the Norman customs which show constant change and adaptation of the rules over more than two centuries suggest that for a time everywhere landowners were busy tinkering with their customs. By the late thirteenth century, however, customary laws seem to have attained definitive, if not final, form. In France regions as close to the royal court at Paris as Vermandois (*c.* 1253) and the Orléannais (*c.* 1270) protected themselves from it by putting their customs into writing. In Germany the precocious statement of Saxon regional custom stimulated the production of a comparable work for Swabia, which also shows that the law was still being modified in the thirteenth century.

England had no statement of customary law to compare with the Norman, but the protests of the barons wrung from King John a list of liberties in 1215, which was the basis of subsequent charters granted by Henry III, as of grace. Constantly reissued throughout the thirteenth century, *Magna Carta* became a basic law. It bound the king to recognize the barons' privileges, on the important understanding that they did as much for their own vassals. Baronial protests at royal infringements of their rights thus regularly involved others apart from themselves; all the freemen gathered for legal business in the various shire-courts wished to uphold the same rule of law. When in due course Edward I saw the advantage of regular consultation about public business, it was natural that he should not only summon his great tenants-in-chief in person but also require spokesmen from the freeholders of the shires. English public law was in a constant state of development throughout the thirteenth century and could not be frozen into formula books. Henry de

Bracton tried to present a coherent account of the rules of common law as applied in the king's court, in his day. This failed to codify the law, as he had hoped.[57] Instead, the legal practitioners evolved their own means of mastering the law and teaching its precepts through the practice of the courts. The Year-Books in their own way also demonstrate that the English legal system had come of age.[58] (Resistance to premature attempts to impose codification is also met with in Castile; Alfonso X, the Wise, himself proposed a royal law-book, but it was not adopted until more than fifty years after his death.)

If England came nearest to being a kingdom with a common law, it should be remembered that in the thirteenth century, even England would not have seemed so different from other lands. Henry III ruled other lordships apart from England, and there was no common law which governed them all. In England itself there were also, of course, different laws for the clergy, townsmen and peasantry while important tracts of territory lay outside the jurisdiction of the king's court and the common law—the palatine counties of Durham and Chester and the March lands of the borders. With these serious limitations, England may be regarded none the less as one political society, made up of freemen with access to the royal courts of law for the settlement of their disputes. Such men, and they alone, were directly concerned about how the king managed these courts and enforced its decisions.

Freemen were in a general sense the landowners, the most powerful men in an agrarian economy; those who made money in commerce had to stay solvent long enough to buy land, if they wanted political influence. Politics turned on the problems and the disputes of landowners, and the geographical limits of their political activities were set by the customary law they worked under. Since for the most part these units were not co-terminous with the lands of kings, the essential activities of the political classes cannot be described at a royal level at all. Within the self-contained regions landowners had no option about engaging in political activity. They could not leave it to others to act as their spokesmen; as lords and vassals, as parents and kin, they had many commitments. The customs that protected their rights obliged them to settle disputes amongst themselves and do right by their dependents. Not even the most arbitrary count could rely entirely on paid officials. Local landowners had to be listened to, and their rights respected. Within each 'unit' of local government, the landowners of Europe concentrated their political efforts at that level to elucidate the 'rules' governing ownership and to maintain the rights they were entitled to. Their political outlook was shaped by their ideas of custom, especially about such matters as inheritance, marriage and tenure. They did not think about the 'state' or other secular abstractions. In as much as they had in some areas to make allowance for monarchy, they saw it likewise, in the first instance, as a great estate, inherited by known rules and governed by established, and preferably unchanging, custom.

The clerical estate

These same interests also influenced their attitude towards the clergy. Though conventionally pious, as landowners they were naturally resentful of churchmen.[59] Not only did ecclesiastical jurisdiction over marriage, probate and inheritance conflict with the desire to manage such matters by their own rules alone. The privileges of the clergy hampered the lords as collators to benefices, since the papacy interfered ever more effectively in this from the mid-thirteenth century. Above all, they resented the fact that, though the churches were great landowners, they were undying corporations whose lands never came onto the market and who paid none of the normal feudal dues on inheritance.[60] Even the greatest lords could do little about this singlehanded. They needed political influence with kings, or with the pope directly to obtain benefices for their relatives and dependents. Collectively, however, they could reinforce the secular power and put pressure on kings to bully the churches. Kings had in the past accepted responsibility for defending the clergy from encroachments. In the late thirteenth century this support turned out to be unreliable. Edward I sent peremptory letters to the archbishop of Canterbury reminding him of his duty to the crown, as he loved the baronies he held of the king, with the veiled threat of confiscating them if the archbishop was found unfaithful.[61] At war, some years later, the king threatened to outlaw the whole clerical community if they refused to pay taxes, though they had papal support for their refusal. In this way the kings demonstrated how much they too had come to share the views of their barons towards the church, using their role as its protectors to coerce rather than succour.

The clergy might well consider kings somewhat ungrateful to repay them for their many services in the thirteenth century by such means.[62] Yet the troubled times that began in the late thirteenth century, which were used to justify unprecedented demands for clerical taxation, had to some extent been brought about by them. The church itself had inspired the kind of programmes for secular rulers that created the political problems of that time. The clergy had intended no doubt to usher in the reign of peace and order by giving rulers a new pious and imperious duty to serve God's purposes in the world.[63] In fact this programme aroused protest and opposition, at home as well as abroad. The clergy also made rulers ambitious and intransigent by dedicating them to good 'causes'. They acted as advisers, and found them resources. Since 'righteous' wars were called crusades they justified taxation. The clergy with privileges in their pockets had confidently assisted in the elaboration of the royal bureaucracies, instilling respect for the Lord's anointed and submission to his just laws. Like all idealists they failed to reckon seriously with the possibilities of opposition.

Louis IX derived from churchmen the laudable desire to make peace between his own family and that of his wife's sister. In the Treaty of Paris (1259), therefore, he received the homage of Henry III for Gascony in order to define their relationship. Whatever the two kings themselves thought of the arrangement as a means of keeping the peace, the treaty became within one generation the seed of discord that damaged Anglo-French relations for centuries. The treaty was interpreted to imply a degree of submission to the royal court in Paris (still in its infancy in 1259), which irked Edward I and was a factor in promoting not peace but war. Is it unfair to blame the clergy for the tendentious interpretations of lawyers? The clergy had encouraged rulers to formulate their political ideas and programmes in writing, so that politics should become not the management of men but the attainment of (divinely inspired) goals. The clergy taught laymen how to live by the letter of the law and by 'logical' arguments from texts, to draw out irrefutable implications that made treaties of peace the excuses for war. In as much as the clergy were the men of learning, they taught kings and advisers to be as cunning as serpents. A similar dispute between Edward I and the Scots arose out of his subtle manoeuvres to obtain recognition of his sovereignty after the death of the Maid of Norway. Edward intended this to guarantee more effective justice in Britain, but it led to wars renewed for more than three centuries. In Italy, the papacy, which had destroyed the disobedient Staufen dynasty, by calling crusades and finding a champion in Charles of Anjou, made him thereby so powerful that a counter-weight was urgently sought, and vainly, by Gregory X. It was the Sicilian barons who disowned Charles (1282) and for twenty years intermittent war in the south made a mockery of the clerical argument that an Angevin dynasty would bring the church peace.

The clergy who lent themselves to the defence of both parties justified their wars in the name of high principles. Educated persons, that is, for the most part, clerics, were used as publicists and propounded views on war derived from the study rather than the battlefield. Warriors enjoyed the encounters, but did not preach the extermination of whole dynasties. Yet this is what the rhetorical letters of defiance issued between Charles of Anjou and Pere II of Aragon over Sicily in 1282 actually propose. Charles boasts that he will bring his lilies by land and sea to exterminate Pere, his friends and the traitors of Sicily, while Pere intends to wipe Charles's kin from the face of the earth, and with his dragon's toxic bites to kill the lion, which had deplumed the eagle's chicks (Frederick II's heirs), and annihilate them so that no memorial of them would be found on earth.[64] The eloquence of learning was thus prostituted for blatant dynastic purposes by both sides in a war to which the papacy itself was committed.

The clergy had not only advocated righteous wars; they helped to pay for them. Society had been basically organized in such a way as to make do without taxation but in the twelfth century the clergy had argued in favour of levies on behalf of the crusade, and the same arguments therefore come in handy later, when the popes had only to call out a crusade against heretics, or Frederick II, in order to claim taxes from the clergy. Since the pope needed secular princes to lead such wars, he offered willing kings a share of the clergy's contributions, and this also made it easier to secure collection. By the end of the thirteenth century it seemed so natural to kings that they should obtain grants from the clergy for 'justifiable' wars, that Philip IV was outraged to be reminded by Pope Boniface VIII that papal approval should be obtained first. The English clergy were sufficiently heartened by this to refuse Edward I aid, but he overcame their resistance by threatening to remove them from the protection of the law; trembling for their privileges, the clergy preferred to pay up. Less than a century before, they had led the way in opposing royal tyrannies. In the thirteenth century, privilege had sapped their capacity to oppose. They depended abjectly on their royal patrons.

Financial expedients

The clergy were not the only ones to suffer, when the king's needs for money made them unscrupulous. However, others turned out to be less easily blackmailed than the clergy; not that their patience was quickly exhausted. It took the oppressions of Philip IV over nearly twenty years to bite deep enough to rouse general protest. By proceeding craftily the king of France could avoid uniting his subjects against him and gull the peaceable citizens into parting with their tax contributions with their own agreement, as the *bailli* of Rouen was advised to do it, offering the excuse of the need to defend the realm. Philip IV's devices for raising money prove the variety of means open to him and the possibility of picking upon defenceless and friendless victims. The Jews, Lombards and Cahorsins simply had to ransom themselves. The king's own bankers, the Templars, had first to be defamed, then tortured and persecuted, so that the king could enjoy their revenues for five years (1307-12). But the king still could not do without more general taxation. He devalued the coinage by declaring in 1295 that the *gros* was worth 15 d tournois instead of 12 — which cut his debts by a quarter, at a stroke. The coinage was a royal right and his subjects could not do more than grumble.

Less excusable were the purchase tax at 2d in the pound (1291), and a wholesale tax on wheat, salt and wine (1295) which had to be withdrawn because of public hostility. Then the king tried to introduce a tax on non-combatants at 1 per cent of property, to be raised in each parish on the basis of local assessments. Neighbours generously estimated these at too low a figure and the tax was raised to 2 per cent and then to 4 per cent for the same reason in 1297. In 1303-4, the king abandoned his effort to tax capital as too difficult and tried an income tax to affect all, nobles included, at 20 per cent, apparently a commutation of military service. All these expedients show that the king was determined to find means of getting his subjects to help him with his financial problems, and their dogged resistance to doing so. At the end of the reign when he continued to collect taxes voted for the Flemish war, after arranging a truce with the Flemings, his long-suffering subjects finally rose against these abuses. They then demanded ratification of their undoubted ancient privileges which they thought would cover them against royal exactions. Until this opposition was roused, the kings had been able to rely on the connivance of their servants and ministers to get their own way. The abilities of these men and their lack of scruple eventually went too far and forced the opposition into the open. The landowners of the communities were confident of their rights in customary law, steadfast in defending them and independent enough to defy exactions. If the king could not pay the costs of settling disputes without financial help he would at least have to come to terms with the real men of power in the kingdom. The encounter between the kings and the spokesmen of the political communities created the new political societies of the fourteenth century.[65]

The opposition
The nobles were great landowners themselves and were well aware that the kings' pursuits of estates and rights, for which they asked taxes, were not on that account alone of general interest. In France, wars against great feudal lords to enforce the authority of the royal courts were not to national, but to royal, advantage. When Pere II of Aragon committed himself to his wife's claims on Sicily, he had to meet the objections of his Aragonese nobles and confirm their privileges of Union (1285), which rudely indicated the legal limitations of his power. (This was sufficiently galling for Pere III to count it as one of his greatest successes that he had been able to suppress it in 1348.[66]) In England, Edward I was desperately engaged in war against Philip IV, when the English barons exasperated by his arbitrary taxes, demanded a confirmation of *Magna Carta* (1297), which they thought the king had evaded illegally. They regarded the war as the king's, not their own, let alone 'England's' and they saw no reason why the circumstances justified suspending traditional liberties.[67]

Emergencies did not change the basis of political right. The barons had no compunction about reminding the kings of the need for mutual confidence, never having forfeited their right to advise the kings for their own good. Whereas in England it was possible for the barons to consider protesting on a 'national' scale, in France, opinion could only be rallied to the defence of provincial rights. This changed nothing essential. The nobles did not hesitate to stand up against the king on whatever legal basis they could find. They were certainly not deceived, as historians may be, by the clerical rhetoric about royal policies as expressions of the public interest. The clergy themselves, when they resisted the payment of taxes, realized that this was not so. Royal wars were often undertaken for reasons that suited the rulers personally and dynastically. The barons were not itching to go to war on any plausible excuse their kings could find. Joinville, in this period, expressed the view that landowners were better engaged looking after their own dependents: *pour mon peuple aidier et deffendre* than going off on crusade. They needed to be convinced if kings claimed to be committed to wars of public concern. Kings discovered that if they could project their schemes as of common profit they might obtain the cooperation they needed. For a time, there was a widespread interest in bringing kings into constant consultation with their subjects.

Representative assemblies
These institutions were from the first royal occasions. They could not take place without royal initiative and the assemblies were managed and the business discussed there, as the king saw fit. Yet because they were also enlarged meetings of the old *curia regis,* they indicate that the king had made some concessions in order to get the imposing assemblies he wanted. He had to approach the communities and get their consent. Who was entitled to speak for the communities? Pope Innocent III had given general currency to a formula of Roman Law *quod omnes tangit ab omnibus approbetur* implying the need for consultation, but it was not interpreted to mean that literally all persons should be represented in public debates, for the business there conducted affected only a very small proportion of the population.[68] Medieval assemblies were in fact properly representative of all those actually concerned in such matters as the kings were likely to raise there: their wars, their finances and the modifications of customary law. Moreover, the king saw that if the assemblies were to serve his purposes they had to be representative of all concerned, for otherwise those who did not come would not be impressed or coerced by the decisions of the others. Medieval parliaments were in some ways therefore more representative than modern ones, since the king insisted on the presence of all persons of any consequence: those

who were too great to speak for the communities were summoned in person: an idea that degenerated into that of an hereditary house of peers.

It would be erroneous to believe that these assemblies conform to a single pattern of the three estates. In France itself, the best known of all early national assemblies, that of 1484, was not organized in three groups, nobles, clergy and townsmen, but in regional groups which mixed all the 'classes' up together.[69] In Flanders, the provincial assemblies comprised representatives of the great Flemish towns, Ypres, Ghent and Bruges, with its district and Walloon Lille, Douai, Orchies and of the district of Lille; the clergy and the nobility were not summoned and made their points of view known to the count of Flanders by other means. The real power of Flanders lay in the towns, and adequate representation of the county was secured through urban delegates.[70] In Castile too, the representation of the kingdom was entrusted to the spokesmen of the towns. In England, the town members heavily outnumbered the spokesmen of the shires in the 'Commons', but here the numbers were less important than the fact that knights of the shire had greater self-confidence. Behind them they sensed the support of their communities, with their regular experience in the courts of cooperating in the king's justice. The landed interest thus dominated both the upper and the lower house and enabled parliament to discover its common sense of purpose in dealing with the common law of the realm. The burgess members, nurtured on borough customs, had, initially, no comparable interest in the law at all.

The delegates were not left in doubt that they had been summoned in the first place to suit the king's purposes rather than their own. It is hardly surprising if the king often used them to obtain votes of supply, because they were in effect only enlarged meetings of baronial assemblies in which the king had in the past asked for 'aids' when he needed them. The estates of Provence are first recorded to have met in 1286 to find the money for the ransom of their lord, Charles II, King of Naples.[71] Assemblies which granted money were in effect passing new laws and modifying the old customs about feudal dues, even if they did not intend the new law to be binding on more than one occasion. By commanding attendance in such assemblies, rulers bound all those represented in it to abide by its decisions. In Sicily, the constitutions of King James II of Aragon in 1288 defined the four occasions when the king might resort to taxation: for defence of the realm, the army, the king's ransom and his marriage. It published regulations about the king's rights over coinage, royal officials and relations between the king and his subjects.[72] The need for such definitions was new. In the past, kings had had domain lands, to be tallaged at will for ordinary revenue, and a few traditional taxes for the expenses of extraordinary occasions like knighting his first born son. As these established rights to money dues came to seem archaic and inadequate, it was right to define new laws, that is to vote new taxes. There was no belief at this stage that the king had any general right to taxation. Taxation thus became a new law, agreed in assemblies competent to modify the customs concerned. The assemblies did not meekly vote what kings demanded.[73] By turning the demand for taxes into new laws, they extracted their tyrannous sting. For example, in England, the king had tried to raise taxes as he needed them by appeals in parliament and elsewhere. Finally in 1334 parliament gave up resisting the pressure and agreed to regular taxation, as the new law, but only by fixing the assessments. A grant of tenths and fifteenths was thereafter frequently voted on request, but ceased to be anything more than a vote of a fixed sum. They had themselves become customary levies and the king had lost the chance to vary the amounts according to his real needs.[74] A similar situation developed in Poland, later in the century. At the change of dynasty in 1374, the spokesmen of the kingdom obtained a promise that there should be no new taxes and that what was voted in the assembly should be collected by persons elected locally for that purpose and not by royal officials. The kings got the money, but lost political control of the machinery.[75] On the other hand, the assemblies which were content to define new customs or laws of taxation also abandoned any chance of continuing to make political headway against the king. The effect on both sides was to draw up new rules, not to embark on constitutional dialogue.

These assemblies usually represented regions of defined common law, so few of them were on a national scale. In England, the general interest of the representatives in the common law made parliament from the first not only a consultative assembly but one with legislative and judicial commitments as well. The king found it convenient, even a necessary part of his ordinary government, summoned it frequently and published in it decisions about law which were given the name of statutes. Expecting regular business of this kind, the members of parliament brought their own petitions for redress of grievance, their suggestions for changes in the law, and eventually came to agree on how to present a united front to the king's government.

The overlap between the representative function and the legal community had quite different consequences in Bohemia where the legal unity of the kingdom was really older than the kingship itself. In 1309, when John of Luxembourg became king, the nobles already spoke for the kingdom, and were in effect able to take over the management of it and persuade the king to spend most of his reign abroad. Their conviction that the Bohemian law was in no need of royal improvements stiffened their resistance to the proposals made by John's successor, Charles, who was also emperor. He planned to codify the law and found territorial lawcourts. Since he had no authority to impose such reforms he had to submit them to the Estates of Bohemia in a general *landtag*. They first demanded (1348) a charter confirming the Bohemian privileges of 1158, 1212 and 1289; then after Charles's triumphant return from his imperial coronation in Rome (1355), they summarily rejected his proposals. The Bohemians were later confident enough of their own rights to jostle Charles's son Wenceslas as king, to keep his brother Sigismund out of Bohemia for fifteen years, and to tolerate or encourage such religious and ecclesiastical reform under the 'Hussites' as scandalized the rest of Europe. The Bohemian nation owed almost nothing of its 'patriotism' to its kings. Yet it did not expect to be politically independent to the point of insisting on a native line of kings or breaking its ties with the empire. The legal community antedated the kingdom and had to be consulted by rulers in need of finding added political strength in the kingdom. But the nobles were so confident of their position that they themselves set the tone of the discussions and gave nothing away.[76] Charles IV came nearest to identifying his interests with those of the Bohemians, yet his most serious attempt to improve the government was opposed out of fear that it would serve the king's interest at the people's expense. The position of the Bohemian estates was too well entrenched before 1300 for the king to extract any political advantages from it for himself.

The Bohemian example proves how self-confident the nobles could be in dealing with their rulers in their own area. If the stand nobles elsewhere took against kings secured them less durable victories, it was because most kings operated on such a broader front than their nobles that they could not be easily cornered. This was obviously the case in the kingdom of France, where the provincial nobles did criticise royal infringements of local liberties, without finding the means to unite their forces and coerce the king at a national level. Whereas Philip IV could not dispense with the advantages of summoning national assemblies, as impressive as possible, most notably to present his case against the pope, the delegates had no national business of their own to bring to the king's notice and simply waited to hear his pleasure. To command a national attendance was in itself a tribute to Philip IV's power; the 'estates' could not have been assembled by Philip II a century earlier. The king's ministers aimed to impress the delegates with the royal majesty and benevolence, in order to overawe or charm them into compliance. Listening to the royal arguments and hearing how the king viewed the problems that had brought them together, the delegates received their first lessons in the national interest. They were tempted to look up from their limited horizons and think of the king as a national figure. If they did nothing but this and reported back what they had heard, they had participated in the process of trying to see the kingdom's concerns from a different angle. The more frequently they met, the more chance there was of persuading them of the king's seriousness. Yet Philip IV who experimented with such assemblies had achieved so little by them at the end of his reign that his final excesses prompted reaction at the provincial, not the national level. It was not until the middle of the century that the Estates General began to respond to the kingdom's problems as a whole, and then intervention in the king's affairs went further than the king wished.

The national response of the delegates in the 1350s was not sustained from behind, as it was in Bohemia, by the sense of representing defined interests with recognizable purposes. In France, the real 'communities' were definitely provincial, and they survived because they could speak on behalf of their members. They did not need princes to speak for them. When the last duke of Burgundy was killed and the duchy reverted to the crown in the fifteenth century, the custom of summoning the local estate was retained. The Burgundian chronicler preferred to see the disappearance of the duchy's status as the first peerdom of France than lose the 'estate': 'la plus belle marque que les Bourguignons savroient avoir'.[77] It was because of provincial loyalties that the kings of France were unable to make much of the Estates General or broaden the basis of their own central government by that means.

The great variety of political communities makes generalization about them undesirable. They had some common features and they developed everywhere about the same time in response to conditions that affected rulers and ruled. The grandiose projects of rulers, inspired by the intellectual currents of the thirteenth century, threatened to founder on the fact that existing political authorities were inadequately supplied with resources to sustain them. Kings had to reinforce their feudal institutions by some form of popular consultation. They summoned to meet them spokesmen of existing local communities, hitherto not bothered by more than local problems. The ability to make these encounters between central and local interests fruitful varied from ruler to ruler, place to place and according to the political problems they had to face. In most of Europe it was not until the late fourteenth century, or even later, that the 'estates' came to be accepted as an integral part of the new and cumbersome machinery of royal government. The problems had become more complex during that time and the estates were given the opportunity to work harder than had originally been intended.[78] In 1476, it was said of Savoy that 'though the duchy has a lord, it is the three estates which in all difficult cases conclude, deliberate and govern this land'.[19] Rulers who had set out confidently to impose their wills and enforce their own rights discovered that they had to compromise to gain their ends, and that by doing so they had to share their programmes with others and take their interests into account. The clergy became relatively less prominent in the political communities, because they had forfeited their real independence in return for royal protection. Pious sentiment kept rulers from pressing their advantages against the clergy, but changed nothing in the relationship. On the other hand, the land-owners had minds of their own, commanded resources that rulers envied and could not be browbeaten like serfs. Rulers had to learn how to come to terms with them, bringing them into national affairs, or conciliating local interests. The nobility did not have books or principles of divine law to help them but they began to work out rules of political activity and force kings to admit that they had responsibilities as well as rights. Politics ceased to be a matter of high-minded theory and became as vulgar as horse-trading, and as difficult to describe historically: there is in every constitution always something that cannot be written.

6

THE
COMMUNITIES
UNDER STRAIN

Christians had accepted for centuries a belief in the existence of pur-gatory, where souls would be punished for their venial sins before being admitted to paradise, but it took a layman, Dante Alighieri, imbued with the learning and literature of his day, to imagine it in detail. He saw it as a mountain rising out of the sea, and himself travelling up it like some knight errant on adventure in Easter week 1300. During the next cen-tury, purgatory became a very real experience for Europeans. The church itself taught them confidently about the after-life, to which as members of the one church militant and triumphant they were bound. They saw to the provision of the needs of souls in purgatory by the singing of masses, conceived of their own lives in the present world as a testing time for their virtues, accepting its agonies as fit punishment for their sins. In order to enter Paradise, men had first to endure the purg-ing flames. Dante, near the end of his journey, was thus summoned by God's Angel into the Garden, through this final ordeal:

> *Come fui dientro, in un bogliente vetro*
> *gittato mi sarei per rinfrescarmi*
> *tant'era ivi lo incendio senza metro.*[1]

The year 1300 suitably inaugurated a long period of European suffer-ing, for the pope Boniface VIII decided to celebrate the thirteenth centenary of Christ's birth by offering a plenary indulgence to all those who visited the Roman churches in that year, repenting and confessing their sins. More than 200,000 pilgrims flocked to the city, in Giovanni Villani's calculation, and it was a matter of astonishment and congratu-lation to him that so many men and their horses could be accommodated and fed there without causing disturbances and disputes.[2] Christendom had never before been so conscious of its effective unity and it encouraged the greatest optimism that Paradise was near at hand. Instead, Christendom had to pass through fire. So, in retrospect the Jubilee of 1300 has seemed the high-water mark of ecclesiastical pretension. It was immediately followed by an ugly quarrel between the pope and the greatest king of Christendom, Philip IV of France. As the century advanced, ever more serious social and economic problems proved the precariousness of European institutions.

The fourteenth century has become known as a period of crisis, of prolonged warfare between England and France, of the Black Death and its aftermath, of violent rebellions—the Jacquerie in France (1358), the Ciompi in Florence (1378), the Peasants' Revolt in England (1381)—and of aristocratic usurpations, most notably in England and the Empire (1399-1400). The church itself was divided by cardinal princes claiming the power to depose the pope and elect another in his place (1378), which started a schism only healed by a general council after nearly forty years (1417). For well over a hundred years the medieval communities were subjected to severe strains. Few of them emerged from their ordeals without mortal injuries. It is hardly surprising that experience deepened understanding of the nature of Purgatory and enriched their discussions of it. Religious experiences and exercises formerly reserved for cloistered monks became in this period matters of urgent concern to all. Their thirst was assuaged by drinking deep of the pious literature written in the numerous vernacular, even colloquial languages of the day, and by gazing at the vivid representations of religious experience devised by painters: the crises of the church made the impact of religion more, not less, profound.

Giovanni Villani himself, however, did not allude to the Roman Jubilee of 1300 with religious enthusiasm. He referred to the money profits made by the Romans and the church from the pilgrims and personally found that the sight of the great buildings of antiquity had inspired him, not with increasing devotion to Rome, but with the idea that his own city of Florence, daughter and creation of Rome, deserved to have its history written up, since it was rising, while Rome was in decline *(nel suo calare)*. Thus for him, this occasion for universal brotherhood had stimulated local patriotism. In other ways this coarse preference for personal and local advantage at the expense of the idealistic may be amply illustrated from the history of the fourteenth century. Many historians have accordingly lost interest in the 'middle ages' at this point, concluding that its creative energies were spent and that there was only decadence to follow, until a new and 'modern' spirit could arise. Others, with more taste for 'social reality' have, on the contrary, heaved a sigh of relief that the fogs of medieval mystification have been blown away by harsh winds of life. They have plunged joy-

fully into the familiar desolation of war, taxation, revolt, social dislocation and fluctuating population. Neither school has done much to show
how the ills of the fourteenth century arose out of the very achievements
of the earlier period, let alone to show how they conditioned the future.
There has been a kind of dumb belief that the fourteenth and fifteenth
centuries were in general for Europe a period of wasted opportunities.
The history of the church may seem like a success story as far as
Boniface VIII, with no real progress thereafter until the Reformation. The
history of the French monarchy moves smoothly to the first climax under
Philip IV and is followed by a disagreeable succession of events, conveniently blamed on England, that prevented any resumption of royal
triumphalism till the late fifteenth century. The medieval history of
Spain, summarily conceived as reconquest of territory from the Muslims,
suffers from a deplorable inertia between the conquest of Seville (1235)
and the final capture of Granada (1492). On the progressive theory of
history, only unfortunate accidents, such as the Black Death, can explain
these years of inactivity.

Some part of this interpretation may be derived from the modern
emphasis on the disruptive effects of warfare and indeed of horror; the
clergy of the fourteenth century lamented the damage and destruction of
war, much as modern writers do. This view does not allow for the no less
important way warfare stimulates technology, gives new opportunities of employment, brings new men to social prominence, and drives
men to search for deeper spiritual certainties. Contemporary writers who
were disgusted by the effects of sudden death by disease show that the
Black Death released a wanton lust for pleasure in the survivors and a
brutal disregard for the claims of charity and mercy to the sick and
dying. Moralists then and now expect, in vain, that men display nobler
emotions than the mere pleasure of survival. The general economic
consequences of reducing the population by disease was to put a higher
value on men's skills, which they were not loth to exploit. Far from
creating conditions of greater squalor or depression, the plague gave
survivors more and better opportunities. And if England and France
were frequently at war, central and eastern Europe had never known
such placid and prosperous conditions. The view that Europeans were
numbed by disasters does not carry conviction.

No one writer of the time was able to view European events as a
whole, let alone attempt a detached assessment of their impact, but the
international commercial network had brought the activities of many
different parts of Christendom and its neighbours within reach of
chroniclers' notice and stimulated a new kind of historical writer. For
the most part, the historians of the thirteenth century were clergy, monks
like Matthew Paris of St Albans or friars like Salimbene, reporting on the

interests of the church, the king and the great. After 1300 such historians become rarer. Writers tend increasingly to be townsmen, often with lay professions; they sometimes write in the vernacular. The most prolific and interesting of these are the Villani brothers, Giovanni and Matteo, whose canvas extends over the whole of Europe known to Florentine business, from Hungary in the east to Tunis in the south. Such writers appreciated how famine in Flanders prompted traders of enterprise to buy up Sicilian grain and sell it at high prices in the north, which at once demonstrates not only the interdependence of the parts of the European economy, but how profitable it was to be well-informed about international events. Writers with an ear for news brought to history more individual interest in miscellaneous information, sometimes of an incidental, inconsequential character, which perhaps indicates that the notices were inserted when received, rather than meditated and incorporated at leisure, as monastic historians had time and taste for. Stuffed though they are also with religious and moral common-places, these notices have the vivacity and colour of immediate experience. Modern readers correspondingly derive from them an impression of life coped with from day to day under threat of imminent disaster, such as newspapers provide now.

The nature of historical sources thus brings disasters into focus, whether or not they actually became more numerous. Why do the sources change? If, on the one hand, the monks and clergy esteemed historical writing less than law and theology — which reflects the academic bias of the fourteenth century — on the other the new religious education of the thirteenth century, particularly in the towns, had created a group of literate laymen eager to record local events. The post-Thomist developments in university thought to some extent also encouraged the observation of all men's activities in the world. Interest was no longer restricted only to those events in which the hand of God could be certainly demonstrated: all events and experience might have value and deserve to be remembered. In the remarkable chronicle of events in his own time, Dino Compagni recalls that he had once hoped others might write of the affairs of Florence, and how he had reined in his impulse to do so himself in imitation of ancient writers, until he realised that what he had seen and heard himself (none of which could have been known better to anyone else) had its own value. Here is a political memoir, written at a moment of extreme anxiety (1311) when the author expected the imminent judgement of God on his wicked fellow-citizens, which in its details exhibits decidedly modern features. No special training or learning was necessary for the keeping of memoirs or scrapbooks about things heard or seen. All that was needed was a belief that such compositions had value. Dino hoped that his work would in later times of prosperity inspire readers to thank God for their own good fortune. The religious reference is still worthy of remark — but it could not be more insubstantial.[3]

The new interest in the experience of unlearned persons makes it possible, rather abruptly from the fourteenth century, to add a further dimension to the historical understanding. Hitherto the predominantly clerical and royal sources suggest a society dominated by intellectual and established institutions. This is certainly misleading: the same sources themselves report the opposition they encountered. The new sources put the spotlight on lesser men: the 'opposition' has learned to speak up for itself, and by so doing, it commanded attention in contemporary affairs. For a time, in some places, it acquired tones of unexpected self-confidence. While the king and prelates of the fourteenth century endured upheavals they could do little to control, leading parts in events fell to commoners — the citizens of Florence, van Artevelde of Bruges, Etienne Marcel in Paris, Cola di Rienzo in Rome, the poet Petrarch. The views of Geoffrey Chaucer or William Langland about their own time are clearer to us than those of King Richard II. It is above all a period of great vernacular literature in which the individual voices of Jean de Meung, Boccaccio, and others, for the only time in the middle ages, may conjure up bustling, hard-headed and earthy communities far removed in spirit from the idealistic souls of the earlier period. Many writers continued to defer to the ancient traditions of Rome, but as with Giovanni Villani, this is mere form: his community of Florence could not honourably boast less distinguished ancestry. Such writers cared little for the ideals of Rome, or the order that it represented. They repudiated the claims of the 'empire' and challenged the religious goals of the Roman clergy. They worked on their own to make good their limited local objectives or to satisfy the interests of their peers.

Until the fourteenth century the constituted authorities of the west had not had to reckon with the force of this much more spontaneous and deep-seated parochialism. The power of churches and kings to organize their dominions had inevitably driven the opposition to speak out. Once they did, a place had to be found for them. They were not everywhere successful, but this does not diminish their importance and in Florence anyway the remarkable succession of writers and artists cannot be regarded as an insignificant aberration. Likewise for generations, English historians who concentrated on the history of parliament appreciated the significance of fourteenth century institutions for the transformation of the English monarchy. Some modern states and nations, like the Polish, the Bohemian, the Hungarian, the Serb or the Catalan owe their revival in the nineteenth century to the memory of these centuries. Rather than see the fourteenth century as a period of disaster, it is wiser to see that it brought into flower the restless energies of European peoples not hitherto given their chance. The astonishing variety of these achievements reveals how resourceful Europe still was, when it gave up believing in order to prefer liberty.

1. THE CHURCH

Rebuilding the church in the thirteenth century proved to be the most solid achievement of intellectual effort and noble aspiration. The papal structure was not easily shaken or taken apart. Institutionally it survived intact till the sixteenth century and its moral and intellectual influence lingered on in both Protestant and Catholic churches after the Reformation. Yet the later medieval church was not smug: it laboured under a profound sense of disappointment, even of failure. Projects for reform burgeoned in every fervent Christian soul, but they did not succeed in recreating the fervour, purity and perfection of the past. Do we see why this was, better than they? Contemporaries do not seem to have suspected that the structure, the organized church, could not of itself usher in the perfect society, for they saw it and its ministers not as human, but divine. They did not suppose that the structure might even delay the arrival of the millennium by making a priority of self-preservation at whatever cost; they focused their attention on the church's ultimate goal and did not see it as an institution, as we are trained to. Nor did they think of the spiritual quest as a constant upward climb, which brought men to a peak, only to reveal a new panorama of unconquered heights above: for them, the best lay behind, with the worst to come, until Anti-Christ should announce the Last Days. In the meantime, the church had attained, in general, the reform programme of the eleventh century: the leadership was left to a duly ordained clergy, educated, disciplined in an impressive hierarchy culminating in Rome. Christians could not believe this structure was not intended by God as the only means of salvation, or that this worldly embodiment of the church was not the providentially realised intention of the Holy Spirit. Most Christians believed with Boniface VIII that there was only one church in which all would be saved and that the bishop of Rome presided over it. This was sometimes inconvenient, but there was no alternative. There was a self-conscious, purposeful and united Latin church, wealthy but generous, centralized but infinitely varied. It had no comparable rival. Did such a church exist now, it would also be difficult to resist its claims. They did not find it perfect, except in principle, but neither the somewhat cynical exploitations of their role by the clergy, who were casually familiar about the structure, nor lay irritation and criticisms of 'abuses' undermined faith in the church's spiritual foundation, for outside it, they glimpsed only the pit of desolation. At least their sights were set high: they were not content with the church they found. Mysteriously the ideal still eluded them. They drew no comfort from thinking their dissatisfaction with the church as it was might be the best proof of the church's continued vitality.

Reformers with the least responsibilities, assuming that reform would operate from the top downwards, concentrated their efforts on the popes, or the curia, since by the end of the thirteenth century the papacy commanded such influence in the church that reform had become unthinkable except with its agreement and by its agency. Most projects of reform were therefore addressed to popes, or aimed at the papacy, which was as frequently criticised as ecclesiastical abuses and as much in need of reform. Popes, needing the services of the curia to effect any changes, saw no need to tinker radically with the apparatus, though some interference with the cardinals, a college too often inclined to be presumptuous and independent, could occasionally be useful. Reform was most needed in local government, where the papacy was least influential. The blame for this was, however, the papacy's. It had sapped the vitality of the local episcopate, for the benefit of central government and Christian uniformity. Local churches suffered in two ways — by turning too often to the popes for trivial business that cluttered up the machinery, and by leaving some business to kings or their prominent laymen, who exploited the timidity of local bishops and the dilatory procedures of Rome. There was no remedy for this state of affairs as long as the most able and ambitious churchmen put the unity of Christendom first and went to the centre to serve the whole church to best advantage. The backward and the poor areas of Christendom gained least from this system, but such disadvantages must be set against the positive gains of all Christendom. The clerical establishment as a whole continued for more than two centuries to believe in the united church. This system depended essentially on the old men elected to the papal office and entrusted with piloting the church through a succession of unpredictable storms.

The burdens of office and the difficulties of finding persons competent to take on its duties showed up alarmingly in the number of long vacancies, as cardinals failed to agree: 1241-3, 1268-71, 1292-4, 1314-16. Pope Celestine V abandoned the papacy after five months of office (1294). Boniface VIII quarrelled irrevocably with some of his cardinals. Successive popes, struggling to preserve a modicum of good sense and moderation, failed to satisfy the rigorous standards of perfection proposed by the spiritual Franciscans. In the battles of words it was natural to pin the blame on persons and wickedness. Now it is easier to see how the responsibilities for the church as a whole, unloaded on to the shoulders of the curia, could not all be borne. The papacy discovered what it could bear and ignored the rest.

The history of the papal church in this troubled period may be conveniently divided into three episodes.

(i) The first and shortest phase led up to the dramatic incident at Anagni when the ministers of Philip IV, King of France, tried to arrest Pope Boniface VII with the idea of dragging him before a church council summoned to depose him. The pope was rescued and carried off to safety in Rome where he died almost immediately afterwards. This outrageous episode is often regarded as marking the beginning of the decline of the medieval church. The metaphor begs the question.

The episode in 1302 concluded seven years of strained relations between the king and the pope. Boniface had political reasons for remaining on good terms with the monarchy; it provided him with his chief political support against his enemies in Italy. Boniface took personal pleasure in gratifying Philip by canonizing his grandfather Louis IX during a lull in their quarrel. But Boniface could not allow the king to brush aside well-established clerical privileges by imposing direct taxes for his war in 1295 and by trying the bishop of Pamiers in a secular court for alleged treason in 1301. On the first occasion, when Boniface denounced him, the king counteracted not only by cutting off the papacy's own revenues in France but by browbeating the French clergy. Boniface had to withdraw and cover his retreat with a formula that left the king to declare the necessity of the realm as his excuse for unauthorized taxation of the clergy. Papal surrender was not abject: the king had been forcefully reminded that the clergy had a fearless champion. After the second provocation Boniface summoned a council to take advice about how to put the French kingdom to rights. The pope secured an impressive contingent of French prelates to his council despite the impediments Philip put in their way. The king's only rejoinder was to summon a national council himself from which the submissive 'estates' wrote letters to the pope protesting against his interference. Both sides disputed for control of the French clergy who did not enjoy the situation and had every interest in preventing a similar occurrence in the future. Though the king had real power to coerce the clergy, his position was untenable. He could not deny the pope's rights to interfere on behalf of the clergy or in his kingdom. At best he could make a personal assault on Boniface's position. Boniface had succeeded the only pope ever to abdicate, Celestine V, so that his constitutional status could be criticised. He was blamed for Celestine's resignation and his numerous enemies in Italy also accused him of responsibility for Celestine's death. All these could be used by Philip, a master of the art of vilification. However, at the time of publishing the bull *Unam Sanctam* in the Rome council, Boniface certainly had the upper hand, for Philip had been publicly humiliated by a Flemish rebellion and the battle at Courtrai. He did not know where to turn. The final decision to seize the pontiff's person came as a desperate measure, when the king saw no other way of avoiding a total surrender to the pope's demands. The idea of a general council to be summoned by the king of France also smacks of expediency, for it was ludicrous to suppose that the king could ever have secured the attendance of more than his own bishops.

The papacy suffered a severe blow at Anagni—of shock and outrage. But it did the papacy no permanent damage. Within eight years a Gascon pope, Clement V, could summon and preside unchallenged over one of the finest medieval councils at Vienne. The council submitted so entirely to his authority that the popes following him dispensed with councils for over a century; not that they feared the outcome: they simply had no need of advice, publicity or assistance. Clement V patched up the quarrel with the king without compromising the future or the papal dignity. Philip IV continued to threaten Boniface with an ignominious posthumous trial, but this was mere bluster, He accused the wealthy military order of the Temple of unspeakable obscenities, seized their revenues and tortured the knights for incriminating confessions. Clement V intervened to little effect on their behalf, though he was eventually able to prise their possessions out of royal hands by prudently dissolving the insulted order and making over their property to the Hospital. Almost immediately the French king was faced with an unexpected revolt by the principal barons of several important provinces and this domestic dispute was succeeded by an unprecedented crisis in the royal family itself, as all three of Philip's sons died within fourteen years (1314-28), leaving no male heirs. Contemporary opinion could not fail to see in this God's vengeance on his outraged vicar.[4] It takes a modern secular outlook to find startling proof of the papacy's weakness that Clement V's successors prudently avoided both the grandiloquence of Boniface and the conciliatory attitude of Clement by concentrating singlemindedly upon their clerical commitments. For this purpose they settled at Avignon.

(ii) This period of church history—the second episode considered in this chapter—still sometimes passes as the Babylonian captivity: a vindictive epithet of obviously Italian origin. There was no ignominious subjection of the popes to the king of France. Avignon was not a city of the French kingdom in the fourteenth century, but of the empire, and it was the see of which Jacques Duèse was bishop before his election to the papacy as John XXII in 1316. The new pope settled in Avignon, and began the building of a palace, in which his successors resided for another sixty years. Admittedly they give the impression of cowering within it, not openly challenging odious tyrants, but offering them diplomatic balm and oil. Such a policy may even befit a Christian pastor, and it proved wise. The Christian community was kept together.

The reputation of the Avignon popes has never been as high as in the present century.[5] The publication of their registers has made plain their application to business, their generally scrupulous management of affairs, their remarkable powers of organization and their diplomatic handling of the involved political problems that beset them in Italy and in France. It now seems unfair to accuse them of abject dependence on the French kings. The ancient alliance between the papacy and kingdom served rather to support the precarious new French Valois dynasty, which had no power to coerce them and much need of sympathy. The popes drew heavily on their own part of southern France for their cardinals and officials. The kings of France gained less than the regions from this favouritism. To staff the papacy with such men, though un-popular in Italy, seems no worse than using Italians at other times. In voluntary exile from Italy, the popes thought constantly of the penin-sula and devoted an exceptional part of their money and diplomatic activity to upholding the papal authority there. The strongest opposition to the pacification of the papal state came indeed from Italian powers like Milan and Florence who feared what effect a strong papal state would have on their own independence. Christendom as a whole found it easier to deal with a stationary and peaceable papacy situated more conveniently for most Christians than Rome itself. It especially suited the royal governments of Christendom who found at the curia officials and procedures similar to their own. The king of England later objected most on the grounds that popes favoured the king of France in the Anglo-French war. The popes had every motive for trying to retain English loyalty, but in as much as they were partial their attitude is surely excusable. They saw France weakened by war and therefore less able to help pope or crusade. They thought Edward III somewhat dis-honest about his claims to the French throne, and reckoned his pretence that he would prefer negotiation to warfare hypocritical. England suffered little from this war, for it was waged almost entirely abroad. The consequences were certainly better understood (and resented) at Avignon than in London. As long as the popes remained in Avignon, however, even the English made no attempt to deny proper obedience.

When so much has been conceded, contemporary Christians were not altogether satisfied with the papacy. The partial criticisms of Italians like Petrarch do not matter very much. A more general feeling of *malaise* indicated lack of confidence in the papal role in the church. Dante at one end and Langland at the other end of the century had no doubts about the fate of some popes in the next world. They did not wish to dispense with the institution, but the faults they found in the heads of the church were sufficiently damning. Accusations of corruption and immorality show that the papacy seemed too much like secular institution. The system pleased rulers and clergy best because it gave them the maximum advantages. The most tactful clergy got the best jobs and managed the church adroitly. The privileges of the church had given it a vested interest in the social structure. It had given up the struggle for a new Jerusalem on earth.

Did popes fear that a repetition of Boniface's attack on rulers would expose how little the church could do to enforce their obedience? Probably not. Their real weakness lay in the fact that as the unquestioned masters of the church, they tended to deal with their problems as other heads of institutions do — at the highest level, on their own authority, according to advice of experts. They issued commands to bishops or monastic superiors. They did not try to command spiritual fervour, suspecting that this cannot be produced to order. They sensibly devoted themselves to what could be done — diplomatic negotiation with kings and efficient management of the clerical hierarchy. Never had they appointed so many churchmen to benefices everywhere; fixing a tariff of taxation that gave them the bulk of their income; making or marring great clerical careers; so regulating appointments that men took their turn according to merit (obvious or advocated). The unsuccessful grumbled but the papacy was not foolish enough to pass over the powerful, the able or the influential. Much of the system survived, so Avignon was vindicated in the end. To organize the clergy into a more or less self-regulating society, allowing secular rulers considerable influence and patronage, but maintaining papal oversight and supremacy represented the real achievement of the Avignon popes.

Rulers who could not deny the authority of the head of Christendom nevertheless got the substance of their demands while the church preserved its theoretical immunity. No secular attack on clerical riches or power was launched by powerful princes and the cooperation between them and prelates bound the church to the social order until the eighteenth century. The defence of churchmen and property might please the hierarchy. It could not satisfy ardent spirits and popes duly forfeited the popularity their predecessors had earned by a bold stand for righteousness and virulent attacks on iniquity in high places. When popes no longer jostled princes on their thrones, other Christians felt religiously inspired to do so: the papacy failed, eventually, to keep fanatics under control.

(iii) The third and most humiliating episode comprised the great Schism which lasted from 1378 to 1417, and the Conciliar epoch, its continuation until 1438. The balance achieved at Avignon did not survive the return of the popes to Rome.[6] Almost immediately Gregory XI died and public demands for an Italian pope influenced or overwhelmed the predominantly French cardinals to elect the archbishop of Bari, a Neapolitan and a subject of the Angevin queen Joanna. This tactful compromise proved a disastrous mistake. The new pope,Urban VI, had no love of cardinals, though he had been a curial official. Within a few months, he had antagonized his cardinals, some of whom withdrew from Rome, declared the previous election invalid (because held in fear of the Roman mob) and elected one of themselves to be pope: Robert of Geneva, who reminded Charles V of France of their relationship in the seventeenth degree. This pope, styled Clement VII, was very shortly afterwards obliged to leave Italy, and returned to Avignon. Charles V, after some consultation, accepted Clement VII; England not surprisingly opted for Urban VI. The division of Christendom generally followed the political alignment of Europe, though pressure had to be applied in some countries like Flanders and Portugal where the general inclinations of the churches ran contrary to the political alliances of the rulers.[7] Since both popes created their own colleges of cardinals, who in due course elected new popes to replace them, the schism was perpetuated. It took thirty years before most of the cardinals of both obediences agreed to summon a general council to restore Christian unity. This Council at Pisa elected a third pope (1409), without being able to eliminate the others. It also encouraged a belief that general reform of the church should be debated and enacted in a further council.

The second council, which eventually met at Constance, did elect a universally recognized pope, as Martin V (1417), but it also voted for certain general reforms of which the most important required church councils to meet frequently. The next council at Siena proved something of a fiasco, so that when the fourth meeting became due at Basel there was considerable zeal in some quarters for making it effective. The pope was less happy about this and declined to attend. He even tried to dissolve it before it really got going and for some years the pope and the council were at loggerheads. Prospects for reunion with the Greeks (who were trying to buy western aid against the Turks surrounding Constantinople), seemed to justify the papal decision to transfer the Council from Basel to Florence, where the theoretical submission of the Greek church to the Petrine supremacy secured the pope a splendid triumph (1438). Only the rump of the old council remained at Basel, and elected a pope of its own, who was recognized in Germany until 1449. This troubled period for the church (1378-1449) lasted longer than the residence in Avignon. It was the final exciting display of medieval energy and ideas.[8]

While Christendom lacked an effective united head and profound debates were conducted as to the proper centre of authority in the church, there was little doubt in the church about the desirability of a pope and no suggestion that the office should be suspended. All parties had such respect for their own pope that they would not doubt his total authority. Each had to recognize, however, that all parts of Christendom were equally certain. In spite of this they felt that Latin Christendom was a whole. But what was the nature of that unity? Did it exist only mystically in Heaven? They ardently willed it to be visible on earth. How could they give it substance? As early as 1380 two respectable canon-lawyers Henry of Langenstein and Conrad of Gelnhausen proposed a textbook solution: the general council in which all Christendom would be 'represented'.[9] But general councils could in theory only be summoned by the pope and all its decisions would need to be ratified by him. Which pope should summon the council? Surely both could do so? In order to secure a common invitation they would have to agree. Even condescending to negotiate was tantamount to admitting equality. The idea of a general council foundered for thirty years on the practical difficulties in getting it to meet. Only the cardinals' arbitrary actions eventually broke the deadlock and the ecumenical assembly at Constance owed most to the Emperor Sigismund who used every means to get the heads of Europe to agree to restore Christian unity. Although unification by council worked in the end, it came therefore only as a last resort, when every other possibility had been tried and found wanting. The cardinals' council at Pisa had even made matters rather worse for a time. Paradoxically the schism showed how papally minded Christendom had become. The unity of the Latin church did in fact literally depend upon one man, without whom it risked falling apart.

The schism occurred by no wish of Christendom and from no resentment of the regime of Avignon. It began with those cardinals who thought they had the right to declare their earlier election improper and to proceed to make a new one. They acted on the assumption that they formed a superior court in the church, able to judge their own acts as well as their elected pontiff.[10] However high-handed their action, it was symptomatic of an attitude of mind found amongst other great lords of the fourteenth century: a surprising readiness to set aside the most hallowed authorities and venture their own arm. The cardinals did not rely on a display of force, even if they canvassed for support amongst secular rulers. They had no justification in law or precedent for their action. At the same time, the action itself, the force it had and the impossibility of going back on it later reveal how much the cardinals' dilemma aroused sympathy. Urban VI had estranged them by temperamental displays of tyranny, but the problem did not remain at the level of personalities. Though goaded into action, they posed the question in abstract terms: if the pope's power in the church is absolute can he behave entirely as he likes? Since it seemed intolerable at the time that a lawfully elected head could be disrespectful of established customs and tradition, it seemed to follow that such rulers must have been improperly chosen. Latent in the discussions of the schism and the councils is the nature of the papal office: to whom should the pope answer for the wellbeing of the church? The papacy had united Christendom to the point where the whole church had itself to take on new responsibilities and find ways of making its officers answerable. At this point in its history the church as a whole faltered and failed to reconstruct the basis of its society. Dismayed by the profound disagreements that began to appear as to how this should be done, the majority agreed to restore papal unity as better than nothing, with a kind of pretence that the clock could be pushed back. The popes resumed their old place with the practical advantage of knowing that alternative systems had been tried and found defective.

During the period of doubt possibilities had been debated. The cardinals would have dearly loved to consolidate the authority of the college. Since the thirteenth century they had several times tried to reduce the scope of papal autocracy by pre-election oaths to prevent popes alienating the lands of the church without their consent, obtain a fixed proportion of papal revenues for the college and forestall new popes from flooding the college with new cardinals. To no avail. Popes depended for their election on the cardinals, but once elected they owed nothing: they could act alone. This discouraged the cardinals and proved unfortunate for the papacy. This irresponsibility of rulers answerable to God alone has in later secular societies procured their downfall, because rulers could not convincingly excuse their tyrannies by such monstrous blasphemies. A later fourteenth-century king like Richard II who used it could be swept aside by his own kinsmen. Unfortunately the papacy could in Christendom more plausibly cover itself in this way: most of Western Christendom believed the pope to be God's vicar. Against the pope's right the cardinals had none: they were his creatures.

During the schism the cardinals continued to work through their own self-importance for the good of Christendom. The Roman cardinals swore in conclave in 1404 and 1406 that whichever one was elected would arrange a joint meeting with the pope at Avignon to issue a joint summons to a council. On both occasions the new popes repudiated their oaths: the pope could not be committed by his own actions as cardinal. So the cardinals once again acted alone: they summoned the council at Pisa and they led the discussions about conciliar government. Out of these proceedings the cardinals emerged as powerless as they went in. They might consider themselves like a Roman senate, but the initiatives and the radical stands they took had no permanent effect in reducing the papal status. On the contrary, once the conciliarist party began to speculate on reform they treated the cardinals as part of the whole Roman curia they wished to condemn or overhaul. For the rest of the church, the cardinals were the pope's creatures, and the role they saw for themselves had no more attractions for the church as a whole than it had for the popes in particular.

In the early years of the schism, Christendom supposed that unity would come by God-given victory in battle. This may seem to us rather an unspiritual way to remedy the evil, but as laymen had lost their right to interfere in the church's affairs, they had only their right arms to lend to their popes. At Avignon, the popes had managed armies in Italy to maintain their authority; Urban VI naturally expected the kingdom of Naples to help him against the cardinals. Unfortunately, Naples was the most turbulent state in the peninsula, chiefly because of its old queen, Joanna I, widow of many husbands but childless. Since the succession was in doubt, Clement VII had no scruples in confirming the succession to one of the possible heirs, Louis of Anjou, younger brother of King Charles V of France and possessed of adequate resources to take the kingdom from Urban's patron. The schism only precipitated the expected war between the rivals for Naples: the fate of the papacy would be sealed by the successful king. In fact the campaigns settled nothing. Louis' initial success was compromised by his sudden death. His rival Charles of Durazzo triumphed for a time but Urban VI then quarrelled with his protector.[11] When Charles was assassinated after adding Hungary to his dominions (1386), the contest in Naples languished until the infant heirs should in due course become old enough to claim their inheritance. Ladislas II, Charles's son, did eventually triumph and then bullied the Roman papacy, but by that time the future of the church had been taken out of the hands of rulers and made to depend on a council meeting north of the Alps. Ladislas died before it met, leaving Naples to his sister Joanna II. Initially however the recourse to arms had seemed likely to produce a solution—not only by warfare in Italy but by campaigns in Flanders and Portugal where successes brought conversions to both camps.

Not until 1394 did Christendom begin to get seriously concerned about the delay in restoring unity. Both colleges of cardinals had by then perpetuated the schism by replacing Urban and Clement with successors. Every bit as adamant as their predecessors they denied that any power in this world could judge them. The University of Paris took it upon itself to propose that all Christendom should renounce obedience, an ingenious idea that left the validity of the papal position untouched, but gave 'Christendom' an independent power to choose its own pope. Attempts to get England to act with France on these lines were frustrated by the political revolution of 1399.[12] The idea represented an ingenious way, however, a typically academic solution which commanded little support even amongst the educated. When eventually tried by the French clergy (1401), it turned out to be a dismal failure. Pope Benedict XIII maintained an impressive dignity, while the defenceless clergy fell into the merciless hands of the lay magnates who no longer feared papal sanctions. Within two years the French church pressed for a return to obedience to the pope at Avignon. The French church, the largest and strongest in the west, could not do without the pope and had no independent power of its own. Thereafter it put on the pressure to get the rival popes to meet and issue a joint summons for a council. Beginning with a belief that a joint meeting was essential, the diplomats concluded that a council had to meet even if the popes did not. By the time the prelates assembled at Pisa 'the conciliarists' called the tune. Over the following ten years, in spite of every obstacle, they acted as the most vocal and single-minded group, only to find in the end that they could hardly agree amongst themselves on any major reform, apart from the need for frequent councils.

The council which met at Constance in 1415 had been summoned by Pope John XXIII, of the 'Pisan' obedience. He was almost immediately deposed (24 May) and the Roman pope then abdicated (4 July). Benedict XIII, held out at Perpignan though only recognized in Spain and Portugal. From this point until the autumn of 1417 the rest of Christendom was united for the first and only time in a representative assembly at Constance. It acted in complete freedom without a pope, not by some republican principle, but of necessity, having to wait until the Iberians should send delegates before they could elect a new pope. The members of the council certainly felt justified in thinking that they more certainly represented the church militant than the Roman curia. As d'Ailly wrote to the cardinals at Pisa in 1409, although the pope as Vicar of Christ can be called in a manner of speaking head of the church, the unity of the church does not depend necessarily or by origin on the oneness of the papacy, because even when there is no pope the church itself always remains one.[13] This church, represented in council, could therefore proceed against the curia and was indeed justified in doing so. From the pope downwards, it was the curials who had made the schism scandalous, so the council should propose drastic reforms while it had the chance, particularly to prevent future popes from causing scandal to the whole church. Considerations of this sort kept alive the conciliar programme and its latent hostility to the Roman curia, until the late 1430s. If in the end the party foundered, it had represented an important aspect of the life of the church for three decades.

The movement voiced a genuine conviction that the curia had itself been responsible for more evil than good. At Constance between 1415 and 1417 it was reasonable to believe that Christendom was more truly united by the council than by the pope and to believe that, as the pope had become more of a hindrance to union than head of the church, the curia should be drastically pruned.

The strength of the conciliarist party came from the clergy of France and Germany with a predominantly university background. They took from this their form of voting in the council, by 'nations' rather than by heads (a form naturally preferred by the very numerous and mostly conservative Italian prelates). It was in the 'national' deliberations that the proposals of reform were discussed. Since the English succeeded in obtaining recognition of their own nation (with less than twenty bishoprics!) on a par with the others, Constance was managed by the three northern nations, until the Iberians eventually turned up to support the Italians.[14] According to the northern nations, serious reform of the church involved a reduction of the size and scope of the Roman curia—with its control of appointments and the power to tax clergy by this means. In these northern nations, papal appointment had notably reduced the powers of appointment by the great lay magnates who alleged that curial officials and friends had been promoted at the expense of the local candidate. From this stemmed such abuses as absentee clergy and neglected duties. The clergy at Constance rightly concentrated on reform of the head of the church, because it was true by this time that the way business was conducted at the curia did affect whatever happened elsewhere. Only by doing this did they remain in agreement about reform. As soon as discussion moved away from this, agreement broke down.

Apart from the papal practice of appointment found everywhere, customs in the different 'nations' were too distinct. And within the nations there were also many humbler clergy (not represented at Constance) who even benefited by papal patronage and feared what might happen if it were removed. The German nation was the one that desired most reform by the council, since there was no question of getting the German king to negotiate effectively with the papacy on behalf of all the princes there. The English nation, however, which was in substance most sympathetic to the German, was least concerned about the council's reforms, for it could exploit the advantage of royal pressure on the papacy, parliamentary statutes, to restrict the use of papal bulls, since the courts of common law could protect both parsons and patrons against papal provision. The great meeting of churchmen to put the papacy in its place and give Christendom new organs of expression thus brought to light the still extraordinary diversity of the churches and the difficulties of securing agreement together. Once the Iberians turned up, agreement proved more elusive than ever. The desperation of radical reformers was increasingly smothered by conservatives wanting to settle the practical issue of the new pope and avoid further theoretical debate.[15]

The diversities of the churches are sometimes held to be a sign that modern national differences had already cleft the medieval church. The truth is probably that the churches had never been more similar than at this time, though the similarities were at the superficial level: the level on which the papacy had operated through the university men who served it and benefited by its operations. When such men thought about reform, their minds turned theoretically to the question of the whole ecclesiastical apparatus. Significantly they were bothered about an essentially clerical conception of the church. The laity left them to get on with it—so much did they respect the clerical immunities that had grown up. The pity was that these churchmen could find no better way of increasing the sense of unity in the church than to summon more councils. When the novelty of the council wore off, all discovered that business was simpler, speedier and more practical through the pope. The conciliarists never really considered how else the church could maintain its unity when the council closed. They seem to have supposed that the pope should be a kind of genial chairman who held the fort between council meetings. Committee men know that when they are not in session chairmen may take important decisions from administrative necessity. The papacy had a millenary tradition of Roman leadership in Christendom, and it was quite unrealistic to expect it to become less forceful. Once a new pope was elected it was his undoubted right to call and dismiss councils, chair their meetings and ratify or annul their recommendations. To function as a pope he needed all the apparatus of the court of Avignon, in his acknowledged place at Rome. Who could tamper with the curia, the pope's own affair? What part could there be for councils in government? This was the pope's concern alone. As long as immediate troubles hid these facts from sight, the conciliarists could dream of how to reform the church. When the papacy was fully restored, Christendom had to choose between the papacy they knew and the ways of council—untried, uncertain and more obviously a product of the academic mind than authorized by scripture or precedent. Christendom preferred the papacy. This can only seem an odd decision to those who think the papacy thoroughly discredited by Avignon and the schism. On the contrary, it had been tried in the fire and come out more finely tempered: it had proved to be indispensable to Christian expectations of a united church.

This long period of criticism and unrest in the church deserves considerable reflection. Some critics may think it unjustified to describe this period as more turbulent or uneasy than others and the contrast between a critical fourteenth-century and an optimistic thirteenth-century papal church may be overdone. Yet in general terms it is fair to point to the confidence of thirteenth-century churchmen and contrast it with the greater reserve of their successors. In part this was due to their scholastic education; in part, to their accumulation of experience. The twelfth- and thirteenth-century church had repudiated the immediate past and set out to build the church anew. By the four-teenth century, from its position of responsibility, it had begun to learn from experience: discovering what could be done and what not. It explored promising intellectual paths and when they led nowhere expected to save futile effort in the future, by barring the entry. Within its own confined world, it even became more confident and authoritative. Holy church had been over the whole ground already; to keep the Christian life flowing in clearly defined channels until the world should end became its unexciting routine.

The criticisms and the crisis of the church between 1294 and 1438 may be considered to have shown three things. First, that despite all its disappointments, the church structure held. The will to restore unity even during the schism was not lost; apart from Bohemia, no part of Christendom broke spiritual contact with the rest. Within the different obediences there was no general loss of confidence in the church. The will to remain a visible single Latin church prevailed. Second, the secular rulers showed remarkable restraint in leaving churchmen to put their own house in order. The Emperor Sigismund, in desperation, made it his duty to help forward the council. Rulers did not hasten to profit from the church's embarrassment. Kings were not above trying to wring concessions from harassed popes, but none of them contemplated national churches or 'nationalization' of church property. The responsibility of putting the church together fell to a comparatively small number of clerical persons. There were some ominous signs that dissenters would have liked to take advantage of the church's embarrassment to try radical change. In England the Lollards drew support from a variety of quarters, but the authorities did not hesitate to suppress them and the enforcement of orthodoxy was not unpopular or resisted. In Bohemia, Wycliffite in-fluence provoked much more radical and widespread opposition to the established church, but this only got completely out of control when royal government also collapsed on the death of Wenceslas (1419). Religious heresies spread from Bohemia in all directions, but elsewhere authority quickly stamped out disaffection. Such ills as Christendom suffered were therefore shown to be confined to its constitution; there was no gleeful escape from the arms of mother church in her hour of agony. Third, within this restricted zone of differences, the clergy who had to find solutions, consistently worked within the existing intellectual framework. The teaching of canon-lawyers had academically provided for the meeting of Christian councils to deal with papal abuses, long before the schism gave an obvious opportunity to apply the theory. No one proved eager for novelties. Though some pressed for the council as a textbook solution, leading churchmen did not want to venture even that far.[16] Some churchmen eventually reacted to the events of the decade 1408-17 by embracing a more extreme doctrine of conciliar government. They never became a confident majority and were not wholehearted enough to impose real restraints on the pope. Clerics did not waver in their belief that the first duty of the general council of Constance was to elect a new pope; once elected, Martin V received the thankful congratulations of all the prelates. Their radicalism had been at best a temporary aberration brought about in the impossible impasse of that crucial decade. Such radical ideas as they then used had the sanction of the university; they invented nothing new for themselves.

Looking back over those years churchmen could, however, draw only limited comfort from it all. Christendom had been reunited under the pope, but only because there seemed to be no other way of doing so. There was admittedly no forgetting that at one point another way had been tried and the papacy prudently concluded that it would be safer not to give councils another chance. Restoration of papal unity had come about as an obvious device *faute de mieux:* it was not an overwhelming vote of confidence for the old apostolic claims. Moreover the disturbances had shown how precarious the stability of the papal church could be. Should the cardinals—a comparatively small group of people—lose their good sense and allow acrimony to prevail, the church could be plunged back into a chaos needing generations of effort to repair. Contemporaries had no stomach for uncertainties and no courage to wrestle with their ecclesiastical authorities afresh. It took many years to restore the papacy, but their debates led to the irresistible conclusion that no other solution was available. It was not perfect, but rather than try to improve on it and risk all, it was better to sit tight for the future and not provoke more trouble: such a cautious *Realpolitik* suited prelates, but not prophets.

The international church was composed of and governed by the best educated men of the day, dedicated to the finest ideals, selected for ability rather than born to office, yet their combined learning and experience failed to find a better or more promising solution than this. There had been both the occasion and the provocation to reform or replace the papal office, and the combined talents of Christendom had baulked at it. As an ecclesiastical institution the church laboured under peculiar difficulties. It was the largest institution known to Europe and there were obvious difficulties about finding a solution as acceptable in Germany as in Spain. As an institution founded by God it could not openly be restructured according to human devices. But the conciliarists had found no difficulty about venturing a plausible and divine authority for their views, while the churchmen in Italy and Spain who were most sympathetic to the papal position were in practice the least submissive and respectful. Some of the clergy had shown at Constance and Basel that they were quite capable of thinking along unfamiliar lines, even if they did not have to face the implications of their reforms as the curia did. The trouble was rather that intellectual solutions did not command universal respect. There was a real need in the newly centralized church to devise adequate supporting institutions if the curia were to remain sensitive to provincial feeling and the prelates alive to their responsibilities as checks on the popes; but instead of doing something about this, the churches agreed to paper over the cracks by restoring the papacy on condition that local conditions were not affected. So criticism of the curia at a responsible level died away. The cardinals took care not to jolt the papacy and the pope presided over a church he could neither control nor reform.

The papacy was the only international institution of Christendom; the pope an elected elderly autocrat, with an average reign of less than ten years. The only long lived popes of the whole period were John XXII and Benedict XIII, both remarkable men whose personalities made their marks on events. As we move from ecclesiastical to secular affairs, so the opportunities for hereditary rulers to mould political affairs over a longer period of their active life might seem to increase, if only on the more limited stage of nations, but such rulers also found themselves immersed in troubles not necessarily of their own making and not within their powers to solve. Philip IV, who began so blithely with policies that were in part original, expired in crisis, bequeathing problems to his successors which were not solved before the second half of the fifteenth century. If such was the fate of the kingdom of France which had made the most remarkable progress in the thirteenth century, how much can be expected of the other nations of Christendom?

2. THE KINGDOM OF FRANCE

Just as the church had created in the papacy a centralizing institution which proved to be a source of difficulties, however valuable in other ways, so the kingdom of France evolved a monarchical form of government which became the cause of unprecedented conflict in the fourteenth century, while remaining the unique source of 'national' unity. The monarchy and the kingdom in some ways suffered more grievous outrage than the church in this period: the whole edifice was anyway more precarious and of more recent origin. Historians have tended to under-estimate the permanent damage done to the monarchy because it apparently emerged so triumphantly from its darkest days. They have tried to present events as though the work of nation-building begun by Philip IV (1285-1314) was simply resumed by Charles VII (1422-61) after a regrettable interval during which the English fought aggressive wars against the French. In this way it has been possible to divert attention from the monarchy's own responsibility for the troubles, miss the crucial differences between the nature of the government before the war and after it, while conveniently blaming the English for the weaknesses they exploited. It seems sensible therefore to examine the nature of the war first.

The war

England was a small kingdom of less than five million people. The French were three times as numerous and correspondingly rich.[17] England was more tight-knit and more subject to royal control, but there is no question of the two parties being equally matched, let alone that England was capable of conducting a long war against France. The nature of warfare also needs to be remembered. Campaigning was generally confined to summer months. There were few pitched battles or even sieges. The English raided across the country, pillaging, burning crops, seizing prisoners for ransoms, driving off cattle. Many years there were no official campaigns at all. Disorder encouraged local lords to indulge their personal hatreds. In some parts of France army captains built up con-centrations of power in their own interest, having only nominal connexions with the kings of France or England. Warfare of this kind is singularly difficult to describe or understand. There were many local incidents set in a framework of political anarchy, over which the French king did not always seem even anxious to impose his will. Individuals distinguished themselves in exploits, heroic and dastardly. Jean Froissart, after the first phase of warfare, began to collect examples of heroism wherever he could cull them.[18] Few writers were concerned to 'understand' the sequence of events or the reasons for conflict. Modern accounts rely on documents from archives and try to piece together incidents in patterns. Contemporaries hardly bothered to do this and even the great men must have been ignorant of what was happening. The unknown Norman officer who kept a record of the campaigns of the 1350s barely noted events outside his own province and was very vague about events south of the Loire.[19] Only two inferior English chroniclers were sufficiently interested in the successful years of campaigning under Edward III to follow them in some detail from 1337 to 1356. These writers also saw the war from the soldiers' point of view, showing up its inconsequential aspect and reporting without compunction the horrors which incidentally attended the violence.[20]

The horrors of war as they impress themselves on civilians were of course as familiar to non-combatants then as now. There were many who suffered from the mere passage of troops through their fields. The clergy, who did not fight, disapproved of wars except against infidels, and, in France, could only suffer; they had nothing to gain from the war.[21] Townsmen resented taxation and the interruption of trade, but their complaints made little impression. One bold burgher, who openly declared his preference for Edward III against the supine Philip VI, found that the French king was at least energetic enough to execute urban dissidents.[22] In the countryside, the anguish endured by the population only once rose to such a pitch that it commanded the awed attention of the chroniclers. Even today it is perhaps remarkable that during the Jacquerie the peasants turned on the French lords who did not defend them, rather than against the English invaders. However disgruntled by the war, the local population was not driven to guerilla activity.

While the majority of the French undoubtedly suffered from the wars, it should not be forgotten that warfare opened up many opportunities for civilians and soldiers, particularly on the English side.[23] Edward III had a natural interest in the French kingdom as duke of Gascony and close relation of French kings; but he had little difficulty in persuading many Englishmen to venture with him. The needs of the army gave merchants the chance to make fortunes by provisioning the troops. The war was mainly fought outside England and seemed to offer only opportunities for profit. When the French retaliated by raids on the Channel ports, the English were indignant and may have lost some of their earlier enthusiasm for combat.[24] Circumstances generally encouraged them to think of the war in France as their great opportunity for adventure.

On the French side, too, there were advantages in the war. It must be remembered that the English could never have gained even a toehold in France had they not found allies who positively pressed them to come in. The English did not create disorder in France, they exploited it. Even as duke of Gascony, Edward III could not have caused anything more than local diversions in the south-west. His effective intervention in France in 1339 depended upon the eagerness of the Flemings to use him for their own ends; in 1343 a dispute about the Breton ducal succession gave him another opening. The most spectacular English victories under Henry V followed the invitation extended to him by both the Armagnacs and Burgundians to join their factions and destroy their rivals. English participation in French affairs was never possible except with influential support. In the circumstances it was the responsibility of the French monarch to keep potential internal enemies separate and sweet, as Charles V in fact did after 1369. It was hardly the fault of the English or of Edward III if other Valois kings were feeble in doing this.

Modern historians seem to suppose that if the kings failed, patriotism should have at least restrained Frenchmen from collaborating with the English. But it is anachronistic to think of the war in national terms at all. The different parties concerned thought of their own partial interests. What was the nation in their day? And who might have the audacity to claim to speak for it, if the king himself faltered? Some incidents have been picked out to illustrate the existence of patriotic sentiment. It is important to avoid confusing this with popular signs of discontent—as with the army of occupation in Normandy during the 1420s.[25] The question is whether patriotism as such was capable of inspiring a sustained policy in adverse circumstances. It is surely significant that Paris, the long-standing chief city of the dynasty, should for more than fifteen years accept the authority of the English king and in 1430 repulse the Maid of Orleans from its walls as a witch. If patriotism could not inspire the leaders of the city and the university to recognize Charles VII, it means that political decisions by political persons were at that time made according to more realistic criteria.

Did patriotism matter more to the English? The wars of Henry V certainly released exuberant displays of triumphant patriotism. The use of English in formal documents was deliberately cultivated in a chauvinistic spirit.[26] But Henry V's own ambitions for a dual monarchy and his brother Bedford's judicious attempts to realize them indicate that English statesmen did not think in a nationalist way. When the war began in the fourteenth century, there was even less room for thinking of it as one between two nations. Edward III spoke French in his own family circle. He was nephew and cousin to French kings, a peer of France as duke of Gascony, and claimed the French crown—his ambition was to unite the kingdoms, not destroy the greater of the two. Public business in his realm of England was conducted in French by all his great men and his officials. At the time French was widely and internationally used in Christendom as the language of the laity and it would have been unusual had England been different in this respect. There was no general use of the unsophisticated vernaculars in official circles and it is difficult to understand that any allegedly national feeling could exist, let alone be expressed. The war was seen differently from each side, and it engendered different sentiments. The English rampaged in France and were cock-a-hoop, while the French were correspondingly despondent. Defeated in France, the English turned vindictively on the traitors at home. They were not inspired with *revanchiste* feelings against the French.

Instead of treating the disasters of France in this long period as the consequence of 'foreign' war, it is safer to abandon our modern viewpoint altogether. How did contemporaries themselves understand the situation?[27] Both the English and the French public assemblies for long continued to insist that the war was the personal interest of their kings. Within the king's own circle it might have seemed axiomatic that what touched the king concerned the 'nation'. However, as long as his subjects could, even for tactical reasons to avoid taxation, hide behind the formula of the king's war, it is obviously impossible to argue that the nation was involved. Edward III who asked for contributions to his wars, did not expect his subjects to advise him about them. The war arose from a dispute within his own family as to the best claimant to the French throne, when Edward III challenged Philip VI's right to be king of France. While the troubles continued within the royal family, the 'nation', had it been able to speak, might well have doubted why it should suffer on that account: it had no obvious reason to prefer one claimant more than another. In the end, France might be united by the dynasty, but in the beginning, the Valois were themselves the source of all discord.

The dynasty

The rift in the royal family was opened by the death of King Louis x in 1316, leaving no son to succeed him, but a pregnant wife. The rights of the child were scrupulously protected by setting up a council under his brother Philip, who thus secured the chief voice in the realm. A boy, John I, was born in due course, but died. Philip then exploited his advantage, excluded Louis' daughter Jeanne from the throne on the specious grounds, unknown to feudal law, that women could not inherit, and became king himself. Jeanne was cheated of her father's maternal inheritance, the county of Champagne as well, because it was too close to Paris and too valuable to be ceded to an infant. The nobles of Champagne were however resentful that they were not consulted about this, while Jeanne, inadequately compensated (and left, of course, with the poor and distant kingdom of Navarre, the rest of her grandmother's dowry) grew up to pass on resentment to her son Charles. He is styled the Bad by those who disapproved of his later attempts to take his revenge.

When Philip v died after only six years, also leaving only daughters, he was succeeded by the youngest brother, Charles IV, who died likewise sonless after another six years. These precedents were used to bar not only the claims of the surviving sister, Isabella, Queen of England, but also those of her son, Edward III, the only grandson of King Philip IV. Philip of Valois was raised to the throne, as the nearest male relation of the previous kings by strictly masculine descent.

The Valois had begun as an apanage family. In 1285, Philip III gave Valois to his younger son, Charles. To this was added in 1293, Perche, Alençon and Chartres, after his marriage to Margaret, who brought him Anjou and Maine as her dowry. It was a great estate and Charles was correspondingly ambitious to make a name for himself in Italy and Germany. But at the end of his life he had not been successful and he became a meddlesome uncle to his royal nephews, increasingly hopeful that he or his line would obtain the French throne. He also became more and more antipathetic to his niece, Isabella. In 1328, when Charles's son Philip became king, the Valois were not universally popular in France and he had no family claim to the loyal sentiments his royal predecessors had enjoyed for centuries.

Philip VI was not a king's son and abstained from royal action until after the coronation ceremony and unction had demonstrated his choice by God. It might have been an ominous sign of the kind of monarchy by divine right that was only to emerge later, but Philip did not begin his reign without energy. In 1328 he resoundingly defeated the rebellious Flemings at the battle of Cassel. However, instead of following this up as Philip IV had done, he restored the count of Flanders to his land and showed his willingness to rule the kingdom by cooperating with the great princes, not by turning against them. After Edward III too had been won over and done homage for Gascony in 1332, it looked as though the Valois had lived down their past and rallied all influential persons to the new dynasty. Its future was assured. Philip himself had a son, John, a boy of nine in 1328, whose son, Charles, was born in 1337. The rule of descent in the male line, introduced to suit Louis X's ambitious brothers, worked to the advantage of their uninspiring Valois cousins.

Philip VI evidently thought that the situation was sufficiently stable to push ahead with plans to launch a new crusade. These idealistic hopes were dashed not so much by the fault of Edward III but of Philip himself, since he seemed to think that the king's responsibilities amounted to so little. If he allowed his great men so much influence in his kingdom, he had at least to dominate them. Instead Philip showed that he could be pushed around by them with impunity. Edward III did not immediately put himself at the head of the vassals with grievances, and did so only with manifest reluctance. He was provoked into doing this when Philip refused to patch up their own quarrels without including Scotland in the terms, which Edward regarded as unwarranted interference in his own business. However had it not been for the willingness of others to admit him into France, Edward's wrath would have burnt out ineffectually. The critical factor in the war was not offending Edward but giving him the opportunity to take his revenge. The most disaffected individual of the kingdom was Robert of Artois, who claimed the county from his aunt by appealing to the new rule of inheritance about the exclusion of women. Denied justice, as he claimed, by the parlement, Robert turned to Edward. He was more of a catalyst than a real cause of war, but he indicated the kind of discontent that rumbled beneath the surface. The most important of Edward's French allies were the rebellious Flemings, who rejected their pro-royal count and preferred the authority of Edward III, who controlled the flow of raw-wool supplies. The Flemings induced Edward to assume the title 'king of France' in 1340.[28] Edward did not intend to be a merchants' king, even if that was how he started. In a proclamation which he sent to the French provinces he promised that if he were recognized as king by the nobles, he would respect custom and law, a pointed indication of his opposition to the tyrannous authority of the Paris parlement, which rankled with Edward, Robert, the Flemings and many others too.[29] The war opened the possibility of providing a government for France more suited to the interests of the constituent parts of the kingdom, which had been flouted in the previous generation for dynastic advantages by the last Capetians and the Valois.[30]

Philip VI might have been expected to receive much powerful support when challenged in this way. It is surprising that so many of his vassals were prepared, if not to join Edward, to take advantage of the confusion in the kingdom to reassert their own rights. Many were troubled by the way kings and lawyers had trespassed upon customary procedures; some welcomed Edward's defiance. The situation was not helped by the fact that Philip VI showed so little courage or ability in defending his crown. His son, John II, was of a more violent disposition and no coward, but was not noticeably more successful in uniting his vassals around him. The aristocracy had no stomach for the chief battle of the reign at Poitiers in 1356 and the king himself was captured and kept in prison until a huge ransom should be paid. The reigns of both kings were marred by several disagreeable political incidents and 'treasons' punished with an arbitrary violence that bewildered the most loyal. Chroniclers comment on grisly public executions, for which there were no French precedents.[31] The new kings were suspicious and they did not inspire loyalty or goodwill.[32] Without these they could not lead or control headstrong princes. The capture of the king in 1356 did not however bring down the dynasty or disrupt the royal government. Though Edward III could never hope to enjoy a better bargaining position, the fact remains that he could not use it to destroy the Valois. The new kind of monarchy fashioned by Philip IV had therefore survived its greatest ordeal and proved its toughness, even if the rulers had not. The reigns of the first two Valois kings brought to the surface the discontents stirred up by the monarchy in a kingdom still basically dependent on princely rule and local rights. Philip VI and John II themselves never realized what their real problems were or how to deal with them. Their own supporters must have often been equally blind. The monastic chronicler of St Denis, the most important commentary on contemporary affairs, consistently viewed events from the monarch's point of view. He maintained a discreet silence about Philip VI's failure to expel Edward III from his kingdom. Summing up the reign after Philip's death he preferred to praise the king for his piety and orthodoxy, as shown in his opposition to the pope himself, John XXII, who had died sixteen years before, as to the nature of the Beatific Vision. The war with Edward III demanded stronger qualities of French kings than this, but until this was realized, the kings were left in charge of a powerful machine they did not know how to look after. It was no longer sufficient to be pious and to hold on; the future of the kingdom was visibly at stake.

The war exposed the weaknesses of the centralizing monarchy which had grown out of the work of St Louis. The basic problem was how to hold together all the assembled lands of the kingdom, many of which had been delegated to apanage princes, granted that they all retained a lively sense of their own individuality. The king's chief instrument for this had become his court of justice, the parlement at Paris, and kings saw that unless the decisions of this court could be enforced against local opposition, their real authority in the kingdom would evaporate.

Provincial protest

The most important part of the kingdom, and near to Paris, where its rulings were defied, was Flanders, and it was therefore in Flanders that a determined stand was originally taken against the king. This began after Philip IV took up the case of the patricians against the count, the last of the independent great northern vassals of the crown. Unfortunately for him, it did not prove as easy to gain possession of the county as it had been for his namesake, Philip II, to seize the duchy of Normandy. Count Guy called in the help of Edward I of England, another powerful and disgruntled vassal of the king for Gascony, because Edward too resented the interference of the parlement in the judicial affairs of his duchy. Philip's apparent success in arresting the count and occupying his lands was checked by a Flemish rebellion at Bruges and the victory of the popular army over the French knights at Courtrai in 1302. The king had not anticipated a provincial rebellion. Instead of dealing with a feudal vassal, Philip found that he had taken on a stronger and more virulent enemy. To this day the independence of 'Belgium' is a reminder that the Flemings were not prepared to become a mere province of the French kingdom.

Flanders was particularly worth having for its great concentration of rich towns and industry. Philip was well known to the townsmen, who had seen what royal policy had done to the formerly flourishing Champagne, which Philip had governed in his wife's name since 1285. The balance of social and political forces in urban areas was much more complicated and delicate than in the feudal lordships of France. Enough townsmen were found to distrust both royal officials and courts of law. They were even prepared to fight for their own liberties. Townsmen made common cause with their count and the English, whose wool-suppliers gave them a lever in Flemish politics. Edward I's participation in military campaigns was only made possible by finding a foothold just across the Channel. He could not have brought pressure on Philip IV by campaigns in remote Gascony.

The war over the Flemish rebellion made Philip IV desperate to raise extra money. It was this that initially brought about the clash with Boniface VIII over the king's right to tax the French clergy. After Courtrai, when the situation became more critical still, Philip was driven to various devices, of trying to rally public opinion, particularly to impress the pope, by calling meetings of the Estates-General and of persecuting the Templars in order to obtain their money (they had been his bankers). At the end of the reign, a tax was raised for the war against the Flemings, and not cancelled when peace was arranged. At this point there was a public outcry, or rather, in several different parts of France, provincial protests against the king's abuse of his powers. The country would take the strain of royal exactions no more.[33]

The resentment against Philip IV arose out of popular feeling that the king was treating his subjects improperly: it did not come from any political judgment about his policy in Flanders. To protect themselves, each province separately demanded a ratification of its own provincial privileges; Normandy, Champagne, Picardy, Languedoc, Brittany, Artois, Burgundy and Auvergne. The people still thought in terms of their regional rights, not how to help the king secure national coopera-tion. The royal charters issued by Philip's successor, Louis X, spell out the points that seemed important at this juncture. The Burgundians and Picards, for example, demanded a clause restoring their traditional right to the duel and freedom from the inquest procedure of the royal parle-ment. The nobles of Champagne suspiciously asked the king to define the so-called *cas royaux* — matters reserved for the king — which was used by royal lawyers to extend royal jurisdiction at the expense of customary law. Louis X had no better answer than this: that the royal majesty is to be understood in those cases which by right or by ancient custom can and should belong to the sovereign prince and to no other. The movement for provincial rights that burst out in these years is therefore only another manifestation of that same distrust of royal law which had started the rebellion in Flanders.

Not all French provinces reacted in this manner, and it was the weakness of their case that they could not even unite in their protests. The provinces with the longest traditions of being governed with consideration by their own princes protested to most effect. Champagne had had its own counts until 1285 and after Louis' death in 1316 still expected to retain its independence under his daughter. Normandy had no duke; nonetheless it was the most self-contained province of France, with its own laws and the will to keep them. Though conditions varied from province to province, there was widespread discontent with the royal government, because of its manifest intention to subvert local traditions.[34] The provinces still constituted the greater part of France. Philip VI himself, as a former apanage prince, may have intended to accommodate provincial feeling in his government, but he had acquired the Capetian monarchy with its own traditions and he was carried along by its momentum. He did not, however, have the same personal authority as the last Capetians over all the princes and, once they realized that they had the chance to shake loose from the centralizing noose, they seized it. This was bound to cause trouble, since the monarchy still had no means of governing without the princes' cooperation, and no established institutions to help it in its government, apart from the parlement itself.

Political consultation

Philip IV's experiments with national assemblies representing the three estates of clergy, nobility and townsmen, had been designed to impress popes Boniface VIII (1302) and Clement V (1308) with the unity of the kingdom.[35] Given the strength of provincial differences it would have been exceptionally difficult to create a French 'parliament' out of them. They met only occasionally and had no regular legal business of their own to present to the king, as parliament had in England. The dynastic crises of the reign, like the political disturbances with the provinces, were settled without them. When the war broke out, it did not occur to Philip VI to consult such an assembly.

It was not even obvious that the king would need to ask for taxes, let alone that the 'estates' should vote them. From the surviving records, it is not very clear how the king's revenues varied from year to year, but this probably reflects the fact that the king himself did not know. A budget was prepared for Philip VI in 1332, when the Crusade was contemplated. Revenue was then estimated at 656,247 livres parisis and expenses at 625,159, which left a surplus of more than 30,000 for the treasury or for largesse. The king apparently made no further enquiries about his financial position until 1344, when the situation had drastically deteriorated. To judge from the situation in 1349, the bulk of the king's estimated revenue was derived from his profits on the royal mint: 522,028 livres out of 781,746. The next largest item was the 64,944 livres from the clerical tenth. On such evidence it must be assumed that the kings expected to meet their expenses from ordinary revenue: their traditional sources of supply were adequate to save them from begging for aid. There was therefore no question of beginning the war by involving the nation in the king's affairs.[36]

In these circumstances it may be easier to see how the war itself could be regarded not as a national one, but the king's alone. His vassals and their subjects ostensibly challenged the dynasty, not the nation. Who, in 1337, could confidently state that the two were inseparable? The problem was in the long run to identify the dynasty of the Valois with the kingdom, without any institutional support, except what was provided by the king's own administration. Until this was done, it might well be true that the kings were no more than despots, abusing public confidence for their own family's aggrandisement. Though men at this time realistically accepted the implications of personal rule and the risk that kings might be drawn into adventures more flattering to their own interests than necessary for the public good, they continued to believe in the crucial difference between a king who was a selfish tyrant and one who was not. The good ruler took great counsel and was ruled by advice. The trouble was that in France the king chose his own advisers without having to consult the great men of the realm at all.

The pious Louis IX had constituted a council of chosen, paid advisers, clerical and lay, sworn to his service to help him discharge his obligations, which were defined by his coronation oath as the confirmation of the privileges of the churches, the promise of peace, justice and mercy to his people and the extermination of heresy.[37] The king was not bound to follow his council's advice; it was intended to help him, not constrain him. Not until Philip IV's reign were there protests about the king's counsellors and then the errors of his last years were attributed not to the king's choice of advisers, but to their personal wickedness. The protests took the unprecedented form of a demand that the king take good advice in the future and Louis X was induced to sacrifice his father's favourites. At this point therefore, serious thought was given to the question of the royal council. The intention was to surround the king with sound advisers and exclude unscrupulous persons who would carry out royal whims without regard for the public interest. The king's council was to be composed of 24 great lords, persons of substance, known to and respected by the king's subjects and of some royal officials, the chancellor, the constable, the marshal, the president of the *cour des comptes* and two bishops. Until 1318 this council was allowed considerable scope in examining the financial accounts, approving grants of revenues, pensions, salaried appointments and clerical benefices — the royal patronage which was most likely to be abused by humble ministers on the make. Then Philip v began to make frequent use of a more intimate advisory council, with less exalted members more willing to work hard at the king's own business. Unfortunately, given the nature of their remuneration, there was a tendency for such men in turn to become great, to claim rights to life membership of his council and so in due course to hamper his freedom of action. To operate effectively the king created committees of loyal servants who learned how to manage royal business in their own way; councillors, prepared to work, became in effect permanent officials. The king then retreated to a yet more intimate coterie of favourites for advice. There was still no public forum for reviewing the activities of the monarch. How could such royal government command the respect of the great princes and the provinces? The only brake on its activities was provided by its own servants.

Bureaucracy

The growth of the royal bureaucracy between the time of Philip IV and Philip VI is not only significant in itself.[38] It makes it easier to understand why the provinces were more and more estranged from the monarchy. They had protested in 1314 and expected a reversion to the good old days of St Louis. The last Capetians found this impossible. They had to go on expanding their central organization to cope with the business of monarchy as they understood it. The provinces were baffled and had no other card to play but revolt against the whole system. They were divided; the monarchy was centralized. For a time it might be stampeded by events, but the armies of dedicated servants were not prepared to give up their advantageous place in central government without a struggle. They had in the end to make themselves indispensable for prosecuting the Valois war effectively.

They had begun as officials of the king's parlement. The number of councillors there rose from 20 to 62 by 1343. In the court of *Enquêtes,* they rose still higher, from 22 to 92; in the court of *Requêtes* from 4 to 29. The number of royal notaries went from 25 to 98; Masters of the Mint from 2 to 6; likewise the king's forestry office: *Eaux et Forêts.* The inflated offices of the crown could no longer move around as easily as the royal household: increasingly the weight of business confined the most routine matters to Paris, the administrative centre. The extension of the royal bureaucracy put a buffer of devoted servants between the king and the nobility, but they also slowed down royal activity and impeded royal initiative by their own rules of procedure. The consolidation of monarchical government was far from representing a simple triumph for personal rule.

The crystallization of the apparatus of the French monarchy was complete when the title of chancellor, which had been in abeyance for more than a century, was revived in 1314. The chancellor was the real head of the bureaucratic machine in Paris and as the first of the king's counsellors in the parlement he was also its effective head. In 1318, the court declared that in any dispute he should not be considered as an interested party: *ipse sit persona publica et domini regis fidelis.* He supervised the other counsellors; apart from the king, he alone had the right to excuse them from duty during parliamentary sessions. He installed new members of the court of *Enquêtes* and acted in the parlement's name during legal vacations. He opened the new sessions every November and took an active part in the appointment of new officials. Philip VI, unlike his predecessors, did not change the chancellor when he became king. In a way it indicated Philip's desire to conciliate great men to his dynasty by acknowledging their rights. Less than ten years later Philip promoted his chancellor to the prince-bishopric of Langres, and instead of retiring from office as previous chancellors had done on promotion, the new bishop continued to act in his old capacity — a precedent that was followed by his successors. Thus the bureaucracy, from being a humble appendage in the king's private service, vindicated its public role and received marks of distinction.

The large writing office or chancery stabilized in the royal palace in Paris, had to function somehow normally, even when the king was not present, which was most of the time. In the year 1332-3, chosen for study at random, the king changed his residence 78 times, moving between 46 different places and spending nowhere longer than a week (at Melun, in July, for the marriage of his son).[39] While the king travelled, his writing office, which had ultimately to deal with all official business, was fixed. The king's chancellor had to be in two places at once. He might even have to be in a third. Philip VI's greatest chancellor, the layman, Guillaume Flote, was an expert negotiator who was in Avignon December-January 1342-3 and in Vienne in the spring of 1343, on the business of acquiring the Dauphinate of Vienne for the royal house. Another chancellor, Guillaume de St Maure, spent three months or more on an embassy in the Spanish kingdoms in 1329. The chancellor took with him the great seal, in order to issue documents in the king's name. Arrangements had to be made for a substitute seal to be used in Paris during his absence. More difficulty arose about how the king should ratify his instructions, while the great seal was not available. Philip VI was obliged to use a secret, or privy seal, a device that was developed after 1332. This enabled the king to send closed letters on his own authority. It has been calculated that the number of letters issued annually after 1333 under the great seal was 20,000 while letters under the secret seal amounted to 15,000. The use of the secret seal in fact enabled the king to effect his private business through the apparatus of the administration, without giving any legal publicity to his actions. This became a notorious abuse and was abruptly terminated in February 1348 (when Philip's regime was replaced by that of his son John), and not revived with Charles V, until the monarchy recovered public confidence.[40]

Financing the war

The war itself added to the work of the government, particularly for the purpose of finding extra money, and at last it exposed the inadequacy of the administration in this respect. Typically expedients had been tried first: the salt-tax *(gabelle)* was introduced in 1341. No public assembly met to discuss the situation until 1343, when an Estates-General representing northern France met in Paris. It was critical rather than anxious, demanding that the king should give up debasing the coinage (another expedient) in return for voting a purchase tax *(maltôte)*. In 1346 a similar assembly in Paris, and one for the south at Toulouse, refused to make any further grants, so the king resorted to summoning numerous local assemblies to ask for help. Such assemblies had still little conception of the interests of the kingdom or nation. They did not think of the king's war as a public matter, still less could they propose to seize the opportunity to take advantage of him politically. After the French defeat at Crécy, a more generous and public-spirited Estates-General met in 1347. The delegates of Normandy and Vermandois again showed their concern for local privilege by demanding the right to elect their own collectors of subsidies, since they did not trust the king's officials to do so honestly. They also criticised the royal advisers. It was this which precipitated the palace revolution, whereby King Philip and his counsellors withdrew from government leaving the king's son John with real power.

After his own coronation in 1351, he summoned an estates-general which refused to vote the king more money in spite of the threat of war, so the king had to negotiate separately with the city of Paris for a grant. No further assembly met till the autumn of 1355 when the war was resumed after nearly a decade of truces; John II asked for advice about how to fill his treasury. The Estates of Northern France which met in December undertook to provide the king with a standing army of 30,000 *hommes d'armes* for one year on condition that the king reform his government and a royal *ordonnance,* immediately published, attempted to do this. There was to be a new egalitarian spirit about the payment of indirect taxation on merchandise (8d in £) and salt: the king and royal family undertook to pay it like everyone else and not allow any exemptions or privileges. Second the estates, adopting the suggestion of the Normans in 1347, planned to supervise the collection of the money by drawing on representatives of each of the three estates who should also organize and pay the troops. Third, the estates asked to be reassembled in the spring and autumn to hear how the levy proceeded and decide if further reforms were required. Fourth, the estates declared their grievances and asked for profound administrative reforms, blaming the king's counsellors for the sorry plight of the realm.

These points show how much the political thinking of the representatives had advanced between 1347 and 1355. The situation of the kingdom had become desperate and the king sought to mobilize all his support if he was to meet the threat of war. On their side the nobles had no intention of letting the king negotiate again with the bourgeoisie of Paris for grants as in 1351; instead they themselves collaborated with the leader of the Paris merchants, Etienne Marcel. The leaders of the estates of 1355 were the prominent prelates and nobles of established status; they blamed the king's advisors for the condition of the realm, and in particular for the bad relations between the king and Charles of Navarre who was negotiating with Edward III to renew the war. The nobles were confident of their right to advise the king and to see that their wishes were implemented. The administration was put on the defensive; at last the issue of politics were openly discussed.

The movement did not fizzle out. In March 1356, the new estates replaced the indirect taxes by an income tax (graduated to favour the rich—thus a man paid £1 on £10 revenue but only £4 on £100 and only £100 on £10,000); in May when they met again, they decided to reimpose the *gabelle* and in June to fix the rate of income tax at 4 per cent on revenues up to £100 and at 2 per cent above £100. By the time the estates met next in October, the king was a prisoner of the English. The kingdom was therefore in the hands of the dauphin. The 800 members of the estates, never before so large or confident, intended to enlarge their contribution to royal government. The estates entrusted their powers to a commission of 80 members who asked the dauphin to change his council, keep the terms promised by his father earlier in the year for better government and to act in accordance with the advice of a permanent commission representing the nobles, the clergy and the bourgeoisie — counsellors with the same authority as the king had to do everything to 'ordonner' the kingdom, as much for appointing and removing officials as others matters. The dauphin eluded these demands and attempted to use the Estates-General for the south at Toulouse to play off the northern discontents. But he was obliged to return to Paris, where the merchants' provost, Etienne Marcel, had forbidden the use of the latest issue of debased royal money in December 1356. Early in March 1357 the dauphin met a new estates in Paris which drew up a new reforming *ordonnance,* appointed a new royal council which would respect the interests of the estates and demanded the meeting of three further assemblies within twelve months; in return they offered to support the cost of 30,000 *hommes d'armes*.[41] The imprisoned King John denounced these estates, but the council they had appointed maintained its position and remained the effective government from April 1357 until the summer of 1358, in spite of the dauphin's objections.

1358 was however a year of great violence. There were disturbances in Paris in January, which flared up into riots during which the dauphin's marshals were murdered in February. The dauphin now called himself regent and prepared to assert his own authority against the council. He left Paris in April and went to Senlis. The next month a violent peasant revolt broke out—the Jacquerie—which was put down with great savagery. At the end of July, Marcel was murdered. When the dauphin returned to Paris, it was as a person of authority and force. The experience and wisdom he had acquired were to stand him in good stead later.

The events of the years from 1355 to 1358 should be considered in their constitutional aspect.[42] In these years the estates-general of northern France met six times. Before ever the imprisonment of King John had created an unprecedented situation, they showed a firm intention to take part in government. In this they went constructively much further than any other similar group in fourteenth-century Europe, yet this movement appeared rather abruptly without any previous build-up of claims.

The interests of the reform party in the estates-general may be reduced to three: first the royal administration of which they demanded specific reform; second, reform of the coinage; and third, good management of the army, including provision for its upkeep, which was to be entrusted to a committee of the Estates-General itself. If we compare these interests with those of earlier movements of protest, such as those of 1315, we must be struck by the extent to which the different social groups, clergy, nobles and bourgeoisie, had come to agree on a coherent scheme of reforms pressed for in successive assemblies in northern France (even if they were not much supported by the relatively insignificant meetings of the estates of Languedoc at the same period). For the first time the cares of the monarchy had come to seem a matter of common concern. The scope of these reforms remained limited: it was confined to the royal administration, which affected all regions equally, however different in themselves, and to the war which had become a scourge since the capture of Calais and the appearance of the 'companies' of soldiers in Brittany after 1347. The public spirit of the estates was such that they were not content to call passively for reform; they intended to keep in touch with government, and considered continuous amendment of their taxation proposals in order to meet objections. One of its enduring achievements was financial reform. The existing clerical subdivisions, the dioceses, were used as the units of taxation for the collection of lay subsidies. Local overseers, *élus* (hence, élections) as originally demanded only by the Normans and Vermandois, were appointed for the whole *langue d'oil* (34 dioceses). These reforms go far beyond anything demanded by that time in England, which had to wait until 1376 before a similar onslaught on the management of royal affairs by royal councillors was launched by the discontented aristocracy.

Both the French and the English constitutional experiments were less important for the permanent gains made than for the affirmation of the public responsibility of the monarchy. The king's problems had ceased to be a private concern, even of his family. The political committees of the realm held themselves to be involved too. The conscience of the kingdom could be effectively voiced; it could criticise the king and his council without dragging down the monarchy; and it helped to stimulate a sense of public responsibility over a range of activities much broader than the area of local legal and judicial responsibility. What then happened to this nascent French constitutional movement?

In the circumstances of the early part of 1358, it is understandable that the royal council in Paris was driven to act independently and in defiance of the regent and the imprisoned king. Yet it was impossible for it to govern long without the cooperation of the monarch. The demand had been for the king to take good counsel; there was no permanent justification for making the council govern in his place. Outside Paris the dauphin found in the spring of 1358 that he retained the affections of the people. Charles did not actually become king until his father died in 1364, but his apprenticeship had begun with his father's capture at Poitiers. Slowly, he learned how he could govern alone. Scrupulously he always listened to the best available advice. But he was not bound by his council to follow their dictates. No French king was better prepared than he for his office: hence his nickname Charles *le Sage*.

Charles V

The capture[43] of King John, which could have meant the end of the Valois dynasty, proved to be the turning point in the fortunes of his house. Edward III could only obtain the heavy ransom of 3 million *livres* for his prisoner, not the kingdom itself. However ingloriously, therefore, the Valois had survived. The vassals of the kingdom had not been able to throw off the incubus of royal sovereignty or usurp the king's place. The dynasty had defended the rules of the royal succession. It also preserved the unity of the kingdom. By the terms of the treaty of Bretigny, large tracts of west France were ceded to Edward III on condition that each territory specifically renounced allegiance to the king of France. Nine years later this had not been completed. The Valois, whatever, their faults, had not effaced the memory of what it meant to claim membership in the monarchy of St Louis. When the war was resumed in 1369, Charles V rapidly had the better of the conflict and the English were soon suing for peace. In his person, the dynasty did more than survive; it triumphed.

Charles responded to events as they occurred, not without good sense, but he was himself unable to set the pace. He had begun his political career obliged to face the Estates-General after Poitiers and desperate to raise the money for his father's ransom. After he became king, his main preoccupation was to overthrow the treaty of Bretigny, without putting himself morally in the wrong: the chronicle of the reign betrays how uneasy Charles himself felt on this point.[44] In dealing with his problems, Charles called upon the best learning of his day, but more important perhaps than their innovations were the traditional elements that still mattered most to Charles and his subjects. For this purpose we may regard as representative a contemporary treatise the *Songe du Vergier* in which a knight and a clerk discuss the nature of power.[45] The knight regards the people as the source of all authority, but the government over them is given by God alone to the king. Nevertheless he is bound to respect ancient customs and serve *la chose publique*. The knight does not propose any way in which the king could be supervised — the traditions of the monarchy merely insisted that the king took good counsel. Charles V himself took the divine nature of his office very seriously. He commissioned a special manuscript of his coronation ceremony in 1365 as a reminder of the supernatural virtues acquired by the monarch at his coronation or *sacre*.[46] The idea of religious duty in kingship placed a curb on the king's personal whims. Charles V did not use his divine mandate to dispense with human advice. On the contrary, the more aware he became of the responsibilities he had taken up, the more concerned he became to discover from his counsellors the best means to discharge them. He was prepared to explore the subject at a somewhat theoretical level. He commissioned translations of Aristotle's *Ethics* and *Politics* into French; he collected books, which he lent to his nobles.[47] The influence of Aristotle was detected in the king's decision to make his council elect a new constable (1370) and a new chancellor (1372-3) and to separate the king's accounting office from the general administration of 1372.[48] But the most important of Charles's reforms inspired by Aristotle was reform of the coinage. Charles's adviser in this was Nicholas of Oresme, his tutor and later his secretary, the translator of Aristotle. From Aristotle Oresme derived ideas about money, which he expounded in a treatise written after the battle of Poitiers. In his view the prince should not regard the money circulating in his lands as his own property, for though the prince struck the coins in his own name, he did so for the public good *(l'utilité commune)*. He argued that the prince should accept fixed legal standards for the coinage and this prepared the way for the royal *ordonnance* of 1360.[49]

Charles's good government according to the best advice tendered for the public good exactly fulfilled contemporary requirements and quenched the raging thirst for constitutional innovation that had developed after 1356, when discontent with the Valois had been most acute. Charles v dealt effectively with the English, consulted the 'polity' and appeared to be a model king, who made the monarchy broadly loved. In a longer reign, or in more settled conditions, his defects might have become more obvious; as it was Charles v, with St Louis, personified all that was best in the French tradition. After the collapse of the reform programme in 1358, although Charles as regent reappointed the officials he had been obliged to dismiss, he also accepted some of the reforms proposed by the council: councillors were allowed to examine all matters affecting the domain and finance, which ultimately had some bearing on how much the king would need to ask for as extraordinary revenue. Charles showed his willingness to act through public channels and not to be secretive or vindictive. His charters likewise received the countersignatures of members of the council and were couched in proper form by the chancery notaries. From the Estates-General he borrowed the innovation of commissioners of taxation. Disputes about taxes were referred to a permanent committee of *généraux* which met regularly in Paris after 1370 and became the *cour des aides*. Though intended to be as temporary as taxation, this became a fundamental institution of the monarchy that survived till 1791. The king's management of extraordinary taxation was secured by this means, though he did not dispense with summoning estates to consent to it. They simply lost their claim to supervise it themselves. The estates' enthusiasm to raise money for the war against the English, first shown in 1355, was displayed again in 1359, when they preferred to prepare for more war rather than accept the terms of peace dictated by the English. Charles v found that in his own reign he could also get financial aid, as in 1367 and 1369 when grants were made three times.

Charles always supposed that taxation would be levied only in emergencies and that the monarchy would have to live from its own domain lands. He saw the desirability of certain changes in conceding lands to his family. In 1366 he changed the terms of apanage made to his uncle, Philip of Orleans, limiting descent to heirs male. For his own children, he introduced a new formula which expressly declared the sovereign powers of the king: the right to strike coins, set up tolls, fairs and markets, ennoble men, protect churches and abbeys. The king justified this by reference to his coronation oath which obliged him to avoid dissension in the kingdom and not to alienate his rights; the Orleans case was brought to the council for its support in dealing with his own family. The definition of royal rights went furthest in the instrument negotiated with Charles of Navarre in 1372: the king resigned the lordships of Montpellier but retained the protection of the church, punishment of crimes of *lèse-majesté,* infringing royal *ordonnances,* false-moneying, carrying of conspicuous and offensive weapons, authority over royal taxes, grants of safeguard, nobility and legitimacy, remissions of crime, lifting the 'ban'.[50] Asked about royal rights in 1315, Louis x had returned an evasive answer. Sixty years later, the king can give a long list of matters over which he has decided to assert a royal monopoly. Charles v reserved these rights and did not concede them to apanage princes or others. The king's resumption of royal rights from members of his own family indicated that a new policy had emerged. It could not be used to cancel the existing arrangements and it was a full century before its effects were really felt. For Charles it was only a tentative step in a new direction, not a major reform.

The biggest problem of his reign was how to set aside the treaty of Bretigny. Charles began with diplomacy and the chance to make war openly did not occur until 1369. In the meantime he had intervened in Spain, whither Edward the Black Prince had marched to the help of Pedro I in conflict with his half-brother, Henry of Trastamara. Charles v, glad to fight the English on foreign soil and hopeful of securing a powerful maritime ally against the duke of Gascony, sent Du Guesclin to Castile. This was not immediately successful, but when Henry murdered Pedro in 1369 and became king, Charles's plans were realized.[51] Even more important was his success in Flanders. Since Philip IV had signally failed to seize Flanders by direct action against the count, his successors had seen the advantages of trying to absorb the count into the kingdom's affairs by gentleness. Marriage alliances gave the counts extensive lands outside Flanders and made them an important dynastic family in their own right, fully conscious of their links with other families in the realm and their place in the whole kingdom. Count Louis I inherited the county of Nevers from his mother and forged the first link between the Low Countries and Burgundy. His son, Louis II, married Philip V's daughter and took her inheritance of Artois. Their son, Louis de Mâle, also eventually inherited the Free County of Burgundy and his daughter, with her prospects in the Low Countries and Burgundy was the most sought-after match in Europe. Edward III negotiated for her marriage to one of his sons, but Charles v intrigued at the papal curia to prevent the grant of the necessary dispensation to marry within the prohibited degrees and pushed the suit of his own brother, Philip. Louis de Mâle demanded the cession of the Somme towns, which he had long coveted to round off his patrimony and Charles v was prepared to make the sacrifice in order to keep Flanders out of the English embrace. The high-handed manner of Philip IV in the Low Countries had been abandoned and it was the count who took lands from the king. By this marriage, the French king was in fact covered against any repetition of those events that had brought Edward III into Flanders and so mesmerized the early Valois, but only for so long as the Burgundian family remained friendly to the royal house. Charles V had no better policy in 1369 and the risk was worth taking, Nevertheless it is significant that the king had in fact surrendered his own power to intervene in the Low Countries, at least for a time, and relied on the Burgundians to manage the king's interests there. The king in fact accepted that Flanders was too big a cherry for him to bite and in the long term the result was that Flanders as a whole was never incorporated into the French state.

With both Castile and Flanders as allies, Charles V no longer hesitated to find an excuse to repudiate the treaty of Bretigny and reopen the war. This promptly turned in his favour. Within a few years, the aged Edward III prepared to negotiate and this gave Charles the opportunity to consider the problems of government at home, without having the war to harass him. But he had very little time to play with and if his policies laid the foundations for the later French monarchy, Charles had not designed them to that end. It was because his reign proved to be the one period of intelligent government in a century of confusion and royal inadequacy that his impromptu arrangements had to serve for something more.

Charles V was by all accounts the most able and attractive king of his whole dynasty. He became king at the age of twenty-seven, already a man of mature political judgment. In a reign of sixteen years, he corrected his predecessors' mistakes, made good their losses and provided a basis for reconstructing the monarchy after the war. He was not a man of great energy or violence; he was not even a dominating personality. He only survived by being devious and shifty in 1356. During the troubles that followed he learned how to dissimulate. The chronicle of his reign, which he himself probably supervised, shows him as devoted to the problems of government. He worked at his kingship with persistence and intelligence, not weighing personal considerations. If he could not offer the kingdom military leadership, he at least had the sense to select Bertrand Du Guesclin as constable. There is no doubt of his mastery of affairs, but he also saw the wisdom of making public gestures of consultation.

The kingdom was still composed of great principalities in loose association with the crown. The state apparatus—the chancery, the parlement and the *cour des aides* served the king, but beneath it the older political and social bonds continued as before. Even in such a novel matter as taxation, the monarchy had taken over the existing divisions of local significance, namely the diocese. What can be detected however about the situation from Charles v's time is that the older France, feudal, regional, with its personal loyalties and acute social distinctions, has at least become hinged to royal government. The great nobles no longer behaved as though they could uphold provincial separatism and remain aloof from the royal court. The greatest danger of the north, the count of Flanders, had become a member of the royal family. Many lords continued to be independent, but they began to expect the king to become active on their behalf, or rather they saw the advantages for themselves in forcing their way into the royal administration. Under Charles v the central government had become a real force in the administration of the kingdom, particularly through taxation, but local government had not lost any of its own energy. If ever the king should himself falter in making his machinery in central government work for his interest, there would be no stopping provincial leaders from trying to obtain control of it, so that it should work for them. The lasting achievement of Charles v was to destroy provincial isolationism and to make Paris the focus of French political life, with all the attendant dangers when the monarch was less capable than he. The 25 years from 1355 to 1380 were specially formative for the subsequent history of France. They were amongst the most tragic years the kingdom ever knew, the consequence of the king's capture at Poitiers, the peace that released active soldiers as idle, brutal brigands and the renewal of the war. Yet the experience of hardship, under those prepared to lead and endure, played an important part in forcing the French to make the best of their political legacy and turn the monarchy into a positive means of uniting the kingdom.

Charles VI
When Charles v died in 1380, the kingdom was entrusted to a minor, Charles vi, for the first time since St Louis and the beginnings of active royal government. Charles vi himself was personally capable of government only for four years between 1388, when he came of age, and 1392, when he had his first bout of madness. The personal monarchy of Charles v was obviously not to be practised under these conditions. It became a question whether the monarchy would survive at all. Its resilience was therefore demonstrated during the years which elapsed after 1380. Not until Charles vii re-entered Paris in 1435 was the kingdom again in capable hands. Fifty-five years is a long time for the ship of state to sail without a helmsman. No sustained attempt was made to find a substitute form of government, by involving the estates, as after 1356. The royal princes improvised in a series of emergencies, as best they could. They

were in no position to improve on Charles v's handiwork, which had therefore to serve in circumstances it was ill-designed for.

No reign of comparable length has been such an unmitigated disaster as that of Charles VI. This is not due primarily to the renewal of the English war, the defeat of Agincourt, the loss of Normandy and the Treaty of Troyes, for Henry V owed his successes to the existing political chaos in France. Earlier English efforts to renew the war after 1380 had come to nothing. By 1395, even the excuse of the schism was given up as an incitement to war. If war came again in 1415, it was the internal condition of France that made it possible. Even in the absence of obvious dangers, the government of Charles VI had proved unable to cope with its responsibilities. The conduct of the king's wife was not above suspicion, which cast doubt on the legitimacy of his children. His uncles and brother disputed their rights to act on his behalf. Yet the king's incompetence inspired no political plan to deprive him of the crown. His right to reign was unquestioned. This was indeed the principal source of trouble, and as before, a pragmatic suggestion about how to deal with the situation came not from France, but from England.

No attempt has been made to write the history of this miserable reign since Godefroy in the mid-seventeenth century collected the materials for it. The principal literary source is still that of the traditional figure of the monk of St Denis, the clerical defender of the dynasty, so the focus remains the pathetic monarch. Yet the reign of Charles VI could be studied as though it were an epitome of the whole *ancien regime:* the rivalries at court, the wasteful expeditions into Italy, the intrigues on the imperial frontier, the war with England, the hated foreign queen, the decadence of court manners, the discontent of Paris and the bloodthirsty mob, administrative incompetence, official peculation: so many features of the monarchy as a whole appear already in this reign.

One of the major sources of trouble was financial corruption. This had not been a problem in the past because until the reign of Charles V there had been no regular taxation and source of ready money. Taxation had then been raised for the war and urgent necessity had spent it without question. On his death-bed, Charles V, moved by pity for his people and suspicion of his covetous brothers, had abolished the *fouages* and two months later, the government of Charles VI had been stampeded by the Estates-General and agitations in Paris into abolishing all other taxes.[52] But within a year, the king's council reimposed the salt-tax and the purchase-taxes, a measure that was greeted by an explosion of protest in the principal cities of the north. But after the royal army had successfully defeated the Flemings at Roosebeke (27 November 1382) the government had more confidence and suppressed dissent. The revival of the *aides* and the *gabelle* provided the government with 2 million *livres.* This was a great deal of money and much of it stuck to many fingers as it passed from the pockets of the citizens into those of the king.

The ordinary revenues of the crown amounted at best to about 200,000 *livres* a year, which was just about enough to cover the expenses of the king's own household.[53] The expenses of his queen, his children and his courtiers amounting to over a million were thus the first charge to be met from the *aides.* Even so there was a lot left over. These taxes were not voted specifically for warfare, as in the past; they were treated as though they were ordinary revenues to be relied on. Exceptional expenses like war or the marriage of his daughter were held to justify a resort to further taxes, the *tailles,* which brought in, on an average, a further 300,000 *livres tournois* a year. Such large sums require careful accounting, if they are to be spent honestly. Financial administration was instead clumsy and easily abused. There was no single treasury account. Extraordinary taxation was always administered separately, on the specious grounds that it was only temporary. There was no means of obtaining oversight of all the king's money which gave too much scope for unscrupulous officials confident that abundant supplies of money should enrich not only the king, but his servants. The bulk of these revenues came from indirect taxation, which was most bitterly resented in the towns and by the *bourgeoisie.* They were aware of the scandals connected with its incidence and loud in their expressions of disapproval. The salt-tax involved corruption over the siting of the salt-barns, which proved a valuable source of bribes for tax-farmers. Some areas were exempt from taxation. In others the *aides* were collected by the princes. Everywhere the collection of taxes fell into the hands of financial managers with a vested interest in resisting reforms and a determination to hand on their lucrative posts to their heirs. The monarchy had found it too easy to extract more than enough to meet the king's needs, but the surplus, which was taken by the officials, inevitably attracted more people than could be satisfied.

The seething protest about corruption boiled over in 1413, but before coming to that it is necessary to say something about the way politics had developed from the beginning of the reign. At that time the schism of the church was still in its infancy. Louis duke of Anjou intended to use the support of the pope of Avignon to win the kingdom of Naples. Philip the Bold, duke of Burgundy had to defend the papacy in Flanders against the Urbanists and their English supporters. Both needed financial help. Was there enough for both their needs? It seemed not, and this started rivalry between them. Fortunately, at this stage, the duke of Anjou died in Italy (24 September 1384) leaving Philip as the principal statesman of the kingdom, since his older brother Jean duke of Berry was a much less able man, more interested in artistic patronage than in government. Philip of Burgundy was able to command influence in the government until his death in April 1404. His death opened up a period of tension between his son, John the Fearless, and Charles VI's younger brother, Louis of Orleans. Despite help from the queen, Isabeau of Bavaria, Louis had to make some room for the relentless John, but their relations did not, and could not, improve. John arranged for Louis' murder on 23 November 1407 and refused to make any reparation for his offence, proudly defending the justice of his action in ridding the kingdom of a tyrant.[54] No one proved powerful enough to obtain satisfaction from him, but the heirs of Louis of Orleans and the party that was built up around them by the count of Armagnac could not accept this ignominious surrender to Burgundian might. In his turn John of Burgundy was assassinated twelve years later: 10 September 1419.

In this quarrel it is clear that the bullying attitude of John is as blameworthy as the desire of Louis to escape from the tutelage of the Burgundians and pursue his own line of policy. As distinct from the problem of assigning moral blame, it is important to recognize that politically John became identified with projects of reform and that neither he nor his party forfeited confidence, although these reforms were not effected, whereas Louis of Orleans, for better or worse, never became associated with this movement for reform. At first his ambitions had been devoted to wresting the direction of the kingdom from Philip of Burgundy, in order to pursue his claims in Italy. After the death of Philip, he was responsible for demanding taxes for an impending war with England. Four *tailles* were raised between 1404 and 1406 which produced about 2 million *livres tournois*, but they were not spent on war. It was generally believed in Paris that the taxes simply enriched the courtiers, for Louis' love of pleasure and luxury were notorious and the conspicuous expenditure of the court unashamed. Contemporaries did not have access to the accounts, but they used their eyes. The author of the *Songe Veritable* sensibly noted how the king's finance ministers behaved in public, what kind of houses they built, the quality of their plate, the magnificence of their hospitality. The constable of France himself, Olivier de Clisson (1380-92), was suspected of having accumulated a personal fortune of over half a million *francs*, though his royal salary was no more than 12,000 *livres* a year. Some officials may have been unjustly suspected of corruption, but their way of life invited criticisms and Louis' own manner of government encouraged the popular belief that he was indifferent to abuses. Such factors as these cannot be neglected when it comes to judging the political issues at stake between Burgundians and Armagnacs. There can be no doubt that both sides when in power dipped into the royal treasury for their own purposes, but it is not sufficient to argue that the weakness of the royal finances under Charles VI was therefore the fault of the great princes, rather than the royal ministers, so loudly denounced as scapegoats.[55] For, whereas the officials were accused of enriching themselves, the money taken by the princes served their policies and their supporters; to judge between the parties, it is necessary to know something of the policies they advocated.

The Burgundian concern for financial reform has already been mentioned. However tenuous, it represented a genuine bid for the support of the townsmen, who mattered very much in the Burgundian lands of the Low Countries. Moreover, because of those lands, the Burgundians occupied a crucial position in all matters connected with the English war. The Armagnac party had no comparable power or interest in the north. The Orleans' interests were in the Loire valley, in the centre and in Italy. The Armagnacs were strong only in the south. If Paris was 'Burgundian' in sympathy for so long, it was because it saw in the duke of Burgundy a royal prince who understood northern French interests. Through his lands in the Low Countries he was able to advance them. Not for nothing did such a prince flaunt an interest in accounts.

In 1413 he became associated with a great reforming movement.[56] The Estates-General met between 30 January and 9 February. No estates general had met since 1381, when the government had been refused its demands for money, but there is no sign that when the estates reassembled after more than thirty years, the members were anxious to take advantage of the government's weakness to demand assurances of being consulted in the future. The parts of the kingdom dominated by the princes of the Orleans faction were badly represented. The meetings of the estates were arranged so that provincial groups could deliberate separately, contrary to earlier custom; as a result only three provinces succeeded in reaching any conclusions The province of Rheims criticised the administration of justice and of finance, blaming the excessive number of officials, their rapacity and their incompetence; the province of Rouen concurred, but emphasized the need of peace in Normandy where the war had recurrently devastated the country; the province of Lyon addressed itself to the king's immediate need of money to prepare for war against the English. They suggested that the king should make his own officials disgorge the money they had made from the royal service; should carry out a complete overhaul of the administration; and should discharge superfluous and dishonest officials, not merely in the financial offices, but also in the parlement itself. These criticisms descended to particulars: individuals of Orleanist sympathies were picked out for denunciation in a predominantly Burgundian assembly, so that political rather than constitutional issues became predominant. The estates were dissolved without receiving more than vague promises that the government would look into the remedies proposed and would not raise any new taxes.

After the estates had left Paris, the university and the bourgeoisie of Paris presented on 13 February a statement about the royal government listing grievances and proposing remedies. The grievances concerned principally the administration of the royal finances by the royal officials, taken to task by name for their deficiencies: the masters of the *chambre aux deniers,* the queen's treasurer, the master of accounts, the *généraux des aides* and the chancellor himself, the last of 25 named individuals. As for the remedies, the first was obviously to dismiss all the officials of finance, to seize their goods and persons and to make them give account of their charges. Second, the king should cancel all grants of pensions and obtain for the future proper accounting of all his revenues; third the king should take the monopoly of all grants of indirect taxation and not concede the levy of certain provincial taxes to the great princes and *apanagistes* (which was the custom); fourth, some 1,500 wealthy individuals should each be required to pay capital levy of 100 francs to help the king when in need; finally, several reforms were proposed, including a reduction in the number of financial and judicial offices, the restoration of the ancient method of recruitment and the election of experienced men to sit with the great princes and other good, loyal and sufficient persons. In spite of the fact that the university and the bourgeoisie could not obtain the cooperation of the lawyers and judges in the parlement to these proposals, the influence of the duke of Burgundy was great enough to secure their acceptance.[57]

Nearly all the officials on the black list were dismissed on 23 February; the commission of enquiry was appointed, which reported three months later. A great *ordonnance* of 258 articles was published on 26-7 May, generally regarded as a model of wisdom; it reviewed the gamut of royal administration, denounced faults and proposed remedies. 'It was in no way revolutionary, it was not even very new. It was a codification of *ordonnances,* amended and brought up to date, the work of *esprits pondérés* which could have been the point of departure for a *roi sage.'* This was expected. On 28 May, Jean Courtecuisse, the king's almoner, university teacher and administrative reformer, addressed the court and the poor king in particular, imagining that Charles V reproached his son: 'Charles, Charles, what has become of the honour and majesty of this realm? where is the panoply of majesty, the fine and rich crown which I forged with much effort? where are the great treasures that I gathered for such a long time?' The inheritance of 1380 had been frittered away by 1413 and the paper scheme, however wise, could not restore it. Within four months it was literally torn to shreds, because reform had become discredited by its association with revolution.

The prospects for reform were clouded while the commission was in session and bleak by the time it reported. The provost of Paris, Pierre des Essarts who had been dismissed in February, returned to Paris at the request of the dauphin and occupied the Bastille of St Antoine from which he threatened eastern Paris. This provoked a popular rising in the city, led by the butchers under Simon Caboche. Paris and the court were at the mercy of the mob for four months from the end of April. The demands of the Cabochiens were not as carefully formulated as those of the *bourgeoisie*. They rose nevertheless to defend the the cause of 'reform' which they believed to be endangered by the attitude of the dauphin, Louis. He was a young man of sixteen, son-in-law to the duke of Burgundy, but resentful of the duke's tutelage and therefore hostile to his political programme. The first impulse of the Cabochiens was to march on the dauphin's residence and demand the surrender of fifty traitors in his service. When this was refused, the hotel was forced and fifteen prisoners, including the dauphin's chamberlain, his chancellor and his cousin, the duke of Bar, were led out. In the evening, several alleged supporters of the Orleanists opposed to reform, were butchered. Nearly a month later, the mob invaded the royal palace and led away the queen's brother and fifteen of her ladies. It was only a few days after this that the reforming *ordonnance* was published in the hope of appeasing the mob. It was too late to serve this purpose. On 10 June, the dauphin's chamberlain, one of the prisoners of 28 April, was executed. More followed. The Cabochiens set up a commission of four to assess the fortunes of the *bourgeoisie* and force them to make appropriate loans, in order to finance revolutionary activities. It became clear that the duke of Burgundy, formerly the darling of Paris, could no longer control the mob, so the court saw no alternative to negotiating with the Orleanist princes outside Paris for relief. Civil war in Paris was only avoided by the flight of the Cabochien chiefs at the beginning of August. The entry of the Orleanists meant the triumph of reaction.

The Cabochien programme had not been as specific as that of the *bourgeoisie*, but it is quite clear what they believed to be the main cause for the collapse of good government: they blamed the courtiers of the households of the dauphin and the queen. They aimed to lead the dauphin from his life of pleasure and debauchery and to persuade him of his serious responsibilities. Perhaps all the reforming ideas failed to probe deeply enough, but it is symptomatic that they were in general directed to financial abuses, for which royal officials and court favourites were held responsible. The emphasis is partly due to the fact that it was the government's need of money, which had brought the estates together. It is nevertheless remarkable that the estates themselves showed no wish to revive plans for creating regular machinery to control the executive. Nor was there any desire to use the parlement as effective protection against the king. On the contrary, it inspired criticisms for its own oligarchical tendencies. The opportunities for general reform were there in 1413, but the discontented concentrated their attentions on finances, because that was where the trouble seemed to lie.

The reformers of 1413, the estates, the university, the *bourgeoisie* and even the Cabochiens themselves for a long period, were patronized by the duke of Burgundy to whom they were in general devoted. Yet it has been pointed out that while the duke used his creatures to secure the denunciation of 'Orleanist' officials for corruption, he himself had been one of those who had taken most from the royal treasure. Between February 1409 and August 1413, he obtained nearly a million *francs*. It seems difficult to concede the force of the Burgundian argument, when the duke himself was a greater predator than the corrupt administrators. No doubt the duke's case was unsound morally. The interesting thing is that he was sufficiently devious to win over support in Paris by this means, and that the Orlèanists, who could have done as well, failed to see the potential advantages of this. If the princes were worse offenders than the officials, this was not due to their selfishness, but to the fact that while the monarchy was in their hands (because of the king's weakness), they were bound to take the king's money and spend it on their political activities. Rather than blame the princes, it is necessary to judge between them as to how wisely they spent the king's money.

Until the death of Philip of Burgundy in 1404, it is agreed that the king's affairs and finances were as well managed as can be expected. The trouble began after his death, because of the disputes between John of Burgundy and Louis of Orleans. They pulled in different directions, but the interests of the kingdom made it more important to conciliate Burgundy, whose power in the north and in the eventuality of war with the English was more weighty than that of Orleans. As to financial corruption itself, there were two remedies: total reform of the accounting system and the abolition of many taxes outright. But those in office and those who gained, or expected to gain, from the availability of so much royal money, had no intention of allowing the source of supply to dry up or of cleaning the channels through which it passed.

The opportunity for reform in the year 1413 was lost and did not return. Civil war between the rival factions was soon complicated by English intervention. The treaty of Troyes (1420) by which Charles VI disowned his son and accepted Henry V, his new son-in-law, as his heir was in its way a pragmatic solution to France's problems. It promised an alliance between the interests of northern France, including the Burgundian lands, and those of the English, and a turning away from the association with France south of the Loire, where the problems of the royal administration caused little anxiety. As it happened, the northern alliance did not bear the weight put upon it. Not that Charles VII after 1422 was able to exploit its weaknesses. It was the miraculous intervention of Joan of Arc in 1429 that brought Charles to Rheims for his coronation and it was another six years before he made peace with Philip of Burgundy and reentered Paris. Slow though this was, his eventual triumph enabled him to recover his authority without making concessions: the dynastic principle had been vindicated. No political compromises had been necessary and the king saw no reason to consider reforms of the administration.

The monarchy alone saved the unity of the kingdom: institutional support was superfluous. It had learned how to dispense with politics in the English sense altogether. Political expediency could not deprive the royal person of his rights, however unsuitable, cowardly, incompetent, mad, or indolent he was. Political solutions proposed for the monarchy's ills were more likely to generate party conflict and civil war. The division of the kingdom and occupation of large parts of it by foreigners did not diminish the true king's credibility and would never be accepted as permanent. The contrast between French legitimism and the English willingness to sacrifice unacceptable kings reflects the different functions of the monarchy in the two kingdoms. In England the king was made to serve established and self-conscious common interests; in France, where regional loyalties still prevailed, the king had to unite the nation and had to be above party. If the king ceased to be the divine instrument of French unity, France itself would fall apart.

By the mid-fifteenth century, the Valois dynasty, like the papacy, could breathe a deep sigh of relief. It had survived and justified itself. The kingdom could not do without it and the monarchy was accepted as the only motor force of its life. The French were exhausted rather than convinced, but the outcome was much the same. Acceptance of Charles VII and his government became the proof of being French. It did not need to stand for anything else.

The papacy and the French monarchy had to cope and eventually compromise with demands for concessions to local interests; they saved the essentials of their centralising achievements without losing all their strength. Their tribulations over this long period obliged them to relax the pressure they had put on the rest of Europe in the late thirteenth century. This meant that authorities there could afford to make more concessions to comparable clamour for local rights. By the time the papacy and the French kingdom emerged from their long tunnel to try and resume their leading role on the continent, the political landscape had completely changed its character. For more than a century the will to build up central monarchies had flagged, while alternative sources of public life enriched most communities. Since the internal disputes of France had most impact on the British Isles and in Spain, these will be considered first. Then follows a discussion of the lands of the empire which were left with a new sense of freedom to pursue their own separate interests.

3. ENGLAND

In the long term, England was more damaged than France by the French war. At the end of the thirteenth century, Edward I was one of the greatest monarchs of Europe. He had conquered Wales and was all set to establish his authority in Scotland too. The united kingdom of Britain under English kings seemed within his grasp. It was resisted then by an un-expected and improbable movement for Scottish independence, under Robert Bruce. Without the diversions of the French war, it is unlikely that English kings would have allowed this situation to endure. French support of Scotland during the war was always adequate to defeat English ambitions. When the French war was over, the independence of Scotland was assured and its institutional differences have been strong enough to resist the consequences of dynastic (1603) and parliamentary (1707) union with England. Whatever nationalist complaints have been expressed against the English, there is no doubt that the United Kingdom has never been as centralized as the French state, or that the unions ever achieved what Edward I might have done before the national revival of Scotland.

The English, left to themselves, by their defeats in France fell to bitter recriminations, as to the cause of failure. The English monarchy had shrunk in European significance to pigmy size, as compared with France and Spain, the new great empires of the continent. Seen from across the Channel therefore the spectacle of English politics between 1307 and 1485 is, in its own way, more dismal than that of France. With no one but themselves to blame, the English conducted their internal disputes with such bitterness that five of nine monarchs perished by violence. None of them had been as cowardly as Philip VI, as hot-tempered as John II, as mad as Charles VI, or as indolent as the young Charles VII—yet all these French rulers died in their beds, respected and mourned. None of the English had been as tyrannical as their French cousins, but in the context of English politics, even their more venial sins were inexorably punished. Henry VI, crowned king of France in 1431, would have graced the French monarchy with another saint; he had a French mother and a French wife. In England he was an utter failure. To sacrifice his ministers did not save him: England needed kings to rule, not pious figureheads.

In order to be obeyed in English political society, kings had to be capable of military success: Edward I, Edward III and Henry V won permanent reputations as military heroes. No French king's hold on his subjects depended on his power to win victories. Philip VI, but only just, survived ignominy and John II personal capture in battle. Charles V, the most successful of the Valois, was an intellectual, whose only military virtue was to recognize the merits of Bertrand Du Guesclin. In England, Edward II was ultimately deposed by the barons, who claimed among other things, that he could not worthily defend his crown in Scotland, Gascony and Ireland. They had tolerated many of his weaknesses, and would have forgiven him all, had his military defeats not tarnished their own reputations. Edward III showed his military gifts early and in what was then the longest reign in English history did not forfeit respect until, in his dotage, his wars went badly.

The demand for martial leadership may suggest a somewhat immature political society to modern eyes. At the time it represented a concern for active kingship, since the barons recognized realistically that a ruler incapable of imposing himself when necessary by force would lose control of strong men's services. Royal commitments to Scotland and Gascony tested the royal firmness of purpose. The barons did not themselves regard these outlying places as no part of their own interests or hope to build up an English political society for the English alone. They were ready for war under kings who sought their cooperation; peace parties were recruited chiefly in the households of unmilitary kings like Richard II and Henry VI. In the country too, war was popular. Civil society was bellicose from top to bottom.

The leading places in baronial ranks were in this period occupied by members of the royal family itself. Edward II had to contend with his cousin, Thomas, earl of Lancaster. Edward III had numerous sons to provide for with great estates. Their descendants, as princes of the royal blood, enjoyed political consideration, irrespective of their abilities and, like the French apanage princes, were so fully persuaded of their devotion to the royal interests that they had no hesitation about urging their opinions against diffident kings, to the point of threatening violence. Richard II was the first king to live with overbearing uncles. Henry VI was treated with more consideration by his, but their own quarrels could not be appeased by such a gentle ruler. The willingness of the royal princes to help run the monarchy was only an advantage when the king himself was firmly in charge of his own family. When he was not, the princes, through their connexions with the barons, their dependents, their townsmen (particularly those of London) and their popular followings, involved all layers of society in the royal problems.

In this respect therefore the pugnacious attitude of the barons in public affairs expresses not the immaturity of soldiers but the determination of politicians to be listened to. The monarchy was seen to be a matter of common interest, which could not be left to mere courtiers, and the involvement of all the leading interests shows how highly integrated English political society had in fact become. The political debates, violence to kings and respect for martial prowess indicate only that in the search for good government, the barons dealt clumsily with an unfamiliar problem.

In France, in similar circumstances, the kingdom threatened to fall apart into its component parts, each of which could, up to a point, cope on its own. In England, this was impossible. The duchy of Lancaster was almost the only provincial entity where one noble enjoyed unrivalled authority, but the dukes would not have enjoyed such political influence had they been remote border lords, like the Percies. They had estates in other parts of England, and in 1399 the duke was generally powerful enough to seize the crown. The duke of Burgundy, when thwarted in Paris, on a comparable occasion, simply withdrew to the Low Countries. All English barons lived in close proximity to one another. As their family holdings grew by marriage and inheritance they stretched out their fingers into more counties and joined hands with more related groups. They did not consolidate regional power. Every county had its own rival factions with allies in other places. Historians have rather fretted about the evidence for local disorder in this period: pressure put by great men on judges and jurors, bands of armed thugs, contests for parliamentary elections, the suspension of the royal eyre and the new role of the gentry as justices of the peace. This is however only the dark side of political changes that brought many more substantial benefits to English government, whereas France, which suffered in the same way, gained nothing. The chief advantage in England was that government by officials was avoided. The monarchy had from the first obliged the knights of the shire to take part in its administration of justice and then found them more eager to run their own affairs than to put up with arbitrary royal servants. In this sense it was no bad thing for public order if responsibility passed into the hands of local notabilities, even if they favoured their friends and tried to bend the rules to suit themselves. They were necessarily more sensitive to their neighbours' opinions than royal servants were likely to be. The greatest men listened to lesser men in their 'parties' and found their most determined enemies in the same social class as themselves. The Lancastrians stirred up the Yorkists by their mismanagement of the government. At least their quarrels were fought out amongst themselves: England never suffered from French armies of occupation. The 'barons' have had a bad deal from the historians. Instead of regarding them as self-centred trouble-makers, it is wiser to ask whether the recurrence of violence over a long period does not suggest another explanation: they were consistently engaged in expressing their profound disquiet with the way political affairs moved.

The earlier disputes between the king and his barons had culminated in 1215 with the formulation of baronial grievances against John and the issue of the great charter. The government of Henry III, warned by John's mistakes, avoided acts of provocation. The barons, for the most part, allowed the king to manage his affairs without interference. They approved the extension of royal justice and left administration to royal servants. Henry III managed to dispense with consulting the barons about his affairs until 1258 when he found himself so deeply committed to helping the pope in Sicily that he saw no remedy except asking the barons to extricate him. Over the next few years, a complete shake-up in the government threatened for a time to put the kingship into commission, but most barons, whatever impatience they felt for Henry himself, were not prepared to suspend him or allow a determined baron, like Simon de Montfort, to rule on the king's behalf. When Simon was killed in 1265, there died with him the old theory that the king's barons might make war on the king to bring him to reason. The royal government was thenceforward seen to be the concern of all. It was not to be improved on by mere *pronunciamentos.*

The problem of how it could be improved, when necessary, was not resolved by Edward I's use of parliamentary discussions as part of the ordinary course of business. In his last ten years Edward ran into serious difficulties in the course of dealing with the Scots and Philip IV, but personally he never lost control of the situation himself, because his age and experience saw him through. It was left for his heir, Edward II, to cope with a difficult situation at home, when the need to be aggressive in Scotland made the government resort to arbitrary methods. Edward II added to his problems by his personal inadequacy for government, and his willingness to trust favourites with great powers. For the most part they exploited this for their own benefit, creating no royal 'party' in the process and profoundly angering baronial opinions. The barons did not rush to arms. They tried a commission of reformers, whose Ordinances (1311) were intended to impose some restraints on the exercise of royal power, while leaving the king and his own ministers the real responsibility. Even these restrictions were not accepted as essential by all the barons and they were abolished by the statute of York (1322). Less than five years later, Edward II was deposed in a political crisis brought about by the return to England of his much-tried queen, Isabella, and the heir to the throne, Edward, duke of Gascony.

No new constitutional limits were imposed on the new king, Edward III, but his father's deposition proved that English kings could not expect a life interest in the crown. The barons tolerated Edward II's incompetence as long as possible. As soon as his heir attained to a reasonable age, he was vested with the kingship, with the minimum of violence. Edward II and his reigning favourites were the only victims. In the next seventy years there was no reckless move to repeat this drastic remedy for royal ills and no sign that kings were frightened by this unfortunate precedent.

Renewed baronial activity in government was however brought about by Edward III's dotage and Richard II's minority, when the king's relations had to exercise political power on his behalf. The senior duke, John of Lancaster, was unpopular and his great personal influence was challenged. Political rivalries were unfortunate but unavoidable when the king's own will was lacking; men looked forward with hope of relief to Richard's coming of age. Meanwhile their experience of taking decisions sharpened baronial awareness of political issues. When Richard began to rule, his conduct immediately aroused criticism. His reaction was to emphasize his royal rights, to act high-handedly, or, weakly, to try and get his way in secret. These reactions proved unwise. They followed from Richard's realization that if the monarchy was to recover the initiative, the precedents of the minority had to be forgotten and his vexed relations, however senior, put in their place. Richard's royal instincts were sound. In fact many of his actions and opinions later commanded much support; in his own times, these sentiments were unacceptable. The princes and barons did not allow him to recreate the monarchy. They expected guarantees that the monarchy would not elude public scrutiny and were prepared to sacrifice Richard himself if he could govern only in his own interest. In 1399, when John of Lancaster died, Richard confiscated his estates, since his heir, Henry, was already in exile and this seemed the best occasion to rid the monarchy of the dangers from an over-mighty subject. Henry did not take this meekly. He returned and finding Richard in his power, swiftly exploited his advantages. He persuaded Richard to tender his 'abdication', and when parliament met, Henry himself 'challenged' the crown. No one contested him and he became king.

These events were, and remain, controversial, but the enormity of setting aside the king and usurping his place in this way must not be underestimated. Henry had seized his chance. Richard's tyrannies were denounced, but there had been no public cry of discontent. Henry himself had originally invaded to claim only his own rights, not to champion a constitutional cause. As king, Henry was forced, like Richard, to defend the royal power, while for a time he had not the same moral claim on men's allegiance as his predecessor.

In the thirty years between the parliaments of 1376 and 1406, the political agitations of the great men of the realm were conducted on a public stage and to the accompaniment of popular applause.[58] One of the main issues of general concern was the royal need for money from parliament and a justified suspicion that the king's ministers were not always honest in using taxes for the public good, or the king's own interests. It was this which had provoked the commons to impeach some of the king's ministers before the lords in 1376 and the device, once tried, served again. But it was an expedient and represented no desire to become permanent watchdogs of the public interest. In 1406, therefore, when parliament ventured likewise to ask the king to present his accounts to satisfy their doubts about his needs, it also petitioned the king to take into his council respected and great lords in no need of feathering their own nests who might be trusted to defend the public interest. By doing just this in the fifteenth century, the kings brought baronial leaders into the inner councils of the kingdom. Contemporaries did not think of the barons as an irreconcilable 'opposition', and the monarchy found its way out of the dilemma of the previous thirty years, and became stronger rather than weaker, by bringing potential critics into consultation.

The kingship, despite the two depositions, did not become the plaything of the nobility, but it did become a public office, to be exercised responsibly by its holders, with the concomitant risk of losing it, if they proved unworthy. Here the English situation must be contrasted strongly with that in France, where the Valois dynasty had clung tenaciously to office. This was in part the 'fault' of history: the 'national' political experience of the English barons was already much longer than the French in 1327. Their commitment to 'national' politics was correspondingly firmer by the fifteenth century, even if the kingdom was for a time convulsed by dynastic rivalries.

It would be a mistake to think that the 'conciliar' monarchy was institutionally weaker than its predecessor: it was much more confident and broadly based. When Henry v died in 1422, the government was managed by the council for fifteen years. The king's uncle, Humphrey of Gloucester, aspired to the title and the powers of regent; he was refused it. The council was not always, or even often, united and it was left to the senior uncle, John of Bedford, regent in France until his death in 1435, to appease its hatreds. The war in France was a constant problem to the two governments on either side of the Channel. The marvel in the circumstances was that conciliar rule proved as effective as it did. When Henry vi came of age, there was some risk of the king reacting as Richard ii had done earlier, but in fact such precedents were not important. If Henry vi was eventually swept away and murdered, as Richard had been, it was not because the royal council had learned how to usurp the royal office, but because of the failure of Henry's foreign policy, and his inability to salvage any of the glorious English conquests in France.

Parliament

The political events of the fourteenth and fifteenth centuries which had turned the royal government into an instrument for the public good had often, if not always, been staged in parliamentary assemblies. Parliament did not as an institution thereby become a potential rival to the monarchy, and, when the strong monarchy reappeared, parliaments meekly resumed their traditional function of carrying out the royal will, with only occasional protests. Had it not been for the friction of the religious passions of the sixteenth century to sharpen its political edge, parliament could have slumped into insignificance as many continental 'estates' eventually did. It was not by its control over the king's government, but by its concern for English law that parliament had become indispensable. Though this may seem too obvious to be worth saying, its significance in the period concerned needs to be pondered. In the time of Edward I the concerns of English law were only a local matter to a king with lands in France and conquests in Wales and Scotland. Not all his vassals were interested in the Common Law and his own business far transcended its competence, even in England itself.[59] By the late fifteenth century, the king's lands had been reduced to the realm of English law. Here the common law was strong enough to have imposed restrictions on the competence of its rivals—particularly, for example in matters of clerical privilege. Free Englishmen were those interested in the common law. The king's lieges, who were not, opted for a different political system. Gascons who would not give up appeal to the French king's court in Paris, as the Edwards had hoped, found themselves shackled to it. The Scots who had renounced the jurisdiction of Edward I's court in 1295, worked up their own system of law. It was partly because the business of government had become such a matter of law, that those with different legal traditions were allowed by English royal governments to slip the leash. The great network of feudal ties had made the English king one of the greatest rulers of Christendom; as guarantor of English law, he had no more than local importance.[60] The political society he presided over for the common good was made up of the freemen with access to his courts who had a common political interest in the body of common law.

The king did not have to use parliament to change legal rules, but parliaments were ideal for securing public attention to legal business. Members took advantage of them to devise common petitions for modifications to the law, as well as to present private ones. They had a lot of legal experience themselves. County members were chosen in the county courts; great lords and prelates had legal responsibilities in their lands and offices; burgesses had experience in enforcing their own borough customs. The formality of legal proceedings and the nicety of legal definitions came naturally to them. They respected traditions and were touchy about respect for rights. They brought to their activities the involvement and persistence of the litigant seeking justice. By the fourteenth century the English common law had evolved its own rules and its own style which made business slow and devious in the courts. By modern standards it may be difficult to believe that justice could be obtained at all. Contemporaries complained; they did not abandon the legal formalities. By contrast to France, where there were still many legal customs, England had only one legal procedure for its freemen and these were the men who met in parliament and found their common interest in the law. The landowners of England, great and small, brought experience of the administration of justice in their own areas to national assemblies. They cared far more for law than for politics, even in the baronial sense.

Under Edward III, in the 1330s, the lords and the commons began to deliberate in two separate places, not together, and this enabled the commons in particular to develop independently, though it is not known that they had a spokesman, or speaker, before 1376. There were certain items of regular business, but even voting taxes became more of a routine matter to be granted or refused once the taxes were assessed at a fixed sum and not voted according to the king's actual needs. At the end of the reign, exasperation with royal ministers stirred the commons to improvise extra-legal procedures for their punishment. The excitement of the occasion stimulated an anonymous author to record the proceedings of the Good Parliament (1376). The high point of parliamentary interference with the king's money came in 1406 and, as has been argued already, this shows its real limitations. The king was prepared to make more concessions to get money than for anything else, but requests were confined to public nomination of the trustworthy persons the king took as counsellors. When Edward IV assured parliament in 1467 that he could live of his own and would not need to summon assemblies as often as his predecessors, the medieval parliament accepted that its value to the royal government had come to an end.

Parliaments could not take real power, because, like church councils, they had no control of their own meetings and no authority to legislate without royal approval. Yet they had met sufficiently often for more than a century to create expectations that in need the king would summon them and that in session they would do business according to agreed forms. They thus became part of the framework of political society. Through them kings demonstrated their desire to keep in touch with public opinion. Richard II's last parliament had met to find the king removed and a usurper ready to take his place. This 'parliament' became the audience for an act of disloyalty based upon trumped-up charges and a claim to the throne by inheritance and by pseudo-conquest. Yet it had nothing to say, but approve. Its behaviour at each change of dynasty thereafter was abject. It recognized rulers who were imposed by non-parliamentary means. But it mattered all the same that these usurpers should make a show of winning public approval; that they manipulated the forms of government; that they maintained an illusion of continuity. The stability of English political life came to depend on these charades. And ever since the most far-reaching changes have been effected by means that helped to mask their nature.

On balance these two centuries of English history sometimes appear rather barren. The expenditure of effort on the continent cost the kings all their great French lands: the pathetic retention of Calais was no compensation for that. The Plantagenet kings who had outshone the Capetians were succeeded by rulers as negligible as the Scandinavian monarchs. Shakespeare gloomily analysing recent history (as it then was) came to conservative conclusions about the lessons of the past. The people should respect their rulers and not usurp their place. Kings who preserved the order of things could expect their reward. The English had gone through a searing experience and they emerged as a whole reconciled to the values of strong government and more deeply aware of how partisan politics could endanger the common interests. They were more prepared to support the government and turn a blind eye to judicial murders. They had no constitutional guarantees, but they had discovered the secrets of political life, all the same.

4. SPAIN[61]

The dynastic union of the Spanish crowns brought about by the marriage of Ferdinand of Aragon and Isabella of Castile (1479) has universally been accepted as inspiring a new period of Spanish greatness. In particular the task of subjecting the Muslims of Spain, which had been suspended since the mid-thirteenth century, was completed by the conquest of Granada in 1492. The intervening period seems by comparison lacking in fervour and a sense of purpose. Yet while Spain laid up its crusading arms, it dealt with its own internal affairs. This is the period of the most remarkable parliamentary activities in both Castile and Catalonia. These developments were less likely to have occurred had Spanish kings been anxious about threats to their security. In particular, the relaxation of French pressure was important. During the fourteenth century, French involvement was limited to providing support for Henry of Trastamara, when his half-brother, Pedro the Cruel, appealed to the Black Prince, as duke of Gascony, for aid. Though Spaniards were not engaged in wars against the Muslims, they were active enough in other respects.

Like France and England, Spain was obliged to get to grips with the problem of its own internal structure. The ruler of the greatest state, Castile, made obvious efforts to impose his will on the whole peninsula, but as in Britain such ambitions encountered valiant resistance. Both Portugal and the Crown of Aragon proved able to defend their autonomy, and the political independence of Portugal, to this day, confirms the view that Spanish problems about unity resemble those of Britain more than they do those of France. The union of the crowns itself, as in the British case, was originally only a dynastic one, and even after many centuries, whatever Castilians may think, the differences between the regions of Spain remain significant. Spain has no national history in the French sense. There dynastic union did not provide Spain with a single ruler until Carlos I (1516), and he almost immediately took Spain into his Habsburg inheritance, the empire (1519). Moreover Spain was already burdened, or enriched, with an expanding American empire. Only in the past century has Spain had no territories far beyond its shores to complicate its political life and without these external commitments, interestingly enough, Spain on its own fell to renewed doubts about its collective destiny: it is far from true that the 'norm' in Spanish history is concentrating on peninsular unity.

The distinct elements of which Spain is composed first showed their invincible determination to preserve their special characteristics during the period from 1252 to 1479, and it is for this reason that it is worth studying. Though the Castilians have been understandably reluctant to concentrate on a period in which the crusade was abandoned, the regions flourishing and Castile itself in disorder, this has not discouraged the Catalans, for whom this is the decisive phase of 'nation' building.

Until the mid-thirteenth century, the main problem of Christian Spain had been to retain the initiative in the wars with the Muslims. The small monarchies of the Cantabrian mountains and the Pyrenees had not made steady progress, but from the late eleventh century, they showed greater determination to overcome stiffening Muslim resistance and Almohad reinforcements from north Africa were eventually defeated at the battle of Las Navas de Tolosa in 1212. This was followed by Catalan conquests of the Balearic islands and the kingdom of Valencia, while the Castilians occupied all southern Spain, from Alicante, leaving the Muslims only Granada as a Castilian vassal state. From time to time in the following two centuries Castilian kings sniped at the Muslim enclave, but the momentum for religious wars had been lost. The anomalous survival of the weak Moorish state emphasized how little the old crusading zeal counted for Spanish Christians in this period. Yet, at the same time, the Catalan kings who found their way blocked by the Castilians to the south turned energetically to the east, creating a commercial empire with bases in Sicily and for a time in the duchy of Athens. They played their part in founding the future Spanish empire in Italy, even if their local independence impeded the achievment of Spanish unity at home.

The united Christian kingdom of Spain had been divided into three parts, Castile, Aragon and Navarra, in 1035. All of them pursued separate courses of development thereafter, for centuries. From the late thirteenth century the virtual independence of Portugal and Granada gave the peninsula a total of five royal states. Castile was the largest, but enjoyed only a primacy of prestige. It had a far less comfortable superiority of numbers and resources than England did in Britain. Navarra was the smallest, but from 1250, when it was inherited by the counts of Champagne, it moved in the orbit of French politics. It did not lose its identity, even when the king of France himself became the king of Navarre, as was the case between 1285 and 1316. In the end it was only brought into the Spanish union by forcible annexation under Ferdinand of Aragon in 1512. The Moorish kingdom which was likewise suppressed by force had shown no signs of withering away. After 1269, when the Berbers captured Marrakesh, the kings of Granada got little help from north Africa, but they maintained their independence and culture without difficulty. They lost both Gibraltar and Algeciras to Castile, but under Pedro the Cruel (1349-69) Castile was markedly receptive to Moorish cultural influence, in architecture and domestic comfort. The Portuguese had to fight more energetically to preserve their separate kingdom from Castilian annexation. Its access to the Atlantic gave it the possibility of seeking distant allies and the English aid in Portugal provided the same prop for Portuguese independence as the Scots found in the French. The English had no direct concern to prevent Castilian hegemony in the peninsula, but the alliance of the Trastamara dynasty with the French was sufficient to justify support of Portugal. Quite apart from the existence of the two important kingdoms of Castile and Aragon, the peninsula was therefore made up of several distinct communities. Five languages, Latin, Castilian, Portuguese, Catalan and Arabic, not to speak of dialectal forms, like those of Leon and Aragon, were in regular use for business and literature. There was no pre-existent cultural unity. It was a situation that might have endured and it looked very different in Barcelona from the way it did in Toledo.

The Crown of Aragon

The county of Barcelona was the heart and soul of the conglomeration of lands, known as the Crown of Aragon. It was reported in England that the first Catalan king of Aragon, Ramon Berengar, boasted of his dignity as count.[62] If so, it represented the view of his house that its future at sea mattered more than its commitments to the barren kingdom of Aragon. Till the early thirteenth century, the interests of the counts of Barcelona stretched along the coast from Tarragona to Provence. King Pere I, the crusader of Las Navas de Tolosa, found himself fighting for the heretics of southern France against northern French crusaders in 1213, in order to defend his claims there. The triumph of the French against the counts of Toulouse and the succession of the house of Anjou to the counts of Provence drove the Catalans from southern France, though they retained till 1659 lands north of the Pyrenees in Roussillon. These campaigns also made them inveterate enemies of the Angevins, whom they pursued in Italy. In the meantime James of Aragon (1213-70), forced out of his birthplace, Montpellier, turned to the south, and made conquests from the Muslims in the islands and in Valencia. For a century and more the Catalans embarked on a sequence of great exploits, all involving campaigns at sea, in the tradition of Barcelona. These exploits were recorded in the four great histories, written in Catalan by James himself about his conquests, by Desclot about Pere II's campaigns in Sicily, by Muntaner, about the Catalan company in Italy and Greece, and by Pere III who wrote his own memoirs of his various activities, mostly military. The Aragonese had little time for the main interests of their kings and until the dynasty of Barcelona died out in 1410 they played a subordinate role in the affairs of the Crown. It was the Catalans who set the pace, politically, commercially and culturally. At a time when the French were dominating the south and the culture of Provence was in decline, the Catalans made the most important contributions to the literature of the peoples of *Occitane*.

The constitutional diversity of the Crown of Aragon did not strengthen the monarchy at the expense of the parts. Pere III had many irons in the fire throughout his long reign (1336-88) and his need of money was exacerbated by the economic troubles of the period: fluctuations of money values, decline of population, agitation for higher wages and unrest in the countryside. Barcelona was the most populous city of Spain and suffered from the same social and economic disturbances as the cities of Italy. The aggressive attitude of Pedro I of Castile after 1352 brought about wars which Pere could only afford by securing grants from the *Cortes*. Like the kings of France and England in the same situation, he thus created political circumstances potentially very damaging to the king. Pere, unlike Edward III, could not expect to make a profit from his investments in war: they were merely defensive. The *Cortes* of Catalonia, which were prepared to be generous, on conditions, so pressed home their advantages that they succeeded in doing what the French estates had failed to do: supervise the collection of the taxes they voted. The *Cortes* thus obtained a permanent committee of *Deputats* (1375) who in effect became the spokesmen of Catalonia and remained so after the Catalans had recognized the Trastamara succession to Aragon (1413). Catalonia confidently believed that its autonomy would be respected because of the *Deputacion*.

The Crown of Aragon, like the Plantagenet empire, comprised many different territories. In the Plantagenet empire, the segments were broken off piece by piece until only England was left: a core that has become too solid to be divided. The Crown of Aragon, on the contrary, was only the beginning of a great cluster of Spanish lands that eventually stretched from Italy to the Philippines. Few pieces of this empire retained any particular interest in the Crown of Aragon, which was only a transitory part of the history. Only Catalonia itself, the most privileged and dynamic part of the crown, which had evolved politically far enough to take a responsible part in the affairs of the whole, emerged by the fifteenth century with institutions capable of surviving in the greatly changed new conditions. But in fact the consolidated custom of Catalonia became in the new monarchy the equivalent of a French 'province'. The needs of government working from a different centre could only erode its privileges, and over a long period the patient loyalty of the province was worn down and outraged rebellions finally obliged the government to abolish privilege all together (1713). The Catalan fate was not uncommon on the continent, where the operations of dynastic marriages brought many lands of diverse custom to one lord. The Catalan success had been precocious and may be explained historically; once it stopped growing, it could not last. As long as the management of political affairs required a broad basis of agreement Catalan institutions proved their worth. In the dynastic governments of the fifteenth century, they already looked anomalous and the conflict between Barcelona and King John II in the 1460s exposed the incompatibilities of tradition and royal authority.

Castile

While the impetus of Catalan self-development continued as long as the dynasty of Barcelona, Castile fell victim to indecision immediately after the death of the crusading king Ferdinand III in 1252. His son, Alfonso X, the Wise, failed to maintain the military pressure and duly ran into difficulties with his warriors. The death of his oldest son raised doubts about the succession, the claims of his grandchildren being defended against those of the second son, Sancho. Alfonso's family connexions with the Staufen and the kings of England encouraged him to pursue an ambitious foreign policy beyond realistic limits. His most famous learned effort, to codify Spanish laws, stirred up suspicions of his desire to subvert local rights and proved unacceptable until long after his death. Under Alfonso X, the monarchy had already lost its power to direct Castilian energies and few of his successors showed greater abilities in this direction.[63]

The fundamental problem of Castile by Alfonso's time was how to exploit the potential of the rich lands taken by conquest between 1212 and 1266, when the territory of the kingdom had doubled in size, but not in population. Tracts of land in Estramadura, La Mancha and Andalusia remained empty. Grants were made to the military orders, as well as to the great nobles and clergy, who in turn offered privileges to attract settlers. Alfonso X already tried to make conditions more favourable for workmen by fixing wages in the south at double those in the north. The compact realm of northern Castile, with its strongholds, lost its homogeneous character. The whole area depended economically on sheep which wandered from north to south and back every year along well-established grazing routes.[64] At various points along the way, local authorities collected tolls from the shepherds, in return for the protection they provided, as well as fines for trespasses on protected woods or commonlands. With the establishment of a single royal government, which could protect the sheep, the justification for the older system lost its force. Alfonso X did not abolish the taxing powers of the town authorities over their districts, for an important part of the royal revenue was derived from the money collected by the towns. Instead he preferred to fix the rates of taxation and grant exemptions for the sheep of favoured towns, monasteries and others. This policy of privilege culminated in the recognition of a national sheep owners' association, the *Mesta,* which acted to defend their interests against the local authorities (1273). Succeeding kings favoured one side or another according to circumstances. The cession of privileges tended to weaken the older collective political elements. The Trastamara dynasty is generally thought to have depended upon the enriched and privileged individuals able to obtain royal favours.

The towns clearly began to feel the pressure upon them from the late fourteenth century, as the divergence of interests between the town communities and the nobility became more pronounced. Already in 1367 the *Cortes* in Burgos asked for permission to set up brotherhoods to defend their interests: *Hermandades*. From 1430 there were also frequent complaints about royal interference in elections.

Playing off the towns against the Mesta did not in fact notably enlarge the royal freedom of action and should not be ascribed to political cleverness. It was rather a consequence of the monarchy's own indecision and its incapacity to impose a real solution. Caught between rival interests, it shifted for itself uncertainly. Castilian history in this period is, for want of other material, chiefly known from the records of the meetings of the Cortes.[65] Even this source does not suggest that the different political elements of which the kingdom was composed found in these assemblies an adequate means of establishing political relationships. Until the decisive accretion of strength achieved by the united dynasty after 1479, Castile remained a kingdom in which the different elements, monarchy, towns and nobility simply remained in balance. Unlike France and England Spain had no urgent problems demanding immediate solutions of some kind, so that the Castilian *Cortes,* which appeared as early as 1258, had to make no decisive constitutional advances. It appeared as a single assembly representing the 'towns' of which the kingdom was composed, often by 'noblemen', and continued to meet as, when and where the king summoned it. The meetings were nevertheless frequent, and continued to be so even under King Philip II, in the sixteenth century. The nobility and the clergy who came to these assemblies played as such no real part in the discussions, which fell to the representatives of the same seventeen towns normally summoned. Apart from Seville, Cordova, Murcia and Jaen, captured in the thirteenth century, the towns represented were the thirteen towns of old Castile and Leon which had been part of the kingdom since the eleventh century. The king's regular royal tax, collected on sheep, and paid annually—though originally approved in the *Cortes c.* 1270—did not need to be re-voted.

The functions of the *Cortes* were advisory and served as useful occasions for airing grievances and publishing ordinances. Legislative changes were bound to be few, since there was no agreed customary law until the *Siete Partidas* were approved in a modified form in 1349. Alfonso XI consolidated a sales tax at 10 per cent to finance his campaigns against the Muslims. The *Cortes* occasionally protested about royal policies over taxation, but it had no authority to vote taxes or scrutinize the royal accounts and remained dependent upon the willingness of the king to listen or the eagerness of the towns' representatives to criticise. Since the nobility and the clergy were exempt from regular taxes, they took no interest in them; rulers who pressed them to pay forced loans did not drive them into collective bargaining, for everyone settled for himself.

Castile was not a monarchy without problems, but in such a large kingdom, where the king disposed in general of revenues adequate to his needs, it was never obvious that finding a common means for political action was desirable. Though there are fragments of chancery registers beginning with Alfonso x, it is remarkable that, until the Trastamara dynasty began to ape the French, the monarchy appears to have bothered little with devising regular machinery for administrative purposes. A royal council was set up in 1371 and remodelled in 1385 to advise the king; a financial chamber and a court of law *(Audiencia)* also appeared at this time. Proposals to set up a royal archive and equip the dynasty with a record of its activities were made in the fifteenth century, though the civil wars of Henry iv's reign destroyed this evidence.

The increasing interest in government shown by the Trastamaras and the nobles who surrounded them is reflected in the first important political history written in Spanish by Pedro Lopez de Ayala, a participant in the events he describes as a courtier (1350-95). Other historians followed this tradition, so that it becomes possible to keep track of what was happening as it seemed to those who were trying to observe some coherence in their disorder. It is surely significant that at an earlier stage, when Alfonso x had attempted to provide a sense of purpose for Castilians by compiling a general chronicle in the vernacular to illustrate the unity of Spanish history, this precedent was not taken up, until the unsatisfactory chronicle of Alfonso's own reign was written in the 1340s. The Castilians were simply not much interested in the history of Spain, or their own special role in it and Alfonso, who in this as in other matters had a sound idea, could not carry his people with him. Until Alfonso's time, concern for Spanish unity had been rather a private interest of the clergy of Toledo, since they aspired to obtain recognition of their church as the primatial see of the whole peninsula. Toledo had antiquarian political associations with the Visigothic kings of all Spain, as known through the works of Isidore of Seville, the distinguished seventh-century Spanish scholar. From the late twelfth century, the clerical historians, Lucas bishop of Tuy and Rodrigo archbishop of Toledo, saw in history a means to establish links between the new Christian kingdoms and the remote past, ignoring the Muslim centuries, but emphasizing the Christian achievements of Castile. It is this tradition that lay behind all the subsequent attempts to base Spanish unity upon the Castilian crusading destiny. But it manifestly failed to inspire Spaniards from the time of Alfonso x himself, either in Castile or outside. The interest of Spanish history in this period lies elsewhere and is no less significant for the future. It is quite untrue to see in this period a mere decline from earlier achievements.

5. 'GERMANY'

The king of France was obliged to attend to his internal affairs just at a time when the disintegration of the empire seemed to offer the most tempting possibilities for the French to take advantage of it. Louis IX's brother, Charles of Anjou, had shown what could be done in Italy. His very success there had, in its way, precipitated the revival of the empire, though it came to look more like a German kingdom. By the time Philip IV's brother, Charles of Valois, tried to exploit the possibilities in Italy and in Germany it was therefore already too late. The French subsequently succeeded in winning over fragments of the empire, but these were only on the borders like Lyon (1310) or the county of Bar (1333). During a lull in the war with England, the king negotiated with the dauphin of Vienne for the reversion of his lands (1349) and, though Charles IV was solemnly crowned king of 'Arles' in 1365, he was so impressed by the dominant role of the king of France in what remained of the kingdom that he made the king his imperial 'vicar' there (1378) and virtually abandoned his own rights. All the same, imperial sentiment counted for something. The Free County of Burgundy, which became part of the lands of the Valois dukes of Burgundy, did not forget its formal membership of the empire, so that when Louis XI seized the duke's lands in 1477, the Franche-Comté reverted to the Habsburgs with the heiress of the ducal line. Only much later was it conquered by France. Despite French successes on the borders, they were in fact mere beneficiaries of the pro-French sentiments of local rulers. French kings themselves were in no position to impose their rule where they were not wanted and the Germans did not, as a whole, offer themselves to the French as defenceless prey.

As against the great authority of the royal dynasty in France, the Germans had no one family with responsibility for resisting on their behalf. There was no ruler east of France with the same claims as the heir of St Louis in France to the deference of his subjects. There were many noble families and it is surprising how well they managed to preserve the German kingdom from the forces that threatened its destruction. Albert of Habsburg, on his father's death (1291), refused to recognize the count of Nassau who was elected to the kingship and eventually vindicated his stand and became king himself. However, the possibility that a Habsburg dynasty would prevail in Germany was averted after 1308, when Albert was assassinated. The Habsburgs were divided amongst themselves and they remained ineffectual and even weak princes for more than a century. In 1308, Count Henry of Luxembourg was elected king and his family's fortunes were made by the acquisition of the kingdom of Bohemia for Henry's son, John on the death of the last native king. After only five years, Henry VII died in Italy. John was not able to secure election in his place, to the considerable annoyance of the Bohemians, though in due course the preeminence of his family was recognized when John's son, Charles, obtained the imperial crown (1347); his direct descendants governed the empire, almost without interruption, for more than four hundred years. In 1313, however, some of the princes had elected Louis of Bavaria, a Wittelsbach, as king. He was a successful soldier who eventually overcame his rival, Frederick of Habsburg. Like all his predecessors, he was a prince from the western part of the empire; his brother was count Palatine. He used his imperial power, as they had done, to strengthen his own family, taking Brandenburg (1322) and Holland-Hainault, when the native lines died out. Thus three of the families of the west, chosen to provide emperors between 1273 and 1313, made their mark by installing themselves in central Germany: Austria, Bohemia and Brandenburg. No clearer demonstration of the shift of political interests eastwards could be asked for. These three families then dominated the kingdom from their new positions of power.

The great families considered even imperial affairs from these quite new points of vantage. There were few families with a direct interest in the old concepts of empire. The Staufen emperors had built up a group of loyal vassals in connexion with the management of their lands, but the extinction of the dynasty dissolved this nucleus of men and estates with specifically imperial concerns. There was no subsequent reconstitution of an imperial domain as such and no dedicated group of imperial officials to animate an imperial policy or coach new emperors in their roles. Building up family power by the accumulation of lands from conquest, sovereignty or marriage is quite a different matter from identifying a particular office as a family right and finding supporters for that concept. On the other hand, few families calculated politically in their pursuit of territories. They were slow to think of their lands as united. They practised division amongst their children, which prevented the family as a whole from combining against others.[66] Even the Habsburg family lands were partitioned in this way both in 1379 and in 1412, so that it took from the emperor Frederick III (1439-79) the best part of his political energy to recover personal control of all the lands of his family. The Luxembourgs were in this respect more fortunate in having fewer children to provide for from their own scattered territories: Luxembourg itself, Bohemia, Brabant (1355) and Brandenburg (1373). The dynasts could not identify themselves with one block of land and their personal empires were no more easily 'unified' than those of the sixteenth-century

Habsburgs or of the eighteenth-century Bourbons.

Internally their estates were also riddled with conflicting jurisdictions. Apart from the king of Bohemia who had received from Frederick II a privilege allowing him to confer bishoprics, the princes had as such no control over the churches of their lands, and did not acquire more influence there until the great schism and the eclipse of papal authority. Many of the towns were imperial free cities, capable of resisting princely encroachments, alone or in league. Most of the 'princes' were anyway prelates with comparatively circumscribed states and little interest in family aggrandisement. Jostled by their own nobles, other churches and towns, they did not seek to break up the empire and risk total self-government. They wanted to keep the empire as an institution.

The records to illustrate the political attitudes of the princes accumulate from the fourteenth century, beginning with those of Berthold archbishop of Trier (1311-13), Henry VII's uncle. The Wittelsbach emperor Louis IV kept registers for the empire and Bavaria, his own duchy; he introduced this practice into Brandenburg when he acquired it in 1336. His cousins in the Palatinate did not begin to keep theirs until 1353. Admittedly the modern survival of records is not conclusive proof of either growth in an orderly approach to government or the first appearance of this tendency. All the same it is symptomatic that the imperial government itself preserved no registers of its own activities earlier than Henry VII. Such documents were personal rather than institutional records and this did not change until Sigismund, a century later, negotiated for the return of his predecessor's register from the Wittelsbach family depository in Heidelberg. It is extremely improbable that individual princely governments had acquired any more sense of system earlier than this. Henry VII's registers were kept in both Latin and French for the king's benefit: 'ut ipse facilius intelligere possit ea que coram eo et dicta proposita fuerint.'[67] With his successor, Louis, German became the principal language of administration. His clerks and advisers helped to develop a spoken and written courtly German acceptable all over Germany, which still lacked cultural homogeneity. Charles IV after him, the priests' king, founded an imperial university at Prague. His chancery encouraged the use of a more dignified Italianate Latin. But Charles also wanted to make his own language, Czech, a standard language of the empire. No one of these various experiments in advancing the interests of the kingdom, was persistently maintained so the effects intended were not achieved.

There can therefore be no question of discussing the history of Germany in the fourteenth century in terms of what the shadowy central authority was doing. Nor in the fourteenth century was there any one group which can be identified with the national interest of Germany.

The several political writers of the late thirteenth and early fourteenth century—Alexander of Roes (1281), Jordan of Osnabrück, Engelbert of Admont (1308-31) and Lupold of Bebenberg (1338) were all concerned with the empire as such, not with the German kingdom or people. Although German was becoming a more familiar language for writing about religious and political matters, there was still no literate German-speaking public to represent German opinion. The dialects retained their hold and still divided the Germans effectively from one another irrespective of political allegiance. It is not possible here to account for the separate histories of the states or a sample of them, but it is desirable to consider seriously what the implications of this are, both locally and at a 'national' level.

The special virtue of the loose structure of the empire was that in no way did it hinder the growth of local authorities. Peace was no condition of urban independence. War provoked further efforts by towns to manage their own defence and to strengthen their leagues, though not all cities could stand the pace. The greatest cities were those involved in international trade—Cologne, Mainz, Frankfurt, Nuremberg, Regensburg, Augsburg, Ravensburg, Basel. In such places the history of the kingdom was written, but from the local point of view.[68] Germany had no one intellectual centre. Until 1348, most students went to Cologne or Paris; after it, more went to Prague. During the great schism princes promoted universities of their own, which gave Germany more of them than any other kingdom of the west; this obviously did not advance a 'national' outlook. The pattern of subsequent German development through many different small governments had been established. Germany had many feet to stand on, just as France was in the throes of opting for the single prop of monarchy.

The essential function of the French monarchical state was to provide an ultimate court of appeal with the means to enforce its decisions. Louis IX's contemporary in Germany, Frederick II, had made a good beginning at the great assembly at Mainz in 1235 at which was proclaimed a general peace to put an end to feuding, as part of his obligations to give peace and justice. As it happened, after that date, the clergy (who might have gained most from it) were involved in the papal move to destroy the Staufen so that the power of the king to enforce the peace steadily declined. Men could not however postpone the doing of justice until political conflict was stilled, so in the meantime, alternatives had to be provided. Responsibility fell particularly on the princes, by virtue of their privileges of 1220 and 1232. When the monarchy was revived for Rudolf of Habsburg, he also conceded the further privilege of not allowing appeals from princely courts to those of the king. In 1356 such a privilege was granted to the electoral princes, who thereby became 'sovereign'. Only if princes were alleged to refuse justice altogether did the king as supreme judge take up the case. The law-books of Germany reflect the changes brought about by these events from the thirteenth century, since by contrast to the Saxon book, the Swabian (1274-5) and the Franconian (1328-38) customs show that localized legal forms were hardening against royal justice and rejecting appeals to his authority. As kings had become ineffectual as immediate defenders of the law, the lawyers realistically strengthened the authority of lesser tribunals.[69]

The very wide spectrum of political activity within the empire does not reflect only a conservative reliance upon existing institutions, as was the case with the numerous prince bishoprics whose origins stretched back to the concessions of Ottonian emperors. There were still men prepared to stand up for themselves and improvise in the new situations. The popular assemblies of Friesland and the beginnings of Swiss independence arose out of more recent events. The growth of the Swiss confederation was a direct consequence of the acquisition of the German throne by Rudolf of Habsburg in 1273. The Habsburg's major family interest became Austria and the Swiss exploited the weakness of absentee landlords to demand concessions. When the Habsburgs failed to hold on to the throne after 1308, the Swiss could happily appeal to the emperor against their lord and it was not until after the Habsburgs regained control of the empire (from 1437) that the Swiss were denied this tactical weapon. By that time the confederation was well on the way to real independence. This case shows how concern for local justice could nevertheless give some 'Germans' a stake in the survival of the empire as a useful concept in contemporary politics. Paralysis of the kingship could not rob Germans of justice altogether.

The result politically was not a complete chaos of distinct sovereign states administering local laws, for the existing law-books came to be used in other areas than originally intended, as an aid to improving local usage. This promoted some homogeneity in the rules. There was also some naive reliance on learned, that is Roman, law, not to subvert custom, but to make it more respectable. Johann von Buch wrote a gloss to the Sachsenspiegel (1325-55) and argued for the fitness of the Saxon rules, by advancing their Roman parallels. Until the foundation of Cologne university in 1388, there was, however, no place in Germany where Roman law was studied, which restricted both the understanding and the use of academic law. On balance, however, the chances for building up forms of centralized law and justice diminished. The tendency was for Germany to break up into several distinct regions of custom.

The emergence of distinct legal districts generally brought to the fore the local nobility who prevailed in them, for the greater princes, while they pursued their family interests, still gave little thought to making themselves masters of discreet territories. Political and legal business was left to the nobles and knights, who used the Länder courts they sat in to discuss public business and limit disorder. Assemblies of 'estates' agreed to local changes in Austria, Bavaria and the lands of the Teutonic Order in the thirteenth century. The three original Swiss cantons, Uri, Schwyz and Unterwalden, which first expressed in writing their common will to cooperate against all their enemies (1291), aimed to exclude outsiders, persons who had bought their office, from the administration of justice. They did not even have a common code of law in the fourteenth century, but they could create a political entity out of their resolution to provide mutual support for the principle of being judged by their neighbours, by judges as free as themselves. This defence of local rights might seem to encourage separatism, but as the case of the Swiss showed, it might also help to keep alive appeal to the mystique of empire, within which local customs continued to flourish and oppressors could be warned off.

The princes were themselves also prominent supporters of the empire. They were not inclined to pursue illusory Romanist ideals in Germany or elsewhere, but they had their own reasons for making the monarchy work. The main problem was to secure agreement as to the imperial candidate elected. Adolf of Nassau (1292-4), like Rudolf before him, had to fight for general recognition. Louis of Bavaria and Charles of Bohemia had the same problem. Civil war was the only means of resolving the disputes. There was also the question of papal rights in the election, and his power to prevent imperial coronation. Did that matter? The German princes declared in 1338 that election by them was sufficient to give their king all the powers of the king of the Romans. This did not prevent the pope from inspiring the election of an anti-king against Louis IV in 1346, but his candidate, Charles of Bohemia, was no less determined than his predecessor to try and prevent disputes about elections.

Charles was the first elector to become king and he proposed to stabilize the German constitution by turning the electors into an imperial college who would act to preserve the unity and dignity of the empire, even if there was no king at all. Like the king they should enjoy sovereignty in their own lands, which were to be transmitted intact by rule of primogeniture. This would avoid disputes about which son should have an electoral vote and help to preserve the dignity of the electorates themselves. In Charles's day there was already some agreement about the number of electoral princes. The ecclesiastical princes had allowed the three archbishops of Cologne, Mainz and Trier to speak on their behalf. There were also four secular electors, the king of Bohemia, the count Palatine, the duke of Saxony and the margrave of Brandenburg: but disputes sometimes arose as to which members of the family might vote. These electors were in 1356, apart from Saxony, members of families who had held the imperial title. Charles negotiated individually with the electoral families for a declaration of electoral rights, as well as with the princes in general, and finally published an elaborate statute, the Golden Bull (1356), which was the most important constitutional amendment in the history of the empire.[70] By defining who the electors were and preventing the division of electoral lands, Charles was able to eliminate the possibility of disputed elections.

It might be supposed that the college would use its powers to strengthen the electors at the king's expense. Charles saw the danger and granted them outright all imperial rights in their own lands. The electors do seem to have taken their duties seriously; before the century was out they actually deposed Wenceslas, Charles's son and successor, for incompetence, replacing him with their own senior member, Rupert of the Palatinate, a Wittelsbach. The college did not repeat this move. It is remarkable that a sequence of men without sons was elected to this office: Rupert (1400), Sigismund (1411), Albert of Austria (1437) and Frederick III (1439), but after 1411 it is perhaps also worth pointing out that the college normally replaced the king with his closest male relative. Though in theory the monarchy remained elective, in practice, it was all but inherited by the Luxembourg family and their heirs general, the Habsburgs. Given the German situation, the college behaved more responsibily in their efforts to keep the kingdom together than their contemporaries in France. Germany was spared the evils one family could do to the kingdom. There was much to be said for the collegiality of the electors in the sprawling kingdom of the fourteenth century.

Just as those princes who wished to keep the empire together found adequate means of implementing their programme, those who did not went their own way. The kingdom began to draw its frontiers around those who were loyal. In the east, the new Angevin dynasty of Hungary resisted German encroachment after 1302. The revival of united Poland in 1320 was intended to reverse German expansion into Polish lands, and though this was not originally successful, it did eventually subject the lands of the Teutonic Order to Polish suzerainty (1466) and define the eastern frontier with the empire. In the west also the kingdom failed to retain its hold both in Burgundy and in the Low Countries. The weakening ties with Germany there encouraged the emergence of 'Dutch' sentiments. It was at this time that both the Swiss and the Dutch began their slow march to independence of the kingdom. No doubt the peoples who remained within the empire were not a nation in the modern sense, but by opting to stay, they continued to experience a common destiny.

Neither Charles IV nor the electors were moved by any frenzied anxieties to reform the monarchy in 1356, the year when the fate of the French king could not have inspired any regrets about German backwardness. The German kingdom would not fall apart if the king were captured in battle. There was no backlog of administrative muddle to inspire constitutional opposition. In the fifteenth century, the prospects looked different. The emperor Sigismund was much concerned about the state of the empire and from the 1430s there was frequent talk of reform. When Nicholas of Cusa reviewed the general state of Christendom in 1433, he included a series of proposals for the reform of the empire as the final part of his book *De Concordia Catholica*.[71] Albert II and his Habsburg successors often raised the question of imperial reform in the diets, urging the need to strengthen royal authority for the administration of justice, the raising of armies and the collection of taxes. The princes resisted these appeals and they have often been blamed since for keeping Germany in a backward condition. Why did Germany appear to need more effective government by the mid-fifteenth century?

Sigismund had first become alive to the desirability of reform as king of Hungary, where he had to face the Turkish advance in the Balkans. A century later, a similar problem stared Charles V in the face. On both occasions the German princes were not much moved and Germany itself was, as it happened, spared Turkish conquest. A less selfish attitude might have saved the Balkans as well and prevented the creation of the Balkan problem, but only by strengthening imperial military power. Sigismund was also concerned about his forces for more personal reasons. When his brother died in 1420, he wished to succeed to the Bohemian throne, but he was unacceptable in Bohemia where he was detested for his part in the burning of John Hus at Constance in 1415. The Bohemian opposition took its stand by the Four Articles of Prague, which gave them the reputation of sharing the same heretical beliefs as Hus. The church preached successive crusades against Sigismund's rebellious subjects. To no avail: all these armies were repulsed by John Zizka's armed peasants. Sigismund's only possible hope was in the empire, from which he aimed to get both men and money. Other German princes were shamed by German defeats in these wars, but they naturally took Sigismund's personal humiliation more lightly.

Discussion for reform in the church which overflowed into the political arena had of course been stimulated in the first place by the schism. The German princes were not so much convinced of the need to restore discipline in church and state, as to exploit the advantages opened up for them personally by the unprecedented collapse of ecclesiastical organization. Royal influence amongst the prince bishops declined. The secular princes moved in. They began to think of consolidating their local power, to unite their family lands, to turn them into autonomous states. They imitated the electors and adopted rules of primogeniture for the succession; as far as they were concerned it was no moment to revive the monarchy.[72] Not until mid-century did Charles VII drive the English out of France altogether and begin to wonder what to do with his professional fighting force and his revenues from taxation. The Emperor Frederick III (1439-79) did not expect to have to take his measure of French power. Rather than argue endlessly with the princes about reform he preferred to do as they did and consolidate his family resources. It was not a courageous or an inspiring programme, but it did eventually pay off. By his marriage alliances, in less than a century, he turned the feeble Habsburg dynasty into the most powerful of Europe, without plunging the empire either into war or political controversy.

The empire of the fourteenth century began to look tired and worn very soon, but its framework survived a long time. It satisfied the demands made upon it and allowed its different territories to find their own strengths. If in the long term it was unfortunate for Germany, even in modern times it can be seen to have had its virtues; in the fourteenth century, it certainly seemed to preserve its peoples from disorder better than the French kingdom did.

6. ITALY

With Italy we reach that part of Christendom which disintegrated politically the most under the pressure of events in the late thirteenth century. No effort was made to preserve even the semblance of unity and no constitutional experiments were tried on a national scale. In the absence of such a framework, Italy was governed by municipalities, military captains and powerful families, each holding its own by force against its rivals. On the death of Frederick II, government fell to those who could exercise it; two centuries later, most of these states had been eliminated in favour of their most powerful neighbours and the affairs of the -peninsula were in the hands of the great five: Milan, Venice, Florence, Rome and Naples. At the end of the century their quarrels had introduced renewed waves of foreign armies, which overwhelmed Italy politically, a fate far worse than anything suffered by Germany.

Yet the miseries of civil war and the humiliation of foreign rule have not succeeded in discrediting the history of these centuries for Italy. The cultural achievements in literature and painting that begin with Dante Alighieri and Cimabue have not only redeemed the political failures but have sometimes seemed to justify them, as though a united Italy could not have flowered so profusely. This is a specious argument. Had Italy done no better than Germany and constituted a *regnum italicum*, as proposed by Gregory X in 1272, it would have been spared some of its worst excesses and been able to nurture culture at least as well as the German towns and principalities did.

Italy had had no princes or electors determined to keep alive the idea of the Italian kingdom. Memories of the empire survived and were stirred by the occasional visits of emperors, but the Italians were content to leave the Germans to elect these kings. Not all Italians were happy with the improvised solutions of their fellow-countrymen. Florentines as different as Dante and Dino Compagni longed for the restoration of imperial government to their distraught city, but what efforts were made to remedy endemic disorder occurred only at the most local level. In the fourteenth century itself most Italians put politics before culture. They would not even have argued that competition between towns stimulated art, for art itself was no more than a craftsman's contribution to his local community. If the Florentines in particular made so much of their independence as to inspire a new school of artists (which is only an hypothesis) it is not obvious that the world's gain justifies Italian political chaos, in a way, for example, that the achievements of Nuremberg in the time of Dürer do not likewise excuse German political weakness. Whatever has been made of these achievements later, and partly to offset the political shortcomings, at the time, solutions to political and social problems in the peninsula seemed the most urgent of Italian tasks.

Pope Innocent IV had deliberately engineered the downfall of the Staufen in Italy, but there was utter confusion about what should re-place them. The successive deaths of Frederick II (1250), Conrad IV (1254), Manfred (1266) and Conradin (1268), which eliminated the dynasty, exposed the problem in hapless detail. After a long interregnum in the papacy, the next pope, Gregory X, could think of no better alternative to the unwelcome dominance of Charles of Anjou than another emperor. He encouraged the German princes to elect Rudolf of Habsburg in the hope of bringing him back to Italy as a desirable counter-poise to the Guelf champion. The idea of the empire continued there-fore to have its importance in Italy, at least until the death of the Emperor Henry VII (1313) who actually returned to the peninsula to claim his rights. All that time Italian political arrangements could be thought of as only provisional, since the emperor would have the right to reject all unauthorized regimes. Only slowly were local governments able to adjust to the idea that the emperor would not come, would not stay, or, if he did, would not restore his government. In the meantime many Italians were nervous about the emperor. In retrospect their fears seem unreal, but this is no reason to discount them all together.

When the last real emperor died in 1250, Italy was aflame with passion, divided between his supporters and his opponents. There was no local vacuum of power at the time, for all Italy was geared to conflict, but it only gradually became apparent what the long-term consequences of imperial collapse would be in any one place. In the long term also, a general solution could only endure if it allowed for the political realities of the peninsula. What were these?

The most powerful single state of Italy was Frederick's kingdom of Naples and Sicily. Efforts to find a substitute for imperial hegemony in the peninsula depended on the hopes of finding a basis for it in the southern Italian kingdom. The papacy had nominal claims to the over-lordship of the kingdom and had tried to lure northern princes into Italy by offering the crown in return for military defeat of the Staufen. Even-tually Charles of Anjou had arrived and defeated Manfred, the reigning king of Sicily (1266). Charles consolidated his success and after the death of Pope Clement IV 1268 was undisputed master of Italy. A single master threatened many Italians hopes of political independence and Charles's success also alarmed many interests in the whole Mediter-ranean from Michael VIII, the restored Greek emperor in Constan-tinople, to Pere II, the king of Aragon, Manfred's son-in-law. The Sicilian rebellion (1282) fatally weakened the Angevins. The island was amputated politically from Naples and twenty years of warfare were unable to reverse this decision. Sicily passed into the keeping of Catalan monarchs. Naples remained under Angevin rulers until 1435. Charles's grandson, King Robert (1309-43), enjoyed consideration as the Guelf champion of Italy. The Florentines in particular cultivated the connexion, since it offered splendid business opportunities in the south, but Villani's eulogy of his wisdom, good sense and learning as a great master of theology and consummate philosopher suggests that politically he was a nonentity.[73] After him, the kingdom passed into the hands of his lascivious granddaughter Joanna, who plunged the kingdom into the worst disorders by her matrimonial problems; she had no children and the future was uncertain. Rival candidates for the succession took up arms even before her death. Occasional signs of effective leadership from Charles III (1381-85) and Ladislas (1404-14) who showed the crude strength of the youthful soldier, proved to be misleading. Ladislas was succeeded by his sister Joanna II (1414-35) no less flighty than her name-sake. Real political leadership over the rest of Italy could not therefore be expected from Naples, and until the Sicilians recovered control of Naples which they did, briefly, under Alfonso V (1442-55), there could be no question of their exercising much influence on the mainland.

The reasons for the failure of the Regno to take advantage of the opportunities in Italy were not merely adventitious. The chances for the Regno were most prejudiced by the remoteness of the southern kingdom from the scene of real turbulence in central and northern Italy. The importance of the south had depended in the past upon its part in the whole scheme of Mediterranean politics, on its power of attracting northern peoples through the peninsula and eventually on its links with the empire, which had coerced the smaller Italian states to the north. Sicily obviously plays a different role if it serves as a stepping stone from Europe into Africa, from what it does as a mere appendix to a continental state, with no outlet beyond. Under Charles of Anjou, the prospects for the kingdom in the Mediterranean still looked rosy. Louis IX's crusade was diverted to Tunis in a sensible attempt to reopen the assault on North Africa (1270). Charles likewise renewed the campaigns in the Balkans and aspired to restore the Latin empire at Constantinople. All these projects failed. Angevin Naples lost Sicily and its ambitions across the seas. The elimination of the crusading states in the Holy Land by 1291 left the Christians with island outposts and commercial concessions which the Neapolitans abandoned to others. Their own land became a 'colonial' territory for northern Italian business. From being the most powerful state of Italy, the kingdom rapidly degenerated into its most backward province: rich still, by virtue of its resources, but poor in proportion to its size and population.

If the lord of Italy was not to be found in Naples, the lord of Rome had the strongest chance of success, but papal leadership has always seemed most desirable to the weakest and least acceptable to those whom the papacy is ill-equipped to coerce. Thirteenth-century popes first demonstrated that they could raise and dispose of effective military powers without moral scruples. This could still inspire sufficient revulsion to make the cardinals choose the hermit Celestine V as pope in 1294. His abdication proved that the papal office was inadequately filled by a mere holy man. Unfortunately the papacy was never able to shed completely the burdens of the international church and concentrate on its ambitions in Italy as a prince bishopric. Being committed to a dual role the papacy argued that a territorial state was necessary for the independence of the spiritual head of Christendom. Though this provided it with local glories, as in Rome itself, this was ultimately one of the reasons for the fission of the universal church. In the 1290s Pope Boniface VIII was without doubt the most successful ruler in Italy, and a great pontiff. The spiritual prestige of the papacy combined with his diplomatic and political gifts made him feared particularly in Latium, which was real proof of his effective power. His success drove his enemies to the desperate lengths of playing upon the humours of the king of France, Philip IV. The imbroglio that followed took the papacy out of Italy altogether. The long residence in southern France (1305-77) was almost immediately followed by the schism and the conciliar epoch, which deprived even the 'Roman' popes of universal respect in the peninsula. While the council of Basel proceeded to deal in its own way with Eugenius IV, the pope himself lingered in Florence, an exile from Rome, with scant resources. Not until his return could the papacy settle down again to make Rome a potential capital for Italy. By that time it was already too late. For nearly a century and a half, Italians had conducted their affairs on the assumption that the papacy had many other preoccupations outside Italy and that they would have to cope without him.

The Italian prejudice against French popes at Avignon, which led to the demand for an Italian pope in 1378, like the impassioned pleas of Petrarch and Catherine of Siena for a return to Rome, reveal how much Italians continued to regard the papacy as an institution belonging to them. They do not indicate that the political authorities of the peninsula desired the restoration of papal leadership. The French popes had so little neglected their military commitments in Italy that they were able to reorganize the papal state under Cardinal Albornoz. The Italians were far from pleased with this. If Milanese objections were predictable, it was much more serious when even traditional papal allies like the Florentines opposed the papacy in central Italy during the War of the Eight Saints (1375-8). They defied papal anathemas and defended the territories they had won for themselves. Florentine presumption went further still. In the first half of the fifteenth century, while the papacy was in eclipse, the Florentines themselves assumed the Roman role offering Italy a cultural centre with high intellectual and artistic standards, which the papacy could not improve upon when it returned to Rome.[74] It began to tempt Florentines away. While the emperor, the king and the pope were excluded from the major roles, the finest phase of Italian history over a period of two and a half centuries was played out in many different centres.

The area concerned lay between the Alps and the Tiber. Though the countryside blossomed as never before, the source of energy was in the towns. The traditions of Roman city life had survived better in Italy than elsewhere; each town had its own bishop and even the 'feudal' nobility had a stake in the towns as well as in the country. Since the twelfth century, towns had been trying to gain a measure of self-government from their local bishops and from the German king-emperors. The success of their campaigns against Frederick Barbaossa (1183) had created numerous semi-autonomous city-states, but only within the continuum provided by imperial government and jurisdiction over the country and the nobility. When the emperor ceased to provide this control, the city councils were the only obvious points of growth for new government, but their practical experience of responsibilities outside the towns themselves was negligible. Many towns were anyway held by Ghibellines, imperial supporters who had to learn how to do without him. In others they were important minorities, exposed to unprecedented difficulties once he could not help them. In the country-side they were also numerous and hostile to pro-papal towns. Those who had consistently opposed the emperor were eager to take advantage of his disappearance. This involved them in determined campaigns to establish their ascendancy over the whole diocese or *contado* if their potential enemies were to be rendered harmless. The problems were new; men in power had no experience; experiments and blunders were inevitable. There was not much faith in compromise and governments were vindictive against their enemies: they executed the intransigent, drove the untrustworthy into exile, and merely disenfranchized the powerful, if they were peaceable. Solutions tended to be impermanent because it was difficult to satisfy all the interested parties. To work at all, they had to bear some relation to what was required. Internal discords had to be eliminated if the government was to retain control of its territory. Conflicts were fought out on the boundaries between states, and those that could not keep them there lost their independence to neighbours. These harsh realities of urban Italy ensured the survival of only the most hard-headed states and promoted the chances of soldiers, bankers and cool politicians supplanting the traditional republican forms of government. Historical attention tends to be lavished on the greatest towns with the most glorious reputations and extensive records, which obscures the effects of their expansion for the smaller towns in their vicinities. To the citizens of such places, however, the loss of their own independence for the greater glory of others was no cause for rejoicing. Their discontent may be less obvious, but it was no less real: it was the price Italians had to pay for keeping out rulers of stature.

The forms of republican government were best preserved during the fourteenth century by the Tuscan cities, particularly Florence and Siena.[75] Until 1250, Florence had no more political independence than any other city of the empire; after 1250, the Guelfs and Ghibellines fought amongst themselves, as elsewhere in Italy, and their fortunes depended upon the successes of their champions. The Guelfs triumphed with Charles of Anjou in 1266, but this did not put an end to the hatreds in the city and it was not until 1280 that the Cardinal Latino was able to recon-cile the factions and pave the way for a new form of government. The new college of Priors, who continued to be the nominal heads of state until 1530, was devised to secure representation of the sectional interests of the city and of the leading professional groups. Changed every two months, it had no opportunity to make itself permanent, and it ex-pressed the republican conviction that the business of government was the responsibility of all persons of substance and that it was more important to rotate office regularly than to rely on men of 'experience'. In the 1290s this system was rendered more workable by excluding certain 'magnate' families from office. Within a generation, this type of government had proved its worth and political agitation was for a time limited to securing recognition of further professional bodies (or *arti*) so that they could share in political office. Between 1343 and 1378 the government achieved the maximum of popular representation though its 'democratic' character should not be exaggerated. A bold attempt to enlarge the 'suffrage' at the time of the Ciompi revolt (1378) precipitated instead an oligarchical reaction. The established interests rallied and increasingly took control of the apparatus of state. Preserving the formal procedures of appointments in rotation, power was nevertheless shared by fewer men and after 1434, the oligarchy surrendered its powers to Cosimo de Medici. The concept of 'liberty' proved remarkably resilient even so. It inspired the restoration of the republic on two occasions when the Medici were overthrown, both at times of political chaos in the peninsula (1494-1512, 1527-1530). Though important in themselves, they are less significant for the history of Florence than the fact that Florence had been obliged to modify its republican principles in order to devise a more effective government. If the republican trappings were preserved it was because Florence was rich enough to afford them and traditional enough to respect them. Even in Florence, the republican city-state was unable to govern in the manner required by the later fourteenth century. Why was this?

The fundamental reason for this change was that to survive this period, Florence, like the other cities, could only do so by acquiring a territorial state, of which it became the 'capital'; it thus ceased to be a city-state and its popular constitution was unsuited for its new respon-sibilities.[76] When the lesser guilds obtained a share in the government (1343) there was already some latent opposition within the governing group between those whose economic interests made them most sensitive to long-distance trade and European affairs as a whole and those whose vision was limited to Tuscany or the city itself. By the 1350s Florence was engaged in a process of trying to consolidate its interests in Tuscany, which involved recurrent, expensive wars. After the treaty of Bretigny when hordes of unemployed soldiers descended on Italy in search of adventure and rewards, Florence had either to hire them, fight them or buy them off.[77] In the 1370s came the war with the papacy; in the next decade, when the oligarchy took power, the limits of the state were pushed as far east as Arezzo; by 1406 Pisa was annexed. The Albizzi faction pursued this policy to the limit by trying to obtain Lucca as well (1429). Its failure to do this discredited the regime and established the Medici, whose conservative policy was to govern the state as it was.

The oligarchs and the Medici believed that their experience of overseas trade, banking and industry enabled them to win and defend the territorial state more effectively than government with popular members lacking experience outside their shops and businesses. The oligarchs could exploit their superior financial resources to raise money by loans and state bonds; they used their knowledge of foreign courts to win friends and plan alliances. It is even probable that the oligarchs felt some reluctance to subvert the constitution in order to retain control of the government for the better interests of the state; republican sentiment continued to cloud their vision. But they also saw that if Florence did not defend itself by creating a state of this kind, it would become a victim of military pressures from outside. It seemed to them better to be 'free' and lord it over others, than to lose freedom under a strictly republican regime. Florence was drawn into the business of state-building gradually, as it were by the force of events. Two main strands in this process may be discerned. The first was that other weaker cities had already been absorbed into the small military empires of distinguished captains, itching to extend their dominions into Tuscany; the second arose from economic circumstances that encouraged, if they did not impose, the transition from city to state.

Within a century of the death of Frederick II, the era of the civic independence was over. Left to cope with government by the elimination of the empire, the cities were not equally endowed to shoulder its burdens, even in their own regions. Already in 1250, cities found that the military captains were powerful enough to suppress some republican ambitions. The Guelf and Ghibelline conflicts played into the hands of the military. Henry VII's invasion, and still more his death (1313), gave his captains their opportunity to clamp down on the towns they controlled. Elected as captain of the people by acclamation, the more successful they were in making themselves masters of one place and leading its armies against local enemies, the more towns they could expect to bring beneath their sway. By the early fourteenth century a number of these military tyrants had been established with a marked tendency to consolidate small territories, in place of the old town units, and to bequeath them to their heirs: the Scaligers in Verona or the Gonzaga in Mantua, the Este in Ferrara. To face up to the threats presented by military captains, Florence had itself to take *signori*. Between 1313 and 1322 it was King Robert of Naples; in 1325 his son, Charles of Calabria, was appealed to; he died in 1328, which put an end to that experiment. More serious were the circumstances in 1342, when Walter of Brienne, duke of Athens, became 'tyrant'. As soon as the consequences became clear, he was driven out. It was at this point that the Florentines tried to salvage the state by giving it a broader electoral basis. Military government might be avoided by stronger political authorities.

The stark alternatives facing the city-states by the early fourteenth century inspired Marsilio of Padua to distil the political wisdom of Aristotle and offer it as an antidote to tyranny.[78] It was however not open to the cities to solve their problems from books. To preserve its independence each city needed a loyal captain of its own, whose ambitions could be only contained by a guranteed income. If the city defaulted on its obligations, the captain could apply force and rule according to his wishes. Until the 1320s the old city militias were still in use, but they retreated before the swelling numbers of professional soldiers. Formerly professional soldiers had been at the emperor's disposal and had served his political purposes. In the new circumstances, the soldiers fought their own battles so that the towns, having acquired the responsibilities of 'sovereignty', had more serious wars to engage in, just when, for political reasons, they had deprived themselves of the services of the 'nobles'. There was a notable falling away in reliance upon the old militias, perhaps because factional conflicts made governments unwilling to keep potentially unreliable citizens in arms, but most obviously because of the expense of military equipment. Rich individual citizens became reluctant to commit themselves to battle in person. Armour cost too much and the risks of being held to ransom were too high. All the towns that could were also engaged in rebuilding their walls and fortifications in self-defence against the engines of war. Professional soldiers exploited their advantages in persuading townsmen to leave such matters to the experts. To cope with them towns needed both stalwart politicians and much ready money. Even if the town could elude the grasp of a military captain, it would still need the services of a much stronger government than the old city regimes.

There were few cities that could pay the price of liberty. If Florence and Venice could do so, it was because they were richer than most. But even the wealthiest cities had to find the political power to coerce the citizens to pay taxes adequate for the military budgets. Florence, despite its able and popular governments, relied on indirect taxation and state-bonds from the early fourteenth century until 1427, when direct taxation of income was at last agreed to in the last years of the oligarchy.[79] Above all the problems of finding enough money were exacerbated by the general economic situation. The towns had grown very fast, without taking thought for the conditions of continuous prosperity. Not merely local disturbances but wars in any part of Europe could directly disrupt Italian prosperity, and the Italians would be powerless to save themselves. The Anglo-French war bankrupted some big Italian businesses even before the plague added to the economic uncertainty.

The needs of large town populations, particularly in the fluctuating circumstances of warfare and disease, made cities more aware of the advantages of drawing their food from their own territories, just when competition for control of such lands made the whole enterprise more costly. The loss of local city-state independence to greater cities had its compensations in the manifest improvement of the countryside. The zones of inter-city friction were removed since conflict was limited to the borders between states. Within the state, citizens and merchants travelled with less hindrance, bought country properties and invested money in them. Tuscany was terraced and planted with vines and olives, fruit-trees and market-gardens.[80] In the Po valley, the canalization of the river waters owed much to the consolidation of Lombardy and the disappearance of the old city rivalries. The price to be paid for these improvements was the rejection of the communal spirit in politics and the growth of hereditary tyrannies.

The earliest and most important example of this development comes from Milan, where archbishop Otto Visconti had to campaign for fifteen years (1262-77) before he was even admitted to his city.[81] As archbishop, his dominion already extended beyond the walls, over his ecclesiastical province. Milan was the metropolis of Lombardy, already a potential provincial capital rather than a walled city. Apart from Rome, Milan had the most distinctive ecclesiastical personality of all Italian sees. Its strategic importance came from its site, where the routes through the Alps converged on the roads radiating across northern Italy. It was by the thirteenth century a major city for banking and industry: the greatest prize of the Italian mainland. The archbishop fulfilled his secular obligations by installing his nephew, Matteo, as Captain of the People. His family retained their hold on Milan and the cities of the province, with occasional disturbances in which another local family, the Torriani, took power. The Milanese were too rich, independent and powerful to accept a petty tyrant from outside. In the fourteenth century the many-branched Visconti family held together several different groups of Lombard towns by family association. By this means some measure of local autonomy was preserved, yet, at the same time, collective security could be realized. Within their towns the Visconti had no need to suppress existing constitutions; the town-councils ceased to matter because executive power was left to the tyrants.

Out in the lagoon, Venice had no direct experience either of the Staufen emperors' government or its aftermath. For centuries, Venice had stood closer to Constantinople than to Italy. Though it had turned against the Greeks by its share in the crusade of 1204, this only deepened Venetian commitments to the Aegean. During the thirteenth century, the traditional forms of government had therefore been under the strain of imperial responsibility. Attempts to strengthen the position of the doge by hoisting him as a demagogue on the shoulders of popular support were, however, thwarted by an alert nobility. Instead of allowing tyranny, they consolidated the oligarchy, subjecting the doge to honourable supervision, entrusting the government to the senior politicians in the *Maggiore Consiglio* (Senate) and the Committee of Ten, closing their ranks to outsiders and contenting themselves with the dull routines of electing all the major officials of the state. The Venetian constitution acquired an envied reputation for stability, because the government was held to account by nobles who renounced power for themselves. During the fourteenth century, the virtues of the regime were tested chiefly by its ability to defend the colonial empire and Levantine trade against Genoese competition. It was not lured onto the mainland in search of land. In outline, however, the growth of responsible government was made necessary by the acquisition of an empire, even if that empire was still overseas.[82]

Venice was brought into Italian politics as a result of the bold attempt by Gian Galeazzo Visconti to impose his will on all northern Italy. He began by eliminating his uncle Bernabo in 1385: the perfect example of a successful coup d'état. He extended his control over other cities and in 1395 bought from the emperor the title Duke of Milan. He was on the point of overwhelming the Florentines when he died suddenly in 1402, whereupon his empire fell to pieces. Some of these were promptly snaffled up by the Venetians who had understood what a united and hostile Lombardy could do to Venetian trade. It is however significant that Gian's son, Filippo Maria, was able to reconstitute the duchy without too much difficulty. The political union of the region was preferable to the chaos of liberty and only Milan was strong enough to give the lead. In the 1420s, Milanese power was sufficiently formidable to frighten the Venetians into joining the Florentines in opposing the insatiable ambitions of the Visconti. By 1430, the Venetians had advanced to the river Adda and thus struck a balance of interests in northern Italy.

The situation that developed in Italy from the late fourteenth century was not the consequence of a few men's ambitions in or out of the city. It grew out of the need to preserve what was possible of the ideal conditions of city life, in a land without king or emperor to keep the peace between rival groups. Those cities that could had to expand to meet the need. They had to improvise and they clung as much as possible to the familiar forms of government. There was no doubt about the difficulties or that expert politicians should be left with the responsibilities for solving them. In most cities, the mind of a single ruler came to seem more desirable than blundering on with divided counsels. Such men had diverse qualities to recommend them. They had to be, or become, wealthy enough to support the charges of government; they needed skill in diplomacy and tact in managing the affairs of their dominions. Already, by the mid-fifteenth century, such men, handing on their offices to their sons, looked no less aristocratic than the nobility of northern Europe, even if they could not claim ancient birth, and had emerged from a system of government originally opposed to noble pretensions. In their own way they aped the dukes of Burgundy, the greatest lords of Europe, with whose lands they had close commercial dealings. They sought marriages for their children in the princely families of the north. In one respect they lacked self-confidence: their 'states' had no traditionally respectable basis of authority, so attempts were made to cover their presumptions by appeal to a remote past, beyond recent memory, and by boasting that in Italy the glorious past of Rome had been recovered. The conquering Romans of the Republic or Empire would have had no time for these rhetorical pretensions, but they have left their mark on the interpretation of the history of this period. Whatever value may be attributed to the achievements of the Italian Renaissance, the creation of the regional states of Italy during this period is the most significant development and this owed nothing to humanist precept or Roman precedent.

7. EASTERN EUROPE

When the English and French could not fight one another directly because of truces in the war, they repaired to Spain or to 'Prussia', where they took part in campaigns against the 'pagans'.[83] In Königsberg (which was in those backward days nevertheless open to visits by the English and the French) old enmities of the west were fought again, as when the Scottish knight, Douglas, was slain by the English Clifford, and avenged by the great French hero, Marshal Boucicault. Yet there was also some genuine interest in the political situation of 'Prussia' for its own sake. Soldiers in search of campaigns responded to the requests for help put out by the Teutonic Order (one of the few military orders of the period on regular active service), though they did not stop to ask about the rights of the case. Men from the west appear to have believed that they were fighting with the Teutonic knights against pagan Lithuanians, when they were in fact participating in a conflict within the Lithuanian ruling family, which the Order hoped to turn to its own advantage. Since those days it has become difficult to write about this kind of campaigning without stirring up the patriotism of Germans and Poles, but there is no way of determining by international or moral law what was right or wrong. If from the west, the affairs of eastern Europe still seemed to belong to an older scheme of war against the heathen, it was because the western political horizon normally extended no further than the empire.

The peoples to the east only intermittently became involved in western European affairs. Enterprising merchants from Italy or Germany, who visited them were the principal sources of information about them.[84] The Poles first became familiar in the west during the Council of Constance, at which they were impressively represented (apparently as part of the 'German' nation). The Czechs who had played a leading part in the affairs of the empire under the Luxembourg kings drew apart during the Hussite period when they forfeited the respect of Christendom. Hungary, a great and rich state grabbed by the Angevin kings in 1302, embarked on ambitious projects for expansion in Croatia, Dalmatia, Bosnia, Wallachia, Moldavia and Galicia. Dynastic alliances that brought Poland to Hungary under Louis the Great (1370-82), in turn took Hungary to Charles of Durazzo and Naples (1384-6), Sigismund of Luxembourg (1386-1437), Ladislas of Poland (1437-44) and only in desperation, to a native prince, Matthew Corvin. In this time this tendency for eastern European states to conglomerate had produced the dual monarchy of Poland-Lithuania under the Jagellons, the largest state in all Europe, stretching between the Black Sea and the Baltic and from the river Oder to the whole Dniepr river-system in the east. Still penned in between the Lithuanians and the Tartars were the Great Russians living a more intense life unto themselves in the fourteenth and fifteenth century. Their opportunity to expand had not yet come. To the south, the Serbian empire, like the Bulgarian before it, swelled like a sponge absorbing water and shrank again when squeezed by the Ottomans.

The glories of their greater days in this period have served in the depressing centuries since to keep alive the hopes of many eastern European peoples for the recovery of autonomy. For since the sixteenth century, the great dynasties have imposed colonial status on eastern Europe. The Polish state just survived until the end of the eighteenth century, but, when the final partition came in 1795, eastern Europe was thereafter divided amongst four empires, Ottoman, Austrian, Prussian and Russian. And since the ideology of the Russian state now prevails not only in Slavonic Europe, but amongst the Magyars and with some of the Germans too (since they have been pushed back over the frontiers they crossed in 1250) this modern 'dominion' as far west as the Elbe transcends the ancient limits of both Orthodoxy and Slavdom. So, Eastern Europe still remains an entity alien to the western imagination, often thought to be uniform in character, by virtue of popular ignorance about its historical diversity. The west has made occasional inroads into those lands, but eastern Europe has in fact more successfully staved off 'westernization' than some other more distant parts of the world. How then should this great territory be viewed from the west?

In the nineteenth century it was assumed that peoples could measure their collective success by their power to create and preserve their own national governments. By this standard, eastern Europe failed. The Poles felt this most keenly and sought comfort in the west, particularly in France, the champion of nationalism. In the mid-twentieth century, however, it is not so certain that national entities, even in the west, are so important. Eastern Europe should not therefore be judged adversely in this period simply because it did not provide suitable opportunities for their growth. Even the states of western Europe were not growing as nations at this time, and there was obviously no existing model for use in the east. The eastern states did borrow such institutions from the west as suited their needs. Indeed the variety of communities that appeared there shows no lack of institutional invention.

The 'problems' of eastern Europe are in the first place geographical. It was access to the sea which enabled the peoples of Europe to draw from the common cultural and economic pool. It was the misfortune of eastern Europe that the further east their peoples lay, the further they lived from the sea. To the south the peoples of the Danube basin were drawn towards the Black Sea. This was only an advantage for Europeans as long as that sea was dominated by Greek shipping. Latin traders in Constantinople used the Euxine not for trade in the Danube basin but solely for the purpose of reaching the western end of the great silk road in the Crimea. There the arrival of the Tartars from the steppes completely sealed off the Russian peoples of the interior from the sea. Eastern Europeans therefore preferred to send their desirable produce down the rivers flowing north into the Baltic. As it happened, however, the mouths of these rivers were by the thirteenth century in the hands of the Germans, who steadily advanced along the northern shores of the great European plain. Once the whole economic system of the European waterways was fully organized in the fourteenth century, the Magyars and the Poles both appreciated the advantages of regaining control of their nearest coasts, but they lacked the resources to do this with ease because both these monarchies found their main strength inland, where noble families had few or no feudal obligations to help their kings. Moreover they had no tradition of discussing or cooperating, even amongst themselves, because their lands, like those of the monarchies themselves, were still relatively unexploited. The nobles' main interest was to attract additional settlers by offering favourable terms to German peasants and townsmen, Italian merchants and Jewish exiles. There was much to be done, but there was no obvious need for ingenuity in politics and no sense of urgency that there might be common interests to be advanced by influencing kings through royal policies.[85] The nobles who were great enough to manage their own affairs by themselves, remained comparatively indifferent to their rulers' dynastic ambitions. So rulers were hampered in their more ambitious programmes and could only become more important by marriage alliances and the chances of inheritance.

The rulers with the most consistent sense of purpose were the princes of the Piast family which had ruled Poland since the tenth century.[86] Poland was originally a Baltic state between the Oder and the Vistula in the great plain (*Pole* is Slavonic for plain), with its ecclesiastical centre at Gnieszno where Boleslav I was first crowned. The princes subsequently lost their control of Pomerania; Casimir I transferred the 'capital' to Cracow before the mid-eleventh century. The Piast princes were soon torn between their interests in the north and their aspirations to take the great city of Kiev, where Boleslav II was crowned in 1076. After the death of Boleslav III in 1138, his dominions fell apart and Western Pomerania was irrevocably lost to others. The princes of Great Poland in the north nursed schemes for recovering their influence from the encroachments of the Germans, but these had little attraction for the princes of Little Poland, who looked east from Cracow towards Galicia and Volhynia. The dukes of Mazovia invited the Teutonic Order to settle and help quell the still pagan Prussians, thus increasing Germanic settlement in the north to the eventual discomforture of the Great Poles. In the west, Silesia was subdivided amongst several descendants of the Piasts. By the late thirteenth century, therefore, the states of the old kingdom were all set upon separate courses of development. In addition to German colonists, there were other predators. The kings of Bohemia, Wenceslas II and Wenceslas III, both obtained the Polish crown at Cracow. Polish independence seemed likely to be totally extinguished in the fourteenth century.

This was averted by the efforts of Przemyslav II of Great Poland and Ladislas the Short of Kujavia to thwart German expansion in the north by reuniting the Piast principalities, though these schemes attracted little sympathy in Cracow. Internal dissensions continued to facilitate the expansion of the Teutonic Order, which was installed in Marienbork; Gdansk was acquired by them from Brandenburg in 1309. Not until 1320 did Ladislas, with Hungarian help, secure his coronation at Cracow and then instigate a legal process at the papal curia against the Order for the recovery of Pomorze (Eastern Pomerania).[87] John XXII favoured his suit because he found Ladislas a useful ally against the Emperor Louis of Bavaria, who in turn supported John of Bohemia, the enemy of Piast influence in Silesia. Bohemian pressure on the principalities there thus prevented the reunification of all the Piast principalities and Silesia remained in the orbit of the German states until 1945. German colonization remained vigorous. Ladislas and his son Casimir III could do no more than stem the flow, despite help from Scandinavia and an alliance with Lithuania.

Like their predecessors they found compensation for their failures in the west by reopening the campaigns in Volhynia and Ruthenia. Cracow was obviously pleased by this change of policy and after Casimir's death in 1370 successfully urged the claims of his nephew, Louis of Hungary, to the throne, since he too was interested in these eastern lands. When Louis died in 1382, leaving only daughters to succeed him, the elder was rejected in Poland on the grounds of her marriage to Sigismund of Luxembourg, the avowed enemy of the Poles, and the throne was offered to the younger, Jadwiga who was married to Jagellon of Lithuania. He became a Christian and took the name of Ladislas. His descendants, by another wife, ruled Poland-Lithuania for two centuries, defeating the Order at Grunewald (1410) and making it a vassal-state of the monarchy in 1466. Pomorze and Mazovia were both incorporated into the dual monarchy, and the Jagellons also extended their influence beyond the Polish frontiers by planting princes of their family both in Hungary and in Bohemia. Dynastic ambition had given the Poles some kind of political purpose in the fourteenth century, but under the Jagellons were subordinated to the interests of Polish family aggrandisement. These Jagellon princes were in fifteenth-century Europe of much greater significance then the Luxembourgs or the Habsburgs, and it is important to consider why this early version of the multi-racial empire proved less durable than its Habsburg counterpart.

Its fragility was probably due chiefly to the fact that it was composed not only of Catholics, but of many Orthodox peoples in Lithuania and the Ukraine, whose loyalties to Catholic princes could not be relied upon, once the princes of Moscow were in a position to play on their sense of what was owed to the Orthodox metropolitan. The significance of religious bonds as such in these multifarious states may not be properly appreciated unless the extent of political division is properly measured.

The many peoples of the empires were initially separated from one another by their different speech. However the Poles, who all spoke one common language, were no less split amongst themselves by region and loyalty. The Silesian princes had once aspired to reunite Poland. Foiled by others, they opted out of the kingdom all together. At Cracow it did not seem improper to the Poles if rulers were taken from Bohemia or Hungary. The princes and the humbler people were in no sense committed even to the Piast kings' interests, and the rulers themselves would have found it difficult to justify their ambitions as national rather than family ones. The rulers did not conceive of their affairs in terms of foreign policy in the modern sense, but as moves in the game of family expansion, to be played by marriages as well as pacts for particular purposes. Admittedly it seems likely that had Casimir III been succeeded by a son, or by his grandson Stettin (as once planned), his more limited kingdom might have acquired more coherence and, by dint of struggling continually with the Teutonic Order, found a means of drawing all the divergent Polish territories into a united effort, comparable to that achieved by the Valois kings in fifteenth-century France. His foundation of a university at Cracow (1364) on the Italian model (which began a period of fruitful contact) might have been intended to promote a broader culture and establish common interests amongst the Polish students who frequented it.

However, the possibilities of building a Polish state were reduced after his death, when Louis of Hungary became king. This was welcomed by the many influential Poles concerned most about the advancement of the landed interest. Even so they were not unmindful of the need to protect local privileges, and in fact successive foreign kings were forced to confirm Polish customs in return for being recognized. The emergence of specifically Polish interests was thus facilitated by the acceptance of rulers from outside the kingdom, even though this meant that the monarchy itself could not be the focus of 'national' sentiment. Under the dual monarchy of the Jagellons in particular, the Poles discovered the advantages of having effective spokesmen to voice their point of view against the Lithuanians. This role however fell to the clergy who in a partly Orthodox state identified Polish interests as a whole with those of Catholicism. Zbigniew Olésnicki, the king's secretary, was the most influential of these. He became bishop of Cracow. Jan Dlugosz, archbishop of Lwow (died 1480), was the first scholar inspired to write an important history of Poland and to view its past in perspective. He began by distrusting the Lithuanian royal dynasty and his sense of the Polish community was affected by the clerical cult of great native saints like Stanislas. Similarly the cult of local saints in other Slavonic lands (John Nepomuk in Bohemia, Sava in Serbia, Serge in Russia) roused a religious patriotism which was quite independent of politics and well able to survive the eventual collapse of the dynasties. Religious patriotism ran deeper than any national sentiment.

Religious passions were inflamed in eastern Europe during the fifteenth century through the wars against the Ottomans waged by the Poles and Hungarians, who were left to shoulder the main burden of resisting the Muslim attacks. The Jagellons were involved not only on the Turkish front, but also in subduing the remnants of northern paganism and encroaching on Orthodox Russia. The Hungarians in particular cultivated a reputation for religious zeal, and their defence of Catholicism in the Balkans gave the Magyars a name for intransigence when dealing with their many neighbours of doubtful orthodoxy. This encouraged the Croats (who differed from the Serbs by religion, though not by language) to make a firm alliance with the Hungarians, otherwise completely alien to them in culture. At that time religion was a more important bond. Only in the nineteenth century, when different criteria were invoked and Latin was abandoned as their common cultural medium, did the Croats and the Hungarians discover how incompatible they were.

Eastern Europe was not peculiar in having peoples of many different kinds thrust into the care of the same rulers. Its misfortune was that no circumstances obliged all the peoples of any one of the dynastic 'states' to opt for religion, or language or princely loyalty in order to bind themselves together definitively by that means. The states remained conglomerations of many different peoples willing their separate survival. The history of western Europe suggests that the most important factor in promoting political coherence there was the growth of communities of 'neighbours'. However variable in size from the canton to the kingdom, many different kinds of person nevertheless wrought a territorial unity out of their common need for agreed rules of law. There was nothing strictly comparable to this in eastern Europe. The discreet princely estates were there sufficiently large for the princes to dispense with consultation or political dealings with their subjects, whom they regarded as mere tenants. Each princely estate could survive by its own efforts and its master never discovered how politics differed from estate-management, a lesson which was difficult enough to learn even in the west. Poland went furthest in devising a political community, but even there the constitution itself came to enshrine the view that the state was no more than a combination of all the interests of the landowners, when it allowed each one of them to impose a personal veto on any act of state.[88] The minority never learned how to accept the unwelcome decisions of the many. There was no bitter need to subordinate private to public interests. Every private interest was a vital fraction of the whole.

The institutional expression of this view was achieved during the fifteenth century by those who thought by this means to preserve Polish interests in the Jagellon state. Regional assemblies met frequently to vote extraordinary taxes which the kings had been obliged to renounce as a royal right. The national *Sejm* (diet) brought together all the nobles not holding offices to discuss the king's business. The Jagellons abandoned to the nobility the real power to speak for Poland within the great dominion and it was no fault of theirs if the nobles representing so many diverse estates and regions did not discover how to speak with one voice.[89] Contemporary France had institutions just as disunited and ultimately stultifying. There was no ready-made formula for success. How many states have ever achieved a satisfactory solution for their institutional problems, or, when they have devised an institution for the purpose, known how to conserve its virtue?

Muscovy

By the union with Lithuania, Poland found factitious strength to deal with the Teutonic Order. Russia which was brutally shaken by the Mongols, had to grow fresh roots over a long period, during which it appeared to be dormant. The period is for Russia without showy display, but in the long term it proved to be one of the most formative in all Russian history. Ancient Russia had been a country of traders and cities, with Kiev as their centre, linking Constantinople, its spiritual home, to the north, which supplied it with corn, furs and timber. After the Mongols sacked Kiev in 1237, the principal survivor of this system was the city of Novgorod. It found a nominal prince in Vladimir, but remained self-governing, with responsibility for a huge tract of territory, supplying raw-materials in demand by Baltic traders. But, since the Mongols had intercepted the Scandinavian shortcut to Constantinople down the Dniepr, Novgorod could be no more than a depot for colonial produce; it had no political potential for Russia as a whole.

The relative decline of trading did not hinder the progress of agriculture.[90] Continuous clearings in the forest-belt of northern Russia indicate that the peasantry were not merely fleeing from the Mongols, but steadily expanding their workforce. As in other parts of eastern Europe, the peasants could profit from their own scarcity-value to organize favourable social conditions for themselves. As they encroached on the forest and laid out their new villages they inevitably took the management of their affairs into their own hands. The Tartars authorised their princely vassals to act on their masters' behalf in exacting taxation from these peasants, who were thus spared direct dealings with the overlords. Churches, particularly monasteries, were able to obtain concessions from the Tartars exempting them from taxation; in return the clergy preached submission to authority. These exemptions attracted many settlers and made the monasteries rich and powerful. Gradually over the fourteenth century a new kind of Russia began to take shape under the Tartar shadow. A land of peasants, princes and monasteries, all Great Russians, who were separated from other Russians, themselves under other protectors.

The hero-prince of this period was Alexander Nevsky, whose military exploits were written up in the thirteenth century both by a warrior retainer and by a monk. Alexander was only warlike in the north against Novgorod, the Teutonic Order and the Swedes; to the Tartars he was submissive, preferring to spare his lands by placating masters he could not defeat. This attitude persisted in his house for more than two centuries. The Tartars remained powerful enough to capture Ryazan as late as 1443 and to take Vasili II prisoner in 1455. However, their grip on Russia began to relax after the fall of the Mongol dynasty in China in 1368; this precipitated the fragmentation of the Tartar empire and the different parts could no longer help one another.

By that time the strongest political leader of the Great Russians had become the duke of Moscow, their holy city, where the Metropolitan preserved the idea of Russian unity. Politically the Russians were split up under the descendants of Alexander Nevsky, though at Tver chroniclers retained some sense of common Russian interests by their concern for the dynasty as a whole. The first duke of Moscow to emerge as more influential than his relations was Ivan Kalita (1328-41), 'Money-bags', so called because he secured the Tartars' exclusive nomination as their tax-collector. Even then Moscow chroniclers did not initially stress the dynastic aspect of their own line of dukes. During the fourteenth century, however, the succession of sons from one generation to another gradually enabled them to establish their ascendancy over the Nevsky family, despite the disadvantages attendant on princes like Dmitri and Vasili II, who succeeded as minors. Yet chronicles written in the circle of Metropolitan Kiprian (1389-1406) continued to concentrate on the Russians as a whole rather than the ambitions of the dukes of Moscow in particular. Significantly, the layman who wrote the life of Dmitri Donskoy, the victor of the battle of Kulikovo Pole over the Tartars (1380), still betrays a very unworldly attitude to political events.[91]

The superiority of the religious concerns may be judged also from the fact that it was from the Metropolitans that rulers of Moscow borrowed when calling themselves Grand Prince of all Russia: the first to do so was Vasili I (1389-1425).[92] The clergy were the most reliable prop of his successor Vasili II (1425-62) whose personal weakness may have encouraged the Russians to try and inculcate more respect for his office: after 1447, he was styled sovereign (*gospodar*). In 1453 Moscow claimed to succeed Constantinople as the third Rome.[93] The independence of the Russian church had been proclaimed in 1441 when the Metropolitan become autocephalous. Ivan III, Vasili II's son took the final step and refused tribute to the Tartars. By defeating Novgorod he also brought all the Great Russians to acknowledge him as Caesar.[94]

The rise of Moscow gave the Russians their characteristic form of government during the period when they were most isolated, particularly from the west. When Peter I moved his capital to the Neva, he brought with him Muscovite traditions which have continued to be important. These were not fully-fledged by 1462. The peasantry had barely lost any of their real independence; the *boyars* had done no more than recognize Vasili II as sovereign; the dynasty itself, if forceful, was not autocratic. As in France about the same time, a new form of government had nonetheless taken shape. The peoples would live with it for centuries, because it had been fashioned carefully from durable materials. Some continuity with the Kievan past was maintained, but there is no need to seek either a Kievan or a Mongol origin for Russian institutions. The Great Russians had lived with new problems, and found ways of mastering them; by the end of Vasili II's reign they were seen to have created something new with promise for the future. The state of Hungary and the bloated state of Poland-Lithuania could not have claimed so much, and over the centuries their power in the east melted away as the Russians became more self-confident. Russia's crisis centuries gave her unlooked-for virtues which proved more lasting than those acquired more easily by her western neighbours.

Throughout Europe for about a century and a half (1290-1440) the local communities had struggled to make themselves heard, to survive tyranny and to find suitable means of preserving their rights. Though they had some intellectual aids at their disposal, they were for the most part obliged to take up the cudgels on their own account. Whereas Froissart tried at this time to record examples of chivalrous exploits, the battles of the Scots, the Swiss, the Serbs, Poles or Russians were desperately earnest and not stylized encounters. Efforts to glamorize some of these local struggles are not convincing and the events of these years have frequently been passed over as times of troubles. The kind of progress that Europe had appeared to be making in the mid-thirteenth century was arrested. There was a vigorous protest from below about the new order promised by the rulers and their clerks. Rulers did not give up without a fight, but they had in the end to recognize that there were powerful interests and sentiments within their communities that could not be silenced. Everywhere they agreed to make concessions to those interests, in order to secure a free hand in matters of greater personal interest to them than their kingdoms: namely their ambitions as dynasts to combine many peoples into family empires.

7

THE PEACE
OF THE
DYNASTIES

By the middle of the fifteenth century Europeans, exhausted by their efforts to devise more reasonable solutions to their problems, for the most part became reconciled to the 'traditional' authorities with the strongest claims of sentiment. Restored to power, the popes and the Valois kings of France recognized that the desire for peace had prevailed over the temptation to find better solutions by experiment. Conflicts had shown up the limitations of government, so rulers saw the sense in not pressing old claims too hard against sensitive subjects. There was an acceptance of an order in which every man knew his place and was expected to keep to it. The temporary governor of Barataria renounced his post with the significant words: 'I was not born to be a governor, nor to defend isles or cities from the enemies who choose to attack them. I understand more about ploughing and digging and the pruning and gathering of vine-shoots than of law-giving or defending provinces or kingdoms. St Peter is well at Rome: I mean that everyone is best practising the trade for which he was born. A reaper's hook comes better to my hand than a governor's sceptre. I prefer stuffing myself with salad to being at the mercy of a meddling doctor who kills me by hunger; and I had rather lie down under the shade of an oak tree in summer and wrap myself in a shepherd's cloak of two skins in winter, with my liberty, than lie between holland sheets and dress in sable skins under the burden of a governorship.' Sancho Panza, the peasant of good sense, speaks for the commons of the new Europe. His political irresponsibility not only mocks the fundamental assumptions of modern democracy; it is no less remote from the stubborn defence of local communal interests shown in town and country during the fourteenth century. In the new society, a few were born to rule and burdensome was their life, defending cities, giving laws and being fussed over in the public interest. But the rest had real freedom, to enjoy summer and winter, protected from enemies and murderers by the benevolent arms of government. Freedom without power was preferred to the worry and cost of self-defence.

As this attitude gradually became more prevalent, European public affairs came to be managed by a handful of crowned heads, with their devoted servants and menials, while the majority of their subjects pursued the trades for which they were born. The numerous neighbourhood communities of the past retreated from the foreground and a new order of political relations emerged.

The outlines of this new order first became clear in the late fifteenth century, a brief period of comparative calm, abruptly shattered in the last decade, when Italy, at the time the stage for the most spectacular achievements of contemporary European culture, suddenly became a battleground for the major political powers. At the same time, tentative exploration by sea beyond European waters abruptly opened up routes across the Atlantic to the New World and round the Cape of Good Hope to India and lands beyond the range of Islam. The affairs of Italy became the concern of all European princes just as the affairs of Europe obtained a world-wide context. It is not easy to resist the view that European history then entered a new phase, so the respite from turmoil in the late fifteenth century seems to separate two different worlds, labelled 'medieval' and 'modern'. Whether this interlude seems more remarkable for what it promised for the future or for what it preserved of the past, in this book it becomes a suitable place to stop, to sum up.

Since the mid-nineteenth century, the secular rationalist outlook has tended to emphasize those features of the fifteenth century which looked forward. Modern historians complacently traced back the histories of modern states to fifteenth-century prototypes and contrasted them to the international medieval church. This contrast will therefore be discussed in the first two sections of this chapter. Even more generally accepted is the view that the Italian or the European Renaissance opened the way for secular culture. The changes in education and the arts will therefore be treated in the last two sections.

1. THE EUROPEAN STATES

The long-dreaded fall of Constantinople when it finally came in 1453 changed little, but signified much. The Muslim advance from the east had never before achieved such a symbolic victory over the Christians. When weaker and poorer, in the twelfth century, Christendom had launched a crusading effort; in the fifteenth century, the papacy, itself no less ardent, summoned Christians to arms: Christendom as a whole remained inert. The Latins viewed with indifference the fate of the Greeks and the consolidation of Ottoman power in the Levant. They found just energy enough in the sixteenth century to keep the Turks out of Vienna. In desperate times cooperation against the infidel was possible and effective, but mere threats proved insufficient to give Latin Christendom a more united political or military front. The Latin emperor gained no extra prestige by the elimination of his Greek colleague and assumed no new responsibilities for the defence of Christendom. In a practical sense Christendom could not have more convincingly demonstrated how much its religious fervour had declined. Yet it would be misleading to leave it at that. Christian sentiments had changed; they had not evaporated. Since the twelfth century the Latin west had concentrated on its Roman Christian capital; the significance of the Eastern holy places had declined; Latins lost patience with schismatic Greeks. Catholic religion also became more intensely spiritual. Though conquering for Christ had not lost its appeal, as subsequent events showed, the hope of defeating Islam by a head-on conflict had melted away. Christians instead set out to surround and suffocate Islam, a policy which proved surprisingly successful down to the twentieth century. It would therefore be premature to conclude that because Christendom no longer reacted to the Ottomans with Crusading fervour, secular considerations already prevailed over religious duty. Yet something had changed: namely the primary duty of rulers had become the government of their own peoples, not military service on behalf of the church universal.

Latin Christendom was by 1453 composed of many small states, for the most part respectful of the spiritual sovereignty of the pope, but otherwise independent and with clearly defined frontiers. They were extremely variable in size and power, but even the smallest had learned how to preserve their independence by skilful use of alliances and diplomacy. The greatest, the German king, had only titular power in a federation of several states. Imperial pretension and conquest had in effect ceased to be the most obvious way of bringing two or more states under one lord: more common were combined monarchies. The constituent elements had such marked individuality, customs and institutions, that they had proved to be indestructible during the century and a half of turmoil. Ambitious rulers could only force different states together by negotiating marriage alliances amongst themselves and relying on the chances of inheritance. Europe already had some united kingdoms in the mid-fifteenth century—Scandinavia, Poland-Lithuania—and others were to follow, most notably Castile-Aragon and England-Scotland. The power of the greatest dynasties had not yet been consolidated, but the Valois dukes of Burgundy showed what was possible by uniting in two or three generations the fragmentary states of the Low Countries. This was one of the outstanding political communities of the continent and would be generally recognized as such, had the union not been broken up a century later by the revolt of the Netherlands against

Philip II. The subsequent history of the Low Countries made it difficult to appreciate the Burgundian achievement, which has been consistently belittled by the nationalist passions of the French, the Belgians and the Dutch. In the mid-fifteenth century it would also have seemed natural to stress the significance of the diverse states of Italy, but Italian patriotic sentiment since has been outraged by the policies of the rulers, which opened the way for foreign oppression of the peninsula. Assessment of the Italian states has been hampered by excessive concern for the unification of Italy, and pride in the vitality of cultural life in the many centres of the Renaissance has only exacerbated criticisms. The political interests and abilities of the greatest fifteenth-century rulers have therefore been consistently misrepresented. They must be appreciated for what they did with their own problems and opportunities, not judged for what they did not contribute to modern nation-building. The fifteenth century had more interesting projects in embryo than the nations of the nineteenth century.

Italy

The Italian states of this period are sometimes thought of misleadingly as city-states of the ancient Greek kind, by historians brought up on ancient history. In some ways, the Italian states were more like the contemporary northern kingdoms of England or France, on a smaller scale. They had their 'capital' cities and they brought together into one state many smaller communities, mainly other towns, with their own customs. Their rulers owed their empires more to conquest than to traditional right and had also to maintain their power more obviously by force, but they justified their office by effective government. Their states survived for centuries, even if the dynastic family itself did not. They preserved internal tranquillity better than the old party rivalries of the communes had. As long as they could also provide protection against outside enemies, they would endure.

By the second half of the fifteenth century, the states had proved their ability to do this. The affairs of the peninsula were left in the hands of a few individuals, sure of their internal authority. One of them was actually a king. Naples was only a shadow of the great Norman kingdom, but under Alfonso the Magnificent, who reunited Sicily and Naples (1442), the Regno began to play a significant part in peninsular politics for the first time since 1343. The crucial political figure of Italy was however the pope. The papal state was an old-fangled concept, the ecclesiastical domain, to realize which many popes had given their best energies. Though it had been made an effective state in the thirteenth century, the sojourn at Avignon and the schism had obscured the papal role. It was not until Eugenius IV was able to return to Rome in 1444 that the papal state could become a powerful force in Italian politics. However anachronistic in form, it looked new in the mid-fifteenth century, and though Christian respect for the pope inhibited criticism of it, both Italians and northerners were baffled by it. The main problem for Italians was that the policies of successive popes were so unpredictable, since there was no continuity provided by a papal dynasty. Each pope could only reckon to advance the interests of the see, as they appeared to him through the eyes of his devoted family, whose sons he used and rewarded in papal service. The change of pope was therefore the most disturbing event to be expected in Italian politics. The other rulers of Italy were particularly anxious to maintain representatives and supporters in the college of cardinals, with the object of covering themselves against eventualities and of promoting the chances of their friends in the conclaves. The outcome, whatever religious importance it had for Christendom, had unavoidable political consequences for the peninsula, which rulers could not squeamishly close their eyes to.

In Venice the election of the doge excited no such anxiety, because the course of Venetian policy was more predictable. The stolidity of the constitution impressed and worried Italians, because it was so unusual. Until the fifteenth century however Venice had not been much drawn into peninsular politics. It was the dangers to Venetian interests threatened by the construction of a united state of Lombardy, under Gian Galeazzo Visconti, that had first alarmed the Venetians. The recrudescence of Milanese power under Filippo Maria Visconti extended Venetian commitment to the mainland, particularly under Doge Foscari (1423-57). By the time of his retirement, the Venetian frontier had been shifted far to the west. The Venetian state was a new creation under a formerly isolated commercial city, with a tough and adaptable constitution. Though Venice was never as formidable as many Italians feared, the new state endured for more than three centuries.

The former city-states of Milan and Florence also became the centres of local empires, both eventually styled duchies, though at widely separated intervals. Gian Galeazzo (1385-1402) had brought all Lombardy under the rule of the duke of Milan (1395). On his death, the Visconti state temporarily disintegrated. Restored by Filippo Maria (1412-1447), it fell apart again, as if to prove that the state was still only the personal creation of the ruler. But the fact that the Ambrosian republic of Milan was a failure, and that Filippo Maria's son-in-law, Francesco Sforza, quickly reunited the duchy, showed that the idea had taken root. The Lombards preferred peace to 'liberty'. Of all the mid-fifteenth-century states of Italy, Milan was the one with the longest continuous recent history. The ruler was a duke of the empire, allied by marriage with the princes of northern Europe; by Italian standards, ancient, respectable, rather tired and conservative: more anxious to preserve than to expand.

Florence, which retained till the sixteenth century its formal republican constitution, had long before this found it necessary to leave the management of its main interests to such persons as could master the arts of diplomacy, warfare and state-finance, whether they held formal office or not.[1] After 1434 the principal burden fell to a private citizen, Cosimo de Medici, a rich banker, who manipulated formal elections to the offices of state through his friends, without offending the republican sensibilities of his fellow-citizens. It is symptomatic of the state of Italian politics that, when Cosimo died in 1464, his non-office was naturally assumed by his son Piero, though he was a sick man. After Piero, his son, Lorenzo, also exercised this responsibility, with more justification. The family right was so much taken for granted on Lorenzo's death, that his son Piero, young, totally inexperienced and foolish, was required to succeed him.

The states of Italy were therefore in the hands of despots and the expected means for perpetuating the advantages of the system was to allow sons to succeed their fathers. Rulers needed more ability in Italy than elsewhere to clear their hurdles, but it was more important still to obtain continuity. Like others, Italians saw the advantages of leaving power to great men and enjoying the security they promised in return. Once these great states had taken shape, the main problem of politics was to preserve the *status quo* in the peninsula, which was done, as far as possible, by diplomacy. For nearly forty years (1454-94) the rulers were left to do this amongst themselves. They relied on professional expertise in dealing with one another, preferring secret negotiation to public debate, in order to make the most of surprise when dealing with well-matched forces. By the sixteenth century, Italy which had once been the stage for the most revolutionary governments of Europe, had its own distinctive aristocratic families and was ready to provide all Europe with models of courtly behaviour, political conduct, diplomatic wisdom —in short, the whole paraphernalia of government.

Whatever the intrinsic merits of Italian experience, Europe could not have benefited had Italian politics been as exceptional as is sometimes alleged. The dynastic pattern in Italy had many points in common with those of northern Europe and Italy was not so insulated against attack from the north as to prevent a renewal of the 'barbarian' invasions. There was gain as well as loss. For once the French were eager to accord the Italians precedence. For the only century of its existence the language of Dante became the international language of diplomacy. Italian achievements in the arts and literature were appropriated by others and turned into the common foundation of European culture. Italians had much to teach, but this did not save their political independence. This was because

Italy, given its basic organization into distinct states, had to accept the logic of the situation and recognize its own place in the European context: it could not claim exemption if it had something of value to teach.

The forty years of diplomatic activity which had left Italians to manage their own affairs were exceptional in the long history of the peninsula, not the norm. Italy had been regularly invaded from the north (except when Roman armies had prevented it), but since the twelfth century Italians had become somewhat careless about calling foreign friends to their aid, because of their confidence in being able to get rid of them without much trouble. Not one of the five major states was so Italian as to dispense with strong alliances of its own outside the peninsula and these mattered more to it than any general fear of foreigners. The king of Naples belonged to the ruling house of Aragon; the papacy was an international, not an Italian institution; Florence owed its prosperity to links with France; Milan was ruled by an imperial duke related to the French king; Venice had its first empire overseas. None of these states could plausibly pose as a national Italian champion or willingly renounce its own foreign allies. They existed to defend their own autonomy and they would not combine against their own friends. While France and Spain still had more important problems to settle at home, no frantic efforts to keep out foreigners were called for, but once the princely dynasts had sorted out their domestic problems, they inevitably turned to Italy to claim their rights there too. The Italian states were centralized under their own dynasts and could be easily annexed. Charles VIII advanced into Italy to vindicate his succession to Naples (1494). The extension of French interests in Italy by his successors inexorably brought the Aragonese back to the mainland to counteract French power. The victorious Spaniards turned against republican Florence, the most obstinate of the French allies in Italy, and reimposed the Medici (who had been driven out at the time of Charles VIII's invasions). Of the several Italian states, only the republic of Venice held out against foreign pressures. Even the papacy was overawed by the emperor Charles V. The Habsburgs dominated Italy, either directly or through the minor dynasties that clustered round the emperor.

The political problems of Italy from the sixteenth century may be described in several different ways. There was resentment at the power of foreigners, like the Spaniards; there was bafflement that Italy's vitality and invention had achieved no political success; there was despair that the intellectual perceptions of such men as Machiavelli or Guicciardini bore no fruit in political life. Such paradoxes are factitious. Few Italians had ever envisaged a united Italian state or cursed the evils of foreign domination. There is no inherent reason why superior culture should provide political wisdom, nor is it obvious that sharp intelligence is essential for political success. The Italian example rather proves how little rationality could contribute to the solution of such problems. The most refined and sophisticated peoples of the sixteenth century lived in the most arbitrary political societies, incapable of uniting men of similar speech or culture and allowing them the least influence in their form of government.

The political shortcomings of fifteenth-century Italy have sometimes been excused by an appeal to the compensating achievements in the arts and sciences.[2] Whatever value has been attached to these since, at the time, they counted for much less. Northern Europe itself was not aware of what it might owe to Italy until the very end of the century.[3] Italians themselves were not so vainglorious as to be unappreciative of northern culture. Paintings and musicians were both imported from the north. In the mid-fifteenth century the court of Burgundy certainly eclipsed its Italian rivals in general esteem. The Italian states cannot expect to be 'excused' on account of their culture.

Burgundy

Burgundian culture has not been claimed as the inheritance of any one modern nation and has not earned the dukes historical justification.[4] Seen without national prejudice, however, the history of this brilliant state casts much light on the affairs of Christendom in this period. It shows how one great dynasty came to defeat its rivals for power in the Low Countries and how unification of the Netherlands, once achieved despite both French and imperial opposition, could survive the death of Charles the Rash (1477) under his Habsburg heirs. It was the birthplace of Charles v (1500) and constituted his basic patrimony.

By the end of the fourteenth century, the many powerful local interests of the Low Countries had already been successfully consolidated by members of the greatest European dynasties: Wittelsbach (Holland-Hainault), Luxembourg (Brabant) and Valois (Flanders). Properly balanced these rivals might have maintained for a long time the division of this wealthy land. However, the dukes of Burgundy, as counts of Flanders, eliminated all their rivals and made themselves masters of the whole. To some extent this was due to the fortunes of the marriage alliances which all the great families negotiated amongst themselves; the Valois dukes unexpectedly benefited by the fortuitous extinction of both the Brabant and Holland lines. But the dukes also acquired a sense of purpose and determination necessary for creating a united Low Countries. This followed their exclusion from the affairs of the French kingdom, as an aftermath of the quarrel between the dukes of Burgundy and Orleans. After Duke John's murder (1419), the new duke, Philip, made an alliance with England, which in effect gave Burgundy political neutrality between England and France for sixteen years. Philip used that freedom to concentrate on his own region. Whereas the Wittelsbachs and Luxembourgs could not operate in the Low Countries without consulting the interest of the whole family, the Valois dukes had only themselves to think of.[5]

The new unity of his dominions was not however a mere product of chance and opportunism. By taking authority into his own hands, the duke eliminated many of the problems of the region, caused by rival jurisdictions. Opposition to ducal unity was naturally strongest where local governments were most confident of their own ability to deal with their own needs. The patricians of the greatest towns, Bruges, Ghent and Ypres, had previously tried to use the French king to thwart the count of Flanders. The dukes of Burgundy cut off this line of appeal. Against the greatest cities, the dukes could also rely on the support offered by lesser towns, who were resentful of the others' arrogance. The dukes who reduced the chaos to order had no historical mould for their state. The ducal territories combined French and German speakers. There were no obvious geographical limits, though expansion was roughly confined to the lands of the old middle kingdom, a transient state of the ninth century. It had rapidly decomposed into many fragments, being the richest and most densely settled area, well able to support many authorities. For the same reason it has always proved the most difficult to reorganize politically. The fact that unity could be restored to the northern end of this old kingdom in the fifteenth century, after centuries of fragmentation, shows how much conditions had changed.

The change of conditions does not diminish the value of the dukes' own contribution. It had to be a personal unity they created, for institutionally the state was only unified through them. They made no attempt to abolish the local customs of their lands: in each one they boasted a different title. The title duke came from Burgundy, a fief of the French crown. When the fief was recovered by the French king in 1477, this was without prejudice to the rights of the heiress in the Low Countries, since it did not affect her standing there. Proposals to set up a kingdom for these lands were fitfully pursued and came to nothing, so the unity remained entirely personal. The duke needed certain offices to assist in his government. In a region of such business activity, the issue of a single money for the duke's lands in 1433 was an important assertion of the ducal prerogative and a lubricant of centralization. The *Audiencia,* a Flemish *parlement* created by Louis de Mâle in 1369 at the time of his triumph over Charles v, was extended by his Burgundian son-in-law to cover all the legal and financial business of his lands (except Burgundy itself) in 1386. Nearly twenty years later, this curia was divided into a financial court of account at Lille and a council for Flanders, under a lay chancellor for judicial business (1405). The duke also summoned an Estates-General of all his subjects, which was confident enough of its standing to declare in 1477, when Charles the Rash died, that it had the right to meet in which place it wished, and to oppose all wars it had not agreed to. The state of Burgundy in the late fifteenth century demonstrates more clearly than others how a great dynasty could assemble in a short time a powerful state out of many fragments, even though the frontiers were ill-defined and government remained a personal matter of the ruler. The Burgundians were chiefly exceptional in making their state the cultural pinnacle of Europe; the credit for this is undubitably theirs.

There were other dynasties at work during the same period. The Jagellons of Poland-Lithuania achieved a similar result. The Trastamara dynasty of Castile, which provided a ruler for Aragon in 1413, eventually united Spain and their dynastic achievement should not be misread as a national one. So far from stopping short at this point, they arranged for the incorporation of the Spanish empire into that of the Habsburg empire, the Low Countries and Germany, not to mention the empire overseas.

To reduce dynastic rulers to the status of national kings does no justice to their historical roles. The dynastic union of lands proved to be an important and even indispensable means of simplifying international politics for many centuries, but as long as it was pursued with family objectives in mind, it did not concentrate royal attentions on solving the internal problems of keeping the state together. The political horizons of the dynasties tended to be too vast to allow their eyes to focus on mere internal politics, for the purpose of increasing their power over any one of their land's resources. The dynastic principle even hindered the growth of political institutions. The great families of the fourteenth and fifteenth centuries often produced many squabbling brothers. Castile suffered repeatedly from the fact that kings died leaving heirs under age—Sancho IV, Ferdinand IV, Alfonso XI, John I and Henry III—so that the continuity of the monarchy was not a means of securing energetic rulers. In England likewise, the monarchy was hardly strong enough to survive the misfortunes of the minorities of Richard II and Henry VI. Worse still the dynastic interest in the royal office also encouraged members of the royal families to see the private right of their family to it before they glimpsed its public character. The Trastamaras and the Yorkists were both prepared to engage in civil war for their personal advancement. This also occurred, in a less blatant form, in France, when the Valois dynasty obstinately clung to office as their family right, despite a lamentable inability to discharge their obligations.

France

France was no exceptional state in dynastic Europe, although the successful outcome of the war against the English has sometimes been represented as a 'national' victory. Joan of Arc is the heroine of this romantic interpretation. She herself, however, declared that her first task was to lead Charles VII to his coronation, in order to vindicate his inherited right to the crown and it was this that she accomplished. Her second task was to expel the English from France, but this she did not do.[6] The coronation proved that God recognized Charles as his father's legitimate heir. His ultimate victory may itself be regarded as an example of dynastic triumph. The Valois finally vindicated their dynastic right to the succession and defeated every attempt to replace them with regimes offering political compromise.

The war was fought to uphold the authority of the Paris parlement against provincial independence, particularly in the critical case of Flanders. Yet Flanders in fact passed into the control of the dukes of Burgundy during the course of the war, and was therefore lost to France, though subsequent kings over several centuries nibbled away at the northern frontier. In this sense the French kings failed to achieve their original objective. Nor did the final expulsion of the English enable the restored monarchy to resume the earlier policy of eroding provincial independence. Though the dynasty had kept the kingdom together, it had only done so by making concessions to the provinces, which were therefore in some ways in a stronger position than before: their privileges were blessed by the crown. Charles VII himself, for example, endowed Poitiers with both parlement and university for its loyalty and did not rescind these privileges when he returned to Paris. The Paris parlement did not therefore enjoy after the war that supremacy which it had claimed before it. As other provinces were taken by the king, they too were allowed to have their own provincial parlements, to protect local custom: Gascony (1453), Burgundy (1477), Provence (1482) and Brittany (1492). Normandy had shown long before that provincial autonomy could be preserved through its own legal system, and it took several centuries before the differences of French customary law had been worn away. Even if the Parisian lawyers continued to work for a unified system, a drag had been attached to their chariot.

The most striking difference between dynastic France and the previous regime was the disappearance of the provincial princes. In this sense France was unified. Local princes were not available any longer to voice provincial feelings. This was in the first place, less an act of deliberate policy in keeping fiefs for the crown, than a fortuitous consequence of the fact that for the next century French kings had so few sons in need of being provided for. Louis XI had to assign some lands to his brother, Charles, and dithered about deciding on Berry, Normandy, or Guienne without showing any will to suppress the system altogether. As it happened, Charles died without heirs, so no new princely house was founded by him. Subsequent kings might have been glad of more sons to support the dynasty, which lurched from branch to branch for over a century (1498-1598) before the Bourbons succeeded to the throne. The fact that the king himself was the direct ruler of all his provinces did not make centralization that much easier, for he was expected to be the zealous supporter of local privilege. Indeed, the strength of the monarchy at first depended upon the differences between the provinces that kept Frenchmen apart from one another and delayed the appearance of national institutions. When Louis XI, who liked gestures, caused the ring of the last duke of Normandy to be solemnly broken, it was as a demonstration that the duchy was irrevocably united to the monarchy. The Normans did not interpret this special relationship as a threat to their freedom. Seen from the provinces therefore, France by 1500 did not look so different from other countries. France was exceptional only in having a single lord who offered privileged protection to all the many separate peoples beneath his care.

Seen however from the king's point of view, France, unlike other states, already disposed of an impressive apparatus of administration, justice, taxation and military force, as well as traditional influence with the churches and towns. Royal servants were installed all over the kingdom to manage royal interests.[7] Instead of faithful vassals, the kings relied on an army of literate underlings to do their bidding. Such servants were no less self-seeking than vassals had once been. They did not openly oppose the royal will, for they were not a military aristocracy given to grandiose gestures. They were nevertheless greedy and dilatory, making nests for themselves and their families in the papers of the royal offices, turning the wheels of the machine to their own advantage, no less than to the king's. The offices of the provincial parlements gave them profitable and influential posts. Taxation officials allowed some of the money that passed through their hands to slip into their pockets. They did not need to defy the system, for they found it could be made to serve their own ends: wealth, influence and family dignity. If feudal vassals had been factious, they were corrupt. The monarchy created the unity of France by their services, but it had to pay their price.

Kings, like all governments, disposed of important patronage and gloried in the multiplication of offices that appeared to enhance their majesty. Apart from the recruitment of noble youths, they found places for experts, particularly for experts in law, who sought notarial offices. These they quickly attempted to make hereditary, or at least transmissible at will.[8] Kings at first tried to resist this tendency to turn royal posts into private rights of office-holders, but they were not able to root out the notion. All office, like any other piece of property in this landowning society, was a life-interest claimed by the deceased's heirs. The only way to prevent the presumption of inheritability was constant reshuffling of posts, such as the Angevin kings practised in English sheriffdoms and the Capetians with their royal *baillis,* but kings came to allow inheritance of offices, though they charged for it. This attitude to office persisted for centuries and should not be too confidently denounced as venal, because office was not thought to be primarily a matter of the public interest. As Loyseau (1561-1627) observed, provostships were more like lordships than offices, seeing that they had attached to them the domain and the emoluments of justice, as lordships did. This admittedly took time to develop. It was not until the reign of Louis XI (1461-83) that the king of France acknowledged that the *baillis* had a life-interest in their offices, with all that this implied for the rights of their heirs.[9] From the king's point of view this meant, in fact, multiplying the number of offices, for the new lords of them regarded office as an investment, not an occupation, so that others actually did the work. The many officers enlarged the royal entourage. The amount of work to be done by any one of them was trifling in proportion to the persons retained for it. Many offices were honorific and the distinguished persons who held titles of honour like that of royal butler discharged them on ceremonial occasions, leaving menials to pour the king's wine on ordinary days. The multiplication of offices served to enhance the royal majesty more than to serve the state, and there was keen competition to obtain sinecures as a family investment in places near the king of influence and profit.

The royal staff of subordinate officials claimed to be devoted to royal interests, but it would be a mistake to regard these as the equivalent of the public good, though royal publicists took it as much for granted as government officials still do that the public could only gain by the extension of bureaucratic influence.[10] In the absence of any form of regular scrutiny of their activities, however, this was not the case and the monarchy became dependent on families with vested interests in the office establishments. Their fulsome adulation of the kings expressed their confidence in royal benevolence towards them and sapped the royal will to interfere with such devoted subjects.

It should not even be supposed that kings or ministers somehow resented the partiality of these public servants for their own private advancement. They had no model in mind of how the kingdom might have been run by dutiful civil servants, as Prussia was in the nineteenth century. For the king, the main problem was not the smooth execution of his orders, but harmonizing the many discordant elements of which the kingdom was composed. The kings were more inclined to be nervous than irate. It was safer to preserve the differences within France in order to prevent the growth of any 'national' challenge, such as had appeared when the monarchy had in desperation needed to appeal for general support after 1355. The estates were not summoned very often and it would have been unwise to provide them with the chance to legislate by creating a national body of law. The survival of the numerous customary laws and the provincial parlements guaranteed that the regions would not unite against the king.

Financial abuses were another matter. Officials aroused constant resentment and every opportunity was taken to denounce them and demand reforms, so that their services could be regarded as a doubtful advantage. They provided much money, but they also took too much for themselves and made the king unpopular. Louis XI was so loudly blamed for the financial abuses of his reign that on his death the new government summoned an estates-general to Tours (1484) and considered proposals for reform in a bid for popularity. The abuses were genuine, but they turned out to be almost incapable of reform. The delegates preferred to put up with the existing system than to learn how to devise a national reform applicable in all the provinces.

As it happens this assembly is the first for which a contemporary account exists. The representative of Rouen, Jehan Messelin, kept a journal of the proceedings, which shows in detail why such an assembly was frustrated in its ambitions to serve the common good.[11] The assembly was not in this case divided into three separate estates. The author explains how each district was represented by delegates chosen at local meetings attended by anyone who wished to do so. These delegates included bishops, nobles, canonists, lawyers, members that is of all the estates, mixed up in one assembly. Business could not, however, be managed in such great numbers (*c.*270 members), so the estates were divided up into 'nations', each defined by the limits of the six financial 'generalities', which was reasonable since the main problems were financial. They were Burgundy, Normandy, Aquitaine, Languedoc— four fairly homogenous entities; and Paris, linked with the territories around it from Orleans and Mâcon to the south together with Champagne, Vermandois and Picardy; and the Languedoil which comprised the rest of northern France. Discussion by generalities, though fitting, was fatal to its effectiveness. Normandy, for example, which was by size and wealth a mere eighth of the kingdom, paid one quarter of the *taille* and the delegates desired to reduce the burden to a sixth, On the other hand, Normandy like the Languedoc enjoyed the privilege of being allowed to approve taxation in local 'estates' and this right was sought by the others. As Messelin himself sadly pointed out when the estates had first met to put the kingdom to rights under their new young king

Charles VIII 'there was amongst us much agreement in words and deeds but money *(denarius)*, this vile thing indeed created to be a means rather than an end, completely divided us and turned us into mutual enemies. Each one struggled on behalf of his own province, trying to reduce its obligation if possible to the least. The struggle between generalities then became a contest between the bailiwicks and seneschalcies and ultimately to disputes between parishes and finally amongst taxpayers.' Messelin himself refers to other delegates like himself who thought of the public interest, but he shows that their efforts were smothered by a political contest in which regional variations were too powerful.

Moreover, many people in the central government also acted to avert radical reform. The king's relations, the tax officials themselves (described as more of a burden than the taxes), the king's council and those who relied on their influence in it rather than on the other delegates, all preferred the system they knew. When the estates went home frustrated and deflated, the royal government resumed its erratic course. The knowledge that such opposition as government provoked in the country was fractioned and powerless persuaded this government, like that of the *ancien regime* as a whole, that reform was better avoided and could be neglected with more safety than otherwise. A sound conclusion, as well-meaning reformers discovered to their cost at the end of the eighteenth century.

The essential function of the state was to preserve the existing order. It was able to assume that there was no real desire within the community to overturn it, because all persons of influence already had their own stake in public office. The old centrifugal tendencies had been contained. The chief dangers came from without, so that royal advisers thought most about armies and diplomacy. The theory was cautious, but in practice rulers were rarely content to repulse their enemies: they were eager to challenge them and strutted out to demonstrate their superiority. Their subjects had no national or natural interests in these royal adventures. Charles VIII dreamed of reviving the crusade against the Ottomans. When he announced his intentions of going to Italy to claim the throne of Naples, as a first step, his barons were unenthusiastic.[12] This made no difference and they nevertheless fought loyally for their rulers, just as others paid, with less grace, for the costly campaigns. The ease with which rulers commanded men and money for profitless wars abroad seems amazing. Perhaps it was simpler to allow rulers to have their way and play at soldiers in another country, than have them stay at home with nothing better to do than play at reforming the state. Certain politicians still often think it is better to be fidgeting with institutions, if not worse, than to leave well alone.

Political realism ·

The business of politics in this period is in its own way more frivolous than the harsh realities of earlier baronial disputes. The latter have been despised by historians, because the barons, unlike the 'courtiers', were not given to the writing of memoirs or pronouncements on the nature of political experience. As the details of courtly intrigue become known from such works, historians have used them to argue that politics in the late fifteenth century acquired a new realism. The *Memoirs* of Philippe de Commynes are often cited to illustrate this.[13] Read carefully they are far from reflecting much credit on his master King Louis XI. Louis' subtleties inspired no contemporary confidence in his cleverness. Commynes as the king's private confidant naturally concentrated on the king's diplomatic activities. When he describes the king as very wise, he means only that he was clever or devious in getting out of some tight corners a more sensible man would have avoided altogether. Louis was timorous and his fears inspired oppressive demands for money to pay for his defence. He upset people by his pettiness and by the freedom of his remarks. He had to spend money lavishly in order to win back those he had offended and to buy loyalty which his person did not inspire. Commynes shows clearly that in dealing with Charles of Burgundy, the king was vindictive rather than crafty. He sought vengeance with such rancour that he lost the greater part of Charles's dominions in 1477, recovering only Burgundy itself.[14] Commynes never implies that Louis's deviousness amounted to a new kind of state wisdom. Were it not for the fact that Machiavelli also appeared to approve this type of secretive behaviour in diplomacy, Louis XI would never have been used as an example of the accomplished politician. Machiavelli's own hero, Ferdinand of Aragon, was more successful, but he was also a soldier, with military victories to his credit in Granada, Italy and Navarra. Talk of the new statecraft sometimes suggests that historians are more impressed by velvet gloves than by hard heads.

When an intellectual interest in politics was revived in the thirteenth century as part of Aristotelian studies, it was the educated clerks who wrote for rulers, spelling out for them the implications of their Christian duty in kingship according to the best secular knowledge of the day. For nearly a century a number of powerful intellects reflected on politics, but it would be hard to show how rulers gained from their speculations and advice. Charles V of France may have learnt something from Aristotle, but how much could any king profit, morally, from the books in dealing with his problems? In general kings showed no consistent interest in acquiring libraries or book-learning. The greatest library of the fourteenth century, that of the scholar Petrarch, was offered to the republic of Venice, but the city never claimed the legacy. Even popes themselves had no important library until the advent of Pope Nicholas v (1447-55) who had been a humanist librarian in his earlier years. Rulers did not find books very useful for their purposes. Did they change their minds as soon as Machiavelli started writing?

Deprived of office by the Medici restoration of 1512, Machiavelli became frenzied by his own political impotence. He brooded over the contrast between the actual spectacle of Italy overrun by barbarians and the historical record of former Roman greatness. Not for the last time did an Italian dream of how that past could be revived. His political opinions were expounded in writing between 1512 and 1527, for the purpose of trying to obtain influence with some prince powerful enough to restore Italian political independence. The politicians of his day did not have to be stupid to find his vision somewhat absurd. Guicciardini too was distressed to observe what had befallen Italy, but he was more of a realist and put no faith in the power of a grandiose inspiration.

It is by no means self-evident that the political wisdom Machiavelli found in Livy is any more helpful than the philosophy of Aristotle for rulers with problems. In Machiavelli's own case, his potential patrons were not immediately struck by his superior wisdom in politics: they chose not to employ him.[14] Real politics seemed to them to have little to learn from the history of the ancient world. It is typical of intellectuals that they have been more impressed than the rulers by the pointing out of historical parallels known from bookish learning. It is even symptomatic of Machiavelli's 'clerkly' outlook that he found in the history of the church examples of the reformation of men's evil ways, when proposing how political communities might be radically restored to their pristine virtue. It could be said that Machiavelli's novelty lay in his hopes of reforming the state, as the church might be, by a return to first principles.[15] Whereas religious inspiration may purify and renew the church by starting new religious orders, attempts to rebuild the state from the bottom up, as in 1789 and 1917, suggest that Machiavelli was justified in his fears that this might prove impossible.

Machiavelli found his ideal in the (mythical) history of the early Roman Republic, as described by Livy. Despite his knowledge of history, it would be a mistake to think that Machiavelli had much historical insight. He can speak of the Gauls and Tuscans as peoples having the same characteristics over nearly 2,000 years, on the most flimsy evidence and in spite of the most obvious objections; he betrays no misgivings that important changes might have been wrought by time.[16] He still views the effects of time according to the moralistic categories of his contemporaries: the purity of ancient ways gets corrupted; periodically there is need for cleaning out the muddied wells. From his reading of Roman history, he was convinced that the republic collapsed because of the prevalence of faction and the decay of self-sacrificing patriotism. Applying the lesson to Florentine history, he blamed the factional politics of the fourteenth century for the growth of the oligarchy and would not see that the passivity and deference shown to the fifteenth-century Medici had marked the real beginnings of decay. Subservience to the idea of the state could not save the republic: it had paved the way to despotism. Such an opinion would have offended Machiavelli's Medici patron, but it was not this that held him back. It was his own unwillingness to accept that republican politics was by its nature disputatious. The revival of the Florentine republic in 1494 had not been due to a new movement of virtue, but to the confusion caused by the French invasion of Italy. As soon as the great powers had reimposed order in the peninsula, the republic was suppressed by the victorious armies of the League of Cambrai, because they preferred to have the Medici rule in Florence.[17] In this they followed their own political instincts. Machiavelli made no allowance for their actual political ideas and wrote of the state of Florence, as of Italy, from a quite different point of view. There was nothing realistic about his ideas because he does not seem to have appreciated the actual conditions of republican success in his day.

Machiavelli deceived not only himself, but many historians, by studying his own times with the categories derived from his reading of ancient history. He was not alone in this, for it was an error of the humanists, like their clerical predecessors, to take the thoughts they found in their books rather than think about the world around them for themselves. While they engaged in wordy debates about tyrants and republics, quoting classical aphorisms out of context and occasionally erupting into political life — as when some enthusiastic scholar republicans murdered Galeazzo Sforza for being a dictator (1476) — the political life of their times was in fact conducted according to much more prosaic notions.[18] Machiavelli had not even to teach his contemporaries how to be double-faced in politics, nor that there was no need to be apologetic about it. He found examples enough of nefarious conduct in the recent history of Italy when men had relied on their wits not on advice.[19] Rulers had little to learn about political treachery from the former Florentine secretary. It would be hard to show that sixteenth-century rulers, whether they read Machiavelli or not, became any more devious and subtle than their predecessors had been. If political activity was described in a more secular manner (in the humanist style), it was because religion was also interpreted in a more spiritual way. Rulers with secular advisers did not cease to listen to their confessors whose political influence continued to be important, and sometimes decisive, until the eighteenth century. It could even be argued that rulers of Machiavelli's day were more scrupulous about their religious obligations; was it perhaps because they did not appear to understand the difference between private and public morality that Machiavelli desperately tried to insist upon it? Nor did the new statecraft prove of much help to political advisers. Diplomats were no more successful than the earlier popes in averting wars, and these became more bitter and more devastating. Subtle ministers did not learn how to cling to power; they were swept away by the passions of sectarian conflicts or the trivial intrigues of courts. Politicians had not learned from books how to be clever.

Instead of hopefully peering for signs of more rationality in the political life of Europe from this time, as Machiavelli has encouraged later generations to do, it is chastening to realize how much less reasonable and more cruel politics became.[20] Popes escaped from the tedious discussions of councils; secular rulers gave up consulting their representative assemblies. Rulers were left with the responsibilities of office and took advice how they wished. Charles V, the Wise, read books, but his son Charles VI mad and inept, was the first ruler to rely on *le plaisir du roi* as sufficient authority for his decrees.[21] Charles VII owed the revival of his fortunes to a simple maid from Lorraine, sent by God, who confounded the wisdom of the Parisians. He had not to show any competence to justify this choice; it was sufficient to demonstrate his legitimacy. Ruling by the grace of God himself, he objected to others, like the dukes of Burgundy and Brittany and the count of Armagnac, who did the same.[22] His superstitious successor Louis XI was gratified by the humanist pope Paul II with the formal title 'Most Christian King' and his Spanish contemporaries had a comparable style, 'Catholic Kings'.[23] Henry VIII earned his title, 'Defender of the Faith' by writing against Luther. God and the pope did much to lift European rulers out of the ordinary and bless their dominion.

The obsequious flattery which Richard II had tried to obtain from his courtiers in an attempt to recover prestige for the monarchy after years of ignominy was lavished without restraint upon the Tudors, whose claims to the throne were dubious, but who benefited from the new sense of respect for God's anointed. Their royal appearances were staged to make pompous impressions of dignified benevolence.[24]

They were also hedged about with religious ceremonies. The new elaboration of church services with choirs and instruments was particularly well-developed in the chapels of rulers. Rulers liked to believe that God had laid upon them the duty of upholding the religion of their states, and since, as men, they disliked those who disagreed with them, they were not unwilling to repress religious dissent, which questioned their own authority. Lay rulers, like most laymen, were profoundly convinced of the truth of their religion. Even had they not been, the piety of their subjects would have obliged them to appear to be. Machiavelli himself admitted that rulers needed to appear to be good, so there were limits to what rulers might do in public. Some rulers of this period are notorious for their impiety and immorality, but it is easy to understand that rulers who joked about religion and mocked the clergy did not permit their subjects to do the same. They took liberties, because they knew the church would prefer not to make an example of them; they were irresponsible libertines, not enlightened innovators. The papacy was still nominally responsible for censuring rulers' morals, but in practice it dealt circumspectly with them if they erred, for there was no longer any question of inciting subjects to reject unworthy kings. Royal appeals to the pope could be sure of a sympathetic hearing. Henry VIII was the only important ruler to be thwarted by the papacy, when it was unable, however willing, to grant the desired divorce. Henry underlined the reasons for papal prudence in dealing with errant rulers when he secured the general assent of the English to his usurpation of the pope's place as Supreme Head of the Church, with only brave, but ineffectual opposition. For his subjects the king was indeed the Defender of the Faith.

The rulers blessed by the church owed their office to inheritance. Even the empire, still nominally elective, in practice became the Habsburgs' lot; the four secular electors inherited their offices and took dynastic rights for granted. Only God could give the heir and the peoples therefore lost their power to scrutinize royal qualifications. The Catalans attempted to contest the succession of Ferdinand of Antequera to the throne of Aragon in 1413, but sold their consent for a confirmation of privileges. A few years later the Bohemians denied Sigismund the succession to his brother's throne (1420) because of his complicity in the burning of Hus. After many years of warfare, he was nevertheless admitted. Even more triumphant was the vindication of Charles VII by the Maid of Orleans, who demonstrated how little God cared for the wishes of Paris or the wisdom of the lawyers and politicians who had surrendered the kingdom by the Treaty of Troyes to the king of England. In England, too, the constitutional depositions of Edward II and Richard II were followed in the fifteenth century by more sanguinary changes of ruler, because the kingship had become too exalted a matter for political discussion. Richard of York dared not object to Henry VI as incompetent. He raised the question of his descent, which, said the judges, was a matter 'so high and touched the king's high estate and regality which is above the law and passed their learning, whereof they durst not venture into any communication thereof for it pertained to the lords of the king's blood and the peerage of this his land to have communication and meddle in such matters'. The Lords, poor wretches, tried to compromise, but their appeasement was an insult to the question of right and the appeal lay to God direct, that is, to force. The victors,

York or Tudor, owed their thrones to God alone and their claims depended on the facts of birth, not the political interests of the community.[25]

Modern politics also knows the urge to trust one man to find or impose the political solution—to cut the community out of the thicket of controversies that chokes its freedom. In the fifteenth century, reliance on the indisputable heir did more than establish despotic government; it imposed legitimacy. Rulers who got their rights were therefore expected to preserve those of others. They might obtain by inheritance many diverse lands, but they were committed to defending the separate customs of each place with impartial devotion.[26] In the eighteenth century 'enlightened' rulers acting on the advice of their tame intelligentsia thought the time had come to treat their territories as a whole, introducing standard procedures, 'rational' administration and 'efficient' government, which, however beneficial, eventually stirred feelings of 'national' protest. Their predecessors, less arrogant and more cautious, had protected the diversities of their lands, keeping up the appearance of personal, fatherly solicitude for each of the peoples they governed, secretly fearful that the subjects would combine against them if they were not kept apart from one another. Thus they fostered a personal loyalty to themselves as rulers, not seeking to create any common political institutions. Thus the notion of personal fidelity originally derived from feudal society, was transformed into the idea of general allegiance by all free citizens.

The rulers' states stretched far beyond the horizons of most of their members. The case of the kings of 'Spain' is the most striking example of the many pieces of which it was composed. Sancho IV at the end of the thirteenth century boasted of his many titles in his instructions for his son. He was king of Castile, Leon, Toledo, Galicia, Seville, Cordova, Murcia, Jaen, Algarve, Algeciras, lord of Lara, Biscay, and Molina.[27] Likewise Alfonso V styled himself in the fifteenth century by the grace of God, king of Aragon, Both Sicilies, Valencia, Jerusalem, Hungary, Majorca, Sardinia, Corsica, count of Barcelona, duke of Athens, and count of Roussillon and Cerdagne.[28] These two inheritances fell eventually to the first king of united Spain, Carlos I, who brought with him claims to the whole Habsburg domain. And America was also his. How could any one group of his subjects consider these lands with the same detachment as Charles V himself?

Personal loyalty to the king could only go so far towards keeping all these peoples happy. Whenever we deplore in our secular societies a lack of common ground in belief, practice or mere behaviour, which makes it impossible to appeal to conscience, law, humanity or patriotism, we may sympathize more with the problems of earlier rulers. While enforcing local customs, they still needed some element to promote concord amongst their subjects, many of whom had been quarrelling with one another in earlier generations. It was at this point that the ruler's favourable relationship with the churches bore fruit, for the clergy, grateful for their privileged status, repaid their debt by placing their resources at his feet, instilling respect for the Lord's Anointed, preaching obedience to his laws, serving in his ministries and providing the channel of communication between the government and the people. By 1500, the church had a representative in every parish of Christendom, whereas governments had no comparable army of reliable agents. All a ruler's subjects were expected to share the same religious allegiance. Dissenters were burned in public ceremonies attended by the crowds, since those who challenged the official doctrines were naturally held to be enemies of society and punished as defiant heretics. Some crowds might have been overawed by such exemplary punishments, but given the inadequacy of secular forces of repression, it would have been dangerous to allow big gatherings had the religious sentiments of the crowd not been predictable. The clergy organized the most numerous and elaborate ceremonies, in times of rejoicing, as in times of woe. It was they who pronounced on the nature of the communities' fundamental values: there could be no secular religion of the state to challenge them.

In the sixteenth century there were still few educated persons who believed that the state should embrace both the secular and the religious content of society. This had been the essence of the ancient idea, and it was canvassed again in Renaissance Italy, as by Machiavelli, but the basic paganism of that notion had no attraction for the educated, the clergy, the pious nobility, the divinely anointed rulers, let alone their ignorant and excitable subjects. The function of the state remained too restricted, at least for as long as the churches themselves were strong enough to control the masses and educated opinion. Royal advisers received no special education in secular affairs to prepare them for their roles. Like the clergy they believed that the loyalty of their lords' dominions was sure as long as they obeyed God's law. This may not be very glorious or original, but men were tired of innovation in politics: they wanted certainty.

2. THE CHURCH

The turmoil and disorder for Christendom as a whole, entailed by the Great Schism and the Conciliar movement, finally subsided in the mid-fifteenth century when the papacy resumed its traditional government of the church. No substantial changes had been effected through conciliar decrees. The French king Charles VII had enforced some of them in his own realm by the Concordat of Bourges in 1438, but even this unwelcome 'Gallicanism' was surrendered to the pope by his successor Louis XI in 1464.[29] No one pretended that the revival of the old order was an unmitigated blessing, but it seemed to augur a better hope for Christendom than constitutional experiments. The papal institutions which had been developed and criticised in the previous period thus survived. They were accepted in a more cynical spirit. This is best exemplified in the hard-headed college of cardinals; though this included a creditable quota of holy and pious men, it operated in Roman and Italian politics with a frank realism that offended more sensitive religious spirits in the north.

Ecclesiastical institutions

The church needed institutions if it was to retain its united corporate life. However unsatisfactory they were, they served nonetheless to teach a religion greater than the one practised by the establishment and capable as such of inspiring greater devotion. Conservatives therefore shrugged their shoulders when it came to considering the abuses of the church. Admittedly in the sixteenth century a few bold individuals were not prepared to leave the structure unreformed, and in some places they carried the day, but in general they failed to persuade all Christendom that their proposals were desirable. As a result, Christendom was irrevocably broken up and the medieval community held together by a common religious bond literally began to disintegrate in the 1520s. The contrast between this period and that of a century earlier is very striking. Despite the abuses of the church and the schism, the medieval church had restored its unity and even survived another round of constitutional debate at the time of the Council of Basel, so that the church newly pledged to the pope had seemingly survived the worst. Less than a century later, the pope, left to preside over the Catholic remnant, had become an odious tyrant to the rest. Was this catastrophe therefore the papacy's fault?

In a very obvious sense it was. When the challenge came, the papacy alone had the responsibility of dealing with it; the ineffectual reaction of Leo X to Luther allowed the situation to get out of control; the moment was lost and the Reformation began. Yet to hold the papacy responsible for the state of the church, as the reformers tried to do, is only possible in the conditions of polemic. If the papacy had had power to reform the church before the Reformation, it would also have had the power to suppress the reformers. In fact it had neither: it had only the responsibility for both. For its fulminations to be in any way effective it needed loyal and authoritative subordinates in every part of Christendom, and though such persons were found in most places they were not found everywhere. How securely the papal thread held the church together in any one place was, however, shown when the link with the papacy was cut: the package immediately fell apart. In England, only the monarchy could keep the church together after 1534 and this proved more difficult than the king and the anti-papal reformers had bargained for. There has been speculation, then and since, about what would have happened if the papacy had been confident enough to summon representatives of the whole church to a council and then been able to confront reform with more confidence and public support. Such a view is not plausible. The papacy was confident, even too confident, in its dealings with Luther and would not have gained more from assembling a council of those who would attend. Its supremacy had been firmly established after the failure of the conciliar movement: a reforming council could only have supported the pope or ineffectually disputed his powers, as had happened at Basel. Had Luther been arraigned before such a council, and condemned, it is unlikely that the outcome in Germany would have been less serious than the consequences of burning Hus at Constance had been for Bohemia. By the mid-fifteenth century, the papacy had vindicated its stand on church government and did not shrink from the consequences. To have summoned a council to deal with heresy would have seemed both superfluous and cowardly.

The popes had never before enjoyed such supremacy in the church. Wrangles about church government had been finally hushed. Even in the college of cardinals, however unseemly their conduct and their bargains, the authority of the pope went unquestioned. The schismatic Bohemians were diplomatically restored to the fold.[30] Popes set about rebuilding Rome as a worthy new capital for Christendom and fostered the artists and scholars who would inaugurate a new age of Christian fulfilment. Beyond the seas, there opened up astounding new possibilities for the Christian missions. The first two decades of the sixteenth century must have been extremely invigorating ones for Christian observers, at least north of the Alps.

Christians were not however complacement or idle. Criticism of the church and the clergy may be an ominous sign in some ways, but before such criticism became an accusation of the papal system, it could also be regarded as proof of a will to reform and an awareness of abuse. In the circumstances these criticisms were never properly formulated, though the Fifth Lateran Council (1512-14) debated the generally corrupt state of the church and suggested remedies.[31] These discussions ranged over many topics without any real sense of urgency, and the curia which inevitably had the responsibility for implementing reforms remained unimpressed by the arguments and dilatory in carrying out what was agreed. Such reforms as were there proposed came at Trent decades later to command more general assent — but it is not likely that they would have satisfied Protestants or averted the Reformation. They assumed rather that the papal system should be maintained and that the papacy should take its responsibilities for the whole clerical hierarchy and the laity more seriously. Such a programme would of course command very general support at the time and, as Trent proves, could have been implemented to a very considerable degree, but only by making the church more centralized than before and giving even more responsibility to the curia. This programme did not really meet the criticisms of all, for it assumed that the curia could become the real and effective dynamo of the church and that its superior wisdom could prevail. This view still commands support, and not only in the church. However, in its own way, it emphasized some of the abuses of the late medieval church, in order to sweep aside others. It was not the only view possible.

It is no coincidence that the period of undisputed papal supremacy in the church coincided with the period of the independent papal state, and the papacy had therefore continually to deal with two distinct problems, not always obviously compatible and yet indissolubly united through the persons involved.[32] This papacy has in fact been governed by Italians with the rarest exceptions and until the present century the college of cardinals has been predominantly Italian. During the fourteenth century the papacy had become very French. This was regarded as an abuse. At least it had the virtue of securing the benevolence of the most powerful Christian king, whereas the growth of an Italian curia exposed the papacy in fact to the full force of rivalries in the Italian peninsula. Conclaves were political rather than ecclesiastical occasions. Popes were partisans within Italian politics from the moment of election and could not retain their real ecclesiastical independence unless they exercised political power. Since they could not contemplate an Italian unity achieved by others or impose one themselves, they were condemned to play politics in Italy. The dual role was inescapable. As long as the curia was staffed and managed by Italians, the affairs of the church were bound to be at the mercy of these Italian clerks and prelates. Reform from the centre thus meant an Italianate church.

The church that these prelates represented and cared for was the church of the influential, the great ecclesiastical dignitaries; their zeal for it brought them into contact with great princes whose interests in the church were similar: a concern for how offices were assigned and conflicts resolved. The popes dealt with kings over the heads of the national clergy themselves, behaving no longer as though the clerical hierarchy had separate interests of its own against laymen, but as though the pope always knew best. Delivered from the constraints of the college and the councils too, the popes came face to face with rulers similarly disembarrassed. There was no hint that the popes would use their power to challenge secular pride — to do so they would have needed local allies, churchmen more independent-minded than the ones they provided to great benefices. Popes used their power rather to deal with other princes like themselves, bargaining and compromising. Loyal churchmen could submit to the superior wisdom of the pope: they had been brought up to serve the church. Laymen only tolerated such Roman decisions when they personally gained by them, as most great kings did, being too important to be alienated. Others, in growing numbers, began to feel that the proper interests of religion were not necessarily or obviously promoted by high diplomacy of this sort.

The church is not an institution to be kept in tip-top working order. Those who deferred to the view that Rome knows best had to regard the church as a machine of which they were replaceable cogs. It is understandable that this view should prevail principally with those who served its administration and that they took pride in their sense of duty and deference, resenting criticisms and disdaining advice from outsiders. In some ways such mandarin service is impressive, wherever it is found. But the devotion of dedicated bureaucrats cannot for long be acceptable. Their rituals and their superiority indicate that they have become divorced from the people they are supposed to serve and that a brutal awakening is imminent. Far back in the twelfth century the reforms to give more honour to the men of God had justified the use of papal authority to defend the clergy. By the sixteenth century the papacy enjoyed such respect that the clergy submitted obediently to all its dictates, even when the papacy pushed them aside to deal with the lay rulers; the means of reform had become a source of abuse. The church was run by great princes, only in name spiritual; in practice no less predatory and corrupt than the great laymen of the eleventh century.

Religious idealism

Whence then could reform come? In the eleventh century itself reform had come from some devout lay rulers collaborating with idealistic clergy. Some protestant theologians revived this model. They were sometimes rather starry-eyed about their lay patrons — the latter-day Josiahs who revived sound religion. All the same the influence of the laity as a positive force for reform on both the Protestant and the Catholic sides suggests a strange reversal of roles over four centuries. It arose from the earlier emphasis on the distinction drawn between the ordained clergy and the laity; it was justified by dissatisfaction with that alleged difference. However, if the laity began to demand higher standards of the clergy, it was from the clergy they had derived their ideas.

Within very generous limits, we can even discern a very widely held belief about the kind of religious life Christendom held to be ideal. There was no general agreement about the need for contemplative religious orders or international societies like the friars, but there was a uniform belief that every Christian community should have within its territorial limits a resident Christian shepherd, more learned than the rest and an example of Christian living, in effect its own bishop, though certain powers might for disciplinary reasons be reserved for regional commissioners by some reformer. Every Christian felt that he had the right of access to all the church's benefits in his own place of work and that it was the duty of Church to supply men of learning and moral authority in their midst. Not all laymen dared interfere directly in the church or demand concessions, but those who took an interest had such expectations and judged churchmen accordingly.

Particularly since the thirteenth century the church had made conscientious efforts to meet these requirements which had first been drawn up at the Fourth Lateran Council. The supervision of the bishops provided a reliable means of controlling both the suitability of the clergy and their good conduct. The foundation of schools, universities and colleges would eventually be adequate for the purposes of educating the clergy and once an appropriate syllabus had been devised it could be taught on a sufficiently large scale. Probably the clergy on the eve of the Reformation had never been better prepared, corporately, for their role; if they failed to give satisfaction it was because the laity in fact expected more than this. For though on the one hand they seemed to want a kind of mechanical perfection from a uniformly perfect man of God, they also looked for a more personal intimation of the profundity of religion. They professed to expect to get this from the most learned clergy, but they could also be satisfied with the inspiration of more ignorant men: and in fact such emotional assurance seemed to be more important. The church must also take responsibility for this. From the thirteenth century there had grown up a somewhat crude emphasis on appealing to the emotions of the laity at the expense of enlarging their understanding, particularly amongst successful preachers, like the Franciscans. For all its dangers, such preaching could have been excused, at the time, as a legitimate means of bringing religion to the people. It rightly made use of men's emotions, for religion cannot be a mere matter of intellectual propositions. At the same time the church had embarked upon the laudable task of assimilating the accumulated wisdom of the ancients for Christian belief and trying to demonstrate the complete rationality of the religious view of life. Not all scholars could accept the Thomistic confidence in natural theology, though it remained an impressive achievement, used by the Dominican order as a basis of their teaching. Alternative systems, more sensitive to the truths of revealed religion, excited the passions of university men and stimulated academic theology. All these duly left their mark upon popular religion too.

As the learned and obtuse debates of the schools impinged upon the laity, they looked for books to strengthen their religious convictions, so that for their benefit, certain theologians and devout men began to provide sermons or meditations especially in the vernacular, capable of stirring devout thoughts in pious laymen, even if cautious theologians suspected them of being heretical. Some well-educated clergy of a conservative outlook certainly disapproved of these attempts to deepen the religious understandings of laymen and thought them dangerous, unnecessary and ill-advised. Yet the amount of such vernacular literature tended to grow, in quantity, if not quality, and the church as a whole certainly did not starve this religious hunger. However, even well-read laymen tended to develop a very different attitude to religion from the clergy, by virtue of their very position.[33] The contrast between learned clergy and pious laymen is unfortunately not often demonstrated. However, in the case of Joan of Arc we can see a girl who trusted her own visions, whereas the theologians doubted their authenticity. Her simple credulity did not seem either admirable or convincing to them yet she believed herself to be a faithful member of the church for which the university defined doctrine.[34]

Against the unreasonable beliefs of the pious, churchmen for all their education, could do little. Their excuses for abuses, their complicated justifications for doubtful doctrines could be written off as so many sophistries. Clergy with no intellectual difficulties about proving the errors of heretics did not convince others, for whom the intellectual propositions of heretics anyway mattered less than their personal fervour, their moral example or the political consequences of their teachings. The clergy had commanded intellectual respect in the thirteenth century when they had called for the destruction of the Cathars; a century later the laity did not leap to the church's call against the spiritual Franciscans; later still, the Czech laity defied the church and joined the Hussites.

For the religion of the laity in the fourteenth and fifteenth century had developed along different lines from the intellectual preoccupations of the clergy without thereby becoming unorthodox. Since the thirteenth century the parochial clergy had stimulated lay devotion by the sacraments, especially the eucharist. Veneration of the host, at mass or on festive occasions like Corpus Christi processions, smack of superstition but passed at the time as expressions of a new and genuine devotion. Characteristically, instead of using the sacraments simply as intended, the devout inclined to spiritualize even their material aspect.[35] Instead of feeding upon consecrated bread, they adored the refined and elevated host, and subsidized the singing of masses for the benefit of souls in purgatory. Their religion had in fact become a matter of internal emotional concentration and they look for occasions when such religious transport could be excited.

The medieval church provided an enormous variety of exhilarating stimulus. The Gothic churches themselves seemed to move, upwards or forwards, with buttresses and decorations contributing cross-rhythms, never in repose. The paintings of the churches set out to stir sympathy, pity or adoration for the emotions of Christ and his saints, realistically portrayed as in life, not symbolically effecting the work of salvation. The paintings of the Italian Renaissance, no less than those of the Flemish school, served to enhance men's religious sensibilities. It is difficult to realize what men made of certain theological ideas before the painters had provided a visual image of them; Raphael's 'Transfiguration', Titian's 'Assumption', like Leonardo's 'Last Supper', permanently affected men's conceptions of religious truth. The technique of perspective which made it possible to project a scene from the point of view of the individual observer 'objectively', if anything accentuated the pious emphasis. Painters turned their devout eyes on the saints, Biblical story or legend and made them as certain and real as though they were present. In painting there was no room for hesitation or reserve. Religious stories had never been portrayed more objectively or carried greater conviction.

Less reflective persons benefited too from the church's efforts. Street performances of religious plays and recurrent festival occasions for processions and spectacles made an assault upon the senses equivalent in modern terms to the combined effect of a travelling circus, a military parade and massed brass bands. Not content with vulgar appeals, the church also provided for the layman's moments of solitary contemplation, when withdrawn from the comforting exuberance of his fellows, the individual Christian might fall into doubt, despair, or self-centredness. Translations into the vernacular of established Christian classics opened the way for original works about the soul's progress in religion.[36]

Against this background it is possible to see how the late medieval church changed its character without being aware of it, and how little the projects of earnest reformers interested ordinary Christians. Conditions across the church varied immensely, but in most places churchmen had found the means to work on men's religious emotions and awaken their personal commitment to God: the clergy found that once roused such feelings could not easily be disciplined.

Personal religion
Intensity in the personal religious life was not entirely new in this period, as the use made of older Christian texts proved. In the past however those who sought Christian perfection had been encouraged to join

monastic communities, where a life of discipline and obedience had tempered enthusiasm and isolated the most fervent from the majority. Monasteries were exceptionally numerous still, but for various reasons they no longer served as a religious refuge for all the most devout laymen. The growth of the parochial ministry had thrust the monasteries into the background: they were places for exceptional people, and not the ordinary place for the religious life. Monasteries tended to recruit monks from rather specialized social groups. There were few townsmen; flourishing monastic communities in this period seem at best to have drawn upon the countrymen of middling station, who lived comfortable lives of a regular routine, divided between singing the divine praise and the management of their affairs.[37] Many monasteries, where places in them were reserved for members of certain families and abbots were appointed *in commendam* by the papacy, naturally declined. The intensity of the earlier struggles waged in them against the forces of evil subsided. Men's spiritual conflicts were fought within their personal souls, and the new learning and piety did not encourage the view that it was better for those in search of Christian perfection to live in communities under regular direction. With women it was otherwise. Some of the most important religious writing and experience of the fourteenth century did still emanate from convents and *beguinages* especially in Germany, where the influence of Eckhardt and Henry Suso provided intellectual guidance. The contrast between the mystical pieties of these groups and the startling visionary experiences of Hildegard of Bingen in the twelfth century might be used to demonstrate how much the religious outlook had changed. Hildegard's visions, recorded with papal approval, and depicted under her supervision, concern the nature of the whole universe. When the created order was handed over for study to the schools, religion concentrated on the problems of personal salvation.

Social conditions of the religious life had also changed. In an earlier age, monasteries had, like villages, lived the self-sufficient life of the group; the piety cultivated there reflected the deepest strengths of primitive solidarity. The erosion of social certainties by 1300 created tensions which drove men to ask the way to salvation. There was in a very obvious sense the disturbing effect of urban growth. By contemporary standards, towns were great sprawling agglomerations of people largely strangers to one another. The town populations grew four or five times within a century and strained the institutional resources of the municipality. The immigrant workers coming in from village communities a few hundred strong were frightened by the anonymity. Townsmen naturally attempted to find alternative human associations within which the familiar qualities of human life could be cultivated. The clergy of the period tried to canalize these sentiments into 'fraternities', clubs with social purposes encouraged by religion, especially care of the sick, honourable burial for members and the relief of their stricken families. These associations might grow out of the life of the town parish, or from the common occupations of workers; some of them arose like modern clubs by individual efforts. Whatever other purposes they might also serve, their religious duties were prominent. The focus of the common life was the church or chapel used for their meetings. Each one had its own patron saint and devotion to the patron owed little to the views of the clerical establishment. The popularity of Saint George in Bohemia, Catalonia and England was not inspired by church historians or clerical instruction. In some cases, social conditions gave new prominence to certain saints like Sebastian or Roch who became popular figures because of their association with protection against the plague. The saints held the little groups together and reassured them of their special relationships with the church triumphant above. The desire to share in such communities did not notably diminish with affluence or disappear with time. In the fifteenth century the richest associations of the towns rebuilt churches and improved the facilities of their groups by constructing halls for festivities, meetings and welfare. Townsmen could not take conviviality for granted, as countrymen did. Nor did they enjoy being alone with their families. They felt socially isolated and needed company; wherever they could they strove to promote sociability.

Although the church helped men to meet their problems, it was also responsible for underlining them. Just as the facts of a man's social isolation came home to him in the town, so it obliged him to face his own individuality as never before, above all, his own personal death. In the country, death and rebirth were constant, inescapable and anyway complemented one another. In the town death was a source of pollution and a proof of decay. Shut in on themselves, townsmen pondered the after-life with feverish anxiety. By 1300 churchmen had persuaded themselves as to the general contours of the after-life, but it was an educated layman, Dante who provided in the *Divina Commedia* a vision of the future reality. It was not a fantasy; he could say with confidence what sins qualified for hell, what should be purged and how the blessed could rise through the heavenly circles. Commentaries on Dante were written during the fourteenth century; his accounts inspired painters. There were no doubts about the nature of the world to come. The uncertainty was where each individual would be consigned in it.

It might seem surprising that earlier Christians had not been equally agitated about the future life of the soul. They inherited the idea of the soul from the pagan philosophers, though not without giving it a new meaning in its religious context, for while philosophers had debated the proper conduct for men in this present life, they had not believed that the future destiny of the soul would depend on right action. During the centuries of monastic dominance it seems to have been assumed that the prayers of the monks would procure the salvation of all those who befriended and served the monastery. The monks themselves believed that the only certain means of eternal salvation was by total renunciation of the world for Christ and life in the cloister: this view encouraged the anxious to become monks. The others relied on vicarious penance, because they still took for granted the notion of the community of mankind.

These clear-cut ideas did not survive the twelfth century. The church itself ceased to regard the way of monks as the only way to heaven. Crusaders were promised remission of penance for their own sins and presumably expected immediate entry to paradise on their death. Over the centuries a great number of different ways into heaven were proposed. The chances of martyrdom notably declined after the conversion of the barbarians. As crusading too became less popular, the likelihood of dying for Christ struck men less than the problem of how to live for him and earn, or at least obtain, the expected reward. Popular preaching brought the problems to general attention. Men were made aware of their sins and tried to obtain remission of the penance they owed. In a world where men travelled for economic reasons, they were likewise prepared to go on pilgrimages to remote places and endure the inevitable hardships for the benefit of their souls. The church offered indulgences for the penances due for a variety of causes. Though it appeared to lay-men and reformers to end up by selling pardons, the doctrine of the papal authority to draw upon the treasury of the church's merits was only a more sophisticated and clerical exposition of the older beliefs in the solidarity of the whole Christian family.[38] The church clearly continued to do what it could to reassure the laity by proposing many ways of atoning for their faults and obtaining divine compassion. Yet men did not seem to be satisfied. They did not feel the state of blessedness they expected. They remained anxious about their prospects after death. Desperate attempts to drown themselves in their communities and dodge the implications of their uniqueness reveal the extent which they were unhappy with their individuality. All the church's comforts could not soften this blow.

Though the church was not alone responsible for the new sense of isolation, and did its best to mitigate its effects, in two ways it had certainly made matters worse. By its own deliberate policy it had divided the church in two, between the clergy who dispensed the sacraments and the laity who received them. For the clergy, anxieties about the future had less force. Monks and clerks who worried and thought about their souls had submitted to a rule of life. Monks expected rewards for their faithfulness to their vows; the clergy fought for the triumph of God's church against its oppressors and had few doubts about their own value. But the laity? How did anyone and everyman get to heaven? They had no particular vocations and no religious communities or corporations to keep them going in steady pieties. In parts of the Rhineland where pious women joined *beguinages* for a common religious life, lay people founded a style of life adapted to their needs; but without institutional form, they were bound to be precarious. Laymen could not expect to find much institutional solace except in the fraternities, and these could never totally appease their religious worries.

Secondly the clergy themselves had taken up a new interest in the problem of the soul in the thirteenth century and their own debates encouraged laymen to be anxious. The prevailing opinion of Neoplatonist Christians like St Augustine had taught that the soul was like a spiritual element within the body which escaped with relief at death as though released from ignominious imprisonment. This doctrine seemed to the scholastic theologians of the Thomist school dangerously similar to that of dualist heretics. More careful exposition of the Christian teaching about creation showed man to be a creature made in God's image, perfect in substance, corrupted by human sin. The struggle for salvation took place within man himself, not between his eternal soul and his mortal flesh. Aquinas used the Aristotelian categories to illustrate the relationship and concluded that the soul could no more dispense with the body than the form with substance; there was an indissoluble bond between the two, as there was between this life and the next; in his body man acquired the experience and knowledge necessary for eternal salvation; by his conduct in the flesh he would earn his rewards.[39] Heroic mortification of the flesh to prove the superiority of the spirit deserved less admiration than intelligent direction of the body by the soul. Since every Christian had a soul of his own, he was individually answerable for it and its eternal well-being depended in the ultimate analysis on his own acts of will. The consequences of *wrong* choice could therefore be fatal; the man who had to save himself might fall. Theologians discussed whether a man could choose the good without knowing what it was and whether he was bound to do the good he knew, but, to save free will, they had to conclude that a man could opt for what he knew to be evil. This gave men's acts of will more importance than his professions of belief. Laymen were duly incited to perform religious acts and to accumulate grace, and tried not to be bothered by fussy distinctions drawn by the learned between grace and merit. They acted as though God were not Himself free to refuse their good works, expecting to earn remission of their sins by their own efforts, whatever lip-service they paid to doctrine. The clergy actually encouraged this sense of 'buying' grace on the market, because they would not abstain from claiming authority over the whole operation of divine mercy. The church had been set up to bring men to salvation and its jurisdiction extended beyond the grave. Even mortal sins could be pardoned. The most categorical rules could be waived by the dispensing power of the church. Many laymen took due comfort from the church's reassurance. Others were doubtful and confused, redoubling their efforts to attain certainty, from the clergy or by other means. A few educated Christians learned to accept the ambiguity of their position as individuals in the world. They gave up looking for perfection in the cloister and made an ideal of working out their own way to salvation through their own personal experiences. Few of them, as yet, wished to stray from the Christian fold, but the gate was open.

Criticism of the church

Sixteenth-century critics themselves imply that the church's different ministries gave great satisfaction to many credulous people, even if some individuals were left without the sense of conviction which was to come from Protestantism. Many parts of Europe were hardly affected by the Reformation at all when it came and some of those that were remained satisfied with the church. It is important to remember that whatever its defects the church did not seem to all men, even the best-educated or holiest, to be in need of Reformation by the sixteenth century. There were criticisms, but these may be regarded more as proof of active concern for the church than of its total corruption. The inadequacies of the church before 1500 were felt and voiced most strongly by literate individuals in the great towns, especially north of the Alps. It was such people who gained most by the Reformation, since it allowed them to express their personal religious convictions and to devise alternative ways of worship and organization. The printing press gave them forms of communication with persons of like mind in distant places. The political situation in both Germany and England permitted discontent to become protest and rebellion.

But even before the sixteenth century the general religious condition of Christendom had not excluded the possibility of dissent altogether. The three centuries before the Reformation are marked by several such outbreaks. At the time of the Albigensian Crusade, the Cathars give the impression of being doctrinally alienated from the church. Dissenting groups after that time seem to arise within the church's own traditions. Doctrines like the poverty of Christ so took possession of men's minds as to lead them to unusual conduct, but it was only in exasperation if in the end they came to clash openly with the ecclesiastical authorities. Religious opinions were exciting but volatile. Men might so easily be carried away by their love of Christ as to be incapable of distinguishing clearly between earthly 'love' and its idealized counterpart. They waxed righteously indignant about the church's wealth but remained naively blind to their own covetousness of church property. Passionate Christians blew hot and cold and the problem of keeping the church together would have been insuperable even before 1500, had there been any general belief that visible unity in the church was unnecessary.

Heresy

At the most critical time in the conciliar epoch when the church's unity was in danger, there were important groups which put their own righteousness first and refused submission to the whole church, partly no doubt because at the time loyal churchmen were themselves in manifest doubt about its real nature. The dangers at the time were worst where the civil government itself was unreliable, as in the Reformation. In England, which was shaken by religious dissenters claiming the intellectual authority of John Wyclif, the monarchy then stood firmly for orthodoxy. The Lollards were dealt with effectively and if they lingered on into the fifteenth century they did so as minority groups. In Bohemia heresy became a much more serious problem, because it was not only the hierarchy that faltered during the schism, but the monarchy as well. The importance of the 'Hussite revolution' has not been generally conceded in the west, apparently as a result of the condescending view that nothing of much significance could happen in a remote backwater like Bohemia. (Likewise in the present century there has been a consistent attempt to feel sorry for the small Czech nation and not face the fact that Bohemia occupies a crucial place in Central Europe and deserves intelligent appraisal rather than sentiment, a fact that the consequences of the Hussite wars themselves did most to obscure.) At this time, however, Bohemia was the principal state of the empire and is therefore highly significant if religious dissent got out of hand, in the special circumstances of the schism. The episode also shows that in the fifteenth century, the taint of heresy was still sufficient to blight a nation's reputation; so Bohemia forfeited the respect of Christendom.

At the time of the schism Bohemia was the homeland of the emperor, the chief defender of the Roman papacy. His capital, Prague, was the cultural and intellectual centre of Europe, with the only university of the empire and the chief theological faculty of the Urbanist obedience, closely allied with the one at Oxford. The gold and silver mines of the country made its king rich and the country prosperous. Its people had obtained recognition of their own laws and customs from the intruded kings of the Luxembourg dynasty. They were developing a vernacular literature of their own. Denunciation of the riches and corruption of the well-endowed clergy proved that the Bohemians were far from complacency and indifference to religion. King Charles IV who became emperor in 1346 encouraged both learning and preaching, but in spite of his benefactions suffered public denunciation as Antichrist by the Moravian preacher John Milic, a former clerk of his own chancery: the end of the world was nigh.[40] Nowhere in medieval Europe were men more frequently reminded of this by popular preachers in both Czech and German, or the clergy more forcefully exposed as corrupt and ignorant. The clergy made their own ripostes, but they did nothing to reform the abuses. The laity flocked to the preachers and intensified their own devotions. The established order at first stood firm after the outbreak of the schism, but trouble began when the German electors, exasperated by the conduct of Charles's son, Wenceslas IV, deposed him from the empire. Wencelas refused to accept this, and tried to bargain with Alexander V, the pope of Pisa, for restoration of his titles; in this he could not obtain support from the Romanist archbishop of Prague and turned for support to the university. By an arbitrary decree Wenceslas increased the representation of the Czech 'nation' in the university to outnumber the Germans, who left Prague in protest, and denounced the Bohemians as heretics.

To all intents and purposes Bohemia was completely amputated from the German confederation though its population remained of mixed Czech and German speech and ancestry. But both in Rome and in Germany the Bohemian church acquired an unsavoury reputation for heresy. Wenceslas had certainly been assisted by Czech scholars favourable to the writings of Wyclif and thought it safer after 1411 to give up protecting the most outspoken of them, Hus. The latter was in due course condemned by pope John XXIII (1412) and later by the Council of Constance, where he was burned (1415).[41] The council naturally assumed that its authority would be respected; however, in Prague, protests against the burning of Hus hardened into defiance of Christendom. Long after the council had dissolved, other Christian rulers led armies against the defiant Hussites: Bohemia repelled them all and proved it could stand out against the whole of Christendom, without any legitimate ruler of its own.[42] The Hussites within the kingdom were not themselves agreed on doctrine, though they had compromised and formulated a joint programme called the four articles of Prague.[43] Their religious unity did not depend on doctrine; it was symbolized by the administration of the eucharist in both kinds to the laity, which revived an old custom of the Slavonic church, emphasized the importance of the sacraments to the 'heretics', and demonstrated the irrelevance of the difference between clergy and laymen.

Such a precarious national religious unity had little attraction outside

Bohemia and it could not last.[44] Religious radicalism alarmed many Czechs. Despite their military victories they could not obtain recognition by Christendom, except by surrendering some part of their peculiarities. Negotiations dragged on for many years. The council of Basel recognized the Hussite practice of administering the communion in both kinds to laymen in order to recover some unity with the Czechs. The moderate party drew away from the extremists. In due course the Catholics became strong enough to reimpose their own formulae. They at least knew their own strength. The Hussites tended to split into divergent groups, since they had no universally acknowledged leaders and no long-established traditional doctrines.

The fate of Hussitism showed the way for dissidents in later times. The Hussites found no national dynasty to make a reality of a national church. Many moderates and even powerful noblemen eventually preferred the universal church, for all its failings, to the risks presented by radical dissenters who disowned all restraints in the cause of religion. Nor did Christendom as a whole show any interest in breaking up its newly found unity to establish other national heresies or admit the rights of enthusiasts to found their own sects. This should not be thought surprising with the Reformation less than a hundred years ahead. Most of Latin Christendom then went on believing in the need for a universal church under the pope, even while pressing the claims of local churches. Difficult though it sometimes is for Protestants to see it, particularly in view of the turn of events since the seventeenth century, the reform was a minority movement even in the sixteenth century and would have taken no root in Germany, or England, its original bases, but for the connivance of the princes and the selfish needs of Henry VIII. Outside the church therefore most men did not expect to find their salvation.

Alternative belief

The inadequacy of the church to satisfy all their demands did however drive men to forms of superstition that the church rather unwisely tolerated, simply because they made no frontal assault on ecclesiastical positions. Amongst these alternatives the study of the occult had a special fascination, for it offered many advantages in a familiar, bookish form, and the border-line between legitimate and accursed knowledge was indeterminate: temptingly, deliciously so.[45] These books stimulated the fantasy, and not only of scholars. Once we leave the certainties of the literate evidence, however, we are at a loss to know exactly what was popularly believed or practised, as in the way of witchcraft. We must allow for general credulity, human vindictiveness, surviving superstitions, as well as some popularly transmitted secret lore, fostered perhaps by the arrival of the gypsies in fourteenth-century Europe and their use of playing cards, the Tarot pack, well known already in Villon's day.[46] Superstitions may be ignored as ignorance or studied as fables, but their prevalence at this time, apparently in unprecedented number, certainly represents at least the feeling that the supreme truths of the established religion were not enough. The most respectable of these supplementary faiths was astrology, the lore of the stars, not as absurd as present-day astrology, since at that time there was no clear line drawn between science and fiction. The source of astronomical knowledge in the thirteenth century had been the Islamic world from which the west derived texts of the astronomers of antiquity like Ptolemy, and astronomical tables. These came however with Arab commentaries designed to relate celestial phenomena to human fortune, through the interpretation of the Zodiac, the divisions of the heavens used by 'scientific' observers. Not surprisingly, the theologians of the University of Paris soon put an end to the more absurd astrological opinions derived from Arab writers, but the confused doctrines found a safer base elsewhere, most respectably at the University of Padua. The astrological teaching of some of the 'scientists' was notorious. Francescho Stabili, (Cecco d'Ascoli) was actually burnt for his errors (1327) without this putting an end to the tradition.

Apart from wishful thinking, contemporaries had good reasons to believe in astrology, and only the church's warning against unhealthy curiosity to dampen their enthusiasm. For all learned men, the clergy included, then believed that the earth was the centre of the universe, a comparatively small affair we might say—created by God for his own purposes but in which mankind was the most privileged (though unruly) creature. The sun and moon, the planets and the stars revolved in their various seasons for God's glory and men's utility. Celestial luminaries were observed with justifiable admiration and legitimate curiosity, when men lived with no other calendars than the sun and moon. All the agricultural seasons would be regulated by these movements. Seamen knew the connexion between the tides and the moon's phases. If northern observations were hampered by cloudy conditions, the learning accumulated in the Mediterranean civilizations, with their astrological additions, could be taken over on trust. There could be no doubt whatever that the heavens did influence the course of the earth. The problem was whether such influence could be known in sufficient detail to yield useful information. And this is the point of the learning: to satisfy individual enquiries about the future: of health, marriages, battles, political intrigues, matters of considerable importance about which churchmen were, for them, unusually non-committal. Since Copernicus, men have become very insignificant quantities in a universe constantly getting larger. Before Copernicus, men thought of themselves as very significant figures indeed. They did not have our powers of controlling nature, but they had something perhaps more important than know-how: they had confidence in their own significance, whereas we can take no consolation in our power to blow the globe to smithereens while the universe goes on as before.

Summing up therefore, the church for all its failings still retained its power and showed few signs of imminent collapse. The abuses denounced by later reformers may be matched by reference to the constant attempts to renew the spiritual life made by reformers in the fifteenth century, like Antonino archbishop of Florence, the Brethren of the Common life, or the monastic reformers of the Benedictine and Franciscan orders.[47] The arrival of printing demonstrated the overwhelming demand of the reading public for religious works, the Bible included, and in the vernacular, as the printers got out the texts of the fathers and the great medieval doctors like St Bernard or Thomas Aquinas. The reformers of the sixteenth century were not all Protestant: Erasmus and More remained in the church they hoped to reform and the roots of the Counter-Reformation went as deep, if not deeper, than those of Luther and Calvin. The reform is another issue. Within the limits assumed in this book, there is no warrant for believing that by 1500 Europe was all set for a nationalist or a secular future.

3. HUMANISM AND LITERACY

The primacy of religious issues in the sixteenth century proves the continued importance of religion for the majority, but revealed the fundamental difference between the medieval and the modern view. Religious leaders themselves, Protestant and Catholic insisted that conviction was more important than unity, so that Christendom was broken up. Europe having once lost the unity given by Rome has never replaced it with another, but it has retained for some centuries a cultural unity, chiefly through its educational system. Those who were formally educated acquired membership of the international republic of letters founded on a knowledge of Latin language and literature. It is now commonly believed that it is somewhat scandalous to have devoted so much effort to the teaching of a dead language. Reformers who advocated the use of the vernacular in worship continued to use Latin for polemics and for scholarship; laymen too were happy to learn the language for their own improvement. For centuries those formally educated in Latin appreciated their advantages in having access to the greatest literature and wisdom then known, written in Latin, with Greek as an increasingly esteemed addition.

This kind of education developed throughout Europe in the sixteenth century from models provided by Italy somewhat earlier, and in both cases it represented the determination of laymen to find a form of training suited to their needs, using the clerical means of reading and writing, but for different purposes. Although scholars read many Latin texts neglected by the clergy in the past, it was not so much the novelties they read as their manner of reading them that created the new education. This may become clearer if we consider what reading Latin had meant in earlier centuries. Twelfth-century clergy admired classical authors, esteemed literature and wrote expressive Latin, without either founding a new kind of education or winning lay converts to their programme. Most of them still relied on anthologies for their favourite quotations, using ancient literature as an adornment to learning, without showing much interest in reading authors whole. The most learned man of his day, John of Salisbury, applied his talents to the menial task of writing elegant letters for his ecclesiastical superiors and advocating papalist attitudes in politics. He wrote better letters because of his studies, but he found no affinity with ancient authors: he reserved his enthusiasms for scholastic logic: as the means for ascertaining truth by the science of reasoning. Twelfth-century 'humanism' was a rather sickly product of the age of Cistercian monasteries and the cathedral schools; before the century was out, the prospects for lovers of Latin literature were bleak. Peter of Blois discerned this and deplored it, but the scholastic future lay with the philosophers and logicians.

The Latin required in 'the schools' for debate and analysis was neutral and 'scientific'. The 'schoolmen' introduced new grammar books of their own and gave up literary affectations, because the weighty subject matter made it seem frivolous to take trouble with writing. The Latin composition of educated persons had become lifeless by Petrarch's day. The schoolmen hardly deserved the obloquy poured out against them since. They thought matter more important than form. They struggled to extract the marrow from the newly discovered works of Aristotle. These works were far from being elegant treatises themselves and they needed a special kind of didactic exposition if they were to be made intelligible. The schoolmen still used Latin as a living language, inventing new words to express new concepts, however abstruse in themselves. Petrarch and the humanists who followed him had no time for excuses. They were intolerant of scientific jargon and scornful of the subject matter. They had a different conception of the nature of language itself and the uses to which it should be put. They did not hark back to the twelfth century but to the ancient world, though the inspiration they found there would have surprised Cicero himself. But they revived the ancient, long dormant tradition of rhetorical education and by wresting the study of Latin from the grip of the clerical, scholastic world, they achieved a major revolution. They dislodged the foundations of medieval learning and proposed another in its place: the study of ancient authors, a wilful and unprecedented archaism. They learned to use language expressively, first only Latin, then Greek. They enlarged their vocabularies, became skilful in composition and adroit speakers and writers. They could describe and explore feelings and experiences formerly neglected, often of a vain egocentric character, but capable of stirring their friends and admirers. The study of classical languages was found to have advantages even for the philosophers since they could study Aristotle and Plato in the original. This gave Plato, who was unfamiliar in the west, a new significance and confirmed the literary character of philosophy since Plato was an accomplished writer, as the scientific Aristotle was not. The humanists discovered how absorbing the study of classical authors through their texts could be and over several centuries justified their reforms.

The first man to pursue such studies was Petrarch, the clerk dispensed from residence, and adequately beneficed by the papal curia at Avignon, which he ungratefully reviled.[48] He was a book-lover, scholar, poet and historian, but prone to leave ambitious literary projects unfinished while he enjoyed the daily study of his books. His numerous correspondents all had much more to do than he, but his example impressed them. His unambitious life in the country surrounded by those eager to discuss literature and ideas came to be the ideal of those who could afford it. The call to public service, arms or business retained its force, but even for the most active of men the attractions of a simple life of cultivated leisure continued to haunt their dreams for retirement or vacation. Indeed in its modern popular form it has never been more taken for granted, though it is obvious that its original virtue has been lost.

Such an ideal for human life only became widespread when societies were rich enough to allow some of their best men to do nothing more constructive than improving their own minds by study. Leisure for this purpose came to count for more than work. The concept has been much derided in an egalitarian age because of its elitism. At the time it represented not an occupation for bored rentiers, but an important new belief that life might be more than a struggle to survive. For centuries men had been busy. Even monks, the most 'leisured' group of the church, had a round of daily offices to perform. Students in twelfth-century Paris began lectures at dawn. They might have taken time off, but they could not expect to get through their courses at the last moment by buying the best books and just reading them over for the examination. They had to be busy about committing their learning to memory. When men were not busy, they were idle; they relaxed, were silly, drunk or boisterous. There was no awareness of the concept of leisure, let alone of learning what to do with it. No one was indolent for long; there was too much else to do. It took a privileged person like Petrarch, the non-resident canon, to show others how to turn the simple life with books into a model for everyone. The attraction of a country retreat for the calm examination of conscience and religious conviction was already well-established and Petrarch's brother joined the Carthusians. But Petrarch's own life was not ruled by religious ideals, whose claims on him he recognized but resisted. He wilfully kept his quiet life for himself, not for God, and this stamped the whole pattern of humanist life thereafter. Men of letters often gave much time to religious duties and contemplation, but they never made a total surrender, as the old monks and hermits had done: 'leisure' was not for God but for the cultivation of their minds or talents: the improvement of the self.

At the beginning of this movement, before any pattern had been established, Petrarch had been strengthened in his way of life by the belief that such had once been the ideal of the ancient Romans. He discovered a text of Cicero's letters to Atticus, in which he glimpsed an ideal of private life, previously overlooked by earlier admirers of Cicero as orator, philosopher or politician. Petrarch, like a medieval clerk, regretted Cicero's public occupations and rebuked his 'friend'. It was fitting for a philosopher to shun such concerns, and better to be without public responsibilities and to live in the world a 'private' life. The pietistic literature of the previous centuries obviously gave Petrarch little help when he came to speculate about the nature of the private life, but in turning further back he found what he wanted.

Ancient literature became his key to understanding the human self, human history and ideas about the nature of human society. Petrarch was interested in people, his friends and his authors. To read was for him a discovery of the writer's personality. This was not, as it is so often in the present, a prurient curiosity, but an acknowledgement of each man's moral worth. The contrast with John of Salisbury is striking. For him the matter he read was always more important than the author and however well he learned to write, style was not cultivated to express his own thoughts and feelings. Petrarch's major literary works were studies of people and he mastered the art of using a man's writings to establish his character. This amounted to the discovery of the inextinguishable individuality of writers, even those long dead. The great writers of the past spoke to him as certainly as his living friends, and as personally. Petrarch naturally wrote letters to them. He did not think of them as crushing authorities for opinions and beliefs, but as personal acquaintances. Since he liked to have his friends always with him he naturally had to amass his own library, with copies of their works. This tradition has been maintained ever since by educated persons. At first the gathering together of manuscripts was a costly, arduous and complicated business; scholars needed persistence to realize their dreams. But they awoke interest in the acquisitions of private libraries and when the press was invented there was already a potential market for printed books. Had men not taken the buying of books for granted by 1450, the press would have been as unprofitable an invention in Europe as it was in China.

The development of classical studies may easily be misrepresented if too much emphasis is put upon its secular or lay aspect. Petrarch and other clergy who followed him, like the popes who later patronized it, were not hypocritical or irresponsible in praising the moral virtues of pagan writers. Like their medieval predecessors, the grammarians, rhetoricians and scholastic philosophers, the 'humanists' believed that the best pagan teachers anticipated and confirmed Christian teaching. The attraction of the new learning in the fifteenth century was that it offered pious minds of the day a more promising basis for their aspirations than the learning cultivated by the 'schoolmen'.

Learning in Petrarch's day had become involved in very high-minded discussions about the nature of God and the universe and in desperate attempts to make them intelligible to human minds. At the same time, the church pandered to the ignorance of the uneducated in its services and cults. Between these two extremes there grew to maturity a body of Christian opinion dissatisfied with both. Whatever theologians and priests may say, the popular prejudices of the twelfth century and since expected the Christian religion to make men better and society more moral. Orthodox monks believed this strongly, if less crudely than heretics. These somewhat naive hopes had therefore formerly provided support for changes in the ecclesiastical structure directed from Rome, but by 1300 Christians were beginning to realize that, whatever the merits of this structure, it had not made notable improvements in moral behaviour. At least one of the reasons for this, they supposed might be that the theologians thought too much in abstractions and too little about how to improve men, while the priests remained too concerned about the theoretical virtues of the sacraments and too little about actual conduct. Many devout Christians, without becoming unorthodox, showed that ritual and speculation did not seem to them to be enough. The value of religion for them was its practical effects; if reasoning did not help to make men better, they should study something else.

This attitude initially appealed to many Italians, in particular. The number of literate laymen was greater in Italy than north of the Alps. The native religious traditions of Italy stressed simplicity and asceticism. Monastic communities were few and mainly small. The theological schools had hardly taken root at all. About 1300 the controversies within the Franciscan order focused attention on the nature of the life led in imitation of Christ. Italians did not falter in their respect for the friars, and the tertiary order encouraged men to consider how they might lead an upright life within the ordinary framework of society. When they consulted the Christian literature on the religious life, they found that in general it assumed or advocated a monastic profession, or at least life by rules. Those in search of guidance about the moral life fell back there-fore upon the moral writers of antiquity, which had been pillaged by Christians for centuries. The very survival of the texts in the Christian period proved that their teaching was not incompatible with the Chris-tian dispensation.[49] Though they could not be of much help with the things of God, their reflections on the affairs of men proved valuable. Their literary force and elegance commended them to educated persons of refinement, masters as well as students; that the teaching of pagan authors was in line with that of the Bible seemed to prove that there were eternal ethical truths for all men, having therefore the force of natural law. The humanists who promoted the study of ancient authors in order to help with the moral education of laymen were not reviving prohibited books. They did not intend to start a renaissance of paganism or of pre-Christian rationalism. When they began, they did not have even the rudiments of an historical understanding that would have enabled them to put Cicero, for example, into the proper historical context of the late Roman republic. They took Cicero as their model of Latin prose writing and the philosophical spirit in action, but the new Ciceronians were scholars, clerks, teachers, intellectuals, not advocates, politicians and statesmen.

Pagan moral advice did not inspire the educated to revive even the old political virtues of Roman republicanism. Leonardo Bruni admittedly wrote as though that were his intention, but the Florentines of the fifteenth century were in practice less active in the government of their city than their less well-educated predecessors.[50] Some of the best men active in the city might have drawn succour from their studies in their arduous responsibilities, but for most educated persons, as for Petrarch himself, the Ciceronian ideal was cultured leisure. In the mid-fifteenth century, Florentine humanists took up a new interest in Neo-Platonist philosophy under the guidance of Marsilio Ficino at the Villa Careggi. In platonic discussions of religion, morals and poetry, they revived the concerns of the Hellenistic world. Yet in fifteenth-century Florence there was still more republican institutional life than in any other city in Europe. If this is what the revival of the classical past meant in Florence, how much could it mean anywhere else?

Humanist interest in pagan moralists was blended in most men's minds with the conventional religious teaching of the church. The lay status of the humanists often indicates their comparative ignorance of theological learning, but not their hostility to religion. When challenged, men of such education invariably recognized the superior claims of Christ. Christian humanism was badly mauled during the Reformation but both Protestants and Catholics continued to value the study of the pagan authors in their universities and schools. The children and students brought up on such fare did not imbibe irreligious sentiments from them. Like the Italian humanists, they knew how to interpret the texts within a context of belief that emphasized the natural support provided by the pagan teachers for the Christian revelation. The conception could be illustrated from painting by reference to Michelangelo's 'Doni Tondo'. There can be no doubt about the importance of the Holy Family in this picture or of the respect with which they are painted, however Amazonian the aspect of the Virgin. The most unexpected feature of the picture is, however, the frieze of naked youths lingering in the background, as it would seem on the very border between heaven and hell[52] Intriguing though they may be, they do not form a rival attraction to the main group: they form a bloodless, elegant justification of the Christian revelation about Love and the Incarnation. There could be no question of setting up paganism as a counter-attraction as long as the church was as powerful and as confident as the best minds of the day made it.

The humanists provided Europeans with a blueprint for secular education.[53] It proved its value over the succeeding 400 years. Now that the pattern it provided is rejected it seems something of a scandal that its principal element was the teaching of Latin. This should not be misrepresented out of some perverse objection to Latin at the present time. In the sixteenth century, it was necessary to know at least Latin, if such subjects as law, science and theology were to be studied at all. However, those who attended universities were not obliged to pursue even these higher disciplines. They found the study of classical literature an education in its own right. The students were not being educated like tradesmen, for some particular career, and they discovered the advantages of a liberal education. It could equip them for anything and enabled them to derive constant pleasure, even in their leisure moments, from reading. It was by this means that all educated Europeans, divided though they might be by their religious persuasions after the Reformation, could share in a common culture, with a mainly secular content. The movement which had begun with Petrarch, a beneficed clerk, thus became the means whereby the laity too acquired an education and a certain esprit de corps, as men of culture. Italy offered educated men posts in the secretariats of governments. Northern Europe found places for them as private tutors and royal advisers. The printing press increased the demand for educated persons as scholars and as publicists. The pamphlet wars of the sixteenth century prove however that religion was still their main interest. They

were absorbed into the cultural pattern of their own day. They did not
suppress the medieval universities or prepare for the triumph of secular
values.

Vernacular literature

The educated did not keep their knowledge of the corpus of classical
literature to themselves. They set about enriching their own vernaculars
and the 'uneducated' by translating ancient books and composing original
works in imitation of the great writers of the past.[54] In numbers and
importance those who could master the arts of reading and writing the
vernaculars greatly exceeded the Latinists, but it still took a long time
for the vernacular languages to accumulate a collection of classics of
their own; in many parts of Europe native vernaculars still have no comparable collection of great literary works. In the sixteenth century it
would have been absurd to pretend that any vernacular language was
comparable with Latin or Greek. Willingness to write original works in
the vernacular did not then represent any discontent with the classics; it
was a modest 'improvement' of reclaimed land. In its own way it re-
sembled an earlier movement in the church which had promoted the
sacramental life and theological teaching in Latin at the same time as popular preaching, prayers and hymns: works for a less sophisticated audience.

Until the languages of Europe attain written form, their character
eludes the historian. We are so accustomed to think of languages as
written that we can barely comprehend the situation of languages that
exist only at a spoken level, though they may be used in a literature transmitted only by oral means, like those of early Irish verse. In Europe,
after the Christian conversion, the use of spoken languages in writing
was unavoidably influenced by the literary written languages of the
church, Latin and Greek. From the first, Christian teaching required
missionaries to learn native languages, to provide them with new words
and to devise forms of writing and spelling. All European vernacular
literatures begin with religious texts in which personal faith is expressed
in the native speech, but it was not inevitable that every speech should
develop a 'written literature' of its own. Even now most dialect speakers
or raconteurs continue to use the standardized language in writing and
compose in it according to conventions generally recognised far beyond
their own dialectal regions. Only in as much as literature is personal
utterance, as it is for religious poetry, may the spoken language become
a literary one. At this level, however, the spoken language has only a
very limited range. In most parts of Europe, with its large political
units, only one of the many dialects was bound to obtain a wider currency, usually by virtue of a ruler's prestige and the influence of his
court. These centres developed literary traditions in that dialect. By the

twelfth century, the royal courts of England, France and Germany had all produced both literary languages and literatures, but they were not necessarily intelligible to all men of the 'national' speech, since they were the sophisticated product of well-educated men with their own social conventions.

These courtly vernaculars did not have much literary future. In Germany, the fine period of Staufen poetry did not survive the elimination of the dynasty; in England, the Anglo-Saxon literature of the Wessex dynasty lost the support of an English-speaking court after 1066, while the new Anglo-Norman literature of the Norman and Angevin kings had a more vigorous rival in France itself. The French literary language itself had a wide diffusion in the twelfth century. It was the *lingua franca* in all the Crusading states, in north Italy, southern France (after 1213) and in England (after 1066). In the fourteenth century it was the language of Marco Polo, Charles IV of Luxembourg and Froissart—but it began to lose its prestige. Its courtly world was divided by rival allegiances and growing particularism. Froissart himself travelled to the provincial centres to gather his stories and his information: without his valiant efforts to keep alive the spirit of chivalry and courtesy, we should have rather the impression of a total disruption of elegant French society. It needed the efforts of Charles V to restore, briefly, a sense of intellectual effort by translation and patronage, mending the broken fences as Alfred had done in Wessex five centuries earlier.

Without the strong control of literary traditions, the spoken languages of Europe in the fourteenth century began to devise popular literatures of a different kind, generally in 'prose' (though the formal distinction between poetry and prose hardly existed at the time). The tradition of writing in the vernacular for religious purposes had become so engrained that there was no question of leaving this popular literature in oral form, though its oral origins remain very conspicuous, in the type of anecdote, funny story or reminiscence that reaches the most sophisticated level in a work like Polo's *Travels* originally written down in 'Venetian-French' and translated for the benefit of others. Such works show an unsophisticated taste for stories, which had in the past presumably been satisfied not from books but from memory. The stories of the great courtly poets were likewise reduced to prose versions for more popular taste. Out of this comparatively unpromising material some writers nevertheless spun literature of the finest quality: Boccaccio and Chaucer. The high style was abandoned. The best poet of the fifteenth century, François Villon, lived as a criminal amongst the coarsest people of his time. During this phase without dominant courtly patronage, any vernacular could be tried out as a literary medium. The Tuscan speech of the Florentine authors came to be the literary medium of any Italian speaker, entirely because of a succession of Tuscan writers from Dante onwards, acting without courts or patrons. Written literature thus lost its predominantly courtly context and came within the range of anyone who could learn to use the alphabet for his own tongue. This was already the situation when printing was invented and the tendency was thus perpetuated: had it been otherwise, printing might well have concentrated on Latin texts altogether.

Printing which concentrated the production of literature in the great centres of book distribution helped to standardize the literary vernaculars. England had numbered several different provincial 'schools' of literature in the fourteenth century; by the sixteenth century, literature had become a predominently London phenomenon: the presses made this so. Popular demand for vernacular works in the fourteenth and fifteenth century had remained unaffected by either good taste or other literary considerations. The vernacular was used especially for devotional or improving books, not valued for the opportunities it gave for self-expression or self-conscious literary composition; ignorance of Latin led to a demand for unpretentious translations of learned works, without interest to scholars, but useful for laymen.[55] When such works could be reproduced mechanically, however, printers naturally preferred to sell them in whatever form of the language had the widest diffusion. Such *koine* were in fact rarely consecrated by established use. Tuscan was an exception, and this had to compete against Latin since high-minded writers preferred the great literature of the Roman past to that of the Florentine newcomers. In Germany, the standardized literary language grew from Luther's Bible, not from the abundant literature of the two previous centuries. In England, Chaucer had written a century too soon for the press; by the time of Caxton's first printings, Chaucer's language was already old-fashioned and could not serve as a model. The rapidly changing vernaculars of these centuries had not been held back by any literary boulders in their course (apart from Dante's *Commedia*); the faster they flowed, the less chance there was for any literary work to become embedded.

Literary historians survey these centuries with ambiguous feelings, picking out very few great authors from a mass of mediocre writing, often commendable only for its picture of social life. However, the social historian learns less from such vignettes than from the fact that the vernaculars were being steadily appropriated for literature, despite their often pitiful inadequacies. Writing had been a clerkly skill; their own example had persuaded others to take it up. The clerks began by talking about God and his saints for all to understand and thus dignified popular speech by giving it potentially elevated themes. Writing ceased to be a clerkly business and was divorced from its Latin associations. When any spoken language could become a language for literature, this too inevitably lost its formal qualities and become a looser, more colloquial matter. This hardly affected 'poetry', since in both Latin and the vernaculars it required a knowledge of metre and skill in its use. The less sophisticated writers naturally wrote 'prose'.[56] Though this might be improved by study, it was normally practised in a naive manner, by those, like Monsieur Jourdain, who hardly realized what they were doing. At this period, the most artless writers appear, sending letters round the family, intended for purely personal perusal.[57] 'Literature' ceases to be public.

Levels of activity despised as illiberal, or at least taken for granted, were forced on the attention of the learned world by those who insisted on writing about them. The most pathetic illustration of this comes from Bertrand Boisset (1350-1414), a surveyor from southern France, who left elaborate instructions for the preservation of the book he wrote, putting his science into vernacular prose.[58] His immortality has not established his book as a work of literature. His modern editors have been able to demonstrate his literary feebleness. Historically his determination to write betrays the anxiety of the formerly inarticulate to attain to the dignity of 'clerkly' status. It had become a social stigma to be illiterate. Craftsmen were no longer sufficiently proud of their own skills — until they had appropriated those of the clerks too. If these humble pursuits were written about, it also became possible to learn at least something of them from books, so 'education' itself might be useful to craftsmen.[59] Skills formerly learned by practice were expounded by internationally reputed teachers in book form. The earliest work on sword fighting was commissioned by Nicholas III of Este from his master, Fiore dei Liberi, who committed the art to verses about 1410. The text was illustrated to make the correct positions clearer.[60] The oldest surviving treatise on the dance belongs to the next generation and was also written in Italy by Domenico da Piacenza about 1440-50.[61]

Writing and reading — the basic elements of learning as we still think — passed from being a clerical monopoly into the potential grasp of all during this period. No knowledge of other languages was absolutely necessary; a man could express his own thoughts in his native speech and acquire translations of desirable works in other languages. Such a situation had never arisen in Europe before. In the past, all literature had been written in Latin or Greek and all would-be readers of books had had to acquire a 'formal' education in order to be able to read the language of the books, even though these literary languages had not been spoken as such since the fall of the Roman empire in the west. The problem of having several compatible vernacular languages only began to appear in the fifteenth century. In England, for example, while French had been the language of high society, English had been only the language of popular speech with different dialect forms all over the country, no one of which enjoyed preeminence. Once English came to be used officially by the government and the leaders of society in writing as well as in speech, the learning of French became a matter of learning a 'foreign' language, only justified for those who had dealings with 'foreigners' or for those interested in reading 'foreign' literature.[62] As the vernacular languages equipped themselves with translations of the best books, and began to develop literatures of their own, Europe started to crystallize into self-contained language groups, potentially quite independent of one another.[63] As long as the church held Latin Europe together, vernacular literatures could not become dominant in cultural life, and learning foreign languages had only a practical, not an educative, advantage.

The novelty of learning to read and write for persons without any clerical or academic ambitions cannot be recaptured now that literacy is not only universally adopted but taken for a natural human right. Perhaps the position would be understood better by comparing the position of musical notation, for the ability to read and write it is still not thought a universally desirable accomplishment and to this day it is only acquired, as writing once was, by those with special reasons for it, while the musical 'public' is still mainly content to listen, not read, let alone write, as was once the case with literature too.

Music

Just when writing itself became more common, music also settled on its modern form of notation, as though to confirm the impression that by the early fifteenth century, there was an irrepressible urge to find a visual form for aural impression.[64] Musical notation made it possible for composers to put their ideas so accurately and clearly into a visual form that performers could from the evidence of the 'score' alone produce sounds to meet the composer's requirements. This enabled the composer and the performers to develop their particular musical gifts independently of one another. Performers could concentrate their art on interpreting other men's music, while the composer, who had no need to introduce his own work to the public, sheltered behind an ever growing number of skilled performers—for the perfection of notation enabled him to write increasingly complex works. The authors of the period wrote more and more for the individual reading alone; in music, writing made possible the harmonization of many talents.

The 'white' notation which made European concerted music possible for the future was not devised for that purpose. It came as the final stage in a long series of experiments conducted over more than two centuries to find a satisfactory means of noting sounds accurately. While those experiments continued, music itself suffered from the inadequacies of its notation and it is no coincidence that once a reliable system had been devised, the most glorious European music became possible. There is a manifest connection between the noting down of music and successful composition.

In traditional Europe there were two kinds of music-making. Strolling entertainers who supplied music for popular singing and dancing had no use for written music. Performers, vocal or instrumental, improvised freely on familiar airs, picking up ideas where they could. They did not study music, or rehearse it; even playing in concert, they relied on professional competence, like jazz musicians, not written instructions. There was however a second kind of music, a learned tradition linked in classical education with the study of mathematics. This was cultivated by the clergy both as a scholastic discipline and as a liturgical necessity, Liturgical music was based on the ancient modes, and according to tradition, classified by Pope Gregory the Great (590-604). Monks were trained from childhood to sing these chants, which were handed on unchanged; for learning to perform them, they needed a trained ear and a good memory. This music was noted in the form of neumes, which was no more than an *aide-mémoire*. It was suitable for indicating the single melodic line of Gregorian chant and was adapted in the twelfth century for noting secular troubadour songs, also with only one vocal line. Performers of such music had no need to keep an eye on parts sung by others or to sing unfamiliar melodies from the musical notation. The length of the sung notes depended directly on the lengths of the vowels of the texts; the rhythm of the verse determined that of the music. When choral singing became more complicated and moved in parallel fourths and fifths, no more elaborate notation was called for. The need for something better was first demonstrated in the twelfth century, when a new concern for singing at the right pitch led to the use of the four-lined stave, which became standard for plainsong. The manner of indicating pitch by progression on the page from left to right was borrowed from writing itself. The rise of the notes on the stave was also derived from writing, in which the acute accent up showed rise in pitch.

Such indications had not been thought necessary to maintain the old traditions in the past. Their appearance in the twelfth century may be connected with the collapse of the former monastic uniformity and the larger number of 'professed' adults in the monasteries. The revival of learning probably had its part to play. By the middle of the thirteenth century there was considerable confusion about the ways of writing music. It was at this point (*c*.1260) that Franco of Cologne performed a valuable service for his contemporaries by establishing a system of mensural notation to fix note lengths exactly, drawing upon scholastic learning in mathematics. The immediate adoption of Franco's reforms suggests that church musicians had for some time been looking for an adequate scheme of notation. Performers had realized this in singing motets, a new form of composition, in which each voice part *moved* differently according to its melodic lines. These would get irretrievably out of step if the notes of each part were not exactly measured. The voice parts were not written out superimposed as in a modern score, but on different sections of the open book, and only concentrated counting of musical units could have ever kept the voices singing together.

We do not know why musicians began to write such works as motets, nor how the chaotic variety of notation permitted tolerable performance of them before Franco. It seems likely that such a change is connected with the ambitions of the better educated cathedral clergy. They knew some musical theory and had less disciplined routines than monks; they were also interested in experimenting with liturgical means of winning the attentions of the laity, in the enormous new churches then being erected. They tried to write music for several voices at once (polyphony). This stimulated their musical invention but also obliged them to consider how to write each part with mathematical exactness. This obviously also had the effect of establishing much greater regularity in the music and reduced the scope for rhapsodic flexibility. The tenor part constituted the core of the work; the other parts were separately composed to combine with it, but not necessarily with one another; they were still written out as parts, not in score. The parts were admittedly sung simultaneously, but they were never conceived, even by the composer, as a harmony, advancing from bar to bar, as came much later.

Between 1260 and 1420 there were many experiments in polyphonic composition. The black mensural notation then in use made it possible to get choirs to sing extremely complicated parts. The exactitude of the notation allowed composers to explore the possibilities of rhythmical complexity, often to excess. Philip de Vitry was the first theorist to advocate the use of other than perfect (that is triple) time in his *Ars Nova* c.1320. Thereafter the mathematicians' influence on the musicians seems to have stimulated composers to elaborate on rhythmical combinations with more learning than artistry. This reinforces the impression that, as in other spheres of learning at the time, the academics were given their head. Interest in notation itself encouraged experimental composition; it did not grow to meet the need to express musical ideas.

After the schism, when the church was reunited c.1420, these extravagances were abandoned. The English composers of melodic polyphony, like John Dunstable, moved into the Netherlands (that is Valois Burgundy) and there launched a new school by blending their melodic traditions with those of the continent. The best-known composers of the fifteenth century were all from this region—Dufay, Ockeghem, Josquin des Prés and Lassus. With them polyphony embarked on its finest period. At this point too, the two schools of black notation, the French and the Italian, were everywhere rejected in favour of the new white notation, still in use. The perfection of this technique made it possible to drop the old part-book and to write out music for each voice separately (the oldest surviving manuscript of such compositions is the *Glogauer Liederbuch* of *c.*1470). The integrated view of music in score was in fact only brought back into use for instrumental music with music for key-board first published in Rome in 1517 with two staves, and the use of bar lines which revived the vertical look in music. Italian sixteenth-century keyboard and consort music was printed in open score, each part with its own stave from 1577. From the seventeenth century all music was written in this way. Bar-lines established rhythmic regularity, which at last made it possible to dispense entirely with the traditional knowledge of how to read off the white notation according to the correct rhythmical conventions for each piece. The score gave all the necessary information for the musical reader. Only the modern key-signature was missing at this stage.

Music thus took several centuries to complete the process of finding a satisfactory means of indicating how a piece could be performed from written signs without a single sound to help the performer. In itself how-ever it is one of the most stupendous of all human achievements, compar-able in importance to the discovery of alphabets, which, unlike this, was done in a remote past without leaving traces of the process. The most decisive step taken in the fifteenth century coincided in time with the putting of the vernacular languages and the craft secrets into written form.

Never had men's eyes been more essential for their education. In music this result was very obviously brought about by fruitful coopera-tion between performers and academics. Music was forced into a rigorous exactitude in note-lengths, in order to achieve harmony and order out of diverse parts. Composers favoured in the great princely courts of the fifteenth century have left examples of music in which many parts were blended to make a new whole, rather as their masters were attempting at the same time to make a harmony out of their diverse dominions. The harmony and sweetness of music are preferred images in social theories. The music of the fifteenth century which first sounded these notes could be regarded as one of the greatest products of the century. Musicians certainly surpassed the writers in achievements. They were celebrities in their own time and, now that their works are once more being performed and finding favour, their true significance for the history of their own times may be appreciated.

4. ARTISTS

European history appears to be dominated by its professionally educated persons, through whose writings alone do we have the means of under-standing society. Yet the arrival of the printing press itself, though it enabled writers to reach an international audience without delay, emphasizes the new role of craftsmen, who then made themselves indis-pensable to the educated. Writers lost something from their own notoriety. Printing made literacy the norm and 'writers' ceased to be excep-tional. Society gave up believing that its greatest treasure was the wisdom of the past accumulated by the scribes, and learned to esteem the capacity to create and invent. Earlier centuries had not despised those with such talents, but as the finest examples of their skills survive to show — those of the stone-masons — their ideas came to them from men of learning. The dependence of artists on intellectuals ceased with printing. The roles were reversed. Artists devised skills of their own without recourse to the learning of others, combing the books, like Leonardo, in vain, because progress could not come by extracting ancient wisdom from literature (as contemporary intellectuals believed) but by invention and ingenious experiment.[65] On the other hand, writers relied on the printing press to obtain recognition. Artists and craftsmen who commit-ted their discoveries to writing could by the same means diffuse a know-ledge of their works: engravings of their pictures; books of their reflections. Learning a craft itself lost some of its traditional character when appren-tices could also learn from technical books. The artist-craftsman, the technician, man the inventor, has become the principal agent of modern European society. Respected by others for his God-like power of creation, proud of his wisdom, treating with intellectuals and rulers at least as equals, emancipated from routines and conventions, he has been able to impose his own terms and go his own way. How did this come about?

The medieval artist was a craftsman, a skilled man, enrolled in a guild which defended the interests of the whole trade and expected collective solidarity. The term 'artist' was later used only of that artisan whose work had value in its own right, to be judged by other standards than its mere utility. Not all craftsmen achieved this distinction at once. Some arts remained minor and their craftsmen humble, until they disappeared altogether with the invention of machines. Some musicians continued to be treated as mere domestic servants in some German courts until the French Revolution. Only recently have actors emerged as artists from the ranks of entertainers. In Europe potters have not yet received the respect accorded to them in ancient China. The value placed upon any one art or craft matters less for the historical transformation of Europe as a whole, than the complete change brought about in the European attitude towards the idea of what art is, which is detectable by 1500.

The achievements of the creative imagination now seem so obviously important that it is easy to forget what different recognition they once received, and how significant therefore is the moment and the place in which their importance was first conceded. The government and the craftsmen of Florence bear more responsibility for this than any other single element. Florence was never at any time a place of significance for academic study. Its 'studio' was not a success; its university was eventually transferred to Pisa in the fifteenth century, as a sop for its loss of political independence, and to suit students who found Florence too expensive to live in.[66] Ficino's 'Academy' for the intellectual enlightment of well-born Florentines was conducted in the country villa at Careggi given by the Medici. In the fourteenth century, Florence's famous writers counted for little in their city. Dante was driven into permanent exile; Petrarch preferred Venice and Padua; Boccacio was old and sick, before the government gave him a pension to lecture on Dante.

By contrast this great industrial and commercial city knew how to honour its artisans and craftsmen. It is possible that the republican government composed of individuals drawn from the major guilds were aware of how much the city owed economically to men of skill, but their own civic pride had most to do with their patronage. They cared for their city's appearance as much as for its reputation. When Giotto was appointed cathedral architect in 1334, the government declared its belief that the building could not be advanced unless a skilled and distinguished person was found and that in the whole world no one more suitable could be found than Giotto himself.[67] Giovanni Villani, whose patriotic history of Florence was inspired by his Roman visit of 1300, brought the same enthusiasm for his city to his office of supervising the casting of Andrea Pisano's bronze door for the baptistery, 'molto belle e di marvigliosa opera e costo'. Were his eyes opened by his patriotism, his office or his knowledge of Roman art? Villani also mentioned Giotto on account of his post as director of cathedral building, though he is praised as 'il piu sorrano maestro state in dipintura che si trovasse al suo tempo e quegli che piu trasse ogni figura e atti al naturale'.[68]

Perhaps the most enthusiastic early account of painting comes from Siena, where the inauguration of Duccio di Buoninsegna's panel painting *Maestà* was the occasion of public rejoicing in 1310. There is nothing comparable for republican Venice. It is ironic that the earliest surviving description of the beauties of the city should be in a poem written in 1442 by Jacopo d'Albizotto Guidi, a Florentine, who thought, in this Tuscan way, to express his appreciation of the city he had lived in since 1427.[69] A glimpse of the artists' own appreciation of life in a city where their activities received critical appraisal comes out in the story that Donatello returned to Florence after years in Padua because he missed the encouragement and alert comments of his fellow Florentines.[70]

In Florence the civic artist grew into a figure of international consequence. He became an individual sought after far beyond his native city
and set free from his patriotic context, whether he was himself a passionate citizen, like Michelangelo, who spent most of his life in Rome, or
like Leonardo, led off to gilded captivity in France, an artist looking only
for a private patron. How had local pride turned artists into demi-gods?

Even in Florence itself the social inconsequence of most painters is
shown by the fact that, until 1380, they were subordinate members of the
druggists guild, by virtue of their common interest in the chemical products from which pigments were obtained. Raw materials used in painting,
like gold leaf and lapis lazuli were still in the late fourteenth century
more precious than the artists' labour, as in the time of Suger. The
workmen had to be prized above their materials, if their daubs were to be
considered valuable in themselves.

In the late fourteenth century Filippo Villani already numbered some
artists amongst the famous Florentines who were thought to have added
to the glory of the city. A different proof of the limited interest artists
had begun to arouse is provided by the recipe book for successful
painting which Cennino Cennini put into writing. It scarcely ventures to
discuss aesthetic questions. It shows that the techniques of the craft are
considered worthy of being written down, and have therefore escaped
from the artisan category into those of men of learning. The book could
not have given adequate instruction to future painters; apprenticeship
remained indispensable. The book might have been a useful work of
reference in a studio, but it is more likely intended for patrons interested
in the artistic process. This is a sign of the coming change.

Florence was a great industrial and commercial city which honoured
its artisans. Its craftsmen beautified the city and earned the thanks and
admiration of their fellow citizens. It is quite understandable that
craftsmen should first attain to public honour in a city of continuous
activity. Though the most important factor in developing the artistic
traditions was the workshop itself, where new techniques were tried out
and quickly consolidated, the public attitudes in Florence itself also
counted for much.

Public interest in the arts received an additional boost in fifteenth-
century Italy from classical scholars. The earliest of these shared the
attitudes of contemporaries and regarded painting as a mere craft, much
inferior to words in its power to portray. Guarino of Verona thought
writers had greater power to inspire the imagination than painters. An
unfortunate opinion, since his contemporaries amongst the painters are
now better known than he. Guarino, like other literary masters, had no
rapturous welcome prepared for picture-makers.[71] For all that, humanists
assisted in three ways to change men's attitudes to art. First, Italian

humanists revived an interest of earlier Greek writers and described works of art, real or imaginary, to enlarge the scope of writing itself: this made them aware of artefacts as objects worthy of detailed study. Second, as part of their interest in learning how to criticise their own art form, literature, they perfected and made familiar a rhetorical vocabulary, surprisingly indebted to the arts and crafts for technical terms. Significantly writers found that it was from artisans that they had to learn, if they were to rescue writing from the exclusively didactic or frivolous purposes it had been made to serve in the recent past. The humanists had little to say (as the modern neglect of their Latin works proves) but they devoted their best energies to learning how to write well, to enlarging their vocabularies, to structure, and to the problem of combining instruction and pleasure in self-contained works of art. They thought about form, criticism, the public, matters of taste, the relation between subject-matter and art. They deserve credit for making their educated contemporaries aware of the work of art as a creation in its own right. And, as they borrowed terms from craftsmen to dignify their own operations, in turn their use of words came to commend the works of artisans. Third, the educated actually encouraged patrons and artists to study ancient examples, to emulate famous artists of antiquity, to take themes from ancient literature or history, and praised their efforts accordingly. This might have encouraged a slavish imitation, but the effects seem to have been less harmful to artists than they were to humanists themselves. Brunelleschi studied Roman architecture, though he built nothing strictly modelled on ancient examples. Donatello collected antique sculpture, though no work of his could be taken now for an 'imitation'. Mercifully there were then no known paintings from the ancient world to tempt 'revivers' of the art and it is probably not fortuitous that it was the painters who took the most decisive steps forward in the fifteenth century: they could not be haunted by classical precedents. The painters nevertheless also deferred to educated taste. They put grandiose architectural settings into their scenes. Mantegna painted men of antiquity in appropriate styles of dress. The scholars by proposing the illustration of ancient myths or philosophies and by praising artists and their work, as Pliny had done, stimulated the painters to greater efforts and patrons to enlightened benevolence. By 1500, the works of painters and sculptors had become potential collectors' pieces. Painters had to be coaxed into doing patrons the favour of carrying out commissions and were in such demand that they could be as capricious as they chose.

Enlightened patronage would in itself have still been insufficient to establish the idea of art. The artists themselves had to imitate the humanists and elaborate the learned aspects of their work. In this way they acquired a confidence in their own intellectual achievements. This is conspicuous in the Florentine school, which laid the foundations for the new aesthetic. The Florentine manner depended upon its own kind of learning. To be an 'artist' involved more than acquiring the techniques of the workshop. It meant reading books, understanding geometry, mastering the secrets of nature and learning how to draw from life. The extensive study of these aspects of his art in Leonardo is a matter of common knowledge, but he followed some important precedents. Artists long before him had expressed their intellectual self-confidence by writing about their subject. Alberti was the famous artist-writer of the first half of the fifteenth century. Ghiberti's *Commentaries* and Piero della Francesca's treatise on perspective are less well known, because they are less stylishly written.[72] Historically they are the more significant, for showing how determined masters of a craft were to write about it. A century later, Giorgio Vasari's *Lives of the Painters* (1550) completed this process of publicizing art in words. Here the history of the Renaissance is presented as the work of the artists, an interpretation which has ever since put the scholastic achievements of the humanists in the shade. This work itself, more perhaps than the artistic productions of the painters, convinced the educated public that painters were greater than writers. This history is built up from a collection of many individual lives, with accounts of their works, beginning in thirteenth-century Tuscany. Vasari only becomes authoritative for the painters of the fifteenth century, when they emerged from the obscurity of the workshops. Vasari's history consecrated the view that the artist was the supremely creative individual.

The first great genius of the fifteenth century was Filippo Brunelleschi, a member of an ancient and distinguished family resident in Florence, who naturally took his turn in the political offices, as was his right, as a member of the goldsmiths' guild, one of the richest and of most consequence.[73] To these advantages of family and position he added an originality and inventiveness of mind. He made his first appearance as a contender in the competition for the doors of the Baptistery, but his dramatic design was turned down by the city committee, which awarded the prize to Ghiberti. He too was a goldsmith. His reflections on art give some idea of how the Florentine attitude to art might have developed, had Ghiberti, rather than Brunelleschi, dominated fifteenth-century Florence. Ghiberti was the accomplished craftsman, proud of his traditions, but generous too in praise of fellow-craftsmen across the Alps. He was not indifferent to book learning. He advocated a type of encyclopaedic education for all competent artists, such as Dürer himself might have received. This kind of technical competence was no substitute for what Brunelleschi supplied: the basis of a new theory of art, as a means of real knowledge.

Brunelleschi's fame followed from his work on the dome of the cathedral, still the most remarkable feature of the city's skyline. In doing this he studied the buildings of ancient Rome and cultivated a personal interest in mathematics to help him. As an architect he had no apprenticeship and he acquired no masons' secrets. He was the man who relied on his own learning. He not only mastered the geometry and mechanics necessary, constructing models and devices to assist his planning. He went on to formulate his findings in such a way that his contemporaries could use them. Before his death, his ideas about perspective drawing had been written up and published by Alberti and their value for painting had been demonstrated by the young Masaccio in the Brancacci chapel in Florence. Brunelleschi was also closely associated with the sculptor Donatello, taking him to Rome, where they both collected statues, and indulging in friendly rivalry with him. The three major 'arts' of fifteenth-century Italy all owed something to this patrician goldsmith. The old separation of crafts by guilds was abandoned. A different conception about art encouraged great masters of one to take up another. The painters of the century received commissions to build and Michelangelo, naturally a sculptor, left major works in all three forms.

To succeed as an artist required much more application to 'learning' than hitherto. Painters opened their minds to all forms of human knowledge with a bearing on their activities. They had more to do than copy their pattern-books and apply their pigments. They had to create a new learning of their own. The art of projecting spatial illusion involved a real and practical knowledge of geometry, such as only architects amongst 'artists' had previously required. After Brunelleschi, this became required knowledge for painters. After geometry, they laboured most at the difficult skill of drawing from the life, particularly of the human body, for this remained the principal element in all their works. They were free to devise their own groupings of figures and there was no human pose, position or stance that might not be of service. Artists brought models into the workshops and made their own studies under direction. Drawing was for these painters and their successors the basic technique of their art, equivalent in significance to the mastery of Latin vocabulary and the writing of Latin prose in imitation of Cicero for humanists. The training of the eye and the hand gave the artist a professional competence and knowledge of the possibilities of his art far beyond the imagination of earlier craftsmen, and more obviously admirable to us than the exercises of scholars. The enthusiasm of Vasari leaves us in no doubt that he was convinced a new kind of learning had been created. Painters offered a 'knowledge' of the world never before suspected.[74]

Renaissance painting did not set out to play on the observer's emotions.

The artist by the technique of perspective drawing placed himself at a given distance from his subject and projected what he saw in proper proportion. The observer standing before the work sees what the artist saw. The artist has conveyed his vision, not his feelings. The essence of the new art was to give the illusion of observing real space, because all the objects of the painting are mutually related as the eye sees them. From the first there was also a tendency towards indicating the temporal element as well. In Brunelleschi's design for the Baptistery door, he showed Abraham on the point of sacrificing Isaac when the angel stayed his hand: the dramatic moment caught by art. The observer could not miss the intensity of the moment, but the artist's skill was shown by not exaggerating the tension for effect. The new art was restrained. There was moreover no element of chance involved, such as would be achieved with a box-camera. The artist composed his scene, the poses were contrived and presented with formal grace. The artist does not see as the casual man might see; he is privileged to see as his art teaches him and the spectator is in his turn privileged to stand before the painting in the artist's moment of truth. So men stood before Michelangelo's 'Last Judgment' in the Sistine Chapel, as Christ lifted his arm to declare judgment.

The patrons of Renaissance painting were however brought up to be learned in ancient literature and to read it with the desire to find its hidden truths.[75] They were not interested in the everyday world and they expected painters also to depict scenes with meanings to be discovered by careful observation. They did not casually glance through the window of the frame at some commonplace occurrence. Paintings were still for reading and meditation. No spectator of the most sensual of all Italian paintings, 'The Venetians', can rest satisfied with the mere superficial beauty of the paint as it strikes the retina. The paintings of Titian pose questions, because it was expected that observers would bring with them their culture and knowledge, not untrained eyes. Pictures had to be interpreted. This may be tiresome for us, since it now requires some knowledge of the literature and symbolism of the period, if such famous pictures as Botticelli's 'Venus' or 'Spring' are not to elude our understanding. Some painters went further in teasing their contemporaries by making esoteric allusions in their works. It was a form of wit that flattered their patrons. If painting was a form of knowledge why should it not naturally provoke as much thought and discussion as literature? Paintings therefore existed on several different levels, proposing pleasure, instruction and meditation. They had to cohere initially as works of art, compositions with their own formal perfections, visually complete; but it was all to the good, if the picture conveyed more to connoisseurs.

If the image is not merely to be seen, but to be interpreted and understood, it is not surprising that painters and sculptors used the unclothed human body as the most eloquent source of the purest and most abstract ideas, for it was universally understood that there was no prurient revelling in nudity for its own sake, until the 1540s when critics of Michelangelo's 'Last Judgment' campaigned for the painting in of decent draperies. The mood had changed. The naked Christ no longer seemed to them like the New Adam clothed as God intended, but undignified and unrespected. They no longer read the painting, and saw only a naked man. It was the end of an epoch. The painters themselves had succeeded in creating illusions; the result was that ignorant men thought looking was enough. Charles v's sculptor, Leoni, could still portray the emperor in the nude to represent him as Virtue, the new-born Adam Novissimus, but he covered him with a decent suit of armour, and the statue is now normally exhibited in that form.

Michelangelo himself had advanced the art of expressing the ideal through the naked male body to a point where the expression he sought proved unattainable. The projects begun and not completed, the figures that he left just breaking out of the block, completely realized but at one with the marble itself, sum up the sublimity and the finiteness of the whole movement. The world of the spirit could not be more fully embodied: the human imagination could not totally vanquish the resistance of the material. The vulgar belief that the rise of the painter produced a pagan art, portraying naked flesh and depicting Renaissance debauchery is so gross a distortion of the truth that it can only arise from the most wilful perversity.

5. CONCLUSION

Contemporary reflections on the experience of recent generations in Europe generally concluded that a long chapter of misfortunes was closed and that a new age of promise had dawned. In England, France and Spain new dynasties encouraged a sense of looking forward. In Italy this hopeful strain ran through a variety of experiences, and, though it proved to be deceptive politically, there was no nostalgia for the recent past. In Italy, and then all over Europe, there was a conscious attempt to revive more ancient glories with a corresponding tendency to despise the intermediate years—the middle ages—for their barbarism and their futility. Of the great writers of the sixteenth century only Shakespeare, reviewing the history of the English monarchy from Richard II to Richard III, came close to showing what the history of those years could teach: the good sense of submission to the established political authorities, if civil turmoil and wasted human effort were to be avoided and if the peaceful arts of mankind were to flourish.[76]

It may therefore seem presumptuous to suppose that there are lessons to be learned from these four centuries of European history. Lessons were certainly not consigned to contemporary historical books to be imbibed as such. But men do learn by experience. They eventually calculate the full cost of repeating the same mistakes. The English at last learned that invading France, once so easy and so obvious, would not again be the means of triumph and riches. Churchmen learned that there are limits to what discussions of reform can accomplish in civil or ecclesiastical business and that differences of opinion, aired at first politely, may lead to violence if pressed home uncompromisingly. Experience also teaches what are the irreducible constants of a given situation. In dealing with the Turks and the Greeks, it became clear that enthusiasm or papal initiative were inadequate to dislodge a great military power acceptable to local interests. These lessons were not learned from books — but experience made men sadder and wiser. They gave up their simple idealism and learned to concentrate upon more limited and rewarding tasks.

The creation of large political states released many Europeans from the obligations of self-government and self-defence, as known to feudal and communal politics. Rulers had never previously been allowed to manage affairs with so little restraint or advice. Representative institutions, such as they were, took no continuous part in government; consulted only on occasions, they fossilized. A few favourites and aristocrats took on the responsibilities of government, while the others, reassured as to their privileges, acquiesced in a life of ease and refinement. Clashes between great states enlarged the scale of wars, but such wars, fought on frontiers, or in other lands, by professionals, came to be regarded as exceptional and so undesirable that 'civilians' paid to keep war out of sight. Europe as a whole passed out of that long phase of its history in which it was taken for granted that a freeman would be regularly engaged in defending his own life and property with the sword.

The princes, whose affairs tend to predominate in historical accounts, had no easy task in maintaining a stable social order. Given the difficulties, they succeeded remarkably well. They protected the privileged, the nobles, the churches and the towns, which thankfully repaid them with adulation. The princes eventually discovered how to promote as well as protect prosperity. Wealth was still unevenly distributed. As ever, many subsisted in poverty. But, as a community, Europe no longer lived in dread of famine or imminent destruction. Only the plague remained of nature's scourges to chasten proud spirits. The majority were not anxious about how to stay alive and were delivered from the problems of self-defence. For a rare period, society existed in such a way as to allow ordinary men to enjoy themselves, as may be seen in the rumbustious scenes of Brueghel. The management of affairs was left to specialist politicians; the rest could pursue their own natural interests. What were they?

For the most part individuals steered clear of both political and religious non-conformity. It was taken for granted that these great communities of peaceable subjects could only endure by remaining loyal to their lord and accepting the moral sanctions of one religion. Some individuals took their religion very personally. Hus at Constance and Joan of Arc at Rouen persisted in believing in their own righteousness in spite of authority, reason and torture, but only exceptional individuals risked their lives for religion, even in the sixteenth century. In a pious country like England, religion obviously remained a predominantly social, not a private matter, to be decided for all by the government. Indifferent to political and ecclesiastical liberty, therefore, most individuals could only use their civil freedom in their own acts of imagination. Whatever the rhetorical conventions of history books may suggest to the contrary, the history of Europe since 1450 has been dominated, not by politicians, but by inventive individuals.

Craftsmen had over the previous two or three centuries steadily extended the capacity of their fellow men to live with their environment. They contributed to improving agriculture as well as mining, building, engineering and cloth-manufacture. They were always trying to invent new machines or adapt them for more uses. Clockwork seemed to have boundless possibilities. The more they invented, the more specialist skills emerged as distinct crafts, and expertise inspired more refinements. This division of labour could only have been viable in a society with a market large enough to absorb their products and services. This market was larger than Christendom itself, since the merchants and bankers who served as middle-men carried trade to the limits of the known world, and brought back materials from lands they had never seen. A market economy on this scale took for granted not merely the use of money and the fact that every object had its price, but the existence of discriminating buyers who would recognize craftsmanship and pay its price. The development of craft skills reflects the organization of their whole society: it was not merely a matter of exceptional genius. A commercial society with discerning patrons stimulated craftsmen to excel and rewarded their talents. The purchaser no less than the artist was able in such a world to demonstrate his individuality as a man of taste.

Civil society and the law of property encouraged men over the generations to accumulate possessions which would pass to their direct descendants and perpetuate the *fama* of their name. They might have piled up their riches indiscriminately; instead they learned to 'create': they built, furnished, beautified and collected not just for themselves, but for their posterity. The patrons relied on craftsmen of all kinds to labour on their behalf and appreciated the deployment of their skills for an increasingly diverse number of purposes. About 1500 the scale of operations was still at a very domestic level. The Borgia apartments in the Vatican, decorated by Raphael, were still comparatively modest in size. The style of courtly life, as caught in Castiglione's *Courtier* is intimate, good-humoured and friendly. The pomp, ceremony and boredom came later. Commissions to poets and painters were arranged as between equals. The Emperor Charles V did not disdain to visit Titian in his studio and the truculence of Michelangelo with successive popes is well-known. Though painters continued to provide great frescoes for churches and palaces, as in the past, the distinctive feature of Renaissance art is the easel picture, eagerly acquired by an appreciative collector from a famous individual painter. Each one was a distinct unit to be moved about the house, taking on fresh significance in each new position and always a personally prized possession of the owner: a portrait or a religious work including his own likeness, a landscape, or other work containing personal allusions or fulfilling personal instructions.

The painters were particularly esteemed as artists, but all other craftsmen in their different ways opened up new areas of human sensibility, and not only for great men. Their professional skill enabled them to transform the raw material into a finished and marketable object: furniture, pottery, metalwork and jewellery. The craftsmen displayed not only practical skill but, even more important, aesthetic sensitivity, sense of form and good taste. And their creations in turn set standards and forced up expectations. Scattered through the museums of Europe they may now be appreciated mainly as objects of aesthetic pleasure; assembled in the mind's eye by historians they are pointers to the way international standards were established by persons who have left no other memorial. Flattered and cajoled by patrons, the craftsmen were nonetheless their own masters, and not always obliging. They worked for themselves and not necessarily to get the most money. Their dependence on a commercial society has come to seem iniquitous in a philistine age. At the time craftsmen accepted this as natural: they themselves were socially derived from the old tradesmen and held no snobbish views about the rewards due to art. They welcomed their new freedom to create on their own account: men made in the image of the Creator.

Likewise, some of their contemporaries, of obscure birth, explored the new world and the orient, opening up splendid opportunities to other adventurers. The European settlement overseas, though carried out in the name of princes, was not the consequence of government initiative, but the ruthless exploitation of the technical resources of society by extraordinary, ambitious, unscrupulous, reckless, disappointed and sometimes idealistic individuals. Such men abandoned their stable continent for doubtful Eldorados elsewhere whereas those who stayed at home to enjoy domestic peace found their adventures in exploring the possibilities they found within themselves.

The individuals with initiative in Europe who transformed the continent in the sixteenth century were usually loners, without the responsibilities of office. The great religious reformers, Erasmus, Luther and Calvin were not men with existing responsibilities: their own ideas led them on. Even more striking are the great writers, like Rabelais, Montaigne, Shakespeare or Cervantes, whose influence on millions has perhaps outlasted that of the reformers, since they gave their vernacular languages an unprecedented and unsurpassed capacity to express the thoughts of individuals. The languages of speech became vehicles of literature. How did such writers acquire a public? They relied on publication and it was the commercial world that gave them a following.

The written word would not have become influential had the printing press not multiplied copies so that books could pass into the personal possession of the educated. While paintings were priceless and inimitable, books were mass produced. In the long run they had a more profound effect on men's general ideas. The book made possible a new style of writing and of communication. Authors no longer wrote for captive audiences of students; nor to flatter and amuse courtiers. They could not even envisage who their readers would be. They wrote for anyone or everyone, for themselves above all. They did not strive to stir up public opinion. The response of readers remained private, even secretive. They accumulated libraries and allowed themselves to think while they read. The schools were no longer in a position to determine the pattern of culture. The most passive subjects were equipped by books to become silent critics and nervous authorities were aware of the dangers from the free circulation of literature, but, once they had lost their power to monopolize information, their only defence against books as sources of alternative wisdom was the clumsy attempt to suppress them.

By their very existence books delivered the literate from the tyranny of ignorance, however powerful; they did not need to be subversive to be revolutionary and they could not be burnt and forgotten. Looking back, it is surely significant that Europeans invented the means to reproduce books for mass-consumption before they harnessed steam-power in basic industries. Printing had no means of transforming the social order, which in many ways continued as before: most men still worked on the land, travelled no faster than horse or sail could carry them, practised the same religion and survived the same politics as their neighbours. But books and reading enabled more of them to escape from the limitations of time and place in order to find a new life of their own in the imagination.

The virtues of this society become more obvious as they become more difficult to realize in present circumstances. Men's confidence in their creative powers eventually prompted them to think that they might remake society, and themselves too, with the industrial resources and wealth they had got. Europeans disowned the idea of a ruling 'class' and declared that politics was a matter of general concern, so 'democracy' has added the burdens of citizenship to every other. Yet men are less well-equipped for it now than they were in the twelfth century, when they fought for themselves and regulated their own local affairs. The purpose of this book has been to show under what circumstances, in other centuries, Europe created out of many local, traditional communities, a single society, superficially divided amongst quarrelsome princes, but fundamentally united for the purpose of enabling creative individuals to realize their potential for the common good.

NOTES

No attempt has been made to annotate every statement in this book; still less to provide a bibliography of sources and secondary literature. The notes that follow aim in the first place to identify the source of documents discussed or alluded to, particularly for the continent (on the assumption that the English material may be more familiar, or more easily traced in other books). Second, there are occasional discussions of points that seem interesting in their own right, but unsuitable for the text itself. Third, there are references to the secondary literature, particularly in English, which is either easily consulted, or the most convenient place to start further reading: they are not intended to be a systematic guide to what is available.

ABBREVIATIONS USED IN NOTES

A.A.S.S.	Acta Sanctorum
A.S.I.	Archivio Storico Italiano
B.E.C.	Bibliothèque de l'école des Chartes
B.E.H.E.	Bibliothèque de l'école des hautes études
B.N.	Bibliothèque Nationale
E.E.T.S.	Early English Text Society
E.H.R.	English Historical Review
H.Z.	Historische Zeitschrift
M.G.H.	Monumenta Germaniae Historica
M.S.A.N.	Mémoires de la Société des Antiquaires de Normandie
P.L.	Patrologia Latina
R.H.D.F.E.	Revue historique du droit français et étranger
R.I.S.	Rerum Italicarum Scriptores
R.S.	Rolls Series
S.H.F.	Société de l'histoire de France
S.H.N.	Société de l'histoire de Normandie
T.R.H.S.	Transactions of the Royal Historical Society

Chapter 1 *Surveying the Field*

1. A fifteenth-century Lombard breviary has an illustration to St Augustine's Sermon LXXV showing the ship of the church, filled with saints; the dove of the Holy Ghost is at the prow, the Father at the helm, and Christ hangs from the mast. Pierpont Morgan Library, Ms. 58 f. 234 v. M. Harrsen and G. K. Boyce *Italian Manuscripts in the Pierpont Morgan Library,* New York 1953, Plate 45, figure 1.

2. Paris B.N. Ms. Lat. 8878 f. 45. The map appears in the copy of the Commentary on the Apocalypse of Beatus of Liébana (*c.*776) commissioned by Abbot Gregory de Muntaner of St Sever (Aquitaine), 1028-72. The map was designed originally to show the spread of Christianity. Although the St Sever version is not the oldest one to survive, it is said to be closest to the original. The material is drawn from the Bible, Isidore of Seville and a Roman provinces' map, like the Peutinger table. C. R. Beazley *The Dawn of Modern Geography* II, 1904, pp. 549-559. M.A.P. d'Avezac Macaya *La mappemonde du VIIIe siècle de saint Béat de Liébana,* Paris 1870.

3. A. Långfors *De miraculis quae in ecclesia Fiscannensi contingerunt,* Annales Academiae Scientiarum Fennice, series B XXV (1), Helsinki, 1930, story 21. A monk *eiusdem linguae peritus Angliae* was needed to intercede with Flemish pirates. Men did not take national pride in their spoken and often unwritten languages; they regarded language as a matter of communication and used whatever was locally convenient. Later, in the commercial town of Bayonne, the civic register, compiled in 1336, included documents written in four different languages: Gascon, Latin, French and Spanish: *Le Livre des Etablissements de Bayonne,* 1892. Medieval society was everywhere polyglot, for the clergy used Latin, the aristocracy was familiar with some courtly lingua franca, often French, and the majority spoke only patois.

4. M. Gouron *L'amirat de Guienne,* 1938, p. 47, estimated that about a thousand ships laden with wine left for England annually. More recently see J. Bernard *Navires et Gens de mer à Bordeaux,* Paris 1968.

5. Der sogennanten Rufus chronik zweiter teil *Die Chroniken der Deutschen Städte,* Vol. 28, Leipzig, 1902, p. 129. J. G. Eccardus *Corpus Historiarum Medii Aevi,* Leipzig 1723, t.II, *c.* 1237-8, says that the king of Castile seized 48 merchant ships.

6. F. Sohr *Le Droit Maritime et son Unification Internationale,* Brussels 1914; J. Pardessus *Us et Coutumes de la Mer,* Paris 1847.

7. P. Döllinger *La Hanse xiie-xviie siècles,* Paris 1964 (English translation, 1970); A. von Brandt 'Recent Trends in Research in Hanseatic History', *History,* 1956, pp. 25-37. H. Sproemberg 'Die Hanse in Europäischen Sicht', *Annales de la Société Royale d'Archéologie de Bruxelles, Mémoires,* t.50, 1956-66, pp. 211-224. J. A. Gade *Hanseatic Norway,* 1951, showed how dependent Norway became on Hanse supplies of grain, and that in the late fourteenth century the Danes gave up their own coinage and used Lübeck's.

8. The Annals of Lübeck *(M.G.H. Scriptores* XVI ed. I. M. Lappenberg pp. 411-29) give some indication of the geographical range of interests in the town from the information about the world thought worth recording there, 1264-1324.

9. R de. Roover *Money Banking and Credit in Medieval Bruges,* Cambridge, Mass., 1948. The Itinéraire Brugeois showed the citizens of Bruges how far it was to all parts of the world from their city. The different routes indicate that travellers could

expect to reach Moscow, Cracow, Nuremberg, Ceuta, Algiers, Tlemcen, Oran, Tunis, Jerusalem and Constantinople as well as Iceland and Greenland. J. Lelewel *Géographic du Moyen Age* Brussels, Epilogue, 1857. pp. 281-308.

10. D. Nicholas *Town and Countryside: social economic and political tensions in fourteenth-century Flanders,* Ghent 1971.

11. *Documents Historiques Inédits des collections manuscrites de la Bibliothèque Royale,* ed. Champollion Figeac II, 1843, pp. 71-121, five treaties of peace and commerce. C. E. Dufourcq *L'Espagne catalane et Le Maghreb,* Paris 1966. C. Carrère *Barcelone centre économique 1380-1462,* Paris, 1967.

12. G. Ostrogorsky *Pour l'histoire de la Féodalité Byzantine,* Brussels, 1954. P. Lemerle, Esquisse pour une histoire agraire de Byzance *Revue Historique* 219, 1958, pp. 32-74, 254-284, *ibid.* 220, 43-94.

13. H. E. Lurier *Crusaders as Conquerors; the chronicle of the Morea,* N.Y. 1964.

14. G. Ostrogorsky 'Problèmes des relations byzantines-serbes au xiv siècle', *Proceedings of the XIIth International Congress of Byzantine Studies,* Oxford 1967, pp. 41-55.

15. M. Komroff *Contemporaries of Marco Polo,* London 1928, gives translations of the accounts of their journeys made by Giovanni de Plano Carpini and Guillaume de Rubruc. The texts are edited by A. van den Wyngaert *Sinica Franciscana* I, Quaracchi 1929.

16. *Recueil des Historiens des Croisades, Documents Arméniens,* t. II, pp. 367-517, Brocard, Directorium ad passagium faciendum.

17. M. Andrusiak 'Kings of Kiev and Galicia', *Slavonic and East European Review,* 1955, no. 33, pp. 342-50. M. B. Zdan 'The dependence of Halych—Volyn Rus on the Golden Horde', *ibid.* 1957, no. 35, pp. 505-23.

18. *Revue de l'Orient Latin,* t.III 'Le Pélerinage du moine augustin Jacques de Vérone', pp. 155-302. His account of Cairo is on pp. 239-40. Philippe de Mézières *Le Songe du Vieil Pelerin,* ed. G. W. Coopland, Cambridge 1969, p. 231, claims that visitors had not seen a badly dressed person in Cairo and no sick persons, since the hospitals were all open and full, with well cared for patients. There is also the account of Lionardo di Niccolo Frescobaldi 'Viaggio in Egitto e in Terra Sancta, 1384' in *Studium Biblicum Franciscanum* no. 6, 1948, pp. 29-90. There is a translation by T. Bellerini and E. Hoade.

19. J. Palmer 'The Origins of the Janissaries', *Bulletin of the John Rylands Library,* 35, 1953, pp. 448-81.

20. O. Lütfü 'Les problèmes fonciers dans l'empire ottoman au temps de sa fondation', *Annales d'histoire sociale* I, 1939, pp. 233-7.

21. B. De la Brocquière *Le Voyage d'Outremer,* ed. C. Schefer, Paris 1892; translation by T. Wright, London 1848.

22. *Recueil des Historiens des Croisades: Arméniens,* t. II, 'Chronique d'Arménie' by Jean Dardel, pp. 1-109.

23. M. F. Hendy 'Byzantium 1081-1204: an economic reappraisal', *T.R.H.S.,* 1970, pp. 31-52.

24. Fidentius of Padua 'Liber recuperationis terrae sanctae', ed. G. Golubovitch, *Biblioteca biobibliografica della terra sancta e dell'oriente francescano,* t. II, pp. 1-60, Quaracchi 1913.

Chapter 2 *Setting the Historical Records in their Context*

1. For examples of medieval jokes still current, see G. Legman *Rationale of the Dirty Joke,* first series, London 1969: Premarital Acts (iii), policeman and priests, and *passim.* B. Castiglione *The book of the Courtier,* translated by Sir T. Hoby (Dent, Everyman, London 1948) reviews the kinds of jesting practised in early sixteenth-century Italy and advocates the cultivation of wit (pp. 134-79) to replace the cruder humour of some contemporary courtiers (pp. 127-8). For an example of burlesque, see the charter of Alfonso V of Aragon (1446) allowing his dwarf to drink without stint. J. L. Villanueva *Viaje Literario* XVII, 1851, pp. 304-5. The educated clergy were naturally prone to mock in their lighter moments. Their fooleries, as over boy bishops and other such ceremonies, were condemned in more serious times. P. Lehmann *Die Parodie im Mittelalter,* 2nd ed., Stuttgart 1963.

2. Einhardi *Vita Caroli,* ed. P. Jaffe, Lib. III, cap. 25.

3. H. Tegnaeus *Blood-Brothers;* Stockholm 1952.

4. One of the most detailed accounts of a medieval brawl, in which a young man who stepped in to help keep the peace was struck a mortal blow, occurs in the *Registre de l'Officialité de Cérisy. 1314-1457,* ed. M. G. Dupont M.S.A.N., série III, vol. X, 1855 nos. 308-9. About twenty different witnesses gave evidence. For the social background to the problem of violence see T. A. Green 'Societal Concepts of Criminal Liability for Homicide in Medieval England', *Speculum,* 1972, pp. 669-94.

5. H. Buchtal *Historia Troiana,* London 1971, p. 12.

6. 'Le Livres des faicts du Mareschal de Boucicault' in C. B. Petitot *Collection Complètes de Mémoires relatifs à l'histoire de France 1825* vol. VI, chapter VII pp. 390-2, where his exercises as well as his strength are commended. The deeds of other fourteenth-century heroes inspired several biographies in the courtly style: Chandos Herald *Life of the Black Prince,* ed. M. K. Pope, Oxford 1910, and Jean Cuvelier *Chronique de Bertrand Du Guesclin.* ed. E. Chassière, Paris 1839.

7. J. Sottas *Les messageries maritimes de Venise aux XIVe et XVe siècles;* Paris, 1938: chapter VIII 'Traversée', pp. 163-183, using the accounts of Fr Felix Fabri (1484), ed. C. Hassler, Stuttgart 1843-9, and Bernardus de Breydenbath *Peregrinationes,* printed in Mainz 1486.

8. B. Castiglione *op cit.* p. 91.

9. R. W. Southern *St Anselm and his biographer,* Cambridge 1963, pp. 70, 72-6.

10. Walter Daniel *Life of Ailred of Rievaulx,* ed. F. M. Powicke. Edinburgh 1950.

11. *Materials for the Life of Thomas Becket: Letters.* ed. J. C. Robertson, R.S., London, 1881-5, letter DCLX XV.

12. *Chronique du Religieux de St Denis.* ed. L. Bellaguet, Paris 1841, vol. III, liv. xxvi, cap. 21, p. 345, and note. cp. *La chronique d'Enguerrand de Monstrelet.* ed. L. Douet d'Arcq, Paris, 1857, *S.H.F.* tome I, pp. 124-5, 156, tome II p. 294.

13. P. Meyer, ed. 'Manière de Langage', *Revue Critique d'Histoire et de Littérature.* 1870, vol. 2. pp. 402-3. Thomas Hemerken a Kempis describes how he shared a room at the Deventer house with Arnold von Schooven, 1398-99: 'simul una camerula unoque lecto ambo contenti', *Dialogus noviciorum libri Quattuor* ed. M. J. Pohl, VII, 1922, pp. 318-9.

14. P. Guiraud *Le Jargon de Villon. ou le gai savoir de la Coquille.* Paris 1968.

15. Bernard of Clairvaux 'De Laude Novae Militiae', cap. II 'de militia saeculari', *P.L..* 182, p. 923.

16. Orderic Vitalis *Historia Ecclesiastica,* ed. A. Le Prérost, Paris t. IV, 1852, pp. 207-9.

17. *Les Grandes Chroniques de France,* ed. J. Viard, *S.H.F.* 1937, t. IX. The monk describes the short robes which showed men's backsides when they bent down 'et ce qui estoit dedenz'... They were so tight that 'leur failloit aide à eulx vestir et au despoiller et sambloit que l'en les escorchait quant l'en les despoilloit. Et les autres avoient leurs robes fronciées sur les rains comme femmes;...et sembloient miex jugleurs que autres gens. Et pour ce ce ne fu pas merveilles si Dieu volt corriger les excès des Francais par son flael le roy d'Engleterre', 1346.

18. William of Malmesbury *De Gestis Regum Anglorum.* ed. W. S. Stubbs R.S. vol. II, 1889, p. 302.

19. 'Gundissalinus De divisione philosophiae', *Beiträge zur Geschichte der Philosophie und Theologie des Mittelalters;* Band IV, 1906, pp. 101-2. 'In proeliis quoque tuba concentus pugnantes accendit et quanto vehemencior fuerit clangor tanto fit ad certamen animus forcior; siquidem et remiges cantu hortantur ad tollerandos quosque labores'.

20. A convenient survey is made by H. Bresslau *Handbuch der Urkundenlehre für Deutschland und Italien,* second edition, Leipzig 1912-31, chapters 4 and 5.

21. *Liber Censuum de l'église romaine,* ed. P. Fabre and L. Duchesne, Bibliothèque des Ecoles Françaises d'Athènes et de Rome, série II no. 6., 1910.

22. G. Leibnitz *Scriptores Rerum Brunswicensia illustrantium,* t. II, pp. 695-8.

23. C. Singer 'The Herbal in Antiquity and its transmission to later ages', *Journal of Hellenic Studies* XLVII, 1927, pp. 1-52. *ibid.* 'Early English Magic and Medicine', *Proceedings of the British Academy* 1919-20, pp. 341-74.

24. *The Bestiary,* Cambridge University Library Ms., I, i 4, 26, ed. M. R. James (Roxburghe Club), 1928, transl. T. H. White, London 1954. Better information about local animals is recorded in the later works of lay sportsmen like Frederick II *(De arte venandi cum avibus* ed. C. A. Willemsen, Leipzig, 1942, transl. C. A. Wood and F. M. Fyfe, Stanford 1943) and Gaston III Phoebus Count of Foix *(Livre de la Chasse* ed. P. Lacroix and E. Jullien, Paris 1880; translated into English by Edward of Norwich, Duke of York (1373-1415) as 'Master of Game', ed. A. W. and E. Baillie, Grohman, London 1904).

25. Adelard of Bath *Quaestiones Naturales,* ed. M. Müller, Beiträge, Bd XXXI, heft 2, Münster 1934. For Gerald of Cremona see B. Boncompagni *Della vita e delle opere di Gherardo Cremonese traduttore del secolo duodecimo,* Rome 1851.

26. L. Thorndike *A History of Magic and Experimental Science,* New York 1923-58; *ibid.* Michael Scot, London 1963.

27. C. Singer, ed. *Studies in the history and method of science,* London 1917, pp. 79-106, 'A study in early renaissance anatomy'. H. P. Cholmeley *John of Gaddesden and the Rosa Medicinae,* Oxford 1912. Sir D'Arcy Power *Selected Writings 1877-1930,* Oxford 1931, pp. 29-47, 'English Medicine and Surgery in the fourteenth century'. The renewed interest in medicine clearly began in the late thirteenth century. As for astronomical knowledge, this only began to improve after the

'Alphonsine' star-tables (*c.* 1272) reached Paris (*c.* 1292) and were translated by John of Saxony into Latin (1327): G. Sarton *Introduction to the History of Science,* vol. II, 1931, pp. 837-8, and vol. III, 1947, p. 118.

28. R. Lopez 'Pisan Merchant Manual' in *Economy Society and Government in Medieval Italy,* essays in memory of R. L. Reynolds, 1969.

29. P. Doncoeur *La minute française des interrogatoires de Jeanne la Pucelle,* Melun, 1952. H. Denifle and E. Chatelain 'Le procès de Jeanne d'Arc et l'Université de Paris', *Mémoires de la Société de l'histoire de Paris,* t. XXIV, 1897, pp. 1-32.

30. 'Haec donatio facta est per unum cultellum quem praefatus rex ioculariter dans abbati quasi eius palmae minatur infigere; "ita", inquit, "terra donari debet".' *Regesta Anglo-Normannorum Regum,* vol. I, ed. H. W. C. Davis, Oxford 1913, no. 29.

31. Hugh of St Victor *The Didascalicon,* transl. J. Taylor, New York 1961, Book VI, chap. 3.

32. Otto of Freising *Chronicon sive Historia de Duabus Civitatibus,* ed. A. Hofmeister, Hannover, 1912, transl. C. C. Mierow *The Two Cities: a chronicle of universal history,* New York, 1928. R. Petry 'Monastic Historiography and Eschatology', *Church History* 1965, pp. 282-93.

33. *Gesta Friderici I Imperatoris,* ed. G. Waitz, Hannover 1912, Lib. I, chap. 47. transl. C. C. Mierow *The deeds of Frederick Barbarossa,* New York 1953.

34. Widukind, monk of Corvey, *Rerum Gestarum Saxonicarum libri tres,* ed. P. Hirsch, Hannover, 1935, Lib. III ch. lvi (956) and ch. lxiii (961).

35. 'Vita di Cola di Rienzo', ed. A. Frugoni, Florence 1957. I. Origo *Cola di Rienzo,* London 1938, notes that in modern times Cola has been hailed as both a nationalist and a pioneer of the proletarian revolution.

36. James I King of Aragon *The Chronicle,* translated J. Forster, London 1883; ch. lxxi on the Saracen angel; *passim* for his attitude to the clergy.

37. Patetta *Le ordalie,* Turin 1890. R. L. Pearsall 'Some Observations on Judicial Duels as practised in Germany', *Archaeologia* XXIX 1842, pp. 348-61. J. W. Baldwin 'The Intellectual Preparation for the Canon of 1215 against Ordeals', *Speculum* 36, 1961, pp. 613-36.
An example of a judicial duel in 960, which went on for many hours, but was inconclusive, is recorded in the *Cartulaire de Beaulieu en Limousin,* ed. M. Deloche, Paris 1859, no. 47, pp. 85-6: 'nam secunda diei hora certantibus usque ad solis occasum neminem quippe cernerent eorum vincere.' The judges therefore declared that both claimants to the possession of the church had lost. The church was awarded to the monks of Beaulieu instead. They naturally made a record of the divine action in their favour. For an ordeal by water with an hilarious outcome in 1045 see *Cartulaire de l'Abbaye de St Victor de Marseille,* ed. M. Guérard, Paris 1857, t. II no. 691, pp. 32-4. The monks of St Victor were in dispute with another monastery and adduced the evidence of charters. Their opponents preferred the appeal to God, but their case was laughed out: 'ibidem cunctis coram hominem mergant in aquam; sed eorum judicio spe injusta frustrato, disruptis lignaminibus et supinatis cruribus risum fecerunt omnibus qui aderant videntibus.' The trial by combat still occurred in sixteenth-century Russia: H. W. Dewey *Oxford Slavonic Papers,* 1959, pp. 21-31.

38. James I *The Chronicle,* chap. DXC.

39. A. E. Levett 'Baronial Councils and their relations to Manorial Courts' in *Mélanges Lot* 1923, pp. 421-41, blamed the influence of the professional legal elements for the decay of the manorial courts, which opened the way for oppression of the peasantry in the sixteenth century.

40. D. Oschinsky, *Walter of Henley and other treatises on estate management and accounting,* Oxford 1971, pp. 61-74. See also note 9 chapter 3.

41. P. Vinogradoff *Roman Law in Medieval Europe,* 2nd ed., Oxford 1929. When Roman Law studies were revived in the eleventh century, the first problem was to establish good texts: this was done by the school of Irnerius. The next stage was to provide commentaries to make them intelligible. This work was completed by Accursius (1182-1260) who composed the *Glossa Ordinaria* on the Code, Institute and Digest during Frederick II's reign. Quite apart from the political implications of adopting Roman Law while the Staufen empire was still powerful, the state of legal studies precluded easy assimilation of Roman Law until the late thirteenth century. cf. note to ch. IV, no. **23.**

42. C. N. S. Woolf *Bartolus of Sassoferrato,* Cambridge 1913.

43. B. Smalley *English Friars and Antiquity in the early fourteenth century,* Oxford 1960, ch. XII.

44. P. Kristeller *Studies in Renaissance Thought and Letters,* Rome 1956, p. 480, n. 19. The commentary by mag. Jacobus de la Lana was translated from Tuscan into Latin by Albericus de Rossata of Bergamo (d. 1354), 'quia talis ydioma non est omnibus notum'.

45. H. Mercurialis *Artis Gymnasticae apud antiquos celeberrimae nostris temporibus ignoratae libri sex,* Venice 1569.

46. W. Wühr *Das Abendländischen Bildungswesen im Mittelalter,* Munich 1950. J. Bowen *A History of Western Education* vol. I 1972, vol. II 1975.

47. N. Orme *English Schools in the Middle Ages,* London 1973. Information about these schools only begins to be detailed in the fifteenth century. C. T. Davis 'Education in Dante's Florence', *Speculum* 1965, pp. 415-35. Conrad Bitschin in the fifteenth century gave some account of what should be taught in school: *Labyrinthis vitae conjugalis* Lib. IV, ed. R. Galle, Gotha 1905. Philippe von Vigneulles (1471-1512) describes his education in his *Gedenkbuch,* ed. H. V. Michelant 'Bibliothek der literarscher Vereins' Band 24, Stuttgart 1852. The difficulties of getting an education in the sixteenth century are vividly recorded by T. Platerus; see the *Autobiography* transl. by E. A. McCaul, London 1839.

48. Orderic Vitalis *The Ecclesiastical History,* ed. M. Chibnall, vol. III, Lib. V — cap. 10, pp. 98-101, Oxford 1969. See also G. Duby 'Les jeuncs dans la société aristocratique', *Annales* 19, 1964. H. Feilzer *Jugend in der Mittelalterlichen Ständegesellschaft,* Vienna 1971.

49. Orderic, Lib. V cap. 14, ed. M. Chibnall, *op. cit.* pp. 150-1. See also pp. 166-71 for Orderic's account of his teacher John, himself the author of historical works now lost. Orderic may not have been happy at St Evroul. His earliest historical work seems to have been his interpolations in the text of William of Jumièges (before 1109). There are hints in Book III of the *Ecclesiastical History* that he had begun to write this about 1114-5 when he was 40 years old, but this book was not completed until after Warin became abbot in 1123. Orderic says that he had begun his history at the command of Abbot Roger (1091-1123), but Roger clearly did little to encourage him. Warin, on the other hand, kept Orderic hard at it and the whole work was offered to him just before his death. Warin was slightly older than Orderic and joined the monastery as a young man of 23 in 1093. He himself wrote up a miracle, which Orderic copied into his own work (III, p. 347). He is described by Orderic in warm terms as a man without pride who listened and learned, *a paribus vel a subditis.* Perhaps he was the man who gave Orderic a new sense of his own value.

50. P. Michaud-Quantin *Etudes sur le Vocabulaire Philosophique du Moyen Age.* Rome 1971, pp. 163-86. chap IX 'Catégories sociales dans les canonistes et moralistes au XIIIe siècle' shows that there was no intellectual recognition of the concept of social nobility until *c.* 1300. The term noble was used till then as an adjective describing persons, kin, seed, blood etc., but not of a class, and not as a noun. The political creation of titles of nobility comes even later. The first English baron to be 'created' by letters patent was Baron Beauchamp of Kidderminster in 1387. The 'peers' first called themselves peers of the realm under Edward II: L. O. Pike *A Constitutional History of the House of Lords,* London 1894.

51. B. Castiglione, *op. cit.* pp. 36-7.

52. *L'Histore de Guillaume le Maréchal,* written 1225-26, shows that the Marshal's moral values, even on his death-bed (1219), were chivalrous rather than Christian. ed. P. Meyer S.H.F. 1891-1901 t. II *ll* 18481-96.

53. G. Favati *Le Biografie trovadoriche,* Bologna 1961.

54. J. V. Fleming *Le Roman de la Rose.* Princeton 1969. N. Cohn *The World View of a Thirteenth-Century Parisian Intellectual,* 1961. Guillaume de Lorris and Jean de Meun *Le Roman de la Rose,* transl. C. Dohlberg, Princeton 1971.

55. R. S. Loomis, ed., *Arthurian Literature in the Middle Ages,* Oxford 1959.

56. The fourteenth-century romance *Ponthus et la Belle Sidoine* describes a relationship of perfect love, in which, however, Ponthus no sooner completes one adventure than he embarks on another. The romance was then concerned with the adventures, not with the knight's repose or dalliance in the lady's bower. F. J. Mather, ed., *King Ponthus and the Fair Sidoine,* Modern Language Association of America, Baltimore 1897.

57. G. Dumézil *Du mythe au roman: La saga de Hadingas, B.E.H.E.,* Sciences Religieuses LXVI, Paris 1953, esp. pp. 132-3.

58. Antoine de La Sale served the Angevin princes for most of his life and eventually became tutor to John of Calabria. For him he began to write in later life a collection of unpretentious stories, so that by reading with pleasure the prince could acquire a knightly education. *La Salade* is edited by F. Desonay as tome I of the *Oeuvres Complètes,* 1955. *Le Petit Jehan de Saintré,* La Sale's most famous work, is edited by J. Misrahi and C. A. Kundson, Geneva 1967.

59. Beha ed din *Life of Saladin,* ed. C. W. Wilson, London, 1897, ch. CXXVIII-IX, CXXXIX-CXL. Joanna the widowed queen of Sicily was to marry Al Malik al Adil, Saladin's brother, with whom Richard was on excellent terms.

60. G. Doutrepont *Les mises en prose des épopées et des romans chevaleresques du XIVe au XVIe siècles.* Académie Royale Belgique des Lettres, Mémoires 40.

Brussels 1930. The cultivation of a literary genre may influence social comportment; it affords no grounds for arguing about 'human nature'. There are 2,500 Provençal lyrics and only 300 English ones earlier than 1399. Such a statistic proves nothing about the sexual proclivities of those two peoples.

61. Fazio degli Uberti *Il Dittamondo e le Rime,* ed. G. Corsi, 2 vols, Bari 1952. Lib. IV cap. xxiii pp. 49-75, describes places in Great Britain mentioned in the Arthurian romances.

62. Instruction in polite table manners is given by the fifteenth-century Paris manuscript, *B.N.* Ms. Fr. 73932. A. Cabanés *Dans les coulisses de l'histoire,* Paris IV 1947, pp. 19-21.

63. J. Aubrey *Brief Lives,* ed. D. L. Dick, London 1958, p. 80 Sir John Danvers: the grand tour on the continent was in part designed to get the young gentlemen away from the servants. cf. chapter III note **49.** I owe this note to the kindness of Professor Norman Blake who came across the passage shortly after we had discussed the substance of this paragraph.

64. E. T. Van der Grinten *Elements of Art Historiography in Medieval Texts: an analytical study,* Nijhoff 1969, p. 83, no. 18. See also P. Frankl *The Gothic,* Princeton 1960, p. 55 n. 2, citing the chronicle of Burchard von Hall where the same architect was responsible for *opere francigeno* and *ad instar anglici operis.*

65. R. Krautheimer 'Introduction to the Iconography of Medieval Architecture', *Journal of the Warburg and Courtauld Institutes,* V, 1942, pp. 1-33.

66. *Gesta Abbatum Monasterii S. Albani,* ed. H. T. Riley, R.S. London 1867, vol. I, pp. 394-5. This is a text composed in the fourteenth century, which may incorporate older material, and was later edited, perhaps by Thomas Walsingham.

67. Suger, Abbot of St Denis, *Oeuvres Complètes,* ed. A. Lecoy de la Marche, *S.H.F.,* Paris 1867, p. 198.

68. J. Fitchen *The Construction of Gothic Cathedrals,* Oxford University Press 1961. L. R. Shelby 'The role of the master mason in medieval English building', *Speculum* 1964, pp. 387-403; *ibid.* 'The education of medieval master masons', *Medieval Studies,* 1970, pp. 1-26; *ibid.* 'The geometrical knowledge of medieval master masons', *Speculum* 1972, pp. 395-421.

69. N. Pevsner 'The term architect in the middle ages', *Speculum* 1942, pp. 546-62. Nicolas de Biart is cited in V. Mortet and P. Deschamps *Recueil des textes relatifs à l'histoire de l'architecture,* t. II, 1929, p. 291.

70. J. S. Ackerman *'Ars sine Scientia Nihil est:* Gothic Theory of architecture at the cathedral of Milan', *Art Bulletin* XXXI, 1949, pp. 84-111.

71. A. Jubinal *Nouveau Recueil des contes dits fabliaux,* t. II, Paris 1842, pp. 96-101: 'Le dit des paintres', from Paris *B.N.* Ms. Fr. suppl. 1132.

72. *The Death of King Arthur,* trans. J. Cable, Harmondsworth 1971, p. 70.

73. There are many examples of complicated texts with surrounding commentaries neatly set out. A fourteenth-century example in Durham Cathedral Library shows that reference between text and commentary was facilitated by using the same decorative motifs in the initials. See also F. Olivier-Martin 'Manuscrits bolonais du Decret de Gratien conservés à Bibliothèque Vaticane', *Mélanges d'archéologie et d'histoire* XLV 1928, Ecole Francaise de Rome, pp. 215-257.

74. M. R. James *The drawings of Matthew Paris in facsimile,* Walpole Society XIV, 1925-6. F. Wormald *More Matthew Paris Drawings, ibid.* XXXI, 1942-3. Matthew Paris *Chronica Majora,* ed. H. R. Luard *R.S.* London 1876, vol. III, pp. 242-4, records the appearance of a celestial phenomenon: 'et quoniam non potest illud prodigiale portentum verbis describi, signo demonstrativo figuratur, ipso caelo sic circinato existente exemplari, immediate multi similitudinem rei sic apparentis pinxerunt, propter rei novitatem admirandum.' Paris also made use of marginal signs for ease of cross reference in his histories. (In the late twelfth century, Ralph of Diss, dean of St Paul's London, had used several conventional symbols to indicate the recurrence of certain themes in his histories.) For a very curious diagram showing the progress of the soul, by descent into repentance and ascent through Christ to the Godhead, see the manuscripts of the fourteenth-century mystic Henry of Suso: *Heinrich Seuse Deutsche Schriften,* ed. D. K. Bihlmeyer, Stuttgart 1907, p. 195 in *Leben Seuses* ch. LIII, abb. 11, from Berlin Ms. 4° 840 f. 82 r. I owe this reference to Dr. N. F. Palmer and would like to acknowledge here the help he has given me with all topics relating to German medieval texts.

75. C. Segre *Li Bestiaires D'Amour de Maistre Richart de Fornival e li response du Bestaire,* Milan 1957, p. 4: 'Diex . . . a donné a homme une vertu de force d'ame ki a non memoire . . . Ceste memoire si a ij portes veir et oir e a cascune de ces ij portes si a cemin par ou on i puet aler che sont painture et parole.' This important text proves that words were still for hearing rather than reading.

76. For example, the pictorial cycles for the Apocalypse: see M. R. James *The Apocalypse in Art,* London 1931. The visions of Hildegard of Bingen, in the twelfth century, were illustrated, probably under her supervision (Wiesbaden Landbibliothek Codex B): see M. Bückeler *Wisse die Wege (Scivias),* Salzburg, 5th ed., 1963. These visions were of rather a different kind from those of St Brigit of Sweden, whose revelations provided direct inspiration for painters able to interpret them in their own terms. Dr. C. M. Kauffmann kindly discussed this matter with me.

77. Vatican Ms. Lat. 1960 'Compendium Chronologica Magna' (1320) of Paolo di Venezia is illustrated with marginal drawings, and many maps: f.13 'requiretur autem mapa duplex picturae et scripturae nec unum sine altero putes sufficere, quia pictura sine scriptura provincias seu regna confuse demonstrat. Pictura autem hic posita ex mapis variis est composita.' *Congresso Geografico Italiano VIII,* Firenze 1921. Atti. vol. II pp. 263-70 A Mori 'Le carte geografiche della cronaea di Fra Paolino Miunorita'.

Chapter 3 *Mundane Business*
1. A. Tolstoy *War and Peace,* book XI, ch. 1.

2. Gregory I *Expositio in Librum beati Job Moralium X,* ch. 13, quoting Job xi, 12, on the man who, like the foal, thinks he is born free, but who has to be bound by discipline like a domesticated animal, if he is to reach heaven *(P. L.* 75, *c.* 933-4). Gregory's point is however missed by Eximenic, who lifts it completely out of its context. Francesc Eximenic (1340-1409), Bishop of Elne, *Crestià libre de regiment de princeps e de comunitat* (1385), edition 1484, ch. 156. G. Franz *Quellen zur Geschichte des Deutschen Bauern-Standes im Mittelalter,* Darmstadt, no. 146: Seifried Helbing. On the other hand a troubadour poet accuses God, in a dream, of giving power and riches to those who use them badly. God should make all men equal. The human desire for social equality is quite a different matter from the theological truth of human equality. P. Meyer: 'Les derniers troubadours de la Provence', *B.E.C.* 1869, p. 281.

3. P. Vaccari 'Le affrancazioni collettive dei servi della gleba', *Documenti di storia e di pensiero politico,* Milan 1939.

4. P. Dubois *De recuperatione terrae sanctae,* ed. C. V. Langlois, Paris 1891; transl. as *The Recovery of the Holy Land,* W. I. Brandt, New York 1956. There is only one fourteenth-century manuscript: Vatican Ms. Regina Christina, 1642.

5. ed. E. Lamond, Cambridge 1893.

6. G. A. Holmes 'The Libel of English Policy', *E.H.R.* 1961, pp. 193-216. The poem indicates that the English were engaged in commerce with lands as far away as Iceland, Prussia, Hungary and Turkey.

7. J. E. Thorold Rogers *A history of agriculture and prices in England,* Oxford 1866-1902, 7 volumes. E. J. Hamilton, 'History of Prices before 1750', *Comité International des Sciences Historiques* XI, Rapports I, 1960 pp. 144-162. R. Mols: *Introduction à la demographie historique des villes d'Europe du xive au xviiie siècles,* Louvain 1956. J. C. Russell 'Recent Advances in Medieval Demography', *Speculum* 1965, pp. 84-101. J. Piquet *Des banquiers au moyen age: Les Templiers,* Paris 1939, gives tables of value for the franc. Ducange *Glossarium Mediae et Infimae Latinitatis* (1895), Volume V pp. 436-8, gives variations in medieval wine measures.

8. F. Lot and R. Fawtier *Le premier budget de la monarchie française: Le compte général de 1202-03, B.E.H.E.* no. 259, Paris 1932.

9. H. Moranvillé 'Rapports à Philippe VI sur l'état de ses finances', *B.E.C.* 1887, pp. 380-95. cf. J. Favier *Les finances pontificales à l'époque du grand schisme d'Occident,* Bibliothèque des écoles françaises d'Athènes et de Rome, fasc. 211, 1966, p. 697: 'La notion même de budget leur était étrangère. La chambre, rapellons-le, était dirigée et servie par des juristes dévoués et efficaces, mais non par des financiers.'

10. J. L. Kirby 'The Issue of the Lancastrian Exchequer and Lord Cromwell's Estimates of 1433', *Bulletin of the Institute of Historical Research* XXIV, 1951, pp. 121-51. A briefer statement had been made in 1421 (Rymer: *Foedera* X, 1710, pp. 113-14) but there is no evidence that an annual review, as proposed by the Walton ordinances of 1338, was ever made. For an example of the meticulous record keeping of the English financial administration in Aquitaine (1370) see J. Delpit *Collection Générale des Documents Français en Angleterre* 1847, no. CCXXIII, pp. 132-76.

11. 'Parliament of 1371', *Rotuli Parliamentorum* II, 303-4, clause 10. Contemporaries cited the case of king David (2 Samuel 24, 1-10; 1 Chron. 21, 1-8) as a warning against proposals to assess kingdoms for taxation purposes.

12. *Le Livre de la Taille de Paris 1313,* ed. K. Michaëlsson, Acta Universitatis Gotoburgensis, 1951.

13. R. E. Glassock *Lay Subsidy Rolls,* Oxford 1975. British Academy.

14. O. Karmin *La Legge del Catasto Fiorentino* (1427), 1906. C. Klapisch 'Fiscalité et démographie en Toscane 1427-30', *Annales* 1969, pp. 1313-37.

15. *Rotuli Parliamentorum* V, 572.

16. *Ricordi di Giovanni di Pagolo Morelli,* ed. V. Branca, Florence 1956.

17. J. Sottas *op. cit.* p. 176.

18. Lopez, in Reynolds *op. cit.*

19. J. W. Baldwin *Masters, Princes and Merchants,* Princeton 1970.

20. F. Novati 'De Magnalibus urbis Mediolani di Bonvicino de Rippa', *Bullettino dell'Instituto Storico Italiano* XX, 1898, pp. 1-176.

21. R. Fawtier 'Comment au début du XIVe siècle un roi de France pouvait-il se représenter son royaume', *Académie des inscriptions Comptes-rendus,* 1959, pp. 117-23; and more fully in *Mélanges offertes à M. P-E Martin,* Geneva 1961, pp. 65-77. The king of France was not interested in the shape of his lands, only in the names of his taxpayers.

22. H. J. R. Murray *A history of Chess,* Oxford 1913, pp. 402-3. The game was known in Europe by *c.* 1000 and had probably begun to penetrate from the east a century earlier. F. Madden 'Historical Remarks on the introduction of the game of chess into Europe', *Archaeologia* XXIV 1832, pp. 203-91, refers to a letter of Peter Damian to Alexander II proving the passion for the game in the mid-eleventh century (*P.L.* 145, col. 454). Bishop Odo de Sully forbade the clerks of Paris to keep games including *scaccos* in their houses (*P.L.* 212, col. 66, n. 29). Jacobus de Cessolis *De moribus hominum et de officiis nobilium super ludo scaccorum,* ed. E. Köpke, Brandenburg 1899, belongs to that period in the history of the game when it was respectable and still popular, that is before the introduction of playing cards provided a more frivolous way of passing the time.

23. T. Rader *The Economics of Feudalism,* ch. 3, New York 1971.

24. Rodericus Sancius de Arevalo Bishop of Oviedo *Speculum Vitae Humanae,* Lib. I, ch. XXI-XXII, Rome 1471.

25. A. Jubinal *Jongleurs et Trouvères,* Paris 1835, pp. 107-109, 'Le Depit au Vilain'. Contrast to this Poems stressing not the coarseness but the poverty of villeins in *Li proverbe au vilain,* ed. A. Tobler, Leipzig 1895, e.g. nos. 52, 71, 74, 86, 105 etc.

26. Alvarus Pelagius *De Planctu Ecclesiae,* Venice 1560.

27. The bishops' registers from the thirteenth century are the chief source of information about the shortcomings of the clergy. Against their incriminating character must be set the fact that from the same period the principal burden of the church's ministry was made to rest upon the priests' shoulders. For a glimpse of parish life in the twelfth century see H. Mayr-Harting 'Functions of a Twelfth-century recluse', *History* LX, 1975, pp. 337-52, especially pp. 346-7.

28. G. Franz *op. cit.,* no. 155, sermon of Br. Ludwig, pp. 412-4.

29. *Paston Letters,* ed. N. Davis, I, 1971, no. 73, pp. 131-4, John Paston to his wife Margaret and others, 27 June 1465: 'Every pore man that hath browt up his chylder to the age of xij yer waytyth than to be holp and profited be his childer.'

30. G. Franz *op. cit.,* no. 169, 1338: *heymanni* were bondmen; *litones,* peasant propietors; *coloni,* tenants; *iurati,* sworn men, perhaps suitors of the law-court. No. 197 concerns Dithmarsch, and no. 205 Eggolsheim.

31. *Quaestiones Johannis Galli,* ed. M. Boulet, Paris 1944, Bibliothèque des Ecoles Françaises d'Athènes et de Rome, fasc, 156, pp. 373-5.

32. W. Levison 'A rhythmical poem of *c.* 1100 by Rudolf of St. Trond', *Medievalia et Humanistica* IV, 1946, pp. 3-25. This deals with abuses including dancing in churchyards. See Reginald monk of Durham *Libellus de Admirandis Beati Cuthberti*

Virtutibus, Surtees Society I, 1835, cap. 1xxxvi, pp. 181-2 for the stag.

33. *Chronicon de Lanercoste,* ed. J. Stevenson, Edinburgh 1839, p. 109.

34. Helinand *De cognitione sui, P.L.* 212, cap. xiii.

35. B. Gilles 'Les développements technologiques en Europe, 1100-1400', *Cahiers d'histoire mondiale* III, 1956, pp. 63-108. M. Bloch 'Avenement et Conquêtes du moulin à eau', *Annales* 1935, pp. 538-63.

36. Frederick I legislated against peasants' sons becoming knights and ordered such knights to be demoted: *M. G. H. Constitutiones* I, p. 318 cl. 20, but Helbling's poem (*Franz* no. 146) suggests that it could not have been totally effective.

37. Jean de Venette *The Chronicle,* ed. R. A. Newhall, transl. J. Birdsall, New York 1953.

38. F. Hämmerlein *De nobilitate et rusticitate dialogus,* Basel 1497.

39. W. Langland *Piers Plowman* B, Passus VI, ed. W. Skeat Oxford 1886 *ll* 3-58, 161-68.

40. John of Monte Corvino *Sinica Francescana Itinera et Relationes Fratrum Minorum,* ed. Anastasius Van den Wyngaert, Quaracchi 1929, pp. 340-55. The mention of horses is on p. 342. Walter of Henley discusses the respective advantages of the horse and the ox in Oschinsky *op. cit.* Arab horses brought back from the crusades improved the strains of horses bred in the west. E. Schiele *The Arab Horse in Europe,* transl. A. Dent, London 1970.

41. J. C. Webster *The Labors of the Months in antique and medieval art to the end of the twelfth century,* Northwestern University 1938.

42. Some monasteries had to buy certain supplies on the market. H. van Werweke 'Comment les établissements religieux belges se procuraient-ils du vin au moyen âge', *Revue belge de philologie et d'histoire* II, 1923, pp. 643-62. G. Duby 'Le budget de l'abbaye de Cluny entre 1080 et 1155: économie domaniale et économies monétaires', *Annales* 1952, pp. 155-71.

43. Oschinsky *op. cit.* Peter de Crescentius (1233-1321) *Ruralia Commoda,* written 1304-07, first printed 1471. L. Frati 'Pier de' Crescenzi e l'opera sua' *Atti e Memorie della Deputazione...Romagna,* serie IV, vol. 9, 1919, pp. 146-64.

44. H. S. Lucas 'The Great European Famine of 1315-17', *Speculum* V, 1930, pp. 343-77.

45. G. Villani *Croniche* (ed. A. Racheli, Trieste 1857, and A. Muratori, *R.I.S.* t. XIII, 1723) lib. XII cap. lxxxiv. Compare the Lübeck annals on this famine in *M.G.H. Scriptores* XVI, pp. 411-29.

46. J. F. D. Shrewsbury *A history of Bubonic Plague in the British Isles,* Cambridge 1970, p. 36. A. B. Falsini 'Firenze dopo il 1348', *A. S. I.* 1971, pp. 425-503. W. M. Bowsky 'The impact of the Black Death upon Sienese government and society', *Speculum,* 1964, pp. 1-34. G. Villani XI CIV, for mortality of 1340; XII, LXXXIV, for 1347.

47. W. Langland *Piers* B, Passus VI, pp. 309-13.

48. Richard Fitz Nigel *Dialogue of the Exchequer,* ed. C. Johnson, Edinburgh 1950, pp. 40-41, where the change is dated to the 1120s. G. E. Woodbine noticed an exceptional case in the early thirteenth century where damages in the courts were awarded in kind, clearly in reparation: *Yale Law Journal* XXXIX, 1929-30, pp. 509-10, citing *Curia Regis Rolls* 1929 IV, p. 289, for Berkshire: 'one cartload of grain, 20 loads of timber and brushwood, 3 shillings worth of hogs' fat and bacon, one quarter of flax'.

49. B. Hauréau *Notices et Extraits de Quelques Manuscits Latins de la Bibliothèque Nationale* IV, 1892, p. 95, from a thirteenth century sermon, *B.N.* Ms. Lat. 14952: 'Rustici filios suos quando parvuli sunt, sublimant et faciunt eis tunicas rudicatas et quando sunt adulti mittunt eos ad aratrum. E contra nobiles viri primo ponunt filios sub pedibus et faciunt eos comedere cum garcionibus; quando sunt magni tunc sublimant *eos';* cf chapter II, note 63.

50. Abu al-Fadl Ja'far ibn Ali al Dimishqi. There is a German translation with a commentary by H. Ritter in *Der Islam* VII, 1917, pp. 45-91. The passage on the beauties of trade is found on pp. 65-6. The work was written before 1174 (the date of the oldest surviving manuscript) and not earlier than the ninth century.

51. Eximenic *op. cit.,* ch. 389.

52. Rodrigo *op. cit.,* Lib. I, ch. xxvii.

53. E. G. Ravenstein *A Journal of the first Voyage of Vasco da Gama, 1497-8,* Hakluyt Society, 1898, pp. 7, 17.

54. Michael of Rhodes 'Autograph Common-Place Book', described in Sotheby's manuscripts catalogue for 11 July 1966, no. 254. M. E. Mallet *The Florentine Galleys in the Fifteenth Century,* Oxford 1967, prints on pp. 207-275 the diary of Luca di Maso degli Albizzi, Captain of the Galleys, 1429-30: an account of his voyage from Florence to London and back. However, he was more a diplomat with naval experience than a seaman.

55. Marco Polo *Il Milione,* ed. L. F. Benedetto, Florence 1928, transl. R. Latham, Harmondsworth 1958. L. Olschki *Marco Polo's Asia,* Berkeley 1960.

56. *Cronaca di Buonaccorso Pitti,* ed. Romagnoli dall'Acqua, Bologna 1905, transl. J. A. Scott. Philippe de Mézières *op. cit.,* t. II, p. 405.

57. L. von Winterfeld *Handel, Kapital und Patriziat in Köln bis 1400,* Pfingstblätter des Hansischen Geschichtsvereins, Blatt XVI, Lübeck 1925, p. 71.

58. I. Origo *The Merchant of Prato: Francesco di Marco Datini,* London 1957. F. Melis *Aspetti della Vita Economica Medievale: Studi nell'archivio Datini in Prato,* Siena 1962.

59. James I *Chronicle op cit.,* ch. cccxcvii. The statutes of a charity in Valenciennes required members to travel in convoys dressed in coats of mail and carrying bows and arrows. H. Caffiaux 'Mémoires sur la charte de la frairie de la Halle Basse de Valenciennes', *Mémoires de la Société des Antiquaires de France,* t. 38, 1877, pp. 1-41, ch. 8-10.

60. *El libro di mercatantie et usanze de' paesi,* ed. F. Borlandi, Turin 1936; B. Pegolotti *La pratica della mercatura,* ed. A. Evans, 1936.

61. G. Zippel 'L'allume del Tolfa', *Archivio della R. Società Romana di Storia Patria* XXX, 1907, pp. 5-51, 384-462.

62. C. M. Cipolla *Guns and Sails in the early phase of European expansion 1400-1700,* London 1965. F. C. Lane *Venetian Ships,* Baltimore 1934. E. Byrne *Genoese Shipping in the twelfth and thirteenth century* Cambridge (Mass.) 1930. G. La Roérie 'Les transformations du gouvernail', *Annales* 1935, pp. 564-83.

63. F. Bourquelot *Etudes sur les foires de Champagne,* Paris 1865. E. Chapin *Les Villes* *de Foires de Champagne, B.E.H.E.* 1937. R. H. Bautier 'Les Foires de Champagne' in *Recueils de la Société Jean Bodin t. V La Foire,* Brussels 1953, pp. 97-145. E. Coornaert, 'Caractères et mouvement des foires internationales au moyen âge et au xvie siècle', *Studi in Onore di Armando Sapori,* Milan 1957, vol. I, pp. 355-71.

64. C. U. J. Chevalier 'Tarif des Droits Perçus aux foires de la ville de Romans au milieu du xiiie siècle', *Revue des Sociétés Savantes* 1872, 5e série III, pp. 62-70.

65. M. de Bouard 'Problèmes de Subsistance dans un état médiéval: le marché et les prix de céréales au royaume angevin de Sicile 1266-82', *Annales* 1938, pp. 483-501. R. Romano 'A propos du commerce du blé dans la Mediterranée des XIV et XV siécles', in *Hommage à Lucien Fèbvre Eventail de l'histoire vivante,* Paris 1953, II, pp. 149-161. M. K. James 'The Fluctuations of the Anglo-Gascon Wine Trade during the fourteenth century', *Economic History Review* 1951-2, second series IV, pp. 170-96. Y. Renouard 'Le grand commerce des vins de Gascogne au moyen âge', *Revue Historique,* t. 221, 1959, pp. 261-304.

66. Villani, Lib. VI, LIV-LV.

67. James I *Chronicle,* ch. cccclxv-vi.

68. *Ordonnances des Roys de France de la troisième race,* ed. M. de Laurière, t. I, 1723, pp. 93-5, for ordonnances of 1262 and 1265.

69. Some strange examples of the effects of shortage of ready cash and small change are given in E. T. Powell *Evolution of the Money Market,* 1915.

70. F. Graus 'La Crise Monétaire du XIVe siècle', *Revue Belge de Philologie et d'Histoire* XXIX(i), 1951, pp. 445-54.

71. Y. Renouard *Les hommes d'affaires italiens du moyen âge,* Paris 1949, *ibid. Les relations des papes d'Avignon et des compagnies commerciales et bancaires de 1316 à 1378,* Bib. Ecol. Ath et Rome, fasc. 151, 1941. Q. Senigaglia 'Le compagnie bancarie senesi nei secoli xiiie e xive', *Studi Senesi* XXIV, 1906, pp. 149-217, and XXV, 1908, pp. 3-66.

72. T. P. McLaughlin 'Teaching of the Canonists on Usury', *Medieval Studies* I, 1939, pp. 81-147. *ibid.* II, 1940, pp. 1-22. R. de Roover *La Pensée Economique des Scolastiques: Doctrine et Méthode,* Montreal 1971. Thomas Aquinas *Summa Theologica,* Pars II secunda pars, quaest. 77-8.

73. William of Malmesbury *Historia Regum,* ed. W. Stubbs, R.S., I, pp. 221-4. Alpert of Metz bears out the importance of the trade with England in his scathing description of the merchants of Tiel *c.* 1020 *(P.L.* 140, *c.* 481).

74. B. Töpfer *Volk und Kirche zur Zeit der beginnenden Gottesfriedensbewegung in Frankreich,* 1957. See L. Huberti *Studien zur Rechtsgeschichte der Gottesfrieden und Landesfrieden,* Ansbach 1892, for texts concerning France. For the empire see *M. G. H. Constitutiones* I, ed. L. Weiland, pp. 596-617: *Recueils de la Société Jean Bodin XIV La Paix,* Brussels 1962.

75. E. Ennen *Die Europäische Stadt des Mittelalters, Göttingen 1972. C. Van de Kieft* and J. F. Niermeijer *Elenchus Fontium Historiae Urbanae,* Leiden 1967: Belgium no.20, charter of count Baldwin of Flanders for Ypres 1116, where the ordeal was replaced by oath-swearing, and no. 11 for le Huy 1066. A Giry *Histoire de la ville de St. Omer,* Paris 1877, pp. 371-5, prints the privilege granted by William Clito count of Flanders in 1127. G. Espinas *'Les origines urbaines en Flandre',* *Moyen Age* 1948, pp. 37-54.

76. Winterfeld *op.cit.*, p. 70-1; charter of 1181, see note 57 above.

77. H. Hauser *Ouvriers du temps passé*, Paris 1899, ch. 5; there are also accounts of shoemakers staying up all night to finish commissions.

78. G. D. West 'The description of towns in old French verse romance', *French Studies* XI, 1957, pp. 50-9.

79. E. Egli *Geschichte des Städtebaues* II: Das Mittelalter, Zürich 1962.

80. P. Lavedan *L'Histoire de L'Urbanisme*, t. I: Antiquité et Moyen Age, Paris 1926.

81. For statutes of the town of Avignon 1243, see V. Mortet and P. Deschamps *Recueil op. cit.* pp. 265-9.

82. *Cartulaire de Mirepoix*, ed. F. Pasquier, Toulouse 1921, t. II p. 18.

83. P. Lavedan *op. cit.* from the Avignon Archives. D. D. Voirie 'Carton des Maitres des rues'.

84. James I *Chronicle*, trans. J. Forster, London 1883 t II ch. CCCIV. This view was approved by Eximenic *op. cit.* ch 111. He objected to what he calls the Italian custom of pulling down the houses of criminals, 'car per aco la cosa publica nes damnificada que per aquello habitacio apres la ciutat nes enlegida en aquella part'.

85. *Liber Albus*, ed. H. Riley, R. S., London 1859, pp. 319-32.

86. *The Marvels of Rome*, transl. F. M. Nichol, London 1889.

87. Guillaume le Breton 'Philippid', *Recueil des Historiens des Gaules*, t. xvii Paris 1818, pp. 117-287; Lib. II, *ll*, 84-148.

88. Eximenic, *op. cit.*, ch. 23-4. J. le Vasseur *Annales de Noyon*, 1633, ch VI, is still prepared to endorse such legends: 'L'opinion qui tient le patriarche Noé fondateur à Noyon est vraysemblable'.

89. William Fitz Stephen *Vita Sancti Thomae*, ed. J. C. Robertson, *R.S.*, London 1877, pp. 2-13: 'Descriptio nobilissimae civitatis Londoniae'.

90. A. J. V. Le Roux de Lincy and L. M. Tisserand *Histoire Générale de Paris. Paris et ses historiens aux xive et xve siècles*, Paris 1867.

91. *Winterfeld op. cit.*, pp. 5-6, for objections to the wealthy plebeian; 'homo pecuniosus et avarus' the 'patricians' were styled 'generosior', 'dives', 'nota et urbana persona'.

92. Brunetto Latini *Li Livres dou Tresor*, ed. F. J. Carmody, Berkeley 1948.

93. *Annales Januenses*, ed. L. T. Belgrano, 'Fonti per la storia d'Italia' 11, 12, 13, 14, 1890-1929.

94. *Die Chroniken der Deutschen Städte*, Leipzig 1862-

95. *Annals of Ghent*, ed. H. Johnstone, London 1951. Written by an unnamed Franciscan in 1308, there is no surviving manuscript and it seems to have been little known in the fourteenth and fifteenth century, yet there is no better Flemish record of the events of 1302, The chronicler's own words hint that the stirring 'historic' events he described did not impress contemporaries as they have historians of the urban revolt against the French nobility: p. 1. Quandoque, aliquibus eventibus demergentibus valde expediens est talia non ignorar'. The defeat of the French inspired a jubilant (and blasphemous) account of the *Passio Francorum*, a parody of the passion story, which was more to contemporary taste than mere records of fact. Adam Usk found it sufficiently entertaining to copy into his English chronicle more than a century later: *Chronicle 1377-1426,* ed. E. M. Thompson, London 2nd ed. 1904, pp. 107-10.

96. A similar conflict between 'els borges majors et prozhomes menors' in Montauban (1254) arose over the assessment of tallage. The king of France was again invoked and after many years (1271-1328) consuls obtained effective power in the town, with royal support. H. Le Bret *Histoire de Montauban,* 2nd ed. 1841, pp. 293-4.

97. C. Higonnet 'Les *terre nuove* florentines du XVe siècle', *Studi in Onore di Amintore Fanfani,* vol. III, Milan 1962, pp. 1-17. M. B. Becker *Florence in Transition* vol. II 'Studies in the Rise of the Territorial State', Baltimore 1965. See also J. Glénisson 'Une administration médiévale aux prises avec la disette: la question des blés dans les provinces italiennes de l'état pontifical en 1374-5', *Moyen Age* 1951, pp. 303-26.

98. E. Fiume 'Fioritura e decadenza dell'economia fiorentina', *A. S. I.* 1957, pp. 385-439; 1958, pp. 443-510; 1959, pp. 427-502.

99. G. B. Depping *Règlemens sur les Arts et Métiers de Paris rédigés au xiiie siècle et connu sous le nom de Livre des Metiers d'Etienne Boileau,* Paris 1837.

100. F. Klemm *A History of Western Technology,* N.Y. 1959, pp. 95-97, from *Chronicken der Deutschen Städte,* vol II, 1864, pp. 507-8.

101. F. Sartini *Statuti dell'arte dei rigattieri e linaioli di Firenze 1296-1340.* Florence 1940.

102. *Cambridge Economic History* vol. II, 1952, ch. VI. The Woollen Industry'. by E. Carus-Wilson, pp. 355-428. H. van Werveke 'Industrial Growth in the middle ages: the Cloth Industry in Flanders, *Economic History Review* 1954, Second series VI, pp. 237-45.

103. P. Bonenfant 'L'épisode de la nef des tisserands de 1135', *Rousseau Mélanges* 1958, pp. 99-109. C. Verlinden 'Marchands ou tisserands: à propos des origines urbaines', *Annales* 1972, pp. 396-406.

104. T. Rader *op. cit.*

105. The legend of St Bénézet of Avignon shows that in the late twelfth century it still seemed preposterous to think of building stone bridges across great rivers. It needed both vision and divine aid to accomplish. M. N. Boyer 'The Bridge building brotherhoods', *Speculum* 1964, pp. 635-50. The first stone bridge over the Thames at London also belongs to this period. The bridge built across the Reuss gorge by *c.* 1200 opened up central Switzerland and stimulated the development of that land in the thirteenth century.

106. J. Wimpheling *Epitoma Germanica* 1502, ch. 64, refers to the German invention of the bombard *c.* 1380: 'Ita non solum Germani nostri (vel ipsis exteris testantibus) bellatores semper fuisse acerrimi sed instrumentorum quoque bellicorum inventores subtilissimi videntur'.

107. K. Huuri 'Zur Geschichte des mittelalterlichen Geschützwesens aus Orientalischen Quellen', *Studia Orientalis Societas Orientalis Fennica.* IX. 3, Helsingfors 1941. compares the situation in both east and west until the west established its definitive technical superiority.

108. L. F. Salzman *Building in England down to 1540,* Oxford 1967. P. du Colombier *Les chantiers des cathédrales,* 2nd ed., Paris 1973.

109. G. Le Bras 'Les confréries chrétiens', *R.H.D.F.E.* 1940, pp. 310-63. There is some evidence of charitable foundations amongst lay townsmen almost from the beginning, but it is not until the early fourteenth century that the proof of concern on a wide scale is overwhelming. Thus the foundation of the fraternity of St Eloi, appropriately enough by two smiths in the diocese of Arras in 1188, was not written up till 1317: P. Bertin *Les Charitables,* Aire-sur-la Lys 1949. See also E. von Moeller *Die Elendenbrüderschafter: ein beitrag zur geschichte der Fremden fürsorge im mittelalter,* Leipzig 1906, and P. Duparc 'Confréries du St. Esprit', *R.H.D.F.E.* 1958, pp. 349-67, 555-85. The evidence for the fraternity of Our Lady at Paris goes back to 1257. It appears that the momentum for charitable foundations gathered speed in the late thirteenth century. There is a fascinating account of tours of inspection at 73 hospitals in the diocese of Paris in the mid-fourteenth century: L. Le Grand *Mémoires de la Société de l'histoire de Paris,* t. xxiv, 1897, pp. 61-362.

110. Hostiensis *Summa Aurea* Lib. v, dist. de magistris, Lyon 1588, p. 288 verso, citing the canonist Placentinus who died at Montpellier in 1192.

111. A. H. Thames in *Calendar of Pleas and Memoranda Rolls 1364-81,* Cambridge 1929, xxxi-xxxv, concluded that the organization of the various trades in London remained very fluid between 1309 and 1423. The situation in the early fourteenth century is known from letter book D, 1309-14 (see R. R. Sharpe *Calendar of letter books,* London 1902) when there were 120 recognized occupations. In 1423 there were 111, but some of these were new.

112. *Die Chroniken der Deutschen Städte* xxxiv, 1929, pp. 39-295.

113. Eximenic, chap. 115: 'habitadors e vehins de la ciutat no son appellats ciutadans ne vehins jatsia que sens ells la ciutat no puxa ben essere car nes fa sens asens e gats e cans e sens altres moltes coses que empero no poden haver nom vehins ne ciutadans de la ciutat'. Compare with this P. von Stetten *Kunst Gewerb und Handwerks Geschichte der Reichs Stadt Augsburg,* Augsburg 1779: 'ich behaupte die Geschichte der Reichstadt Augsburg sey vor der Geschichte anderer Städte vorzuglich in Ansehung der Künste die darin seit langer Zeiten blüheten, besonders merkwürdig'.

114. C. L. Kingsford *Chronicles of London,* ed. C. L. Kingsford 1905; *The Chronicle of Fabyan.* ed. H. Ellis, London 1811.

115. *A Parisian Journal 1405-1449,* transl. J. Shirley, Oxford 1968.

116. *Arezzo Archivio di Stato: Statuti 1385-1506,* f. 184: 'Guilielmus Guelfi de Montecatino comitatus Florentie nunc habitator Aretio in burgo . . . dixit dicto Cauti camerario . . . verba iniuriosa . . ."tu sei uno guittoncello anche serrai pagato delle toi cattivazze" et postea predictus Guilielmus altiavit pannos a parte posteriori et mostravit sibi pudibenda nature dicto camerario et in despectum dicti camerarii et contra eius voluntate et contra formam iuris stat, statutorum civitatis Areti'. He was fined £3 12 shillings.

Chapter 4 *The City of God*

1. F. Nietzsche *Beyond Good and Evil,* transl. R. J. Hollingdale, Harmondsworth.

2. 1973, p. 66. cp. Milton *Il Penseroso ll,* 158-166, on the exaltation induced by looking at a religious building.

3. Peter Damian *P.L.* 144 *cc.* 378-86, *Epistolae* Lib. vi, 5; and *ibid.,* 145, *cc.* 857-60, from the miracles of St Hugh of Cluny. Orderic, ed. Chibnall, Vol iii pp. 150-1,

Lib. v, 14.

4. *Libellus de diversis ordinibus et professionibus qui sunt in aecclesia,* ed. G. Constable, Oxford 1972.

5. *The letters of Peter the Venerable,* ed. G. Constable, Harvard 1967; ep. 28 deals with the Cistercian criticisms.

6. Otto of Freising *Chronicon,* Lib. vii.

7. C. Dereine 'L'élaboration du statut canonique des chanoines réguliers', *Revue d'histoire ecclésiastique* 1951, no. 46, pp. 534-65.

8. Orderic, ed. Chibnall vol III, pp. 216-7, Lib vi, c. 2, Gerold of Avranches: chaplain to Earl Hugh of Chester.

9. M. Aubrun *Vie de saint Etienne d'Obazine,* Clermont-Ferrand 1970. This life illustrates some difficulties surrounding reformers in this period.

10. The earliest confirmation of the *Carta Caritatis* by any pope, that by Calixtus II in 1119, is, curiously enough, lost.

11. Gregory VII *Registrum,* ed. E. Caspar, Berlin 1923, Lib. iv, *c.* 20. cf. M.G.H. Scriptores VII, p. 540.

12. Peter the Venerable *Contra Petrobrusianos hereticos,* ed. J. Fearns, Turnholt 1968. The church of Liège wrote to Lucius II about a similar group, *P.L.* 179, *cc.* 937-8. R. Moore 'The origins of medieval heresy' *History* 1970, pp. 21-36, and (forthcoming) a collection of documents to illustrate the beliefs of heretics in this period.

13. *P.L. 182, cc. 676-80.*

14. B. Smalley *The Study of the Bible in the Middle Ages,* Oxford 2nd ed. 1952.

15. N. R. Ker *English Manuscripts in the Century after the Norman Conquest,* Oxford 1960.

16. *The story of Abelard's adversities,* transl. J. T. Muckle, Toronto 1964. Bernard was brought into dispute with Abelard by William, Abbot of St Thierry, whose Disputatio adversus Petrum Abelardum (*P.L.* 180, *cc.* 249-82) demonstrates the hostility Abelard's teaching aroused in the late 1130s. For this see also A. V. Murray *Abelard and St. Bernard: a study of twelfth-century modernism,* 1967.

17. G. Makdisi 'The scholastic method in medieval education: an enquiry into its origins in law and theology', *Speculum* 1974, pp. 640-61, has called attention to Islamic parallels and suggests that because Islam had no universities there were no institutional means of fostering the scholastic method there.

18. John of Salisbury *The Metalogicon,* trans. D. D. McGarry, Berkeley 1955, Lib. iv, c. 6.

19. Peter Lombard *Libri IV Sententiarum,* Quaracchi 1916. About thirty years later the prior of St Victor, Gautier, still upholding earlier traditions in theology, lumped Lombard together with Abelard and others, and accused them of sowing confusion in men's minds: 'Contra Quatuor Labyrinthos Franciae', *Archives d'histoire doctinale et littéraire du moyen âge,* 1952. xix, pp. 187-334, ed. P. Glorieux.

20. E. Vinaver *The rise of romance,* Oxford 1971, pp. 23-32.

21. *P.L.* 161.

22. P. Fournier *Histoire des collections canoniques en occident depuis les Fausses Décrétales jusqu'au Décret de Gratien,* Paris 1931-2, 2 tomes.

23. P. Vinogradoff *Roman Law in Medieval Europe,* Oxford 2nd ed. 1929. The earliest teacher of law in Bologna was Pepe, mentioned in 1076. Irnerius lectured there from *c.* 1088 and began to restore the text of civil law by gathering and comparing manuscripts. He was followed by the glossators, whose concern was to try and make sense of the text.

24. *Decretum magistri Gratiani,* ed. A. Friedberg, Leipzig 1879. He too needed commentaries. Hugh of Pisa (Huguccio) wrote his, 1188-90. The Glossa Ordinaria by Johannes Teutonicus Zemeca was completed *c.* 1215-17. The great *summa* by Henry of Susa (Hostiensis), begun in 1239, was finished in 1253: *synthesis utrumque ius.*

25. Lucius III was dragged into a row between the proctor of Capua and an acolyte, Sergius, who had goaded the proctor into striking him in the face, *leniter.* Lucius sensibly referred this petty matter back to Capua, but he had still been bothered by an obviously trivial case. W. Holtzmann 'Kanonistische Ergänzungen zur Italia Pontificia' in *Quellen und Forschungen aus Italienischen Archiven und Bibliotheken* xxxviii, 1958, p. 131, no. 172.

26. C. R. Cheney *From Becket to Langton: English Church Government 1170-1213,* Manchester 1956, pp. 58-9, cites the case sent by Roger, Archbishop of York, to Alexander III for a ruling: what was to be done about the man who confessed to fornicating, at her instigation, with the mother of the girl less than ten years old whom he had married. The marriage had not been consummated.

27. Since it had no special resources of its own to meet the additional expenses of caring for all the churches of the west, the papacy naturally made those who forced it to attend to their business pay up for their privileges. Visitors to Rome therefore complained and criticised Roman greed. The earliest extensive example of such a denunciation is, however, satirical, and shows that the author ridiculed the clergy in search of dignities as much as the curia: *Tractatus Garsiae,* ed. R. M. Thomson, Leiden 1973. The criticisms became more bitter in the late twelfth century, and more conventional. They should not be read as expressing dissatisfaction with Roman government as such, only with some of the more disagreeable consequences of it. Whatever the cost, litigation at Rome was deemed necessary by disputatious clerics. Satire flourished because they evidently thought a spiritual government should cost them nothing.

28. C. J. Hefele *Histoire de Conciles,* transl. H. Leclercq, 1907, t. v. 2, canon 13; Ne nimia religiosorum. On Innocent III's love of order see M. Maccarone *Studi su Innocenzo III,* Padua 1972, pp. 334-7.

29. Such is the impression left, for example by M. D. Knowles *The Religious Orders in Medieval England,* Cambridge 1948-59, whereas in the *Monastic Order in England,* Cambridge 1940, which dealt with the years before 1216, Knowles was able to show how the monasteries had played a leading part in the church's affairs. What might have been true of England, however, or of other parts of western Europe, does not have the same immediate effect in central Europe. It was only in the thirteenth century that the Cistercians began to colonize Bohemia. In such matters it is of course difficult to speak for all Christendom at once.

30. The pathetic Lollard petition to the English parliament of 1410 fancifully imagined how religious property could, if confiscated, be assigned to worthy secular purposes. It commanded so little sympathetic attention there that no record of it appears on the parliament roll: C. L. Kingsford *Chronicles of London*, 1905, pp. 65-8, from Cotton MS. Julius BII.

31. Suger *Oeuvres*, pp. 151-209. G. Duby *Annales* 1952, pp. 155-71 for Cluny. A. Chèdeville *Liber Controversiarum S. Vincentii Cenomannensis*, Paris 1969, p. 35: the first cartulary of the house, 1080-1120, describes the growth of the domain; the second, 1190-1220, shows its defence and stabilization.

32. W. Map *De nugis curialium*, transl. F. Tupper and M. B. Ogle, London 1924.

33. M. E. Reeves *The Influence of Prophecy in the Later Middle Ages*, Oxford 1969.

34. J. H. R. Moorman *A History of the Franciscan Order*, Oxford 1968; P. Sabatier *Vie de Saint Francois d'Assise*, Paris 1931.

35. T. Manteuffel *La naissance d'une hérésie: la pauvreté volontaire*, Mouton 1970, shows that the church encouraged individuals to practise poverty but never advocated it for groups.

36. M. Dufeil *Guillaume de St. Amour*, 1972.

37. The Inquisition was only introduced to inquire into heresy about 1230 and definitely organized by Innocent IV in 1252: *Ad extirpanda*. The evidence for the survival of heretical beliefs a century later is found in *Le registre d'Inquisition de Jacques Fournier, evêque de Pamiers*, ed. J. Duvernoy, Toulouse 1964. For the unpopularity of Dominican inquisitors see C. Compayré *Etudes historiques et documents inédits sur l'Albigeois et le Castrais*, Albi 1841, nos. 62, 65, 69.

38. *Aucassin and Nicolette*, transl. P. Matarasso, Harmondsworth 1971.

39. Andreas Capellanus *The art of courtly love*, transl. J. J. Parry, from *De Amore libri tres*, New York 1941.

40. H. Caplan *Of Rhetoric*, Cornell 1970. Alan of Lille wrote a *summa de arte praedicatoria P.L.* 210, *cc* 111-98. The Dominican Humbert of Romans wrote a treatise on preaching, which has been translated by W. M. Conlon, 1951. J. Hus in 1412 endorsed the view that preachers counted for more in the church than prelates: *Letters*, ed. H. B. Workman and R. M. Pope. London 1904. As preaching became more common in the later middle ages, it was generally assumed that more exhortation, rebuke or instruction would make men better and that more preaching was an unmitigated blessing.

41. Mortet *op. cit.*, pp. 203-4.

42. O. Lehmann-Brockhaus *Schriftsquellen zur Kunstgeschichte des 11. und 12 Jahrhunderts für Deutschland*, Berlin 1938, no. 3053. cf. Radulphus Glaber *Historia sui temporis*, *P.L.* 142, c. 651.

43. G. Mollat 'La restitution des églises privées', *R.H.D.F.E.* 1949, pp. 399-423. M. Chibnall 'The monks and pastoral work', *Journal of Ecclesiastical History* 1967, pp. 165-172. Gratian Decretum *op cit* Causa XVI, discusses at much length the case of an abbot who appointed a monk to a parish; it was one of the three or four most complicated problems in his textbook. See also O. P. Clavadetscher *Die geistlichen Richter des Bistums Chur* Basel 1964 p. 1, where the bishop of Chur authorized a monk to serve a church of his diocese when the parishioners challenged it, on the grounds that the abbot had the right of presentation: 'diximus monacho de iure

licere divina ibidem populo celebrare', from *Bündner Urkundenbuch*, ed. E. Mayer-Marthaler and F. Perret, Chur. vol II, 1973, no. 496: 1201.

44. Gregory VII *Registrum op. cit.,* t. II, pp. 546-62, Lib. VIII no. 21.

45. *ibid.* t. I, pp. 66-7, letter of 29 March 1075. Eadmer *Historia Novorum in Anglia* ed. M. Rule R.S. 1884, pp. 141-4. Alexander III ordered an enquiry into the case of a priest accused of having taken back his concubine and given her children, after she had married another. W. Holtzmann *Quellen und Forschungen,* 1958, p. 138, no. 182. The celibate clergy began to make much of the common lay vice of *Luxuria carnis* which they had ostensibly overcome. See for example Adam de Perseigne. *Lettres* ed. J. Bouvet, Paris 1960, letter xiv, 'Inter ceteras autem horum criminum pestes eminet quae magis imminet luxuria carni'.

46. There were always local exceptions. In the time of Alexander III special rules applied in at least the three kingdoms of England, Hungary and Sicily. Frederick II's 'Constitutions of Melfi' (1231) show that benefit of clergy did not cover accusations of treason. J. M. Powell: *The Liber Augustalis,* Syracuse, New York 1971, pp. 37 (no. lxviii) and p. 44 (no. xlv).

47. *Liber Antiques de ordinationibus vicariarum tempore Hugonis de Welles Lincolniensis episcopi 1209-35,* ed. A. Gibbons, Lincoln 1888. For the proof of the thoroughness of episcopal visitation in the thirteenth century see Odo Rigaud *Register,* transl. S. M. Brown and J. F. O'Sullivan, New York 1964.

48. Hefele *op. cit.,* v. 2 canon 21. Alexander III ordered suspension of a priest accused of blabbing about what a man had confided to him in confession of his sexual offences. W. Holtzmann *Quellen,* 1958, p. 148, no. 187. The significance of confession and absolution given by the priest only becomes clear when the new situation is seen in contrast to the old. Formerly the priest had carefully examined the penitent and then imposed on him the appropriate penance prescribed by the penitential tariffs, finally praying that God absolve the sinner. By 1200 penitents expected the priest himself to pronounce absolution, the tariffs were abandoned and the penance could anyway be performed vicariously or 'indulged'. A. Lagarde 'Le manuel de confesseur au xie siècle. *Revue d'histoire et de littérature religieuse* 1910, pp. 542-50.

49. Gregory IX laid down a ruling in 1231 that there was to be no repetition of the sacrament of ordination, even if it were not conferred at the proper time. This brought ordination into line with the exemplary sacrament of baptism which could be given once only and was indelible. Potthast *Regesta Pontificum Romanorum,* Berlin 1874, no. 8832. *Enchiridion Symbolarum,* H. Denzinger, 32nd edition, A. Schönmetzer, Herder 1963, no. 825. Ordination was first defined as one of the seven sacraments of the church in the profession of faith required of the Greek Emperor Michael VIII, Paleologus at the Council of Lyon II, in 1274. *Ibid.* no. 860.

50. J. F. McCue 'The doctrine of transubstantiation from Berengar through Trent', *Harvard Theological Review* 1968, pp. 385-430.

51. J. A. Jungmann *The Mass of the Roman Rite,* transl. F. A. Brunner, London 1959. Archbishop Reynolds of Canterbury required the parishes (1313-17) to supply the service books, vestments, altar-furnishings etc. necessary for the spiritual life of the community. Such evidence as there is for the fourteenth century shows that efforts were made to meet his standards. For example, see *Inventory of Church Goods in the archdeaconery of Norwich,* ed. Ailred Watkin, Norfolk Record Society XIX, 1947-8.

52. Robert de Sorbonne on marriage in B. Hauréau *Notices et Extraits* I, 1890, pp. 188-202, from Paris *B.N.* Ms. Lat. 3218.

53. D. Wilkins *Concilia Magni Britanniae et Hiberniae,* 1757, t.II, pp. 51-61. Robert Grossetest *Epistolae,* ed. H. R. Luard, London 1861, (*R. S.*) pp. 155-7.

54. L. Boyle 'Oculus Sacerdotis', *T.R.H.S.,* 1954. pp. 81-110. J. Dietterle 'Die Summa Confessorum', *Zeitschrift für Kirchengeschichte* Bände, nos. 24-7 (1903-06), several articles. Y. Lefèvre *L'elucidarium et les lucidaires,* Bibliothèques des écoles françaises d'Athènes et de Rome, no. 180, 1954: this is an early twelfth-century work of elementary theology much used in Latin and in translation throughout the next four centuries. It indicates a much less sophisticated attitude to theology than the teaching of the thirteenth-century schools. For the religious instruction of laymen see M. D. Legge 'Pierre de Peckham and his "Lumiere as lais" ', *Modern Language Review* xxiv, 1929, pp. 37-47 and *ibid.* xlvi, 1951, pp. 191-5. C. V. Langlois *La Vie en France au moyen âge d'apres des moralistes du temps,* Paris 1925.

55. The clergy themselves thought the same. This is one of the main concerns of the fifteenth-century letter collection described by W. A. Pantin 'A medieval treatise on letter writing', *Bulletin of the John Rylands Library* XIII, 1929, pp. 326-82.

56. L. Boyle 'The constitution *Cum ex eo* of Boniface VIII', *Medieval Studies* xxiv, 1962, pp. 263-302. E. F. Jacob 'English University Clerks in the later middle ages—the problems of maintenance', *Bulletin of the John Rylands Library* xxix, 1945-46, pp. 304-25. For colleges see A. L. Gabriel *Student Life in Ave Maria College,* University of Notre Dame 1955, and A. Cobban *The Medieval Universities,* London 1975.

57. W. O. Ault 'Manor Court and Parish Church in fifteenth-century England', *Speculum* 1967, pp. 53-67, and *ibid.* 'The village church and the village community', *Speculum* 1970, pp. 197-215.

58. B. Hauréau 'Mémoire sur un commentaire des Métamorphoses d'Ovide', *Mémoires de l'Académie des Inscriptions* vol. xxx, 2, pp. 45-55: a commentary by Pierre Bersuize O.S.B., a friend of Petrarch.

59. R. W. Southern *Medieval Humanism,* Oxford 1970, pp. 105-32.

60. W. and M. Kneale *Development of Logic,* Oxford 1962.

61. An interesting example of the application of Aristotle and other pagan writers to theological problems appears in learned opinion about the nature of the virgin birth of Christ. The Thomists used Aristotle; the Franciscans preferred Galen when elucidating these mysteries. K. E. Bórresen *Anthropologie Médiévale et théologie mariale,* Oslo 1972.

62. M. de Bouard 'Encyclopédies Médiévales', *Revue des Questions Historiques* CXII, 1930, pp. 258-304.

63. Peckham's predecessor at Canterbury, the Dominican Robert of Kilwardby, was prominent in this affair: F. Ehrle 'Der Augustinismus und der Aristotelismus in der Scholastik' *Archiv für Literatur und Kirchengeschichte des mittelalters* V, pp. 614-32.

64. Jean De Jandun in 'Le Roux de Lincy', *op. cit.* Contrast this with the mockery of university learning shown in Pierre Michault's poem *Le Doctrinal du temps present* (1466), ed. T. Walton, Paris 1931. An underground school is run by Falsity and the teaching begins under Masters Boasting and Vainglory. The course terminated fittingly with a graduation ceremony: pp. 9-40, 140-44.

65. *P.L.* 182 'De consideratione': the phrase comes from Leo I, letter 14.

66. M. Maccarone *Vicarius Christi: storia del titolo papale,* Lateranum XVIII, 1953.

67. The special loyalties of the Roman clergy to their own particular churches are well illustrated by the tracts written, at least in part, in the late twelfth century, describing the buildings, services and traditions of St. Peter's (*AASS* June, VII, pp. 37-56) and St. John Lateran (*P.L.* 194, *cc* 1543-60). K. Jordan 'Die Entstehung der Römischen Kurie', *Zeitschrift der Savigny Stiftung* Band 59, Kanonische Abteilung 28, Weimar 1939, pp. 97-152.

68. Philippe de Mézières denounced the multiplication of offices. *op. cit.* II, pp. 224-6. C. Lux *Constitutionum Apostolicarum de generali beneficiorum reservatione 1265-1378,* Breslau 1904, pp. 51-4: Ex debito (1316) Extra Comm 1. 3. G. Barraclough *Papal Provisions,* Oxford 1935.

69. *Rotuli Parliamentorum* III, 301, 465.

70. The papacy was drawn into opposing Frederick II in Italy for such reasons, but it could only excommunicate him for spiritual ones: Gregory IX had therefore to try and justify himself when writing to Louis IX of France, a sound Christian but traditionally allied to the Staufen Frederick. The pope alleged that 'Cum enim pugnare pro eripienda Terra Sancta de manibus paganorum sit perpetua vita meritorium, multo magis (!) merito esse creditur si eorum qui exterminium fidei in qua salus totius mundi consistit et ecclesiae machinantur generalis excidium impietas expugnetur.' L. A. Huillard-Bréholles *Historia Diplomatica Friderici II,* Paris 1852-9, vol. V, p.460, 21 October 1239.

71. Boniface VIII *Registre,* ed. G. Digard, t. III no. 5382, Lateran 18 November 1302.

Chapter 5 *Lay Dominion*
1. H. Mitteis 'Rechtsgeschichte und Machtsgeschichte' in *Wirtschaft und Kultur (Festschrift Dopsch),* Baden bei Wien 1938, p. 565. F. Kern 'Recht und Verfassung im mittelalter,' *H.Z.* 120, 1919, pp. 1-79.

2. K. G. Cram *Iudicium Belli: Zum Rechtscharakter des Krieges in deutschen Mittelalter,* Beiheft zum Archiv für Kulturgeschichte Heft 5, Münster 1955.

3. P. J. Proudhon *La guerre et la paix: recherches sur le principe et la constitution du droit des gens,* Brussels 1861.

4. Eadmer *op. cit.* p. 69.

5. V. D'Alessandro *Fidelitas Normannorum,* Note sulla fondazione dello stato normanno e sui rapporti col papato, Palermo 1969.

6. Guillaume de Poitiers *Histoire de Guillaume le Conquérant,* ed. R. Foreville, Paris 1952.

7. Suger Oeuvres, 1867, pp. 5-149; transl. H. Waquet *Vie de Louis VI.* Paris 1929, cap. xxviii, pp. 218-31.

8. William of Malmesbury *De Gestis Regum Anglorum,* ed. W. Stubbs, R.S. vol. II, 1889, pp. 368, 369-71, 373-4.

9. Orderic *op. cit.,* ed. M. Chibnall, II, pp. 310-15, Lib. IV c. 14.

10. *Chronicle known as Benedict of Peterborough,* ed. W. Stubbs, R.S., London

1867. Now usually regarded as the work of Roger of Hoveden and known as the *Gesta Henrici.* See D. Stenton 'Roger of Hoveden and Benedict', *E.H.R.* 1953, pp. 574-82. This identification is doubted by A. Gransden: *Historical Writing in England,* London 1974, p. 230.

11. *Recueil des Actes d'Henri II,* ed. L. V. Delisle and E. Berger, Paris 1916. T. A. M. Bishop *Scriptores Regis,* Oxford 1961.

12. *Letters of Thomas Becket,* ed. J. C. Robertson R.S. London 1881-5. The complaints about York carrying his cross in the province of Canterbury occur in several letters e.g. ep. xxvii, xli, xlii, xliii.

13. *ibid.* no. xiv See also A. Saltman 'Two Early Collections of Becket Correspondence', *Bulletin of the Institute of Historical Research* xxii 1949, pp. 155-6.

14. *ibid.* ep. xxiii.

15. A. Werminghott 'Ein *tractatus de coronatione imperatoris* aus den vierzehn-Jahrhundert', *Zeitschrift der Savigny-Stiftung für Rechtsgeschichte Germanische Abteilung,* xxiv, 1902, pp. 380-90.

16. E. Martène and U. Durand *Veterum Scriptorum et Monumentorum Amplissima Collectio,* t. vii, Paris 1733, col. 198, cap. xi.

17. M. G. H. Legum t. iv, 2, pp. 241-7.

18. H. Sproemberg 'La naissance d'un état allemand au moyen âge', *Moyen Age* 1958, pp. 213-48, argued against the view that the Staufen were founders of a specifically German state.

19. Jordan of Osnabrück *De praerogativa Romani imperii,* ed. H. Grundmann, 1930.

20. A. Nitschke 'Friedrich II, ein ritter des hohen mittelalters', *H.Z.* 194, 1962, pp. 1-36.

21. C. C. Bayley *The formation of the German College of Electors in the mid-thirteenth century,* Toronto 1949.

22. M. G. H. Legum IV, *Constitutiones et Acta Publica Imperatorum et Regum,* ed. L. Weiland, Hannover 1896, pp. 89-91, 211-13.

23. G. Post. 'Two Notes on Nationalism in the middle ages', *Traditio* 1953, pp. 281-320.

24. F. Lot and R. Fawtier *Histoire des Institutions Françaises au moyen âge* t. i *Institutions seigneuriales,* Paris 1957. P. Feuchère 'Essai sur l'évolution territoriale des principautés françaises', *Moyen Age* 1952, pp. 85-117, emphasized that the principalities were not merely political creations, but grew out of the basic pattern of social organization.

25. F. Lot and R. Fawtier *Le Premier Budget de la Monarchie Française, B.E.H.E.* 259, Paris 1932.

26. B. Guénée 'L'histoire de l'Etat en France à la fin du moyen âge', *Revue Historique* 232, 1964, pp. 331-60.

27. 'Recueil des Historiens des Gaules et de la France', t. xxiv, Paris 1904. *Les Enquëtes Administratives du règne de St. Louis* ed. L. V. Delisle.

28. W. Berges *Die Fürstenspiegel,* Leipzig 1938.

488   *The Medieval European Community*

29. Vincent of Beauvais 'De morali principis institutione'. Merton College Oxford, Ms. 110 ff. 352b-374b, summarized in Berges *op. cit.*

30. H. F. Delaborde 'Le texte primitif des Enseignements de St Louis à son fils', *B.E.C.* 73 1912, pp. 73-100, 237-62. Sancho IV of Castile also wrote advice for his son in 1293: 'con ayuda de cientificos sabios ordene fazen este libro para mi fijo', which was appropriate not just for the prince, but for all lords and *siervos* great and small. *Castigos e Documentos para bien vivir,* ed. A. Rey, Bloomington *(Indiana) 1952.*

31. Most of the Latin texts subsequently translated for use in the *Grandes Chroniques de France* were copied into a manuscript written in Louis's time: Paris B.N. Ms. Lat. 5925.

32. H. Bordier *Archives de la France,* Paris 1855.

33. Odofredo of Bologna (died 1265) is discussed by N. Tamassia in *Atti e Memorie della R. Deputazione di Storia Patria per la provincia di Romagna,* 1892-3, 1893-4. See also G. Post 'The theory of public law and the state in the thirteenth century', *Seminar* VI 1948, pp. 42-59.

34. J. Archer 'Notes sur le Droit Savant', *R.H.D.F.E.* 1906, 30, pp. 138-78.

35. *Coutumes de Beauvaisis,* ed. A. Salmon, Paris 1899, ch. 49.

36. The 'Gravamina Ecclesiae Gallicanae' recorded by Matthew Paris in his *Chronica Majora* R.S. VI pp. 99-112, list the complaints of secular lords against the encroachments of the papacy. For the relations of the king with churchmen see G. J. Campbell 'Clerical Immunities in France during the reign of Philip III,' *Speculum* 1964, pp. 404-24.

37. C. V. Langlois *Registres perdus des Archives de la Chambre des Comptes de Paris.* Notices et Extraits des Maunscrits de la Bibliothèque Nationale, t. 40, Paris 1917, pp. 33-380.

38. Jean, sire de Joinville, *Vie de St. Louis,* ed. N. de Wailly, transl J. Evans, Oxford 1938. *Les Olim,* ed. A. A. Beugnot, 1839, 4 tomes.

39. T. Rymer *Foedera, Conventiones etc.,* T. I, London 1704, pp. 776-8.

40. R. Cazelles 'La guerre privée', *R.H.D.F.E.* 1960, pp. 530-48. H. Morel 'La fin du duel judiciaire', *ibid,* 1964, pp. 574-639.

41. *Ordonnances des Roys de France, op. cit.* 1733, t. II, pp. 219-24.

42. *Ordonnances* t. I, p. 502. Philip IV set this up at Orléans.

43. *Coutume, Style et Usage au temps de l'Echiquier de Normandie, M.S.A.N.* second series VIII, Caen 1847, cap. xxv-xxvii.

44. P. Petot 'Le droit commun selon les coutumiers', *R.H.D.F.E.* 1960, pp. 412-29. J. P. Dawson 'Codification of French customs', *Michigan Law Review* 1940, pp. 765-88. On Jean Boutillier, see A. Paillard de Saint-Aiglan in *BEC* ix, 1847-8, pp. 89-143. C. Loyseau *Traite des Seigneuries,* 1610.

45. James I shows the variety of laws enforced in his own courts, *Chronicle, op. cit.* cap. cccxcvi.

46. C. Bornhak 'Römisches und Deutsches Recht', *H.Z.* 159, 1939, pp. 1-21, stresses the variety of laws in medieval Germany where all Germans did not live under the

same laws; the clergy, nobles, towns and peasants (according to locality) all had their own. Germany was not in this respect exceptional.

47. K. S. Bader *Dorfgenossenschaft und Dorfgemeinde,* Cologne 1962; *ibid.* 'Bauern-recht und Bauern Freiheit in späteren Mittelalter: *Historisches Jahrbuch* 1941, 61, pp. 51-87. The canonist Henry of Susa (Hostiensis) quotes with approval the bold remark of an English peasant: 'quilibet dominus dicitur rex rerum suarum quod ostendit regi Anglorum Ricardo Anglicanus rusticus habitans in foresta.' N. Didier 'Henri Suse en Angleterre', *Studi in onore di Vincenzio Arangio Ruiz,* Naples t. II pp. 333-51. For village customs see the interesting example printed by F. Moulenq 'Albias et ses Coutumes', *Bulletin de la Société Archéologique du Tarn et Garonne* 1869, pp. 97-112, 129-133.

48. E. J. Tardif *Coutumiers de Normandie, S.H.N.* 1881.

49. J. Balou 'les fondements du régime foncier au moyen âge', *Anciens Pays et Assem-blées d'Etats* VII 1954, p. 158, defends the coherence of the evolution of the medieval land law and speaks of the génie de ces hommes qui, à la mesure des évènements stupénants qu'ils ont eu à vivre tout au long de l'effondrement de l'empire ont su concevoir un droit nouveau et en déployer l'ordonnance à travers tant de siècles.'

50. K. Lehmann *Das Langobardische Lehnrecht,* Göttingen 1896, 2nd ed. K.A. Eckhardt 1971. The fullest version of the law, the 'Vulgate', was complete before 1233.

51. H. Pelz, H. Grauert and J. Mayerhofer *Drei Bayerische Traditionsbücher aus dem xii Jahrhundert,* München 1880: Codex Falkensteinensis.

52. G. Friedrich *Codex Diplomaticus et epistolarius regni Bohemia* t. II, Prague 1912, no. 234, pp. 222-25: a confirmation by King Ottokar I (1222) of Conrad-Otto's privilege. F. Graus 'Origines de l'état et de la noblesse en Moravie et en Bohème', *Revue des Etudes Slaves,* 39, 1961, pp. 43-58.

53. K. Bosl (ed.) *Handbuch der Geschichte der Böhmischen Länder* I, Stuttgart 1967.

54. F. W. Maitland *Select Pleas of the Crown,* Selden Society vol. I 1887, p. 139.

55. R. Schroeder in *Zeitschrift der Savigny Stiftung für Rechtsgeschichte 24 Germanis-tische Abtheilung* XI. 1890. p. 244. R. Schroeder in Zeitschrift, p. 244, review of K. Lamprecht: *Deutsches Wirtschaftsleben.*

56. O. Brunner *Land und Herrschaft,* 3rd ed., Brünn 1943.

57. Henry de Bracton *The laws and customs of England, transl. S. E. Thorne,* Cambridge (Mass.). 1968.

58. W. S. Holdsworth *A History of English Law,* London 1923, 3rd ed. vol. II pp. 525-56, book III part I, ch. 5.

59. e.g. Philippe de Mézières *op. cit.* II, pp. 300-01.

60. Hence J. Wyclif *Tractatus de civili domino,* ed. R. L. Poole and others, Wyclif Society 1885-1904, lib. I, cap. xxxv etc.

61. *Registrum Epistolarum fratris Johannis Peckham archiepiscopi Cantuariensis* ed. C. T. Martin R.S., vol. I 1882, ep. cxcv-cxcvi, 28 September 1281.

62. They frequently aired their grievances but in spite of their complaints they had played an independent, important and respected role in thirteenth-century

England. Never again were they to be so influential or effective as a group. W. R. Jones 'Bishops, Politics and the two laws: the Gravamina of the English Clergy 1237-1399', *Speculum* 1966, pp. 209-45.

63. A different way of expressing this idea may be found in F. Borkenau *Der Ubergang vom feudalen zum burgerlichen Weltbild*, Paris 1934. Aquinas had shown that the social order had its part to play in the divine scheme of things, and the better educated clergy came to recognize that it was part of their clerical duty. to help rulers fulfil the duties God had laid upon them.

64. H. Finke 'Nachträge und Ergänzungen zu den Acta Aragonensia', *Spanische Forschung* IV 1933, pp. 428-33.

65. A. Landry *Essai économique sur les mutations des monnaies dans l'ancienne France*, Paris 1910. A. Grundzweig 'Les incidences internationales des mutations monétaires de Philippe le Bel', *Moyen Age* 1953, pp. 117-72. R. Cazelles 'Quelques reflexions à propos des mutations de la monnaie royale française, 1295-1360', *ibid.*, 1966, pp. 83-105.

66. James I shows that the troubles with the Aragonese began before 1282: *op cit* chp. cccxcv-vi. *Chronique Catalane de Pierre IV d'Aragon, III de Catalogne*, ed. A. Pagès, Toulouse 1941, pp. 239-290. Quart Capitol.

67. H. Rothwell 'The Confirmation of the Charter 1297', *E.H.R.* 1945 LX, pp. 16-35, 177-91, 300-15.

68. Justinian, Code V 59. 5. 3 used by Innocent III in Decretals I, xxiii, 7 (Canon Law c. 7. X. 1. 23). G. Post, 'A Roman Canonical Maxim: 'quod omnes tangit' in Bracton *Traditio* IV 1946, pp. 197-251.

69. Jean Messelin *Journal des Etats Généraux de France tenus à Tours en 1484*, ed. A. Bernier, Paris 1835, pp. 499-505, reports an interesting discussion of the theory that representatives only spoke for the 'class-interest'. Some of the clergy and nobles claimed that they defended the people more effectively than the third estate did. In general for the problem of representation in the Ancien Régime see E. Lousse *La société de l'ancien régime*, Louvain 1943.

70. *Etudes sur l'histoire des assemblées d'états*, Paris 1966, pp. 118-19.

71. *ibid.* p. 171.

72. F. Giunta *Anciens Pays et Assemblées d'Etats*, XXXVI 1965, pp. 87-102.

73. H. Prentout *Les états provinciaux de Normandie*, t. II, Caen 1925, ch. V and VI showed that the Norman estates resisted requests for aid.

74. R. E. Glassock *The lay-subsidy assessments of 1334*, Oxford 1975. By the fifteenth century the Lancastrians had to resort to borrowing to meet their needs. The situation was not improved until the Yorkists were once again able to live from the revenues of the crown domain. For the period to 1369 see now G. L. Harriss *King, Parliament and Public Finance in Medieval England*, Oxford 1975.

75. K. Gorski 'The origins of the Polish Sejm', *Slavonic and East European Review* 44, 1965-6, pp. 122-38.

76. K. Bosl *op. cit.* (v. supra. n. 53). For Hungary see G. Bonis *Anciens Pays* XXXVI 1965, pp. 287-301.

77. *Etudes*, 1966 *op. cit.* p. 179.

78. *Anciens Pays* 1964, XXXII, pp. 3-13: A. Maravall showed that in the 'Speculum principum ac iustitiae' (Paris 1530) Petrus Belluga, the Valencian lawyer who served Alfonso V of Aragon, gave a sympathetic exposition of the rights of assemblies: cap. XXXVI.

79. *Anciens Pays,* XXXVI, 1965. L. Marini argued, however, that this was somewhat partisan: pp. 103-38.

Chapter 6 *The Communities under Strain*
1. Dante *Purgatorio* XXVII, 49-51. The church's teaching on purgatory only developed in the second half of the thirteenth century. Opinion in 1243 is represented by Geoffroi de Paris in *La Bible des Sept Etats du Monde* who described purgatory in book 4 by translating the twelfth-century De purgatorio S. Patricii by Henry de Saltrey (P. Meyer 'Notice sur...' *Notices et Extraits* XXXIX 1909, pp. 255-322). Innocent IV required the Greeks to accept the Latin name 'purgatory' for the place assigned for the dead while they purged the venial sins that could have been pardoned in life. He assumed that the purging would be by fire (6 March 1254: *Enchiridion Symbolarum,* H. Denzinger, 32nd ed., A. Schönmetzer, Herder 1963, no. 838 pp. 271-2). As a result of the elaborated teaching of the canonists and theologians on penance, the church became more confident in dealing with purgatory. Hugh of St Cher (1200-63) expounded a theory of the treasury of merits from which the church could draw to pay the penalties for sins, so that indulgences were not so much 'pardons' as 'credit'. Bonaventura argued in his commentary on the Sentences (*In Quartum Librum Sententiarum,* Venice 1580, p. 318, IV, 1,1.) that advantages could be obtained for souls in purgatory by those who could help pay the debt. At the Council of Lyon, Gregory X, after listening to the arguments of another Franciscan, John Paraston, agreed that the souls in purgatory might be helped by the prayers of the faithful and the celebration of masses. Plenary indulgences were until the late thirteenth century, issued only in connection with the crusades, but Nicholas IV (another Franciscan) granted them for visits to the Roman churches, and this opened the way for their use in the Jubilee year of 1300. No papal grant of indulgences for souls in purgatory is known earlier than 1457 and the earliest surviving document of papal indulgences for them is the Franciscan Pope Sixtus IV's grant of 1476. In the meantime, however, popular belief in the efficacy of the church militant's intercessions on behalf of those in purgatory outran the more cautious pronouncements of the learned world in general. I have benefited from the reading of an unpublished paper on this matter by my friend Mr. D. A. R. Forrester.

2. G. Villani *Cronache* VIII, XXXVI.

3. Dino Compagni *La cronica,* ed. L del Lungo, *R.R.I.I.S.S.* IX 2 1913; transl. E. C. M. Benecke and A. G. F. Howell, London 1906.

4. Villani, VII, cap. XXXVI.

5. G. Mollat *The Popes at Avignon,* transl. J. Love, London 1963.

6. N. Valois *La France et le Grand Schisme d'Occident,* Paris 1896-1904.

7. The schism had a number of curious consequences at a local level, as may be shown by considering the case of the Abbess of Montivilliers who took advantage of the situation to establish her complete independence of the archbishop of Rouen. In 1378, the archbishop, Philippe d'Alençon, quarrelled with Charles V and went over to Urban VI, who gratefully made him a cardinal. The abbess therefore sought exemption from his schismatic jurisdiction, which was graciously conceded

by Clement VII in 1384. From then until 1789, the abbess in effect ran her own diocese. P. Le Cacheux *L'exemption de Montivilliers,* Caen 1929.

8. J. N. Figgis *Studies of political thought from Gerson to Grotius 1414-1625,* Cambridge 1900; E. F. Jacob *Essays in the Conciliar Epoch,* 2nd ed., Manchester 1953.

9. B. Tierney *Foundations of the Conciliar Theory,* Cambridge 1955.

10. Philippe de Mézières approved of this and took their right to do so for granted: 'lesdiz cardinaux ont plaine puissance de retraictier leur deffaulte sans autorité d'autruy et faire nouvelle ou nouvelles elections valables selon le droit divin et positif', ed. Coopland I, p. 370.

11. See the curious documents printed by H. B. Sauerland 'Aktenstücke zur Geschichte des papstes Urban VI', *Historisches Jahrbuch* 1893, pp. 820-32.

12. E. Perroy *L'Angleterre et le Grand Schisme d'Occident,* Paris 1933.

13. E. Martène *op. cit.* VII pp. 909-10. F. Oakley *The political thought of Pierre d'Ailly,* New Haven 1964.

14. It is curious that in England, however, this division by nations was at the time interpreted in a secular way, as proving that the English had matured sufficiently to be recognized as a nation (J. S. Davies *An English Chronicle,* Camden Society, London, 1856, p. 44). It is evident, however, that the chronicler valued the approval, as though without it, the nationhood of England might have been in doubt.

15. L. R. Loomis *The Council of Constance,* New York 1961.

16. J. B. Morrall *Gerson and the Great Schism,* Manchester 1960, showed how slowly Gerson was won over to the conciliar position.

17. E. Perroy *The Hundred Years' War,* transl. W. B. Wells, London 1951, pp. 36, 51. Perroy makes approximate estimates of 10-12 million Frenchmen as against 3½ million English: barely a third of that of France.

18. J. Froissart *Chroniques,* ed. Kervyn de Lettenhove, 1867-77. He began writing only after the battle of Poitiers (1356); in 1360 when he came to England and showed Queen Philippa, his compatriot, his work, it was still in the form of a rhymed chronicle. His serious interest in writing history developed over the next forty years, when the finest English exploits of the earlier phase had become a matter for wistful memories. Jean Le Bel, a canon of Liège, composed a chronicle (ed. J. Viard and E. Deprèz, Paris 1904) which was Froissart's chief source for the earlier part of the war.

19. *Chronique Normande du XIVe siècle,* ed. A. Molinier, *S.H.F.,* Paris 1882.

20. Geoffrey le Baker *Chronicon,* ed. E. M. Thompson, Oxford 1889. Robert of Avebury *De gestis mirabilibus regis Edward III,* ed. E. M. Thompson, R.S. 1889. In the 1420's and 1430's there appears to have been no continuous interest by the English in recording the fortunes of war. Only one narrative on the English side deals with Norman affairs (Cotton MS Cleopatra C.IV, ed. C. L. Kingsford, *Chronicles of London* 1905, pp. 117-52). On soldiering see more recently H. J. Hewitt *Organization of War under Edward III,* Manchester 1966. M. Keen *The Laws of War in the late Middle Ages,* London 1965.

21. H. S. Denifle *La désolation des églises monastères et hôpitaux en France pendant*

la guerre de cent ans, Paris 1897-9.

22. *Grandes Chroniques de France,* ed. J. Viard, IX, 1937, pp. 269-70.

23. M. M. Postan 'The Costs of the Hundred Years' War', *Past and Present* 27, 1964, pp. 34-53. K. B. McFarlane 'The investment of Sir John Fastolf's profits of war', *T.R.H.S.* 1957, pp. 91-116. *ibid.* 'A Business Partnership in War and Administration 1421-45', *E.H.R.* 1963, pp. 290-310.

24. For example Adam of Murimuth records in 1338 raids on Southampton, Harwich and elsewhere. The French reappeared in 1340 and again much later in 1377 and 1380. Interesting instructions for the French navy when an invasion of England was planned in 1340 were incorporated by Adam of Murimuth into his *Chronicle* (ed. T. Hog, London 1846, pp. 94-9).

25. P. Le Cacheux *Actes de la Chancellerie d'Henri VI concernant la Normandie sous la Domination anglaise 1422-35, S.H.N.,* Rouen 1907, t. I pp. xv-xvi: 'L'impression qui s'en dégage est celle de la misère du menu peuple, rançonné tour à tour par les gens d'armes anglais et les partisans français'. R. Jouet 'La résistance à l'occupation anglaise en Basse-Normandie (1418-50)', *Cahiers des Annales de Normandie* no. 5, 1969.

26. R. W. Chambers *A Book of London English 1384-1425,* Oxford 1931. The documents of London show that English became the language of most official documents somewhat abruptly during the 1420s.

27. J. E. Barnie *War in Medieval Society: social values and the Hundred Years' War 1337-99,* London 1974, attempts to do this from the literary evidence on the English side. R. Boutruche *La crise d'une société—seigneurs et paysans du Bordelais pendant la guerre de cent ans,* Paris 1947, examined one French region in depth, using mainly archive materials.

28. Robert of Avebury *op. cit.,* p. 308. Edward III's mother-in-law, the abbess of Fontenelles (formerly countess of Hainault) who was also Philip VI's sister, acted as negotiator of the truce of 1340. When the Flemish leader Artevelde reminded Edward III not to leave the Flemings out of the terms, she burst out 'Lord God have mercy. All the noble blood of Christendom will be shed for the word of a "vilain",' *Grandes Chroniques* IX p. 207. It is unlikely that Edward III cared more for his merchant allies than he did for the approval of his relations. The Flemings were anyway not much loved in England. Their unpopularity in fourteenth-century London is attested by the Brut Chronicle *(E.E.T.S.)* vol. II 1908, pp. 582-600. For Flanders see H. S. Lucas *The Low Countries and the Hundred Years' War,* 1929.

29. Avebury *op. cit.,* pp. 309-10. The manifesto was sent on 8th February 1340.

30. P. Wolff 'Un problème d'origines: la guerre de cent ans', *Eventail de l'histoire Essais pour Lucien Febvre,* Paris 1953, t. II, pp. 141-8: 'La guerre est avant tout une crise de croissance de l'Etat français.'

31. *Grandes Chroniques op. cit.* IX pp. 269-70. The execution of Simon Pouilliet was so barbarous that even the pious royalist chronicler commented that it was 'une horrible justice ne onques mais n'avoit esté fait semblable on royaume de France'. The loyal Norman chronicler was likewise perturbed at the way the count of Eu had been summarily executed: 'ne il ne fut mie declairé au peuple la cause pourquoy le roy fist mourir le dit conte d'Eu et il ne fut pas mort devant le peuple ains fut decolé en la tour de Nesle'. This comment was also made when Harcourt and others were executed in 1355: 'qui ne furent point jugez devant le peuple mais

tantost qu'ils furent prinz furent decolez', *op. cit.* pp. 96, 109.

32. The guileless chronicler of Philip VI's reign reports that the king was so mystified by men's disloyalty about 1343 that he began to enquire about its possible cause. *Grandes Chroniques* IX, p. 248.

33. A. Artonne *Le mouvement de 1314 et les chartes provinciales de 1315,* Paris 1912. *Ordonnances op. cit.* I, p. 606.

34. At this point the great princes had to maintain lawyers to defend their interests at the parlement of Paris. Guillaume de Breuil served Edward II in this capacity, 1314-18, and was involved in the affair of the Artois inheritance in 1329, for which he was suspended. Obliged to enter upon a period of unwelcome and unprofitable leisure, he decided to write a little work explaining the arcane mysteries of the workings of the parlement for the benefit of litigants. To judge from the number of surviving manuscripts this was much appreciated. If the parlement had reason to regret this unusual breach of professional reserve, the historian is grateful. *Stilus Curie Parlamenti,* ed. F. Aubert, Paris 1909.

35. G. M. R. Picot *Documents relatifs aux Etats Généraux et Assemblées réunis sous Philippe le Bel,* Paris 1901. *ibid. Histoire des Etats Généraux,* Paris 1888.

36. J. B. Henneman *Royal Taxation in Fourteenth-Century France,* Princeton 1972. E. A. R. Brown 'Customary Aids and Royal Fiscal Policy under Philip VI of Valois', *Traditio* XXX 1974 pp. 191-258.

37. N. Valois *Le conseil du roi aux XIVe, XVe, et XVIe siècles,* Paris 1888.

38. F. Lot and R. Fawtier *Histoire des Institutions Françaises au moyen âge,* vol. II, Institutions Royales, Paris 1958.

39. R. H. Bautier 'Recherches sur la chancellerie royale au temps de Philippe VI', *B.E.C.* 1964, CXXII pp. 81-176; 1965, CXXIII pp. 311-459.

40. R. Cazelles *La société politique et la crise de la royauté sous Philippe de Valois,* Paris 1958. *ibid.* 'Les mouvements révolutionnaires du milieu du xive siècle et le cycle de l'action politique', *Revul Historique* 228, 1962, pp. 279-312.

41. *Ordonnances* III pp. 124-46, March 1357.

42. A. L. Funk 'Robert le Coq and Etienne Marcel', *Speculum* 1944, pp. 470-87. E. Faral 'Robert le Coq et les Etats Généraux d'Octobre 1356', *R.H.D.F.E.* 1945, pp. 171-214.

43. R. Delachenal *Histoire de Charles V,* Paris 1909-31.

44. *ibid.* ed. *Chroniques des règnes de Jean II et de Charles V, S.H.F.,* Paris 1910.

45. J. P. Royer *L'église et le royaume de France an XIV siècle d'après le Songe du Vergier,* Paris 1969.

46. Charles V revised the coronation ceremonial of 1365. The text (B.M Cotton MS Tiberius B VIII) was edited by E. S. Dewick for the Henry Bradshaw Society, London 1899, vol. XVI. L. V. Delisle 'Notice sur un recueil de traité de Dévotion ayant appartenu à Charles V', *B.E.C.* 1869, pp. 532-42. Extracts from Jean Golein's 'Traité du Sacre' from his translation of Guillaume Durand's 'Rational des Divins Offices' in M. Bloch *Les Rois Thaumaturges,* Strasbourg 1924, Appendice IV pp. 478-89.

47. L. V. Delisle *Le Cabinet des Manuscrits de la Bibliothèque Impériale,* Paris 1868, I, pp. 43-51.

48. G. Dodu 'Les idées de Charles V en matière de gouvernement', *Revue des Questions Historiques* CX 1929, pp. 5-46. The reference is to Aristotle's Politics VI, 12.

49. N. Oresme *The De Moneta,* transl. C. Johnson, London 1956. E. Babelon 'La théorie féodale de la monnaie', *Mémoires de l'Académie des Inscriptions* XXXVIII/1 1909, pp. 279-347.

50. *Ordonnances* t. V, pp. 477-80, from Archives Nationales Xa, 8602. See E. Lavisse 'Etude sur le pouvoir royal au temps de Charles V', *Revue Historique* 26, 1884, pp. 233-80.

51. P. E. L. R. Russell *English Intervention in Spain and Portugal in the time of Edward III and Richard II,* Oxford 1955.

52. H. A. Miskimin 'The last act of Charles V: the background to the revolts of 1382', *Speculum* 1963, pp. 433-42.

53. M. Rey *Les finances royales sous Charles VI: les causes du déficit 1388-1413; ibid. Le domaine du roi et les finances extraordinaires sous Charles VI 1388-1413,* Paris 1965.

54. A. A. Coville *Jean Petit: La question du tyrannicide au commencement du XVe siècle,* Paris 1932.

55. Philippe de Mézières was outraged that 'le filz d'un pauvre homme, aujourduy simple tresorier des guerres et de cellui du peuple qui doit estre converty en la guerre du royaume aura plus grant estat que ung des ducs du royaume en vaisselle en joyaulx, en mules, en chevaulx, en ornement, et en oultrageulx disners', *op. cit.* I p. 458. Rey *op. cit. Finances* p. 610, admits that for many years' Les oncles ou le frère de Charles VI n'addressent aux finances que des demandes modérées.' Compare the advice given to the new duke of Milan about the same time: 'Quod precipiat curialibus suis quam strictius potest quod non presumant impedire exactiones dirrecte vel indirecte. Et hoc si non facit magis possibile est asinum volare quam possibile fuerit suum statum conservare', N. Valeri 'L'Insegnamento di Gian-Galeazzo Visconti' *Bollettino Storico-Bibliografico Subalpino* 1934, pp. 452-87.

56. A. A. Coville *Les cabochiens et l'ordonnance de 1413,* Paris, 1888.

57. Mézières had much to say about the corruption of the parlement *op. cit.* pp. 91-103, 462-507.

58. The first extensive account of parliamentary activity in the chronicles is given in the *Anonimalle Chronicle 1333-81,* ed. V. H. Galbraith, Manchester 1927. The proceedings of 1399 are given in the *Rotuli Parliamentorum* t. III, pp. 415-32, and of 1406, *ibid.* pp. 567-603.

59. A similar situation existed in the Crown of Aragon. James I makes it clear how tiresome he regarded the assemblies of his particular dominions, which did not see his affairs as broadly as he could. All the same, he showed some skill in managing them: *op. cit.* chaps. CCCLXXX-CCCXCVII.

60. The Brut Chronicle makes the strange comment on the troubles of the early fourteenth century that they should not be thought surprising since the great lords of England were 'not all of one nation but were melled with other nations, that is for to say, some Britons, some Saxons, some Danes, some Picts, some Frenchmen, some Normans, some Spaniards, some Romans, some Hainaulters, some Flemings and of other diverse nations': *The Brut or the Chronicles of England* Part i, ed. F. W. D. Bric, *E.E.T.S.* London 1906, p. 220. London, from being an international community in the thirteenth century, became a very English town, using only English in its records. The first tax on foreigners as such was not imposed until the parliament of 1439 and became permanent in 1453, as English attitudes hardened into xenophobia.

61. J. F. O'Callaghan *History of Medieval Spain,* Cornell 1975.

62. William of Newburgh *Historia Rerum Anglicarum,* ed. R. Howlett, R.S. 1884 vol. i pp. 123-5. For Catalonia see P. Vilar *La Catalogne dans l'Espagne Moderne,* Paris 1962. James i emphasized the importance of Catalonia in his dominions: *op. cit.* chap. cccxcii.

63. E. E. S. Procter *Alfonso X of Castile,* Oxford 1951. The learned Alfonso transmitted some of his interest in learning to his successor Sancho iv, who provided for the composition of a book instructing his heir in his duties: see chapter v note **30.**

64. J. Klein *The Mesta: a study in Spanish economic history 1275-1836.* Cambridge (Mass.), 1920.

65. There is some evidence of assemblies, comparable to the Cortes, meeting in Leon before the mid-thirteenth century, but only from the end of the century do they become regular, and at times annual occasions. There are no surviving official registers of these meetings, apart from the records sent to various towns or clergy and often still to be found in the local archives. During the fourteenth century many towns sent procuradors to the Cortes, but by the fifteenth century only seventeen towns regularly expected to send representatives, though others did so from time to time. Manuel Comeiro wrote two volumes of introduction and commentary to the published records of the Cortes 1883-4. *Cortes de Leon y de Castilla* vol. i 1020-1349 (1861); vol. ii 1351-1405 (1863); vol. iii 1407-73 (1866); vol. iv 1479-1537 (1882). The *Actas de las Cortes de Castilla* 1877-8 cover the meetings from 1563. Apart from these Castilian records, only the proceedings of the Catalan Corts have been published. These are much more voluminous: 27 volumes for the years from 1064 to 1479 published by the Real Academia Madrid, 1895-1919.

66. R. Folz argued that Wittelsbach Bavaria should not be considered a state, but as family lands, until the parts, first divided into two in 1255 and then into four in 1392, were reunited in 1504; *Anciens Pays* xxxvi 1965, pp. 163-91. This impression is confirmed by the records of the different local assemblies: F. von Krenner *Baierische Landtagshandlungen in den Jahren 1429 bis 1513,* Munich 1803-05.

67. M.G.H. *Constitutiones* iv, pp. 968-9, nos. 933-41.

68. H. Angermeier *Königtum und Landfriede in deutschen Spätmittelalter,* Munich 1966.

69. R. Schroeder *Lehrbuch der Deutsche Rechtsgeschichte* 1966, Period iii, ch. 2, para. 49, 3. There was no book of Reichstaatsrecht until Peter of Andlau, a professor of canon-law, produced in 1460 his *Libellus de Caesarea Monarchia:* ed. J. Huerbin *Zeitschrift der Savigny-Stiftung für Rechtsgeschichte,* 1891-2, xxvi, Germanische Abteilung xii pp. 34-103, xiii pp. 163-219. The encroachments of Roman law were resented and opposed. One of the Bavarian estates asked that no

obstacle be put in the way of the law and ancient customs of the country, and that tribunals composed of honest and capable judges be taken from the nobility and country peasantry: F. von Krenner *op. cit.* Bd. VII, Munich 1804, pp. 103-4, 268-9, for the requests of the Landtag of Landshut-Ingolstadt in 1461 and 1471.

70. K. Zeumer *Die Goldene Bulle Kaiser Karls IV*, 1908; *ibid.* 'Ludwig des Bayern Konigswahlgesetz "Licet Iuris" vom 6 August 1338', *Neues Archiv* XXX 1904, pp. 85-112.

71. Nicholas of Cusa *De Concordantia Catholica*, ed. G. Kaller, Hamburg 1963. Book III is devoted to Sigismund's empire.

72. Only one of these principalities has been written about in English: H. J. Cohn *The government of the Rhine Palatinate in the fifteenth century*, London 1965.

73. Villani XII, X.

74. G. A. Holmes *The Florentine Enlightenment*, London 1969.

75. G. A. Brucker *Florentine Politics and Society 1343-78*, Princeton 1962. W. Bowsky 'The Buon Governo of Siena 1287-1355', *Speculum* 1962.

76. M. B. Becker *Florence in Transition: I The Decline of the Commune*, Baltimore 1967; *II Studies in the rise of the territorial state*. 1968.

77. D. M. Bueno di Mesquita 'Some Condottiere of the Trecento', *British Academy Proceedings*, 1946. M. Mallet *Mercenaries and their Masters*, London 1974. Guillaume de la Penne wrote a metrical chronicle on the Bretons who campaigned in Italy in the 1370s: Martène *op. cit.* III, 1457-1504. This is in the spirit of the chivalrous histories of warfare written by Muntaner and Froissart. An impression of the sufferings of Italy in this period and the barbarities then familiar may be derived from reading the chronicle of the Novarese lawyer, Peter Azarii, *R.I.S.* XVI, 1730, pp. 299-424.

78. Marsilius of Padua *The Defensor Pacis*, ed. C. W. Previté-Orton, Cambridge 1928, transl. A. Gewirth, New York 1956. For the problems facing the cities see P. J. Jones 'Communes and Despots', *T.R.H.S.* 1965, and for Padua in particular J. K. Hyde *Padua in the age of Dante*, Manchester 1966.

79. E. Fiume: see chapter III note **98.**

80. *Storia di Milano*, Fondazione degli Alfiere vol. IV-VII, 1954-6.

81. D. M. Bueno di Mesquita *Gian Galeazzo Visconti duke of Milan 1351-1402*, Cambridge 1941. D. F. Dowd 'Economic Expansion of Lombardy 1300-1500', *Journal of Economic History* XXI 1961, pp. 143-60.

82. For a recent single volume history in English, see W. H. McNeill *Venice, the hinge of Europe 1081-1797*, Chicago 1974.

83. *Chronicon Henrici Knighton*, ed. J. R. Lumby R.S. vol. II, 1895, p. 27: 'et exinde multi Angligenae et Francigenae transierunt ad Spruciam ad bellum campestre assignatum (1342-3); p. 69: Henry duke of Lancaster went there in 1351, while the war with France was in suspension; p. 314: his grandson Henry of Derby went, 'cum armata manu mille electorum militum armigerorum et valettorum arripuit iter versus Pruciam et mense aprilis rediit cum magni honoris tripudio et omnibus Christianis excellenti gaudiflua expeditione'. See also L. T. Toulmin-Smith *Expeditions to Prussia and the Holy Land made by Henry Earl of Derby*, Camden Society 1894.

84. *Anonymi descriptio Europae orientalis,* ed. D. Olgierd Gorka, Cracow 1916. Written by a clerk knowing the Balkans and Hungary at first hand, the book suggests that the author's knowledge of Bohemia and Poland came from travellers and earlier descriptions. Only about a quarter of the whole is devoted to these two countries.

85. P. Skwarczyński 'The problem of Feudalism in Poland', *Slavonic and East European Review* 34, 1956, pp. 292-310. K. Gorski 'Les structures sociales de la noblesse polonaise au moyen âge', *Moyen Age* 1967, pp. 73-85. J. Blum 'Eastern Europe and the Rise of Serfdom', *American Historical Review* LXII 1957, pp. 807-36.

86. W. Reddaway and others *Cambridge History of Poland* vol. I, 1950.

87. P. W. Knoll *The Rise of the Polish Monarchy 1320-70,* Chicago 1972.

88. W. Konopczynski *Liberum Veto,* Paris 1930.

89. K. Gorski 'The origins of the Polish Sejm' *op. cit.* (see note chap V, 75) and *Anciens Pays* XXXIX 1966, pp. 67-83, XL 1966, pp. 45-58, XLVIII 1968, pp. 39-55. K. Kadlec *Introduction à l'Etude Comparative de l'Histoire du Droit Public des Peuples Slaves,* Paris 1933.

90. G. V. Vernadsky *History of Russia,* revised edition, New Haven 1954. N. L. Chirovsky *A History of the Russian Empire,* vol. I: *Grand-ducal Vladimir and Moscow,* 1973. J. Blum *Lord and Peasant in Russia from the ninth to the nineteenth century,* Princeton 1961. R. E. F. Smith *The enserfment of the Russian Peasantry,* Cambridge 1968.

91. For some discussion of the chronicle evidence see J. L. I. Fennell *The Emergence of Moscow 1304-1359,* London 1968, Appendix A.

92. G. P. Fedotov *Russian Religious Mind* vol. II, Harvard 1966.

93. G. Alef 'Political Significance of the inscriptions on Muscovite coinage in the reign of Vasili II', *Speculum* XXXIV 1959, pp. 1-19.

94. J. Raba 'Fate of the Novgorod Republic', *Slavonic and East European Review,* 45, 1967, pp. 76-124.

Chapter VII *The Peace of the Dynasties*

1. N. Rubinstein *The government of Florence under the Medici 1434-94,* Oxford 1966.

2. E. H. J. Gombrich has examined the Medici reputation for artistic patronage and arrived at some unexpected conclusions: 'The Early Medici as Patrons of Art', *Italian Renaissance Studies: a tribute to the late Cecilia M. Ady,* ed. E. F. Jacob, 1960; reprinted in *Norm and Form* 1966.

3. For the English awareness of Italian cultural life in the fifteenth century see R. Mitchell *John Free* 1955, and G. B. Parks *The English Traveller to Italy,* Rome 1954. For the influence in Germany see L. Bertalot *Humanistisches Studienheft eines Nürnberger Scholaren aus Pavia (Lorenz Schaller) 1460.* Berlin 1910. Based on Jena University Library MS. Cod. Buder, q. 105 which blends medieval and renaissance Latin P. Joachimsohn 'Frühhumanismus in Schwaben' *Württembergische Vierteljahrshefte für Landesgeschichte* n.f. 5 (1896), pp. 63-126 and texts, pp. 257-288.

4. O. Cartellieri *The court of Burgundy,* transl. M. Letts, London 1929. J. Huizinga *The Waning of the Middle Ages,* transl. F. Hopman, London 1924. R. M. Tovell *Flemish Arts of the Valois Courts,* Toronto 1950. R. Wsngermée *Flemish Music and Society in the fifteenth and sixteenth century* 1968.

5. R. Vaughan *Philip the Bold,* 1962; *John the Fearless,* 1966; *Philip the Good,* 1970; *Charles the Bold,* 1973.

6. *Procès de Condamnation de Jeanne d'Arc,* ed. P. Tisset, Paris 1960, t. I pp. 221-2.

7. F. Autrand 'Offices et officiers royaux en France sous Charles VI', *Revue Historique* 242, 1969, pp. 285-338.

8. R. Fédou *Les hommes de loi lyonnais à la fin du moyen âge,* Annales de l'université de Lyon, IIIe série, lettres, fascicule 37, Paris 1964. Inheritance of office began with the notaries. War caused confusions about which king had the right to nominate to some offices, but disputes showed that the idea of a right to succeed to offices had already taken root: L. Caillet *Les relations de la commune de Lyon 1417-83,* 1909, pp. 413-16, no. cxxiii bis, document of 1432.

9. Pierre de Bourbon invested a son with his father's office of 'juge des appellations du Beaujolais à la part du royaume et de l'empire' in 1497: L. Aubret *Mémoire pour servir l'histoire de Dombes,* 1868, III, p. 134. G. Pagès 'La vénalité des offices dans l'ancienne France', *Revue Historique* 169, 1932, pp. 477-95.

10. For complaints made by the citizens of Valencia about officials see *Bulletin de la Real Academia de Buenas Lettras de Barcelona* no. 79, 1923, t. II, pp. 70-79.

11. Jean Messelin *op. cit.* p. 369 on officials, p. 458 on money and the apportionment of taxes.

12. F. Delaborde *L'expédition de Charles VIII en Italie,* Paris 1888, pp. 320-1, showed how little support Charles could count on in France.

13. Philippe de Comines *Mémoires,* ed. J. Calmette, Paris 1924; transl. I. Cazeau, New York 1963, book I cap. X.

14. C. H. Clough 'N. Machiavelli: political assumptions and objectives,' *Bulletin of the John Rylands Library* 1970, 53, pp. 30-74. N. Machiavelli *Il Principe,* ed. L. A. Burd, 1891.

15. N. Machiavelli *The Discourses,* transl. L. J. Walker, London 1950, Lib. III cap. l. on reform of religion and states.

16. *ibid.* Lib. III, cap. 43, on the Gauls.

17. F. Guicciardini *Storia d'Italia,* Bari 1929.

18. The murder was inspired by reading about the Catiline conspiracy and by the humanist Cola Montano: E. Casanova 'L'uccisione de Galeazzo Maria Sforza e alcuni documenti fiorentini', *Archivio Storico Lombardo* 1899, pp. 299-332, espec. p. 307.

19. N. Machiavelli *Istorie Fiorentine,* In the Proemio, Machiavelli claimed that the existing histories of Florence to 1434 had neglected internal politics to concentrate on foreign wars. Half of his own history was therefore devoted to Florentine politics up to 1434; the other half concerns the years of the Medici 'despotism', 1434-92. C. Benoist 'L'état italien et la science politique avant Machiavel', *Revue des Deux Mondes* XXXIX, 1907, pp. 164-88.

20. Although it is difficult to generalize about such a matter as the growth of cruelty, it is arguable that changes in the normal legal processes which authorized the use of force and approved barbarous treatment of accused persons put the violence of the authorities in this period into quite a different category from the unpremeditated horrors of earlier times. The new legal systems, having rejected the appeal to God, needed rational evidence. It was believed that confessions were the most certain proof of guilt or innocence and torture was therefore used in the expectation of discovering the truth. Pope Innocent IV recommended its use in cases of heresy in 1252. Moreover, punishment of offences against the new arbitrariness of secular rulers required spectacular cruelties, notably in England from the time of Edward I. The cruel executions in fourteenth-century France were still thought a horrible innovation (see chapter VI, note **31**). Such symbols of the new style of government repression as the Bastille, built in Paris in the 1370s, and the rack, introduced into England by John Holland, fourth duke of Exeter, as constable of the Tower of London in 1447, indicate a change in men's attitude to the use of force. In the past, men had defended themselves in fair fight. Hereafter they were at the mercy ⌒f the forces of public order.

21. A. Giry *Manuel de Diplomatique,* Paris 1894, p. 769: 'Après avoir ainsi comporté un certain nombre de variantes, cette clause s'est fixée au commencement du XVe siècle dans les formules: car ainsi nous plaît-il être fait et car tel est notre plaisir.'

22. Giry *op. cit.* p. 319, note 3.

23. Giry *op. cit.* p. 323. 'Dans une lettre addressée à Charles VII, le pape Pie II déclara que ce titre de roi très chrétien *christianissimus* lui appartient par droit d'héritage. Ce ne fut cependant qu'à dater du pontificat de Paul II et sous Louis XI que cette expression devint en vertu d'une concession expresse du saint-siège la qualification propre des rois de France.'

24. The need for impressive show of royalty is artlessly proved by the Great Chronicle of London in the scornful account of Henry VI's parade through London on his restoration in 1470: 'the which was more like a play than the showing of a prince to win men's hearts, for by this means he lost many, won none or right few, and ever he was showed in a long blue gown of velvet as though he had no more to change with', ed. A. H. Thomas and I. D. Thornley, 1938, p. 215.

25. *Rotuli Parliamentorum* V, 376.

26. James I recognized the need to do this; see chapter V note **45**.

27. See chapter V, note 30.

28. This pompous style is found in the humorous charter whereby Alfonso V granted his toothless court dwarf Mossen Borra permission to drink as much wine as he could for the rest of his life; see chapter II, note **1**.

29. N. Valois *Histoire de la Pragmatique Sanction de Bourges sous Charles VII,* Paris 1906.

30. F. G. Heymann *George of Bohemia King of Heretics,* Princeton 1965.

31. H. Jedin *A History of the Council of Trent,* trans. E. Graf, Nelson 1957, from the German of 1949. N. H. Minnich 'Concepts of Reform proposed at the Fifth Lateran Council', *Archivum Historiae Pontificae* VII, 1969.

32. P. Partner *The Lands of Saint Peter,* London 1972.

33. The mockery of religion, priests and ceremonies which are the reverse side of the pious image should not be misconstrued as blasphemous or rationalist in the manner of the eighteenth century. They were mischievous, not savage, and they relieved religious tensions, much as modern caricatures of politicians on the stage, or in the newspapers, help men to laugh when they feel more like weeping. Such humour does not imply a disbelief in 'politics' or in all 'politicians' and even the faithful party supporter laughs to see his chiefs mocked in his own newspaper. It is a healthy society that subjects those put on pedestals to public raillery. Only so, is it possible to bear with the oppressions of politics and the sombre truths of religion. See above chapter II, note 1.

34. See chapter II, note 29.

35. In a very material way: F. Clark 'Bleeding Hosts', *Heythrop Journal* I, 1960, pp. 214-28.

36. The development of pietistic writing in all the European vernaculars of the fourteenth century has not been conveniently summarized in one book, since specialists are invariably philologists concerned with only one language or one group of related languages. For the problems of enriching the colloquial languages with the necessary psychological and theological terms see P. Hodgson *Deonise Hid Divinite, E.E.T.S.,* London 1955. For the turning of even abstruse theological works into the vernacular seek K. Ruh *Bonaventura Deutsch. Ein Beitrag zur deutschen Franziskanermystik und Scholastik,* Bern 1956. For English mystical writing see E. Underhill *Medieval Mysticism,* and in *Cambridge Medieval History* vol. VII, 1932. D. Knowles *The English Mystical Tradition* 1961.

37. For one monastery in this period see: R. B. Dobson *'Durham Cathedral Priory 1400-1450'* Cambridge 1973. J. Leclercq and F. Vandenbroucke *The Spirituality of the Middle Ages* London 1968 part II sets out the evidence for the spiritual life of the monasteries in this period.

38. Hugh of Neufchateau, the Franciscan, denounced the traffic in indulgences in the first half of the fourteenth century, when they were still in their 'infancy' (see chapter VI, note 1). He was astonished that learned bishops allowed ignorant pardoners to impose on the devout, and get away with it: B. Hauréau *Notices et Extraits des Manuscrits de la Bibliothèque Nationale.* Paris 1896, XXXVI, pp. 332-8, from B.N. *Ms. Lat.* 16089. A. Landgraf: Grundlagen für ein Verständnis der Busslehre der Früh-und Hoch-Scholastik *Zeitschrift für Katholische Theologie* Band 51 1927 pp. 171-194.

39. T. Aquinas *Summa Theologica Pars* I, q. 89 art.1.

40. Matthias de Janov 'Dicti Magister Parisiensis' *Regulae Veteris et Novi Testamenti,* ed. V. Kybal, Innsbruck 1908-26, vol. III p. 361, in Narracio de Milico cap. 7.

41. The Cardinal d'Ailly answered Hus's appeal from the council to God with the exasperated comment of a reasonable man: we cannot give our verdict according to your conscience, but according to the evidence: *The Letters of John Hus,* ed. H. B. Workman, London 1904. D'Ailly pointed out that as Hus accepted Wyclif's metaphysics, as a realist, he was logically committed to Wyclif's interpretation of the eucharist. Hus denied this, but his position looked unconvincing to the Fathers at Constance, whatever the Bohemians made of it: 7 July 1415. M. Fox 'John Wyclif and the Mass', *Heythrop Journal* III, 1962, pp. 232-40, argued that Wyclif denied Christ's substantial presence at the eucharist, and asserted his real presence, virtual, spiritual and sacramental.

42. F. Seibt 'Die Hussitenzeit als Kulturepoche' *H.Z.* t. 195, 1962, pp. 21-62. H. Kaminsky *A History of the Hussite Revolution,* Berkeley 1967.

43. The four articles of Prague comprised clauses allowing freedom of preaching, the communion in both kinds for laymen, relieving the church of all lordship in temporal goods and burdening those in responsible positions with the punishment of offences formerly dealt with by the clerical courts. The precise meaning of the first and fourth clauses is obscure, by intention: it was a formula allowing for different interpretations. The third clause enriched the nobility; the second earned the moderate party the name of Utraquists.

44. O. Odložilik 'Wyclif in Central Europe', *Slavonic and East European Review* 1928-29, 7, pp. 634-48.

45. D. P. Walker, *Spiritual and Demonic Magic from Ficino to Campanella,* London 1958. W. Shumaker *The Occult Sciences in the Renaissance,* Berkeley 1972. J. B. Russell *Witchcraft in the Middle Ages,* Ithaca N.Y. 1972. H. Kramer and J. Sprenger 'Malleus Maleficarum (1486)' transl. M. Summers, 1928. For a late fourteenth-century manuscript combining politics and the occult see Bodley MS 581 written for Richard II in 1391 and comprising a section on the duties of kings, the significance of visions seen in dreams and a Libellus Geomancie compiled from Peter de Abano.

46. Playing cards came into Europe from the Muslim world in the late fourteenth century and quickly supplanted chess as the most popular of medieval domestic games. H. R. D'Allemagne *Les cartes à jouer du xive au xxe siècles,* Paris 1906 L. A. Mayer *Mamluk Playing Cards,* ed. R. Ettinghausen, Leiden 1971.

47. R. R. Post *The Modern Devotion,* Leiden 1968. For the Benedictine revival see P. Schmitz *Histoire de l'ordre de St Benoît,* t. III 1948, t. VI 1949, and for the Franciscans J. H. R. Moorman *op. cit.*

48. E. H. Wilkins; *Life of Petrarch,* Chicago 1961. The letters to Cicero are found in his letter collection the *Familiares,* Book 24, ep. 3, ed. I. Fracasetti, Florence 1859-63.

49. St Basil, Bishop of Caesarea, had compared the Christian love of poverty with that of Zeno and Diogenes; see *Letters,* ed. R. J. Deferrari, London 1926, vol. I, letter IV to Olympus in 358. Alan of Lille in the twelfth century had used the ethical teaching of Seneca, for example in his summa on preaching. *P.L.* 210, *cc.* 161-2.

50. H. Baron *Leonardo Bruni Aretino Humanistisch-philosophisch Schriften,* Leipzig 1928. *ibid. The Crisis of the Early Italian Renaissance,* Princeton 1955. Cf. E. Garin *Italian Humanism,* Oxford 1965.

51. P. Kristeller *The Philosophy of Marsilio Ficino,* 1943.

52. Mirella Levi d'Ancona 'The Doni Madonna by Michelangelo; an iconographic study', *Art Bulletin* L, 1968, pp. 43-50.

53. W. H. Woodward *Vittorino da Feltre and other Humanist Educators,* Cambridge 1897.

54. They also began to analyse their own languages and construct grammars for them: see S. B. Meech 'Early Application of Latin Grammar to English', *Publications of the Modern Language Association of America,* vol. 50, 1935, pp. 1012-32. I owe this reference to Dr. A. I. Doyle, whose learning has been of incalculable benefit to me in many matters treated in this book.

55. Mézières *op. cit.*, pp. 223-4, was already worried about reliance on translations, such as Charles VI's father had encouraged: 'Car il y a en la saincte escripture certains et plusieurs motz en latin qui du lisant percent le cuer en grant devocion, lesquelx translatez en francais se treuvent en vulgal sans saveur et sans delectation.'

56. Examples can be found in the numerous common-place books: e.g. L. Toulmin-Smith *A Common-Place book of the fifteenth century,* London 1886.

57. In addition to the *Paston Letters, op. cit.,* there is the letter collection of the *Stonor family,* ed. C. L Kingsford, 1919, 1923. For Italy there the letters of a mother to her exiled sons: Alessandra Macinghi degli Strozzi *Lettre di una Gentildonna Fiorentina del secolo XV ai figliuoli esuli,* ed. C. Guasti, Florence 1877.

58. B. Boisset 'Traité d'Arpentage', ed. P. Meyer, *Romania* XXI, 1892, pp. 557-80, XXII pp. 87-126, and F. Novati *Romania* XXI, pp. 528-56.

59. Painting itself was still at the artisan stage when Cennino Cennini wrote his account of the craft about 1400: *Il Libro dell'Arte,* text and translation by D. V. Thompson, Yale 1932-3, 2 vols.

60. F. Novati *Il Fior di Battaglia di Maestro Fiore dei Liberi da Premariacco,* Bergamo 1902. Wrestling was however still probably too vulgar to be written up. The hero of Le Petit Jehan de Saintré, *op. cit.,* says that as knight 'onques je ne fus luicteur, et ces seigneurs moynes en sont les maistres, aussi de jouer a la pauline gecter barres, pierres et paulz de fer et tous autres essais quant ilz sont a leur privé.' There is an early printed book, *c.* 1500, giving demonstrations of the holds in wrestling (W. L. Schreiber *Manuel de l'Amateur de la gravure,* Berlin 1891, IV, pp. 445-8, no. 5097-8, and VIII pl. cxx) and it is well known that in the sixteenth century even kings did not despise the art. But the courtier (B. Castiglione, *op. cit.* p. 98) discusses the matter with mixed feelings. He speaks well of the accomplishment and some arguments in favour of it as a manly sport cutting across social barriers are expressed forcefully, but his conclusion seems to be that it was improper for gentlemen to wrestle with carters.

61. Domenico da Piacenza wrote *c.* 1440-50 the earliest manual of dancing to survive (Paris B.N. *Ms. Ital.* 972). A. Michel 'The earliest dance manuals', *Medievalia et Humanistica* III, 1943, pp. 117-31, esp. pp. 119-24.

62. J. Koch 'Der Anglo-Normannische Traktat von Walter von Bibbesworth in seiner Bedeutung für die Anglistik', *Anglia* LVIII, 1934, pp. 30-77. This is the oldest English grammar of French *c.* 1285. For evidence of how William Paston studied French, 1450-54, see *Paston Letters op. cit.* pp. 150-3 no. 82.

63. R. L. Poole noticed that Wyclif wrote worse Latin than William of Ockham and supposed that this might be explained as a consequence of Wyclif thinking in English. This would represent a serious change in the intellectual habits of the schools: see Poole's edition of Wyclif's *De civili domino op. cit.* As for laymen, the thirteenth century Romance from Kent *Arthur and Merlin,* ed. D. D. Macrae U. Gibson, *E.E.T.S.,* 1973, Auchinleck Ms. V. 9-26, suggests that many English nobles even then only understood English. According to the Parliament Roll, (Rot. Plt. II p. 268) the chancellor opened the session of 1362 with a speech in English but the first recorded English speech in parliament is Bolingbroke's claim to the throne in 1399. The important question is not however when English first appeared in the records, but when it was no longer taken for granted in sophisticated circles that Englishmen would be conversant with other languages than English.

64. Apel *The Notation of Polyphonic Music 900-1600,* Cambridge (Mass.) 1949. C. Parrish *The Notation of Medieval Music,* London 1958.

65. Mariano di Jacopo detto il Taccola *Liber Tertius de ingeneis ac edificiis,* ed. J. H. Beck, Milan 1969. *ibid. De machinis: The Engineering Treatise of 1449,* Wiesbaden 1971. Taccola wrote to the Emperor Sigismund asking for employment. J. H. Beck 'The historical Taccola and the emperor Sigismund in Siena', *Art Bulletin* L, 1968, pp. 309-20.

66. A. Gherardi *Statuti dell'universita e studio fiorentino dell'anno 1387,* Florence 1881. These documents prove how fitfully the studio operated between 1349, when it was recognized by Clement VI as a *studio generale,* and 1472, when it was transferred to Pisa. R. Abbondanza has more recently published further documents for the year 1388: *A.S.I.* 1959, pp. 80-110.

67. G. Gaye *Carteggio inedito d'artisti dei secoli XIV, XV, XVI,* t. I, Florence 1839, p. 481.

68. Villani X, CLXXVI.

69. V. Rossi 'Jacopo d'Albizzotto Guidi e il suo inedito poema su Venezia', *Nuovo Archivio Veneto* t. V, 1893.

70. G. Vasari *The lives of the painters, sculptors and architects,* transl. A. B. Hinds, London 1963, vol. I, p. 308.

71. M. Baxandall *Giotto and the Orators,* Oxford 1971; *ibid.* 'Guarino, Pisanello and Manuel Chrysoloras', *Journal of the Warburg and Courtauld Institutes* XXVIII, 1965, pp. 183-204.

72. L. B. Alberti *On Painting and on Sculpture,* ed. C. Grayson, London 1972. *Ten Books of Architecture,* transl. J. Leoni, London 1955. L. Ghiberti *Commentaries,* ed. J. von Schlosser, Kunstgeschichtliches Jahrbuch Bd. 4., 1910. Piero Franceschi *De prospectiva pingendi,* ed. G. N. Fasola, Florence 1942.

73. A. Manetti *Vita di Filippo di ser Brunellesco,* Florence 1927, transl. C. Enggars, University Park 1970. F. O. Prager *Brunelleschi: studies in his technology and inventions,* 1970. G. C. Argan 'Architecture of Brunelleschi and the origin of Perspective Theory', *Journal of Warburg and Courtauld Institutes* IX, 1946, pp. 96-121.

74. E. H. J. Gombrich *Art and Illusion,* London 1960.

75. E. Wind *The Pagan Mysteries in the Renaissance,* revised edition, Harmondsworth 1967. R. Marcel *Marsile Ficin 1433-99,* Paris 1958. A. Chastel *Marsile Ficin et l'art.* Geneva 1954. *ibid. Art et Humanisme à Florence au temps de Laurent le Magnifique,* Paris 1959. E. Gombrich. 'Botticelli's Mythologies', *Journal of Warburg and Courtauld Institutes* VIII, 1945, pp. 7-60. Donat de Chapeaurouge 'Aktporträts des 16. Jahrhunderts', *Jahrbuch der Berliner Museen* Band ll, 1969, pp. 161-77.

76. G. Wilson Knight 'This sceptred isle: a study of Shakespeare's kings', 1940-56, in *The Sovereign Flower,* London 1958, pp. 11-91; for key speeches see *Richard II,* 3 ii-iii; *Henry IV (1),* I iii, 3 i, 4 v; *Henry VI (3),* 2 v; *Richard III* 5 v.

INDEX